Yugoslavia: A State that Withered Away

Central European Studies

Charles W. Ingrao, senior editor
Gary B. Cohen, editor

Yugoslavia: A State that Withered Away

Dejan Jović

Purdue University Press
West Lafayette, Indiana

Copyright 2009 by Purdue University. All rights reserved.

Printed in the United States of America.

Library of Congress Cataloging-in-Publication Data

Jovic, Dejan.
  Yugoslavia : a state that withered away / Dejan Jovic.
    p. cm. -- (Central European studies)
  ISBN 978-1-55753-495-8
  1. Yugoslavia--Politics and government. 2. Yugoslavia--Ethnic relations--Political aspects.
  3. Nationalism--Yugoslavia. I. Title. II. Series.

  DR1255.J68 2008
  949.702'4--dc22

                                            2008013563

Contents

Introduction 1

Chapter One: Analytical Approaches to Studying the Disintegration of Yugoslavia

1.1. A Critical Assessment of Existing Approaches in Analyzing the
    Disintegration of Yugoslavia 13
    1.1.1. The Economic Argument 15
    1.1.2. The Ancient Ethnic Hatred Argument 18
    1.1.3. The Nationalism Argument 19
    1.1.4. The Cultural Argument 23
    1.1.5. The International Politics Argument 25
    1.1.6. The Role of Personality Argument 28
    1.1.7. The *Fall of Empires* Argument 30
    1.1.8. The Constitutional and Institutional Reasons Argument 32

1.2. The Analytical Approach of this Book 33

Chapter Two: The Kardelj Concept: Constructing the Fourth Yugoslavia (1974-1990)

2.0. Introduction 47

2.1. Four Constitutive Concepts 48
    2.1.1. King Alexander's *National Unity* Yugoslavism (1918-39) 48
    2.1.2. Prince Paul's *Sporazum* Yugoslavia (1939-41) 51
    2.1.3. Tito's *Brotherhood and Unity* Federalist Yugoslavism 54
    2.1.4. The Emergence of Kardelj's Concept 62

2.2. The Elaboration of Kardelj's Concept 68
    2.2.1. A Biographical Note on Kardelj 68
    2.2.2. Kardelj's Interpretation of Marxism 72
    2.2.3. The Notion of State in Kardelj's Concept 77

2.3. Conclusion 81

Chapter Three: The Constitutional Debate 1967-1974: Why did Serbia accept the Kardelj concept and the 1974 Constitution?

3.0. Introduction 95

3.1. Did Serbia Accept Kardelj's Concept Voluntarily? 97
    3.1.1 Relationship between Tito and Republican (Serbian) Leaders 97
    3.1.2. Serbian Leaders and Serbian National Interests in the 1967-74 Debates 103
    3.1.3. The Serbian Leaders and the Lack of Democratic Legitimacy 106

3.2. The Serbian Leadership between Ranković and Kardelj 108

3.3. Two Visions of Serbia and Yugoslavia Within Serbian Politics in May 1968 113
    3.3.1. Discourse One: Ćosić and Marjanović 115
    3.3.2. Discourse Two: The Majority of the Serbian Central Committee 119

3.4. Conclusion 124

Chapter Four: The Economic Crisis: The (Lack of) Response of the Yugoslav Political Elite to Economic Crisis in the Early 1980s

4.0. Introduction 141

4.1. "Boalization": Associated or Disintegrated Labor? 142

4.2. Debating the Causes of the Crisis 147

4.3. Government and Economists vs. Party Leadership and Republican Leaders 150

4.4. The International Factors 155

4.5. The Response of the Elite: Kraigher's Long-Term [sic!] Program of Stabilization 159

4.6. The Source of Regime Stability: the "Syndrome of Radical Egalitarianism" 162

4.7. Conclusion 164

Chapter Five: The Political System Reexamined: The Serbian Question and the Rise of the Defenders and Reformers of the Constitution (1974-1984)

5.0. Introduction 171

5.1. The *Blue Book* of 1977 172

5.2. The Kosovo Crisis	176
5.2.1. The Background of the Kosovo Crisis (1981)	176
5.2.2. The 1981 Protests in Kosovo: the Beginning of the State Crisis of Yugoslavia	183
5.2.3. The Reaction of the Elite	186
5.2.3.1. Discourse One: The Federal Political Elite Reaction to the Kosovo Protests of 1981	188
5.2.3.2. Discourse Two: The Serbian Political Elite Reaction to the Kosovo Protests of 1981	191
5.2.3.3. Discourse Three: The Provinces	196
5.2.3.4. The Position of Slovenia and Croatia: the "Defenders of the Constitution"	197
5.3. The First Direct Conflict: The Case of Draža Marković (1982)	200
5.4. Constructive Criticism and Critical Analysis of the Political System	205
5.5. Conclusion	213

Chapter Six: The Emergence of Alternative Concepts and the Reaction of the Political Elite in Serbia (1984-1988)

6.0. Introduction	226
6.1. Intellectual Dissent in Yugoslavia	226
6.1.1. The Rise of the "Critical Intelligentsia" as a Political Counterelite (1981-84)	228
6.1.1.1. Political Engagement	228
6.1.1.2. The Literature of Apocalypse	231
6.2. The (Croatian) Political Elite's Reaction: The *White Book* (1984)	234
6.3. Serbia between the *White Book* (1984) and the Memorandum (1986)	239
6.3.1. The Martinović Case and the Emergence of Public Protests in Serbia	239
6.3.2. Stambolić's Initiatives	244
6.3.3. The "SANU Memorandum" and the Reaction of the Political Elite	248
6.4. Slobodan Milošević's Discourse in 1984-1987	253
6.5. From Divisions to Unity: the Emergence of Institutionalists and	

Revolutionists within the LCS (April-September 1987) 258
   6.5.1. The Kosovo Polje Speech 258
   6.5.2. The Student Case: "Differentiation" Within the Elite 261
   6.5.3. The Paraćin Case and Its Interpretation 263

6.6. Institutionalists vs. Revolutionists-Toward the Last "Palace Putsch" in Yugoslavia 264
   6.6.1. The Institutionalists 265
   6.6.2. The Eighth Session of the LCS Central Committee (24-25 September 1987) Victory for the Revolutionists 268
   6.6.3. Milošević's Interpretation of Titoism: Return of the third concept of Yugoslavia 272

6.7. Why Did the Others Support Milošević? 274

6.8. The Aftermath: Toward the "Antibureaucratic Revolution" 282

Chapter Seven: Slovenia and Serbia: the Final Years of Yugoslavia (1988-1990)

7.1. Constitutional Changes and the "Antibureaucratic Revolution" 308

7.2. Slovenia and Serbia: Divisions between the Intellectual Elites 312

7.3. The Slovene National Program (1986-87) 314

7.4. Reaction of the Slovene Political Elite 322

7.5. The "Slovene Spring" 1988: Army vs. Slovenia 327

7.6. The Consequences of the Slovene Spring for the LCY 331

7.7. The Final Battle: Changing the Rules of the Game 332

7.8. The LCY Membership Divided 343

7.9. The Last Hours: the 14th (Extraordinary) LCY Congress 349

7.10. The End of the Party and the End of the State 351

7.11. The Last Hope: Marković's Attempt to Unite Yugoslavia Without the LCY 353

7.12. Conclusion 361

Bibliography 375

Acknowledgments

This book has been long in making, and thus many people and institutions have contributed to the final product. Its main bulk was completed during my doctoral research at London School of Economics and Political Sciences in 1995-1999. I am very grateful for generous advice and guidance I received from my two supervisors, Professor Dominic Lieven and Dr. Chris Binns, and from the two examiners of the thesis, Professor Stevan Pavlowitch and Dr. Wendy Bracewell. Their encouragement and curiosity about the main argument helped me not only to complete the project, but also to understand more about the nature of doctoral research in general.

When published in both Zagreb and Belgrade in 2003, this book appeared to be the first academic book published jointly by one Croatian and one Serbian publisher. I would like to thank the publishers of the Serbian and Croatian edition, Dejan Ilić (Fabrika knjiga, Belgrade) and Božo and Neda Rudež (Prometej, Zagreb) for their courage to break the ice, and for their comments and assistance in what was my own ice-breaking endeavor.

I am also very grateful to a number of people who worked on this American edition of the book. I owe gratitude to Professor Charles Ingrao for his patience with the timetable and for his agreeing to include this book in his distinguished Central European Studies Series, as well as to James T. Keating and Katherine M. Purple for their help with the editing of the book. In particular, I am grateful to Professor Sabrina Ramet and to the late Professor Dennison Rusinow for their very detailed and enormously useful comments on the first draft of the manuscript.

During all these years, many colleagues and scholars have commented on my main argument or various parts of the book, and I would like to thank them wholeheartedly for that. Among them, Dr. Jasna Dragović-Soso and Dr. Dejan Djokić (now both distinguished British academics) stand out as the source of endless and selfless encouragement and support. Much of what I have learned about the period(s) I wrote about in this book originated in our regular friendly discussions throughout our four London years and much beyond that. I have greatly benefitted from the intellectual interaction with the late Mr. Desimir Tošić, Professor Aleksandar Pavković, Professor Ivan Prpić, Professor Jovan Mirić, Professor Todor Kuljić, Dr Nebojša Vladisavljević, Dr. Eric Ringmar, Dr. Chun Lin, Dr.

Abigal Innes, Dr. Vesselin Dimitrov, Dr. Nick Sitter, and Dr. Predrag Marković, to mention but a few.

The word of thanks should also go to a large number of interviewees quoted in this book, whom I interviewed during the course of my research. Most of them were participants in Yugoslav politics in the period I focus on here. I know that for many of them to talk about what happened must have been a personal—and sometimes emotional—experience, yet they kindly agreed to give their views and sometimes even to grant access to their personal archive. None of these people, of course, bear responsibility for any shortcomings of this book.

Several institutions and some individuals enabled my research by providing generous financial and institutional support. Without such support from the late Mr. Vane Ivanović, I would have not been able to begin the research in the first place. I am proud to have been supported by this noble Yugoslav. Of institutions that supported me, I would like to thank the Overseas Research Support Grant Scheme of the Vice-Chancelors and Principals Association of the United Kingdom, the London School of Economics' research grants schemes, as well as Open Society Institute in Croatia (Soros Fund) for their trust in my work and for all support they provided. The book would not have been completed without the encouragement of my colleagues at the University of Stirling, who allowed me to use sabbaticals for final editing. I am also grateful to Jean Monnet Fellowship scheme, which enabled me to enjoy the beauty of Florence, as well as a vibrant and very supportive academic environment of the European University Institute, where I was a post-doctoral research fellow in 2000.

Finally, I am indebted to my friends (wherever they are) and to family in Zagreb, who have encouraged and supported me throughout this (and other) project(s).

—Stirling, September 2008

Foreword

We are proud to welcome Dejan Jović to the long list of European scholars who have published with Purdue University Press's Central European Studies series. This is also the fourth series volume to be republished in English in revised and expanded format.[1] It is certainly a good fit, given its analysis of the attempts to establish and legitimize a state structure that could accommodate a multicultural society.

Specialists of Europe's multiethnic eastern half will have much to compare here with the experiences of political elites elsewhere in the continent's Tsarist, Ottoman, and Habsburg spheres. Certainly one common theme that they will recognize is the need for continuous readjustment in the country's political institutions. Habsburg historians reading Jović's account of the four "constitutive concepts" implemented in succession by King Alexander, Prince-Regent Paul, Marshall Tito, and Communist party ideologist Edvard Kardelj will recall the series of governmental constructs that the imperial regime enacted a century earlier. Nor will students of twentieth-century central Europe's other abortive experiment in multiethnicity fail to recall the repeated adjustments that political leaders in Prague and Bratislava made in reconstituting—and ultimately dissolving—Czechoslovakia. Perhaps the message for the social engineers in Brussels is that constant institutional innovation is the common currency of supranational states in an age of multicultural democracies, without which they face the inevitable bankruptcy that befell the Ottoman and Soviet empires' claim to political legitimacy.

Which is not to say that ideological and institutional innovation guaranteed the success of the Yugoslav state idea any more than it did the survival of Czechoslovakia and the Habsburgs. Readers will note the author's emphasis on the roles that the party's political elite played both in creating the Socialist Federal Republic of Yugoslavia (SFRY) and in tearing it down. Despite all of the forces that contributed to its demise, Jović rightly focuses on the human agency of the federation's elites. Indeed, since the beginning of modern times, no opposition movement or revolt has ever stood a chance of achieving a revolutionary agenda without their leadership and ability to articulate an ideological argument. The party's failure to sustain a consensus stands out amid the multiplicity of contributing causes that Jović presents. In characterizing himself as a "moderate intentionalist," he joins the chorus of scholars who have rejected the inherent inevitability of Yugoslavia's dissolution, even though the shape that it had assumed in the 1974 constitution rendered it more susceptible to the centrifugal forces that helped destroy it.

Those of us who have studied the creation and ultimate demise of so many multinational states over the past century may very well share Jović's appreciation for the penultimate, Socialist phase of the Yugoslav experiment. He is doubtless correct that at least the SFRY never quite fit the definition of "empire" since no single group dominated. While it lasted, the country's stability was insured both by a balance of power between the federation's constituent peoples and by a genuine desire of Serbian and other party leaders to accommodate the concerns of those nations and minorities that felt weak or threatened. Alas, multiethnic polities can never make a conclusive claim to success in their integrative mission, only to ongoing success in sustaining the process. Hence, the experiment's abrupt end once Slobodan Milošević had destroyed the spirit of accommodation and upset the balance, thereby returning Yugoslavia to a prewar state in which a single ethnic group could once again make good its claim to lead and dominate it.

—Charles W. Ingrao
Senior Editor

Notes

1 Jugoslavija - država koja je odumrla: uspon, kriza i pad Četvrte Jugoslavije - 1974-1990 Prometej, Zagreb, Samizdat B92, Belgrade, 2003.

INTRODUCTION

Hundreds of books and probably thousands of articles have been written on the collapse of Yugoslavia. Why is yet another needed? How different can it be from those already written on the same subject?

As chapter one of this book analyzes in detail, most of the recent analyses of the disintegration of Yugoslavia are focused either on the long-term macrostructural factors that have made the country unstable ever since its creation in 1918 (Lampe 1996; Ramet 1992; Sekelj 1993; Vučković 1997; Pavković 1996; Denitch 1994; Irvine 1997; Dyker 1997; and others), or on the role of personalities (such as Josip Broz Tito and Slobodan Milošević) in the last two decades before disintegration. A great many of these studies have focused on the actual disintegration of the Yugoslav institutions and the causes of the post-Yugoslav wars in the 1990s (Woodward 1995; Samary 1995; Silber and Little 1995; Van den Heuvel 1992; Crnobrnja 1994; Glenny 1992 and 1993; Cohen 1993; Magaš 1993; Stojanović 1997; Meier 1999; and others). Some of them analyze the role of international politics in the Yugoslav crisis (Gow 1997b; Williams 1998; Owen 1995; Rose 1998; Zimmermann 1996; Bildt 1998; Holbrooke 1998; and others). This book, however, focuses on the elite perceptions of reality and of a desirable future, which evolved in the period analyzed here. It has three objectives: to explain reasons for the emergence of the last political compromise in Yugoslavia (of the 1974 Constitution); to provide an explanation for the crisis of this *constitutive concept*; and to explain reasons for the breakdown of this ideological and political consensus in the late 1980s. Therefore this book is about the emergence, crisis, and breakdown of the elite ideological consensus from 1974 to 1990.

The politics of Yugoslavia in the period under scrutiny were the politics of its elite. Although Marxist ideology was in its teaching antielitist, the Communist regimes were in reality constructed on the Leninist notion of the Party being the vanguard of society. It was guaranteed a leading (and de facto ruling) role because of its vision of the future that was built on its ability to understand the *General Laws of History*, to see further into the future and thus to construct reality according to this vision. The Party (i.e., its leadership) was the main interpreter of the aims of social development. Its mission was to lead society toward a true communist (classless, stateless) form of social organization. Thus while in theory the Socialist societies were antielitist, in political reality only the (Party) elite mattered. The main political conflicts in Socialist Yugoslavia were intraelite conflicts.

The basic contradiction between the declared goals (in the Yugoslav situation, self-management as the form of direct democracy) and political "necessity" in the transitional period (displayed in the guaranteed role of the Party as vanguard) was a source of permanent contradictions in all Socialist states. On the one hand, the elite occupied the main locus of power, and on the other it declared direct democracy to be its main aim. The contradiction was resolved by the notion of the transitional period between the old regime (of political, party democracy) and the communist society in which the ideals of direct self-government would be fully implemented. The Socialist period was a period of permanent reform of the political system, aimed at reducing the role of the institutions of the old regime, in the first place of the state, which was to wither away at the end of this process. In this process of the state's withering away, the Party (as the elite) had the leading and irreplaceable role.

The period analyzed in this book was the last attempt to reform the Yugoslav political system toward these goals. The ideological and political consensus within the Yugoslav political elite was based on the Marxist notion that the state should be permanently and gradually weakened and direct democracy strengthened in the transitional period. The processes of "Socialization of the state" and of "de-etatization of society" was at the core of Socialism as a "transition period" toward Communism. This general conclusion was formulated primarily in various books, articles, and speeches by Edvard Kardelj, the main ideologue of Yugoslav self-management, and was adapted to Yugoslav reality through major debates in the 1967-74 period. The members of the Yugoslav political elite, being Marxists themselves, largely (though not unconditionally) agreed on Kardelj's interpretation of reality and social aims. The 1974 Constitution was an expression of this agreement. The "constitutive concept" of post-1974 Yugoslavia transformed the Yugoslav interpretation of Marxism into new legal provisions and political actions. It decentralized the institutions of the federal state not only to *resolve* the national question (of which the Yugoslav Communists were aware), but also to make a further step forward toward the withering away of the state and its replacement by self-management as an alternative.

Of course Yugoslavia did not collapse only because of the ideology promoted by its political elites. Other factors–economic, geopolitical, national structure, international politics, and the role of personalities, to name but a few– were just as important. However, no explanation of the collapse would be complete without including the perceptions of the political elite in the period that immediately preceded it, without an analysis of its ideological beliefs and of the mechanism by which these beliefs were transformed into political action. Despite the ever-existent long-term problems, the Yugoslav political elite in the period 1967-74 found a way to preserve the unity of Yugoslavia. Fifteen years later, in circumstances that looked much more promising, they were unable to secure its further existence. The aim of this book is to explain why these long-term problems were successfully sidelined in one period, though in another they formed an insurmountable obstacle. The difference was, it is argued here, in the breakdown of the elite ideological consensus, which was based primarily (but not exclusively) on Kardelj's interpretation of Marxism. The ideological vision of objectives and the shared interpretation of reality that existed in 1974 were no longer there in 1989. The *constitutive concept* that linked the elite consensus on ideological issues with their legal and political actions gradually collapsed as the vision became blurred.

In its final two decades (and especially after the new constitution was introduced in 1974), Yugoslav unity was built more than ever on specific ideological grounds (i.e., on a specific interpretation of Marxism), and less than before on the nationalist notion of the unity of South Slavs. Perhaps paradoxically, Yugoslavia seemed to be more ideological than its East European neighbors, to which ideology was largely imported (from the USSR) and not conceived at home. The ideology on which the Yugoslavs sought to build their unity after World War II (and especially since the mid-1960s) was based on the notion of the withering away of the state. By its letter and intention – it was an antistatist ideology. At the core of the Yugoslav problem, I argue, was the long-lasting (but not much debated) question: can a state survive if based on an antistatist (and antinationalist) ideology? Is a Socialist state a contradiction in terms? Does more Socialism mean less state? And – does any further advancement of Socialism in fact lead to the weakening of a state? Although the Kardelj concept offered some answers to these questions, it ultimately failed to resolve this basic dilemma.

Yugoslavia shared these dilemmas with other Socialist states, which all found themselves in crisis in the last two decades of the 20th century. Having advanced more than any of the others in the development of an alternative to the state (in the form of self-management), Yugoslavia found itself only facing these dilemmas more directly and with a much greater intensity. Moreover, it also faced additional hurdles, such as stronger nationalist, authoritarian, and liberal challenges than in other East European countries (because of a much more open and developed civil society in comparison), an economic crisis, a complex ethnic structure, and a dramatic change in its international political environment.

The collapse of Yugoslavia shows that the more that states base their unity on ideology, the more vulnerable they are to a collapse of that ideology, which forms the basis of their identity. The less flexible they are about adapting their ideological narratives to the realities and challenges of the time, the less protected they become from a possible collapse. The Yugoslav project-to an even larger extent than other Socialist projects in Europe-was based more on the notion of representing the ideal future than the not-so-ideal reality. In that sense, it was more ideological than representative. Its institutions were created primarily on ideological grounds and less on the necessity to represent the existing ones. This is one of the main reasons that the key institutions of the state and society (including those that appeared to be rather powerful, such as the army, secret police, and the Party) in fact looked more like a "tower of sand" once the ideology had collapsed.

Furthermore, ever since Yugoslavia's break with Stalinism in 1948, the very essence of Yugoslav political (and to some extent also national) identity was modeled in opposition not only to the liberal West, but also to the statist Socialism of the Soviet Union. Treating Soviet Socialism as revisionism, the Yugoslav (Kardeljist) interpretation of Marxism linked elements of the national tradition with a strict implementation of the Marxist notion of the withering away of the state. The new Yugoslav identity was therefore linked to a new and largely unique interpretation of Marxist ideology. The existence of the "Soviet Other" was soon to become (and to remain for the whole pre-Gorbachev period) one of the pillars of the new Yugoslav political identity. To be a good Yugoslav meant to be loyal to the ideology of Socialist self-management and nonalignment, both of which emerged as alternatives to Soviet Socialism. Subsequently, once the Soviet Other began to crumble, it carried with it the very essence of what it meant to be a good Yugoslav. Unlike other East European countries, whose elites followed ideological interpretations made by somebody else (the Soviet Communists), the Yugoslavs had no one but themselves to blame for the failure of their own project of Communism. Unlike, for example, the Polish or Hungarian anti-Communist movements, which were in their essence anti-Soviet but not anti-Polish or anti-Hungarian, anti-Communism in Yugoslavia was to a large extent organized in opposition to the concept of good Yugoslavism, as imagined by Yugoslav Communists.

Here we come to another unresolved paradox at the core of the Yugoslav ideological narrative. On one hand, the Yugoslav Communists could not have imagined any other form of Yugoslavism except one that was based on Socialist principles. At the same time, however, Communism was not nationalism and was not meant to construct a Yugoslav nation. On the contrary, Yugoslav Communists argued that any attempt to create a Yugoslav nation would be not only futile, but also ultimately undesirable. They argued that Communist Yugoslavia made sense only if it was no longer a prison of the nations. But where, exactly, is the border between a state that is unacceptable (a prison of the nations) and one that is viable and desirable? The arguing on this issue has never ceased throughout the existence of Yugoslav Socialism.

The manner in which Yugoslavia collapsed set the stage for what followed. In the antistatist ideological narrative of self-management, one may find the seeds of the later fascination with statehood by the anti-Communist movements and parties in the post-Yugoslav states. As opposed to self-management as an antistatist doctrine, the anti-Communist movements were often ultrastatist. As opposed to the antinationalism of the Yugoslav political elite in the last Communist period, they were often ultranationalist. The collapse of Communism and the emergence of nationalism were therefore not two separate lines of events. It was not that Communism collapsed because of nationalism or that nationalism emerged on the ruins of Communism. The relationship between the two was more complex: they always existed separately, yet they constructed themselves by reacting to one another. As a result, both doctrines (Communism and nationalism) in Yugoslav circumstances each contained elements of the other. Once the turning point took place in the late 1980s and early 1990s, only those who had disregarded the complexity of Yugoslav politics in its last 20 years were taken by extreme surprise. This is why I argue that it is impossible to understand what happened after 1990 without analyzing what happened before the collapse of Yugoslavia. Only within the existing political context can political events be understood, events that were the result of the long process I follow in this book. For this reason this book aims at underlining the importance of analyzing these events within their context.

It proposes that political change be analyzed by focusing on the political actors and their (subjective) perceptions of the (objective) factors that constitute the context in which they act. To explain political action, we need to take the actors and their beliefs, intentions, motives, and explanations seriously. Political actors, especially in Communist politics, do not simply act as representatives of various social groups (such as nations and classes); they also act (and even primarily) as representatives of their ideas and perceptions. To reconstruct their perceptions, the approach presented here relies on Quentin Skinner's (1988) proposals on how to analyze political action. As Skinner argues, one of the most frequent mistakes that political analysts are tempted to make is a result of analyzing past events from the comfortable position of the known outcomes of these events. Knowing that we cannot fully exclude personal attitudes or simple knowledge of what happened after the period analyzed in this book, we should nevertheless aim at analyzing the events as they happened in their own context, not in the context of their consequences. The main focus of this book is thus on the perceptions of the political actors and their reasons for action at the moment they acted, not what we or they today think they should or should not have done to achieve certain goals. The purpose of political analysis is not to condemn or justify, but to explain why the actors acted as they did. Not much more and no less. Personal judgments about how *sensible* their actions were are left to every reader. Having no universal grounds for condemning or justifying political actions, political analysts and historians should have no monopoly on judging them.

This objective thus dictates the book's methodological approach and the range of sources relied on. Since the archives for the period analyzed will remain inaccessible for at least a decade, we should rely on semiarchival sources, such as published and unpublished Party documents, minutes from Party and state leadership sessions, analyses of political events prepared for various sessions of party institutions, speeches by leading Yugoslav politicians, public statements, newspaper reports from sessions of the Central Committee and other Party institutions, interviews with members of the political elite conducted by journalists and published in the periods in which the actions had taken place, video-recorded minutes of Party meetings, and various other sources of reliable information.

A large proportion of this book relies on the memoirs and recollections of the leading members of the Yugoslav political elite in the 1974-90 period. Political leaders, especially in Serbia and Slovenia, have provided us with substantial help by publishing their speeches in the period analyzed and have given many interviews explaining their role.

As a journalist in the last period analyzed in this book, I interviewed some of the key participants in Yugoslav politics for various newspapers I had been writing for since 1984. My early career in journalism enabled me to attend many Party meetings, to collect minutes, and to have direct access to the main politicians. For this book, I used my personal archive along with the personal archives of dozens of politicians who kindly permitted access to their correspondence and other documents, such as the minutes of main debates conducted behind closed doors (some of which have not long ago been classified as state secrets). I also used notes in my diary, which I had occasionally taken to record my informal conversations with politicians, journalists, and other analysts of the events as they were unfolding.

Furthermore while working on this book I have conducted interviews with leading members of the Yugoslav political elite in the 1970s and 1980s. The transcripts of these interviews are almost equal in size to the book itself. The interviews I conducted have enabled me to cross-reference their statements with documents and other sources from the time when the events took place. Only with reference to archival documents and their own statements in the actual context (i.e., at the time of the action) do I use political actors' present recollections as relevant. Most of these sources are presented in footnotes as evidence for and illustration of my argument, which is stated in the main body of the work. Although somewhat longer than one would normally expect them to be, these footnotes make a substantial part of my argument. They also tend to guide the reader through the various streams of arguments presented throughout the book.

It is my hope that one day, when the archival sources are fully available, the actors' explanations of their own motives for certain actions will represent a valuable contribution toward an even more complete picture of Yugoslav politics in the last fifteen years preceding the disintegration of the state. Taking into account the nature of Communist regimes, in which many decisions were taken informally with no written trace to constitute evidence or a source for future historians, we can assume that the archival sources alone would be insufficient to map out the extreme complexity of intraelite relations. The reconstruction of the elite thinking would then perhaps prove to be not only an additional, but also an unavoidable, source of historical research.

Before moving to the main text of this book, I wish to present a few words about the use of some key concepts in the text. Based on the conclusion that to reach our goal accurately and effectively we should always approach the political actors themselves, their way of thinking and their motives, the book uses certain key concepts in the meanings they shared, not in the ones we would share today, in a different ideological and temporal context. What is necessary is to explain the reasons for action as seen by those who acted in certain ways. We can never do so if we simply dismiss their way of thinking as irrational, incorrect, and therefore illogical. On the contrary, only if we approach the actors' way of thinking as closely as possible will we be able to explain their reasons for their own actions. This is why I do not attempt to correct Yugoslav political leaders when they use certain concepts in ways different from how most readers (or indeed the author) would normally use them today. We should, however, be aware of the differences in regard to the main concepts. A detailed exposition of the key concepts used by Yugoslav Communists is developed in chapter two, in which the Kardelj constitutive concept is analyzed. I shall therefore limit my explanation here to only a few key concepts in order to prevent initial confusion.

In the Yugoslav Communist vocabulary, for example, the word *nation* (nacija, narod) signified the *constitutive nations* (konstitutivne nacije) of Yugoslavia (Serbs, Croats, Slovenes, Muslims, Montenegrins, and Macedonians). *Nationality* (narodnost) was a term used to describe the special status of the Albanians, Hungarians, and other *nonconstitutive nations* to distinguish them from *nations* and from *national minorities* (nacionalne manjine), as they were previously named. The Yugoslav state is often referred to as a *federation*, since the word *federative* was in its name since 1943. However, one may notice that in the period I here analyze, Kardelj's conclusion that Yugoslavia was neither a classic federation nor a classic confederation was accepted by all political leaders. The word *state* (država) and concept of *statism* (etatizam) were used with negative connotations, as something opposed to *self-management* (samoupravljanje). A *statist* (etatist) was an enemy of self-management. Among other words used as labels of anti-Socialist behavior were *bureaucracy* (birokracija), *nationalism* (nacionalizam), *liberalism* (liberalizam), *techomanagerialism* (tehno-menadžerizam), and (as perhaps the most dismissive) *counterrevolution* (kontrarevolucija). Since Yugoslav self-management was opposed to Soviet *state-Socialism* and interwar Yugoslav unitarism, words such as *unitarism* (unitarizam), *hegemonism* (hegemonizam), *centralism* (centralizam), *Great-State tendencies* (veliko-državne tendencije), *Greater-Serbian domination* (veliko-srpska dominacija), and *Stalinism* (staljinizam) were also high on the list of political disqualifications.

The Yugoslav politicians, like those of other East European countries, named their political system *Socialist*, but often emphasized that their Socialism was not statist, but *self-managing* (samoupravni socijalizam). The word *Communism* (komunizam) was used rarely and only when related to the Party, which was in 1952 renamed the *League of Communists* (Savez komunista, SK) to emphasize both its roots in Marx's ideas and a difference with the Communist Party of the Soviet Union. Although the state was *Socialist*, the party was *Communist*, because it was representative of the future of society (i.e., full Communism), not of its present. Communism remained a goal of the Party's activities. Real Communism, at least at a symbolic level, existed only within the Party: its members addressed one another as equal regardless of their ranks and positions. Even with Tito, they used the familiar *Ti*, rather than the formal *Vi*, emphasizing that one day, when Communism came, this perfect equality would be extended to the whole of society. The Party was a *vanguard* (avangarda), and its members were *morally and politically suited* (moralno-politički podobni) to educate others and guide society toward Communism. Although the earlier phrase *people of a special mold* (ljudi posebna kova) was not used in the period analyzed here, the Party members were the *politically conscious* (politički svjestan) part of society. The Party itself (together with four other official organizations: the Socialist Alliance of Working People; the Alliance of Socialist Youth; the Union of Fighters of the National-Liberation Struggle; the Alliance of Trade Unions) was the *subjective force* (subjektivna snaga) of society. By definition, to be a member of the Party meant not only to be admitted to a privileged club of those who are conscious and suitable to educate and lead others, but also to be recognized as a subject (i.e., an active element), rather than an object of practical politics. Thus on the other hand, expulsion from the Party meant not only that such privileges would be lost, but also that the person being expelled would be demoted to object, from subject. He or she would be publicly stripped of recognition of being conscious and suitable and would therefore be humiliated and excluded from public life. The Socialist societies (including Yugoslavia) were divided between those *included* and those *excluded* from politics more or less along the lines of Party membership.

In the vocabulary of Yugoslav Socialism, the word *ideology* was used mostly with a negative connotation, as *false consciousness* (lažna svijest). The Party was not professing an ideology, but a *scientific world view* (znanstveni pogled na svijet). Marxism was not ideology either; it was *scientific Socialism* (znanstveni socijalizam). Instead of being called *ideological*, Party commissions in charge of ideology were named *ideopolitical commissions* (idejno-političke komisije). Terms like *commissars* were also avoided as being too closely reminiscent of Soviet practice. In the army, the *commissars* were replaced by *officers for ideopolitical education*. In the state structure, neither *commissars* nor *ministers* were used. The *federal* (*republican, provincial*) *secretaries* were members not of *government,* but of the *executive councils.*

The construction of a new reality (as Socialism defined its objective) demanded the replacement of old terms linked to the existence of the state with new ones that belonged to the *self-management* glossary. Some of these words are almost impossible to translate into any West European language, since they were invented to describe institutions uniquely linked to a new form of social organization. Terms such as the *basic organization of associated labor* (BOAL or OOUR in Serbian/Croatian) and *self-managing community of interests* (SIZ) soon became trademarks of Yugoslav antistatist Socialism. The term *nationalism* was used as a synonym for *separatism* and *chauvinism*, and *unitarism* meant Yugoslav state-nationalism, a doctrine and practice that denied the federal character of Yugoslavia and/or the existence of its constitutive nations and their republics (states). In the official vocabulary of Yugoslav Socialism, *nationalism* and *unitarism* were anti-Socialist practices/doctrines and were thus to be defeated. Although in public rhetoric all nationalisms were treated as equally dangerous, in intraparty debates the nationalisms of the largest nations (in particular the Serbs and the Croats) were treated as more dangerous than others. Furthermore, Serb nationalism was somehow *naturally* identified as the closest possible ally of *uni-*

tarism and a potential ally of Soviet hegemonism and was therefore considered to be the most dangerous. Unless it is obvious from the context or explicitly stated, these terms are used here in their original meaning, i.e., as they were used by the Yugoslav political elite.

In this text I introduce several new concepts that need to be explained here. By *constitutive concept* I mean a set of ideas and beliefs about the nature of the state on which a basic consensus is created within the (ruling) political elite, which forms a more or less internally consistent whole that is then transformed into political and legislative action. As explained in chapter two, I identify four major *constitutive concepts* in the whole period of Yugoslavia (1918-92), the last of which (here called the *fourth*, or the *Kardelj* concept) is the main object of my analysis. The *constitutive concept* is a term that links ideology (here Marxism), its dominant interpretation (in this case Kardelj's interpretation), with the main initiatives by which the political elite attempted to implement it through legislation (the 1974 Constitution) and political action. The *constitutive concept* therefore forms a linkage between ideology and practice: it is a means of the transformation of ideology into legal regulation and political action. The formulation of the *constitutive concept* occupies a central place in the politics of highly ideological societies. As Socialist Yugoslavia illustrates, major political conflicts took the form of constitutional debates. In highly ideological societies, the wording of social aims is the main substance of politics. Yugoslav domestic politics were almost exclusively organized around constant constitutional debate, which resulted in four constitutions (1946, 1953, 1963, and 1974) in the four decades of its existence, and in a decade and a half, i.e., in the period analyzed here (1974-1989), it was in a permanent process of reforming the last constitution. Such a situation of permanent reforms and changes in the constitution was primarily an expression of the belief that Socialism is a transitional period in which institutions and political culture are in permanent transition from their old, pre-Socialist forms toward new Communist ones. Although constitutional changes were not independent of the pressures placed on political leaders by internal and external political factors, they were initiated from within the elite to further push *reality* toward *Communist* ideals. The changes of the period analyzed here were therefore not only a pragmatic response to the existing challenges that the elite faced from within and from outside the country but also an effort to further improve the Socialist character of Yugoslavia.

This book is about political elites, and thus the meaning of this term should also be explained. In Socialist societies it is sometimes difficult to identify the members of the elite, since politics often take place as informal activities, and the criteria for inclusion in or exclusion from the real decision-making processes are very different from those established in representative democracies. By elites, I refer to the not-very-strictly structured body of Party, state, and military leaders who have real influence over the formulation and implementation of political decisions in Yugoslavia. For the entire period from 1945 to 1980, Josip Broz Tito was the key member of the Yugoslav political elite. After the dismissal of Tito's deputy, Aleksandar Ranković (1966), and until his death in 1979, Edvard Kardelj was clearly the main creator of the *constitutive concept* expressed in the 1974 Constitution and the political action that followed it. In this period, the leaders of the republics and provinces increased their influence, playing a much more independent role than ever. After 1974, the influence of the army in Yugoslav politics also increased. On the other hand, the importance of state functionaries, such as the head of the Yugoslav government, the various state secretaries (except those directly linked with Tito), and even the members of the Yugoslav Central Committee (except its presidency, which represented their republican/provincial organizations) decreased. In the post-Titoist period, as explained in chapter four, the Yugoslav government unsuccessfully tried to occupy the central locus of power, but it was the Party that remained the most important institution until its actual disintegration in January 1990. The main political conflicts in Yugoslavia were intra-Party conflicts. Finally, the disintegration of the Party led directly to the disintegration of the state. By the political elite here, therefore, I refer to the inner circle of the Yugoslav leadership, whose core was the Party leadership at the federal level and in the republics and provinces.

Lastly, the structure of the book follows its main objective. In chapter one I analyze the current attempts to explain the disintegration of Yugoslavia, relating my analysis to their main conclusions. I identify eight different sets of explanations, seven of which (with the exception of the ethnic hatred argument) are helpful to our understanding of the problem.

The core of this book is structured in three parts, each containing two chapters. The first part (chapters two and three) analyze the rise; the second part (chapters four and five), the crisis; and the third (chapters six and seven) focuses on the decay and fall of the Fourth Yugoslavia.

Chapter two explains the main elements of the Kardelj concept, which was in constitutional terms formulated during the constitutional debate of 1967-74. This concept was to a large extent a genuine attempt to accommodate the differences between the various segments of the elite within a system that would still remain Socialist in its character. This chapter analyzes the main aspects of Kardelj's concept in detail, and chapter three examines the reasons why his concept was accepted by various groups in Yugoslavia, and especially by the Serbian leadership. The *Fourth Yugoslavia*, just like the three previous constitutive concepts, was a complex compromise between the various segments of its political elite. I argue that the *constitutive concept* was the result of complex negotiations among those *included* in real politics, i.e., the members of the political elite.

Chapters four (on economic crisis) and five (on political crisis) examine the political actions taken to implement the constitutive concept agreed on in the 1967-74 constitutional debate. In these two chapters, politics as the struggle for the *real meaning* of Kardelj's concept is analyzed in detail. During the period 1974-86 Yugoslav politicians interpreted the text of the constitution and the intentions of its authors in such different ways that the fragile compromise reached in 1974 became seriously endangered. It was also in this period that the *supreme arbiters* (Tito and Kardelj) died, leaving Yugoslavia to its divided regional elites. The context in which the constitution was to be implemented was gradually becoming very different from the one in which it was agreed on. The *objective factors* had changed as a result of economic crisis, foreign involvement, and the first signs of organized opposition to the regime.

Chapters six and seven analyze the emergence of alternative constitutive concepts in Serbia and Slovenia in the last four years of Yugoslavia (1986-90), and the reaction of the political elite to this. The division of the elite into "defenders" and "reformers" of the constitution polarized the Yugoslav political elite, whose Slovenian and Serbian parts moved closer to their electoral constituencies. At the end of this process, Kardelj's concept of Yugoslavia, terminally wounded by the disintegration of the LCY (League of Communists of Yugoslavia) in January 1990, ceased to exist. Many participants in Yugoslav politics, ousted in the mid-1960s for their opposition to Kardelj's concept, now came back, playing a significant role in Yugoslavia's overthrow. Detailed analyses of Slovenian and Serbian nationalism and of other alternative concepts (such as *civil society* in Slovenia and *antibureaucratic revolution* in Serbia) may be found in these two last chapters of the book.

The structure of the book in its main lines follows the central message: the disintegration of Yugoslavia should be analyzed through the interaction between the constitutive concept and the context in which it was implemented.

CHAPTER ONE

Analytical Approaches to Studying the Disintegration of Yugoslavia

1.1. A Critical Assessment of Existing Approaches in Analyzing the Disintegration of Yugoslavia

Why did Yugoslavia collapse? Was its disintegration unavoidable? Was it the result of impersonal (objective) factors such as economic crises, social cleavages, complex ethnic structure, changes in the international environment, or processes of modernization and globalization? Or was the collapse of Yugoslavia primarily the outcome of actions taken by political elites in Yugoslavia itself, thus of personal (subjective) decisions, beliefs, and intentions? And if it were, what were these beliefs and intentions? How did they emerge, and why did they prevail over the forces of integration?

Broadly, recent literature on this subject identifies eight major types of arguments on the reasons for the collapse of Yugoslavia: (1) the economic argument; (2) the ancient ethnic hatred argument; (3) the nationalism argument; (4) the cultural argument; (5) the international politics argument; (6) the role of personality argument, (7) the fall of the Empires argument, and (8) the constitutional and institutional reasons argument. With the exception of the *ethnic hatred* argument, which in this book is rejected in its entirety, all other approaches offer useful elements for explaining the reasons for the disintegration of Yugoslavia. However, they sometimes tend to reduce its complexity to a single cause. They also often neglect the subjective, the perceptions of the relevant political actors, and their beliefs and stories they tell about themselves and others. Sometimes they fail to take ideology seriously, that is, the complex system of beliefs and ideas that influenced the Yugoslav political elite so much. The disintegration of Yugoslavia had many causes, not just one. Among them, the commitment of the Yugoslav political elite to the Marxist ideological tenet of the withering away of the state throughout the existence of the Socialist Yugoslav Federation-and especially in its last twenty years before the collapse-has been among the most significant. However, in the existing literature this has been a somewhat underestimated factor. Only by analyzing the relationship between beliefs developed by the relevant political actors and their actions can we understand the events that followed. In Socialist Yugoslavia, ideology was not an empty word, a ritual in which nobody believed. It was the main motivator of political action. After the break with the USSR in 1948, the Yugoslav political elite did not simply paste and copy Soviet models when imagining and constructing Yugoslav identity and the institutional structure of the new Socialist Yugoslav state. The elite indeed followed Marxism, but the way they interpreted its meaning was to a large extent authentic. Yugoslavia was constructed as a Socialist state, but the meaning of both Socialism and state differed from the one promoted by the USSR and its closest allies in Eastern Europe. Yugoslavia perceived itself as a Socialist state, but its Socialism was not meant to be statist.[1] The notion of self-management, promoted by its elite in the aftermath of the 1948 conflict with the USSR, was a fundamental element of the new Yugoslavia's identity. It was at the core of political action for the remaining 40 years before Yugoslavia collapsed (in 1991). Because of the authenticity of this interpretation and because of the unattractiveness of its alternative (Soviet Socialism), the Yugoslav ideology was seen by many-both within the country and abroad-as an attractive alternative to both the capitalist liberalism of the West and the statist Socialism of the East. Because of its ideological alternative to both East and West, Yugoslav self-managing Socialism presented itself as a third way, a possible compromise in an ideologically and politically divided world.

However, its consequences in real political life were ambiguous. On one hand, Yugoslav ideology was accepted as a better alternative to East European Socialism (Doder 1977), but on the other it contributed to a weakening of institutions and of the legal system, which in turn increased the sense of insecurity and the fear of chaos among a large segment of the population. The last years of Yugoslav Socialism, when the concept of antistatist (self-managing) Socialism was promoted almost as the single source of Yugoslav identity, were also the years of chaos, fears, and anarchy. Yugoslavia as a state was withering away at the moment when many wanted protection from the possibility of a "war of all against all" in a nonstate situation. In statists such as Milošević, Kučan, and Tudjman, many found a response to their worries and hopes for protection.

This book introduces ideology as a serious, perhaps crucial, factor among those already mentioned in various debates as the reasons for the collapse of Socialist Yugoslavia.[2] It argues that this collapse cannot be explained without reference to the Marxist concept of withering away of the state, which the Yugoslav political elite implemented, paradoxically, with some success. Although other elements contributed very significantly to the process of the disintegration of Yugoslavia, its collapse in the first place was not the result of some ancient hatreds or of international conspiracies and interventions, or even economic crisis and disputes over the leadership. The collapse of Yugoslavia was primarily a logical, though perhaps unintended, consequence of political actions taken by its elite, and these actions were largely based on the ideology of a withering away of the state. It would be unfair to say that any of the main political leaders of the Communist period deliberately aimed at dividing Yugoslavia into several separate nation-states. But by remaining committed to ideology, which had in its heart the concept of a withering away of the state, they decisively contributed to its weakness, and ultimately to its inability to respond to challenges it faced in a new, post-1989 world. Yugoslavia was not destroyed from the outside, and it did not collapse as a result of internal ethnodemographic complexities. Although the change in the outside world and the reemergence of ethnic nationalism (including even its most extreme and violent forms) contributed to its collapse, these contributions emerged more as a consequence of the weakness of the Socialist project and of the state than as a cause of this weakness.

Before I develop this argument further, I will first discuss other existing explanations, relating them to my own argument.

1.1.1. The Economic Argument

The economic argument is based on the assumption that the economic crisis that occurred in the late 1970s and the widening gap between the developed and underdeveloped regions (republics and provinces) made the further existence of Yugoslavia impossible. The most developed republics, such as Slovenia and Croatia, demanded independence for reasons of their further development. They also opposed attempts to limit the achieved level of economic autonomy, as provided by the 1974 Constitutional compromise. The economic theory is based on the assumption that political decisions are influenced by the interests of political participants, which are primarily economic. Kosovo and Slovenia, although being at the two opposite poles on the scale of economic development, both came to the point of seeing no incentive to remain further in Yugoslavia. In 1987, for the first time, Slovenian public opinion indicated that Slovenia would have better economic chances outside of Yugoslavia than within it (Toš 1987). Kosovo, however, saw no economic benefits to remaining any longer in Yugoslavia when its GDP, though permanently increasing in absolute terms, when measured per capita had fallen to 26 percent, from 47 percent, of the Yugoslav average in the postwar period.[3] The cases of Slovenia and Kosovo, the most- and least-developed constitutive units of Yugoslavia, indicate the relevance of the "separatism of the extreme" explanations.

One may indeed accept that economic factors played a significant role in creating the context to which the narratives of political leaders were forced to respond. As Woodward (1996) argues, the economic crisis in the late 1970s and early 1980s triggered constitutional conflict, which resulted in the crisis of the state itself. I follow this chain of events by analyzing the response of the political elite to the economic crisis (chapter four) and constitutional issues (chapter five) to arrive at an analysis of the emergence of alternative political concepts in Serbia and Slovenia (chapters six and seven). Yet the question remains: was the economic crisis in itself sufficient to destroy Yugoslavia? Despite its severe economic difficulties, Yugoslavia was still the most prosperous country among all European Communist states and was by no means entirely unsuccessful in economic development. Furthermore, as Bojičić argues, "the intensity of collapse in the Yugoslav region does not follow from the scale of the economic and political troubles in which they found themselves at the end of the 1980s (1996:77). Contrary to the arguments of the economic-based explanations of the collapse, Yugoslavia in fact disintegrated at the moment when the economic reforms of Ante Marković's government were showing their first positive results, accompanied by the elimination of inflation and a sharp increase in the personal income of Yugoslav citizens.[4] As Pleština points out, the resignation of an ineffective government in December 1988 and the selection of the new market-oriented prime minister, Ante Marković, in January 1989 were signs of hope for the future of Yugoslavia, rather than of its collapse:

> The inflation rate, which for the month of December [1989] had climbed to 56 percent, had by the end of January [1990] fallen to 17.3 percent; by February it was down to 8.4 percent, by March to 2.4 percent, and for April it registered only 0.2 percent. Foreign-currency reserves, which at US$5.4 billion in December [1989], were strong enough to permit the convertibility of the dinar, had increased by January [1990] to US$6.5 billion and by May [1990] to US$8.5 billion. Industrial productivity has also increased, and foreign loans have been secured to aid the restructuring of the economy.... Marković has managed to galvanize a degree of support and energy after a decade characterized by cynicism and apathy. (Pleština 1992:166)

At that time political reforms were also gaining momentum. Freedom of expression and also the possibility of independence from the state in economic and political terms were rising, not falling. Yet what seemed to be "hopeful like a new beginning was but a very brief lull before the proverbial storm" (Pleština

1992:155). It was at this moment, when the first hopes for a democratic and economically stable society emerged, that the state collapsed. The economic argument has failed to explain this paradox.

As will be argued in chapter three, the political reforms of the federation in the 1967-74 period were even less motivated by economic failure. On the contrary, to a large extent they were encouraged by economic success, which promoted Yugoslav self-management as a possible alternative to both state Socialism of the Soviet type and capitalist societies, which both faced deep crises in 1968. In the same way, the economic factor played no main role in the last phase of negotiations about the future of the country, when the three main leaders of the Yugoslav republics (Milan Kučan, Slovenia; Franjo Tudjman, Croatia; and Slobodan Milošević, Serbia) declined an unofficial offer by the European Community to find a political compromise in return for substantial economic support.[5] In terms of modernization, despite the significant setback of economic and political crises, Socialist Yugoslavia was not a disastrous failure and did not have to collapse. Thus while one should not deny the importance of economic factors in the disintegration of Yugoslavia, we should also notice that this importance is not per se, but indirect. An economic crisis triggered debates and exposed problems of the Yugoslav Socialist ideology: its failure to deliver what had been promised. It also provided a context in which arguments on exploitation and injustice within Yugoslavia could occur. The failure of Yugoslav Socialism to close the gap between those most and those least developed in the country undermined the main claim of Socialism, that there cannot be political equality without economic equality. The sense of inequality (and of injustice) was thus strongest in Kosovo, the least developed region of Yugoslavia. Many Kosovars consequently turned toward Enver Hoxha's radical egalitarianism, which attracted them not only (and perhaps not primarily) for its ethnic dimension, but also (and perhaps primarily) for the notion of equality.[6] The same notion (of inequality and injustice) was then shared by others in Yugoslavia, resulting in economic nationalism in Slovenia and Croatia, and also elsewhere. The failure of Socialism to deliver on its main promise-economic equality and social justice-served as fertile ground for alternative ideologies. Soon, everyone in Yugoslavia was claiming to be disadvantaged and that somebody else was privileged. The economic element truly played an important role in generating demands for changes from within both the political elite and the population. However, economic reductionism can never explain political phenomena completely because it leaves out the human element, i.e., the perceptions and actions of political actors. It was only when and only because it undermined the narrative the Yugoslavs used to tell about themselves that the economic factors became important.

1.1.2. The Ancient Ethnic Hatred Argument

The argument often referred to as the ancient ethnic hatred argument is very popular in debates that are not strictly academic, such as those found in the media[7] and with politicians, soldiers,[8] writers,[9] and others. It is perhaps best summarized by former U.S. President Bill Clinton, who justified military intervention against the FR Yugoslavia (March – June 1999) when saying this:

> Under Communist rule, such nations projected a picture of stability, but it was a false stability imposed by rulers whose answer to ethnic tensions was to suppress and deny them. When Communist repression lifted, the tensions rose to the surface to be resolved by cooperation or exploited by demagoguery.[10]

This book strongly rejects the ethnic hatred argument in any form. The Yugoslav conflict, I argue, did not begin as an ethnic conflict. Ethnic hatred was not ancient and ever-existent, but it had to be created before what started very far from the level occupied by the average citizen of any of the nationalities was transformed into an ethnic war.[11] Although the lack of openly expressed nationalist views in the first part of the period I analyze here was certainly the result of tight control of the media by the elite, it is still not accurate to say that Yugoslavia was held together by a brutal political dictatorship or by pure suppression of national sentiments.[12] But once the constitutive concept of the Fourth Yugoslavia started to disintegrate, there was a tendency (initiated primarily by nationalist groups within both the intellectual elite and the population) to revert to stereotypes and behavior characteristics of an earlier period, i.e., World War II and before. Once the previous "others" to which the elite referred (such as class enemies within the country and both East and West outside the country) disappeared as a realistic danger, new "others" had to be invented.

As numerous public opinion surveys conducted in the last years of the 1980s demonstrate (analyzed in the last two chapters of this book), political protests in Serbia and Slovenia were in their first phase primarily concerned with injustice and the bureaucratization of the political elite. But the elite successfully redirected these protests against new "others."[13] The Serb demonstrators were worried about the disintegration of the country, for which "the others" (such as Slovenes, Croats, and various international institutions) were made responsible. The Slovenian intellectual elite and media also argued that "the others" were responsible for greater-Serbian expansionist demands, for the economic exploitation of Slovenia, and for the unitarist suppression of the national identity of the Slovenes.[14] By redirecting popular protests toward the others, the political elites in Serbia and Slovenia survived at the cost of undermining Yugoslavia. In other republics, in which political elites of the late 1980s refused to do the same-primarily in Croatia and Bosnia-Herzegovina-they found themselves defeated by newly emerged nationalist parties.

The hatred to which the supporters of the ethnic hatred argument refer was not ancient. Indeed, it had emerged in the course of the Yugoslav wars of succession, i.e., after the breakup of Yugoslavia. As an explanation of the actual disintegration of Yugoslavia, it is as irrelevant as it is inaccurate. Moreover, the argument that the Yugoslavs have always hated one another serves as a convenient alibi for those who disturbed stability and peace in this country. If various ethnic groups in Yugoslavia have always hated each other, then it was inevitable for this country to disintegrate. If something were inevitable, political leaders were then in fact powerless to prevent it and thus should not be held responsible for the consequences of the breakup. Therefore such an interpretation is rather convenient for political leaders of the post-Communist period who are keen to blame other people, but not themselves, for the violent character of the breakup.

At the same time, however, we should avoid an argument to the contrary-that the Yugoslavs lived in perfect harmony with one another, in a situation of some imaginary "ancient ethnic love." Although unburdened with moral issues related to an attempt to avoid responsibility for violence in the aftermath of the breakup, this interpretation is also naïve and highly misleading.

1.1.3. The Nationalism Argument

Although popular in current debates, the ancient ethnic hatred argument can easily be dismissed as inadequate. Nevertheless, it is certainly more difficult to object to the nationalism argument, widely present in academic debates on the disintegration of Yugoslavia. Nationalism, here defined as the primacy of the national interest over any other interest in political activities and as a doctrine that at its core has the creation of a nation-state, as homogeneous as possible, does not always develop into ethnic hatred-or even animosities-toward the other. Although ethnic hatred between Yugoslav nations did not exist to any greater extent than might be seen within other multiethnic states, nationalism was always present as a political doctrine in its many forms. As Djilas (1995) argues, nationalism in Yugoslavia was stronger than liberalism, and thus was the main alternative after the fall of Communism. Occasionally, such as in the 1967-72 period with the Croatian crisis, or, as Burg calls it, the Yugoslav crisis, or with the 1968 and 1981 protests in Kosovo, nationalist doctrines and actions caused ethnic tensions and an instability of the country. However, it is difficult to accept the somewhat *fatalistic* conclusion that nationalism and hatred had to prevail over other doctrines once Communism was defeated. Along the lines of many other authors, I argue that in its most dangerous form in which it emerged in the late 1980s, nationalism was created by the intellectual elites and then adopted as an alternative ideology-often blended with elements of other ideologies, both liberal and nonliberal-by certain segments of the political elite, primarily in Serbia and Slovenia.

The causes of nationalism in Yugoslavia were indeed many: historical, economic, and cultural differences being among the most important. Yet in the period analyzed, it was the ideological narrative that made the nationalism of Yugoslav nations (including that of the Kosovo Albanians) both weak and strong at the same time. The weakness of Yugoslav nationalism in the period we analyze in this book (the Kardelj period) was the result of the antistatist ideology on which Yugoslavia was restructured following its 1974 Constitution.[15]

Kardelj's concept (explained in chapter two) projected self-management as an alternative to the state. More than other Socialist states, the Yugoslav state was, at least at an ideological level, in the process of withering away. The antistatist rhetoric had enormous consequences for the (de)construction of Yugoslav institutions and of Yugoslav high culture (to use Gellner's term). The complex system based on Kardelj's antistatist ideology made Yugoslavia economically and politically atomized. It prevented fast and decisive responses to economic and political crises when they appeared in the early 1980s.[16]

In real terms, however, Yugoslavia remained nevertheless united by its ideological narrative, formulated by Kardelj and accepted by other members of the political elite. It was Kardelj's narrative, not the ethnic similarities among the Yugoslavs (South Slavs) or the political equality of its citizens that the elite saw as the glue that bound Yugoslav differences into a whole. Paradoxically, therefore, the Yugoslav state itself was based on an antistate ideological conception. This paradox is one source of the Yugoslav state's crisis in post-1974 Yugoslavia.

By treating Yugoslav constitutive nations as completed (as Kardelj formulated it in 1970) and their republics as sovereign states (as formulated in the 1974 Constitution), the ideological narrative of Yugoslav Communism in practice-and perhaps unintentionally-shielded and promoted nationalism in its constitutive nations. At the same time that Yugoslav nationalism and the Yugoslav state were being weakened, the nationalism of the constitutive nations was getting stronger. The same concept that had kept Yugoslavia together by consensus between its leaders held in itself also a destructive and disintegrative potential. This trend was in fact also the result of the Kardelj concept, which was constructed as a radical alternative to both interwar Yugoslav *unitarism* and Soviet *statist centralism*. Being based on a fragile political compromise between segments of the elite, the stability of the Yugoslav state depended heavily on the interpretation of the real meaning of this concept rather than on formal procedural rules and effective representative institutions.

Besides this, by promoting a nonethnic base for Yugoslav unity, the elite made nationalism the main rhetorical antipode to the dominant ideology of the regime. During the same time, by naming many who opposed the regime nationalists, the regime in fact promoted such nationalism as the main alternative to itself. By excluding it from the public sphere, Kardeljists both weakened it in public and made it stronger underground. The weakening of the state made nationalist demands for a strong state plausible (whether Yugoslavia or separate nation-states of constitutive nations). This is how one can explain why nationalism (and not, for example, the liberalism of the minimal state) grew as the main alternative to the self-managing system. Contrary to popular interpretations that link the existence of strong states run by Communists with people's demands for strong (nationalist) states after Communism, this book argues that it was the weakness of the state that provoked calls for an alternative. Post-Communism (as anti-Communism) was about establishing the state that had been missing, not about preserving one that already existed. In the case of ethnically more homogeneous Socialist states, such as Hungary and Poland, the 1989 revolution meant establishing themselves as states by means of liberation from Soviet tutelage. While the Hungarians and Poles perceived the Soviet Union as the main obstacle to creating a proper state, the new narratives developed after the fall of Communism among the Croats, Slovenes, and Albanians in Kosovo perceived Belgrade as this obstacle. Paradoxically, Yugoslav independence from Moscow thus proved to be a disadvantage for preserving the country's unity, since there was no possibility of blaming an external power for the crisis.

The demand to establish a proper state that did not exist (because of the semianarchic character of self-managing society) was what the nations and nationalities in Yugoslavia shared. Of course they disagreed fundamentally about whom this/these new state(s) should belong to and where their borders should be drawn. At the end of the 1980s, public protest, in its new form of overt nationalism, was a result of the country's democratization. The minority rights of the Kosovo Serbs and Montenegrins united the democratic and nationalist segments of the Belgrade opposition, the strongest opposition in the country. The elite was confronted by massive protests by the Kosovo Serbs and Montenegrins, and also by public demands for political reforms from the Slovenian and Serbian critical intelligentsia. At this time, Slovenian public opinion was united by the fear that their status as a constitutive nation would be downgraded to a minority. These fears stemmed from the consequences of the country's democratization, which demanded a new set of rules and a new constitutive concept for Yugoslavia. Political leaders in Slovenia and Serbia decided not to use force against the demonstrators and intellectuals, but to accommodate their demands. Despite their originally antinationalist intentions, this is how they became tolerant of nationalism, causing a split in the LCY (League of Communists of Yugoslavia) and the Yugoslav state. Although neither Milan Kučan nor Slobodan Milošević were originally ethnic nationalists, their political pragmatism and the context in which they acted led them to act like "someone who has jumped onto the tiger of nationalism and is finding it difficult to get off again without the tiger eating him" (Owen 1995:129).

But it did not need to happen this way. For as long as they remained committed to the Kardeljist concept, political leaders in Yugoslavia rejected coalition with ethnic nationalists and sought an intraparty compromise. They even hesitated to criticize the members of the elite in other ethnic groups and republics. Once this rule was abandoned, another set of rules had to be invented to keep Yugoslavia united. But it was difficult, if not impossible, in circumstances in which the political elite developed entirely different notions of democracy and of the political unit to which it should be applied.

What the nationalism argument fails to explain is the growing sense of Yugoslavism among the population at the time ethnic nationalism was increasing. The two parallel processes that characterized the period are analyzed here: (1) the (re)emergence of a Yugoslav culture[17] and the first demands to establish institutions of representative democracy, which were likely to result in the creation of a Yugoslav political nation; (2) the reaction of ethnic nationalists to this. The struggle between the forces of integration and those of polarization was what the Yugoslavs increasingly witnessed as the 1980s wound to a close. This new Yugoslavism was above all a reaction against the accelerating trend in favor of fragmentation in the last 20-30 years of Yugoslavia. A Yugoslav culture was emerging in the younger and more educated generation.[18] A direct result of this was a significant growth of declared ethnic Yugoslavs in the decade from 1971 to 1981: from 273,000 to 1,219,000. The share of Yugoslavs in the total population in this decade increased to 5.4 percent, from 1.3 percent, but the share of all constitutive nations (except Bosnian Muslims) decreased: for example, Serbs to 36.3 percent, from 39.7 percent; Croats to 19.8 percent, from 22.1 percent; Slovenes to 7.8 percent, from 8.2 percent. The Croatian historian and politician Dušan Bilandžić estimated that the share of the Yugoslavs would further increase in the 1981-91 decade to approximately a fifth of the total population, a trend that displeased and worried ethnic nationalists in all the Yugoslav nations.[19] The realistic chance of Yugoslavia soon becoming a member of the EEC, in which case national identities would have found themselves under two supranational lids (Yugoslav and European), additionally augmented the sense of danger among the ethnic nationalists.[20] In its essence, the nationalism that emerged in various Yugoslav countries was largely antiurban,[21] anti-European, and to a certain extent motivated by romantic and antirationalistic ideas. It was based on fears (primarily among the intellectual and political elites) that the status of their ethnic groups would be decreased from one of completed constitutive nations (as recognized by the 1974 Constitution) to one of a minority in the new democratic structure of the country.[22] Consequently, the nation-states were seen not only as desirable, but as a necessary protector against this trend.

Although it correctly points out the importance of nationalism for the disintegration of Yugoslavia, the nationalism argument often overlooks the ambivalent relations between Communism and nationalism. It also tends to underestimate the complexity of the situation in which members of the political elite found themselves in the late 1980s. Lastly, it neglects the importance of personal beliefs and perceptions by the elite and the population. Arguing that it has always been present, only somewhat frozen during the Socialist era, the nationalism argument denies the importance of the subjective. By not taking into account the context in which nationalism reemerged as an alternative to antistatism under the circumstances of a weak state and high uncertainty, this argument fails to explain why nationalism became an attractive alternative to so many people throughout Yugoslavia.

1.1.4. The Cultural Argument

The cultural argument on the disintegration of Yugoslavia is an applied and broader version of the ethnic argument. In various attempts to explain the collapse of Yugoslavia, it has been argued that the diversities of the traditions and cultures of the Yugoslav nations (based on the ancient divisions between Eastern and Western Christianity, and also between Christianity and Islam) played the major role in the failure to constitute a Yugoslav culture, nation, and state. The argument relies on John Stuart Mill's discussion of nationality in his *Considerations on Representative Government* (1865). Representative government, Mill argues, is best established on "the sentiment of nationality," whose existence is "a prima facie case for uniting all the members of the nationality under the same government, and a government to themselves apart." Thus cultural diversities (primarily religious and linguistic differences) made nations and promoted members' desires to live separately from others in their own states. Cultural, religious, economic, linguistic, and historical differences among the Yugoslav nations were simply too large to allow the creation of a Yugoslav nation, which permanently destabilized the Yugoslav state. Fragmentation of the country was thus inevitable and somehow natural.[23]

In its recently most famous version, the cultural argument has reappeared in Samuel P. Huntington's *Clash of Civilizations* thesis. Although his book focuses on international politics after the end of the Cold War, it was much used by nationalist politicians in the post-Yugoslav states (especially by Croatian President Franjo Tudjman)[24] to legitimize and justify not only the breakup of Yugoslavia, but also the conflicts between Christians (Orthodox and Catholic) and Muslims in Bosnia-Herzegovina. [25] It has also been used to explain tensions between Serbs and (predominantly Muslim) Albanians in Kosovo.

Even if we were to accept this argument, we would not have immediately explained to us why the Yugoslav mosaic of diversities survived for at least 45 years after World War II, only to collapse so suddenly after the Cold War when cultural diversities in the world, including in Yugoslavia, were decreasing, rather than increasing. Yet the cultural argument proves to be closer to the main thesis of this book than many other approaches. The book examines the breakdown of the ideological consensus within the Yugoslav political elites. Ideologies are part of what can be broadly called culture. In the current literature on the subject, the importance of people's beliefs, which were largely created by opinion makers and ideologues, is largely underestimated.

A different type of example that relies on cultural factors in explaining the collapse of Yugoslavia is Andrew Wachtel's study of the relationship between the Yugoslav idea and the creation and disintegration of the Yugoslav state (1998). His analysis is based on the same assumption this book is: that the collapse of Yugoslavia (like the collapse of states in general) must be analyzed primarily through the collapse of the constitutive concept (as I call it here) or the concept of a Yugoslav nation (as he says in his book). I share Wachtel's view:

> The collapse of multinational Yugoslavia and the establishment of separate uninational states…were not the result of the breakdown of the political or economic fabric of the Yugoslav state; rather, these breakdowns, which manifestly occurred and have been copiously documented, themselves sprang from the gradual destruction of the concept of a Yugoslav nation. (1998:4)

To a certain extent, we can accept his conclusion that the "various causes that have been cited for the collapse of Yugoslavia were secondary to the disintegration of the very concept of the Yugoslav nation, and it is to that cultural process we must turn if we wish to see how existing deep-seated rivalries and hatreds were at various times overcome and encouraged and how they have reemerged triumphant" (1998:17).

Yet Wachtel's exclusive reliance on cultural factors resulted in underestimating the contextual framework in which the concepts (including the concept of Yugoslavism) emerged defeated or triumphant. Although he correctly points to the importance of the "text" of his narratives, he also neglects the many factors in real life that strongly influenced the narrative. Constitutive concepts (or, as Wachtel would prefer, narratives) are not once-and-for-all fixed sets of beliefs and ideals, but flexible compositions of elements. It is for this reason that we cannot take the concept alone in attempting to explain action. The other "objective" factors that influenced it must always also be seen. In Skinner's words, one needs to "exhibit the dynamic nature of the relationship that exists between the professed principles and the actual practices of political life" (1988:108) by asking what the actors were doing while they were saying something. Ideas always need to be situated in their practical context. My argument here is that precisely because the existing constitutive concept (as interpreted by its main representatives) was incapable of providing an adequate response to the challenges of the objective factors, Yugoslavia ultimately collapsed. Consequently, new constitutive concepts were created in reaction to both economic and political crises in the 1980s.

It would therefore be inadequate to analyze these two (the concept and its context) separately. True, the economic and political crises were to a large extent the results of attempts by the political elites to see their constitutive concepts implemented at any cost. But they were also catalysts for the further revision and, indeed, the abandonment of certain elements of the ideology. The answers to some of the key questions surrounding the collapse of Yugoslavia are to be found in the dynamics between ideas and practice. Because of these dynamics it is somewhat difficult to accept Wachtel's idealist conclusion that a nation is "not a political entity, but a state of mind." This book accepts that the narrative indeed ultimately defines a nation at any given moment, but this still does not imply that "no matter how heterogeneous a group of people might appear to an observer, there is a level at which its members could choose to see each other as belonging to one nation" (1998:2). Nations are neither fixed communities defined once and for all by, inter alia, linguistic, anthropological, political, and economic factors, nor are they simply imagined from nowhere by intellectual and political elites. If anywhere, this is obvious in the Yugoslav case. The attempts in Yugoslavia to create or imagine a nation, despite the reality, by neglecting or underestimating the importance of already existing differences, generated political tensions and-within a certain context-set up a framework in which the breakup of the state was possible.[26]

The cultural analysis is a good basis for the analysis of the Yugoslav collapse, but only when certain elements of other explanations are also applied to explain the context in which culture operates.

1.1.5. The International Politics Argument

The international politics explanation of the collapse of Yugoslavia insists on the importance of one or several factors in the international arena in the rise and fall of Yugoslavia. It is argued that Yugoslavia was created (in both 1918 and 1945) with significant help, or even as a creation of the great powers whose balance of power substantially helped Yugoslavia to preserve its existence and independence.[27] Yugoslavia's strategic position between the two military-political blocs in Cold War Europe and its politics of equidistance in both ideological and political terms could not survive the collapse of bipolar structures at the end of the Cold War. Yugoslavia was the victim of the fall of the Berlin Wall. In a strategic sense, it lost its importance when compared with other areas of the world and, consequently, was no longer able to attract economic and political support from the West. The insensitivity of the Western world to the new position of Yugoslavia was evident, as Woodward (1995) and Zimmermann (1996/1999) argue, in its failure to support the economic reforms of the Marković government (in 1988-91). Even worse, the pressure on Yugoslavia from the IMF (International Monetary Fund), already in the early 1980s, made the Yugoslav reformist elite incapable of performing its functions and opposing growing social disorder. The economic hardship produced a constitutional crisis, which in turn helped ethnic nationalists to undermine what was even by Western standards a rather stable and plausible project. As Woodward argues, Yugoslavia collapsed because of neither ethnic hatred nor the breakup of some political dictatorship, but because of the disintegration of the international order by which Yugoslavia was strongly influenced.

> Critical to its breakdown was change from the outside, in the foreign economic and strategic environment on which the country's stability had come to depend. Contrary to the myth that has formed since Yugoslavia's demise, the cracks in the system were not the fault lines between civilizations that came together in the Balkans, but those that defined the country's domestic order and internal position during the Socialist period. (1995:22)

Drawing from what they define as "the seminal work of Susan Woodward and others," Gokay and Fouskas (2005:166) argue that "in the final instance, the external rather than the internal environment was responsible for the collapse of the country and the displacement of so many innocent civilians, either by nationalistic aggression or U.S./NATO bombing."

Woodward's argument is also echoed in Yugoslav domestic debates on the causes of the disintegration. Former Yugoslav Defense Secretary General Kadijević (1993) argues that the collapse of the Soviet Union left Yugoslavia vulnerable to pressure from the West, which encouraged anti-Communist and nationalist forces in traditionally Western-oriented areas (Slovenia and Croatia) to increase their demands. The failure of Communism in the USSR and Eastern Europe undermined the country's (and especially the army's) ideological basis.

Kadijević saw the "new world order" as the ultimate danger for Yugoslavia's independence and survival.[28]

Although international factors always played a significant part in Yugoslav politics, we should not exaggerate their importance in Yugoslavia's last phase. Yugoslavia was not a member of either of the two military-political structures. Promoting "self-managing" rather than "statist" (Soviet) Socialism, its leaders saw *perestroika* and *glasnost* as a victory rather than as a defeat for their own model of Socialism.[29] With very few exceptions, the Yugoslav Communists welcomed the policy of detente between East and West, even seeing in it yet further recognition of the success of the Yugoslav road to Socialism. The reforms in Eastern Europe were not seen as a threat, and by no means did the Yugoslav leaders feel endangered by these changes. Neither did the Yugoslav political elite follow the IMF's instructions exactly. As chapter four will demonstrate, the Party leadership was successful in blocking the attempts of four successive federal prime ministers (Djuranović, Planinc, Mikulić, and Marković) to implement a program of serious economic reforms, as demanded by the IMF and other foreign creditors. The prime ministers, not the Party leaders, regularly lost these intraelite battles, being either marginalized (Djuranović and Planinc) or forced to resign (Mikulić).[30] Being a leader of the nonaligned group of countries, Yugoslavia had a fairly independent foreign policy. Although this proved to be the main reason for the country's favorable position during the Cold War, in the late 1980s it somewhat blinded the political elites, making them unaware of the immediate and long-term consequences of political changes in Eastern Europe.

Instead of seeing the collapse of East European Socialism as a danger for its own international position and internal cohesion, the Yugoslav leaders and citizens concluded that with the collapse of the Brezhnev doctrine, the most serious threat to Yugoslavia's security was eliminated. The Western states certainly did not want Yugoslavia to disintegrate, and even less did they wish to see instability in the turbulent region. Yugoslavia was considered to be the first East European country that would join the European Economic Community (EEC), and already in the late 1970s it had signed the first documents on cooperation with the EEC. Throughout the final crisis of Yugoslavia, the United States and the EEC both remained committed to a policy of a "united and democratic Yugoslavia," as formulated by U.S. Ambassador, Warren Zimmermann. On these grounds, the European Community decided on 1 November 1990 to include Yugoslavia in the PHARE (Poland and Hungary: Assistance for Restructuring their Economies) program.[31] Furthermore, the German minister of foreign affairs, Hans-Dietrich Genscher, expressed Germany's full support for Yugoslavia's prospective membership in the European Community after his meeting with Yugoslavia's foreign secretary, Budimir Lončar, on 2 September 1990.[32] The policy of firm support for the unity of Yugoslavia altered only in the aftermath of the military conflict between Slovenia and the Yugoslav army-and only after the Yugoslav state presidency (on 18 July 1991) decided on its own will to withdraw JNA (Yugoslav People's Army) troops from Slovenia.

At the moment of its disintegration, Yugoslavia had very few if any enemies in the international community. It would therefore be incorrect to argue that the intervention by Western states and organizations was the main reason for the country's collapse. True, when the international community reacted, it demonstrated its lack of understanding of the context, thus contributing to further disastrous developments in the Balkans. But Yugoslavia was already at a very advanced stage of its disintegration when (in July 1991) foreign involvement took place for the first time. Even then it was hesitant and, as Gow (1997) has noted, showed "a lack of will." Yugoslavia was, as Perović (1993), Lukić and Lynch (1996:113), and Djilas (1993:109) argue, "defeated" from within, not from the outside.

1.1.6. The Role of Personality Argument

Many authors emphasize the role of personalities in the collapse of Yugoslavia. The two personalities most often mentioned in this context are the former Yugoslav President Josip Broz Tito[33] and the former Serbian leader Slobodan Milošević.[34]

In short, the attempts to explain the collapse of Yugoslavia by focusing on Tito's personality emphasize that Tito was the only real decision maker, the real sovereign in Yugoslavia. He identified the state with himself and concentrated all real power in his own hands. During his life, Tito was the key arbiter in political disputes. It has often been argued that despite the formal decentralization of the country following the 1974 Constitution, Yugoslavia remained united and centralized because of Tito's personal role. He was above the law and outside the law. This was especially so after 1974, when the constitution declared Tito "President of the Republic without limitation of office,"[35] therefore outlawing any attempt to replace him for as long as he was alive. He was no longer just the supreme politician, but also the state itself (Tepavac 1997). The main areas of state politics (such as defense, foreign affairs, and state security) were considered to be his personal domains. His cult of personality was never so omnipresent as in the last couple of years of his life. Furthermore, the constitution prevented anyone from replacing Tito after his death. When he died in May 1980, there was no one to reconnect the broken bonds or to make decisions regarding the conflicts of interest within the country. Yugoslavia, weakened to one person-Tito himself -died together with its ruler.[36]

The other person who decisively influenced Yugoslav disintegration was Slobodan Milošević. Many authors see the Serbian leader as a person who wanted to replace Tito by occupying the empty space of power vacated after his death (Vejvoda 1993). By doing so, Milošević distinguished himself from the other post-Titoist leaders, who continued marching along "Tito's path," favoring collective leadership as constructed by Tito himself. It was Milošević, they argue, who disturbed the newly achieved balance between republics and provinces and who destroyed the tranquility of Tito's moribund successors. At this time, Milošević also introduced the masses into politics, using them as a source of pressure in the intraelite conflicts. Although many authors share this conclusion, perhaps none has explained it better than Lukić and Lynch:

> Had Slobodan Milošević not emerged as *Duce* in Serbia, Yugoslavia might have evolved gradually after the end of the East-West geopolitical division of Europe into an asymmetric federation or confederation.[37] (1996:114)

The *role of personalities* approach is part of a wider argument between intentionalist and functionalist historians. The two schools developed their arguments during the 1980s when analyzing Hitler's role in the rise and fall of the Third Reich: the intentionalists focus their research on the minds and intentions of political actors, the functionalists argue that structures and institutions, or the system's automatic mechanisms for "cumulative radicalization," could explain the politics of the Third Reich better than Hitler's personal beliefs and intentions.[38] Several moderate versions of these two schools emerged in the debate, such as Browning's "moderate functionalism" and Burrin's "conditional intentionalism."

In this book, an attempt to articulate a moderate intentionalist position is made. I share Browning's conclusion that the two contrasting positions are unduly polarized. In reality, the interaction between a personality and an institution is unavoidable, and it is thus difficult to understand actions taken by personalities without understanding the institutional and ideological context in which the action has been conceived. Tito and Milošević (and any other political leader) can be understood only within the context of the political processes that brought them to power and enabled them to influence politics in such a powerful way. They were just as much "products" as they were initiators of political trends. They had to take into consideration the interests of other participants in politics and to find a compromise between their own views and interests and those of others. As this book illustrates, it is the complexity of intraelite politics that we must not neglect when analyzing Yugoslav politics. The *role of personality* argument often does exactly this.

Milošević came to power as a representative of the main trends in Serbian politics before him, and in many respects he followed a policy of continuity with his predecessors. The historical context in which Milošević emerged as the undisputed leader of Serbia is often underestimated. This neglect has resulted in the failure to properly understand his intentions, (as demonstrated, for example, during the 1999 NATO war against Serbia over Kosovo). In this book some suggestions are offered on how to read and understand Milošević's past actions. They are based on reading these actions within their context. Failure to do so, I argue, is due to several methodological mistakes, such as, for example, the *ideal type* mistake, the *prolepsis* hypothesis, and the *coherence* hypothesis, as explained by Skinner (1988).

While focusing on Milošević, we should also not lose sight of other actors in Yugoslav politics who influenced his actions. Post-Titoist politics were to a large extent conducted on an antipersonality-cult rule. It was an attempt to prevent the emergence of strong leaders. Many politicians attempted to resolve the growing economic and political problems before Milošević, and this book also devotes some attention to them.

1.1.7. The Fall of Empires *Argument*

The *fall of empires* argument formulated by Eric Hobsbawm[39] argues that instead of becoming a nation state constructed by liberals (as was originally planned, following the idea of the self-determination of nations), Yugoslavia developed as a multiethnic "empire," much on the model of the Austro-Hungarian and Ottoman empires that had prior to her creation included its main regions.[40] The concept of an empire was much more successful in the postwar period under Tito, "the last Habsburg" (as A. J. P. Taylor called him), who was much less identified with any ethnic group than King Alexander because of the internationalist ideology he professed. As a Communist, to whom national allegiance was secondary to ideological affiliation, Tito became a supranational arbiter in interethnic conflicts. Legitimized by the internationalist ideology and not in parliamentary elections, Tito was not a representative of any existing group, but primarily of a specific vision of the future.[41] The gradual replacement of the ideological leadership with more representative leaders of republics and provinces meant the abandonment of this supranational position at the top of the "empire." Unlike Tito and Kardelj (in the ideological sphere), the rulers of post-Titoist Yugoslavia could not be seen as impartial arbiters, but more as representatives of their segments of society, i.e., their nations and nationalities. Without an impartial arbiter in both ideological and political conflicts, it became more difficult than ever to maintain the fine balance on which the stability of the Yugoslav mosaic had been built and preserved under Tito. The transition from an empire-like ideological structure to a fragmented semiconfederalist system was in part institutionalized by the 1974 Constitution, which treated Tito as a constitutional exception. The 1974 Constitution was to large extent the beginning of the de-Titoization of Yugoslavia, which in real terms started even before 1974, only to intensify after his death six years later. The system was projected to prevent anyone else from becoming a new supreme (and perhaps absolutist) arbiter in the post-Titoist period. Indeed, in this respect Tito was not only "the last Habsburg," but he had now become (at least officially) "the only true Yugoslav."[42] Milošević's ambition to replace Tito in the late 1980s was indeed impossible, since the space of power occupied by Tito was now not only empty (Vejvoda 1994), but also de jure deleted from the political map of Yugoslavia's institutional structure. It was against the spirit of the ideology of decentralization and against the letter of the constitution to even attempt becoming "a new Tito." Moreover, the existing political elites of republics and provinces had no desire to continue with the model that would continue to reduce their powers and subject them to the often unpredictable political will of somebody who had neither Tito's charisma nor Tito's international and domestic stature.

In this respect, Milošević's attempt to become the new Tito (which is how his supporters initially saw him, and also how he liked to be seen) was by definition anticonstitutional and an attack on the essence of the ideology of decentralization and self-management. To succeed in becoming the supreme arbiter of this quasi-empire, Milošević had to change the constitution and destroy the existing political system of semiconfederalism. But unlike Tito, Milošević could not have been seen as impartial. He did not profess an ideology that would make him supranational. On the contrary, identifying himself closely (indeed, exclusively) with only one ethnic group (the Serbs), he was viewed as insufficiently Yugoslav (in the Titoist sense of the concept) by others. Milošević was a representative of the Serbian political elite and not a person without links with any separate ethnic group prior to his (potential) accession to the Yugoslav throne. Milošević was thus a Tito in reverse. To become a real Tito, he needed to turn the whole system upside down. When he attempted to do this, the others decided to leave.

Although the fall of empires argument links various elements of other approaches and has some merits in explaining Yugoslav politics, it is still somewhat difficult to see how Yugoslavia can be compared to real empires, in which there generally was a dominant nation and which used colonial expansion to lower tensions inside the metropolis. Yugoslavia was perhaps an ideological empire, but in this approach similarities with real empires of the past are certainly exaggerated.

1.1.8. The Constitutional and Institutional Reasons Argument

The last set of explanations presented insists on constitutional and institutional reasons for the collapse of Yugoslavia. The main argument here is that Yugoslavia disintegrated because of this or that set of institutional or constitutional rules, which were either so complicated or simply so impractical that they made it impossible for a united and "normal" state to be created. In particular, this approach emphasizes the importance of the 1974 Constitution of Yugoslavia. The constitution, it has been argued,[43] made it impossible for federal institutions to function properly and thus aided the disintegration of the whole system. Being insufficiently clear and already the result of compromises with various nationalist groups in the republic and provinces, the constitution has often been described as a "blueprint for secession." Not surprisingly, say the promoters of this approach, the separatist forces in the late 1980s and in early 1990 based some of their actions on the text and spirit of the 1974 Constitution. Because other main laws (such as, for example, the Associated Labor Act of 1976) followed constitutional logic, they too contributed to the disintegration.

The other key institutional factor that is often described as harmful for Yugoslav unity was a decision to organize democratic elections in 1990 only in republics and not at the level of the federation. This argument is presented by Linz and Stepan (1992). Had the first democratic elections in 1990 been held at the federal level rather than in the republics, the federal institutions would have received democratic legitimacy before the republics and provinces. This in turn would delegitimize separatists in the republics, who often argued, rather convincingly, that they were the only true democrats, while their opponents were illegitimate Communist authorities. Linz and Stepan based this argument on a comparison with Spain, which survived as a united country despite strong separatist currents in its constituent parts during the transition from authoritarianism.

This argument has its validity. Constitutional and institutional arrangements are important. However, we should not forget that constitutions are always a result of a certain balance of power between those who make the decisions. Constitutions are the outcomes of political processes and rarely ever are the main cause of political events. The Yugoslav constitution of 1974 is no exception. More than any before, this constitution was the result of long and often very conflicting negotiations between republics and the federal institutions (including Tito) over the future institutional and structural setup for Yugoslavia. Had it been possible to write a different constitution, there would have been no obstacle for political leaders to do so. But because the constitution provided for a "loose" federation with a weaker, rather than stronger, federal center, it was only an illustration of what was possible at that particular moment. Whoever blames the constitution for the disintegration of Yugoslavia should be advised to take a step back and analyze the processes and actors involved in writing it. This leads us back to some other approaches that were analyzed earlier in this chapter.

The same counterargument is valid in the case of the 1990 elections. The real question here is not whether it would be different had the federal elections preceded those in republics and provinces. It is this: Why was it impossible for political leaders of republics and provinces to agree on proposals by then Federal Prime Minister Ante Marković, who favored this order? The fact that this was impossible already indicates that no elections in themselves would have saved the unity of Yugoslavia-it was already too late to agree on that solution. In short, instead of treating institutional setup and constitutional arrangements as a cause of disintegration, they should be treated as direct consequences of the climate produced by the political elite.

1.2. The Analytical Approach of this Book

Although all the approaches analyzed above (with the exception of the ethnic hatred argument) have added some valuable contributions to our understanding of the disintegration of Yugoslavia, they have sometimes neglected the element of interaction between the external (or "objective") factors (such as economic crisis, ethnic structure of population, and international politics) and the perceptions of these elements by political actors themselves and their resultant actions. Much misunderstanding of the actual events leading to the breakup of Yugoslavia was the result of the underestimation of the importance of the subjective in politics. Politics is a field of human interaction and not just the reflection of some external, objective elements, such as economic, demographic, or geopolitical trends. Although political actors normally do not act entirely independently from these objective factors, how they perceive and react to them depends on their beliefs, perceptions of interests, values, and personal characteristics, among other things. These subjective factors are exposed to permanent change and are thus unstable.[44]

For this reason this book is based not only on an analysis of political events, but also on analyses of political concepts and ideas that influenced participants in the political debates that preceded the disintegration of Yugoslavia. In Kedourie's terms (1996), it is a political history and intellectual history at the same time. The analysis of a Communist system is incomplete if it does not include both dimensions. In Communist systems, perhaps more than in others political actions were attempts to implement a set of ideas in political reality. To a large degree, politics in Communist-led societies was, to use Voegelin's expression (1952:70), a "representation of truth" defined by certain texts and interpreted by the Party (the subjective force of Socialism) just as much as it was the representation of certain interests or preferences of its main participants, the political elites. Communist politics was about the realization of "the truth," in which the Party, as Edvard Kardelj explained, has the role almost of a scientific institute.[45] The Party was a collective intellectual,[46] and thus we cannot possibly understand its role and actions without taking ideology seriously.

The intellectual debates within the political elite were, if not the main acts of politics, then certainly the most suitable medium of real political struggle. As Irvine argues, "control over the actual meaning of language became essential to those regimes' ideological and symbolic sources of legitimation" (1997:6). Political conflicts in the Socialist societies of Eastern Europe had often been expressed as a linguistic debate over the "correct" interpretation of Marxism.[47] Although certain variations have been allowed, the main idea behind these conflicts was that there is essentially only one correct way of understanding Marx's message and that the Party was entitled to act as an arbiter between conflicting interpretations when they occurred. In reality, however, many interpretations emerged, struggling for the status of the official one. The level of liberalization of a Communist system was indicated by the presence (or absence) of alternative (nonofficial) interpretations of Marxist ideology. Since no other (non-Marxist) ideology was allowed to compete with Marxism, the intraparty debate on the real meaning of Marxism covered a much larger spectrum of issues than an observer in ideologically pluralized societies would expect. In stricter times, when liberalization was in retreat, defeat in the struggle for the "correct" interpretation resulted in expulsion from public life, or even persecution, under the label of "revisionism."

The main question I am addressing in this book is this: Why did political actors act as they did? Why did their actions make sense to them? What were their rationales, their motives for action, and their intentions? If we really want to understand the rationale behind the actions of the Yugoslav Communists, we need to take their beliefs seriously. What is relevant here is not whether these actions make sense to us, but whether they made sense to them, to those whose actions we analyze and to the relevant segment of the political body on whose approval the existence and stability of the regime depended. It is not the aim of this book to judge the actions taken by the Yugoslav elite in either favorable or unfavorable terms, but to explain them by understanding the reasons the actors had for them. I am attempting to reconstruct and present these reasons.

In doing so, I rely on Quentin Skinner's theory of analyzing the meaning and understanding of words and actions in their mutual interaction.[48] It is also in Skinner's warnings about possible problems of historical analysis that we can find useful guidance.

Skinner warns about two extremes in analyzing intellectual history: one is linked to overestimating the context in which a text occurs; the other is doing the opposite, neglecting the context by arguing that the text itself can be understood without much reference to the context. When it comes to the context, this book aims at correcting inaccurate interpretations of the intentions and actions of the main Yugoslav politicians based on the *myth of coherence* and the *myth of the ideal type*.

The myth of coherence is an outcome of methodological error that can best be described as an attempt to find consistency in one's ideas and actions at all costs. Coherence may be found in time "horizontally" or "vertically." When horizontal, the coherence is sought in actions by the members of a group, even if they differ in most relevant matters. When vertical, it is sought in actions of the same actor over time. The myth of coherence, therefore, neglects or underestimates changes that occur over time and denies plurality within social groups. Having said this, we should not, however, assume that all political actors (or even most of them) act incoherently. The world, especially the highly ideological world of the Cold War, was (and to a large extent still is) full of fanatics and dogmatists who are unprepared to change, even when and if the context in which they act has changed dramatically. They lose touch with reality. Regardless of what it looks like from the outside, however, the fanatics and dogmatists are rarely ever representative of the mainstream body of political actors. Even in political systems that are not based on the principle of popularity (i.e., public support), political elites rarely ever remain unmovable by the context in which they find themselves. The coherence hypothesis ignores this change to the detriment of the quality of political analysis offered by its main advocates.

The myth of the ideal type is an outcome of an attempt to reconstruct the meaning of intentions and actions in accordance with previously constructed ideal types, such categories as nationalists, Communists, liberals, and democrats that have been defined in certain ways by social scientists. The ideal types are constructed on more or less exact observations, but they can also be influenced by stereotypes and prejudices about certain groups and actors. Even when they are not, they can rarely ever explain all aspects of any particular case and they are thus useful-but only to a degree. This book is about the disintegration of a particular state. Because of their heavy reliance on ideal types, social science explanations on the disintegration of states in general can be of only limited assistance.

Both types of myths linked to context in reality use the methodological apparatus of mainstream social science (especially of scientific naturalists, as Ricci names them, 1984:92) to construct generally applicable models of analysis. In doing so, they more often than not blur our understanding of a particular event.

For example, once we label a person X as a "nationalist," there is a danger of attempting to retrieve the meaning of what this person said, or did not say, from what one expects a nationalist to say or not say. These two mistakes (the *coherence* and *ideal type*) are the basis on which controversies or changes of mind are often dismissed as yet another cosmetic change, or as just a tactic, almost as if there is always some "real" (and often hidden) agenda that in fact determines people's actions. Therefore, for example, when person X publicly dismisses nationalism-regardless of how strong the statement might be-many are still inclined to believe that this is only because that person had to hide some true beliefs, not because the statement was the result of true feelings. Even if someone does something contrary to what is expected from a certain ideal type of person, this would be taken as merely a "tactical move," not a real indication of change. Although these analysts focus their research on the subjective, they still make the mistake of not looking at changes over time and of trying to situate actors within certain ideal-type categories.

In this book, I try to avoid the myths of coherence and of ideal types, arguing that we need to take political actors seriously if we want to understand them. To take them seriously, however, does not imply that we should believe only their words; on the contrary, we should never neglect the context in which these words were expressed and the actions that came before and after them. Actions need to be understood in the historical and contemporary context in which they happened. This is why this book is not a pure discourse analysis. It goes further by situating discourses in the context of practical politics.

Another methodological mistake this book warns about is identified by Skinner as the *myth of prolepsis*. It is committed when a person relies on his or her interpretation of events that happened after the political decision was taken, assuming that there was a causal link between the action and its result. The assumption here is that the results of somebody's action was always intentional, and that once we know the results (or even, more precisely, only then), we can fully understand the real intentions, the real meaning of the words and actions that "caused" such results. In other words, the assumption here is that we can "read back" the intentions of actors from the outcome of their actions. If the breakup of Yugoslavia was a consequence, then it had to be the result of the intentions of the main political actors involved: domestic and/or international. Or, to take Skinner's example, if totalitarian ideologies of the twentieth century claimed they were based on Rousseau's writings, then Rousseau's writings were somehow responsible for totalitarianism. Intentionalists would claim that very few events in history, if any, happened unless people intended them to. In the context of the disintegration of Yugoslavia, this explanation is often described as a "conspiracy theory." Its main representatives offer simple explanations for the breakup of

Yugoslavia-for them it was an intended result of actions planned in "political laboratories" of the White House, the International Monetary Fund, the Vatican, Germany, or, simply, the capitalist West. Some would go so far as seeing this state collapse as a long-term strategic goal of the (long-dead) Communist International (the Comintern), or of a joint action by two or more of these institutions! On the domestic front, the conspiracists are quick to point the finger of blame at this or that republic (most often Serbia, but also Slovenia), or Kosovo. Some would explain the collapse of Yugoslavia as an intended outcome of actions taken by the Yugoslav Communists in general, or some of them in particular, for example, Josip Broz Tito, Edvard Kardelj, Slobodan Milošević, or Milan Kučan.

I am far from dismissing the importance of any of these actors, institutions, or states. Their actions (and inactions) have been crucial indeed for the line of events that preceded the breakup of Yugoslavia. However, did they have a plan to destroy it? Did they intend to partition it? The analysis offered here suggests a different conclusion. An in-depth analysis of the speeches and actions of the main Yugoslav politicians in the fifteen years before the actual disintegration of Yugoslavia shows that not many political actors (and especially not many of those within the political elite) really wanted Yugoslavia to collapse. On the contrary, most of them intended to save it by either reforming or preserving various elements of its constitution and political practices. Furthermore, an analysis of the politics of the main international actors involved in the Yugoslav crisis (which is not within the limits of this book) also shows that back in 1990 no country wanted Yugoslavia to disintegrate. On the contrary, the main global powers-the US, the EU, and the USSR (then collapsing)-stood firmly in support of its unity, even when the first conflicts in Yugoslavia had already begun. It was not before January 1992, that is, when the conflict in Slovenia was already over and the one in Croatia resulted in the destruction of Vukovar and the heavy bombardment of Dubrovnik, that the EU changed its policy and recognized the fragmentation of Yugoslavia. To most of the political actors, as to many analysts, the disintegration of Yugoslavia came as a surprise, not as an inevitable result of their premeditated actions. Yet once it happened, many claimed they "knew" it would happen, or even that they had wanted it to happen. Sometimes, when reminded of historical sources (such as speeches or actions by politicians), the radical intentionalists would claim this was only a public statement, though the "real" intentions were something else.

Lastly, yet another set of methodological mistakes that Skinner calls the *mythology of parochialism* should be rejected: attempts to apply our own criteria to another culture without sufficient effort to approach the meaning of actions from within the context in which they happened. This was perhaps the most frequent mistake by Western policy makers in the Yugoslav crisis. An assumption that

Yugoslavia would not disintegrate, because its disintegration would be "irrational" for the interests of the main participants, was based on the pure extension of our understanding of rationality to an area in which different criteria of rationality were valid. To be fair, the Western observers and policy makers were not the only ones who made this mistake. Many Yugoslav intellectuals, also basing their analyses on excess of rationality and underestimation of nonrational factors (such as emotions, fears in particular), argued that Yugoslavia would not collapse because that would be irrational. It is always a mistake to neglect the actual context in which an action takes place. And it would be an even greater mistake to understand this context incorrectly. The context in which action happens is never an intellectual seminar or a perfect social-science laboratory. It is also influenced and created by the irrational, inexplicable, spontaneous, and affective. This is perhaps why some of the best representations of various wars and other disasters are authored by artists, not social scientists. Not only in situations as extraordinary as conflict and war, the instincts and emotions are often more important factors than cold-headed rationality.

Without entering into a debate on meaning and understanding in anymore detail than is necessary to explain the methodology and the main argument of this book, I shall now conclude by saying that if we wish to understand action, we cannot simply concentrate on the words alone. The analysis of the rhetoric of the main political actors is always only a first step-necessary, but not sufficient. We need to study the situations in which the words are used and what the author was doing in saying or not saying something. Ignoring the practical context of political actions will not help us to understand them.

This book aims at following the interaction between Kardelj's interpretation of Marxist ideology and the political context in which this concept was implemented. As Tully (1998) argues, to place the text in its political context means to treat it in interaction with "the collection of texts written or used in the same period, addressed to the same or similar issues, and sharing a number of conventions." Such interaction will help us to reveal the intentions of the political participants when they spoke or acted in a certain way. It is for this reason that in many places of this book the main discourses by participants are presented and analyzed. It is only within their context that the reader will understand the actions that followed.

In saying this, we must be aware that no explanation of people's real intentions can be perfect if by "intentions" we understand the thoughts of the political actors. Political analysts surely hold no key to an actor's mind. But as Skinner concluded, "When we claim to have recovered the intentions embodied in texts, we are engaged in nothing more mysterious than this process of placing them within whatever contexts make sense of them." It is not that we try to reach peculiarly inaccessible mental causes operating in the privacy of the mind, but only to explain the reasons behind behaving in certain ways "to exhibit certain skills and capacities in conventional ways." Unlike Derrida, Skinner points out that "the intentions with which anyone performs any successful act of communication must, *ex hypothesi*, be publicly legible" (1988:279).

> Suppose I come to understand that the man waving his arms in the next field is not trying to chase away a fly, but is warning me that the bull is about to charge. To recognize that he is warning me is to understand the intentions with which he is acting. But to recover these intentions is not a matter of identifying the ideas inside his head at the moment when he first begins to wave his arms. It is merely a matter of grasping the fact that arm waving can count as warning, and that this is the convention that he is exploiting in this particular case. Nothing in the way of empathy is required, since the meaning of the episode is entirely public and intersubjective. As a result, the intentions with which the man is acting can be inferred from an understanding of the significance of the act itself. (1988:279)

In this way I understand the meaning of the intentions in this book. For Skinner, some intentions really may be irrecoverable, but this is simply on account of there being insufficient information about their context to permit an ascription of intention in a particular case: "Some utterances are completely lacking in the sorts of context from which alone one can hope to infer the intentions with which they were uttered" (1988:280). Most intentions are normally identifiable, but only if we make an effort to understand the context in which they occur.[49]

We sometimes must admit that some things we cannot explain, because even the actors themselves often cannot explain their own actions; however, this should not prevent us from accomplishing this goal as much as possible. Not even the most radical positivist approaches to the study of politics would claim we can explain everything. The point made here is that we are more successful when avoiding these methodological mistakes.

In the next chapter I will focus on the historical and ideological context that influenced the development of the Kardelj concept, the original Yugoslav interpretation of Marxism on which the Yugoslav political system was structured in the period this book analyzes. Without an understanding of this concept, I argue, we would fail to understand the actions that followed. In chapter three these actions are analyzed in relation to the concept itself. Then I move on to explaining the failure of Kardelj's concept (in chapters four and five) and then the emergence of alternative concepts, most explicitly in Serbia and Slovenia (chapters six and seven). I argue that the breakdown of the ideological consensus within the Yugoslav political elite during an extended period of almost two decades was important (in my opinion, perhaps the most important), yet an often-neglected reason for the actual disintegration of Yugoslav institutions.

Notes

1 For main differences between the Yugoslav and Soviet ideologies, see Jović (2004).
2 For a very useful overview of these debates see Ramet (2005).
3 For the economic argument, see Žižmond (1992), Zdunić (1994), Vojnić (1994), Ferfila (1991), Uvalić (1992), Gapinski (1993), Horvat (1992), and Horvat (1993).
4 As Denitch (1990: XIV) notes, Yugoslavia's international debts were reduced to US$16 billion, from US$24 billion, under the government of Ante Marković (1989-91). The last U.S. ambassador to Socialist Yugoslavia, Warren Zimmermann, says that in less than a year in office, the prime minister had quadrupled Yugoslavia's foreign exchange reserves, bringing down annual inflation from 25,000 percent to zero (1996/1999:49). However, as Djilas points out (1993:139), Marković overestimated the importance of economic factors in "saving" Yugoslavia. He had no clear political vision (a "constitutive concept") and believed that everyone would realize that it was "irrational" to separate from Yugoslavia. Political decisions, however, did not follow the logic of economic rationality.
5 In an interview I had in June 1996 with Macedonian President Gligorov, he confirmed that Jacques Delors, then the president of the European Commission, offered US$5.5 billion to support the transformation of Yugoslavia toward a looser Union of Yugoslav States, which would be admitted to the European Union. Milošević and Tudjman were angry. Tudjman said, "You cannot buy us with promises. We don't need your money." Milošević was even angrier: "You Europeans want to cheat history. There are big and small nations," he said. "You had better keep your money. We are capable of deciding about our future." Gligorov repeated this conversation in his interview with the Italian newspaper *Corriere della Sera*; see *Vjesnik* 20 January 1997.
6 This is why almost all relevant groups of Albanian separatists in the 1980s used such words as "Marxism-Leninism" in their names. For division between Hoxhists and Titoists among Yugoslav Albanians, see Maliqi (1998) and Judah (2000).
7 For example, Patrick Bishop in the *Daily Telegraph* 20 January 1999, says this: "Folk memories are long, and an inability to forget the hatreds of the past has condemned successive generations to perpetuate them.... The countries that make up the former Yugoslav Federation are split by deep political, religious, and ethnic fault lines, left over from the days when the region was divided between the rival empires of Turkey and Austria-Hungary" (Bishop 1999).
8 See Michael Rose (1998).
9 Kaplan (1994).
10 *The Sunday Times*, 18 April 1999.
11 Oklobdžija (1993:92); cf. also Pavković (1997) and Woodward (1995).
12 For example, research on social distance between members of Yugoslav ethnic groups conducted in 1987 (Pantić 1987) indicates that Albanians were the only group that preferred not to enter marriages with members of other groups, and vice versa, that members of other groups had a problem in marrying an Albanian. In relationships between members of Yugoslav constitutive nations, the largest social distance was of Slovenes

toward Muslims (not vice versa). In all other cases, more than 50 percent of respondents expressed the view they would not have a problem in marrying members of other ethnic groups, though in all cases respondents preferred a member of his/her own group. Most important, 74 percent of Serbs said they would not mind marrying a Croat, and 72 percent of Croats said the same for a Serb. Significantly, neither Serbs nor Croats expressed many problems about marrying a Slovene (76 percent and 72 percent, respectively), but the Slovenes hesitated more toward these two groups (59 percent and 60 percent, respectively). The research certainly does not confirm any conclusion about high levels of social distance between members of Yugoslav nations, with the noticeable exception of Albanians.

13 For an excellent elaboration of this argument, see Gagnon (2004) and Gordy (1999).
14 Relations between Slovenian and Serbian intellectuals and the political elites in these two republics are analyzed in chapters six and seven of this book and in an excellent book by Dragović-Soso (2003).
15 In this book I present data on very low cross-Yugoslav mobility, especially among students and workers, who almost exclusively remained in their own republics, unless they were members of minority ethnic groups in this republic. Institutions were created in such a way that no all-Yugoslav political force could emerge: there were, for example, no Yugoslav-wide elections, no Yugoslav media. Officially, Yugoslavia had not even a national anthem, since the republic and provinces could not agree on its words. An interesting debate on this issue was conducted in Yugoslavia in the 1980s. The Albanian representatives opposed using the word *Slav* in the first verse of the text, while Slovenia and Croatia did not agree to change it to *Yugoslav*. Economic systems were clearly built to suit the self-sufficiency of the republics and provinces. Terms such as national working class were coined to describe the national (not Yugoslav) character of the main political substance of Yugoslav society. In general, the failure to construct a Yugoslav political community indeed could be explained by the lack of a "centralized educational system supervised by and often actually run by the state in question, which monopolizes legitimate culture almost as much as it does legitimate violence, or perhaps more so" (Gellner 1983:141). The Fourth Yugoslavia was an example of having neither a central culture nor a central state, two conditions Gellner pointed out as crucial. As Lendvai (1991) argues, in a political sense, Yugoslavia was left without Yugoslavs.
16 All three multiethnic Communist federations proved incredibly weak and incapable of protecting themselves once their constitutive stories collapsed in 1989. But it was precisely Yugoslavia that went the furthest of the three in its attempt to implement an antistatist ideology, inventing self-management and decentralizing the entire system. By doing this, Yugoslavia's Communists aimed at denouncing the Soviet version of Socialism as dogmatic, statist, and practically revisionist. They claimed a monopoly over the right interpretation of Marxism, denouncing the others as revisionists. Ideological commitment to Marx led them to eliminate the state to a larger extent than was the case in both Czechoslovakia and the Soviet Union. Apart from ethnic structure and historical and geographical circumstances, it was also for this reason that Yugoslavia collapsed in a more dramatic way than the other two former Socialist federations, especially Czechoslovakia. Unlike Czechoslovakia, Yugoslavia linked its identity more closely to its own original constitutive concept. Consequently, the collapse of this concept made the existence of Yugoslavia much more difficult. Finally, in Yugoslavia there was no one else to blame for the failure of a concept that was created by the Yugoslavs

themselves. Other East European countries had a perfect scapegoat in the existence of the Soviet Union, which was perceived as the oppressive other. But in all cases the collapse of the constitutive concept was the main reason for the disintegration of even the strongest institutions (such as the army or secret services) of what seemed to be among the most powerful states in the world. The institutions collapsed once they were left without the constitutive concept that kept the system together. For the differences between the Yugoslav and Soviet understanding of the state, see Lapenna (1964) and Ferdinand (1991).

17 The real bearers of the Yugoslav culture of the 1980s were people such as film director Emir Kusturica and rock musicians Goran Bregović, Johnny Štulić, and Vlatko Stefanovski, who in fact opposed the official doctrine of semiconfederalism, often clashing with politicians and ideologues. Ramet (1992, 1996) offers an excellent analysis of the Yugoslav rock scene. Both Bregović and Štulić left the country after its disintegration in 1991. So did Kusturica and some of the most popular Yugoslav film actors and actresses from Zagreb and Sarajevo, such as Rade Šerbedžija and Mira Furlan. Bregović and Kusturica supported Ante Marković's party at the 1990 elections in Bosnia-Herzegovina, and Šerbedžija took part in antiwar protests a few days before the war in this republic in 1992. Many Yugoslav writers (such as Dubravka Ugrešić, Slavenka Drakulić, Filip David, Bora Ćosić, and David Albahari) found themselves in exile.

18 As Cohen (1993, 1995:49) points out, the fivefold increase in the number of declared Yugoslavs, especially in ethnically mixed areas (Vojvodina, Croatia, and Bosnia-Herzegovina) and among the younger, urban, and more educated generation, was in sharp contrast to an increasing aversion to the LCY (League of Communists of Yugoslavia) in the same segments of the population. Surveys conducted by Flere (1988) and Katunarić (1988) showed that by 1985 the level of Yugoslav identification had further increased as a form of protest against the political fragmentation of the country.

19 An interesting debate on the real meaning, causes, and significance of Yugoslavism occurred in Yugoslavia following the 1981 census (see Matvejević et al.).

20 The globalization theory, as expressed by Giddens, argues that ethnic separatism is a reaction to the processes of globalization. Applied to the Yugoslav case, separatism was a reaction to the growing sense of Yugoslavism and the emergence of a Yugoslav culture, as explained above. But however accurate globalization theory is in pointing out the link between the two trends, it fails to explain the existence of nationalism in earlier phases (before the end of the Cold War). Further, the collapse of multiethnic Yugoslavia does not support the optimistic vision of the future Giddens promoted. Globalization theory is a typical social-scientific attempt to explain the *General Laws of History*, which are based on objective factors. Being universalist and revolutionary, the globalization theory tends to underestimate the importance of cultural and contextual elements and to subsume all nationalisms under one type of antiglobalization: fundamentalist traditionalism.

21 For the antiurban character of nationalism (especially of the Serbs in Bosnia-Herzegovina), see Vujović (1996). The destruction of Dubrovnik and Sarajevo from the hills above them, Vujović argues, was a symbol of the hatred developed by Karadžić's Serbian nationalists against the cities. One of the reasons was the large number of ethnically mixed marriages in the urban centers, as compared with rural environments. In 1981 in Bosnia-Herzegovina, 15 percent of all children were from mixed marriages, in Sarajevo, 40 percent. Karadžić himself wrote a poem about the burning of a city (presumably Sarajevo) and obsessively advocated the division of the Bosnian capital. "Our

vision of Sarajevo is like Berlin when the wall was still standing," he told the American ambassador, Warren Zimmermann (1995:20). The antiurban character of Croatian nationalism is best represented in the literary works of Ante Pavelić, the head of the Ustasha Independent State of Croatia, and his education minister Mile Budak. In more detail, these discourses are analyzed in Čolović (1997) and Žanić (1998).

22 For ethnic status see Horowitz (1985). The sense of losing an already existing *ethnic status* was permanently present in the discussions of Slovenian intellectuals in the late 1980s, and also among the Albanians in Kosovo, following the 1989 change in the Serbian constitution. It also emerged among the Serbs and Croats outside Serbia and Croatia (with almost equal strength), who feared they would become a *minority*, not a *constitutive nation*, especially in Bosnia after the declaration of the independence of this state, and also because of demographic trends. This is also why the ethnic nationalists blocked Marković's initiatives to organize federal elections and reconstruct federal institutions in order to represent the citizens of Yugoslavia. The making of (political) Yugoslavs would be the decisive step toward making Yugoslavia a unitarist state, instead of a federation as it was in the whole post-war period. As will be clearly demonstrated on several occasions in this book, the ethnic nationalists of the Yugoslav nations rated democracy second to issues of national identity. On these grounds, one can also explain why the critical intelligentsia emerged more strongly in the late 1970s in Serbia than in Croatia or Slovenia, whose nationalist intelligentsia were less critical both of the lack of a Yugoslav-wide democracy and the ideology of decentralization via self-management than Serbian dissidents were.

23 A good overview of cultural theories of nationalism (Herder, Schleiermacher, and others) is given by Kedourie (1993:48-52).

24 See Tudjman's interview with Vjesnik 13 September 1997.

25 On several occasions during 1996 and 1997, Tudjman quoted Huntington in connection with the Croat-Bosniak conflict. In his interview with the *Feral Tribune* on 10 November 1997, the former Bosnian ambassador to the UK, Muhamed Filipović, said it was "by no means accidental that Huntington should appeal precisely to Tudjman....The theory about a clash of civilizations suits Tudjman, because it justifies his actions....He cannot find (justification for the war) in either the realm of politics or that of international law, but only in the sphere of ideology-which is why Huntington's thesis about the clash of civilizations serves his purpose."

26 In saying all this, we can entirely agree with Wachtel on several other points that he has made in such a convincing way. For example, with his opposition to the "inevitable" conclusions, which, as he says, "assume that the outlooks of individuals and groups are immutable" (1998:17), Wachtel's historical classification of the attempts at nation building in Yugoslavia as (1) Serbian, (2) multicultural, and (3) supranational models is among the best short accounts of different approaches to the Yugoslav national question. However, Wachtel-typically a representative of a cultural approach that somewhat underestimates the context-does not precisely explain why Yugoslavia collapsed in the 1980s, when Yugoslav identity was getting stronger in the cultural sphere, but weaker in the political sphere.

27 In the Communist interpretation of history, the first Yugoslavia was "the creation of Versailles." Croatian historians of the Communist past (like Tudjman and Bilandžić) are still committed to this interpretation. Tudjman argues that international factors played an absolutely crucial role in the creation of Yugoslavia and its development. For a debate on the Yugoslav question within the CPY (Communist Party of Yugoslavia) in the interwar period, see Vlajčić (1978, 1984, 1989) and A. Djilas (1991).

28 On these grounds, the Yugoslav army led by Kadijević supported the failed August 1991 military coup d'état by the Soviet generals. They hoped that the overthrow of Gorbachev would help reestablish a bipolar structure that would consequently make the fragmentation of Yugoslavia impossible. There were also ideological reasons for this support.
29 See Milošević's toast to Gorbachev in March 1988 (Milošević 1989:198-200), the opening speech at the 2nd Session of the CC LC (Central Committee League of Communists) Serbia (12 January 1990) by Tomica Raičević (IB CKSKS, 1/1990) and Štambuk's article in *Nin,* 29 January 1989. A more cautious approach to the consequences of *perestroika* for Yugoslavia is expressed by Bebler (1989).
30 This is the main reason for Marković's legendary comment on the breakup of the LCY: "This country will survive the breakup of the Party. It does not depend on it." In fact, he saw the breakup as the best opportunity to implement economic reforms.
31 *Delo,* 18 July 1990 and 1 November 1990. Yugoslavia was to receive US$47 million through PHARE. Greece was the only country that opposed this decision.
32 *Delo* 3 September 1990.
33 Josip Broz Tito (1892-1980) was the undisputed leader of Yugoslavia from 1945 to 1980. From 1937 he was head of the CPY (LCY after 1952), in 1945-53 the Yugoslav prime minister, and from 1953 to 1980 the president of the SFR (Socialist Federative Republic) of Yugoslavia. The most useful biography of Tito in Serbo-Croat is Dedijer (1953 and 1981) and in English those of Pavlowitch (1992) and Djilas (1981). West (1994) and Ridley (1995), Gow (1997), and Tepavac (1997) are useful too. Good guidance to literature on Tito is offered by Pavlowitch (1992).
34 The full titles of Milošević's posts since 1986 were: president of the presidency of the Central Committee of the League of Communists of Serbia (1986-89); president of the presidency of the Socialist Republic of Serbia (1989–90); president of the Republic of Serbia (1990-97), and president of the Federal Republic of Yugoslavia (1997-2000). Shorter versions of these titles are used in this book. For Milošević, useful sources are Cohen (1997), Djilas (1993), Djukić (1994), Ramet (1991), Vujačić (1995), Thomas (1999), and Sells (2002).
35 An exceptional treatment for Tito was introduced already in the 1963 Constitution. Article 220 of this constitution limits the time in office for a president of the republic to two consecutive terms, but it adds this: "There is no limitation in the case of Josip Broz Tito" (Petranović and Štrbac 1977:III:73).
36 Immediately after Tito's death, a slogan was invented by the political elite: "After Tito-Tito." In a joke it read "After Tito, Titanic."
37 This thesis is also popular in all parts of the former Yugoslavia that seceded, or would like to secede: it was Milošević who made the whole difference. This interpretation insists that the role of Milošević in Serbian politics was absolutely crucial. The conclusion is in its most direct form expressed by Wheeler (May 1999).
38 The terms were coined by Mason (1981). More about this debate in Browning (1992) and Breitman (1991).
39 In an interview with the author in June 1996. Along these lines, during an interview I conducted in May 1996 (published in *Arkzin* in June 1996), Tolis Malakos argues that the idea of the nation-state, imported from the West to the Balkans, produced conflicts both in the interwar period (with the attempt to create a Yugoslav nation-state) and in the aftermath of the 1991 disintegration of Yugoslavia. He argues that Yugoslavia had a chance only as a new "Ottoman Empire," a multiethnic entity, not as a nation-state.

Malakos, being a Marxist himself, comes close to Kardelj's understanding of the national question in Yugoslavia.

40 Kedourie (1991) points out similarities in the new world (dis)order following the fall of the Austrian-Hungarian and "Soviet" empires. In both cases, Kedourie says, small states emerged as a result of the principle of self-determination, but it soon proved that not many among them were democratic.

41 Religious differences were also abandoned among the Communists. Furthermore, unlike King Alexander, Tito was not a member of the ruling elite before he became the Yugoslav leader.

42 Reportedly, Tito realized this too late, in 1978 when his wartime General Vukmanović Tempo told him that there was no Yugoslavia any longer, and no Party. The Yugoslav former Foreign Secretary Mirko Tepavac (ousted as a liberal in 1972) recalls a conversation with Tito in autumn 1971, when Tito said, "If you saw what I see for the future in Yugoslavia, it would scare you" (1987:73). In 1973, Tito told Dara Janeković that if all that she had reported to him about the situation in the country was true, then he had "spent [his] life in vain" (interview with Janeković April 1998).

43 See, for example: Koštunica (1987-88) and Dimitrijević (1996). For a good academic analysis of the Yugoslav Constitution of 1974 and its consequences for further development in Yugoslavia (especially in Bosnia-Herzegovina), see Hayden (2000) and Vučković (1997).

44 Pizzorno (1984) points out how common it is that over time a person loses interest in something for which he or she was once ready even to die. The Yugoslav example also demonstrates how much people can change their political beliefs: not only "ordinary" people, but also (perhaps even more) members of the political, economic, military, and intellectual elites. The political elites in Eastern Europe were taken by surprise when various "revolutions" happened in their countries, no less than Western observers. Perhaps the best example is Romania's Ceaușescu, who convened a public rally to support his position, only to find that he had lost all support "practically overnight." Similarly, Slobodan Milošević was so convinced he would win the public vote at presidential elections in 2000 that he brought them forward and changed the constitution in order to enable a direct vote for president. In fact, revolutions-*per definitionem*-always take rulers by surprise. But in fact, none of these changes came overnight, as the participants and some analysts sometimes argue. As this book demonstrates, the disintegration of Yugoslavia was only the end result of a long prelude in which most of its elements had been tested and fully developed.

45 More on this will be said in chapter two.

46 As Stipe Šuvar pointed out in an interview for this book, the leading Yugoslav party ideologues (Edvard Kardelj and Vladimir Bakarić) were influenced by the ideas of Italian Marxist Antonio Gramsci and wanted to introduce some institutions derived from the Italian Communist Party. It is for this reason that the main conflicts between the elites and dissidents in Communist societies took the form of a conflict between the politicians and the intelligentsia. This was equally the case in Central and Southeastern Europe, where intellectuals traditionally played a "messianic" role in nationalist movements. In the Yugoslav case, as illustrated in the last two chapters, the new (nationalist) visionaries saw their chance after the death of the previous generation of (Communist) visionaries. Among them was Dobrica Ćosić, who said that the writers and intellectuals in nondemocratic states had "assumed the role of the conscience of the nation and society, the role of prophet and spiritual savior, as they did in the age of

national romanticism" (1992:18). In Serbia, in which Ćosić himself was first the most prominent member of the "critical intelligentsia" and then the first president of the FR Yugoslavia (1992-93), they "have been bringing about the spiritual rebirth of Serbian society" (1992:20). For an excellent analysis of the role of intellectuals in Serbia and Yugoslavia, see Dragović-Soso (2003). Similar examples could be found elsewhere in Eastern Europe.

47 The Eighth Session of the CC LC Serbia (analyzed in chapter six) is an example of this. Excellent sources on the importance of language in Communist politics are Waller (1972) and Bogdanović (1988).

48 The interpretation of Skinner's position in this section is based on his essays edited by James Tully and published in Skinner (1988).

49 For a debate on Skinner's position, see Skinner 1988 and McBride 1996.

CHAPTER TWO

The Kardelj Concept: Constructing the Fourth Yugoslavia (1974-1990)

> The unity of the nation is not possible unless based on a clear platform, on a clear outlook for the future development of society.
>
> **Edvard Kardelj**
> **(1977:263)**

2.0. Introduction

From the very beginning of the *Yugoslav idea*, and in all attempts to create a Yugoslav state, the main question was to be asked again and again: *What is Yugoslavia*? To what extent was it *an association of communities* and how far a *community in itself*?

There were four different constitutive concepts regarding the main question of (co)existence between Yugoslav nation(s) from 1918 to 1990: (1) the model of national unity; (2) the model of *Agreement* Yugoslavism; (3) the model of brotherhood and unity federalist Yugoslavism; and (4) the *Kardelj* model, which could be best described as a model of "associated labor international Yugoslavism." In this chapter we first briefly analyze the three earlier models, only to focus on the last: the fourth constitutive concept of Yugoslavia, formulated during the constitutional debate of the 1967-74 period. The three previous constitutive concepts provided the historical context for the fourth. Kardelj's concept of Yugoslavia was an attempt to construct reality in a different, and for most of its content, an opposite way from what had been in any of the three previous phases. In Skinner's terms, Kardelj (and Yugoslav Communists in general) cannot be understood without knowing the contexts available to him. The first step we need to take in analyzing political actions based on ideological concepts is therefore "to situate the text in its linguistic or ideological context: the collection of texts written or used in the same period, addressed to the same or similar issues, and sharing several conventions" (Skinner, 1988:9). The ideological context for understanding Kardelj is Marxism. The concepts against which he constructed his own alternative were (1) interwar Yugoslavism (national unity) and (2) the Soviet interpretation of Marxism. This chapter addresses the question of what the author was doing in writing a text in relation to other available texts that made up (these two) ideological context(s). To a lesser extent we shall also address other questions proposed by Skinner, such as what the author was doing in writing a text in relation to viable and problematic political action that made up the political context. This question will be discussed in the following chapters in which we further examine the relationship between the Kardelj concept and the political action that aimed at implementing it in reality.

2.1. Four Constitutive Concepts

2.1.1. King Alexander's National Unity *Yugoslavism (1918-39)*

According to the doctrine of *national unity*, the Serbs, Croats, and Slovenes were on their way to forming a single Yugoslav nation. The existence of three *tribes* (plemena) (as the official ideology treated Serbs, Croats, and Slovenes, but not any other ethnic group within Yugoslavia, such as the Bosnian Muslims, Montenegrins, and Macedonians), who had lived in different empires (Austria-Hungarian and Ottoman) and had different religions, was recognized as a transitional fact. Yugoslavia would be a vehicle for the development of a *Yugoslav identity* and a *Yugoslav nation*. The ideas of separate political identities should be suppressed and eliminated from political life. The constitutional structure of the *Kingdom of the Serbs, Croats, and Slovenes* (as the first Yugoslav state was called) was constructed to help the transition of identities from tribal separateness to *Yugoslavism*. The country was first administered in 31 units, deliberately organized to transmit these identities, then in nine counties (*banovine*), none of which was named after a dominant tribe.

This idea corresponded basically to the nation-state vision of Yugoslavia, with a Yugoslav nation being only in the process of being built. The Yugoslav idea as it emerged among the South Slavs in Austria-Hungary was a nationalist idea. The emergence of the Yugoslav state in December 1918 was the result of a particular interpretation of the principle of self-determination, and also of the understanding of its main creators, that the South Slavs (both those within the former Austria-Hungary and those in the South-Slavic regions that for centuries had belonged to the Ottoman Empire), were definitely becoming one nation. Once they had created their own state, they would have been expected to strengthen their *oneness*. The state institutions were in the first place *constructors* of a Yugoslav identity. As soon as this identity emerged, the country could be fully democratic, but in the meantime it should be *guided toward this goal*. The idea of a guided democracy was by no means specific or unique to the newly created kingdom. For most of Central and Southeast Europe, democracy was a relatively untried concept, often seen as being far too utopian to succeed. This was especially so in countries with a very low level of general education, where society remained rather traditionalist and authoritarian. After all, the concept of Yugoslav unity, linked with self-determination and democracy, was "invented" by modern intellectuals, but it succeeded only when it was wedded with the political interests of various elites. Tensions between the concept and political realities were there from the beginning. Although the very idea of Yugoslav unity emerged among intellectual elites in the nineteenth century, the state-once created-became an instrument of the Yugoslav idea promoted from "above," often by pragmatic elites interested more in Realpolitik than in intellectual concepts. Its contents came to be decided at the top of the social pyramid and to be transmitted to the base.

But this idea met with strong opposition from both Croatian and Serbian nationalists who could not simply accept the disappearance of the separate identities of their respective *tribes* and *nations*. The Croats warned that the Serbs were overwhelmingly dominant in Yugoslav institutions from 1918 to 1941. In the 268 months of the First Yugoslavia, Serbs held the Office of Prime Minister for 264 months, the Office of Minister of the Army and Navy for the entire 268 months, the Interior Ministry for 240 months, and that of foreign affairs for 247 months, finance for 216 months, education for 236 months, and justice for 237 months. The Orthodox (Serbs, Montenegrins, and Macedonians) formed 86.5 percent of the prewar Yugoslav generals and 70.2 percent of the entire number of army officers. At about that time, their share of the total population was 49.3 percent. Some of these disparities were a consequence of the outcome of the World War I, which Serbia ended victoriously, but Croatia and Slovenia (being part of the Habsburg Empire) found themselves on the losing side. However, the question of fairness soon emerged. Was it then really an impartial and *Yugoslav* policy, or only an extended Serbian policy under the name of *Yugoslavism?* Moreover, if the new state is indeed a democracy, why were the Slovenes and Croats so much underrepresented?

Ultimately, Yugoslavia was unified on terms closer to the Serbian proposals for a new Kingdom, which was to be organized on the idea of national unity and therefore centralized to a large extent. The readiness of the Croatian political elite (not necessarily the Croat population because a referendum on unification was never held) to agree to Serbian ideas was largely determined by the fears of Italian, Hungarian, and Austrian *revanchism,* and it seemed that they were united more by *negative considerations* (what would happen if they did not unite?) than by *positive bonds*.

Once that it seemed Croatian interests had not been treated with respect, the Croat question became the fundamental issue of the First Yugoslavia. To Yugoslav integralism, the Croats soon opposed their own Croatian integralism; to Yugoslav nationalism, their Croatian nationalism; to the project of *Yugoslav unity*, their own project of Croatian rights to their own state or at least a high autonomy within the existing state. This was a conflict of two emerging polities, which could not grow up together because they feared that the very existence of one would necessarily endanger the identity of the other.

On the other hand, many Serbs also had a problem in accepting Yugoslavism or centralization. Having a state of their own before unification, some of them challenged the very reasons for unification and the benefits it would provide them. The political conflicts in the new country split Serbian public opinion into *pro-Serb* and *pro-Yugoslav* policy orientations. This division characterized the Serbian political scene and society throughout the 20th century.[1]

Negotiating with both Serbs and Croats, King Alexander entered into occasional conflict with both sides, though in view of the nature of Croatian demands and the strength of their manifestation, he clashed more with the Croats than with the Serbs. His rule became more autocratic than any side wanted. His *Yugoslavism* conflicted with the reality of strong nationalist support for the Serb and Croat hard-liners. All of this only helped to build separate national identities for the Croats, Serbs, and Slovenes-a goal completely opposite to the wishes of the *integralist Yugoslavs*.

In such circumstances, Yugoslavia went from one crisis to another. Formed as a result of World War I, its very existence was challenged by the revisionist claims coming from neighboring countries, both in Central and Southeast Europe. Powers that were traditionally influential in the region but excluded from the Versailles negotiations, Germany and Russia (since 1922: Soviet Union) questioned the Versailles structure of Europe, of which Yugoslavia was part and in which it played a prominent role. Unable to find an acceptable path of internal cohesion, Yugoslavia seemed to be kept together more because of the common fear their constitutive tribes felt in the face of external threats than because of the internal pressure for unity. However, it should not be forgotten that the tradition of Serb-Croat cooperation, developed first between the Serbs and Croats in the former Austria-Hungary, did not completely vanish. Both the opposition and the government were of multiethnic composition. Although the national question was a serious and unifying force (especially for the Slovenes and Croats), the vote for each of the largest parties was still derived from various parts of the country (Banac 1984:389). Coalitions between parties were also transethnic.

When the Croat leader Stjepan Radić died after being shot by a Montenegrin (Serb) nationalist, member of Yugoslav parliament Puniša Račić, in the chamber of the Yugoslav Assembly in 1928, Alexander declared a personal dictatorship, abrogated the constitution, banned political parties, and announced a new wave of Yugoslavization. The country was finally named Yugoslavia, with an army general as prime minister. Although Alexander intended to further strengthen Yugoslavism by banning all separate national parties and renaming the country, his action was also an act of recognition that only ten years after the all-embracing unification, the Yugoslavs were brought to defend their state unity by a royal coup d'état. Being defended by a dictatorship, the Yugoslav idea could not expect to win approval among the Yugoslav democrats. Although Alexander's authoritarianism was not a unique phenomenon in interwar Eastern Europe (nor should it be compared with the dictatorships of Hitler and Mussolini in the 1930s), the first attempt to build a democratic Yugoslavia had clearly failed. The symbolic death of this concept of national unity was to be seen in the assassination in October 1934 of the unifier, King Alexander, by Croat and Macedonian separatists in Marseilles.

2.1.2. *Prince Paul's* Sporazum *Yugoslavia (1939-41)*

King Alexander's cousin Prince Paul reigned from 1934 to 1941 on behalf of the late king's son, Peter, who was still a minor. The fear of internal dissolution and external threat to the security of Yugoslavia made him think of a new constitutional arrangement between the country's constitutive nations. Since the *Croat question* was the most important issue and increasingly threatened to become an international issue as well as an eternal obstacle to any sustainable internal unity, Prince Paul moved toward a policy of a new agreement between the Serbs and the Croats.

After several failures, he succeeded in softening the radical demands of both groups. On the Serb side, he had to secure support for a substantial change to the integral Yugoslavism doctrine. On the Croat side, the ideas of separatism (which were encouraged by foreign forces, particularly by Italy) had to be defeated.

The final agreement was reached in August 1939 between Yugoslav Prime Minister Dragiša Cvetković (the prince regent's personal representative, a leader of the Yugoslav Radical Union) and the leader of the opposition, the Croat Vladko Maček. According to the *Agreement (Sporazum)*, the Croats were given autonomy within the administrative unit called *Banovina Croatia*. Both the name of the newly established unit and the competencies given to it (all but foreign policy, financial policy, the army, and transport) indicated that the crown acknowledged Croatian separateness and its right to be defined as a political entity. By this recognition, the official Yugoslav project was redefined from one of *Integral Yugoslavism* to *Agreement Yugoslavism*. Yugoslavia was no longer projected as a country that would nullify ethnic differences between its tribes, but as a common framework within which at least one (Croatian) separate entity should be recognized.

An acknowledgment of the autonomy of only the Croats produced new political and social antagonisms between the country's different ethnic groups. The Serb intellectual and political circles argued that *Agreement Yugoslavia* was to the advantage of the Croats and to the disadvantage of the Serbs (Dragnich 1983:123-134). It is difficult to agree entirely with such a conclusion. First, because Yugoslavia was still a country in which the Serbs retained the most important positions, such as the monarchy, the army, the police, and the main political posts. Second, because the agreement really made the common institutions stronger. Although the Croats earlier had no policy for Yugoslavia, considering it almost to be only an area of Croat foreign policy (A. Djilas 1991:134), they now accepted some responsibility for the future of the country. However, various Croatian political elites still remembered throughout the whole duration of Yugoslavia, including its later Socialist phase, that the Croats had achieved more in direct negotiations with the crown than through the democratic elections of the 1920-28 period. For Croatian leaders, the agreement was a message that democracy in a multiethnic country does not always mean fairness and justice. Sometimes more can be achieved by direct negotiations with authoritarian rulers than by democratic procedures. This lesson of history would resurge in the last phase of the Yugoslav crises in the late 1980s and early 1990-when the Croatian political elite strongly argued in favor of regionally based democratization, but opposed the all-Yugoslav elections. They feared that these elections could lead to an institutionalization of the dominant position of the largest nation at the expense of these smaller ethnic groups

However, the opposition to the agreement was sufficiently strong to check its implementation wherever possible. There were several sources of criticism. First, the *integralists* (with strong support in the military) argued that it led to Croat separatism and that it was basically unconstitutional. Another group of critics was organized within the previously *United Opposition*, which considered Maček's agreement with the ruling party a betrayal of the opposition. They were basically right when they argued that Maček was not interested in democracy as much as in the solution of the Croat question. Lastly, two groups that were not very influential at that time (but that played an important role later, during World War II) also opposed the agreement. The Croat separatists, located then in Italy and Hungary under the command of Ante Pavelić (later the head of the Independent State of Croatia) saw the agreement as nothing but a lifeboat for Yugoslavia that was to be sunk in the new world order promised by the Nazis and Fascists. On the other hand, the Communist Party (CP; the fourth strongest Yugoslav party in the 1920 parliamentary elections, outlawed a year later) had an ambivalent attitude toward the agreement. It welcomed the abandonment of integral Yugoslavism and Prince Paul's move toward the real politics of ethnic separateness. But it considered the new compromise to be only an agreement between two national bourgeoisies that had nothing to do with the real problems of the people. For the Communists, the real problem was that of social revolution. The real solution of the national question, Communists believed, could come only when exploitation ended. For both problems-the social and the national-there was only one solution-and that was revolution (Kardelj 1939).

All three opponents of the agreement (separatists, Communists, integralists) had been awaiting a suitable moment to attack it. When the government signed the acceptance of the Tripartite Pact (on rather good terms for Yugoslavia, and only in April 1941, at which time the rest of Europe had been either already occupied or was under severe attack from Germany) (Balfour, MacKay 1980:215-40), they saw their moment. The integralists, led by the air force commander, General Dušan Simović, overthrew the government in a coup d'état on 27 March 1941. Prince Paul was replaced by King Peter II (still a minor) and forced to leave the country. Crowds on the streets of Belgrade claimed *Better War than the Pact* (Bolje rat nego pakt), a slogan that entered the Yugoslav (especially Serb) mentality and remained there for years. The British Prime Minister Winston Churchill declared that the Yugoslavs had found their soul. But soon afterward they lost their country. After 17 days of resistance, the Yugoslav Army surrendered to the overwhelmingly stronger forces of occupiers, whose aim was not only to defeat Yugoslavia militarily, but also to dismember it.

The other two antiagreement forces-the Croat separatist Ustashas and the Yugoslav Communists-came also onto the stage. The latter group soon organized and began a liberation war, and also at about the same time (and sometimes with even greater intensity) a civil war with two other groups: the Croatian Ustashas and the Yugoslav but overwhelmingly Serb integralists (under the command of General Draža Mihailović-linked with the royal government-in-exile). Although the divisions were to a large extent also between ethnic groups, they often crossed ethnic lines, especially with the emergence of almost the only all-Yugoslav military and political force – the Partisans, Yugoslav antifascists led by the Communist Party of Yugoslavia (CPY). It should be stressed that though they differed in their stands on foreign occupation, the largest difference between these three forces was that they had different answers to the main questions: *What is Yugoslavia?* and *Should there be a Yugoslavia at all?*

2.1.3. Tito's Brotherhood and Unity *Federalist Yugoslavism*

Emerging out of the liberation struggle led by the Communists, the *new Yugoslavia* contrasted fundamentally with the Yugoslav Kingdom. As early as 1943, the king was temporarily banned from returning to the country, and from November 1945 he was permanently banned. His troops on the ground (the Yugoslav Army in the Fatherland-also known as Chetniks, under the command of General Draža Mihailović) were considered to be his main internal enemies (Djilas 1981:12; Seton-Watson 1985: 118-131).

In the years immediately after the Yugoslav unification (1918), the Communists had some specific difficulties regarding the Yugoslav idea and the Yugoslav state itself. They had changed their views on Yugoslavia several times from 1919 to 1937, regularly being a step behind the current Comintern policy. On the one hand, they argued that Yugoslavia was a product of the Versailles order, which was an expression of imperialist intentions. Yugoslavia was a product of the anti-Soviet policy of containment and also the Great-Serbian bourgeoisie, whose policy was driven by its imperial goals of exploiting other ethnic groups and classes in the country. On the other hand, though, Yugoslavia was a chance for the working class to unite beyond the ethnic borders. The unification of the South Slavs was therefore considered as a positive step, provided that the second phase of revolution (the proletarian one) followed the first: the bourgeois revolution of 1918. At one time, the Yugoslav Communists saw the future Communist Yugoslavia as the core of a future Balkan federation, which would be a step toward the worldwide revolution, ending in a worldwide Soviet Union of Socialist Republics.[2] Another source of controversies was the internationalist orientation of the Yugoslav Communists. As defined by the national unity concept, Yugoslavia was an instrument of Yugoslav (South Slav) nationalism. Its main purpose was to create a Yugoslav nation. Being internationalists and recognizing the separateness of the various constitutive nations of Yugoslavia, the Yugoslav Communists opposed such a concept. However, exactly because they were internationalists, they also supported the notion of cooperation and unity between (South Slav) nations within a wider framework of Yugoslavia. The controversy over cooperation between Yugoslav nations on the one hand and fears of the unitarist concepts, creating one single nation out of the various Yugoslav ethnic groups, on the other remained present throughout the existence of the postwar Yugoslav state.

The other reason for the skepticism of the Yugoslav Communists toward the existence of Yugoslavia was to be found in the Marxist and Leninist doctrine that the state should "wither away" as Communism approached. The very success of the CP could be measured by the level of the state presence in reality. Now, if the state was withering away, did this mean that the Yugoslav state would also disappear? Therefore how could patriotism be reconciled with Communism? These dilemmas regarding Yugoslavism caused continual conflicts and purges within the CPY from 1919 to 1937.³

The Communist Party was banned in the Law on the Protection of the State (1921), after which the police took severe measures against its members. Therefore, ever since 1921 the Yugoslav Communists had no reason to even think about working with the monarchy. One of their main objectives was to oust it once and for all. Starting as the fourth largest political party in the first Yugoslav elections (1920) with 198,376 votes (Banac 1984:389), they were reduced to no more than 700 members in 1924 (Pavlowitch 1992:119). In the late 1930s the CPY had 1,500 members, most of whom were either imprisoned or had emigrated from Yugoslavia. However, being internationalists and having their supporters from various parts of the country, the Yugoslav Communists were the most ethnically pluralistic political group. But the members of the CPY were not really representatives of their national groups. They were united in revolutionary action by the international proletariat. For the Yugoslav Communists, the national question was the main potential source of revolution. Linked to the peasant question (in the policy of the main opposition Croat Peasants Party), it became the weakest point of the regime in the 1930s. In the whole interwar period, and especially after the assassinations of CPP leader Stjepan Radić (1928) and King Alexander (1934), the national question became the main source of popular discontent. Encouraged by Prince Paul's moderate policy toward the opposition and by the Comintern *Popular Front* policy (1936-39), the Yugoslav Communists (from 1937 effectively led by Josip Broz Tito) strengthened their ranks by paying special attention to the national question. At the Fourth Party Conference in 1934, Tito reportedly held the view that the Communists "must take the lead in the national-liberation movement." Consequently, in what was seen as "the inauguration of the course toward creating a people's revolutionary party instead of an isolated, sectarian one,"⁴ two years later (1936) a separate Communist Party of Slovenia (CPS) and in 1937 the Communist Party of Croatia (CPC) were created by the CPY leadership. This was already a significant change toward recognizing the ethnic separateness of the Slovenes and Croats as a political fact two years before official Yugoslav politics moved toward the same recognition in the Serb-Croat Agreement.

It was no surprise that Tito and Edvard Kardelj, the two leading men of the new CPY leadership after 1937, were opponents of integral Yugoslavism and Pan-Slavism. Not only because they themselves were a Croat and a Slovene,⁵ but because as Communists they had no reason to be fascinated by a policy that outlawed their party and imprisoned their comrades and themselves. But more important than anything, they saw the national question as the main potential starting point of the social revolution in Yugoslavia. And also, they firmly believed that the national question could not be solved without a social revolution. In their minds, the Great Serbian bourgeoisie was the common denominator for both types of exploitation: it exploited the working class as a bourgeoisie and concomitantly exploited the small Yugoslav nations for the sake of the Great Serbian ideology.

By the formation of the two national Communist parties within the Yugoslav CP, the leading Yugoslav Communists demonstrated their belief that the class and national questions were linked. Slovenia, for example, could not be freed unless the Great Serbian bourgeoisie was overthrown. Integral Yugoslavism and Pan-Slavism were not much more than a cover that had hidden the great Serbian nature of the new state. The Slovene bourgeoisie, Kardelj said in his speech at the constitutive congress of the CPS, were concerned not with Slovene interests, but with their own class interests. The best it could offer, he concluded, was cultural autonomy within Yugoslavia. But the national question was not only a cultural or linguistic issue; it was a political issue as well. Consequently, the Slovene question could be solved only when the Slovenes formed their own state with the full right to self-determination as to whether they wanted to be united in a larger multinational state such as Yugoslavia.[6] And they could remain a part of Yugoslavia only if and when they were not exploited, but treated as an equal people in their own state. The bourgeois character of the state, Kardelj argued, was the main reason why the Slovenes had no more positive feelings for Yugoslavia than for the former Austria-Hungarian or Italian state. They were, the Declaration of the Founding Congress of CPS said, divided among four countries (Italy, Hungary, Austria and Yugoslavia) by the Versailles peace accord, becoming, therefore, one of the main victims of postwar European imperialism.[7]

When Yugoslavia was occupied and divided into various administrative regions supervised or directly governed by the occupier in 1941, Kardelj's conclusions about "bourgeois treachery" were easily seen as a good prediction. One royal government signed a treaty with Hitler, and another went into exile as soon as the first bombs reached Belgrade.[8] There was no such option for the Yugoslav Communists, and when the Soviet Union was attacked on 22 June 1941, they invited the Yugoslavs to fight against the occupation.

But the Yugoslav Communists did not fight for just any Yugoslavia, nor did they think the old idea of Yugoslavia was worth fighting for.[9] They promised a fundamentally new Yugoslavia, one in which their constitutive peoples would be equal and free and in which social justice would be achieved. In Tito's words, expressed as early as 1942:

> The words *national liberation struggle* would be nothing but words, and even deception, if they did not have, together with their meaning in the over-

all Yugoslav context, a specifically national meaning for each people individually, if they did not mean, together with the liberation of Yugoslavia, the liberation at the same time, too, of Croats, Slovenes, Serbs, Macedonians, Arnauts [Albanians], Muslims, and the rest; [the words would mean nothing] if the national liberation struggle did not contain the substance of effective freedom, equality, and brotherhood for all the peoples of Yugoslavia. This is the real essence of the national liberation struggle. (Tito 1942:3)

The new type of Yugoslavism, the vision of a federation of equal nations, motivated many non-Communists (especially in areas outside Serbia) to join the Communist-led Partisans. At certain moments, it looked as if the idea of national emancipation was emphasized much more strongly than the idea of social justice and revolution. In doing so, the Yugoslav Communists demonstrated not only political pragmatism, but also loyalty to their major allies in Moscow and London, who urged them to eliminate or suppress their revolutionary notions for the sake of Yugoslavian liberation. For a long time, the Yugoslav Communists, including Tito himself, hesitated to reveal their ideological background, speaking only of Yugoslav patriotism (Seton-Watson 1981:220). The slogan of "brotherhood and unity" expressed this notion in the most explicit way. Along with an open rejection of the "old Yugoslavia" and its main institutions (foremost the monarchy), the idea seemed appealing to non-Serbian ethnic groups in the country. Yugoslav orientation and the courage of the Partisans demonstrated in battle against the Ustashas in the first place attracted many Serbs at that time (especially those from the territories within the Independent State of Croatia-in today's Croatia and Bosnia-Herzegovina) to Tito's Partisans. In fact, as Gow argues (1992:54), by the end of the war the Serbs made up 75 percent to 80 percent of the National Liberation Army, followed by 15 percent to 20 percent of the Croats and less than 4 percent of Slovenes. The balance between Serb dominance in its rank-and-file and Tito (Croat) being the supreme commander offered certain hopes to all constitutive nations that the new Yugoslavia might indeed respect their interests.[10] This was especially so as Tito presented himself not as a Croat or indeed a Communist, but primarily as the leader of an all-Yugoslav "liberation movement," whose primary interest was to liberate the country and secure peace.

The new Yugoslavia was formed in November 1945 as a federation of six republics and their five constitutive nations (Bosnian Muslims were not at that time recognized as an ethnic group and were treated as ethnically undeclared until the late 1960s). The three *tribes* (Slovenes, Serbs, and Croats) were now recognized as nations, as well as two entities (Macedonians and Montenegrins), whose separate identities were not earlier recognized. But closely copying the Soviet blueprints, in reality the whole country remained centralized in regard to the most important functions, such as defense, foreign policy, economic and financial policies, transport, ideology, and culture. With time, the Communist character of the new Yugoslavia became ever more obvious. As a Communist federation, it was firmly led by the Communist Party leadership. Despite its federalist claims, and though the leadership comprised people from different nations, in practice Yugoslavia developed a political system that allowed no more than "regional cultural autonomy combined with the most rigid political centralization" (Seton-Watson 1981:339).

This situation created a new paradox: in words and indeed in ideological justification, the Yugoslavism of the Yugoslav Communists was fundamentally (i.e., revolutionarily) different from that of the interwar period. Yet it was equally centralized and equally undemocratic (in the sense of representative democracy) as the Yugoslavism of King Alexander and Prince Paul.

It is often emphasized (Bunce 1999) that unlike most other East European Party leaderships, this one had the legitimacy of a successful liberation movement supporting it. The whole legitimacy of Socialist Yugoslavia was built on victory over foreign forces and internal "quisling" forces. The bourgeoisie was identified as the source of internal betrayal in the war. Tito used the evils of civil war to legitimize and strengthen his power.[11] He considered opposition to his rule to be rooted either in the integralist Yugoslavism of the prewar bourgeoisie or in the quisling forces during the war. He justified the one-party system by interpreting the old multipartism as the main cause of the Yugoslav dissolution in World War II. In Tito's interpretation, multipartism was the road that led directly to fraternal slaughter.[12] The new Yugoslavism the Yugoslav Communists promised would guarantee no return to the past.

Yet despite their opposition to "Pan-Slavist and Yugoslav illusions" (Kardelj, 1962:138), in the first postwar years Tito hesitated to abandon the South Slav dimension of Yugoslav cohesion. As people who knew him later witnessed, deep in his heart he still believed that the South Slavs should be in one country because they were South Slavs (Dedijer 1980:76). This idea of South Slav unity motivated him to propose closer links with the only South Slav country outside Yugoslavia-Bulgaria.[13] Not only did the two countries share South Slav ethnic origins, they were also united by the common goal of building Socialism. If the South Slav concept and the revolutionary idea were the two cohesive elements for the Yugoslavs, why should Bulgaria remain outside such a country? Yugoslavs and Bulgarians therefore entered serious negotiations, signing an agreement on a new federation in 1948 (Kardelj 1982:94-97), which was immediately vetoed by Stalin.

The hesitation of the Yugoslav Communists, however, to entirely abandon the South Slav concept of Yugoslavia caused serious problems with the Albanians, the only non-Slav group living on the compact territory of Kosovo, in the south of Serbia. The Albanians felt alienated from any concept of South Slav Yugoslavia. Although in the war and in the first three years afterward, the Yugoslav Communists had a very close relationship with the Communists in Albania, and in spite of Stalin's proposals that they should effectively control Albania if they liked, the de facto unification between two countries never happened. A federation between Albania and Yugoslavia would definitely have disturbed the South Slav concept of Yugoslav unity. The preference that Yugoslav Communists gave to their links with Bulgaria over links with Albania was a strong indicator of their (ethnically-based) brotherhood and unity concept, which did not abandon the South Slavic dimension.

Being expelled from the community of Socialist countries in 1948, the Yugoslavs had to find a new road in a complex world situation, and a source of new legitimacy within the country. On both fronts, their cohesive ideas were challenged. If they dropped revolution from their programmatic agenda and relied only on South Slav brotherhood and unity, how different were they becoming from Alexander's or Paul's Yugoslavism? If they abandoned the concept of South Slav unity for the sake of international revolution, this would have weakened popular support for Tito and enlarged foreign support for his opponents.

Hypothetically, there was a third way, that of a democratic republic, sufficiently different from Alexander's authoritarianism on both accounts-as being democratic and as a republic. This meant a complete change of rhetoric and practice on the part of the Yugoslav leadership. But this was impossible without a re-institutionalization of representative (parliamentary, multiparty) democracy and the abandoning of Communism.[14] Although the first signs indicated that some of the Party leaders might have been willing to move toward a partial if not a full democratization (for example, Milovan Djilas), and in spite of being encouraged from the West to do so, they never reached the point of a break with the one-party monopoly and revolutionary logic. The ideology was for Yugoslav Communists always more than just a formal justification of their political actions-and it was for this reason that they found it impossible to abandon it. They instead tried very hard to show that it was the Soviets and not they who had deviated from Marxism. To the accusation of being "revisionists," they replied with the same counteraccusation against the Soviets. The Yugoslav identity was now created against not only the past concepts of Yugoslavism, but also against the Soviet concept of Socialism. These two *others* (the interwar bourgeois Yugoslavia and the Soviet type of Socialism) became the two landmarks against which the Yugoslav mirror image was to be created. The new Yugoslavia became constructed as an antipode to its own past and to the other model that claimed to be the blueprint of Socialism.[15]

Tito's ambitions to unify and lead all the South Slavs (and one day, if Georgi Dimitrov's "incautious" remark about an "East European Federation" were to be realized-possibly all East European Slavs or even all East Europeans) made Stalin think that Tito was primarily a nationalist and a rival Socialist leader (Dedijer 1980:167-8; Kardelj 1981:104-12). In Tito's hesitation to abandon the ethnic dimension in the new Yugoslavia's identity, Stalin recognized a deviation from internationalist principles for the sake of South Slavic (Yugoslav) nationalism. At the same time, the revolutionary dimension of the new Yugoslav identity distanced Tito from the other world power "entitled" (by the Moscow Conference in 1944) to control the region: the British. Being left on their own and isolated, Yugoslav Communists were pushed toward thinking of alternatives. Now willing to abandon Marxism, they embarked on reading the original texts by Marx and Engels (rather than various interpretations by Stalin and other Soviet leaders). They soon came up with a specific interpretation of Marxism, which would become known as "Socialist self-management."

A new reading of Marx proved to be extremely fruitful for the new identity-building of the new phase of Socialism in Yugoslavia. In 1952, the name of the Party was changed to the League of Communists of Yugoslavia, based on the example of Marx's Communist League of 1848. The idea of self-management appeared out of this reading in 1950. It was not a finished project, but more like a slogan for the new Yugoslav road to Communism. However, it had a relevant symbolic value in the early fifties. Finally, as regards foreign policy, Yugoslavia accepted the idea of nonalignment (formulated from 1956 to 1960), which gave Tito and his country what he always wanted: a distinctive and prominent role, this time in the world arena. The concept of brotherhood and unity had now been complemented with the idea of Yugoslav Socialist patriotism, a clear indication of the Socialist character of South Slav unity. Now that its borders had become safer as a result of the world power balance, and that internal enemies had been finally defeated, the existence of Yugoslavia was no longer in question. It was a time for social change, which would definitely eliminate the last vestiges of the national question. What the resistance to foreign occupation during World War II and to the Soviet Union in its immediate aftermath did in terms of the external legitimation of Yugoslavia, Western economic and military support did in terms of the internal legitimation of its leadership.[16] Being encouraged by Western loans and having an increasingly important say over the main problems of international relations (such as the Middle East Crisis, Cuba, and East-West relationships), Yugoslavia entered its *golden age*. In the sixties, she was the most developed of all the Socialist countries, with a promising level of GDP growth. The Yugoslavs felt more independent and wealthier than any of their Eastern neighbors, and more so too than any of their Balkan neighbors. It seemed that internal conflicts had been put aside. Tourism, which started in the mid-sixties, encouraged limited private initiative and small family enterprises throughout the Dalmatian coast. The borders were relatively open. The war was mostly forgotten. The repression of the first years of revolution (1945-50) had been stopped. The Yugoslavs dreamed their dream of prosperity and international influence.

However, it soon turned out that economic development also reopened questions that the leadership believed had been answered once and for all. The development of tourism, mostly along the Croatian coast, had a crucial significance. Encouraged by the main principles of self-management (which argued that the workers should decide on the results of their labor) and by market reforms launched in the mid-1960s, many Croats in particular started thinking economically-whose money was earned in tourism? How much of it went to Belgrade, and why was it proportionally distributed to all republics and provinces? Was this not an unfair redistribution? Should not money earned in Croatia be distributed from Zagreb, rather than from Belgrade? The same argument applied to remittances sent by Yugoslav Gastarbeiter, which also started in the mid-1960s.

The other parts of Yugoslavia had an argument against such proposals. Yugoslavia was one country, and without Serbian agriculture and the Bosnian work force, Croatian tourism would not be successful. However, twenty years after the Socialist revolution, the Croatian question seemed to return to the agenda, reminding many of the interwar disputes between ethnic segments of the bourgeois political elite. At the same time, all the developed areas (Slovenia, Croatia, and Vojvodina) questioned the necessity and efficiency of supporting the less-developed areas of Yugoslavia-Macedonia, Bosnia-Herzegovina, Montenegro and particularly Kosovo. For the first time after the war, the unity of the political elite seemed to be cracking on issues of social justice, national equality and the further development of Socialism. Discussions were held on several levels, but the main dimension was between centralizers and decentralizers. On the other side, among those who agreed that Yugoslavia had to be decentralized, the argument was whether it should be decentralized to only ethnic or also (and primarily) to functional units of various communities of self-managing interests.[17]

This conflict within the elite was fueled by the facts that President Tito was approaching an advanced age (he was 70 in 1962), and that he had already been in office 17 years (plus the 4 war years). Legally, it was no longer possible to elect him president once again. The extensive intraparty struggles for at least the No. 2 position, if not openly for the succession, were becoming stronger.[18] Although nobody openly challenged his undoubtedly exceptional position, everyone was thinking of the post-Tito period, trying to secure the best possible starting position. As early as 1960, this serious question appeared for the first time: What would happen to Yugoslavia after Tito?

2.1.4. The Emergence of Kardelj's Concept

The first discussions on this issue had already occurred in the late 1950s. The Party's long-term ideologist, Edvard Kardelj, was the most explicit, maintaining that the leadership still had too much power, that self-management was more or less a paper house without real roots in society, and that bureaucratism was growing above the sustainable level. But his main objections were about the illusion that a new Yugoslav nation was emerging out of the Yugoslav state. Socialism itself (just like any other ideology) can neither make nor deny the existence of nations, Kardelj wrote in the preface to the second edition of his book (1957), *The Development of the Slovene National Question,* originally written in 1939.[19] In 1961 he warned that "our federation is not a framework for any new Yugoslav nation, nor for any national integration about which in their time some advocates of hegemony and denationalizing terror used to dream" (Kardelj 1979:237).[20] For Kardelj, Pan-Slavist and Yugoslav illusions were the main potential danger for the future of Yugoslavia. They were the product of the epoch of bourgeois expansion and nationalism and therefore had to be defeated by the Socialist revolution. But also-and even more dangerous-they were potentially attractive to dogmatic forces and the new Socialist bureaucracy, which was pursuing a policy of Great-State Centralism, Kardelj's favorite term for what in essence was pro-Soviet or even pro-Stalinist tendencies within the country. Kardelj said clearly that there was a danger from Great-State ideology when the old revolutionaries passed away. In *The Development of the Slovene National Question*, Kardelj wrote that the Communists were the only force that could offer a viable solution of the national question in Yugoslavia. But also, in the new circumstances, it was from the ranks of the Communist bureaucracy that the main potential danger came. It is therefore the struggle with bureaucracy that should be given high priority in Party and state policies.

As early as the beginning of the 1960s, Kardelj concluded that even the idea of Socialist Yugoslavism was no longer feasible, since the Yugoslav nations had became fully constituted nations.[21] Yugoslavia had helped them to reach the level at which they wanted to have their own nation-states, staying in Yugoslavia as long and only as long as it suited their common interests. These interests, Kardelj concluded in 1970, could arise mostly in three areas: first, in the common defense policy; second, in the common goals of the revolutionary transformation of the country; and third, in developing a common market area. In all other areas, Kardelj said, the countries of Yugoslavia had become mature enough to take care of their own interests.

Consequently, Kardelj argued that Yugoslavia should make a decisive step forward from a centralized, nation-making state to a *federation of sovereign nation-states*. It was only then that both the interwar concept of Yugoslavism and the Soviet model of the centralized state could be defeated in reality. Furthermore, it was only then that the Yugoslav Communists could truly deliver on their fundamental promise of a genuine and fair federation of nations and thus become revolutionary-different from a prewar structure that failed to solve the national question in Yugoslavia. The interests and identities of the constitutive nations should be the basis for a genuinely new Yugoslavia. A multiethnic state that would not protect the independence and state structures of small nations would not be in their interest. Although Kardelj was an advocate of the existence of a Yugoslav state, Yugoslav unity in his concept now became conditional on the agreement of its constitutive parts. Already in 1957, Kardelj used words such as "today" and "at this moment" when concluding that Yugoslavia was in the interest of all Yugoslav nations (1957:47,62). And it existed because nations were "complete national organisms wishing to live in a community with all other peoples, and especially with the Yugoslav peoples" (1969:226). But Yugoslav unity was a matter neither of ethnic similarities nor of ideals, but one of interests and historical necessities. Furthermore, this unity was more an expression of internationalism than any South Slav (even less, Pan-Slavic) nationalism. Yugoslav nations, in Kardelj's interpretation, were open for global cooperation with other nations, and for this reason of course with one another. It was the internationalist character of Communism that linked them together: the ethnic similarities could help, but should not become the main source of their unity.

> The unity of the peoples of Yugoslavia is not based so much on their ethnic relatedness as on joint interests deriving from a common destiny, and above all on their joint struggle for Socialist relations among men and nations. (1975:141)

In fact, the existence of Yugoslavia was desirable "provided [that the state] was founded on the free will and equality of all peoples." Kardelj believed that the Socialist character of Yugoslavia, and not ethnic similarity, was the main unifying force of the country. He was in favor of a Socialist Yugoslavia also because he believed that small nations could not remain independent in the world of imperialism.

> Unity was to their advantage not only because of their momentous bonds from the past or from the standpoint of the brotherhood of nations in the future, but also in terms of shared economic interests and the interests of Socialism. Above all, unity was to their advantage in safeguarding their very existence and independence. In the modern world, the power of the reactionary force of imperialism and political hegemony is still extremely great. The Yugoslav nations would need one another's support to be able to guarantee their economic and political independence. (Kardelj, 1967:54)

Separatists and ethnic nationalists, whom Kardelj often criticized, were "cutting the branch on which they themselves were sitting" (1969:237) and "killing the ox for a pound of meat" (1969:238). In the world of the two powerful political and military blocs, it would have been virtually impossible for any Yugoslav nation to be independent to the degree that it was in Yugoslavia. In 1967, Kardelj referred to American policy toward Vietnam as a good example of what would happen to small independent states after the potential disintegration of Yugoslavia. They would become "a provincial appendage of the imperialist world, which is today again showing its true face in Vietnam" (1967a: 203). At the same time, however, he warned the Yugoslav unitarists not to provoke ethnic separatism but to allow any nation to create its own state within Yugoslavia. Only when the Yugoslav nations secured their own states within Yugoslavia, when they really governed themselves, would ethnic separatism be finally defeated.

> For a free decision of a nation on the form of its cooperation with other nations, it is first necessary that this nation has control over itself, and only then can it make a free decision. (1957: 47)

Kardelj's writings and speeches in the 1957-66 period met if not with open criticism, then certainly with serious resistance among the advocates of (unconditional) Yugoslavism and South Slavism within the party and state leadership. The most prominent among these critics was his main rival in a discreet battle for the succession of Tito, the state vice president, Aleksandar Ranković, who controlled home affairs. Although a Serb himself, he was recognized as more of a Yugoslav Centralist than a Serb representative in the federal leadership. For the democratic and liberal opposition, but also for many true believers in the concept of self-management from within the Party, Ranković was the embodiment of central state power. As a Party practitioner (the organizational secretary of the LCY and the main controller of the state security services ever since the end of the war) and not an ideologist (as Djilas and Kardelj both were), he was a symbol of the bureaucracy and state apparatus. In Kardelj's criticism of Great-Statist tendencies and bureaucracy, he therefore recognized himself. Although seemingly very loyal to Tito, Ranković was widely perceived as responsible for the belief that Yugoslavia meant more than just the sum of the six republics and that it was necessary to keep the federal institutions (especially the Party, the army, and the security forces) independent of the influence of republican leaders.[22] He feared decentralization, which he saw as a step toward the disintegration of Yugoslavia. The conflict between the two options for Yugoslavia intensified from 1962 to 1966. Since Kardelj and Ranković (together with Tito and the once-jailed Djilas) were considered to be the core of the war and first postwar leadership, their conflict was perceived as the conflict between the only possible successors of Tito. In this conflict, Ranković seemed to have a few important advantages over Kardelj: he was a party practitioner (not an ideologist) with a finger on the pulse of the party and the state cadre policy. He was also very popular in the army, Party, and state security institutions and was considered to be more acceptable than Kardelj to the Soviet Union, despite his radical action against the Cominformists (Soviet supporters) in the 1948-53 period. Ranković's rare public addresses were uttered in simple words, which was in sharp contrast to Kardelj's long and rather unattractive theoretical discourses. Lastly, Ranković was a Serb, a logical choice for leadership after the Croat-Slovene Tito in a country in which the balance of power was traditionally based on the relationship between the Serbs and Croats. But at the same time, all these advantages-and especially the last two-were somehow also disadvantages. In a highly ideological society, the second most powerful position was often reserved for the main ideologist of the regime. Furthermore, even though he was in charge of the state apparatus of coercion and repression, this would not automatically qualify Ranković as a successor in a country that proclaimed self-management and antistatism as its main ideology. The Soviet commendation too was more of a "kiss of death" in a country that viewed the Soviet Union as a danger and threat rather than as a friendly Socialist nation.

From 1962 to 1966, Tito seemed to switch his support from Kardelj to Ranković, then back and forth a few times. Deep in his heart, says Djilas, Tito believed that one day all the differences between the Yugoslavs would disappear, in both the social sense and the national sense. Milovan Djilas, once his *enfant terrible* and then his best-known prisoner, recalls a discussion on Yugoslavism with Tito in 1953:

> Tito believed that the nationalities of Yugoslavia would ultimately merge into one true nation. When I remarked that King Aleksandar Karadjordjević thought so too, he retorted: "Ah, but there was no Socialism then." (Djilas 1981:134)[23]

But crucially, Tito was now taking Yugoslavia down the path of reform, which was aimed at creating a country based on decentralization and self-management. By then he was an experienced politician, well aware that the national question could have been easily manipulated by opponents-both domestic and foreign-of his concept of Yugoslavia. Tito was now thinking of a long-lasting legacy of his rule. Resolution of the national question once and for all, if possible, was how he wanted his period to be remembered. The future of Socialism he now linked with the concept of equality among the nations of Yugoslavia. What were the prospects for Socialism if the nations of Yugoslavia were not satisfied regarding their national demands? And what was the future of Yugoslav independence if Yugoslavia was unable to create an effective and radical alternative to both prewar Yugoslavism and Soviet state Socialism?

The series of internal Party discussions from 1962 and 1966 showed a deep divide between the two options for the future of Yugoslavia. This debate, in which Kardelj won over Ranković (who was ousted from power in July 1966), determined the course of events that constituted the prelude to the disintegration of Yugoslavia in the last two decades of its existence. Kardelj's main argument in this debate-the one that finally swayed Tito to his side-was that Yugoslavia would not be different from the two *antipodes* (prewar Yugoslavism of King Aleksandar and Soviet statist Socialism) unless it further decentralized. The main goal of Socialism was that everyone decided on the results of their labor. This principle applied also to nations.[24] The decentralization of Yugoslavia was a precondition for self-management to work. Since self-management was the only real democracy, decentralization was a precondition for democratization too. On the other hand, the continuation of a centralized Yugoslav state would endanger both the *national* and *Socialist* dimensions of the Yugoslav revolution. Lastly, Kardelj underlined that the state was *withering away* in the *transitional period* and that the model of governance should be transformed toward direct democracy. Socialism was not about state itself; it was not a statism. Between Socialism and statism there is a permanent tension. The Socialist project is about replacing the state (an institution of the period of the bourgeoisie) with a self-managing society. Thus any attempt to preserve a centralized, strong, powerful state would be detrimental to the main purpose of Socialism. Indeed, it would be anti-Socialist.

Tito agreed with this interpretation, which was entirely in line with the Marxist concept of the "withering away of the state." He believed that the key to Socialist transformation lay in the Party, not in the state, and thus accepted that the state should be decentralized, but he requested that the Party should remain united. Tito now agreed to strengthen the Party and to weaken the state. If the Party were sufficiently strong to lead society as its vanguard, the stability of Socialism would be guaranteed. The national question-which Tito viewed as the remnant of old class-divided society-would be solved too as social inequalities in general diminished. Nationalism is not something endemic to Yugoslav nations, but a product of circumstances in which they found themselves. These circumstances were characterized by long historical foreign domination and domestic inequality often linked with nationality. The purpose of Socialism is to change these circumstances once and for all. Once this is done, the national question will no longer pose a threat to Yugoslav unity.

Furthermore, Tito shared Kardelj's argument that the dissolution of Yugoslavia was not a realistic option because it would change the whole international balance of power. If this were so, nationalism and separatism had no chance as long as the Communists remained in power. And this would be so for as long as the Communists demonstrated they could offer more independence to nations than either "the imperialist forces" of the western world or the forces of (Soviet) statist Socialism. Since in principle there could be no "return to the past," the real danger originated in a different, statist type of Socialism.

> For, as I have already stated, the alternative here is not whether Yugoslavia will survive or not, but whether it will continue to develop as a Socialist, self-managing, and democratic community of equal peoples, or whether it will fall into the hands of hegemonic forces in any political or ideological guise. (Kardelj 1981:228)

By "hegemonic forces," Kardelj meant Soviet-type Communists or any other type of great-statist ideology that would "naturally" rely on the strongest nation, the Serbs or perhaps even the two strongest: Serbs and Croats jointly. Kardelj insisted that these forces must be denied any possibility of succeeding to the presidency and that Tito's role in achieving this was crucial. No other "social critics" (as Kardelj called them in his 1965 book) represented such a real danger to the Yugoslav project of Socialism as those who advocated different "directions of the development of Socialism."[25] Because the *old society* "had absolutely no chance of success, it may be claimed that today the...choice [is] between Socialist self-management...and the system of bureaucratic-technocratic statism" (1973:286). The future of Yugoslav Socialism depended-in both its national and its class aspects-on who would define and lead Socialist policy. Neither the liberals nor the nationalists could succeed, because of the "objective laws" of social development and because of international and domestic reality. The future of Yugoslavia thus ultimately depended on "subjective forces," among which the Party played an exceptional role.[26]

In this conclusion, Kardelj had the support of the younger cadres, the newly elected leaders of the republics and provinces. Not only did they share his enthusiasm for further changes of the bureaucratized system, but they also sought more autonomy for their republics and more security for their positions in the post-Tito era. Since none of the Republics (not even Serbia) had a majority of votes to control the federal leadership on their own, all of them preferred the second best option: to have as much autonomy as possible in their own territories and to prevent any drastically unfavorable outcome. Since the federal leadership was firmly in Tito's hands, they were all expected to be only republican representatives. Increasingly, the leaders of the republics focused on doing exactly what was expected of them-to conduct only "republican" politics, thinking of Yugoslavia in a way increasingly similar to that of the prewar Croat leader Stjepan Radić-as an arena for their republics' "foreign" policy.[27]

The victory of Kardelj's concept over the one symbolized by Ranković in 1966 marked the end of the third *constitutive concept* of Yugoslavia and introduction of the fourth, which is often referred to as Kardelj's concept of self-managing decentralized Yugoslavia. The new concept, based on Kardelj's interpretations of Marxism and of Yugoslav political reality, was defined in the 1967-74 constitutional debate and codified in the 1974 Constitution. As both Tito and Kardelj admitted, the changes introduced on this occasion had a *revolutionary character*.

2.2. The Elaboration of Kardelj's Concept

2.2.1. A Biographical Note on Kardelj

Edvard Kardelj (1910-79) was the most prominent ideologist among the Yugoslav Communists throughout the Tito period, for more than forty years from 1937 to 1979. When Ranković was ousted in 1966, Kardelj remained the only member of Tito's closest wartime leadership still in power. Tito himself considered him his closest political aide, and "an illuminating figure [who] will be an inspiration to generations to come as an example of a consistent Communist, tireless revolutionary, and a wonderful man" (Tito 1979:385).[28] His Slovenian origins, Yugoslav political orientation, and Marxist beliefs provided the major context in which Kardelj's actions in the post-Ranković years should be analyzed. Although a Slovene, Yugoslav, and Marxist, Kardelj opposed Slovenian nationalism, Yugoslav unitarism, and Soviet state Socialism, building up his own interpretation of Slovenian interests, the Yugoslav constitution, and Marxist principles. Although Kardelj's views on these three major issues had been developed in almost thirty years of his writings prior to 1966, it was only now that he saw the real chance to transform his beliefs into a new constitutive concept and make it the pillar of the new (fourth) Yugoslavia. Unrestricted by any other member of the political elite except Tito himself, Kardelj proceeded to see his ideas transformed into the constitution, laws, and political decisions, creating what would become, in essence, *Kardelj's* (already post-Titoist) Yugoslavia. Before I move to expound his views in detail, a brief biographical note is necessary to explain the origins of Kardelj's ideas.

An event that, as he himself later explained, "decisively influenced" his decision to join the Communist Party was the conflict between the Communists and members of the Organization of Yugoslav Nationalists (ORJUNA), which occurred in his youth in the Slovene mining town of Trbovlje. While a student at the

Teachers' Academy in 1928, eighteen-year-old Kardelj joined the antiunitarist and the antimonarchist forces. His first public appearances were indeed closely linked to discussing the national question in the light of Marxist theory. In his first article ("The National Question as a Scientific Question," 1932), Kardelj concluded that "every nation has the right to an independent life, but such freedom will be won only by the constant struggle of the working people, because-as we have seen-the national problem is in its essence not a cultural but a social problem" (Filipović 1979:154). This idea was further developed in Kardelj's 1939 book on *The Development of the Slovene National Question,* which marked a turning point in the Communist understanding of the national question in Yugoslavia. After several years of illegal political activity in Slovenia and several prison sentences (some of which-the most extensive ones[29]-were served in Belgrade prisons), in 1934 he went to Moscow to attend courses and teach the history of the Comintern at the Communist University of the National Minorities in the West (KUNMZ), and at the International Leninist School. After two-and-a-half years in Moscow, he returned to Yugoslavia in February 1937, when he joined Josip Broz,[30] who was soon appointed general secretary of the CPY by the Comintern. Kardelj remembered Broz from Broz's spectacular 1928 trial in Zagreb, when he was jailed for five years for having attempted to organize an uprising there.[31] They soon became close, fighting against the "factionalism" and "sectarianism" of the CPY. The new political leadership of the CPY, Kardelj said from a distance of 30 years in 1967, "dropped sectarian slogans" and offered "the unity of democratic forces in the struggle against the antidemocratic regime and against the growing fascist menace" (1967:12-3). There were, he acknowledged, four major focuses of the Party's new policy: (a) the fascist threat-especially after the Austrian *Anschluss* in 1938; (b) the economic situation and increasing poverty of the working class and masses; (c) the antidemocratic political system; and (d) the national question. But as much as the Communists later emphasized Tito's autonomous role in consolidating the Party, it was nevertheless a fact that these four issues were entirely in accordance with the new approach favored by the Comintern itself. This was the time of "the popular front" policy, which urged the Communist parties to approach and cooperate with other "progressive" social and especially national movements in their respective countries. Antifascist fronts, of which the Communists were a part, had been formed in France and Spain at the same time. Within the Comintern, as well as within almost every one of its national sections, the supporters of the old policy of the struggle of "class against class" were replaced by the supporters of the new policy of the "popular front against fascism."[32] The internal Party conflict between the two approaches to Fascism was also strong in the Yugoslav Party and was not resolved until the Fifth Party Conference in Zagreb in 1940. At this conference, Tito was confirmed as the Party secretary, and

Kardelj was elected to the Politburo. Tito and Kardelj, therefore, came to the top of the Party as Comintern loyalists and as exponents of less sectarian and more open politics for the renewed Communist Party of Yugoslavia.

During the war, Kardelj was among the main organizers of the Slovenian Partisan liberation movement. Practicing the policy of a wide antioccupation and antifascist coalition of the main political forces in the country, the Slovenian "Liberation Front" (*Osvobodilna Fronta*) became a unique political formation. It was not led by a Communist, but in fact by a man who started a public polemic with Kardelj's book in 1939.[33] But Kardelj himself was its vice president. The formation of the "Liberation Front," containing representatives of the three main currents of the political spectrum (Christian Socialists, Liberals, and Communists), was a sign of wide cooperation with the Communists from the beginning of the occupation. Partly, it was also an expression of the Slovene political tradition, which is often characterized as "corporatism."[34] But it was Kardelj's 1939 book that made many believe that the Communist movement did care about Slovene national interests and that the liberation struggle would result in a Slovene state (though perhaps recognized only internally, rather than internationally) based on social justice and national freedom.

From 1941 to 1945, Kardelj was also the most prominent Slovene representative in Tito's headquarters. He was one of the two main creators of the 1943 AVNOJ Declaration (the other being Moše Pijade), which declared the wish of the Yugoslav Partisans to establish a federation after the war. In 1943 Kardelj became vice president of the newly established National Committee of the Liberation of Yugoslavia (NKOJ), effectively the Partisan Government. He drafted the agreement between NKOJ and the Yugoslav Royal Government in 1944 (the Tito-Šubašić Agreement). In 1945 he became vice president of the Yugoslav government and minister for the Constitutive Assembly. He was Yugoslav foreign secretary and head of the Yugoslav delegation at the Paris Peace Conference.[35] He was also one of the main participants in talks with Stalin in Moscow from 1945-1948.[36]

In the whole postwar period, Kardelj was in charge of the structuring of the political system and ideology. Milovan Djilas, his colleague in the Yugoslav party leadership, remembers that Kardelj was-together with him-the main creator of the self-management doctrine. Writing about the first days after the conflict with Stalin in 1948, Djilas says that Kardelj and he had to convince Tito "that without an ideological squaring of accounts with the Soviet system, without ideological backing for our positions, we would lose our bearings, our confidence, and our stability" (Djilas 1981:33). In Djilas' words, Tito accepted self-management only after initial hesitation and "was never exactly passionate about it" (1981:76).

On the contrary, Kardelj was-on Djilas' account-a genuine democrat within the Party. He belonged to a liberal group within the Party's leadership (1981:157), not only immediately after 1948, but also later, from the early 1960s. As such, Kardelj was, more than any other member of Tito's inner circle, a target of frequent attacks by Soviet Marxists and politicians. By the Soviets he was seen as the leading critic of their own system, which Kardelj often attacked as too statist and bureaucratic.

But although Djilas remembered Kardelj as "resourceful, clever, tolerant, civilized, and cunning" (1981:159), he had a chance to experience Kardelj's political realism too. In 1954, a year after Stalin's death, Tito was showing signs of wavering about self-management. Milovan Djilas was the first victim of the new circumstances. In January 1954 it was Kardelj who claimed that Djilas was a revisionist under the "anarcho-liberal" influence of the ideas of Bernstein. More like Tito, Kardelj believed that "without organization and without power, ideas are little more than a pipe dream" (Djilas, 1981:159).[37] Although Kardelj "cherished a secret desire for what is democratic," Djilas believed he was "without the guts to fight for it, to sacrifice for it" (1981:149).[38]

Djilas' characterization of Kardelj explains his wording of the program of the LCY, which was accepted at the Seventh Congress of the LCY in 1958, never to be changed or even amended by the Party until its disintegration in January 1990. Because of its severe criticism of the Soviet one-party system, the program became the source of constant dispute between the Yugoslav and Soviet Communist Parties. Consequently, Kardelj was considered to be the main anti-Soviet in the Yugoslav leadership until his death.[39]

Within the state leadership, Kardelj held the post of chief lawmaker and, especially, of constitution writer. His most important job, for which he will be remembered in all the Yugoslav republics, was that of the chairman of the Constitutional Committee for three Yugoslav constitutions (1946, 1963, and 1974). Being in charge of the constitution, Kardelj formulated the normative elements of Yugoslav Socialism. He did it not only through his speeches and public addresses, but also in a dozen books.[40] His last book, *Ways of Developing the Socialist System of Self-Management,* (written a year-and-a-half before his death in 1977) was accepted as a "part of the ideological and political guidelines for the League of Communists" in preparing the 11th Congress of the LCY in 1978.[41] Together with Tito's concluding speech at this Congress, it represents the unofficial political testament of the two leaders of Yugoslav socialism.

For all these reasons, it is not difficult to understand Tito's words, that Kardelj was a key participant in the "strategy making of [our] movement" (1979:383), and that he was his "closest aide" in foreign policy and in formulating a new "theory of the national question" (Tito, 1979:383). It is therefore justified to take Kardelj as one of the most reliable sources to reveal the Yugoslav Communists' story, their intentions, and the policies that led to their realization.

2.2.2. Kardelj's Interpretation of Marxism

As I have already argued, there were two *antipodes* to the new project of Socialism, as Kardelj's writings suggested: (1) interwar Yugoslavia, which was considered to be unjust in ethnic and social terms; and (2) the Soviet type of Socialism, which was treated as revisionism from Marxism following the split between the USSR and Yugoslavia in 1948. We have already discussed the Kardeljist alternative to interwar Yugoslavism. This part of the chapter focuses on Kardelj's interpretation of Marxism and the differences between the Yugoslav and Soviet models.[42]

The Yugoslav Communists claimed that their project of Socialist revolution was a "practical implementation of Marxism in society" (Tito 1952, in Dedijer 1984:610). When asked about Titoism as a new doctrine, Tito fiercely rejected its existence:

> Titoism as a separate ideological line does not exist....To put it as an ideology would be stupid....It is simply that we have added nothing to Marxist-Leninist[43] doctrine. We have only applied that doctrine in consonance with our situation. Since there is nothing new, there is no new ideology. Should Titoism become an ideological line, we would become revisionists; we would have renounced Marxism. We are Marxists; I am a Marxist, and therefore I cannot be a Titoist. (Dedijer 1953:432)

As Marxists, the Yugoslav Communists believed that socialism was a transitional phase from capitalism to Communism. The notion of transition remained a stable part of Kardelj's concept. "The times we live in are a typical transitional period between two historical epochs. Elements of both historical epochs exist and are operative within the frameworks of each individual country," said Kardelj in his 1955 speech at Chatham House in London (1955:69). More than twenty years later, in 1977, in his last important study, *Ways of Democracy in Socialist Societies*, Kardelj repeatedly concluded: "We are living in a typical period of transition" (1977:18).[44] Transition was a long-term project, that began only with the Socialist revolution.[45] It was also a complex project of social, economic, and political changes.[46] These changes are permanent and revolutionary in their character. They mean the "gradual acquisition of positions in society by the working class" (Kardelj 1977:104) and destruction of the last remnants of the bourgeois system.[47] Socialism is a time of building a "future world" that would reduce social antagonisms to a minimum, fully developing "each individual's creative will" (1955:20). The end of the process is known: Communism.

Kardelj had a clear vision of the future world and was convinced that a vision of the future was a gift granted to exceptional politicians, such as Tito was. However, not only the top politicians, but also the Communist rank-and-file were expected to be clear in their goals and "must build [the society] in anticipation of such a future" (1977:185). The whole idea of politics in a Socialist society was linked to this final aim. The very formulation of the concept of the future was the prime political activity. It involved a selection of the "new," which should be protected and helped by the party to develop, and of the "old," which should be equally "helped" to "wither away." In the order that claimed to represent the future, the political prophets (visionaries, in Kardelj's words) were creating reality. As formulated in the LCY Program (1958:266), the "historic task" and "ultimate goal" of the Yugoslav Communists were to "transform the contemporary social scene, which bears all the marks of the transition period, into one in which classes and all traces of exploitation and the oppression of man by man will disappear," to create "a society without a state, classes, or parties" (1958:267).

What politics also involved, the Yugoslav Communists argued, was to convince as many people as possible about this vision of the new society. It was the *scientific character* of Marxism that could help them in doing so.[48]

> Following a critical Marxist analysis of social trends, the League of Communists has arrived at scientific data about the essence of social processes. On this basis it established the directions of the further development of the revolution, ensuring its continuity. At the same time, it armed the working class with these data, making it the conscious subject of Socialist development. (Tito 1978:65)

As Tito said in his report to the 11th Congress of the LCY (1978), self-management was "the cornerstone of the scientific theory of the classics of Marxism" (1978:66). Marxist science and philosophy[49] were therefore an essential help to Socialist forces in contemporary Yugoslavia. These forces should base their activity "on scientific knowledge" (Tito 1978:68).[50] On the contrary, "those social sciences that are under the influence of bourgeois science would hardly be in accordance with our Socialist trends" and should therefore be subjected to "ideological struggle."[51] In Kardelj's words, change from one epoch to another was the result of organized political action, which was "based on science and specialized knowledge, placed at the service of…the masses" (1972:45).

Such a change was inevitable, and it meant a progression.[52] Socialist societies were "an important historical advance" when compared with the "political pluralism of bourgeois society" (1977:165). The main difference between the two was not primarily in the model of government as much as it was in the types of interests they protected and promoted. In general, politics was about interests. A state protected and promoted the interests of the ruling class regardless of the form and political system it developed.

> The only difference [between "our society" and "bourgeois democracy"] is that...our defense of the system is in the interest of the overwhelming majority of working people, whereas in a bourgeois democracy there is often a hypocritical cover-up of its being the political system best suited to the capitalist mode of production. (1977:216)

Such a cover-up was impossible in the long run and would therefore inevitably underpin the internal conflicts immanent to a bourgeois society. Kardelj had no original thoughts about it that had not already been expressed in Marx's or Lenin's notion of dialectics. However, he explicitly underlined that to be "in the interest" of the majority does not necessarily mean to be supported by the same majority. The majority might be unaware of its own best interests; it might be blind to them. This is why a vanguard was needed to show the proper way and to educate the masses. This was why the role of the Party as the *collective intellectual* was crucial in the *transitional period*. "Communists," says the program of the LCY, "must educate the working people to take a greater, more direct, and more independent share in the management of society, and to think and act in a Socialist manner until the very last citizen has learned to manage the affairs of the community" (Program 1958:128).[53] There is no doubt that the Communists were seen as not only capable of this task, but as a predestined force for it.

> That democracy is not synonymous with rule by erratic impulse and that it is not the Party's role to act as a programmed executor of the "will of the majority" are fundamentals never forgotten by the Party, despite its consistent commitment to democratic goals and the masses. If the Party meant to remain the leading force of society, it had to see deeper and further than the broad mass of the people and the majority. The Party had to perceive the principal historical meaning of its leading ideological and political role in elaborating the long-term goals of progressive social action and in persevering in its work of transmitting its progressive learning to the broad masses of the people. (Kardelj 1967:47)[54]

Socialist democracy, Kardelj argued, was not only superior to "political" (capitalist, liberal) democracy, but it was the only real form of democracy because it included economic equality, not only political. Socialism was a definite break with any exploitation, both within countries and between them. Ultimately, democracy is possible only when exploitation has been abolished.[55] Democracy is not only a procedure. It is not a system either. It is not acceptable per se, but only if it is Socialist. Socialist democracy is, as the Program of the Communist Party of the Soviet Union (CPSU) (1961/1962:32) declared, "a new type of democracy-a democracy for the working people." There could be no genuine democracy in a capitalist society because democracy was primarily the possibility to fully decide on the results of one's own labor. In Tito's words, "only in Socialism could an individual be regarded as totally equal, because equality always has an economic basis. The economic basis makes democracy in Socialism real" (Tito in Dedijer 1984:610). This was why both Tito and Kardelj believed that self-management was the highest realistically possible level of democracy applicable to Yugoslav experience. Self-management was the key to connect "real individual liberty," which "is made through the economic process" (Tito in 1952, Dedijer 1984:611) with the freedom of social groups, such as class and nation. On both accounts-as a strategy for social justice and national equality-self-management was seen to be the perfect solution. In contrast to prewar Yugoslavia, in which centralization meant both national and class exploitation, the new Yugoslavia was, at least in theory, based on the principle of full autonomy in deciding the outcome of one's own labor.

Kardelj made a significant effort to explain self-management as the result of Yugoslav political tradition, which was not that of the developed capitalist mode of production. The (relative) autonomy of the Yugoslav Partisan movement from Moscow, and also its relatively broad scope among the population, was now used as the main sources of new system building. Kardelj also emphasized that the Yugoslav bourgeoisie left no significant heritage of democratic institutions, characterized by strong parties, parliamentary tradition, or impressive records of human and political rights. But even if it had been much different, a Socialist country could not just simply take over the institutions of bourgeois society without readjusting them to new social goals. Of course, it had even less reason to establish them where they did not previously exist. The institutions of bourgeois society, Kardelj says, in fact "blur the true class nature of the system" (1977:108) when claiming they represent "abstract citizens" or "the whole society." In reality, however, a citizen had no say in bourgeois democracy dominated by political parties. In fact "he often feels as though he were living in a jungle in which there is a constant struggle going on between interests and forces that are alien to him and incomprehensible, so that he retreats into the only world that is left to him, the world of the "lonely consumer" (Kardelj 1977:112). However progressive it was in previous periods of social development, political democracy was now only a farce, a false and misleading external picture, a façade of capitalist society[56] that promoted a real economic and political inequality among its citizens.

Parliament and political parties are the main institutions of such a system. Kardelj rejected them both. In his conception, parliament was an embodiment of the representation of abstract citizens. Thus it was no more than a place for the stabilization of class power, which was concentrated outside it, in many circles of "extra-parliamentary power."[57] In short, the parliamentarianism of representative democracy was there to represent and preserve society as it is. The Socialist system had a completely different purpose: to radically change reality. The old system was there to represent "what is," the new one to represent "what ought to be."

Subsequently (and from this conception, of course, logically), Kardelj attempted to build the Yugoslav political system on exactly the opposite grounds to those of representative democracy. Yugoslav Communists, he says, have no reason to buy "secondhand" clothes from the bourgeoisie. They had no interest in rebuilding political parties that had never found their roots among the people and that were not "the last word" in social development (1977:130). Parties and parliaments were products of the bourgeois phase of social development: they did not exist before, nor will they necessarily exist after it. Kardelj was convinced that one day when Socialism became the indisputable and dominant system in the world, we would look at political parties in the same way as we did now at the institutions of feudalism.

What makes Kardelj most different from the Soviet critics of bourgeois democracy, however, is his criticism also of one-party systems.[58] Kardelj refutes the Soviet-style one-party system as incompatible with self-management, and indeed with Socialism.

> Furthermore, the one-party system becomes more vulnerable to deformations the farther it gets from the initial stages of revolution. (1977:118)

In a powerful attack on one-party systems, Kardelj went so far as to conclude that in Eastern Europe one party had taken over the role that was performed by many parties in the West. And that was all. This very change, however, had not changed much. This was in fact a regime change, not a revolution. Certainly it did not open the doors to direct, economic, self-managing democracy, which was Kardelj's ideal. Politics had not become more accessible to the people, but was controlled by the top leadership of the party. It was all contrary to what self-managing democracy was intended to be. Kardelj's criticism of the Soviet model was as strong as his rejection of Western democracies.[59] For Yugoslavia, he was constructing a *third way* in what he considered to be a real alternative to both sides of the Cold War divide.[60]

The attempt to offer an alternative to East European models and the Western democracies was the reason behind the *revolutionary* restructuring of the Yugoslav political system. The old parliamentary structures were destroyed. New "delegate assemblies" were created, and thousands of people really became members of such groups as delegations, working councils, and self-managing interest communities.[61] Instead of professional politicians as in parliamentary democracies (who were declared "subservient to extra-parliamentary class power"), the assembly delegates were only spokespersons of their delegations. Usually they had to vote as they were instructed, and they were replaceable at any time. A complex electoral system was introduced that abandoned equal representation of citizens, replacing it with functional representation of social groups.[62] The Party still kept the *leading role*, but without being named a *party* (since 1952: the League of Communists), and was supposed to run society by persuasion of the workers and citizens (assembled in the Socialist Alliance of Working People), not directly. The system of self-management was to replace the state, which was decentralized on its way to withering away. After 1968, even the defense system was, in theory, replaced by the concept of the general people's defense.[63] Eventually the functions of the Yugoslav Federal State were drastically reduced, while the functions of the republics were increased by the new constitutive concept. The reform of the federation in the 1967-74 period was a logical consequence of the introduction of Kardelj's concept, which was accepted by almost all relevant participants in Yugoslav politics. Here I argue that we cannot understand the motives of political actors in the 1967-74 constitutional debate without understanding the narrative they had followed. This narrative was based on Kardelj's interpretation of Marxism, which included the notion of the gradual decentralization of state toward its dying out at the end of the transitional period toward Communism.

2.2.3. The Notion of State in Kardelj's Concept

On both accounts-as a supranational body and as a potential "nest" of bureaucrats-the federal state had been increasingly seen as a potential danger. Apart from this, if the Yugoslav Communists wanted to offer a real alternative to both the interwar Yugoslavism and Soviet Communism, they had to make a significant step toward further decentralization of the federal state. It was in this belief that we must look for the motives of the constitutional reforms.

Kardelj was not an anarchist, and he was a severe critic of "theories of spontaneity," which he (incorrectly) associated with anarchism.[64] He believed that the state had an important and progressive role in securing the results of the revolution, especially in its immediate aftermath. But the state was still a product of the past historical epoch, which was inevitably to be substituted at the end of the transitional phase. It was not the aim of Socialism to "create a state-sponsored democracy, but rather to socialize state functions and to promote self-management and self-managing democracy" (Kardelj, 1977:140). Once direct democracy is promoted, the "state apparatus will turn into a specialized public service of the self-managing society" (1977:140).

Contrary to the Soviet optimistic predictions of the Khrushchev period that the state would wither away in 20 or 30 years,[65] Kardelj thought that it would take several generations before that happened. But the process of the "withering away of the state" was relentless. And it began with the revolution itself. The promotion of the Yugoslav model, therefore, demanded transformation of the state by transferring its functions to society.[66] In 1969, Kardelj declared that the Yugoslav state was not a "classic" state,[67] but a "self-managing community of working people, nations, and nationalities"; therefore terms like "federation" or "confederation" were no longer applicable to describe the new Yugoslavia.[68] Although the state was still named the "Socialist *Federative* Republic of Yugoslavia,"[69] federation, Kardelj said, was an "outdated category that can solve nothing in our system" (1969:246). The same applied to the term "confederation."

> Both the federation and the confederation...represent categories of the multinational state, which was a form of bourgeois political society in the capitalist epoch. (1969:246)

These forms of state played a progressive role in their time, but just as parties and parliaments, they were unsuitable for the new epoch.

> Briefly, present-day Yugoslavia is no longer a classical federation, nor can it be a classical federation, but it is a Socialist self-managing community of peoples, which in many respects represents a substantively new category in relations among nationalities. (1969:248)

Lastly, it was not only that words to describe the institutions of the new Yugoslavia had to be invented, but that the entire structure of the state was unique. The functions of the Yugoslav federal state were drastically reduced mainly to common defense and foreign policy, but even in these areas the federation itself became "more the initiator, executor, and agent of adjustment...than an autonomous decision maker" (Kardelj 1974:292).[70] And these areas were left to Tito himself, who acted almost as if foreign and defense policies were his private domain.[71] However, in domestic politics (including the nationalities policy) the federation had very little say, and Tito himself was seen more as a mediator and ultimate arbiter than as a decision maker. As of 1969, Tito's meetings with delegations of republics and provinces closely resembled those he had with foreign state delegations. According to Kardelj's interpretation of the national question, the federal state had no autonomy in itself, but was only a tool of the working class (by then already divided) and the nation-states. Federal bodies were not independent of the republics, but formed directly by them. The republics handed over to the exercise of the federation only these powers they "explicitly determined in the federal constitution," which could be amended only with the consent of all members of the federation. "The power of the federation...derives from the republics, not the other way around" was the principle realized in the Yugoslav legislature (Kardelj 1973:279).

Consequently, Yugoslav citizens as such were not directly represented in any of the federal institutions. As Zagreb Professor Žarko Puhovski said (1984), they were fictive political beings:

> And since the system of representation through federal units, which means through ethnic identities, has been taken to be decisive for any political participation, there can be no place for those who have canceled their belonging to such a system.

Another professor of politics, Jovan Mirić (also from Zagreb), concluded:

> As long as a citizen remains an outsider, an unrecognized element of the community, the awareness of belonging to this community will not develop. A community (in contrast to a society) can be built and destroyed in our own minds. It cannot be constructed externally, from somewhere outside ourselves. (Mirić 1985:45)

But the concept of citizenship that both Puhovski and Mirić had in mind was a liberal concept and therefore was not acceptable to Kardelj. As he explained in his "Notes on Social Criticism" in 1965, the Yugoslav political system should not be based on the liberal notion of abstract citizens, because an abstract man is nonexistent (1965:74). He existed only in liberal models that "try to transform man into a god" instead of accepting that man's life was dependent on both society and nature. Instead of basing their criticism on man as he was, they criticized him from the position of man "such as he ought to be" (1965:73). On the contrary, Kardelj believed that his concept should enable representation of existing interests, making sure that the interests of the majority (i.e., *working people*) were satisfied. It was because of these beliefs that he saw no problems in basing the entire structure of the Yugoslav political system on separate interest groups, rather than on the equality of abstract citizens.

The fact that the citizens of Yugoslavia were politically nonexistent was therefore the logical result of Kardelj's Marxist beliefs as well as of his views on the national question. Since the idea of a Yugoslav nation was condemned as "great-state, nationalistic, unrealistic, and profoundly harmful and reactionary," people who wanted to declare themselves as ethnic Yugoslavs could in the 1971 census register only as "undeclared/Yugoslavs," not as a separate ethnic group. Unlike the recognized "constitutive nations," and even the "nationalities" and "national minorities," they were not represented in politics.[72] This was a legal expression of Kardelj's belief that "Socialist forces would be making a big mistake if they allowed themselves to be carried away by futile ideas of creating some new kind of nation," since "this would only intensify nationalism and chauvinism in the existing nations" (1957:127).[73]

One of the greatest controversies in Kardelj's writing (and in the ideology of Yugoslav Communism) was his argument against the federal state when republics were declared states themselves. Why was Yugoslavia on its way to *withering away* at the same time the separate nation-states of its *constitutive nations* were to be created and strengthened? Was it because he still considered Yugoslavia to be an "artificial creation," as the Comintern had argued for almost the entire interwar period?[74] Was it because he believed that multiethnic states were in principle only a *transitional creation*, an incubator that helped small nations to become *completed*, and then subsequently to create their own separate states? In the decades to come, Kardelj's critics (especially those from Serbia) pointed to this controversy as the main evidence of his (Slovenian, ethnic) nationalism. What they often overlook, however, is that republics and provinces were also "withering away," and that their leaders often complained about too much "localism" and "logic of self-sufficiency." Thus the system was fragmented not only from the federal level to the level of republics, but from republics down to municipalities, or even further. Once Kardelj's concept was implemented, in the 1980s, leaders of the republics found it in fact more difficult to keep control over their own territories-not because of the pressure from "above," but from various autarchic tendencies from "below." Serbia was only the most drastic example because of its specific character as the only Yugoslav republic with two provinces (Kosovo and Vojvodina) within its borders. But this was by no means the only example. After all, when Yugoslavia collapsed in the late 1980s, all of its republics (with the possible exception of Slovenia) collapsed too: various regions and even municipalities went their own ways and rebelled just as the republics as a whole rebelled against the federation. It was only by force (of nationalism as political doctrine, as physical military force) that they defeated separatism on their own territories.

Nevertheless, the controversy over the "withering away" of the federal state at the same time nation-states of republics were given more authority remained. Kardelj himself offered only a few explanations of this controversy. As has been already mentioned in this chapter, he believed that no supranational state (such as the Austria-Hungarian or the Yugoslav) could create a "supranation," especially when its constitutive nations had been "completed." The failure of the concept of national unity, which attempted to create a Yugoslav nation in interwar Yugoslavia, was the main historical lesson to be learned by the Yugoslav Communists. Nations would gradually be transformed into "something else" as the world approached Communism. But in the meantime, they were a reality and should be treated as one.[75] Socialist society should be a step ahead, a better alternative to a liberal-led melting pot of nations. Multiethnic federations made sense to their constitutive nations only if they increased "the feeling of security of the peoples" that constituted them (1975:148).

The recognition of republics as nation-states followed yet another of Kardelj's arguments about the future. In an expression very reminiscent of the present-day *globalization theory*, Kardelj argued that the international process of integration constituted "the present and the future of mankind" (1975:175). This globalization is an inevitable result of technological revolution and a "natural result" of "scientific and technical progress" (1969:246), which would bring about new communication and cultural links between nations. Kardelj was convinced that this was a sufficient guarantee for the future of Yugoslav togetherness.

> It is beyond any doubt that Yugoslav society, all Yugoslav people and in all situations, will find enough strength to resist all disintegrating tendencies. (1969: 228)

This argument was only strengthened by the global political situation in which the two blocs were clearly opposed to any disintegration of Yugoslavia. On the other hand, the eventual disappearance of the two world military and political blocs would be very much a confirmation of the farsightedness of the Yugoslav nonaligned policy.[76] Whatever happened would thus only confirm Kardelj's belief that "the alternative here is not whether Yugoslavia will survive or not, but whether it will continue to develop as a Socialist, self-managing, and democratic community of equal peoples, or whether it will fall into the hands of hegemonistic forces" (1969:228).

Now, with the existence of Yugoslavia guaranteed, Kardelj turned to satisfy the needs of its nations within the globalized world. The creation of nation-states within Yugoslavia was Kardelj's attempt to find a new balance between increasing globalization in the world and the wish of the Yugoslav nations to protect their national identities. In Kardelj's concept, to increase national feelings was not incompatible with globalization: as long as they were well balanced, these were two sides of the same coin. Problems would emerge only if globalization went too far: this would necessarily increase nationalism and the separatism of Yugoslav nations. Without a balance between *globalization* and *securing national identities,* the whole Yugoslav house was endangered.[77] He saw discontent with the possible violation of national rights as the main potential danger for the future of Yugoslavia. Although the main conflict even in Socialist society was still a class conflict and not a national one (1975a:268), the national question, Kardelj warned, could be used to undermine Yugoslavia in the same way it was used by the Communists in the interwar period against the bourgeois government. Twenty years after the disintegration of Yugoslavia, we can safely conclude that this was one of the very few of Kardelj's predictions that did indeed materialize.[78]

2.3. Conclusion

The Yugoslav political system underwent revolutionary political changes from its third to fourth (Kardelj) constitutive concept, following the new interpretation of reality that was expressed in Kardelj's texts after 1957. The new concept was the result of Kardelj's interpretation of Marxism, and also of contextual circumstances, such as the attempt to construct a system that would be an *antipode* to both interwar Yugoslavism and the Soviet model of Socialism. Once it had been formulated as a more or less internally coherent vision of reality, Kardelj's interpretation became a blueprint for political action. It became a new *platform*, a Party line to be followed by all Yugoslav Communists. In a society in which politics was primarily a representation of ideals and not of reality, the dominant interpretation of *truth* was to be protected by the state apparatus and implemented in reality, despite all resistance. Any opposition to such an interpretation was treated as "contrary to the truth of history" and would be defeated as "a representative of untruth in history" (Voegelin 1952:59).

But in the Marxist conception, the purpose of knowledge of the *truth* is to change reality and to construct the new world. Knowledge makes sense only if it becomes action.[79] Revolutionary theory is a weapon in the revolutionary transformation of societies. This is why Kardelj's interpretation was so crucial to the political events that followed in the last two decades of Yugoslavia. To use Voegelin's description of *Gnostic societies*, his interpretation of reality and vision of the future presented "a dream world that itself is a social force to motivate attitudes and actions" (1952:167). Within this conception the transition meant the denial of one reality and the construction of a new one, which should come as close as possible to the ideal, nonexistent, dream world. The Communists were entitled to lead such societies not because they were the only ones who could interpret the existent, but because they represented the *future*, which would inevitably one day become reality.[80]

But even if the *future* works, present reality might not. In fact it is characteristic of *Gnostic societies* to neglect reality for the sake of the future. By neglecting reality, however, they often fail to recognize the need to react to it in a real and adequate way. Being convinced that the future must come in the way they predicted, Communists actually underestimated the real danger from the real world. Their vision of the future blurred their ability to view the present. Their almost religious belief in the power of words and beliefs made them react by moral condemnation, resolutions, and propaganda, rather than by measures that belonged to the world of real politics. They therefore engaged in endless criticism of deviations. They "reformed" the system relentlessly to be more efficient than both Western representative democracies and Eastern "state Socialist systems." But they also allowed an almost anarchic situation under the name of self-management. As will be demonstrated in detail in chapters four and five, the disintegrative processes were a direct consequence of their belief that the state should decentralize in order to "wither away."[81] Instead of supporting "integration across borders," the system collapsed into various small units, all becoming more and more "autarkic." Instead of enabling direct democracy within "self-management," it became more bureaucratic than ever.

Although Kardelj's concept had materialized in the laws and political actions of the Yugoslav Communists, the results of these actions were different from what he had intended. His own disappointment about the reality only three years after the new constitution had been introduced[82] offers a good example of failed predictions, which were entirely based on what he believed was the *scientific* analysis of politics. In reality, instead of being a *vanguard* of further globalization, the Yugoslav party elite became an ally of the forces of disintegration. It was because of his loyalty to the Marxist interpretation of the *General Laws of History* that Kardelj failed to see this danger. Although he perhaps understood reality better than any of his contemporaries in the Yugoslav leadership (including Tito), it was still his own vision of the future that prevented him from taking reality as the basis for his action.

In the next chapter I analyze why other relevant participants in Yugoslav politics accepted the Kardelj concept and how they transformed it into the institutional and constitutional structure defined in the 1967-74 constitutional debate. I argue that the main reason was to be found in their beliefs and perceptions about political realities. These beliefs were best expressed by Kardelj himself. Of course they interpreted some of his ideas in their own ways, depending on the context in which they operated. But the cohesion of the Yugoslav house was possible primarily because the relevant political participants shared the same concept of what Yugoslavia was, what it was not, what it should become, and what was to be prevented. In the fourth and fifth chapters, I analyze the political actions of the Yugoslav Communists who tried to change reality to fit their vision of the future. I argue that in doing so they clashed with reality and failed to react to the challenges they faced in real politics. On the contrary, they reacted in the way described by Voegelin: by condemnations and resolutions only. In the meantime, the problems in reality remained unresolved. Defending their vision of the future, the Yugoslav Communists in the end lost touch with the present. Once they realized the vision itself was inadequate to explain and change reality, they had lost both present and future.

Notes

1 For this, see Pavković (1997), and also Ćosić (1992) and Popović (1985). More on the debate between Serb and Yugoslav groups within the Serbian political and cultural elites in chapters three and six of this book.
2 Remnants of this thinking could be seen in Tito's policy toward Albania, Greece, and Bulgaria during 1945-48, and later in the Balkan Pact with Greece and Turkey in the early 1950s. As Dragosavac says in the interview conducted with the author in April 1998, Tito was the key figure in Balkan politics throughout the entire postwar period.
3 More on this in Vlajčić (1984). Vlajčić (1978) and A. Djilas (1991) are good sources for understanding the CPY policy toward the "national question" from the first days of the CPY (1919) throughout the interwar period.
4 This assessment was given by an official document of the 11th LCY Congress in 1978: "Three decades of the struggle of Yugoslav Communists for the Socialist transformation of society and for new relations in the world" (1978:107-86).
5 Actually, Tito's father was Croat and his mother Slovene. He was born in a village next to the "border" between the two "countries" and spent the first seven years of his life with his family in Slovenia.
6 This view was upheld by Slovenian politicians throughout postwar Yugoslavia and only reemphasized with Milan Kučan (1986). Slovenian membership in Yugoslavia was conditional on the preservation of Slovene national identity.
7 The four countries being Hungary, Italy, Austria, and Yugoslavia. Slovenian efforts to reunite their national territories within the new Slovenian republic (by including Carinthia and Trieste) characterized the whole postwar period until the mid-1970s. The resolution of this problem was also linked to the prevalence of Kardelj's concept, which claimed that borders between states would eventually disappear and that Yugoslavia would then become an example of various ethnic groups living peacefully together. (See more on this further in this book).
8 The accusation of treachery was the reason why the Yugoslav Communists considered General Mihailović's Chetniks to be their most dangerous internal enemy. If successful, Mihailović's troops would not only bring the old bourgeois system back, but it would also show that this charge was unfounded. Moreover, Mihailović's troops were also the most radical exponents of the Great Serbian ideology.
9 This view was repeated in the late 1980s by Josip Vrhovec, the Croatian representative in the Yugoslav Federal Presidency, and on several occasions by Milan Kučan, the Slovenian Party leader. Unlike the day of unification (1 December 1918), the day of the Second Session of the AVNOJ (Anti-Fascist Council of People's Liberation of Yugoslavia-29 November 1943) was a national holiday. It was on this day that the new Yugoslavia was conceptualized as a federation.
10 At the same time, however, the imbalance between overwhelming Serbian participation in the military and their underrepresentation in the highest echelons of politics of the Party sowed the seeds of the future rhetoric of the "Serbs: winners in wars, but losers in peace." The imbalance continued in the postwar period. As Gow argues (1992:54), although in 1972 the Serbs made up 60.5 percent and the Croats 11.7 percent of the full-officer corps in the YPA, the structure of its high command was very different: 38 percent were Croats and 33 percent Serbs. The Serbs, therefore, concluded that even in the army they were in fact disadvantaged, since their chances of being promoted to higher positions were much lower than those of members of other nationalities. Many Serbs thought that Slovenian complaints about the "unbalanced structure of the Yugo-

slav People's Army" in the late 1980s entirely ignored the overwhelming dominance of Serbian fighters in the Liberation War of 1941-45. Furthermore, the arguments about Serbian control over the army were seen as not only unreasonable, but also insulting.

11 For this purpose, the already high numbers of war victims were multiplied for ideological reasons, and the memory of the war was kept alive by state propaganda. This produced a reaction among the nationalists (for example, Tudjman) that influenced the events in the late 1980s and the wars in the 1990s.

12 This was a misinterpretation, since it neglected the failure of the Yugoslav idea to disappear with the occupation of Yugoslavia. Quite the contrary, this idea proved to be strong enough to launch at least one (and possibly even two) significant liberation movement(s). Tito's interpretation also neglected Yugoslavia's not having a proper political pluralism after 1929, since it was a "guided democracy" with limited possibilities for political association.

13 In his speech at the Founding Congress of the CP of Serbia on 11 May 1945, Tito said: "With the Bulgarians we are trying, and they are trying as well, to make our relationship of brotherhood and unity firm. We have deeper ambitions with the Bulgarians, and we have wanted to realize them, but the English and the Americans have not allowed it. Fine; we shall not (do it) now. But no one can stop us in this. We are Slavs, and they are also Slavs, and they have always been in the hands of reaction. It is up to us, the Yugoslav Communists, to develop the consciousness that we need to live with the Bulgarians in the closest relationship so that between us and the Bulgarians there should be no greater contradictions than between Serbs, Croats, and Slovenes. We shall act so that the Bulgarian people will be happy, as we shall be too, when we unite in a country of the South Slavs" (Tito 1945:214).

14 However, we need to ask if there was really such a possibility for Yugoslavia in the by then already strictly divided spheres of influence within Europe. Would it not have been just another proof that Stalin was "right" when accusing the Yugoslavs of being "hidden capitalists" under a "Communist mask"?

15 This had enormous consequences for the final years of Yugoslavia in the 1980s. Once the Soviet model ceased to represent a real threat, only the fear of a renewal of interwar Yugoslavia remained. In Milošević's attempts to reunite Yugoslavia, Slovenia and Croatian leaders saw such an intention.

16 In the period from 1950 to 1959, the Yugoslavs received more than US$1.5 billion of economic assistance. Further, US$724 million was given as military aid (Warner Neal 1962: 3). Lampe concludes that from 1950 to 1964, U.S. aid covered up to 60 percent of the deficits in the Yugoslav balance of payments (quoted by Denitch 1990:137). For more on American assistance to Yugoslavia, see Lees 1997.

17 Among issues debated within this dilemma were whether the Federal Assembly should be composed of two or three chambers, the third being the Chamber of Associated Labor, and also whether the Party organization should be structured along "functional" or only "territorial" lines (see Rade Končar's amendment rejected by the 12th LCY Congress in 1982). The territorial (and thus to a large extent ethnic) argument won over the "functional" argument.

18 For the importance of succession in Communist regimes, see Bunce (1999) and Keeler (1993). More on the struggle to "replace Tito" after his death in 1980 can be found in chapters five and six of this book.

19 In this conclusion, the second edition (1957) differs from the first (1939). Although in 1939 Kardelj fully shared Stalin's definition of the nation as the result of the bourgeois epoch, which is present in Socialism only as a remnant of this old epoch, in 1957 he

defines nation as a "product of the socioeconomic relations of the epoch of capitalism" which is a product to "the social division of labor." Since under Socialism the division of labor still exists, so does the nation. Kardelj himself admits that the second edition dropped elements of Stalin's influence. For the importance of this change, see Filipović (1979:157).

20 He repeated an almost identical sentence in his speech to the Federal Assembly on 20 September 1962 (1962:138).

21 Kardelj used the term completed or fully constituted nations (završene nacije), emphasizing that the republics in Yugoslavia became states after the Socialist revolution in 1945. Observing from his Slovenian experience of living in two multiethnic states that treated their ethnic groups as cultural but not political entities (Austria-Hungary and the Kingdom of Yugoslavia), Kardelj was a strong opponent of any similar attempts in postwar Yugoslavia. For relations between Kardelj and the Austro-Marxist tradition, see Nečak (1991).

22 To be fair, by the very fact of being the main Serbian politician, Ranković was in an unenviable position of being almost automatically suspicious of hegemonism and great-state (or potentially even great-Serbian) tendencies. Serbian politicians (as will be explained in chapters four and six of this book) have often felt uncomfortable with what they saw as an unjust burdening of them with legacies of prewar Yugoslavia, dominated by the Serbs. In the 1980s, Slobodan Milošević tried to ignore this trend of accusing all Serbian leaders of hegemonism, but the way he was doing it served only as evidence in favor of this accusation. For more on the perceptions of Ranković in the 1980s, see chapter six.

23 In his memoirs, the former Yugoslav Foreign Secretary Mirko Tepavac concludes that "Tito was a Yugoslav in the good meaning of this word, and even a unitarist. To him, even Yugoslavia as it was, was somehow too small" (1998:154).

24 This explains why Yugoslavia refused to accept Soviet supreme authority and to join the Warsaw Pact. Since Yugoslav nations were "completed," Yugoslavia itself came close to becoming a "pact" between the newly created national states on its territory. It is not only that various republics therefore spoke of Belgrade (the federal center) as a supranational force with no right to intervene in their domestic affairs, but Kardelj himself contemplated Yugoslavia more as an international conglomerate than as a state in any classic sense. Once it arrived in 1991/1992, full state independence was perceived by the non-Serbian republics of Yugoslavia (primarily Slovenia and Croatia) in rather similar terms to the non-Soviet countries of the bloc, as "liberation" from a supranational center. For the Serbs, of course, this was not a valid comparison, since they certainly did not see themselves as "the Soviets" of the Yugoslav "bloc." On the contrary, they argued they were disadvantaged in Yugoslavia.

25 In his "Notes on Social Criticism in Yugoslavia" (1965), Kardelj analyzed four types of opposition: (1) bureaucratic [or Stalinist]; (2) nationalist-separatist; (3) "the radical left" [Praxis philosophers]; and (4) liberals. It is in his Marxist belief in the "general laws of history" that we need to find the explanation for Kardelj's conclusion that nationalists and liberals had no real chance of overthrowing Communists. "A man who would today try to make gold following the recipes of medieval alchemists would be considered a charlatan or a ridiculous ignoramus," said Kardelj, concluding that the same rule of natural science should apply to the social sciences, where the creation of an "ideal society" was attempted "with the aid of an alchemical mixture of abstract eternal truths about humaneness and freedom, in disregard of the objective laws that govern social life and regulate the relations between man and nature" (1965:64). Kardelj's criti-

cism of liberals and right-wing critics was a typical example of the scientific rhetoric of the Yugoslav Marxists, who claimed that Marxism was scientific Socialism.

26 Ironically, Kardelj's belief that the future of Yugoslavia depended on the future of Party and-ultimately-on the Yugoslavs themselves today sounds almost like prophecy. Despite the optimistic predictions of the last Yugoslav prime minister, Ante Marković, and of most Western analysts, the disintegration of Yugoslavia indeed followed the collapse of the Party in January 1990.

27 On a symbolic level, a good illustration of this shift is the decision of Edvard Kardelj to move from Belgrade to Ljubljana in the early 1970s. The main Croatian leader, Vladimir Bakarić, had never moved his residence to Belgrade, but always, even when he was member of the Yugoslav Presidency (1974-83), lived in Zagreb. In the 1970s, Belgrade was left to Tito, federal ministers, and federal administration (largely domestic, i.e., Serbian), while the real politics shifted to republican (and provincial) capitals.

28 Several sources confirm that Tito considered Kardelj as his potential successor. West (1994) and Dedijer (1981) say that in a situation of despair after the first unsuccessful actions of the Yugoslav Partisans in Serbia in December 1941, Tito offered his resignation from the post of Party general secretary and proposed Kardelj as his successor. Ridley (1994:332) mentions that Kardelj was "acting president" during Tito's visit to India in 1953. However, the Tito-Kardelj relationship had its bad days as well. In the early 1960s, Tito supported the hard-liner Ranković and not the liberal Kardelj. In December 1962, Kardelj went on a private visit to London without telling Tito that he was going. Tito thought that Kardelj had deserted him (Ridley 1994:371). It is not clear why Kardelj spent almost two months in London, but Kardelj's wife told me in 1987 that this was for health reasons. In summer 1962, Kardelj had been shot and injured by a leading member of Serbian political leadership, Jovan Veselinov, in a hunting expedition and needed to recover. The Croatian historian Bilandžić told me in an interview conducted in December 1995 that the tense relationship between the two lasted from 1961 to 1964, when Tito finally changed his mind. Ridley explains why and how. From then on, Kardelj was undoubtedly Tito's closest political ally. However, in an interview I conducted in October 1997, Stipe Šuvar, once president of the LCY Presidency, said that Tito and Kardelj disagreed about the future of Yugoslavia even in their last years. According to Vidoje Žarković, the Montenegrin representative in the Party and state leadership, they addressed each other formally ("Vi," not "Ti") by the end of their lives. The texts discussed in this chapter were written mainly between 1965 and 1979.

29 A detailed description of Kardelj's imprisonments is given in Dedijer (1953:70-81).

30 Kardelj first met Broz (later, Tito) in Ljubljana in 1934. On this meeting, see Kardelj's interview with Veljko Bulajić on 26 February 1977, recorded for a documentary on Tito and published as "My First Meeting with Tito" (1980:209-55). Tito's memories of his first meeting with Kardelj are recorded by his official biographer Dedijer: "Comrade Kardelj was a calm, quiet man, and it was just his equanimity that impressed me most. He was an honest revolutionary at a time when many were corrupted by factionalism" (Dedijer 1953:96).

31 About the Bombaški process, see Sobolevski (1977). At this trial, Broz publicly declared his Communist beliefs and refused to recognize the legality and legitimacy of the Yugoslav Royal Courts. In fact, he said, "I do not recognize this court. The only court I recognize as relevant is the court of my Party."

32 On the "class against class policy," see Vlajčić (1989).

33 Josip Vidmar. Vidmar was not a Communist, and in his criticism of Kardelj in 1939 he opposed his Marxist views on the nation.

34 For this, see Lukšič (1994).
35 On this period of his political activity, see Kardelj's *Reminiscences* (1982).
36 Like Djilas, Kardelj published several accounts of his talks with Stalin. Some are in his *Reminiscences* (1982) and in Dedijer's *Tito* (1953).
37 Some would see Kardelj's last book (1977) as a return to Djilas. But as Šuvar said in the interview conducted for this book in October 1997, this view is certainly an exaggeration.
38 According to Djilas, Kardelj was privately very sorry about this split between the two. Before the session of the party leadership in 1954, he even told Djilas that nothing had been as difficult in his life as to write a political platform against him (Djilas, 1981).
39 For more on Soviet-Yugoslav relations, including the ideological dimensions of the dispute, see Clissold (1975) and Mićunović (1980).
40 His published opus has about 6,000 pages, but there is almost the same amount of unpublished material, some of which is used in this chapter, courtesy of the late Mrs. Kardelj, who gave me access to some of Kardelj's manuscripts back in 1987. The private archive of the Kardelj family, containing 64 boxes of correspondence and other sources collected from 1928 to 1992, is now part of the Slovenian State Archive. It is, unfortunately, still inaccessible for detailed research.
41 The decision was taken at the 13th session of the Presidency of the Central Committee of the LCY; see Dolanc 1978:13.
42 Although both sides in the conflict-Yugoslavs and Soviets-exaggerated the differences between their interpretations of Marxism, these differences were far from being entirely insignificant. For this, see Zukin (1975) and Lapenna (1964).
43 Back in 1953, Tito still used the phrase Marxism-Leninism to name the doctrine he followed. This phrase was later proscribed as a synonym for dogmatic Marxism, especially for the Albanian official interpretation of Marxism as formulated by Enver Hoxha. Following the 1981 unrest in Kosovo, many Albanians were convicted for joining Marxist-Leninist illegal organizations. Indeed, several groups of Albanian separatists were named Marxist-Leninist (Mertus 1999). At that time, Hoxha called Yugoslav revisionism "Titoism" (1982).
44 The notion of transition (i.e., the transition to Communist society) was the basic assumption of the program of the LCY, whose draft was made by Kardelj. To some extent similar to the program of the Communist Party of the Soviet Union (CPSU) (1961), this was a program for the Party in the transitional period.
45 Kardelj's argument was in this respect not much different from the one expressed in guidelines to Communist Parties issued at the December 1961 meeting in Moscow. In this document, the process of transition was described in ten steps (Wilczynski 1981:604).
46 The triple transition to Communism could be compared with the post-Communist notion of triple transition (Offe 1991). Although their conclusions on the nature of the end result are totally different, many elements of the Communist and post-Communist transition rhetoric are similar: both talk about revolutions, after which the false and unnatural course of history was reversed; they both saw the trend as inevitable in the long run, though allowing the possibility of the set-back (counterrevolution) in the short term; they both rely on a scientific approach to history and on the idea of progress in history; they both use the notion of transition (transitional period); and they both have a strong vision of the future (liberal democracy, Communism).
47 This is why the Yugoslav society and all other Socialist societies were in a state of permanent "reform." Yugoslavia changed four constitutions (including the 1953 Con-

stitutional Law) in the 28 years from 1946 to 1974. The necessity of permanent changes could be understood only within the logic of transition.

48 About the scientific character of Marxism, see Waller (1972:29); Graham (1966/73:65); Marx's writings in his *Economic and Philosophical Manuscripts;* and Engels' *Anti-Duehring.* The scientific character of Marxism was in line with the arguments of the main enlightenment authors to which Marx referred in his writings.

49 Tito urged Marxist philosophy to "do much more to research the character, factors, and development of Socialist society" (1978:66). This was no different from the way in which the program of the CPSU urged the Soviet social sciences to "constitute the scientific basis for the guidance of the development of society" (CPSU Program, 1961/1962:223). This was the main motive for the later (1985) invitation of the Serbian president, Ivan Stambolić, to the Serbian Academy of Sciences and Arts to join the political leadership in resolving political and economic crises in the country. Although the nationalist intelligentsia was condemned, constructive criticism of the regime from within the progressive forces of the intelligentsia was tolerated and supported.

50 Accordingly, in the 1970s Marxism entered school curricula as a compulsory course. Political schools at all levels were established to promote Marxism to the members of the LCY and the general public. Political science, heavily based on Marxism, became a university study after four Faculties of Political Science were opened. In Skinner's words, we can describe this as an attempt by the ideology to control the instruments of dissemination (1988:15).

51 This explains the tougher stand against philosophers and some radical left and liberal social scientists and philosophers (such as those around the Praxis journal) in the 1970s. Also, it explains the reasons behind the permanent conflict between the Party and the humanistic intelligentsia (dissidents), not only in Yugoslavia, but also elsewhere in Eastern Europe. Both groups believed they were entitled to a monopoly over truth. For politics as the struggle for truth in "Gnostic societies," see Voegelin (1952). This book also argues that politics in Yugoslavia was to a very large extent a struggle for the right interpretation of truth that took the form of the struggle between the right interpretation of Marxism and revisionism, both internationally (with the Soviets) and domestically (with the various left groups opposed to the official interpretation).

52 The idea of post-Communist transition is also based on the notion of inevitable progress from authoritarianism to democracy following the 1989 revolutions. Anthony Giddens, for example, argues that these changes were inevitable and are irreversible, since they are the results of deeper structural reasons (see my interview with Giddens in June 1999).

53 An almost identical formulation of the role of Party could be found in the CPSU Program: "The Party considers that the paramount task in the ideological field in the present period is to educate all working people in a spirit of ideological integrity and devotion to Communism, and cultivate in them a Communist attitude to labor and the social economy..." (1961/1962:202). Statutes of other organizations of the Yugoslav regime, such as the Socialist Youth Organization, or the Socialist Alliance of Working People, used the word "education" to define the goals of these organizations.

54 Only by understanding this can one explain why the Party mattered more than the state in a Socialist society. It was the position of the general secretary of the Party, not the state president, who held real power. When thinking of resigning his post as state president in 1971, Tito wanted to remain Party president-not vice versa (Tripalo 1991). Tito could accept the federalization of the state, but not of the Party. The federalization of the Party would mean real federalization, not a symbolic one. All political conflicts in

Yugoslavia took the form of intraparty divisions. Even as late as 1987, the Serbian state president considered it unthinkable to use his state position to act independently from the Party (more in chapter six). In its final phase, the LCY Central Committee became the real parliament of Yugoslavia. Ultimately, this explains why the disintegration of the Party meant the end of Yugoslavia as a state.

55 The link between "man's emancipation from exploitation, which is what primarily constitutes social justice," and democracy is established also in the CPSU Program (1961/1962:40).

56 The whole bourgeois system "gives the masses the illusion that they are in charge of society or that at least they have an opportunity of running society, even though in fact society is being managed by the top echelons of the political parties and the state executive, and above all by the leading forces of extra-parliamentary class power" (Kardelj 1977:109).

57 "By extra-parliamentary power, we mean the real power that is exercised by the ruling class by virtue of its right to private property" (Kardelj 1977:109).

58 In Tito's words soon after the split with Stalin (1952, dialogue with Dedijer): "The role of the party is historically limited to a certain period...The party withers away gradually. That does not mean that a one-party system will be superseded by a multiparty system. It merely means that the one-party system, having superseded a multiparty system, will in turn vanish...Therein lies the very difference between our view and that of the Soviets" (Dedijer 1953:430-1).

59 Having this in mind, it was not surprising that strong criticism of state Socialism and statism was not only permitted, but encouraged by the elite. Criticism of Soviet models of state Socialism (or even Stalinism) was a major problem in relations between the USSR and Yugoslavia. In the late 1980s, Slobodan Milošević attempted to reaffirm the role of the state, but this was immediately recognized as state Socialism and Stalinism. The most loyal supporters of Kardelj's concept recognized in his demands exactly what Kardelj criticizes most: great-statist tendencies coming from a person who was at the same time appealing both to promoters of great-statism and to great-Serbianism.

60 This is how one can explain nonalignment as the main foreign-policy orientation of Yugoslavia. Kardelj believed that Yugoslavia could offer a model of national independence and social justice to the Third World. This definition of national interest was based on these ideological premises.

61 In 1977 there were about 75,000 delegations altogether, comprising more than a million citizens; thus nearly one in five of Yugoslav adult workers were directly involved in the process of self-management (Wilson 1978:255).

62 More on the new structure of the Yugoslav political system in Potts (1997) and Cohen (1989).

63 On the GPD concept see Gow (1992). More about what happened in reality will be said in the following chapters of this book. It was not only that the system was never fully put into practice (since it would have seriously destabilized the real pillars of power, including Tito's and Kardelj's role), but the results of actions that were taken were often directly opposite to the declared intentions. A system that claimed the working people to be its cohesive force became divided into thousands and thousands of small units. Bureaucracy was not defeated either in its size or in its real power. On the contrary, the possibility of manipulation increased, both because the new "delegates" had no political experience or adequate education, and because they had no courage to voice their own opinions, since they were always accountable to "delegations" they had to represent. The system of government became extremely expensive and complex. Millions of

anonymous self-managers were formally responsible, and extra-parliamentary centers held real power. Instead of moving toward "direct democracy," voters in Yugoslavia had an opportunity to elect only members of delegations, not even a delegate herself. The whole structure soon became an example of real disenfranchising, which made many people feel manipulated and powerless.

64 Although Marx believed in the inevitability of progressing from capitalism toward the classless society, he also argued that this process could not be the result of its autonomous logic, but could happen only if the "subjective forces" organized and led it. In his pamphlet, "What Is to Be Done," Lenin wrote this: "All worship of spontaneity of the working-class movement, all belittling of the role of the conscious element…mean… strengthening the influence of bourgeois ideology on the workers" (Lenin, Works V:354). This was the main argument Kardelj used against Djilas's proposals to reduce the role of the Party back in 1953-54.

65 The official CPSU gazette *Komunist* declared in 1959 that the "main elements [of the transitional period] should be completed within the next fifteen years" (De Koster 1964:151).

66 This process was called the "Socialization of state" (podruštvljavanje države). Instead of state property, social property was introduced, and administrative units (such as municipalities, regions, republics, and the federation) were named sociopolitical communities. This was all done to demonstrate the differences between "social self-management" and "statist Socialism" as practiced in the USSR. An excellent account of the debates between Soviet and Yugoslav Marxists on the "withering away of the state" is given in *Lapenna* (1964). For "Socialization of defense," see Gow (1992).

67 As Bettelheim argued (1971:34), the Socialist state was "no longer completely a state because it is the instrument of the exercise of power by the working masses themselves," and not an instrument of control and repression against them. I argue that the incredible weakness of the Yugoslav state to resist the pressure it faced in the late 1980s had its deep roots in this "antistatist" rhetoric and action. It was precisely in Yugoslavia in which the state "withered away" faster than in other cases in Eastern Europe that the consequences of this process were most obvious.

68 Kardelj's concept introduced many new words into the Yugoslav political vocabulary. Old words were considered unsuitable to describe the new reality. Creating new words was in fact the first step to changing the world. In this book I prefer using the official (Yugoslav government) English translation for these terms, if it exists. I realize that outside of their ideological contexts, some of these terms are easy to misunderstand.

69 Interestingly, it was reported that Slobodan Milošević, then a student at the Law Faculty in Belgrade and later the main political leader of Serbia, was the member of the LCY who proposed that the country be named the Socialist Federative, rather than (as Kardelj originally had suggested) the Federative Socialist Republic of Yugoslavia. The emphasis on Socialism, rather than on the form of the state, somehow suited both Ranković's and Kardelj's concepts. Within the concept of the Third Yugoslavia (pre-1966), the Socialist character of the state was emphasized; in the fourth concept (Kardelj's), the form of the state was to be rated second to the "form of social order." Rating "federal" (character of the state) second to "Socialist" (type of social order) was therefore in their common interest. Milošević's proposal was accepted by his Party organization (Law Faculty in Belgrade) and later by the Party leadership itself.

70 Republics increased their influence over the appointments of ambassadors and intensified their bilateral relations with foreign states. (This included the relations between Kosovo and Albania, and between Slovenia and its neighbors Austria and Italy.) In

defense policy, although the army was highly centralized and under Tito's full control, the republics were allowed to form units of territorial defense, and the military strategy reemphasized the partisan (local) tactics as opposed to frontal army activities only. The territorial defense units would a decade-and-a-half later become the main source of the emergence of separate armies in the republics, and the concept of self-defense via Partisan war in fact provided suitable training of civilians, many of whom used this knowledge in the post-Yugoslav wars.

71 Tepavac remembers that although the ministers of defense and foreign and internal affairs were in constant personal contact with Tito, the speaker of the parliament and the prime minister could not see him even after repeated requests. "However, Tito's direct contact with the republic governments and LC leaders became more important as their autonomy increased. With these leaders he met regularly, if not frequently...republican delegations officially reported to Tito and increasingly turned to him for the approval of many measures they believed could not be adopted through constitutional channels. Furthermore, Tito was inclined to agree with everybody. When a problem arose between two or more republics, republican leaders learned to approach Tito separately instead of meeting together. Tito would often satisfy the parties individually, sometimes at each other's expense, and without resolving the underlying issues" (Tepavac 1997:74-5). This explains why Tito's death left Yugoslavia without effective federal government.

72 On this issue, Tito and Kardelj seemed to disagree. Although in 1964 Tito for the first time declared himself a Croat (rather than a Yugoslav), at the 8th LCY Congress elections he opposed "witch hunts" against Yugoslav patriotism. This he repeated in his passionate speech against Croatian nationalism in December 1971. What did it mean to be against Yugoslavism, he rhetorically asked his colleagues in the party leadership? "If it means to be against the old Yugoslavism of King Alexander, then of course I am against this sort of Yugoslavism. But if it means to love my country, to feel as a Yugoslav in the first place and to be proud of it, then I must tell you that I am Yugoslav. Of course, as you know, I am from Croatia, but I am also a Yugoslav, and I have spent all my life working for Yugoslavia." But Tito was already an exception, both in constitutional and in real political terms. No other politician would escape the label of "unitarist" if he repeated Tito's words. At the same time that Tito declared himself a Yugoslav, Kardelj was writing that the illusion of Yugoslavism represented the greatest danger to Yugoslavia itself.

73 A similar type of argument was later used by Milošević and Kučan. They were both "saving Yugoslavia" by "satisfying" national demands, to "prevent" ethnic nationalists from taking power and destroying Yugoslavia. Milošević was also "saving" Yugoslavia from "anarchy," arguing that anarchy would lead to a totalitarian response.

74 In an interview conducted for this book in December 1995, Dušan Bilandžić, the Croatian politician and historian, recalls a talk with Kardelj who told him in 1971: "We have tried every possibility so far to preserve Yugoslavia: first, it was a unitary state, then it became a federation, while now we are moving toward a confederation. If this proves to be yet another unsuccessful attempt, then it remains only to admit that the Comintern was right when arguing that Yugoslavia was an 'artificial creation' and that we, the Yugoslav Communists, have made a mistake."

75 In 1970 Kardelj declared that Socialism had not significantly changed the nature of the nation and the character of its demands (1970/1979:270). These views were somewhat different from what Tito said on several occasions, that the national question had basically been solved after the Socialist revolution. Many Yugoslav Communists-as Milka

Planinc said in an interview I conducted with her in April 1999-believed the same as Tito and were surprised when the national question reappeared in the 1960s.
76   For this, see his 1970 speech at the 12th Session of the LCY Presidency (Kardelj 1970). In fact, Kardelj was thinking of Yugoslavia as a multinational corporation, as a core of the prospective wider integration in the region, rather than as a state. When the time came, Yugoslavia would be an ideal example of different nations in different states living under the same roof. Yugoslavia was once again (not only in an ideological sense, but also as a state) meant to be a transitional entity, as something that might well be transcended in a broader post–cold-war political structure of Europe. More on the views of other Yugoslav leaders about the prospects for Balkan and other regional integration in the late 1960s will be said in the next chapter.
77   Anthony Giddens's conclusion on fundamentalist traditionalism as a reaction to globalization comes close to Kardelj's views (see the interview I conducted with Giddens, published in *Acque & Terre*, 4-5/1999, 77-81.).
78   In his last public addresses, Kardelj uttered some pessimistic predictions about the future of the Yugoslav project. At a closed session of the Party leadership in 1974, he warned that the Chilean scenario could happen in Yugoslavia if the country did not immediately stop taking loans (unpublished papers, and also Šuvar, interview for this book, April 1998). In his dramatic speech at the 11th LCY Congress in 1978, though already suffering from terminal cancer, he concluded that social consciousness had not changed much and that it was still equivalent to that of prewar Yugoslavia (Documents 1978). This meant that the main task of the Party-to change people's consciousness-was far from being achieved. Indeed, Kardelj earlier even said that "many democracies collapsed because they could not control their internal contradictions and antagonisms and defend their own social system from the pressure of contrary tendencies, either revolutionary or reactionary" (1969:219). I heard from several of his colleagues in the Party and state leadership whom I interviewed for this book (such as Jure Bilić, Josip Vrhovec, and Dušan Dragosavac) about Kardelj's disappointments in the last years of his life with what had been achieved.
79   As Marx famously explained: the point is not to describe reality, but to change it.
80   A pleasing illustration of this belief is to be found in a report of a certain Lincoln Steffens after visiting Russia in 1918, as quoted by Sweezy and Bettelheim (1971:80). Steffens, a Communist, said: "I have been over into the future and it works." Communists often referred to Communism as the "bright future," or the "future of mankind." Some of this rhetoric is preserved in Slobodan Milošević's speeches in the 1984-87 period, analyzed in chapter six.
81   In this respect, we can only share the conclusion of Warren Zimmermann, the last American ambassador in Socialist Yugoslavia, who asked himself why the other Socialist countries of Eastern Europe succeeded while the Yugoslav reforms failed? "The key reason is that those countries had strong central governments; Yugoslavia did not" (1999:49). Indeed, as I argue in chapter four of this book, economic and political reforms in the 1980s both failed for this reason.
82   In 1977 Kardelj accepted criticism by the Serbian leaders, recognizing that the way the constitution was implemented in reality produced results opposite those desired. His wife Pepca Kardelj told me of his disappointment with the general situation in the country in the final years of his life. He felt sidelined and misunderstood by his colleagues in the federal leadership. Also, he felt that Tito had lost the ability to change things anymore.

CHAPTER THREE

The Constitutional Debate 1967-1974: Why did Serbia Accept the Kardelj Concept and the 1974 Constitution?

> Ranković's whole line was conservative. In Serbia, we felt him to be a heavy burden....Tito exercised full control over foreign policy and the army, while Ranković controlled the Party and police. We wanted to put the lid on this.... Everything that Kardelj initiated and promoted in our political system distinguished us from the East, and it was a guarantee that we would not return to the past. In general, he was a reformist and a Yugoslav.
> **Petar Stambolić, 1992**

> At no other time and in no other place was the mistake of granting more rights and wider possibilities (than necessary) for the development of smaller nations and nationalities committed. History never records that such a "mistake" has been committed toward the nationalities and national minorities.
> **Marko Nikezić, June 1968**

3.0. Introduction

Kardelj's concept was transformed into legislation during the long constitutional debate in which members of the Yugoslav political elites representing the interests of republics and provinces engaged from 1967 to 1974. In this chapter I examine this debate to show why the Yugoslav republics (and especially Serbia and its political elite) agreed on the proposed compromise and accepted the 1974 Constitution.

When discussing the 1968-74 constitutional debates, most authors focus their research on the "Croatian Spring," the reformist attempt of the Croatian leaders that reopened the Croatian question. The focus here, however, is not on Croatia, but on Serbia. More precisely, I focus on the reasons behind the decision of Serbia's leaders to accept the Kardelj concept and the constitutional compromise of 1974. The reason for this is provided by the further course of the events that preceded the disintegration of Yugoslavia. First, although the Serbian leaders initially agreed on the Kardelj concept, they soon voiced dissatisfaction with the implementation of this constitutional compromise. Subsequently, the "Serbian question" (both in its internal dimension, the question of Serbia's relations with its two provinces, Kosovo and Vojvodina, and in its external aspect, its relations with other republics and the Yugoslav federal center) had already emerged in the late 1970s, only to intensify in the 1980s. This question, though not the sole reason for the breakup of Yugoslavia, no doubt fueled Serbian nationalism, raising tensions that would lead not only to disintegration, but also to post-Yugoslav conflicts. Ultimately, it was first in Serbia that the 1974 Constitution was rejected by the political elite (though not before 1989), which had an enormous impact on the final stages of the Yugoslav crisis.

Although this chapter focuses on the reasons for Serbia's acceptance of the 1974 Constitution, its conclusions also address the other Yugoslav republics. It is today widely accepted that these republics accepted the 1974 Constitution because it offered them better status in terms of national rights and autonomy than any previous concept of Yugoslavia. But although national issues played a significant role in the constitutional debate, it was also the context of the Kardeljist interpretation of wider social goals (such as, above all, social self-management as the main element of Yugoslav identity when compared with both the East and the West) that made the leaders come to support it. One should never forget that leaders of Yugoslav republics and provinces at that time were Communists-not nationalists. It would thus be misleading to reduce all reasons for the acceptance of the 1974 Constitution to the national question. The main motive for their decision was to be found in their firm belief that the state should gradually be weakened and decentralized, as explained in chapter two. Lastly, by neglecting the ideological dimension of the debate, we would necessarily fail to explain why Serbia agreed to the constitution.

Chapter two focused on the emergence of Kardelj's concept within its historical and ideological context, and this chapter places this concept in its practical context, that is, "the problematic political activity or relevant characteristics of the society the author addresses and to which the text is a response" (Skinner 1988:10). It addresses the question of "how ideological change comes to be woven into ways of acting and analyzes the relations between political ideology and political action. It also focuses more closely on the then-dominant Serbian interpretation of Kardelj's concept, which has been permanently contested within Serbia itself, only to be replaced by alternative concepts that emerged in the 1980s.

3.1. Did Serbia Accept Kardelj's Concept Voluntarily?

Three frequently stated arguments on why Serbia (or indeed other republics) agreed to the 1974 Constitution need to be discussed before I offer my own argument.

First, that the republics (including, or even especially, Serbia) had to accept everything that Tito and Kardelj dictated because of the nature of the authoritarian (or even autocratic) system in which any opposition (primarily) to Tito would be marginalized and purged. Consequently, it was Tito (and Kardelj) who imposed the 1974 Constitution on Serbia, contrary to its interests and regardless of the real wishes of its leaders.[1]

Second, that the Serbian politicians of the time were not interested in Serbian national interests, but were either a-national (as Communists, also internationalist) or too opportunistic to risk their personal privileges.[2]

Lastly, that the Serbian elite was illegitimate in democratic terms, and therefore they did not reflect the political preferences of the population, which were significantly different from those represented by the elite itself. In this respect, it was irrelevant whether the elite itself agreed or disagreed with Tito and Kardelj, since their decisions lacked (democratic) legitimacy.[3]

It is important to examine these three arguments, since they influenced the political actions of the Serbian leaders in the late 1980s and throughout the 1990s. Although there are elements of truth in all of them, these three arguments still disregard or greatly misrepresent the motives of the relevant political actors in accepting the 1974 Constitution.

3.1.1. Relationship between Tito and Republican (Serbian) Leaders

We should first examine the statement that Tito was too authoritarian to be opposed by republican elites. Available primary sources (interviews with Tito's former aides and memoirs of the leading Yugoslav politicians in the late 1960s and early 1970s) confirm that Tito indeed had an extraordinary and central role in Yugoslav political decision-making processes. Such a position was the result both of his personal role in the formation of Yugoslav institutions (the army, the reorganization of the Party, the formation of the Yugoslav Communist Federation, and the role of Yugoslavia in international politics) and of the offices of the president of the republic (which he held since 1953) and of the Party (since the late 1930s). But none of this had really prevented other politicians from being critical of his initiatives, especially in face-to-face or more confidential debates. This criticism was particularly strong during the 1967-74 constitutional debate, when it originated mostly from the Serbian leaders (such as Koča Popović, Mijalko Todorović, Latinka Perović, Marko Nikezić, and Petar Stambolić).[4]

This criticism of Tito's position by Serbian leaders (perhaps even more than that by other leaders) sometimes (and not only on subordinate issues) influenced Tito's further decisions. His closest aides say that far from initiating conflict, he tried to avoid disputes with other leaders whenever possible.[5] He spent four crucial years (1962-66) trying to reach some compromise and resolve the issue within the closed circles of the political elite before taking an active part in the conceptual disputes that emerged within the closest circle of his aides, between Edvard Kardelj and Aleksandar Ranković.[6] Throughout the first phase of the constitutional debate (1967-71), Tito hesitated to take a direct part in it, avoiding direct confrontations with either side. In such moments of wavering, all the participants tried to influence Tito, and some were more successful than others. The compromises Tito suggested were therefore the result of interaction between him and republican leaders, as well as between him and Kardelj, and not simple proclamations of his personal views. This is how Tito reaffirmed his central role without antagonizing the republics and provinces too much-though there was indeed a lot of tension between him and local leaders. During this time, however, by promoting direct talks between himself and republican leaders, Tito reduced the role of other federal institutions (the Federal Party Presidency and the Federal Assembly) and prevented any collective action by two or more republics against others and against himself.[7]

Available sources indicate that Tito's relations with the Serbian leadership were especially strained throughout the constitutional debate. In his diary (published in two parts, one in 1987 and the second in 1988), the leading Serbian participant in the constitutional debate, Draža Marković, describes several occasions in which the Serbian leaders opposed Tito.[8] When we sum up Marković's recollections, we find the following list of disagreements between Tito and the Serbian leaders:

First, the Serbian leaders initially thought that Tito favored the Croatian leaders (especially when compared to the Serbian leadership).[9] The Serbs felt that Tito publicly criticized what he saw as deviations in Serbia's politics while he kept his criticism of Croatian politics (then already developing its Croatian Spring policy) hidden from the public and restricted to inner circles of the federal leadership, or even restricted to *tête-a-tête* talks with the Croats. The Croats also believed that Tito was the main political ally of the (otherwise fairly isolated) Croatian leadership, which made the Croats tough participants in the constitutional debate. The impression of the Serbian leaders that Tito was the main sponsor of the reformist fraction of the Croatian League of Communists that led Croatian Spring was shared by other republics (including Slovenia's Kardelj, the main critic of the Croatian leadership's *avant-gardism*). It is not surprising that Tito in the end accepted Serbian demands that he should act more resolutely to bring Croatia back to negotiations. The Serbian leaders felt that without his support, Croatia would be much more willing to negotiate[10] with others in Yugoslavia during the constitutional debate.[11] However, it is not clear to what extent Tito really wanted to replace the leaders of the Croatian Spring and how much he was really forced to remove them by those (unnamed) persons who had told him "either them or you," as Tripalo recalls Tito's words.[12]

Second, the Serbian leaders also objected to Tito's harsh public criticism of many Serbian institutions (such as Belgrade University, the *Student* newspaper, and the Belgrade media in general), of Serbian intellectuals (the Praxis group and others), of Serbian politicians (such as Koča Popović and Mijalko Todorović), and of the general political situation in Serbia. Tito's criticism of the Belgrade *čaršija*[13] was seen as criticism of the Serbian political leadership and its inability to prevent anti-Socialist activities.[14]

Third, the Serbian leaders were dissatisfied with Tito's inclination to make concessions to the demands of the two Serbian provinces-Kosovo and Vojvodina. Serbian politicians believed Tito was too soft on Kosovo and Vojvodina and ready to accept political compromises with them even when this was clearly against the main principles of the new constitution. In this respect, they considered Kardelj to be much more principled than Tito.[15] To some extent, it is correct to say that Serbia's (and other republican) leaders preferred building up institutional politics with clear rules rather than leaving too much power to Tito personally. But for many reasons, this was not a realistic option. They had to adapt to Tito's extraordinary position, though they used any opportunity to influence him.[16]

Fourth, in line with the previous objection, Serbia's leaders (and also those of other republics) were suspicious of Tito's tendency to use his enormous influence with the security and military apparatus and to take advantage of his charismatic status with the broad Yugoslav population to stop or reverse political processes in the republics and the country in general.[17] They feared Tito's personal links with the masses, as well as his support in the international arena, both of which enabled him to act as a fully independent participant in Yugoslav politics.

Fifth, the Serbian leaders (even more than others) objected to the violation of intraparty rules and procedures by Tito, especially when it came to the selection of Serbian candidates for various federal posts. Serbian leaders asked Tito to clearly state that some of the Serbian cadres in the federation (such as

Defense Secretary General Nikola Ljubičić and Foreign Secretary Miloš Minić) were his appointees and not those of Serbia's.[18] Serbian leaders were even more dissatisfied with Tito's attempts to decide even on cadres for various positions in Belgrade and Serbia, including civil servants (mostly Serbs) in the president's private office.

Sixth, all Yugoslav republics, again especially Serbia, were suspicious of Tito's acceptance of his closest associates' manipulation of his name and authority, especially after 1972. In this year, when Tito was 80, the newly created collective leadership of the federation moved to take over several of Tito's duties and to restrict access to the ageing (and ailing) leader. An inner circle of leading federal functionaries that kept daily contact with the president was reduced to not more than ten people (the foreign, defense, and home secretaries, chairman and secretary to the Party's Central Committee, vice president of the federal presidency, Kardelj, and Tito's chief of cabinet).[19] However, Tito maintained contacts with his personal friends, mostly from his early Party career or his wartime generals, who now influenced him more than the political leaders. Marković's memoirs reveal Serbian dissatisfaction with the role played by many of these friends (such as the Croat Ivan Krajačić Stevo, whom they considered to be a Croatian nationalist) and those played by Tito's wife, Jovanka Broz,[20] the chiefs of cabinet, and other semiofficials among his entourage. Other republics were also discontented with this, but none of them as much as Serbia. To a degree (and since the fall of Ranković in 1966 with only limited success), Tito was also influenced by the secret police reports that he relied on. Many political struggles in the 1970s were fought to gain control over the state security apparatus.

In many respects, 1971 was the most critical year in Serbian relations with Tito. Since 1968, Serbian leaders had tried to persuade Tito to influence Croatian politicians, who isolated themselves in the constitutional debate. By April 1971, the Serbs felt that the Croatian demands in the constitutional debate had become intolerable and that only Tito could stop them, and thus had to. They were not prepared to accept, as they said in a conversation with Tito on 15 May 1971, the permanent suspicion under which Serbia and institutions in Belgrade had been kept by the other republics and the federal center. During an extremely open meeting, the Serbian leaders told Tito that before the fall of Ranković they had been suspected of being the "basis of conservatism," and they were now accused of "technocratic deformations." They told Tito:

> We are identified with unitarism and centralism, though our position on these issues is very clear and principled; we have been treated as the bearers of resistance to the changes [constitutional amendments], though today all the others have greater reservations about them than we do. (Marković 1987:284)

Marković describes the tense atmosphere in the president's office:

> The tone was occasionally sharp, very unpleasant. Tito told us a few times: "Well, you came here to attack me, didn't you?" We denied it, arguing that we did not want to attack anyone, but to inform and to clarify certain points. This was accepted and respected....At the end of the talks, we concluded that a full stop should be put to all this, and that we should all together move toward serious tasks ahead and look to the future, rather than to the past. (Marković 1987:284).[21]

However, when talks like this became almost a regular practice, Tito concluded that some Serbian leaders represented a "different concept, a different policy" (Marković, 1987:357), and he initiated changes in the Serbian leadership. Clearly, the Serbian leaders' independence indicated that Serbia was not a passive, but a very active participant in the constitution-making process (1967-74). However, Tito's decision to remove some leading Serbian leaders in 1972 raises a question: does it not prove that Serbia had to accept Tito's proposals (including the constitution), regardless of their disagreements and opposition to them?

To answer this question, we should emphasize the following facts:

It was true that Serbia changed leading politicians more often than any other republic from 1966 to 1972 (Ranković was removed from power in 1966; Ćosić and Marjanović in 1968; "the liberals" in 1972; also there was the "silent removal" of the executive secretary of the LCY Presidency, Mijalko Todorović, in 1974 and the withdrawal of Koča Popović, the former vice president of Yugoslavia after Ranković, in protest in 1972). It is also true that similar changes occurred in all the Yugoslav republics, except Montenegro.

Because so many Serbian politicians were forced to leave politics does not yet mean that Tito did not command substantial support for his position from the majority of each of the republican political elites and from the large segment of general population in each of the republics. Political conflicts in the late 1960s and early 1970s were not only (and not even in the first place) between Tito and the leadership of Serbia and Croatia, respectively, but also (and at certain moments even more so) between groups within each of these two political elites. Tito used existing differences to support the side that seemed to be less independent and more loyal to him. He exploited internal party pluralism, which offered some space for various interests to be represented in the political elite, fearing unanimity such as was shown by the Serbian leaders in his talks with them on 15 May 1971. It was precisely intraparty diversity that enabled Tito to make pacts with various factions, both at the federal level and in republican politics. He needed to send no one from the federal leadership to introduce and implement his politics in "disobedient" republics:[22] it was sufficient to rely on some existing "cadres."[23] Relying on a majority in each particular republican leadership and on the mass support he enjoyed among the population, as well as explicit support from abroad (especially in 1970-1972) Tito managed to strengthen his already independent position and to use it to eliminate those republican leaders he disagreed with.

Furthermore, when it came to crucial issues in relations within Yugoslavia, there were no major differences between the various conflicting groups in either the Serbian or the Croatian leadership. In both, differences arose over how to treat non-Communist political actors; these became public in the late 1960s as a result of the general democratization of political life in Yugoslavia. The Croatian leadership remained united on the Croatian position in Yugoslavia and on the arrangements for a desirable constitutional structure of Yugoslavia.[24] None of the Croatian leaders of the time was an anti-Titoist, and not many of their opponents in the various cultural, semipolitical, or academic institutions were. On the contrary, their rhetoric was very much pro-Titoist.[25] Contrary to many current interpretations, the main idea of the Croatian Spring was not to challenge Tito's power, but to present itself as the only force in the country that truly understood, followed, and supported Tito's concept of equality among the Yugoslav nations and the self-management of the Yugoslav workers.[26] The Croatian League of Communists insisted on describing itself as a progressive force, pushing forward in the same direction as Tito, facing the same obstacles he was facing. They tried to convince Tito that their critics were in fact targeting him when criticizing them. Furthermore, it was not the Croatian leadership that initiated conflict in 1971, but Tito himself.[27] Tito was for a relatively long period (more than three years) the main protector and sponsor of such *avant-gardism*.[28] When he decided to withdraw his further support, as one of the most prominent Yugoslav and Croatian leaders of that time concluded,[29] he started reemphasizing his Croatian origins.

To conclude: the change of leadership in 1971 in Croatia was only a partial replacement of various (minority) factions within the republican leadership, in which the majority (including the leading Croatian politician Vladimir Bakarić) not only survived, but were also promoted to higher posts. Most of the Croatian Central Committee and the vast majority of the Croatian political elite in general supported Tito and not the ousted leaders.[30] Lastly, the political and personnel changes in Croatia changed the Croatian position neither in regard to the constitutional issues, nor Tito in general.[31]

The same applies to Serbia, as can be documented by even more sources available at the moment.[32] Two main actors, one of whom (Latinka Perović) was forced to resign in 1972 as the secretary to the Serbian LC Central Committee, and the other (Draža Marković) in 1972 became the leading Serbian politician over the next fifteen years, both confirm that differences had been significant not on the issue of the status of Serbia within Yugoslavia, but on the relationship toward the inner or external opposition to the regime.[33] Even when the Serbian leaders disagreed on the issue of the Serbian position in Yugoslavia, this was also a result of their soft or hard approach toward the opponents of the regime.

In his account of points of disagreement between his group and the "liberals" (Latinka Perović, Marko Nikezić, and Mirko Tepavac), Draža Marković lists the following elements:

First: Freedom of the press in Serbia (the liberals advocated more media freedom, while Marković accused them of having a media monopoly because they controlled the main Serbian daily *Politika*);

Second: The replacement of one generation of leaders (Partisan Veterans, still committed to the concept of pre-1966 Yugoslavia and somewhat displeased with the removal of Ranković) with another (the young "technocrats"[34]: Marković saw this as unnecessary, but the liberals argued it was a *sine qua non* for modernization);

Third: Control over some important institutions in Serbia (primarily the police forces);[35]

Fourth: Some ideological disagreements, expressed in mutual accusations of being "liberal" or "conservative."

From this account, we could conclude that the two groups in the Serbian leadership fought primarily over the issues of the *democratization* and *liberalization* of Serbia and Yugoslavia and much less over the Serbian position in Yugoslavia.[36] At the end of July 1972, Marković wrote in his diary that "the issue of Socialism or non-Socialism was at stake" (23 July 1972; 1987:378). For a Communist, there could be no more important issue than this one. To conclude: the fall of the Serbian liberals in October 1972, therefore, did not mean a radical change in the Serbian position on the constitutional debate, but it did mean a change in treating opposition and opposing various anti-Socialist activities and groups. Both factions of Serbian politics (conservatives and liberals) accepted the constitutional changes when the reform of the federation was debated, and thus the objection that the reform was imposed on them by Tito or by other federal units proves to be incorrect.

3.1.2. Serbian Leaders and Serbian National Interests in the 1967-74 Debates

The second question to be discussed here is this: Were Serbian politicians at all interested in Serbian national interests,[37] or were they concerned only with remaining in power, showing no concern for public issues, such as Serbia's position in Yugoslavia? This question reappears throughout any political analysis. In chapter one I argued that Communist politics was very much an attempt to implement visions in reality. The analysis of the differences between Serbia's leaders and Tito in this chapter shows that Serbian leaders were surprisingly negative toward Tito's pragmatic politics, adhering to principles as they understood them and avoiding too many political compromises. But in their views, the principles they followed did not clash with the real interests of Serbia and Yugoslavia. It was by following these principles (based on a Marxist interpretation) that they argued the interests of each Yugoslav nation could be best served. To separate interests and principles was impossible for them and thus should prove unproductive as an approach for us. Principles drove their action, but this action was also held to be in the interest of those they believed they represented.

The Serbian leaders (and others) could perhaps have found a much more convenient means of securing personal power than by opposing Tito on so many occasions that he finally decided to remove some of them from office. Yet their beliefs drove them to such a situation.[38] They were not soft negotiators, nor were they ready to accept everything Tito and the other republics asked them to accept. They had been very firm in not accepting Kosovo as the seventh Yugoslav republic, for example. They had also been interested in securing sufficient autonomy for Serbia within Yugoslavia, with which Serbia had been identified in the perceptions of other republics for much too long: during the whole interwar and to some extent even in the postwar period until 1966. Finally in March 1971 they came very close to realizing that other arrangements for Serbia might also be in the Serbian best interest.[39] Only Tito's move against the Croatian *mass movement* (which was to a large extent initiated by "Serbia standing up for herself," as Tito said in April 1971) convinced them to rethink the consequences of such a move.

For this reason, neither the position of the Serbian leaders nor that of the other Yugoslav leaders in the constitutional debate can be understood without explaining the main principles of Communist nationality policy, shared by all Communists. This is especially important, since it was over these principles that political elites argued during the constitutional debate. The central question was this: Was it possible to be at the same time an advocate of Slovenian, Croatian, Serbian, and other national interests and also a Communist? Although the advocates of pre-1966 Yugoslavia found it extremely difficult to reconcile the two, thus always yielding precedence to *Communist* over *national* affiliations, the new concept (Kardelj's Yugoslavia) argued that the two not only did not clash, but always went together. As will be shown in the following sections of this chapter, most of the Serbian leaders in the constitutional debate accepted Kardelj's argument, believing that national and Communist did not exclude each other.[40]

The second important principle in the Communist movement was that the Communists were expected to oppose nationalism primarily in their own nation and only later (or, in practice, almost never) in other nations. This necessarily drove the Serbian Communists to act against Serbian nationalism, leaving aside Albanian, Croatian, and all other nationalisms. In such a situation, however, to the Serbian public it seemed that the Serbian Communists overstated the presence of Serbian nationalism while underestimating the danger of other nationalisms, especially the growing Croatian and Albanian nationalism of the late 1960s and early 1970s. *Mutatis mutandis*, the same was felt by other Yugoslav nations-that the Communists overestimated the danger of "domestic" nationalism. Paradoxically, by fighting nationalism in the ranks of their own nations, the Communists now found themselves under the accusation of being the "gendarmes" of their own nation. In return, this only added to the arguments by nationalist forces, which now found it easier to promote their conclusions about the "treacherous" role of national Communists.

Of course, the Serbian Communists (just like the others) expected Communists in other nations to fight their nationalisms. But in the late 1960s, it seemed that more autonomy for the republics might lead to a situation in which not everyone in Yugoslavia would have the same criteria about what nationalism was and how to fight it. It was the rather mild stand of the Croatian Communists toward the Croatian Spring that displeased the Serbian leaders. At that time, they felt they were losing the institutional and political tools to do anything to change the situation.

Also, the Serbian politicians were aware that the position of Serbia remained somewhat specific; since the Serbs were the largest nation in Yugoslavia, the one with the historical burden of interwar Serbian domination strongly felt on its shoulders. This specificity did not allow Serbia to revise its position toward Serbian nationalism. The Serbian Communists felt that their opposition to Serbian nationalism must be unconditional and forceful, since, as Petar Stambolić, the president of the Serbian Central Committee said in May 1968, the Serbian nation was the only one that could "realistically become hegemonic" (1968:142).[41] Belonging to the largest Yugoslav nation, many members of the Serbian elite felt disadvantaged in opposing ever new demands by the smaller Yugoslav nations.[42] The Serbian Communists thus found themselves more than any others caught between the principles in which they believed and the reality they faced. Disappointed by what they saw as the reluctant reaction in the past of other Yugoslav Communists to nationalism in their own nations, and unwilling to offer additional arguments to those who argued that the only realistic danger for the Yugoslav decentralized system came from "great-Serbian hegemonism"[43] (either in the form of a renewed interwar bourgeois Yugoslavia, or as a Soviet-style centralization), Serbian Communists found themselves in a frustrating situation between two fires. This frustration would remain a permanent source of political crisis in Serbia and Yugoslavia throughout the 1970s and 1980s.

3.1.3. The Serbian Leaders and the Lack of Democratic Legitimacy

Ultimately, the third objection to the view that Serbian politicians voluntarily accepted the 1974 Constitution relates to the issue of the legitimacy of the Serbian political elite. This objection could equally be raised about the political elites in Yugoslavia in general, including the elites in those republics where the issue of legitimacy regarding the acceptance of the 1974 Constitution has never been raised. The Croatian and Slovenian leaderships were not more legitimate than Serbian in this respect. Perhaps surprisingly for those who argue that Communist systems lacked legitimacy, the Yugoslav case shows that between the elite (especially Tito himself) and a wide range of the population there was a degree of a tacit agreement on basic political issues.[44] This can be illustrated by recognizing that whenever Tito wanted to remove the political elite in one or another republic, he would rely on the direct link between himself and the population.[45] Even in the moments of crises (such as, the protests by students at the University of Belgrade in 1968, or the Croatian Spring of 1971), he was still capable of securing wide support from the population, in which sense he really was a populist. Importantly, when facing criticism from the population, this would more often be from positions of radical egalitarianism than from a demand for greater democratization or more national rights.[46]

Tito's personal popularity among the masses had its origin in several factors, extensively examined in the relevant literature on Yugoslavia. *The Washington Post* correspondent in Belgrade (1973-76), Duško Doder, writes about his talks with the Yugoslavs:

> Out in the country, Tito has a real hold on the people. It was my impression that if by some miracle free elections were suddenly held in Yugoslavia, Tito would get a majority of the votes, even if his Communist party would not. (1978:118)

Doder quotes from various Yugoslavs he spoke to about the reasons for such support. When we sum up what they said, one main reason appears central-the fear of Soviet domination. Tito was seen as the guarantor of Yugoslav independence and the chief defender against the Soviet Union. Doder quotes a textile worker from Pirot, a small town on the border between Serbia and Bulgaria. When Doder asked him why would the Russians come to Yugoslavia, the worker "motioned eastward toward Bulgaria" and said, "Ask them, over there" (1978:118). He received a similar answer in Slovenia from a Roman Catholic clerk: "God bless his [Tito's] soul. Had it not been for him, we would have been another Bulgaria or Czechoslovakia today" (1978:118). Or in Zagreb: "I do not like him. But I guess we all respect him for having stood up to the Russians and kept us out of their clutches" (1978:118). All other reasons were derived from the comparisons with the Eastern neighbors of Yugoslavia.[47] Tito was praised for being a mild ruler, for not murdering his political foes, for allowing private initiative in the country, for importing goods and encouraging consumerism, for keeping the country peaceful, united, and respected, and for promoting the "third way" between the two blocs. Based on Tito's resistance to Fascism and Stalinism, a myth of the special place that Tito held for Yugoslavia in world politics was promoted by the media. The facts of life seemed to support this myth: Yugoslavia's leader was the most prominent figure within the nonaligned movement, while maintaining reasonably good relationships with both East and West. Yugoslav economic successes and political stability were widely admired, and Tito was seen as the main guarantor of Yugoslav stability. Were there any reasons for the Yugoslavs not to share this belief?

Although the political and intellectual elite (who knew that Tito was-for all his historical achievements in struggles against Stalin-less critical of the USSR than some other politicians, such as Kardelj and Koča Popović) expressed some criticism of Tito's role and of the system he had shaped, a wide range of the population proved to be far less critical and much more supportive of Tito. There is no better illustration of this than a diary note by Dobrica Ćosić (the leading Serbian anti-Titoist) on the day of Tito's death in May 1980. Describing the reaction of the Serbs to the news of Tito's death, Ćosić says:

> With my anti-Titoist feelings, I am here alone....I felt desperation and coldness walking on the opposite side of the street from the people; I felt alone, completely detached (from them). For the first time in my life I felt this loneliness, detachment from the people of my country. (1992:22-23)

When a week after Tito's funeral Ćosić saw queues several miles long of people waiting to see Tito's mausoleum, he wrote (on 13 May 1980):

> All anti-Titoists are confused by the way people are reacting to Tito's death. Such grief, especially among the young people, is confusing. (1992:39)[48]

The popularity of all the Yugoslav leaders was largely dependent on Tito, and not the other way around. Several groups of Serbian leaders had been removed from 1966 to 1974, but no serious political strike was organized in their support, nor even did any civil disobedience to the Titoist system gather strength.[49] The only exception to this was the 1968 Belgrade student demonstrations, which did not seek to stop, but actually to speed up, the removal of the bureaucrats (all but Tito) from their offices. The only real outcome of these protests was the strengthening, not weakening, of Tito's position in the country. They had a negative effect on the process of liberalization, which had started a few years before 1968. The protests of 1968, like later protests in Kosovo (December 1968) and Croatia (1971), only helped Tito to send a clear signal to local leaders-that their position and the stability of the country ultimately depended on him. The public protests helped the president to restore his position, somewhat weakened by the pressure from republican elites and the federal apparatus. A leading Serbian liberal politician, Latinka Perović, had this to say:

> Tito could once again say that only he himself expressed authentically the interests of the masses. [In 1968] he once again accused his fellow leaders of being unwilling to listen to his advice. Such overwhelming [plebiscite] support, he would say, could be compared only with his popularity immediately after the liberation of the country. There was nothing he could not do. In fact, he was rather economical with his own power. He was more cautious than those who were inviting him to use it.[50] (1991:59)

In conclusion: the Serbian leadership was in tune with the mood in Serbia when supporting Tito's proposals for the reform of the federation, but it also showed significant independence (both from Tito's views and from its own population) when defending what they saw as the best interests of Serbia. They considered the proposed reforms to be in the Serbian interest, though they objected to several ideas, asking Tito and others to change their original proposals and to offer more guarantees for the equality of Serbia in Yugoslavia. By doing this, they found themselves permanently squeezed between two sides: Tito and the mass of the population on the one, and the intellectual opposition (*critical intelligentsia, dissidents*) on the other. In what was a process of negotiation beneath the surface of unanimity, they tried to satisfy all sides, but ended up being denounced as "liberals" (by radical egalitarians) and as "traitors to Serbian interests" (by nationalists). Still, though they differed on issues of democratization, the Serbian leaders remained fairly united when the issue of the Serbian position in Yugoslavia and the reform of the Yugoslav federation came onto the agenda.

3.2. The Serbian Leadership between Ranković and Kardelj

The position of Serbian leaders with regard to constitutional debate must be situated in the context of their acceptance in 1966 of Tito's removal of Aleksandar Ranković, the most prominent Serb in the Party leadership since the 1930s. Why did the Serbian leaders (handpicked for offices not without Ranković's explicit consent) agree on this?

Twenty-five years after this event (when it became extremely unpopular to criticize Ranković and the concept he symbolized), the then (1966) Yugoslav Prime Minister Petar Stambolić explains:

> Ranković's whole line was conservative. In Serbia, we felt him to be a heavy burden. I remember my talk with Milentije Popović [another leading Serbian politician] in 1963. Both of us concluded that it would be a great misfortune if Ranković replaced Tito. One should remember that everything that happened at that time was linked to the issue of the Russians, because we feared very much that they would again draw us into their bloc....There was a time when I thought we would join them. It is at this time that there was a lot of debate about Tito's successor. It is in this framework that one should situate the Ranković case. Tito exercised full control over foreign policy and the army, and Ranković controlled the Party and police. We wanted to put the lid on this. (Djukić 1992:212-14)

The Serbian leadership saw the fall of Ranković in July 1966 as a unique chance for the emergence of a modern, democratic[51] Serbia, relieved from the permanent suspicion of being a "guardian" to everyone else in Yugoslavia. The young generation of Serbian leading politicians hoped to decrease federal influence over Serbia to the same extent as over all the other republics (Perović, 1991:42). They saw their acceptance of the decentralization of Yugoslavia as the ultimate evidence that Serbia was not and did not want to be a "tutor" in the country. Not unlike Communists in other parts of Yugoslavia, the leading Serbian politicians believed that any centralization was contrary to Serbian interests, since there was a temptation to identify Yugoslav centralism with Serbian hegemony. Because the Serbs in Socialist Yugoslavia did not in fact dominate (neither Tito nor Kardelj were Serbs), the accusations on this account were, they believed, unjust and incorrect. But the old perception of Yugoslavia as the "Serb-dominated" country was still alive in other republics and in Kosovo. Sometimes this perception would resurge also in intraelite debates, especially in moments of crisis, where other republics' interests clashed with Serbia's. Serbian leaders felt that this negative image of Serbia as republic that could potentially destroy the equality of all Yugoslav nations and return to policy in which it would dominate over others was unfair. But they knew they should address it and do what they could to eliminate this image.

The best way to do that was by accepting the decentralization of Yugoslavia, which would bring more autonomy also to Serbia. The constitutional changes of 1967-74 were acceptable "because they also strengthened the position of Serbia as an equal among equals, thus reducing further pressures on her and minimizing the chances for the renewal of hegemonic tendencies in the political, economic, and cultural areas in Serbia itself," says Latinka Perović (1991:268). It is easier to understand the logic of such reasoning once we know about Serbia's dissatisfaction with some of Tito's decisions. A looser Yugoslav federation, the Serbian leaders believed, would mean a weaker position for federal institutions, which were in fact reduced to being tools of Tito's personal politics. This would also secure more independence for Serbia, enabling her to develop as the real center of a modern, democratic Yugoslavia and as the strongest promoter of reforms in a post-Titoist Yugoslavia.[52] Serbia, they felt, had to change her image. From being a rural, conservative country, suspected by everyone, it should become the center of democratic transformation in Yugoslavia, a modern and technologically developed republic. As Draža Marković said, the Serbian post-Ranković leaders were "constructing Serbia with a different face and different qualities," which would be "closer to the Serbia of the future than to the Serbia of the past" (1 March 1970; 1987:180-81). To a large extent, they were successful in doing this. Not only in the late 1960s, but even later, right up until Milošević, Serbia was perceived as a democratic stronghold in Yugoslavia.[53] This made Serbia think of keeping the central role in the future process of the democratization of Yugoslavia. As Marković wrote in his diary on 17 January 1971:

> Although a democratization of the country today seems impossible, since real democratization in society is not really wanted, the trend of democratization cannot really be halted for good....I think that Serbia is precisely the republic with the greatest chances to give the strongest boost to such a development. We should firmly remain on this orientation. This is where our strength lies, both for Serbia and for Yugoslavia as a whole. (1987:253)[54]

It was not as the result of pressure or against their understanding of Serbian interests that the Serbian elite supported the constitution, but because of their firm belief that the constitutional arrangements were in Serbian interests. For these reasons, the Serbian leaders respected Kardelj, the main architect of the new explanation of Yugoslav reality. If their relations with Tito were defined by pragmatic reasons, their relationship with Kardelj was influenced much more by sharing the common ground of ideology. In the summer of 1991, Petar Stambolić, by then a retired and heavily criticized (but in 1967-74 still central) figure of Serbian politics, said that he had been and remained Kardelj's supporter, since "Kardelj's mistakes were also mine." Stambolić repeated the most common argument of the Kardeljists:

> Everything that Kardelj initiated and promoted in our political system distinguished us from the East and was a guarantee that we would not return to the past. In general, he was a reformist and a Yugoslav.[55]

To some extent, the Serbian leaders criticized Kardelj less than Tito, since they believed that Kardelj was a man of principles, but Tito was a pragmatist, ready to give too many concessions to other republics, and especially to the provinces.[56] The difference between the two became obvious in the case of the *Blue Book* (1977): while Kardelj supported the Serbian demands, Tito inclined toward the position of the provinces.[57] Although Kardelj acted from the principle that "only the republics are sovereign; thus only they decide which elements of this sovereignty they would delegate to the federation and which to lower sociopolitical communities, such as provinces" (I. Stambolić, 1995:70), Tito was motivated by the pragmatic need to avoid confrontation within the political elite in what he felt would be his last years in power.

Marković's diaries reveal that his relationship with Kardelj had undergone a serious transformation in a positive direction during the constitutional debate. Although he was very critical of Kardelj in the beginning (19 October 1971, 21 January 1971, and so on), considering him intolerant, dogmatic, and "schematic" (10 October 1970), as time went on Marković understood that Kardelj was not a priori hostile to the Serbian point of view. On the contrary, he witnessed several situations in which only Kardelj supported Serbia, when she was either isolated or ignored by other republics. This was especially so with regard to the Serbian provinces, which the other republics treated as a Serbian internal question, leaving Serbia to struggle alone with their demands, being again constantly on the verge of new accusations of hegemonism. In such situations, Kardelj was an invaluable ally of the Serbian leadership. The extent to which they appreciated such support is described in Marković's words (24 January 1976):

> Sometimes one wonders-what would happen without him? Can the whole system be based on the authority and intervention of one man? For now, this is so. One must, however, live after him, and without him. I do not see how.[58]

In January 1978, a year before Kardelj's death, Marković wrote in his diary:

> I have learned to like him. He is the right man....clever, open-minded, a democrat. Tolerant in discussions, wide in his views. (6 January 1978; 1987:426)

Kardelj also liked Marković. The leading Croatian politician of the time Jure Bilić recalls a talk with Vidoje Žarković, the Montenegrin representative to the state (1974-84) and Yugoslav Party Presidency (1984-88). Already on his deathbed, Kardelj told Žarković that among the Serbian leaders, Marković was the most loyal to his concept. "He is as nationalistic as any other Serbian leader, but he is more committed than others to the concept of self-management."⁵⁹

To conclude: the dominant explanations of the reasons for the Yugoslav disintegration underline the interrepublican and interethnic conflicts as the main cause of the state and regime failure. But the sources we have quoted in this chapter show a high level of understanding and cooperation between the Slovene Kardelj, the Croat Tito, and Serbian leading politicians. In what follows, it will become clear that the main conflict was within republics and not primarily between various ethnic groups and territorial units. The political conflicts in Serbia were primarily between members of the political elite belonging to the same ethnic group, as will be shown by the example of the debate between the majority of the Serbian Central Committee and two other members (both Serbs) in May 1968. The same applied to the other Yugoslav republics.

Second, contrary to later dominant interpretations, the leading Serbian politicians firmly believed that Kardelj's concept projected Serbia as a republic equal to others and offered her much more autonomy than she had before. In fact, they believed that Kardelj satisfied two main goals of Serbian politics: to preserve Yugoslavia and to secure the autonomy of Serbia within it. While Yugoslavia still remained united (despite permanent political differences between its regions), Serbia's extensive autonomy ("statehood") was now fully recognized as a permanent and undeniable fact. As to the other Yugoslav republics, the principle of "not intervening in its internal affairs" was also recognized by the federal constitution as applying to Serbia.⁶⁰

The "ethnic nationalists," "liberals," and "Stalinists," three groups the Yugoslav Communists aimed to suppress in public life, were left dissatisfied with the 1974 Constitution.⁶¹ The republics did not exactly follow ethnic lines in Yugoslavia, nor did democratic elections take place constituting a (liberal) democratic Yugoslavia.⁶² The proposed concept was a further step away from the East European, especially the Soviet institutional setting, and West European political systems, based on representative democracy. But the Serbian politicians in the late 1960s and early 1970s were neither ethnic nationalists nor democratic Yugoslavs in the West European meaning of the word. Still less were they pro-Soviet in the sense of being dissatisfied with Kardelj's ideas on these grounds.⁶³ Like other Yugoslav Communists, they shared the self-managing concept, adapting it to the Serbian situation. It was their interpretation of Kardelj's ideas that defined Serbian identity in the last twenty years of Yugoslavia. This interpretation is analyzed further in this chapter.

3.3. Two Visions of Serbia and Yugoslavia Within Serbian Politics in May 1968

Even more explicitly than other Yugoslav republics, Serbia understood that the change of concept (after the fall of Ranković) urged her to reconstruct her own discourse in Yugoslavia. I shall examine the creation of this new Serbian discourse in the light of the polemics between two defenders of the pre-1966 concept of a Third Yugoslavia (Dobrica Ćosić and Jovan Marjanović) and the majority of the Serbian Central Committee, which took place at the 14th CC LCS session on 29-30 May 1968. This debate had important consequences for several reasons:

(1) The Serbian Communists once again confirmed their commitment to constitutional changes, offering new arguments in their support; by doing this they in fact defined Serbia's political discourse, which remained valid until the late 1980s;

(2) The debate indicated the existence of long-term divisions between factions of the Serbian party, which now entered a new phase; these divisions cannot be entirely described by terms such as "conservatives" and "reformists," or "internationalists" and "nationalists," since they were rather complex ideological explanations and visions of the future;

(3) The debated issues, such as the position of Serbia in Yugoslavia, relations within Serbia and with the provinces, recognition of ethnic and political diversities, and others, entered the main agenda of Yugoslav and Serbian politics to stay there, only to be redefined again with Milošević twenty years later;

(4) One of the main participants, Dobrica Ćosić, became the leading figure of the opposition in Yugoslavia and also the first president of the Federal Republic of Yugoslavia (Serbia and Montenegro) in 1993; in this respect the debate was equally formative of the views of the Serbian opposition and the Serbian elite since 1968.

The debate between the two concepts (sometimes referred to as the *Pre-Brioni* and *Brioni*)[64] showed deep differences in understanding the new Party politics, as presented in an internal Party paper, "On the tasks of the League of Serbian Communists in the realization of the policy on national equality in SR Serbia," proposed by the Serbian leadership to the Central Committee of the LC Serbia at its 14th Session (29 and 30 May 1968). The document clearly suggested that a "new phase" in the policy on the national question had begun with the fall of Ranković two years earlier. In the earlier phase, the document admits, the "bureaucratic forces had in practice violated the main principles of the LCY's policy on national questions. An especially grave form of this violation was permanent suspicion of the *nationalities* (narodnosti),[65] and the obstruction of the politics of national equality." This was especially so in Kosovo-Metohija, with regard to the Albanian nationality. The document explicitly denounced the previous policy of "bureaucratic forces" in Kosovo as "a drastic form of anti-Socialist chauvinist practice" (minutes of the XIV LC CCS Session, 1968[66]:18).

The new phase was intended to fully realize the equality of Yugoslav nations and nationalities in line with Kardelj's abandonment of the Slavic character of Yugoslavia. Since Yugoslavia was no longer based on the ethnic similarities of its constitutive nations, but on their common interests, non-Slavic Albanians should not be treated differently from others.[67] Apart from this matter of principle, there were more pragmatic reasons for this change: Albanians had now become the fourth largest Yugoslav ethnic group (smaller than the Serbs, Croats, and Slovenes, but larger than the Bosnian Muslims, Macedonians, and Montenegrins), with a growing intelligentsia. They thus became a typical example of an emerging nation, fitting into Leninist theories of social development. Before the eyes of Yugoslav Communists, an ethnic group now developed the characteristics of a fully developed nation, demanding what every nation demands for itself: its own state. The same, of course, applied to the Slavic nations of Yugoslavia; they now became "completed nations" (as Kardelj concluded), willing and ready to form their own states. Yugoslavia was there to acknowledge and support this historical process. In granting more autonomy to Yugoslav constitutional units (both republics and provinces), Yugoslav Communists believed they were acting in a truly Marxist way – recognizing what was an inevitable result of the historical process.

The Serbian Central Committee, acknowledging the new development, invited the relevant institutions to pass additional measures to reduce differences in development between Kosovo and the rest of Serbia and to speed up the education of the Albanians so that they themselves could take responsibility for the further development of Kosovo (Minutes 1968:25). The political equality of nations and nationalities could not, the Serbian Communists argued, be achieved without economic equality, since it was the economy that formed the base of the political suprastructures. Equality, on the other hand, was the fundamental value of Socialism. Without equality, no society could pretend to be Socialist.

The new phase, the Serbian Communists admitted, carried with it the danger of nationalism. For this reason, the document invited the Communists of Serbia (regardless of their nationality) to block any action by nationalist and chauvinist elements in their own nations. In opposition to the interpretation that some (i.e., Serbian) nationalism was "defensive" and only a reaction to the "aggressive" nationalism of other nations (i.e., Croats and Albanians), it was stressed that "each nationalism had its own origins in a particular nation or nationality" and nationalism should therefore be fought within that nation by the Communists of the same nation. There was no such thing as more or less dangerous nationalism and no "defensive" nationalism should be tolerated.

3.3.1. Discourse One: Ćosić and Marjanović

Dobrica Ćosić, however, did not accept the strong criticism of the "old phase" of Yugoslav Socialism. Ćosić, a partisan himself and a writer who had helped Kardelj to word the Program of the League of Yugoslav Communists in 1958, came under suspicion after sending a letter to Tito in which he opposed the removal of Ranković in 1966. Now, two years later, he again voiced his disagreement with criticism of the Ranković period, saying that "since the Republic of Serbia was established up until the present, the leading political forums of the Republic of Serbia have, in general and in historical perspective, conducted a democratic and internationalist policy" (Minutes 1968:105). If there were a reason to be worried, it was because of the most recent events. "The unity of the working class and of the nations of Yugoslavia is undermined at its roots by strong social and national differentiation and growing economic inequality." This was all, Ćosić said, the result of "bureaucratic nationalism that keeps replacing Marxist internationalism and universalism," as well as of "the ideology that equates Socialist self-management and national, i.e., state sovereignty" (Minutes 1968:102). This trend made many people worry about the future of Yugoslavia, which might well result in various nationalist tendencies.

Ćosić was supported by Jovan Marjanović, another member of the Serbian Central Committee and one of the main historians of the Yugoslav World War II period. Marjanović criticized what he saw as the abandonment of "Socialist Yugoslavism" and Yugoslavism in general and opposed innovations in the ethnic structure of Yugoslavia (recognition of a separate Muslim nation and of the existence of a separate Montenegrin culture, for example). Both Ćosić and Marjanović said that a debate on the state of the Serb nation had been avoided, despite the "serious anti-Serb atmosphere, which has been widely manifested in certain areas, especially in Croatia and Slovenia," where Serbs were perceived as those who "want only to dominate, govern, and control" (Minutes 1968:103). Accusing other Communists of being tolerant toward anti-Serb nationalism, Ćosić refused to follow the rule of nonintervening in other republics' internal affairs. He especially refused to leave Hungarian and Albanian nationalism to Communists in Vojvodina and Kosovo, respectively, warning of "Hungarian segregationism and the bureaucratic autonomism[68] of the Vojvodina bureaucracy." Marjanović asked why the Slovenian League of Communists defined itself as a "national organization" in its statute (Minutes 1968:91). He argued against the recognition of the Muslim nation, since this would-as he said-lead to new ethnic conflicts in Yugoslavia. This decision, as well as the recognition of the cultural separateness of the Montenegrins (as opposed to their Serbian background), were two examples of bureaucratic nationalism that was opposed to "the free development of Yugoslav Socialist awareness, and of a sense of belonging to the Yugoslav Socialist community" (Minutes 1968:98). The bureaucratic forces that made these decisions "used violence to halt any process of integration and unification of the Yugoslav nations and their segments." Yugoslavia thus found itself in "the absurd and comic situation that despite the proclamation of the right to self-determination, one could not declare oneself a Yugoslav, while many honest fighters for Socialism experience humiliation as people without nationality, being treated almost as displaced persons," said Marjanović. It was not true, he emphasized, that people did not want to be Yugoslavs. They were discouraged from being so by the political elite that "paid much more attention to elements that make us divided and different in national terms rather than to those that integrate and bind us together" (Minutes 1968:97).

But it was Kosovo that divided Marjanović and Ćosić most in the Serbian Central Committee from the advocates of the new-phase approach. Despite the dominant rhetoric according to which the rights of Albanians had been violated under the Ranković regime, Marjanović and Ćosić now claimed that the Serbs and Montenegrins in Kosovo suffered in the new phase. They had been pushed out of jobs and pressurized by the Kosovo Albanians. Therefore they had begun to leave the province.[69] The Provincial Committee of the LC of Kosovo "did not attach appropriate importance to the struggle against Albanian chauvinism and irredentism, coming out with mere political phrases" (Minutes 1968:107). A policy that replaced class with national criteria and that understood the self-managing rights of *nationalities* as their right to statehood and sovereignty could be fatal. In opposition to Kardelj's rather loose understanding of sovereignty and of statehood, Ćosić argued that in Kosovo there could be either Albanian or Yugoslav sovereignty. "A combination of both is impossible without negative results, at least in today's circumstances," said Ćosić (Minutes 1968:108). One of these outcomes could be the revival of the "old historical aims and national ideals of the Serbian nation-to unite itself into its own state" (Minutes 1968:111). This could have unimagined consequences.[70]

Ćosić saw the solution in the strengthening, not the abandoning, of Socialist internationalism, which would eventually lead to a Balkan Federation of Socialist countries. National conflicts could be prevented only by truly internationalist politics, which would result in the "formation of an internationalist community of nations...bound together on the grounds of common class and economic and social aims and interests, regardless of national allegiances and borders." In such an association, "class, societal, and individual interests should always have priority over national and state allegiances." A federation of Balkan nations, "as an organic part and form of the processes of global integration," would "not be a pure alliance of nations or states, but would tend to become an alliance of free people and working associations...not of supranations" (Minutes 1968:115).

Ćosić was convinced that such an association was possible and feasible.

> If this is impossible and only a fiction, then Socialism itself is a fiction and an unfeasible ideal. If our intentions to realize this goal should be postponed for better and more suitable times, then the revolution itself should have also been initiated in more appropriate and better times. But I think neither that this...is impossible to achieve, nor that it (or the orientation toward this aim) should be postponed. Quite the contrary. (Minutes 1968:115)[71]

In his speech, Ćosić stressed that the Albanian and Macedonian questions were the most complex parts of the Balkan problem, since these two nations were divided between several Balkan states. It was true, he said, that in certain circumstances those who argued for the unification of all Albanians within a single state could become perceived as "a historical vanguard and could also have a certain Socialist program and revolutionary slogans" (Minutes 1968:13).[72]

> "In principle, we have no right to ignore or to hide from ourselves the sentiments of the Albanian nation for its own unification." Rather, this reality should be "seen in correlation with the past and the future of relations between Serbs and Shiptars [Kosovo Albanians], and in the spirit of Socialist internationalism."

Ćosić, in fact, invited members of the Serbian Central Committee to openly debate the question of Kosovo:

> The Serbian nation is aware and has enough power and willingness to understand the democratic national feelings of the Shiptars of Kosovo-Metohija and to support all their aspirations if they are democratic in form and content, if they do not endanger peace in the Balkans and the independence of the Yugoslav community, that is-if they do not realize their national sovereignty by nationalist methods, endangering the existence, freedom, and integrity of the Serbs in Kosovo-Metohija. (Minutes, 1968:113-4)[73]

But we also should not forget that 300,000 Serbs and Montenegrins "certainly cannot and will not accept becoming a part of a less developed sociopolitical community and one less civilized than that to which they belong by all criteria" (Minutes 1968:114). For this reason, Ćosić said, any abandonment of "a really internationalist policy," that would lead to a Socialist federation of the Balkan people as "an organic element of the processes of the world's integration" would be a fatal mistake.

Both speeches were an open attack on the main ideas of the new phase of Yugoslav Socialism. But their criticism comprised heterogeneous elements that could hardly make up a consistent political alternative. Their approach, in fact, used some elements of the *national unity* rhetoric, merging them with the *pre-1966* discourse of Socialist Yugoslavism.

Yet Ćosić and Marjanović openly pointed to facts that the political elite in Serbia and Yugoslavia wanted to ignore or to hide from public debate. With the democratization of public life after 1966, nationalist tendencies were indeed more represented in the debate. This was especially so in Croatia and Kosovo, regions that for historical reasons Serbian nationalism often referred to as anti-Serb. A year before Ćosić's speech, the leading Croatian cultural institutions and the most distinguished intellectuals had demanded the recognition of a separate Croatian language in the *Declaration on the Name and Position of the Croatian Literary Language* (1967). Their Serbian counterparts replied with the "Proposition for Consideration." As Ćosić himself experienced after his polemics with Slovenian author Dušan Pirjevec (in 1961), by the mid-1960s, hardly any common sense of Yugoslavism remained between intellectuals from various parts of the country.[74]

Ćosić's warning about the possibly dangerous consequences of the new policy in Kosovo could have also been supported by facts. The fall of Ranković in 1966 was followed by public criticism of his (largely anti-Albanian) politics in the province. Massive purges in the security structures, especially in Kosovo, affected many Serb and Montenegrin civil servants in the province. The "new phase" now promised even further "positive discrimination" in favor of the new Kosovo (Albanian) intelligentsia, which was idealistic and to some extent nationalist. In 1967, for example, a historian, Ali Hadri, published an article on "Kosovo in the Kingdom of Yugoslavia," in which he offered an "Albanian point of view" that certainly provoked Serbian sentiments linked to Kosovo (Hadri 1967; Dogo 1997).[75] In Kosovo, where the relation between the two ethnic groups had often been seen as one of master-servant rather than of two equals, the Serbs now increasingly felt they were becoming "servants" of new masters-the Albanians.[76] This launched a large wave of emigration from Kosovo, already by far the least developed region of Yugoslavia. From 1961 to 1981, it was reported that 100,000 Serbs and Montenegrins left Kosovo. Together with the much larger birth rate of the Kosovo Albanians, this in reality changed the ethnic structure of the province, in which the share of the Serbs had fallen in these 20 years to 13.2 percent, from 23.5 percent. Interviews conducted with the migrants, as well as research into their economic backgrounds, show that the sense of inequality and political pressure after 1966 was by and large the most important reason for migration (Petrović 1992; Blagojević 1997 and 1998).[77] Ćosić was indeed the first Serbian politician to warn about these trends, at a time when nationality issues were still somewhere between a taboo and an open issue.[78]

It is no surprise, therefore, that the debate that followed their speeches at the 14th CC LCS Session had a strategic importance not only for the Serbian position in the constitutional debate, but for the course of events in the late 1980s. It was a clear choice between various concepts of Serbia and Yugoslavia. The majority of the Central Committee declared in favor of Kardelj's concept. Next in this chapter we follow the arguments that the majority used in polemics with Ćosić and Marjanović.

3.3.2. Discourse Two: The Majority of the Serbian Central Committee

The Vojvodina Party leader, Mirko Tepavac, argued that if Ćosić's approach were accepted, the Albanians would have no alternative but to feel "like subtenants in a Serbian national state, to acknowledge that they are second-rate citizens, to accept that only if they accept Serbian domination they could remain where they are" (Minutes 1968:141). For Draža Marković, "the idea that everything, including national feelings, should be subordinated to the notion of unity is not a new argument," but an old Stalinist idea. "However, even fifty years after the October Revolution, the national question could not be put off the agenda by any talk of *unity*," as the Czechoslovak case explicitly proved.[79] This case was used by Milojko Drulović, who asked what the reason was that the Czechs and Slovaks "had only now come to the conclusion that the relationship between them should be organized in an entirely different way" (Minutes 1968:195). The main reason was in their previous commitment to the Stalinist tradition of resolving problems between nationalities, which neglected the complexity of this issue in a Socialist and multiethnic state. The president of the Serbian assembly, Miloš Minić, speaking for more than two hours, went a step further than the main group of Serbian politicians[80] when he proposed that even the most radical proposals of the Kosovo leaders in the constitutional debate should be accepted. Minić accepted the new name of Kosovo (without mentioning Metohija),[81] the change of the name to "Socialist Autonomous" (instead of previously only "Autonomous" Province),[82] and the wide use of a new flag of Albanian *nationality*.[83] On the other hand, Minić criticized Marjanović for his mentioning of the Ustasha crimes against the Serbs in the context of this debate.[84] Serbia had no reason to be afraid of granting wide autonomy to "its nationalities" and regions. On the contrary, it was precisely because of the large differences between regions in Serbia (and especially between

Vojvodina and Kosovo) that "autonomy should be created even if it has not previously existed-and very wide autonomy, because otherwise we will not be able to solve such different problems without making bureaucratic centralism stronger," concluded Minić.

However, the speeches of the three most influential members of the Central Committee-its former, present, and future presidents, Dobrivoje Radosavljević,[85] Petar Stambolić,[86] and Marko Nikezić[87]-defined the Serbian mainstream interpretation of Kardelj's concept on the national question. Formulated in opposition to Ćosić and Marjanović, this platform remained almost unchanged in the next two decades, until the 8th CC LCS Session in September 1987, when Slobodan Milošević defined a new program.

Here are the main ideas of the Serbian mainstream discourse during the period from 1968 to 1987:

First, the existence of nations is a reality that should be acknowledged.

Even though they were products of the bourgeois epoch, nations had not withered away and would remain in existence for much longer than Stalinists believed. In itself, this is not necessarily an obstacle to the successful development of Socialism. The Communist Party of Yugoslavia, said Dobrivoje Radosavljević, had long ago (and especially during World War II) abandoned dogmatic views on nations. Radosavljević said:

> Yugoslavia is a multiethnic community...and no political forces of the old (prewar) Yugoslavia could have resolved the national question. No revolutionary movement, no Socialism that did not at the same time deal with the national question, no Communists that disregarded the existence of the national question would be able to do anything. (1968:237).

On the contrary, it was because they addressed the national question that the Communists became popular and were accepted by the Yugoslav nations. The Party became strong only when it proved itself as a force from within the nation, as a part of a nation, not something that was imposed on the nation from the outside. The aim of the Party, especially in a complex multiethnic community such as Yugoslavia, was to secure the free development of nations according to Socialist principles, and not to deny or neglect the national question. In this context, Ćosić and Marjanović's argument that the Party overemphasized differences and neglected similarities between Yugoslav nations was rejected.

Second, one could not *resolve* the national question, even if one wanted to, by unitarist formulas or by pressure on existing nations. Past failures in building up a Yugoslav nation (in the *First* Yugoslavia) and the Stalinist experience in the East European countries (especially in Czechoslovakia) were instructive enough. The national question reappeared in its full force, regardless of the Yugoslav

Communists' naïve wishful thinking that it would disappear after the revolution[88] (Stambolić, Minutes 1968:303; Radosavljević, Minutes 1968:242, and others). The politics of *Diktat* and pressure on nations from above in a state, as Marko Nikezić said, were no longer acceptable to anyone, including, of course, Serbia. "New relations have become needed by everybody," he said, and this was the reason why all republics in Yugoslavia had accepted them. "To dictate at a time when it is no longer historically inevitable, which means when it can no longer be justified-this is hardly acceptable," especially to the more developed regions of Yugoslavia (Minutes 1968:212). When it came to nations, the Serbian politicians concluded, it was much better to give more rights rather than fewer rights. It was "better to be too generous, in terms of concessions and flexibility toward national minorities, than to fall below real needs" (Minutes 1968:242).[89]

Third, even if Serbia advocated the centralization of Yugoslavia and a unitarist approach to the national question, she could find no political support for this policy in Yugoslavia.[90] The only potential allies of unitarists were outside the country-in the USSR and East European countries. Bearing in mind the context of the Czechoslovak crisis, to Serbian (and other) leaders it was clear that a defense of the unitarist concept of Yugoslavism would lead to the endangering of Yugoslav independence.[91] Petar Stambolić argued that the notion of Socialist internationalism, when combined with demands for unity, could "serve as a cover-up for a claim that we are all Communists, that we therefore have internationalist obligations, and consequently that we must subordinate our actions, for example, to some conclusions reached at some global meeting of world Communists" (Minutes 1968:303). The Yugoslav Communists defied such attempts when they split with Stalin in 1948, arguing that they were responsible to their own country, their own working class, and the people they led in the revolution.

Marko Nikezić (then the Yugoslav foreign secretary) argued that the crisis of the Western Democracies was so intense that in practice only Socialist (Communist) ideas were left in the political arena. Demonstrations in Paris, the Vietnam War, and antiwar action in the United States provided the confirmation of what all Marxists believed-that capitalism was the epoch of the past, which was to be replaced by Socialism, as a transitional phase to Communism.[92] "Thus it seems that the question is neither Socialism nor no Socialism, but what type of Socialism."[93] Consequently, Ćosić's and Marjanović's ideas, being Socialist (but in a different sense from Kardelj's Socialism) presented a greater danger than any capitalist alternative.

> It seems to me that there is a realistic danger that the Socialist future becomes in reality discredited by elements of the old models. For we have already seen societies that expropriated the rich classes and that even organized industrial development, but that nevertheless failed to improve the liberation of

man. I must say that we have already attempted to do this, we have already been there...but fortunately, we were moved from there,[94] and now we do not want anyone to push us back to these ideas. (Nikezić, Minutes 1968:214-5)

In Nikezić's words, if Ćosić's and Marjanović's ideas were supported, Yugoslavia would move to "statist concepts," while in its nationality policy it would return to positions that many other Socialist countries (for example, Czechoslovakia) wanted to leave by any means. Furthermore, it made no sense for Yugoslavia to move toward centralism at precisely the same moment everyone else realized that this system provided no grounds for the development of Socialism.

Fourth, the majority of the Serbian Central Committee argued that Ćosić and Marjanović misinterpreted the notion of Yugoslavism, which emerged as an expression of the demands of the South Slavs in the Austro-Hungarian Empire for their national individuality. Petar Stambolić said:

> "When they had no strength to achieve their national freedom individually, they relied on each other, and all South Slavs, creating a certain strength in order to achieve independence." (Minutes 1968:303).

Accordingly, no one wanted to be a Yugoslav to deny or even less to suppress their own national existence; to the contrary, they invented Yugoslavism to make their own national existence possible. The same motive mobilized the Yugoslav nations during the war for national liberation, which they did not fight for the slogan of unity, but for their own freedom, impossible without their being united (Nikezić, Minutes 1968:214). A unity that would endanger the freedom of the Yugoslav nations was therefore unacceptable. Stambolić remarked:

> For the reason of our relationship with other Yugoslav nations, we in Serbia must be very clear about this. We must deal very carefully with all these expressions of Yugoslavism, and this is what creates a political problem here.

Fifth, the main enemy of Serbian national interests was Serbian nationalism, which the Serbian Communists must oppose with all their strength. "No force in society is more reactionary than nationalism and chauvinism," concluded Miloš Minić. "If we wanted to test a Serbian Communist on nationalism, we needed to ask him what he thought of Kosovo-Metohija," he said.

But what was Serbian nationalism? Serbian Communists (as well as other Communists) became extremely sensitive on nationalism and "nationalism," leaving the threshold for labeling a person as a nationalist rather low, especially in ethnically mixed areas and where Serb-Croat relations were at stake. On one hand, taken the horrific nature of World War II in Yugoslavia, one can understand that the Communists were enormously sensitive on any appearance of nationalism and extremism. On the other hand, once a person became labeled as nationalist, this immediately led (at least) to his complete exclusion from official political life. To Petar Stambolić, Ćosić's warning that the Serbs were leaving Kosovo as a result of political pressures seemed strange, since it basically originated in the doctrine of Serbian nationalism. "It is strange when Communists of Serbia, debating nationality issues in 1968, look at who inhabited an area before others," he said. Replying to Marjanović's criticism of the recognition of Muslim national and Montenegrin cultural specificities, Stambolić invoked the CPY practice of treating Muslims as a separate entity in all wartime declarations, recalling that the Muslims had 45 *national heroes*.[95] The statehood of Montenegro was older than that of Yugoslavia; the separate (as distinct from the Serbian) culture of the Montenegrins had been developed over the past several decades in Yugoslavia. In general, the Serbian Communists believed that "one does not need to do more to harm Serbia today, at this moment of our real differentiation on nationality issues, than to preach Serbian nationalism" (Tepavac, Minutes 1968:141).[96]

Sixth, for historical reasons, Serbia needed to be careful when opening up national issues. Serbia did not want to be permanently suspected and blamed for dominating others in Yugoslavia. She was satisfied with the widespread perception among the others (especially Kardelj) that she had acted responsibly when accepting the removal of Ranković in 1966. Emphasizing this positive perception of Serbia in Yugoslavia, Petar Stambolić also argued that any fears that Serbia might be endangered in Yugoslavia were senseless:

> First of all, could anyone today say that it would be in the interest of the Serbs if the *nationalities* did not enjoy the same rights as we do, or if other nations did not have the same rights as us?...No one wants to say this, and no one can. Second, are we really endangered by the *nationalities*?[97] I do not know of any case when one could be endangered by a *nationality*.[98] It is only the majority that can put pressure on minorities, and therefore the problem of the minority is not a problem for the minority, but for the majority. And this is why we take these decisions regarding Kosovo-Metohija-it is in our own interest, in the interest of political stability and the strength of Serbia.

Lastly, majority in Serbian leadership believed that the new constitutional structure not only would not lead to the disintegration of Yugoslavia, but that it was the only way to prevent it. The unitary Yugoslavia of the prewar period, the Serbian (and other) Communists argued, disintegrated not only because of the military attack by the occupying forces in April 1941, but also because internal tensions had previously weakened its defensive strength. The third concept of Yugoslavia, of "brotherhood and unity," although promoting a federation, it also failed to eliminate and/or resolve the national question. Even though successful in preventing further ethnic conflicts in the aftermath of the war and in granting more rights to smaller national groups in Yugoslavia than they ever had, this model "could no longer secure progress, and the consequence of this conclusion was that after serious consideration, we have taken conscious action to move further on," said Nikezić. It remained to be seen if integration could be secured on other grounds[99] by the enlarged autonomy of nations and their republic-states. "This is not a disintegration; this is an integration because integration can be successful only if it is voluntary," concluded Petar Stambolić (Minutes 1968:309).

3.4. Conclusion

The Serbian political leadership accepted the 1974 Constitution because its members saw Kardelj's concept as a step toward the realization of the main Serbian national interests: to preserve a self-managing and Socialist Yugoslavia in which Serbia would have substantial autonomy without being suspected of suppressing the free development of other nations and "nationalities." The decentralization of Yugoslavia, under these conditions, meant greater autonomy for Serbia and thus was not against, but in favor of, Serbian interests. The Serbian leadership wanted to use this autonomy to modernize Serbia, and to some extent to liberalize its political system. By doing this, the Serbian leaders believed that they would increase the influence of Serbia on political decision making in the country, especially after Tito's departure. They also hoped to advance a self-managing (decentralized) Socialism, which they saw as the only realistic alternative to both "parliamentary democracy" and "state Socialism." Serbian Communists did not seek and did not want to accept an alliance with Serbian nationalists and Yugoslav unitarists, since they believed that these two alternative ideologies represented the main threat to Serbian long-term interests. Yet they did not like to see constant attacks by other republics and the federal leadership on Serbian nationalists and on other negative tendencies within Serbia, considering this to be an "intervention in their internal affairs." They expected Communists in the other Yugoslav republics (and two provinces) to reject any coalition with nationalists in the ranks of their nations. In this context, it was entirely understandable that the issue of Albanian nationalism was left to the Albanian Communists (predominantly in Kosovo), while the Serb Communists were expected to condemn, prevent, and reduce the strength of Serbian nationalism. Besides the already explained Communist beliefs that the state should decentralize in the "transitional period" in order to enable direct democracy (self-management) to replace its main functions, the decision of the Serbian Communists to accept Kardelj's constitutional proposals seemed perfectly logical.

In analyzing the intra-Serbian dispute over what Serbian interests were and how they should be defended, one should notice again that the greatest political conflicts in Yugoslavia were for a long time neither interethnic nor interrepublican; they were about the vision of society and therefore ideological. To the majority on the Serbian Central Committee, the Slovene Kardelj was much closer than the Serb Ćosić. Even more so, they preferred Kardelj, the architect of a loose structure of Yugoslavia, to Ćosić, the defender of the strong Socialist and united Yugoslavia that, as he believed, developed before the dismissal of another Serb and Yugoslav: Aleksandar Ranković. Lastly, they abruptly rejected Ćosić's argument that the Serbs had become unprotected and that the "anti-Serbian" nationalism of the Croats, Macedonians, Bosnian Muslims, and especially the Albanians was entering a dangerous phase. Instead, the Serbian leaders argued in favor of greater autonomy for Kosovo and Vojvodina, fully supporting further decentralization not only of Yugoslavia, but equally of Serbia itself.

Reading this today, we can only ask: how was this possible? But after-the-fact attempts to explain past actions tend to go wrong if they fail to understand the reasoning of the relevant actors within the relevant context. Within the discourse of Serbian nationalism, it is impossible to say anything else about this "impossible" coalition of Serbian leaders and the Slovene Kardelj except that it was a "betrayal" of national interests.[100] But in the discourse of the Communists of Serbia in the 1970s, the nationality of the political actors played a secondary role compared with ideological agreement. As Kardelj argued, it was "the common vision of society," not ethnic similarities, that bound Yugoslavia together.

Unable to situate events in their context, the Serbian nationalist discourse today offers no other explanation of the "pact" between the Serbian population and the Croat-Slovene Tito, the "greatest enemy [of Serbia] in this century"[101] (as Dobrica Ćosić called him on the day of his death), but the one advanced by Ćosić himself in 1989. Speaking in Budva (Montenegro) immediately after Milošević's successful overthrow of the last Titoist leadership of the smallest Yugoslav republic, Ćosić concluded:

> The reasons for this [i.e., for Serbs supporting Tito] were not primarily political or objective, but anthropological; they may be found in the anthropological nucleus of our national being....In our *ethos*, there is an existential incapability of being rational when it comes to ourselves and the world in general; there is an inclination to self-destruction, a permanent tragedism in our historical existence.

It was because of this "tragedism" that the Serbs simply "had no power to recognize the enemy" or to recognize it only too late (Ćosić 1989/1992:246).[102]

Of course Ćosić's explanation of Serbia's support of the 1974 Constitution in terms of anthropological or ethnogenetic reasons falls short of any understanding about what really happened. However, this interpretation became popular in Serbian political discourse of the late 1980s and the 1990s. In the following chapters I will analyze why.

Notes

1 Borisav Jović, the president of the Serbian National Assembly in March 1989 when the 1974 Constitution was significantly amended, talked about the "imposed constitution." The SANU Memorandum (1986) uses the word "prescribed [by the leader]" (*oktroirani*) to describe it. "Serbia must openly say that this order [of the 1974 Constitution] was imposed on Serbia" (Krestić 1986/1995:145).

2 Antonije Isaković, the chairman of the commission for the SANU Memorandum, says that the SANU academicians thought Ivan Stambolić, the president of Serbia (1986-87), was a "traitor to his own people" (interview conducted in April 1996). Similarly, Slobodan Milošević said in June 1989 that "no nation would tolerate such weakness in protecting its national interests as was demonstrated by leading Serbian politicians in the past" (Politika, 29 June 1989).

3 This argument was presented by various groups of dissidents and those opposed to Communists in Serbia. For more on the discourses developed by the opposition, see Dragović-Soso (2002).

4 For direct criticism of Tito by other members of the political elite, see Tepavac's account of the dispute between the vice president of Yugoslavia, Koča Popović, and Tito (1998:127); of the argument between the Yugoslav ambassador to the USSR, Veljko Mićunović, and Tito in 1961 (Tepavac 1998:134); and of the dispute between the Macedonian politician Lazar Koliševski and Tito (Djukić, 1989:117-20), among others. Many examples are to be found in Draža Marković's memoirs, frequently quoted in this chapter.

5 For this, see Tepavac (1997:74-5).

6 Leon Gršković, one of the two main constitutional lawyers who cooperated with Kardelj and Ranković in writing the 1963 Yugoslav Constitution, said in an informal conversation with Mladen Babun that Tito's hesitation to take a stand on the differences between the two men resulted in a constitution that had to be replaced immediately after the overthrow of Ranković three years later.

7 In an informal conversation I had with Miko Tripalo (then a member of the Federal Party Presidency for Croatia) in 1993, he said that Tito and Kardelj were "mediating between Serbs with Croats, but in such a way that they really did not want them to act united." He thought Tito had decided to move against both Croatian and Serbian leaders in April 1971, when the Serbo-Croatian agreement on confederalization seemed to become more realistic than ever. Tito and Kardelj feared not only for the future of Yugoslavia, but also for their position if this happened.

8 Marković, at the time president of the Serbian Assembly (the highest "state" position in Serbia), describes conversations of 15 May 1971 (1987:284), 26 June 1971 (1987:288), 4 July 1971 (1987:289), 30 November 1971 (1987:317), 14 May 1972 (1987:357), 5 November 1972 (1987:399), 14 April 1973 (1987:433-4), 10 June 1973 (1987:446), and many others after the 1974 Constitution had been enacted, which is not the subject of this chapter. Another important Serbian politician, Latinka Perović, the secretary of the Central Committee of the League of Communists of Serbia, describes some of her talks with Tito during 1971. Although in 1972 Marković and Perović went different ways in intra-Serbian political divisions, there is no major disagreement between these two accounts. For talks between Tito and Croatian leaders, see Tripalo (1990), Bilić (1988), and Dragosavac (1988).

9 Marković, 1987: 6 March 1971; 15 May 1971; 26 June 1971; 30 November 1971; 10 December 1971; 15 November 1972; and others.

10 Perović (1990:141) and Marković (30 November 1971).
11 It seems that Serbian criticism initiated a change in Tito's views on the Croatian leadership of Savka Dabčević Kučar and Miko Tripalo. Marković reveals that ten days after a difficult talk he had with the leadership of the City of Belgrade, Tito sharply criticized Croatian politicians, giving them a "final warning" at a closed meeting in Zagreb and Brežice, 4 July 1971. He asked them to act more resolutely against Croatian nationalism. On the very day of his meeting with the Croats, Tito spoke to Draža Marković for more than two hours. Marković recalls, "He was very worried about the situation. He spoke about the attacks on him: he talked about himself, his past, emphasizing that he had devoted his whole life to the cause of the working class, to revolutionary struggle; he was very critical about the situation in Croatia and the LC of Croatia. He told me he would leave for Zagreb that day and that he would be absent from Belgrade for two months. He was interested in my assessment of the situation in Serbia and Belgrade; almost directly he asked for guarantees of stability and security in this period" (4 July 1971; 1987:289).
12 Tripalo 1990:187. Tito, for example, tried to convince Tripalo not to resign, saying that he did not have to. However, he resigned in protest, saying to Tito that the attacks on the Croats were in fact directed at him, and that once he (Tito) had left the scene, the forces that had initiated the removal of the Croatian leaders would "publicly hang us both."
13 *Čaršija* is a word of Turkish origin, used to describe semipublic but influential circles among Serbian intellectuals that used to criticize the regime at various private and semiofficial gatherings. Tepavac says that "Serbia always worried Tito more than any other republic, because he sensed the volcanic potentiality of Serbian nationalism" (1998:154). Tito was kept informed of their views by secret police reports. This gave the impression of a massive surveillance of leading Serbian intellectuals and left room for speculation about how much the role of the secret police had really changed after the dismissal of Aleksandar Ranković (1966). Several affairs involving police information emerged during the constitutional debate, most of which were used to try to blacken its participants in Tito's eyes.
14 In return, this helped Serbian leaders and the opposition to build some bridges between them, since they both felt attacked by Tito. This explains why the political elite tried to soften Tito's demands for legal prosecution of the leading Serbian intellectuals. Marković's diary reveals his frequent contacts with some of them, such as Antonije Isaković and Dobrica Ćosić. The Serbian (and other) intellectuals were not really dissidents in the sense in which this word was used in other Eastern European countries. They always managed to find a segment of the political elite to act as their protector.
15 This is how Petar Stambolić describes Kardelj and Tito (Djukić 1992:241).
16 In an interview conducted for this book, Milka Planinc, who was the president of the Croatian Central Committee (1972-82) and the Yugoslav Prime Minister (1982-86) told me that "leaders of all republics would meet Tito separately to avoid direct discussion between them, and when they returned, they would argue that Tito had supported their position, not that of the other republics." This was in accordance with Tito's tendency to appear impartial and not deeply involved in political arguments between republican elites in Yugoslavia.
17 The direct link between Tito and a wide range of the population is explained in Županov's theory of "social contract between the highest and the lowest positions in society" (see further in this and following chapters).
18 Tito did this in the case of General Ljubičić. In proposing him for a third term as defense secretary in 1978, he disregarded the rule that banned anyone from being elected

to such a post more than twice, but on Serbian insistence he clearly stated this was his decision. Tito's other appointee, Miloš Minić, was removed from politics two years after Tito's death.

19 This list was composed after interviews with Josip Vrhovec, Jure Bilić, Dara Janeković, and Dušan Dragosavac, who-at least in some periods-had direct access to Tito.

20 Dissatisfaction of the closest circle of political and military elites with the role of Jovanka Broz resulted in her separation from Tito in 1977. Immediately after Tito's death in May 1980, she was forcibly evicted from all state estates and kept under surveillance (see Toma Fila's interview in Globus, 20 September 1999). Jovanka Broz blames General Ljubičić and Stane Dolanc for "misinforming Tito about the real situation in the country" to which she reacted, but was stopped by the closest circle of political dignitaries. Dara Janeković, a journalist very close to Tito and Jovanka Broz, confirmed this interpretation in an interview I conducted in April 1998. Janeković says Dolanc and Ljubičić prevented Tito from giving her an interview in 1978, despite his previous intention to do so. The case of Jovanka Broz remains a mystery even today, almost 30 years since Tito's death.

21 Latinka Perović writes that Tito commented on this meeting to a Montenegrin politician and his wartime friend Veljko Vlahović in the following words: "The comrades from Serbia came to talk to me. They made me very angry at the beginning. No one has talked to me like that in the past 30 years. But it is good that we have people like them in our Party" (1991:263). Tito was surprised to see the Serbian leaders united in opposition to his recent statements and actions. He decided to accept some of their criticism, but, as Latinka Perović said, he never forgave them for such an independent way of thinking (1991:263). In this and many other conversations, Perović finds the main reason for Tito's decision to eliminate both Croatian and Serbian leaders in 1971 and 1972.

22 The possibility of sending healthy forces from the federation was debated immediately after the Croatian Spring in 1972. In an interview I conducted with him in October 1997, Stipe Šuvar confirmed that it seemed that Tito would send three prominent Croatian leaders from Belgrade back to Zagreb as his "commissars": Mika Špiljak, Marijan Cvetković, and perhaps also General Ivan Gošnjak. All three politicians had at that time been treated as "unitarists" by the Croatian leader Vladimir Bakarić, who did not allow them to take a direct part in Croatian politics, but sent them to federal posts in Belgrade. However, there was no need for their return, since Tito could rely on Bakarić and a clear majority of the CC LC Croatia. It is often forgotten that ultimately neither the Serbian nor the Croatian leaders ousted by Tito in 1971/1972 secured a clear majority in their leaderships. For example, in the five months following the 21st session of the LCY presidency (1 December 1971 to 30 April 1972), only 741 members (out of 214,614) of the LC Croatia were expelled from the Party (which comprises about 0.2 percent of its total membership). A total of 131 people were forced to resign, and another 280 resigned "voluntarily." Among them were 3 members of the LCY presidency and its conference, 9 members of the Croatian Central Committee and its executive committee, 5 members of the LC Croatia Conference, and 37 secretaries of the basic organizations of LC Croatia. Eighty-five people were removed from their state positions (at all levels) and 52 were ousted from managerial offices. Among those expelled from the Party, 4 became CPY members before 1940, and 31 joined the Party during the war. The Partisans totaled 91, of whom 19 joined Tito's troops in 1941. As a consequence of the Croatian Spring, 23 basic organizations (totaling 715 members) were suspended (Official Report 1972).

23 A good illustration of this technique is again to be found in Marković's diary on 21 October 1972. At the meeting of the Serbian leadership in October 1972, Tito interrupted the Serbian leader Mirko Čanadanović when he said he wished to argue against Draža Marković: "You may argue against him, but you would then argue against me as well because I agree with Draža" (1987:392). This was how Tito supported one group against another in all the republican leaderships.

24 Tripalo (1990:117-26 and 163-9), the leading politician of the Croatian Spring, says that groups within the Croatian leadership differed on the importance of occasional incidents that had occurred at public rallies, on what measures should be taken against the anti-Socialist forces, and on what endangered the system more: nationalism or unitarism. They differed on how to approach the opposition, but not on how to structure Yugoslavia. In this sense it really was a conflict between reformists and conservatives within the LCY, but not between confederalists and federalists, or centralists and federalists, as often occurred.

25 An excellent example is Savka Dabčević Kučar's toast to Tito in Zagreb, in September 1971. She said, "I raise this glass to the man whose personality most vividly expresses the glory, unity, and successes of our past, the revolutionary Socialist strength of our present, and the bright prospects of our future; to a great revolutionary, thinker, and statesman; to a real fighter for workers, national and human rights, and freedoms; to the greatest son in the history of Croatia and all our other nations and nationalities; to our dear Comrade Tito and to Comrade Jovanka" (Perović 1991:296-302). This toast was proposed less than three months before Tito decided to remove the Croatian leadership (headed by Savka Dabčević Kučar) for being inactive in the fight against Croatian nationalism.

26 Serbian leaders complained about Croatian avant-gardism. Interestingly, the term *avant-gardism* held a negative connotation, though the Party itself was treated as the vanguard of the working class.

27 An interesting parallel could be drawn between the current interpretations that the Croatian leaders split with Tito's autocracy, and Tito's claim that it was he who split with Stalin, in 1948. Both interpretations are incorrect, but both entered public discourse, producing important myths.

28 A myriad of examples of this could be found in Tripalo's book. He describes Tito's personal participation in writing the conclusions of the Tenth CC Croatia Session in 1970, which subsequently became the turning point in the emergence of the Croatian Spring (1990:112). Stipe Šuvar (in an interview of 11 October 1997) confirms that Tito's role in supporting the Croatian leadership of Savka Dabčević Kučar and Miko Tripalo was crucial and to some extent directed against Vladimir Bakarić.

29 Jure Bilić, in an interview I conducted on 9 January 1998, said, "I would not say that Tito was biased, but I think it is true that he felt better in Croatia than anywhere else in Yugoslavia....I could even say that Tito became 'more' Croat after 1971 than he was before. For example, I remember him telling me that he proposed that Franjo Herljević (Bosnia-Herzegovina) should take up the post of the federal minister of the interior. He told me: 'You know, he is a Croat!' In these words exactly! It was perhaps true that he felt more obliged to protect 'Croatian interests' after 1971 than before." Miko Tripalo in his book (1990) recalls his conversation with Tito in May 1970. Tito criticized the Croatian leaders, but he also said, "I think you understand my position very well. You know that I am from Hrvatsko Zagorje, which is the cradle of Croatia. And, when it becomes needed, I shall give you my support" (1990:117).

30 Support for this conclusion may be found in the growth of the LC Croatia membership to 350,513 in 1982, from 206,985 in 1972. Only when the economic and political crisis in the country emerged in the early 1980s did the Croatian League of Communists (just like the others) start losing its membership. In 1984, for example, the LCC lost 12,050 members, while only 6,653 were admitted. This year, 77.7 percent of the LCC basic organizations did not admit a new member (73.2 percent in 1983) (IP CK SKH, 5/1985 and 6/1985).

31 It is often asked to what extent the ousted Croatian leaders participated in the process of constitution writing before 1974, and whether the constitution was not the result of their pressure. The 1974 Constitution was certainly not written by the Croatian leaders ousted in 1971, but as we have said, their successors did not differ from them when it came to the main issues treated in the constitution. Also, we need not forget that the main directions for the new "constitutional concept" were drawn up in the 1967-72 amendments to the 1963 constitution.

32 Dušan Dragosavac disagrees with this conclusion, saying that Perović's "liberals" acted more on the line formulated by (Serbian 19th century social-democrat) Svetozar Marković, for which reason the Croatian leadership preferred them to the much tougher stand taken by Draža Marković and Petar Stambolić' (interview April 1998). However, Dragosavac admits that both Marković and Stambolić proved to be antinationalists in the late 1980s, opposing Milošević's new nationalism. In an interview for this book, Dragosavac said: "They proved they were not ethnic extremists, although they had been perceived as Serbian nationalists by other leaderships in Yugoslavia." Dragosavac's comment shows how easy it was to become perceived as nationalist, even if one was a member of the highest state leadership. In fact, both in the 1967-74 period and in the late 1980s, "liberals" and "conservatives" both opposed what they saw as Serbian nationalism and Yugoslav unitarism.

33 Although showing much more respect for the liberals Perović and Nikezić than for the Tito loyalists Marković and Stambolić, Dobrica Ćosić still criticizes them for accepting the constitutional amendments of 1967-72 and for not protesting against the methods used in purging Ranković in 1966 (Djukić 1989:225).

34 To eliminate the conservative veterans from important positions, the liberals issued a recommendation that only those having higher education could occupy executive posts in factories, state organs, and similar. This met with strong opposition from the Partisan generation, exemplified by Marković (17 June 1972; 1987:368).

35 Marković opposed the liberals' attempt to control the Serbian Interior Ministry, which was the stronghold of conservative forces in the leadership (15 July 1972, 1987:372).

36 In his diary, Marković explicitly confirms this, saying that "the liberals" had not been at all interested in the constitutional debate. When they could not entirely avoid debating these issues, their contribution was counterproductive for Serbian interests, since they made "too many concessions to the provinces, especially to Kosovo." They were also "indifferent toward the Yugoslav center." But more important, they ruled out ("were not prepared for") any use of "administrative measures" against "the groups of enemies" in any situation.

37 The concept of "Serbian national interests" is not, of course, an objective, fixed, and once-and-for all agreed concept, but-as we can see from this chapter-not much more than a perception of these interests by the relevant political elite. However, nationalist criticism of Serbian leaders for their acceptance of the 1974 Constitution insists on their "betrayal" of Serbian national interests, as if they were fixed categories.

38 The same argument goes for Tito and, indeed, for Milošević two decades later. As Tepavac, the Yugoslav foreign secretary in the late 1960s and early 1970s, argues in some of his controversial foreign policy decisions, Tito "was not a slave of Russian pressure, so much as he was a slave of his own ideological beliefs" (1998:60). As examples, Tepavac lists the diplomatic recognition of Eastern Germany and the breaking up of diplomatic relations with Israel in 1967. As I argue in chapter six, it would be too simplistic to treat Milošević as a "pragmatist," as if he had no ideological beliefs. On the contrary: I argue that it is lack of pragmatism and firm ideological beliefs that have often driven him to conflicts with many others.

39 According to Tripalo (1990), in April 1971 the Serbian and Croatian leaders were close to agreeing on a more confederalist structure for Yugoslavia. This possibility moved Tito and Kardelj to act against both republics.

40 A good illustration of this belief was offered at the 14th session of the Serbian Central Committee by Milojko Drulović, who used an example from the Paris student demonstrations that took place at this time: "The rioting masses, and Communists among them, raised both red flags and French national three-color flags; the masses were singing both *the Marseillaise* and *the Internationale*. I ask you: Why would it be a problem for French Communists, when they demonstrate, to feel at the same time both French and Communist?" (1968:195). In this context, it was argued that it was these Serbian Communists who argued in favor of Kardelj's concept that showed more concern for the national question than those who stood for the (pre-1966) concept of brotherhood and unity and Socialist Yugoslavism.

41 This attitude remained unchanged until 1987, when Milošević introduced a new rhetoric in LC Serbia. Already in 1984 he had said, "For a long time, and for no reason, a complex of unitarism and a sense of guilt over the behavior of the Serbian bourgeoisie in the past have been imposed on Serbian Communists...Serbian Communists have always been in a situation to remove this shame, which does not belong to them, and to acquit themselves when it came to issues of unity and the Yugoslav state, just to avoid being accused of unitarism. We have no reason whatsoever to bow our heads to anyone" (1984/1989:34).

42 To some extent this could be compared with the position of the Czechs in Czechoslovakia and even the Russians in the USSR. However, there is an important difference: while the Czechs and Russians were the majority in their respective states, the Serbs (though the largest ethnic group) made up less than 40 percent of the total population. Further, the Yugoslav system was much more decentralized than the Soviet and Czechoslovak systems at the time. This all decreased the chances of Serbian domination. However, it did not eliminate the wariness of other Yugoslav nations toward the Serbs.

43 As explained in chapter two, Kardelj avoided the term "greater-Serbian," using great-state hegemonism instead, except when explicitly referring to prewar Yugoslavia. However, it was a common understanding that the two terms were synonymous.

44 The reasons for this agreement are explained in chapter four of this book (personal network of survival) and in Županov's notion of the pact between the elite and the masses.

45 A month and a half before ousting the Croatian leaders, Tito took a trip throughout Croatia, and a month before replacing the Serbian leaders he did the same in Serbia. Tito's personal popularity was especially strengthened after the 1968 student demonstrations in Belgrade, when he briefly sided with demonstrators against "bureaucracy." The idea of antibureaucratic revolution, promoted by Slobodan Milošević in 1988, had

its origins in Milošević's attempt to reestablish the direct link between himself and the population against the bureaucracy as Tito used to do.

46 Draža Marković describes the exceptionally favorable perception by the Serbian population of Tito in his diary on 30 October 1969, 14 May 1972 (1987:148, 358). He also writes about the expression of discontent the workers of the Ivo Lola Ribar factory conveyed to Tito when he visited them in 1972. The workers demanded radical measures against bureaucracy and inequalities in society. To restore support from the masses of the population, Tito issued two letters to party organizations and the general public in 1972 and 1973, insisting on more equality and social justice. Although they were reminiscent of Mao Zedong's rhetoric of the time, the letters were very well received by the population.

47 The *Eastern* danger was also stronger than a *Western* danger among members of the elite, as Petar Stambolić's explanation of the reasons for supporting the fall of Ranković reveals (Djukić 1992:212-14, quoted later in this chapter).

48 I should here also mention very positive views on Tito expressed in the West. See more in Pavlowitch (1992).

49 Certainly, one must not neglect that public criticism of Tito was impossible, since the regime, which situated Tito in its center, was in absolute control of the media. It is, however, impossible to explain the *tacit* consent between the population in general and Tito only by coercion.

50 A similar conclusion was drawn by Miko Tripalo (Croatia), who says that the "already hesitant leadership" used the 1968 demonstrations to halt any radical reforms in the economic sphere and in terms of democratization of the country (1990:89).

51 As explained in the Introduction, the terms democracy and democratic should be understood in the context of self-managing, not of liberal democracy. Liberalism, as the removal of the "liberals" in Serbia illustrated, was a proscribed doctrine, almost to the same extent as "nationalism."

52 It should not be forgotten that Tito was already 80 when he decided to replace the Croatian and Serbian leaderships (in 1971 and 1972, respectively). As with Djilas (1954) and Ranković (1966), the large-scale replacements in the early 1970s were another episode in the permanent struggle for the succession. Tito ended this struggle by being granted a possibility (but not an automatic promise) that he could remain the president "without limitation of term" (Article 333 of the 1974 Constitution, finally formulated by Serbian leader Draža Marković), and promoting collective leadership in state and party institutions (in 1972 and 1978).

53 For this, see Doder (1978). The positive image of Serbia was in sharp contrast with the terrorism of émigré Croatian separatists, who organized several hijacks of Yugoslav planes; bombing campaigns at railway stations, on airplanes in flight, and at cinemas; and assassinations of Yugoslav diplomats. Consequently, the Croatian nationalist opposition to the regime was identified with this terrorism. The old images of the Second World War Ustasha atrocities reemerged in the international press. Furthermore, the Croatian nonterrorist (nationalist) opposition refused to join its Serbian and Slovenian counterparts in united action against the regime. This made Belgrade and Ljubljana (Slovenia) the two centers of antiregime activity, with Zagreb falling into silence. In this respect the situation paralleled the one in Czechoslovakia, where the main opponents of the regime came from Prague, not from Bratislava (Innes 1997). One should here notice that the Serbian leaders had good reasons to tolerate and even protect the opposition in Serbia in the face of criticism from Tito and from other republics. This was what they indeed were doing. The same applies to the Slovenian leadership, but

much less to the Croats. Consequently, the division between the regime and opposition in Croatia was sharper than in other parts of Yugoslavia, which would seriously radicalize the Croat opposition by the late 1980s.

54 Not only the Serbian, but most of the other republican elites had the same ambition: to take the central role in a post-Tito Yugoslavia. Since the late 1960s, and especially after 1972, Yugoslav politics were full of struggles for the best possible positions in the post-Tito period.

55 After all that has been quoted in chapter two about Kardelj's views on Yugoslavia as a "transitional community of people," it seems illogical that Stambolić believed he was a Yugoslav. But both Stambolić and Kardelj understood that what was meant by "Yugoslavia" was the new, post-1974 Yugoslavia. They both believed that it was in the interest of the Yugoslavs to live together, and that this interest, not ethnic origins, was the reason for being together. To Ćosić, Kardelj's conclusions meant abandoning Yugoslavism, since in Ćosić's concept (of the pre-1966 Yugoslavia), the Yugoslavia of Kardelj was no longer Yugoslavia. Speaking from different discourses, Ćosić and Stambolić understood Kardelj differently-one as an anti-Yugoslav, the other as a Yugoslav.

56 This relates to Tito's views on Croatia during the Croatian Spring and on Kosovo after the *Blue Book* of the Serbian leadership in 1977 (chapter five). For Croatia, see Marković's diary on 6 March 1971, 15 May 1971, 26 June 1971, and 15 and 19 September 1971; for Kosovo, see Petar Stambolić's interview with Slavoljub Djukić (Djukić 1992:212-14) and Ivan Stambolić's interview with Slobodan Inić (1995).

57 For Kardelj's and Tito's position on the provinces, see Marković's diary on 13 November 1975, 24 January 1976, 12 and 28 February 1977, and 29 May 1977. Petar Stambolić also says that Kardelj was acting out of principle to a greater extent than Tito when it came to the provinces (Djukić 1992:241).

58 Indicatively, Marković writes of Kardelj (not of Tito) as the key figure in Yugoslavia, which only confirms our conclusion that the post-1974 Yugoslavia was based on Kardelj's concept. It also offers an argument for the importance of his personal views in the legislative decision-making and constitution-writing processes. Contrary to this pessimism in Marković's diary, public statements by Yugoslav politicians were extremely optimistic. They kept repeating that nothing would change after Tito.

59 Bilić, in the interview conducted in January 1998. I did not have a chance to check out Bilić's interpretation with Vidoje Žarković. However, Marković indeed became the strongest opponent of the nomination of Slobodan Milošević for the leading Party post in Serbia in 1986. Ivan Stambolić described Marković's reaction to the election of Milošević: "Immediately after Milošević was selected (as the only candidate), Draža told me that history would never forgive me this choice, and that the Serbian people would never pardon me for pushing Milošević through, for Milošević would spoil everything....Frankly speaking, I would feel less guilty today if Milošević had managed to blind Draža as well. It would be easier for me now. But he could not outplay the old fox" (I. Stambolić 1995:148-49).

60 One can ask: Was this solution not against the interests of Serbs outside Serbia, since the principle of nonintervening ruled out their more extensive links with Serbia. But it was always clear to Serbia that the problems of the Croatian Serbs should be resolved in Zagreb, not in Belgrade (Serbia), as Marko Nikezić told the Croatian Serbs on several occasions. This arrangement was made on the understanding that both Croatia and Serbia were Socialist republics and that Croatian Communists would fight Croatian nationalists, protecting the equality of Serbs and Croats in Croatia. Some Serbian leaders, such as Draža Marković, however, felt that the Croatian Communists were not doing

this, but they were also aware that raising this issue would be understood as intervention in Croatian affairs. After talking to a Croatian Serb on 26 October 1974, Marković wrote in his diary: "I am more and more convinced that there is something defective, something bad in this. On behalf of what principles should we promote such relations? Why should I be indifferent about the position of the Serbs in Croatia, Albanians in Macedonia, and so on if-as a Communist and a citizen-I am not indifferent about the Turks in Cyprus and the Irish in Great Britain?" (Marković 1988:58) The principle of nonintervention was violated for the first time when Slovenia supported the Kosovo Albanians in 1989, to be continued with Serbian support for the Croatian Serbs in 1990.

61   Nevertheless, one should acknowledge that some democratic Yugoslavs in emigration proposed the reorganization of Yugoslavia in a very similar form to the one accepted by the 1974 Constitution (see Ivanović, 1996:84-93). Already in 1963, the *Democratic Alternative*, a group of Yugoslav like-minded émigrés mainly from the UK, in their *Stansted Declaration* projected a Union of Yugoslav peoples, each of which would be entitled to form its own state. This was the result of the conclusion, which the Yugoslav democrats in emigration reached "with a heavy heart" (as the leading person of the group, Vane Ivanović, said), that "the Yugoslavs are today a small minority in our country" (1970/1996:95). In this respect, one should take *cum grano salis* the criticisms of Kardelj's concept as being an invention of his personal "Slovenian nationalism" (as stated by Koča Popović in *Nenadović*, 1988).

62   Marković openly admitted that "regardless of all declarations, the real democratization of society is not wanted. The main obstacle to this is those people who have been sitting in the forefront of the state and society and who have identified with them, who have merged together...positioning themselves at the center of all that happens. This is also continued by some new people who do not want a really democratic discussion" (17 January 1971; 1987:253).

63   It was, however, out of the political elite itself that these three opposition groups had been created. In chapter six we examine the transformation of some of the losers of the intraparty conflicts in the late 1960s into prominent leaders of the anti-Kardeljist opposition in the post-Titoist period (Dobrica Ćosić in Serbia and Franjo Tudjman in Croatia being the most obvious examples).

64   The *Pre-Brioni* corresponds to the third and the *Brioni* to the fourth constitutive concept of Yugoslavism, as described in chapter two. The names are derived from the holding of the constitutional debate at Tito's summer resort on the island of Brioni (Istria, Croatia).

65   The use of the terms *nationality* (narodnost), *nations* (narodi), and *national minorities* (nacionalne manjine) is explained in the introduction. An interesting debate developed on the usage of narodnosti and nacionalne manjine between Petar Stambolić and Dušan Dragosavac in July 1983 (letters in possession of the author).

66   Reference (Minutes 1968) is further along in this chapter used for quotes from the authorized Minutes of the 14th LC CCS Session, as published by *Komunist*, Belgrade 1968.

67   It soon proved, however, that the abandonment of the Slavic basis for Yugoslavia necessarily led to the Kosovo Albanians' demands to be treated as equal to other Yugoslav nations, which meant as a "constitutive nation" with the right to form a republic, rather than as a "nationality" without the right to self-determination. Kardelj's refusal of these demands had been seen as an indication of the unwillingness of the Yugoslav leadership to secure political equality for Albanians in Yugoslavia.

68 This is how the term *autonomism* (autonomaštvo) appeared in the Serbian political vocabulary. When it was repeated by Špiro Galović at the Serbian Central Committee session on 6 May 1981, the leaders of Vojvodina accused the Serbian leadership of borrowing labels from Ćosić, by then the most prominent opponent of the regime.

69 Many of Ćosić's conclusions were indeed based on facts. The situation in Kosovo after 1966 is analyzed in detail in chapter five of this book.

70 Ćosić's warnings on the danger of the emergence of Serbian nationalism, as well as the whole tone of his speech, show that at this time (1968) he was more a defender of the *Pre-Brioni* Yugoslavia than a promoter of "greater Serbia" or even the prewar concept of national unity. His criticism was for this reason even more dangerous for the political elite, which could not easily label him a nationalist. A Croat Praxis Professor Predrag Vranicki came to the same conclusion in his review of Ćosić's 1982 book. However, what he saw as the lack of commitment of other Yugoslav nations to Yugoslavia, and his conviction that Kardelj's Yugoslavia abandoned the main principles of the Partisan Struggle, made Ćosić so disillusioned that he moved toward Serbian ethnic nationalism, whose patriarch he gradually became in the late 1970s. Ćosić then became one of the very few Serbs to argue that Yugoslavia was not in Serbian interests. The evolution of Dobrica Ćosić from a Ranković supporter in the 1960s to the main patron of Serbian nationalist ideas in the 1980s is paradigmatic for a great many Serbian intellectuals and indeed for a large section of the Serbian population. See also Pavković (1998).

71 If we wonder how it was possible to dream of Balkan associations in the circumstances as they were in 1968, we should be reminded that Kardelj himself was talking (though cautiously) of a "future cooperation in this region" (see chapter two). Tito, who saw himself as the central figure of Balkan politics in the whole postwar period, could have been only supportive of this possibility. The idea of a Balkan Federation, however, was older than Tito (see the ideas of Svetozar Marković and Dimitrije Tucović, the leading Serbian Socialists of the 19th century), and it continued after him (see, for example, Branko Horvat's proposals for a Balkan Federation as the only possible solution for the Balkan national questions (*Feral Tribune*, 6 April 1998), or similar proposals by the Kosovo Albanian leader, Adem Demaqi).

72 The already difficult problem with Kosovo and the Albanians was only intensified because Albania was another Socialist country, with a separate interpretation of Marxism and a domestically rooted and legitimated leadership. All these elements made it additionally dangerous in ideological terms, since-as Kardelj argued-the real danger for Yugoslav Socialism lay only in an "alternative form of socialism," not in liberal democracy. Albania, being different from Soviet state Socialism, represented an example of such a danger.

73 In the 1990s, Ćosić moved toward proposing a division of Kosovo into Serb and Albanian parts, with the possibility for the Albanian part to join Albania. Ćosić has also championed the unification of (ethnic) Serbs in the Union of Serbian Lands: Serbia, Montenegro, Republic of Srpska (Bosnian Serbs), and-until August 1995-the Republic of Serbian Krajina (Croatian Serbs). For Ćosić's views on both the Albanian and Serbian questions in 1990, see Borisav Jović's diary, 11 September 1990 (1995:191-94).

74 A good example of the controversies between Serbian, Croatian, and Slovene intellectuals may be found in a conversation between Antonije Isaković and Miroslav Krleža in the early 1970s. According to Isaković (my interview), Krleža claimed that "Yugoslavia did not exist any longer" and that cooperation between writers could not change this fact, since "it was all too late already." For debate between Pirjevec and Ćosić, see Milojković-Djurić (1996).

75 Muhamedin Kullashi (himself an advocate of the "Albanian point of view" in Kosovo historiography) now admits that textbooks used to teach history in Kosovo were "to some extent nationalistic." But, he said, quite accurately, that this was a "phenomenon common to all historiographies in Yugoslavia" (Kullashi 1997:58).

76 An interesting analysis of the master-servant relationship in Kosovo is presented by Kofos (1998).

77 Serbian migration from Kosovo became the central issue of Serbian politics in the mid-1980s and significantly influenced the rise of Milošević and the return of Ćosić to Serbian politics. We shall return to this question in chapter six of this book. The Albanian discourse will be explained in chapter five.

78 This is how one might explain his enormous influence on the Kosovo Serbs in the 1980s. Ćosić was the key figure in linking them with the Serbian elite (see Hudelist 1989).

79 This refers to the Prague Spring of 1968, which reached its peak in the days of the 14th CC LCS Session. Marković here talks about the federalization of Czechoslovakia, for which Dubček (1993) is a good source.

80 Minić did not make many friends among Serbian politicians with this speech. Draža Marković (2 June 1968; 1987:68) considered Minić to be ready to make too many concessions to provinces. After Minić's speech at the 14th Session, the gap between him (on the one side) and Marković and Petar Stambolić (on the other) became ever wider. The conflict between them culminated in June 1982 (see chapter five for "the case of Draža Marković"). Marginalized after 1982, Minić became the first of Tito's confidants to sense the change in policy of the Serbian leadership after Tito's death. The conflict between Minić and Marković is only one of the many intraelite conflicts in Serbia, which confirms that ethnic elements did not play a primary role in the politics of the Kardelj Yugoslavia.

81 On the importance of this change, see Simić (1998:201).

82 Serbian politicians at that time opposed this change (for reasons, see Marković, 20 October 1968; 1987:92). A compromise solution was reached on 4 November 1968 (see Marković, 6 October 1968; 1987:98). However, already in May 1968, Minić concluded that the word "Socialist" should be accepted to distinguish Socialist provinces from "the classical political autonomies of bourgeois-parliamentarian and some other political systems, where autonomies exist....without being democratic in the Socialist sense" (1968:272).

83 The issue of national symbols in Kosovo was very controversial. Minić believed that the free use of the flags of the nationalities (Albanians, Turks, among others) in Kosovo was a civil right, and that the flags would not in themselves create problems (1968:272). The debate continued long after 1974, reaching its peak in the 1980s. (See correspondence between Dragosavac and Stambolić, July 1984).

84 Emphasizing that he was the former military prosecutor in the trial of Draža Mihailović, Minić said, "All slaughters were terrible, because they were (the result) of a bestial madness, but the most terrible one to me was when five thousand Bosnian Muslims were slaughtered on a bridge in Foča...Entire Muslim villages were exterminated by Serbian Chetniks. [Thus] I would prefer very much if Joca [Marjanović] had taken any of the many cases of the Serbian Chetniks' slaughter, leaving the comrades in Croatia to talk about the slaughter committed by the Ustashas" (1968:275). This attitude of Minić's represents the main line of Communist policy on the national question-that it was the duty of Communists in all Yugoslav nations to attack nationalism in their own

nation. The Yugoslav Communists did not accept the "Brezhnev doctrine" of "fraternal help" in internal Yugoslav relations.

85   Radosavljević was the CC LCS president from July 1966 to March 1968. Latinka Perović describes him in these words: "I profoundly agreed with him on two issues-on his understanding of the development of Socialist democracy, and on his genuinely internationalist policy on the national question....He was the only person I sincerely missed once circumstances detached me from the people I had worked with" (1991:51).

86   Petar Stambolić, the wartime Party leader of Serbia, was a "caretaker" in the post of the president of the CC LCS from March to November 1968.

87   At the time of the 14th Session of the CC LCS, Nikezić was the Yugoslav foreign secretary. Very popular as Tito's mouthpiece in the period of the Czechoslovak crisis, Nikezić was elected president of the CC LCS in November 1968. This move was also an attempt to normalize relations with the Soviets after their intervention in Czechoslovakia. He remained in this post until October 1972, when he was removed after Tito's attack on liberalism in Serbia.

88   Milka Planinc offers a good illustration of this belief. In an interview I conducted in April 1998, she said, "We were all, including myself, Yugoslavs, and we did not have, even in our most private thoughts, the idea that Yugoslavia could disintegrate. I remember how shocked I was when it was reported that Vladimir Bakarić, a very experienced politician, said somewhere in Belgium in the mid-1960s that what we were doing was restructuring Yugoslavia, but that only the future would show how long it would last as a common state. To me, this statement came as a big surprise. I asked myself: 'How could he say this? Does he really think that there could be something else but Yugoslavia?' We all believed that, in principle, the national question had been resolved and that the misunderstandings we occasionally had would decrease as economic development progressed." Other members of the leadership, regardless of their ethnic or republican origins, shared the same belief. For example, Dušan Dragosavac (the leading Serb politician in the Croatian Communist leadership) believed the same, as he told me in April 1998.

89   Serbian and Yugoslav politicians often quoted this from Lenin: "There is nothing that halts the development and growth of proletarian class solidarity more than injustice on the national front, and there is nothing that members of a small nation feel more sensitive and hurt about than a sense of inequality and the violation of equality, even if in negligence, even in the form of a joke, when it comes from their comrade proletarians. This is why, in this particular case, it is better to be too generous, rather than not flexible at all. This is why in this case the basic interest of proletarian solidarity, and thus the interest of the proletarian class struggle, demands that we abandon a formal (bureaucratic) approach to the national question." This paragraph is from the 14th Session, quoted by Dobrivoje Radosavljević (Minutes 1968:242). It was also used by Dušan Dragosavac at the presidency of the CC LCY Session in July 1984, when he argued in favor of the wide use of the flags of nationalities in Kosovo.

90   Nikezić said that Ćosić and Marjanović did not count on political alliances because their speeches did not intend to open a dialogue with others, but to reintroduce a system of monologues. "This speech is a monologue, sometimes even an insulting monologue. But the time of monologues is expiring everywhere, and in our country it has already ended. The monologue is always an expression of a political monopoly, which we have left behind us by now" (Minutes 1968:220).

91   The time of the 14th Session was characterised by extensive Yugoslav worries (both of the leaders and the population) that the USSR might intervene in Czechoslovakia, and

subsequently in Yugoslavia, because Yugoslavia not only supported Dubček's reforms, but it also promoted a much more liberalized version of Socialism than was the Czech program. The fear of Soviet intervention had permanently preoccupied Yugoslav public opinion, but it reached its peak in 1968 (Tripalo 1990). This may be illustrated by the discussion at the emergency session of the Yugoslav political and military leadership on 2 September 1968, seven days after the intervention of the Warsaw Pact units in Czechoslovakia. According to Miko Tripalo (a Croat participant), the army leadership admitted that Yugoslavia would be able to resist a USSR attack for not more than three days. An additional problem was that the core of the Yugoslav army was stationed on its Western borders, not its Eastern borders. Koča Popović (the vice president of Yugoslavia, Serbia) then attacked the defense secretary, Ivan Gošnjak (Croat), and indeed (as Tepavac witnesses in 1998:127), even Tito himself for the ideological dogmatism that created the grounds for such a decision. The situation was so tense that the Croat leader Bakarić said he would not sleep at home, since the army commanders in charge of Zagreb were pro-Soviet. He accused the army (led by another Croat-General Gošnjak) of being responsible for the situation in which Soviet troops would reach Rijeka (the Adriatic port) in two days. Tepavac argues that at this moment, only 1,000 soldiers protected the territories between the Yugoslav border with Hungary and the Vojvodina capital Novi Sad (1998:127). On 5 September 1968, the British newspapers *Daily Telegraph* reported on the preparations of the Yugoslavs for Partisan war against the Soviets. The concept of "people's self-defense" was developed as the consequence of this debate. The situation was only worsened when the Romanian leader Ceausescu three days after the invasion (24 August 1968) sought formal permission for his army to retreat to Yugoslavia if attacked. Tito agreed, on condition that they left all weapons on the borders (Tripalo 1990:104).

92 This belief would be only strengthened in the next six years, before the final acceptance of the constitution. In the early 1970s, an economic crisis hit the West, and in 1974 the Watergate affair underlined the "moral corruption" of Western democracies, and so on. Consequently, too many (left-wing) intellectuals in West (and in the East) Yugoslavia looked like an "oasis of stability and progress in Europe."

93 This conclusion is in agreement with Kardelj's views. As explained in chapter two, Kardelj was convinced that the only real and long-term danger came from an alternative type of Socialism, i.e., from "Stalinism" (state Socialism) and to some extent from the type of Socialism advocated by the Praxis philosophers. The basis for such thinking is a linear understanding of history, as explained in chapter one of this book.

94 This is a very carefully worded allusion to the expulsion of Yugoslavia from the Cominform in 1948. Interestingly, Nikezić had chosen the passive form ("we were moved from there"), rather than repeating Tito's interpretation that Yugoslavia broke with Stalin.

95 The argument based on participation of ethnic groups in Socialist revolution was often used in relation to their status. One of the main arguments against the status of a Republic of Kosovo in 1945 was the poor participation of Kosovo Albanians in the Partisans (Horvat 1998; Vickers 1998). On the other side, Stambolić used what he claimed to be a high participation of Muslims (Bosniaks, as they now prefer to be called) in the Partisans as an argument in favor of changing their status in the new structure of Yugoslavia. However strange this argument seems today, it was logical for those who believed that the Communist revolution was the beginning of the "real history" of the Yugoslav nations. It was also based on the notion that its Socialist character bound Yugoslavia much more than the ethnic similarity of its "constitutive nations" (see chapter two).

96 The Serbian Communists took this line even during Milošević's first years in office, but now they violated the rule of nonintervention that Minić insisted on when objecting to Marjanović's "Ustasha example." Milošević and his aides denied neither the existence of Serbian nationalism nor the necessity to oppose it, but they now claimed that only Serbian Communists were fighting their nationalism, while all other Communists (and especially Kosovo Albanians, Croats, and Slovenes) made a tacit or even open coalition with the most prominent nationalists in their nations. They also argued that Serbian nationalism was only a reaction to other, at this particular moment, more dangerous nationalisms (see my interview with Radoš Smiljković in 1989). Milošević's statement at the end of the Eighth CC LCS Session (September 1987) illustrates this: "We have often failed to react in an appropriate manner to other forms of ideological and political pressure on Socialist self-management, pressure created by bourgeois and statist ideas that were put forward by their protagonists. But we have always considered our nationalists as first-class enemies. And it was not without reason. Serbian nationalism today is not only intolerance and hatred of another nation or other nations: it is a real snake in the bosom of a Serbian nation" (Milošević 1987/1989:171-72).

97 It is obvious that Stambolić here deliberately avoided the word "minority," although this word seems to be more appropriate for what he wanted to say. However, at the time of this speech, it was already politically correct to use "nationality" instead of "national minority." Later Stambolić revised his position. In his letter to Dragosavac of 20 June 1983, he used the word "minority," explaining that this word fit into "how the world talks about it." (See Stambolić to Dragosavac, 20 June 1983, and Dragosavac to Stambolić, 27 June 1983; copies are in my possession.)

98 Marko Nikezić concluded similarly to Stambolić: "At no time and in no place was the mistake of granting more rights and wider possibilities for the development of smaller nations and nationalities (than necessary) committed. History never records that such a 'mistake' has been committed toward the nationalities and national minorities" (1968:143). Dragoslav Marković was, however, of a different opinion when he spoke (13 years later) at the CC LC Serbia Session immediately after the Kosovo demonstrations (6 May 1981). Marković then said that the policy that the provinces should be given more rights than the constitution instructed resulted in reducing the rights of Serbia. Therefore, he advised, "everything is anticonstitutional, which is not in accordance with the constitution, whether more or less than the rights secured by the constitution" (1981:103).

99 This scepticism Nikezić obviously shared with Kardelj. As Tepavac witnessed, Tito's views on the future of Yugoslavia were also pessimistic. In November 1971 he told his political aides in an informal conversation on the train between Bucharest and Belgrade: "If you only knew how I see the future of Yugoslavia, you would be shocked!" (1998:153).

100 Ćosić says that the Serbian leaders were nothing but "Tito's obedient servants" (1982/1992:58). In an interview I conducted in April 1996, Antonije Isaković (a longstanding political and personal friend of Ćosić's) described the Serbian leaderships before Milošević as "opportunists of the worst kind" and "traitors to their own country." These statements are still representative of the dominant discourse among Serbian nationalist intellectuals.

101 This is how Ćosić describes Tito on the day of his death, 4 May 1980. Excerpts from Ćosić's diary (published in 1992) illustrate Ćosić's obsession with Tito and his alleged "anti-Serbianism." Although he admits reediting his scripts to eliminate the most radical expressions, he still authorized this one. Ćosić's anti-Titoism is the key to understand-

ing why he (and many other Serbian nationalists) supported Milošević. They saw him as "the most successful destroyer of Tito's order, the fittest person to achieve Serbia's abandonment of a half-century-long subordination to the anti-Serb coalition, a Communist who reestablished a Serbian state that was annulled by the Serbian Communists, a politician who aroused the historical consciousness of millions of Serbs and who reestablished Serbia as a political factor" (Ćosić 1991/1992:168). Ironically, Milošević originally tended to promote himself as the new Tito who would unite Yugoslavia (more in chapter six).

102 A similar explanation is offered by Croatian nationalist Franjo Tudjman, the president of Croatia, when he says that the Croats lived in the dark ages of Communism, without being aware of their national interests, all the way through to the establishment of his party-the Croatian Democratic Community in 1989. Ćosić and Tudjman, as well as Kardelj, are all visionaries; all three had a mission of bringing light to the dark age that preceded their existence. To all of them, the real history of their nation began with them; everything else should be burned and forgotten. "The future revolution in this country, over which Communists, Stalinists, and Titoists ruled, ought to begin with the burning of their papers! The burning of all books, all texts and newspapers written by Communists under their governance....Our literacy must go back to the evangelism of Miroslav," says Dobrica Ćosić (1982/1992:70). More on Ćosić's position in the 1980s in chapter six.

CHAPTER FOUR

The Economic Crisis: The (Lack of) Response of the Yugoslav Political Elite to Economic Crisis in the Early 1980s

> The Party presidency was a big problem to me, but at the same time I knew I would not be able to operate without their support...To secure their support, I had to convince them that the market was not against self-management. I argued that the market was a limitation of state, the same as self-management, and that therefore they could go together, since they are both opposed to statism. The debate on this was going on and on for all four years of my term in office.
>
> **Milka Planinc, Yugoslav prime minister (1982-86)**

4.0. Introduction

The acceptance of Kardelj's concept by the Serbian leaders in the 1967-74 constitutional debate, I argued in the previous chapter, was the result of their commitment to Marxist ideology and of their perception of Serbian interests. In this chapter, I follow the response of the Yugoslav political elite to economic crisis in the late 1970s and in the 1980s, arguing that the same two reasons-commitment to ideology and the perception of the interests of various segments of society-motivated their actions. Communist societies, as I argued in chapters one and two, favored a vision of the future rather than the imperatives of reality. Yet their vision of the future was based on their perception of the interests of those they were "entitled to lead." As Kardelj argued, it was not for reasons of ethnic similarity, but because of common interests in developing a self-managing community of nations that the Yugoslav nations decided to remain in Yugoslavia. The interests of the Yugoslav nations were not opposed to Marxist ideology: on the contrary, they could be best served only by following it.

The economic crisis, which began in the late 1970s, represented a serious challenge to the link between ideology and interests. Two groups emerged within the leadership: one (primarily in the federal government) argued in favor of a more pragmatic and less ideological approach, and the other (mostly linked to Party leadership) remained often dogmatically committed to the ideology, even when the economic and political situation was causing concern among experts and foreign observers. In this conflict, the "ideologues" in the Party prevailed over the "pragmatists" in the government. Although they made a significant effort to accommodate the ideology to the circumstances in which they operated, in any serious clash between ideology and reality the Communist leaders ultimately favored the vision of the future rather than the imperatives of reality. The Party as the *representative of the future* was therefore predestined to win over the government, an institution of the state that would *wither away*. Although the elites were genuinely concerned with the economic crisis in Yugoslavia, their confidence in the ideological vision of the world, which they were attempting to construct, blinded them to the economic and political reality and to the consequences of their actions in reality.

4.1. "Boalization": Associated or Disintegrated Labor?

The Yugoslav economic system was reconstructed following the main ideas of Kardelj's concept. Among the aims of the reform, normatively prescribed in the 1976 Associated Labor Act (ALA), were (1) to enable workers even in large enterprises to take direct part in decision making; (2) to enable workers to control not only the factories, but also the whole "social reproduction"; and (3) to further decentralize the state by reducing its control over the economy and transferring many of its functions to "workers' councils" and other alternative institutions. The ALA (consisting of 671 articles) was to replace the state constitution once circumstances allowed it. It was therefore to even greater extent than the constitution itself an ideological document. Its main ideas were in line with the idea of transforming society into an "association of free producers." *Associated labor* was imagined to be an integrative factor in the complex Yugoslav multiethnic society. It was also an alternative to Soviet *state Socialism*, characterized by a larger role of the state in the economic sphere.[1]

To enable workers to control the factories, the complex system of Yugoslav economy was divided into small functional units, the *Basic Organizations of Associated Labor* (BOALs, or in Serbian/Croatian, OOUR). Although the BOALs could remain autonomous units (self-organized enterprises), they were usually too small to remain independent. Therefore, at least in theory, several BOALs "associated" in one *Work Organization*. A typical Work Organization (RO) had three to four BOALs and one *Work Community* (RZ, administrative unit). The final forms of *associating* were the Complex Organizations of Associated Labor (COAL, SOUR), which sometimes had even more than 100 BOALs.

However, in practice the organizational reform meant that the existing large enterprises were divided into smaller units. Four years after the declaration of the ALA, 94,415 BOALs were created in Yugoslavia.[2] In large enterprises, for example the [Yugoslav] Post and Telecommunications (PTT), there were no less than 291 BOALs, 2 Work Organizations without BOALs, 26 Work Organizations with BOALs, 4 Work Communities or BOALs, and 22 other Work Communities.[3] Even Air Traffic was organized in not less than 52 different units, 21 of which were BOALs.

Outside observers did not take long to realize, however, that instead of the development of *associated labor*, the Yugoslav economy was disintegrating and fragmenting. True, many more workers now became members of governing bodies in their own BOALs and COALs. But instead of running the factories and the whole process of social reproduction, they participated in decision making only in their small units, not at any higher level. And the BOALs themselves were powerless to change the conditions of production. Even if the workers formed a majority in these bodies, they often felt powerless and not competent to face the large amount of legal and economic decisions they were asked to take. They therefore leaned heavily on the technomanagers and administration. Instead of the "debureaucratization of society," a sea of new regulations was issued to support and explain new structures.[4]

The new system was based on the ideological notion that the working class was pluralist within itself, but that its historical role remained an integrative factor for the various separate interests that could emerge within it. "Social agreements" (*društveno dogovaranje*) between BOALs were promoted as the main instrument of potential conflict resolution. But instead of uniting to promote "working class interests," the BOALs started to fight with one another to protect the small interests of their workers against those working in another BOAL of the same company. In some factories the situation became so paradoxical that physical barriers were raised to separate workers in two BOALs.[5] A complex system of consensus (unanimity decision-making requirement) made possible a situation where half of the workers in one BOAL practically vetoed thousands of other workers in their BOALs if they voted against the majority decision.[6] Since BOALs were the basic units of decision making in industry, the invention of Kardelj and Tito and also a symbol of working class power in Socialist Yugoslavia, it was extremely difficult to overrule their decisions. This was especially difficult at the state level, since in the ideological concept promoted by Kardelj, the state must follow, not obstruct, the interests of the working class. In the end, the state would wither away at the end of the process. The workers' self-management was therefore institutionally protected to a level that the state was not. Statism was seen as the main obstacle to its further development (Kraigher 1985:76).[7]

The whole idea, however, showed itself to be inefficient, expensive, and disintegrative very soon after the first steps to implement it were taken. The Yugoslav system resulted in the creation of an autarkic and divided working class. It was not so much that the *Yugoslav* working class was now divided into *working classes of republics*[8] (this was already explained by Kardelj's notion of *completed nations* and Bakarić's of *national working classes*), but that not even within the republics could the process of disintegration be terminated.

Still, the republics were in a position to do much more about the reintegration of their economic systems than the federation. In the end, they controlled their own plans and therefore had the final say on issues of investment. The leaders of the republics and provinces had an additional motive to do so: fearing the *social pact* between Tito and the *working class,* they were interested in satisfying the needs of *their* workers in order to legitimize their own power.

Paradoxically, to prevent a total disintegration of the system and to preserve political power that was formally increasing, but practically decreasing, in the last years of Tito's life, the republics aimed at centralization within themselves while decentralizing Yugoslavia as a federal state. This trend again found its support in the new understanding of the nationality question in Yugoslavia, which was expressed in the 1974 Constitution by which the republics became *sovereign states* of their *completed nations*.

The Yugoslav republics, being recognized as sovereign states, significantly reduced their mutual trade. While in 1970, a total of 59.6 percent of goods and services were traded within the republics in which they were produced; in 1980 this rose to 69 percent. Only 21.7 percent of goods and services were exchanged between Yugoslav republics, and 9.3 percent went to foreign export. Not infrequently, one republic would import goods while another republic would be exporting the same kind of goods. Thus one republic would be paying more for imported goods that were already available on their domestic market (Korošić 1988:72). This, for example, happened with electricity: four regions with electric power production resources (Bosnia-Herzegovina, Slovenia, Serbia proper, and Kosovo) exported it, while another four (Montenegro, Croatia, Macedonia, and Vojvodina) were importing it from neighboring countries. Consequently, the price of electricity varied in 1983 from 89 percent of the Yugoslav average in Bosnia-Herzegovina to 121.4 percent in Kosovo.[9] The same happened for similar reasons with other prices, which varied from 20 to 30 percent across the regions. Living standards, already several times lower in the underdeveloped regions of Yugoslavia, now also differed from region to region. Average salaries in Slovenia in

1986 were about 40 percent higher than the Yugoslav average, and in Macedonia they were 30.6 percent lower. The ratio was 1:2. The rents of state-owned apartments in Bosnia-Herzegovina, for example, in 1985 were 39.5 percent lower, but in Slovenia they were 76.8 percent higher than in Croatia.[10] Little was left of the Communist promise to reduce the differences between the poor and the rich regions of Socialist Yugoslavia. On the contrary, the differences were growing, which is evident from the following chart.

Table 4.1: GDP per capita in Republics and Provinces 1952-89 (Index 100 = Yugoslavia's average)

	1952	1962	1972	1982	1989	1989:1952
Slovenia	182	189	194	193	196	+ 14
Croatia	121	121	126	125	126	+ 5
Serbia (total)	93	92	90	91	92	- 1
Vojvodina	90	107	112	119	119	+ 29
Montenegro	88	70	74	76	74	- 14
Bosnia-Herzegovina	86	71	67	68	68	- 18
Macedonia	71	61	69	67	65	- 6
Kosovo	47	34	32	28	26	- 19

(Source: Vojnić 1994:263)

As demonstrated in this table, both the biggest winners and the biggest losers of Yugoslav economic development were situated in Serbia, in its provinces. Although Vojvodina was the only region of Yugoslavia that had successfully transformed itself from an "underdeveloped area" (below the Yugoslav average) to a "developed" one, the other Serbian province, Kosovo, even further decreased its economic level when compared with the other republics and Vojvodina. In 1952 the ratio in GDP level between Kosovo and Slovenia was 1: 3.9, and 30 years later, despite large investments in Kosovo, the ratio had doubled to 1:7.9. Although Croatia and Slovenia (and especially Vojvodina) raised their level of development, all the others (and especially Montenegro, Bosnia-Herzegovina, and Kosovo) saw no relative improvement for themselves in Yugoslavia.

The growing gap between the developed and underdeveloped regions in Yugoslavia created a problem for an ideology that claimed there was no real equality between nations without economic equality. Not only did this process reopen the issue of economic exploitation, it in fact also presented the case described in Kardelj's warnings about the potential problems for national equality in Yugoslavia. The events were, however, following a different path from what Kardelj defined as necessary in the *transitional period*. The inability of the Yugoslav Communists to reverse these trends produced a growing sense of inequality and economic exploitation in Yugoslavia. It further promoted a policy of protectionism within the more-developed republics, particularly Slovenia. Although no laws banned employees of other regions of Yugoslavia from moving and finding a job in Slovenia or Croatia, they somehow increasingly felt unwanted in the more-developed regions. The "Bosnians" (*Bosanci*, a term used in the Slovenian colloquial vocabulary for "Southerners," Serbian/Croatian speaking manual workers in Slovenia) felt this in Slovenia, although the Kosovo Albanians had the same experience anywhere in Yugoslavia.[11] In a situation of economic crisis and with the increasing tendency to "autarky," the Southerners became "foreigners." Gradually, the general public began to recognize them as culturally, religiously, politically, and ethnically *different*. The economic differences thus increasingly became social and political. The sense of exploitation and of undesirability was growing. Sticking with one's own republic, and in some cases (when, as in Kosovo and the underdeveloped regions of Croatia, Macedonia, and Bosnia-Herzegovina, they were inhabited by a minority ethnic group) with one's own people, was a viable alternative. It was now more and more true that the antinationalist rhetoric of the regime was in sharp contrast with the results of the system built on the same ideology. As in other areas of life, ideological rhetoric and reality were growing apart from one another.

In the last years of Tito's life, the already low social mobility across the borders of the republics decreased still more. In 1976 only 2.1 percent of Work Organizations had one or more BOALs in a republic other than where its seat was. But even such a small number fell to 1.6 percent in 1981 (Korošić 1988:76). However, each republic had its own aluminum factory, dozens of tobacco factories, an electroindustry, and car factories, even when they had no basic conditions to make them productive. Many of these were actually "political factories," a pure expression of the political fears of being dependent on others in Yugoslavia. Yugoslav industry, paradoxically, found it sometimes easier to cooperate with non-Yugoslavs than with partners in other republics. It seemed that fears of being dependent on others in Yugoslavia led Yugoslav republics to increase their dependency on international banks. This trend was also supported by the government's encouragement of exporters: they were now additionally looking for partners abroad, rather than within the country. But the protectionist measures in Western Europe, as well as the low quality and high prices of the Yugoslav products, made this attempt fail. Many young unemployed people also found it easier and more promising to move to West European countries than to try to find jobs elsewhere in Yugoslavia.[12] This was also because a student, for example, in Zagreb had more chances to learn English or German than Slovenian, Albanian, or Macedonian language, and to obtain a British scholarship than to be supported by the Yugoslav federal government for studying in Skopje (perhaps also because there was no federal ministry of education: education was a matter for the republics and provinces).[13] Not even federal officials (army officers, customs officers, federal politicians, and bureaucrats) spoke more than their own native language, unless it was not Serbian/Croatian.[14] Both the underdeveloped and the most developed now asked: What was then left of the equality of nations in practical terms? Was it all just a fiction, an unfulfilled promise? The economic crisis now provided a context in which the wider issues of the political system reemerged in the 1980s.

4.2. Debating the Causes of the Crisis

The main question, however, is what prevented the Yugoslav leaders from obtaining a consensus on an effective program of economic rescue, and at the same time ensuring that everyone would adhere to such a program? The main reason, again, is to be found in their commitment to Kardelj's concept. Not only did the ideological commitment provide a pre-text from which reality was *read* in a specific way, but the elite also believed that economic problems were only the result of incomplete or inadequate implementation of Kardelj's concept in reality, not of the concept itself. They criticized *autarky* and *disintegration*, but it never occurred to them that both the *autarky* and *disintegration* were to a large degree outcomes of the *self-managing* and *antistatist* ideas and practices promoted by the dominant ideology itself.

Analyzing reality from an ideological platform, they find it difficult even to recognize that the Yugoslav economy was facing great difficulties. The first to identify the problem were economists, not politicians. In the mid-1970s, they warned the Yugoslav politicians that three problems had appeared in full strength: (1) the low efficiency of Yugoslav industry; (2) a high rate of inflation; and (3) high foreign debts (Korošić 1988:55). When analyzing how to respond to these three problems, Yugoslav economists found that a response was rather difficult in the circumstances of economic fragmentation that had emerged since 1967.

Yugoslav economic experts offered two explanations for the causes of the crisis: one insisted on objective causes and the other subjective ones.

Among the objective causes, the global economic problems of the 1970s were mentioned most frequently. From 1973 (with the global oil crises)[15] to 1981, Yugoslavia borrowed in foreign banks and institutions about US$16.5 billion. Its foreign debt thus increased to US$21,096 billion, from US$4,663 billion. When its loans to other countries were deducted from this sum, US$19,511 billion of net to debt still remained in 1981. Another unfortunate circumstance was that many short-term loans (amounting to more than US$11 billion) were taken up in the 1977-80 period, when interest rates (for the loans taken out in the United States) rose to 16.8 percent, from 5.5 percent. These short-term (five-year) loans were due to be repaid in the 1982-85 period. The international oil crises and the increasing interest rates in the United States, as well as the prices of technology coming from the West European countries, proved to have disastrous effects for a country that was rich neither in oil nor in technology. These external causes of the crises left Yugoslavia almost with no choice but to take more new loans to "preserve some level of production and income to satisfy basic needs and to return loans," as Yugoslav Prime Minister Veselin Djuranović concluded in his 1985 analysis of the causes of economic crisis (1985:207).

Among the subjective causes of the problem, however, the decentralization of power and the disintegration of the Yugoslav market were listed as two of the most important. Yugoslav economists argued that these processes were the result of the "subjective" decision of the Yugoslav political elite, which was based on ideological and not economic reasons. Until 1961 only the federal government had been authorized to decide on foreign loans. After 1961, however, the "right to receive loans" was given first to specialized banks and after 1967 also to work organizations. By 1975 the federal institutions had lost control over the amount and structure of foreign loans taken out by various economic subjects. After 1971, the republics had full control over their economic plans, and they planned unrealistically. The notion of national economies, promoted firmly by the Croatian leader Vladimir Bakarić, was frequently quoted as an ideological justification for this. In practical terms, the decentralization of the country, following the 1974 Constitution, was an important contributing factor to the Yugoslav economic disintegration. The Yugoslav economists pointed out that the federal government warned the republics in 1975 to be cautious about foreign debts, but in vain (Kraigher 1985:201). Kardelj even mentioned "the Chilean scenario" as a possible dangerous outcome of the situation in which "no other solution would be possible as a result of high inflation, low living standards, and the anarchic situation in the country" except for the reintroduction of "firm-hand" governance.[16] But the interests of the republics and provinces in continuing their autonomous roads were so strong that in the social plan for 1976-80 they sanctioned only each other's overambitious investments. Tito was still there, but he was rather hesitant to stop what looked like a great prospect for a new boom of the Yugoslav economy. Although evidently worried about the political situation in the country and especially in the Party as he neared the end of his life, the aging leader proudly announced great economic successes of the Yugoslav economy in his last address to the LCY Congress in 1978.[17] The biggest problem, however, was again in the irreconcilable controversy between the ideological background and demands for recentralization. How could the fragmentation of the Yugoslav economic system be stopped without recentralization? Kardelj and his successors found it simply impossible to answer this question. But no political elite of a republic or a province wanted recentralization, which would reverse the achieved level of autonomy both of *constitutive nations* in their *republics*, and of the *self-managers* in their BOALs. Yet without such a recentralization, how could the negative trends of *autarky* and *anarchy* be stopped?

During all these years, the economic situation in the country was becoming worse. In 1965, a total of 73.8 percent of Yugoslav imports were covered by exports, but in 1979 this share dropped to only 55.9 percent (Djuranović 1985:214). The country's dependency on the import of electrical power increased to 42 percent in 1979, from 30 percent in 1970 (Djuranović, 1985:215). And at that time, people were spending in money terms eight percent more than they produced. Public investments were growing fast. From 1974 to 1978, the annual investment rate grew by 12.7 percent each year. The share of investments in the total social product rose to 40 percent in 1978, from 29 percent in 1974. The wave of investments spread throughout the country. Since decisions were taken by the political leadership, or "in close links between the inner circles of the political elite and commercial banks" (Djuranović 1985:220), even insolvent enterprises started investing. "Investomania" characterized the Yugoslav economy during the last years of Tito's life. The reason for this could also be found in ideology. Yugoslav society, after finally finding the *golden key* of social development, had to prove its successes also in economic terms. Moreover, the new leaders of the republics now wanted to demonstrate that the federal centralism they were finally being freed from really was the main obstacle to the rapid development of their own republics and provinces, and that the ousted pre-1972 leaders were not only politically, but also in economic terms, inferior to them.[18] For various reasons (such as the wish to modernize the economy, to show the advantages of decentralization, to reach the level of the more-developed regions, and to demonstrate that Yugoslav Socialism was economically successful, among other things), a new wave of investments was launched in the late 1970s. The "autarkic tendencies," enhanced by the 1974 Constitutional arrangements, now significantly contributed to an intensive and (from an economic point of view) an irrational increase of foreign debt in the second half of the 1970s as well as to high inflation in Yugoslavia during the 1980s (Kraigher 1983/1985:201-03). In 1978 there were 40,000 new projects in which investments were made.[19] Decisions on them were often informal, taken by the political leadership at various levels and not by the self-managing organs in BOALs or COALs. But everyone was happy to see libraries, factories, television centers, hotels, and roads built, not asking where the money came from. The Party Congress in 1978 therefore concluded in a very optimistic tone, rejecting any notion of crisis. This was Tito's last congress, and though they were aware of the problems,[20] the leaders hesitated to make them public in such a situation.

4.3. Government and Economists vs. Party Leadership and Republican Leaders

The first segment of the political elite that recognized the problem was the one that was directly involved in economic policy-the Yugoslav Government (Federal Executive Council, [FEC]). In a Communist society, the government was no more than an *economic council* and thus had a secondary role to the ideological headquarters, the Party leadership. Being in everyday contact with the economic data and facts of economic life, the Yugoslav prime minister (FEC president), Veselin Djuranović (1977-82, Montenegro), warned in the late 1970s that the external causes of the world oil crises left Yugoslavia with almost no choice but to take loans to "preserve some level of production and of income to satisfy basic needs and to return loans" (Djuranović 1985:207). In a later account of the causes of the economic crisis, Djuranović admitted that many subjective causes, originating from domestic policy, had contributed to it. The Yugoslav economy was "autarkic, inefficient, and inflexible with a long-standing orientation toward the domestic market and not exports, with an ever-growing level of dependency on imports, and with a permanent and significant trade deficit." For all these reasons, Djuranović argued, the Yugoslav economy was simply incapable of resolving the problems that had occurred as a result of the international oil crisis (1985:207).

To reverse these negative trends, the FEC (advised by its economic experts) proposed a much more realistic approach to investment in the 1980-85 plan. However, though speaking with Tito's full support (in 1979), Prime Minister Djuranović was unable to persuade the members of the Yugoslav Assembly to accept his government's measures for strict austerity.[21] The federal government had no choice but to withdraw in front of the "sovereign" republican elite.

The prime minister then proposed the devaluation of the *dinar* to support exports. But Tito, who was particularly sensitive on the issue of the national currency for symbolical reasons, rejected this demand.[22] Djuranović then simply had no alternative but to increase inflation by printing money, which was lacking both for investments and for returning the foreign loans that were already due to be repaid. In the four years from 1977 to 1981, capital was artificially created by printing 350 million dinars, said Ivo Perišin, chairman of the Federal Advisory Board for Economic Development, in June 1981.[23]

The economic crisis, however, could not be hidden from the general public. In the late 1970s, the government introduced reductions in the electrical supply to households. The imports of tropical fruits, coffee, washing powder, and chocolate were reduced, which caused the first queues on the streets of Yugoslavia. In May 1979, Djuranović introduced restrictions on car use and increased gasoline prices in the country.[24] The "ordinary man in the street" in Yugoslavia now for the first time after the short postwar period experienced restrictions on his consumerism. This was a serious political challenge to the regime, which was by then very much based on the consumerist culture. The Yugoslavs, who tended to believe that their living standards, much higher than those of other people living in Communist countries, were the product of their better work and of their unique self-managing system, which managed people's needs better than Soviet "administrative Socialism," wondered what had happened. As a reaction, shopping abroad in the neighboring countries of Austria and Italy increased. In 1979 every second Yugoslav citizen traveled abroad at least once, and in all, they crossed the border 24 million times. About US$2 billion was spent in these "shopping tours" in that year.[25] This became an additional problem for the reputation of the country. While more than one million of its workers already worked in the West, an additional 12 million people buying soap powder and coffee in Austria and Italy did not promote a good image of Yugoslav Socialism.[26] Nevertheless, both measures helped the regime to dissipate potential revolt in the country.

When Tito died in May 1980, Djuranović took a new initiative to alert the leaders. On 6 June 1980, only 32 days after Tito's death, he devalued the Yugoslav dinar by 30 percent.[27] On 2 July 1980, he presented a report to the National Assembly meeting, admitting several serious economic difficulties that threatened to weaken the stability of Yugoslavia. With an openness that-as the Western reporters noticed-went "beyond anything taking place in the other Communist countries,"[28] Djuranović detected the basic causes of these difficulties in "insufficient economic motivation and a highly buoyant domestic market, which has discouraged exports while stimulating imports; [in] unrealistic development ambitions, that could not be satisfied by raising indebtedness abroad; and [in] inconsistent and inadequate application of some systematic solutions in this sphere." He announced "radical measures" to accompany the devaluation of the dinar.

Djuranović did not, of course, touch on Tito's personal responsibility for the economic difficulties. But in his next public speech in November 1980, he made it clear that "there were dilemmas and hesitations earlier, and this was precisely one of the basic causes of the problems that have finally led us into such an unfavorable economic situation."[29] Djuranović's statements and actions were indeed the first sign of a "new policy," which thus appeared surprisingly soon after Tito's death.

The "silent rehabilitation" of Kiro Gligorov,[30] the creator of the 1965 economic reforms, who disappeared from the public scene when his term in office as Federal Assembly President ended in 1978, was another indication of the "new economic policy." In June 1980, Gligorov reappeared as the foremost critic of the subjective causes of the Yugoslav economic difficulties. The existing problems, Gligorov argued, were only partially influenced by the international economic crisis. On the contrary, the crisis originated "from our domestic difficulties and contradictions." In his interview with *Nin* in June 1980, Gligorov said that "in the past, some people claimed we would solve our difficulties in a relatively easy manner, that no great sacrifices were needed, sacrifices that would inflict only harm and demoralize our workers." He argued in favor of radical measures, which would carry out "a revision of all currents of our economic life and do so at all significant points."[31]

Gligorov's criticism was even sharper in November 1980. The present difficulties stem, he said, directly "from suppressing market laws and operating in a subjectivist way in which social and economic goals and plans were formulated not on the basis of our realistic possibilities, but rather on what our Socialist society would like to achieve." The economic problems were, in other words, a consequence of "forgetting realities in Yugoslavia."[32] The main Yugoslav economic experts, such as Croatian Professor Marijan Korošić, supported Gligorov and Djuranović. Already in June 1980, Korošić demanded the introduction of "energetic measures and even shock therapy." These measures should aim to "change economic policy radically."[33]

However, the warnings of Djuranović, Gligorov, and Korošić did not disturb regional leaders. In November 1980 they simply carried on with the 1981-85 Social Plan as if almost nothing had happened. In July 1981 they basically ignored a letter from the state presidency to the Federal Assembly, in which the state leadership insisted that "foreign credits could be taken out only to increase exports and to improve the country's balance of payments."[34] In September 1981 they turned a blind eye to the warning of Dobroslav Ćulafić (Montenegro), a member of the Yugoslav Party presidency, that "the greatest part of the leadership, of the organizations, and of the members of the League of the Communists of Yugoslavia up to the present day were unable to understand or to accept that our country is undergoing great economic difficulties."[35] They acted as they publicly "swore" when Tito died: as if nothing at all would change after his death.

It is in fact striking and not entirely clear how it was possible that the federal leaders used such strong rhetoric of "radical changes" while the republics they represented in the federal leadership acted differently. Even more striking was that the republican leaders (with some exceptions) did not publicly disagree with this rhetoric. What, then, was the invisible obstacle to the implementation of the changes? The federal leaders kept talking about unnamed obstacles, addressing everybody and nobody. They argued against the bureaucracy as if they were not in charge of it. They were critical of autarkic tendencies as if they had no control over the republics they represented in the federation. They complained of "investomania" without doing much to stop it. Who were they in fact directing their complaints against?

In an interview I conducted much later (in 1998) with Milka Planinc, who in June 1982 succeeded Veselin Djuranović as the Yugoslav prime minister, she said:

> The Party was the main obstacle. The members indulged themselves in laments about the ideological and political situation, about the enemies of Socialism, and other things. They always tried to find reasons against fundamental economic reforms because they were skeptical about the market. On the other hand, I was responsible for the economic situation, and I tried to find quick and efficient ways to improve it. The Party presidency was a big problem to me, but at the same time I knew I would be unable to operate without their support. They controlled the votes in the Federal Assembly and in all the republics and provinces. To secure their support, I had to convince them that the market was not against self-management. I argued that the market was a limitation on the state, the same as self-management. And that therefore the market and self-management could go together, since they were both opposed to statism. The debate on this was going on and on for all the four years of my term in office.

Planinc's assessment of the main conflicts within the leadership confirms that the main lines of division were not ethnic, and not even strictly between republics, though-as Planinc admits-the divisions were often between *the developed* and the *underdeveloped*. On this particular issue and in the first post-Titoist years, the main conflict was between the *ideological* and *pragmatic* approach within the Yugoslav political elite. It was because they lost the battle for a more pragmatic approach to politics that the four successive Yugoslav prime ministers in the analyzed period (Djuranović 1977-82, Planinc 1982-86, Mikulić 1986-88, and Marković 1988-91) left politics disappointed and disillusioned about the prospects of Yugoslavia. In the 1998 interview, Planinc said, as follows:

> The Party was supposed to be a cohesive force, but by then [1982] it had become, on the contrary, the main source of conflicts and conservatism in Yugoslav society. In Tito's time, changes were still possible if Tito was convinced they were necessary. But after him, it was much more difficult. There was no money anymore to satisfy everyone's needs. And the federal government had no instruments to run affairs on its own. It had to rely on the republics, on the federal presidency, and on the Party presidency. When members

of the Party leaderships became the main defenders of their own republics, Yugoslav cohesion became impossible.

Paradoxically, it was the main promoter of national economies, the Croatian leader Vladimir Bakarić, who proposed Milka Planinc for the post of prime minister in 1982, in order to stop Djuranović's attempts to recentralize the Yugoslav economy. Planinc, who from 1972 to 1982 held the post of Croatian Party president, was a Party appointee. But once she became the federal prime minister, it took little time for her to change into a promoter of the market economy and Yugoslav economic unity.

> When a person holds this office, she or he changes a lot. This happened to me, and also to my successor, Branko Mikulić [Bosnia-Herzegovina]. All the way through, as a member of the federal presidency, he was my hardest critic. During the 1984-86 period, there was no session of the federal presidency at which he would not criticize my policy, demanding administrative regulation, state intervention, and the suspension of the market. But when he became the prime minister in 1986, he needed only one year to change his position and to become even more radical than I was. Only when one faces the pressure from the republics, from abroad, from your colleagues in the Party, only then can one appreciate the real difficulty of the situation.[36]

However, although all four Yugoslav prime ministers in the post-Tito period changed their ideological positions for more pragmatic ones, the Party leadership remained largely committed to Kardelj's concept. Although they tried to reform the system from within, the federal government had no instruments (and perhaps no courage) to face the real problems: political provisions, ideological barriers, and the habits produced by them. Although dependent on the republics and provinces, as well as on Party leadership, the government showed substantial independence from them. But it did not make the last step: to challenge the political system, which made radical changes impossible. A program of economic stabilization conceived under the slogan "economic reforms, yes, political reforms, no," said Josip Županov, "simply could not yield any serious results because the attempt was being made to deal with the consequences rather than the causes of the crisis."[37] And the cause of the problem was in the political system. The confederalized system of "consensus policy" was described by Korošić (1988:68):

> Only those changes that satisfied [all] political interests were generated. The result was that there were no fundamental changes. Every group of interests was capable of blocking a reform. This was because the economic results were not, in fact, what mattered: they were taken into account only incidentally, as an excuse for changes if and when [politicians] had already accepted them. In other words, the political system dominated over economic ratio-

nale; its aims were decisive while the economy remained subordinated and unimportant. Since the resistance to political changes was even growing, the economic system was waiting in line. Concomitantly, the rest of the world was marching at a fast pace out of the 20th century.

Not only did ideological obstacles prevent any radical change, but institutions were set up to stop it. Djuranović's position was so weak by July 1981 that the international commentators wrote: "Had it been possible for members of the two chambers of the Yugoslav National Assembly…to have held a vote of confidence, Djuranović would have been defeated immediately."[38] He ended his mandate in June 1982 marginalized and unpopular. However, it was soon proved that his successors in the office of federal prime minister had every reason to envy him: they were publicly criticized (Milka Planinc in 1985), forced to resign (Branko Mikulić in 1988), and rendered nonexistent in a political (and almost a physical) way (Ante Marković in 1991). They all faced the same opponents.

4.4. The International Factors

In her book *Balkan Tragedy*, Susan Woodward argues that the foreign influence on what happened in Yugoslavia was enormous and started with the IMF (International Monetary Fund) intervention in 1982-83. In her analysis, Woodward identifies the Western financial pressure on Yugoslavia as damaging for the stability of the country. Indeed, the IMF intervention in the Yugoslav economy was of great significance. But taking into account the context of internal conflicts within the elite, we can conclude that the IMF intervention may have had ambivalent, rather than exclusively negative, consequences.

Had there been no obligation to repay foreign loans, the status quo would have certainly prevailed over any attempt to reform the economic system. The resolution of the 12th LCY Congress in 1982 still talked about "acute problems and contradictions,"[39] though even members of the state presidency agreed that the situation was "dramatic" and needed an urgent and systematic response. But in 1982 the loans came up for repayment, and the republics suddenly realized they were simply not capable of doing this.

Croatia, whose level of investments was (largely because of political reasons related to a need of the post-1971 leaders to endear themselves to the Croatian public) the highest in the country, was now the first republic to face the wall of bankruptcy. "If Croatia is not helped by the other republics, it will not get out of its present economic crisis," declared Croatian top politician Jure Bilić at the CC LCY session in October 1982.[40] He said that without such help, "Croatia would be compelled to take new foreign credits, or would be threatened by a complete halt of its whole economy."[41]

At the same time, the IMF demanded federal guarantees for the repayment of the loans. The Planinc government reacted to this not only by introducing new measures of austerity, but also by proposing a tight control over foreign currency. She saw this as her chance to win the support of the republics and provinces at a time when it had become unavoidable to introduce some economic reforms. A year earlier, in May 1982 a new law was proposed with the effect of centralizing foreign currency earnings in the country. The law was meant to reduce the almost unlimited rights of BOALs and Work Organizations to dispose of foreign currency earnings as they pleased. But the Slovenian leadership reacted most sharply to this idea. Andrej Marinc, the newly elected president of the Slovenian Party Central Committee, said that this proposal "contradicted some of the very foundations of the system of Socialist self-management, and was against the position of workers in associated labor and against the constitutional system."[42] Vojvodina also objected to this "ideologically and politically unacceptable centralization." These regions in the end forced the federal government into a compromise: the law was withdrawn, and only a partial centralization was imposed by government decree for a period of one year only.

But the situation was different after IMF pressure. In July 1983, the federal government finally succeeded in breaking through the barrier of separate republican interests. It looked as if the marathon session of the Federal Assembly on 2 and 3 July 1983 should have in this respect been considered as "a turning point in the country's modern history" and "a beginning of the real post-Tito era" (as the RFE/RL commentator said immediately after it).[43] Milka Planinc demanded from the federal parliament the approval of several laws written in cooperation with the IMF, which aimed at making the Yugoslav state its federal bank and making its government guarantee all the credits received by the various Yugoslav institutions. To the shocked delegates of the Federal Assembly, the federal prime minister openly declared that Yugoslavia "would not be able, even with the greatest effort, to repay the debts falling due in 1983," and that "unless we find other possible means, we are without any doubt in a situation in which we will have to proclaim a moratorium and embark on a general rescheduling of our debts to foreign countries." The "other possible means" were presented through legislation proposed by the federal government and supported by the IMF. "We had to accept these conditions," Planinc said, precisely because "owing to our earlier conduct and even our conduct this year, owing to a lack of discipline in repaying our foreign debts...our negotiating position was very weak. For this reason, we had to accept the provision that the National Bank of Yugoslavia should be not merely a guarantor, but also a direct debtor and that the federal state should guarantee all the credits that the whole country received, regardless of who took the loans."[44]

Pushed into a corner by the threat of resignation of the federal government and faced with a "moratorium" that would include immediate confiscation of all Yugoslav property abroad, the delegates accepted the laws. But the opposition to "radical reform" was stronger than ever. Not only some republican leaders, but also many veterans' organizations throughout the country opposed it for different reasons. The veterans, as well as a large part of the Yugoslav army, saw in the IMF a representative of Western capitalism that had seriously undermined Yugoslav independence. Sergej Kraigher, a member of the Yugoslav presidency (representing Slovenia), who was in charge of economic reforms, had to justify the IMF-backed legislation to members of the army general staff on 29 July 1983. His message was simple: there was no alternative.

> Analysis has shown that if the International Monetary Fund denied us [financial] resources, and without loans from foreign banks, production would fall by 15 to 20 percent. This means that we would no longer be capable of sustaining the level of employment as it is, and especially-we could not create new jobs. (Kraigher, 1983/1985:192)

And all this happened less than three years after Tito's death, at a time of high ethnic tension in Kosovo, following the 1981 unrest. Watching the TV news from Poland, the Yugoslavs could not avoid comparison with another deeply indebted country, in which political unrest had led to martial law in December 1981.[45] The Yugoslav leaders were urged to act quickly and resolutely to reach a solution. But they were "willing hostages" of their own constitutional provisions and ideological beliefs, indecisiveness, and megalomaniac ambitions, especially at the regional and local levels. They also feared losing control over their own republic/province's "inner affairs" and thus opposed any significant recentralization of Yugoslavia.

After decades in which GDP growth was among the highest in Europe, Yugoslavia entered a period of stagnation that resulted in 0.6 percent GDP growth from 1981 to 1989, compared with 5.6 percent in 1976-80 and 5.9 percent in 1971-75.[46] But even in this situation, a great many political leaders were not willing to change their positions. They did not publicly oppose any implementation of measures aimed at the reintegration of the Yugoslav economy, but they did actively obstruct it. Ideological commitment to Kardelj's doctrine, as well as more pragmatic reasons linked to their own republics and provinces-their own "electoral units"-were much more important than economic results.

Despite the declarative support they offered to Djuranović's and Planinc's radical measures," when discussion began on the 1984 budget in the same assembly four months later, the republics and provinces opposed every single measure aimed at further reform of the economic system. A "radical reform" was simply impossible. The Yugoslav finance minister, Jože Florijančič (Slovenia), resigned in protest against this stalemate. Florijančič's resignation was motivated by the still chaotic situation in the foreign currency market, because of which US$700 million was lost in 1983 alone.[47] Although a Slovene himself, Florijančič did not want to compromise on these issues. For this he felt under strong pressure from his own republic, as a result of which he left politics and withdrew to business.

For the same reasons in 1983 Milka Planinc offered her resignation to the federal Party presidency.

> They all looked at me suspiciously, many convinced I was an IMF *spy* in their ranks. I publicly said that the IMF initiative was welcome because many people at home were against reforms. I had in mind the LCY leadership, though of course I did not say this explicitly. But they knew whom I was criticizing. Another incident occurred when I told the IMF representatives that I appreciated their efforts because this was exactly the same direction as the one proposed by my government. The Party Presidency was so angry that they almost formed a separate commission to discuss my words. When I offered my resignation in 1983, the president of the Party Presidency, Ali Shukrija, said there was no need to discuss it, since I was only a member of the Central Committee, and only the CC should discuss it, not the presidency. Only because of the scandal this would produce did they decide not to accept it. But when I resigned again in 1985, they agreed, asking me to remain a caretaker until the end of the normal term in office, the following year.

The inadequate reaction of the Yugoslav Party leadership to Planinc's initiatives urged Marijan Korošić to conclude the following:

> The bureaucrats have taken the program of stabilization into their own hands, interpreting it in their own way....I was optimistic in July when the government announced radical changes, but am not any longer. Everything seems to be reduced to only "cosmetic corrections"...Because of ideological disunity in preparing changes in the economic system...everything has resulted in no changes at all.[48]

Contrary to Woodward's conclusion, therefore, the IMF initiative was in fact welcomed by the reformers within the Yugoslav political elite. Furthermore, at some point it looked as if they could use it in the internal struggle against the conservatives. However, it is perhaps fair to say that Milka Planinc did not realize how far-reaching political changes would be had they been really launched at that time. In her 1998 interview for this book, she complained about the deadlines imposed by the IMF on her government:

> Our main problem with the IMF was the tight deadlines they wanted us to follow. What they asked us to do in three years, we could have done in ten years without a problem. But they insisted on short deadlines.

The IMF intervention, therefore, can only partially be blamed as a factor in Yugoslav disintegration. Although the pressure on the Yugoslav economy narrowed its ability to satisfy all groups competing for political power and therefore provoked further conflicts, it did not in fact much move the Yugoslav party elite, which was still largely committed to Kardelj's concept.

4.5. The Response of the Elite: Kraigher's Long-Term [sic!] Program of Stabilization

The unwillingness of the elite to accept significant changes was obvious in the 1,500-page Program of Economic Stabilization (not reforms!), which was, after two years of debate, formulated by the federal leadership.[49] The Kraigher proposal, as the program was named after its main author, the Slovenian representative in the Federal State Presidency, was just another "feasible" compromise subject to various possibilities of interpretation. Here are the main points of Kraigher's views, as expressed in his speeches from 1980 to 1985, and in two interviews I had with him in January 1986 and February 1988, respectively.[50] Since Kraigher's program was accepted in its initial draft form as an official document of the 12th LCY Congress in 1982 and then-as a long and completed document-on several later occasions by the LCY Central Committee, the Yugoslav Presidency, and the Yugoslav Assembly, we can safely assume that his views represented the dominant discourse of the Yugoslav political elite in response to the economic crisis in the early 1980s.

First, Yugoslavia remained committed to self-management, to which there was "no real alternative," either in liberalism or in state Socialism (Kraigher 1982/1985:104 and 1983/1985:209).[51] Kraigher opposed Keynesianism and monetarism (1983/1985:180,211), the two economic doctrines that had proved "incapable of solving the economic problems of modern capitalism" (1981/1985:66, 1983/1985:260-1). In a surprisingly ideological rhetoric for the 1980s, Kraigher argued that "the general crisis of capitalism was deeper than ever, and with no viable prospect of being resolved" (1981/1985:66). Although it was widely perceived that historically the self-management project was a reaction to Stalinism after 1948, its renaissance after 1971 Kraigher saw as a response to growing liberal tendencies in Yugoslav society. The reemergence of self-management in its present form Kraigher saw as the alternative to the technomanagerial and liberal tendencies of the purged republican leaders (in the 1971-72 period), especially in Slovenia, Croatia, and Serbia (1983/1985:194). But these forces (*liberals* and *technomanagers*) had not yet been fully defeated (1983/1985:204,245), and this was where Kraigher saw the main focus for further action. The main problem was neither in the new Yugoslav constitution, nor in the Associated Labor Act, but in their insufficient or incomplete implementation. If BOALs were organized in accordance with the constitution (not only in letter, but also in spirit), they would not be elements of economic and political atomization in the country (1983/1985:180). But, Kraigher concluded that technomanagers and liberals, who still kept the key posts in the economy and politics (1982/1985:87-9), were the main promoters of autarkic tendencies. Even 30 years after self-management had been introduced, decision making was still limited to narrow circles (1983/1985:196) in which economic and political powers were linked (1982/1985:111, 1983/1985:160).[52] Although his analysis criticized the political elite for promoting autarkic principles, Kraigher opposed witch-hunting, calling for unity in implementing his stabilization program rather than for differentiation among the political leaders (1983/1985: 240-41).

Second, Kraigher acknowledged that the Yugoslav market was seriously fragmented, but he warned that "one should not exaggerate" this (1983/1985:211; 1984/1985:326,363). The centralized federation, as it had been before the constitutional changes, had produced even worse conflicts over the redistribution of economic goods via federal institutions (1983/1985:211). It was true that autarkic tendencies must be prevented, but not by any recentralization of Yugoslavia. By repeating Kardelj's notion of self-management as both a solution for the national question and a Socialist vision, Kraigher argued that recentralization would in fact destroy both the equality of nations and self-management (1981/1985:37). It was true, Kraigher argued, that the process of interrepublican negotiations in Yugoslavia was difficult and slow, but this was also a result of the unavoidable "pluralism of self-managerial interests," as promoted by Kardelj (1977). Responding to increasingly critical public opinion that was calling for the government to meet its responsibilities, Kraigher opposed the idea that the state leadership (such as the federal government) should take the whole responsibility for the economy, since this would again reinforce statist structures (1983/1985:166). On the contrary, power should be devolved from any statist power center, whether federal, republican, or municipal, to self-managing employees (1983/1985:177).

Third, the workers, Kraigher argued, were not "naturally" prone to a self-management orientation (1983/1985:253). In a rhetoric that again repeated Kardelj's attack on the theories of spontaneity (1983/1985:167; 1984/1985:324), Kraigher warned that the key to the workers' actions still lay in subjective forces (i.e., in the Party). He shared and extended Kardelj's view on the Party's new role. The Party (which he criticized at several places for being too closely linked to the state and too distant from the workers) should act as the main promoter of self-management in the BOALs (1983/1985:230). This was where he saw the new place of the LCY in the political system.

Fourth, Kraigher concluded that some "minor modifications" were necessary in the political system. They should be "corrections of our practice, and probably of some elements in the system itself in terms of its further clarification, but not of the system as such" (1983/1985:209). Kraigher emphasized that no fundamental change of the political system could be expected. But, for example, political objections to "small private enterprises"(coming from the conservative Partisan Veterans) were in his opinion undesirable. Small-scale industry (crafts and small private businesses) could not endanger Socialism (1983/1985: 224, 270) and should therefore be allowed and further developed. Kraigher's criticism of the regime did not go much further than to acknowledge that Socialism was much more endangered by privileged members of the economic and political elite than by potential investors in small enterprises. His criticism was directed at various hesitations and at the lack of will to implement good ideas suggested in previous attempts to reform the Yugoslav economy. In the interview I conducted with Kraigher in January 1986, he said this:

> We hesitated [in the 1965 reform] to develop a suitable economic system and to implement a suitable economic policy. It all went too slowly. Now, we still lack consistent and synchronized measures that would lead to implementation of the program. The main problem has always been that we were too slow and too late. All other things are just the result of this indecisiveness. We spent huge amounts of energy and many hours in reaching a compromise, instead of spending this time creatively in the implementation of our program.

Kraigher warned political leaders that the key to the solution of the economic crisis still resided with them, but he was not even in favor of changing the political elites that were "slow" and "inconsistent" in implementing the good political program. Without changing the system, and with the old elites still in power, how could one expect to change anything?[53]

It was not surprising, therefore, to see that already in 1984 the Kraigher Program was collapsing. Instead of the planned 10 percent, inflation increased to 75 percent per annum in 1985. The living standards of the population fell by 34 percent from 1979 to 1984. About 40 to 45 percent of households earned less than the poverty line. The 850,000 new employees (hired from 1979 to 1984) did not manage to increase total production by anymore than 0.8 percent for the entire period of five years. This meant that labor productivity was in fact decreasing as personal income was rapidly falling. Although in 1979 the price of a kilogram (2.2 lb) of bread was equal to payment for 14 minutes of work for an average worker, in 1984 more than twice that much paid time (29 minutes) was needed (Bilandžić 1986:116-19). The foreign trade deficit was indeed reduced and even eliminated in 1984, but mostly because imports were reduced, not because exports were increased. Exports, however, did increase significantly, but to COMECON and not to the West European market.[54] As a consequence, Yugoslavia was cutting itself off from the world market instead of increasing its participation in it. Ideological barriers made even minor recommendations of the Kraigher Program neglected or even rejected in practice: to many low-ranked conservative apparatchik's small enterprises, as well as foreign investments (including those of the Yugoslav Gastarbeiter), were just potentially dangerous promoters of capitalism. Even an attempt to loosen restrictions on land ownership by farmers met with resistance by ideologically correct opponents. Moreover, no serious investors would take the risk of running enterprises according to the Associated Labor Act and the tons of regulations that followed it.

4.6. The Source of Regime Stability: the "Syndrome of Radical Egalitarianism"

From the traditional *economic approach* to analyzing the stability of regimes, it is certainly a paradox that the economic crisis met with no major revolt among those whose position was obviously worsened: workers. Why was this so? At least a partial explanation is offered by Croatian sociologist Josip Županov, who in the early 1980s (as one of the first Yugoslav academics to recognize the depth and seriousness of the crisis) authored the phrase *"the syndrome of radical egalitarianism."*[55]

> For our workers, it is not disastrous that they live badly; it is a tragedy if someone else lives better. This is quite a different system of values [than in the West]: in our society, it is a catastrophe if someone is rich and not if somebody is poor. With such views you cannot expect workers to go on strike...Since conflicts do exist, however, they are expressed in another way, for instance, in the form of a vast amount of sick leave, which, economically speaking, is worse than strikes.[56]

Justice was a word used for equality in restrictions. In an interview I conducted with Županov in December 1995, he said,

> When the "even and odd" system of bans on car driving was introduced, people saw that the measures applied equally to everyone, regardless of how wealthy one was. Let me use my personal experience: I could tolerate sitting in complete darkness in my flat every Tuesday and Thursday as long as I saw my neighbors across the street in the dark on Mondays and Wednesdays. But if I saw some of my neighbors' bulbs switched on when I was in darkness, I was ready to rebel against the state.

Only the corruption of elites could have resulted in riots. But the elite in fact corrupted the masses by what Županov calls "a pact between manual workers and political elite." The pact was based on self-management rhetoric, which favored the working class in its "fight against state bureaucracy and technomanagerial forces." In a pragmatic compromise between the elites and workers, the latter agreed not to protest against the regime, which tolerated various *alternative means of survival*.[57] Although the level of efficiency at work was lower than ever, no person lost a job for not working. "They could not pay me as little as I can work" was the favorite proverb of Yugoslav workers in the 1980s. It was Kardelj's concept of self-management that guaranteed that workers had a right to work and to participate in decision making. They were not employed by a boss or a manager: they associated their labor with other workers. The workers could fire a manager if they were not satisfied with him/her, not the other way round. It was this concept that created the crisis. But it also prevented any social protests from emerging.

During that period, the state turned a blind eye to the massive violation of regulations, while the citizens tolerated elites incapable of managing the country's deep crisis. If Yugoslavia ever was a firmly run state in which citizens feared state repression, it was now on its way to slipping into anarchy.[58] In people's minds, no obligations to the state needed to be met, since the state would simply not react to any infringement.[59] Weakened by the antistatist rhetoric, the state was now in reality withering away under pressure of both the ideology and the practice of self-management. By tolerating personal networks of survival, the state was, however, blind to the breaking of laws, which became the rule rather than exception. But the elite also benefited from the whole situation. It hoped that the people would avoid any collective action that would endanger their private projects for survival. Losing any confidence in the institutional way of changing things, people became indifferent. Even those dissatisfied directed their efforts at building up their personal networks rather than opposing the whole system. However, Županov was right in saying that the social deal between the elite, which was "closing its eyes," and ordinary citizens, "who tried to find their own ways of surviving the crisis," could not last ad infinitum. "The conflict will emerge in an entirely different area," he concluded wisely in January 1985.[60]

This other area was in politics, more precisely on ethnic issues. The sense of injustice, triggered by the different levels of economic development of various Yugoslav regions, resulted in violent collective action in Kosovo, the Serbian southern province, in March 1981. The causes of Kosovo's problems were many and will be explained in detail in the next chapter. But the sense of inequality in economic, political, and ethnic terms was the most important one. Županov's conclusion that it was not so much the sense of being poor, but of others being wealthy, that triggered the discontent with the system will then be used again.[61]

4.7. Conclusion

The debate on the economic crisis in the early 1980s had the following five characteristics:

First, the conflict crossed republican lines, both among politicians (Djuranović was Montenegrin, Kraigher Slovene, and Planinc Croat) and among economists (Korošić, a Croat, was the most stubborn supporter of economic unity). In general, it did not follow the divide between the more and less developed republics, since both Slovenia and Kosovo, the most developed and least developed regions in Yugoslavia, were opposing recentralization of the system, even when it became obvious that it had entered a deep crisis.

Second, the conflict was more vertical than horizontal: between central government and the republics/provinces, rather than between republics on the horizontal level. The economic disputes in the early 1980s were not ethnic disputes. Although some republics (Slovenia and sometimes Croatia, and the province of Vojvodina) more often than others obstructed federal policy, the others also used or threatened to use their veto rights to make sure their interests were properly taken care of (Bilandžić 1986).

Third, there was a relatively high level of unity within the federal government, whose members managed to put themselves above their respective republics, or at least to be more than just their mouthpieces. This was also the case with the federal presidency, whose members were reelected in 1979, still under Tito's supervision. To some extent, the same could be said of other federal institutions (the Party and state presidencies), which saw their prime task to be replacing Tito, not in representing the republics and provinces.[62]

Fourth, for the same reasons it was no surprise that the Yugoslav leaders showed a remarkable loyalty to Tito's legacy, even when facing serious economic and political crisis. They remained committed to the basic values of Tito's policy, three of which were emphasized: self-management, federalism, and nonalignment.

Fifth, the changes they introduced were made out of necessity, not by way of the introduction of a new ideological or political concept. And they were not met with enthusiasm; in fact they were even opposed as much as possible.

Lastly, among the pressures they faced, those coming from the international environment were feared more than those originating from within the country.[63] The loss of independence and the advances of liberal democracy or state Socialism worried Yugoslav politicians more than the economic crisis itself.

It was because of the ideological concept they shared that the Yugoslav politicians created an institutional framework that made any radical changes impossible. Despite their revolutionary rhetoric, in the immediate post-Titoist period they became rather conservative. The basic discrepancy between dramatic conclusions about reality, which did not change in accordance with proclamations, and inadequate actions taken to change it continued throughout the 1980s, despite several attempts to introduce radical measures. All four Yugoslav prime ministers in this period (Djuranović, Planinc, Mikulić, and Marković) attempted the same, only to face the same insurmountable opposition from autarkic republicanism and ideological dogmatism. In 1985 the new federal presidency practically dismissed Planinc's policy. In December 1988, Branko Mikulić was forced to resign as prime minister under the same pressure. And finally, the last years of Yugoslavia were characterized by the same conflict between the attempts of the last Yugoslav prime minister, Ante Marković (backed even more strongly by international financial institutions than Planinc was in 1983), to reform the system and the various ideological and separate national interests that opposed any re-centralization. The great difference, however, was that the lines of the conflict in the late 1980s matched first the borders of republics, and then more and more the "borders" between ethnic groups in the country.

Notes

1 Speaking of this system in 1995, Ivan Stambolić said that its main idea ("however ideological") was an expression of an "orientation that was not wrong: that before any party, state, and before politics in general there was a 'world of labor.' To us [political leaders] it meant, above all, basing ourselves in the world of labor, rather than basing our power on force and the authority of one political party" (Stambolić 1995:45).
2 In Bosnia-Herzegovina, 16,207; Montenegro, 1,813; Croatia, 20,038; Macedonia, 6,002; Slovenia, 10,836; and Serbia, 35,519, out of which 12,846 were in Vojvodina and 3,356 in Kosovo. *Statistički Bilten* 1286, SZS, Belgrade, 1980.
3 *Statistički Bilten* 1986:22.
4 From 1.25 to 1.50 million directives, orders, contracts, and other obligatory acts were enacted throughout the system in the first few postconstitutional years (Bilandžić 1986:39). The Croatian sociologist Slaven Letica calculated the costs of the new legislation to be equal to creating 150,000 new jobs. The Belgrade political scientist Vladimir Goati says that by 1988, the Yugoslav political and economic life was directed by 8 million directives, laws, and legal acts. The number of employees in the administration increased 44.3 percent from 1972 to 1978 (1989:43).
5 Stambolić, 1995:46; Čkrebić in *Politika*, 31 December 1985.
6 Stambolić offers an example: "Seven thousand workers voted for a decision on referendum, but the BOAL of the Catering Services voted 31 against and 29 for: because of this two-vote difference, seven thousand workers could not realize their self-managing will" (Stambolić 1995:44).

7   This was, however, one among many controversies in the Kardeljist project. The states were to be replaced with self-management, but the statehood of republics was recognized in 1974. The way out of this paradox was found in the self-managing concept of the states, and in the "new role of the party," which was theoretically directed at managing self-management. Even the politicians themselves, however, admitted this was an illusion.
8   For example: the Assemblies of Republics and Provinces had their *Chamber of Associated Labor*, but the Yugoslav Assembly had no such chamber. Several proposals, mainly by the Serbian leaders, to form one were rejected always on the basis that there was no such thing as a *Yugoslav* (supranational) working class.
9   *Ekonomska politika*, 1691, 27 August 1984.
10 *Danas*, 30 July 1985.
11 For "Bosnians," see Mežnarič (1986); for the social distance between Slovenes and Albanians, see Kuzmanić (1989).
12 In October 1979, as many as 1,185,000 Yugoslavs lived in West European countries. Of these, 695,000 were employed and 490,000 were dependents (including 250,000 school-age children). In non-European countries, mostly in the U.S., Australia, and Canada, but also in some Latin American countries, there were about 300,000 people with Yugoslav passports, and 62 percent of the Yugoslavs living in Europe were from 18 to 35 years of age. The largest part of them (about 240,000) were from Croatia. The large majority (70 percent) had no professional training. Among European countries, Germany had the largest number of Yugoslavs-in 1977, 405,000 (RFE/RL 18 October 1979). During the 1980s, the Yugoslav workers held about US$21 billion in Western banks, but only US$1.2 billion went to Yugoslav banks.
13 *Statistički godišnjak Jugoslavije za 90/91*, 1991:599. It was not surprising, therefore, that in all the Yugoslav republics the number of students studying in their own republic was about 90 percent: in Bosnia-Herzegovina 88.4 percent, in Montenegro 91 percent, in Serbia 91.4 percent, in Croatia 91.5 percent, in Macedonia 96.3 percent, and in Slovenia 96.8 percent.
14 This fact was used by ethnic nationalists (especially in Slovenia) to illustrate ethnic inequality in the late 1980s.
15 The damaging effect of the oil crisis for the Yugoslav economy may be illustrated by the fact that during the three years of 1979, 1980, and 1981, Yugoslavia average annual spending on oil imports was US$2,335 million (more than US$7 billion in total). But in the three years before that period (1976, 1977, and 1978) the annual bill was on average US$934 million, thus US$1,422 million a year less (Djuranović 1985: 208).
16 Several years later, Slobodan Milošević used the same argument in his fight against anarchy. He proclaimed he was in fact fighting against the "strong hand" (recentralization with the elements of Soviet Socialism) that would be the logical result of anarchism and the fragmentation of the Yugoslav economic and political system.
17 As described by Tepavac (1997) and Perović (1991) and explained in chapter three, Tito tried to avoid conflicts with other politicians. Since 1972, he had tried to please local leaders by accepting almost all proposals that did not endanger his personal position. The economy, for which he had not much interest, was the area in which he could accept many compromises without many problems.
18 This was particularly important in Serbia, Slovenia, and Croatia, where the replaced leaders had put great stress on economic issues. Especially in Croatia, where the ousted leader of the CC LC Croatia-Savka Dabčević Kučar-was a professor of economics.

19 *XI Congress of the LCY: Documents.* It was not before 1984 that the Federal Assembly managed to suspend the investments projected by the 1981-86 Social Plan.
20 That they were aware of them was shown, for example, at the joint session of the Party and state presidency with the presidents of the republics and provinces in November 1979. The top leadership debated the "threats of further deterioration" (RFE/RL 30 November 1979).
21 RFE/RL, 28 December 1979.
22 Interview with Dušan Bilandžić in December 1995.
23 RFE/RL, 30 June 1981. Perišin was against the "revival of any unitarianism and centralism while favoring a "unified Yugoslav market."
24 RFE/RL, 30 April 1979.
25 The regime significantly liberalized regulations for traveling abroad: out of 2.4 million applicants for passports in 1979, "only" 26 thousand applications were rejected, and 1,644 people were compelled to return their passports (RFE/RL 26 September 1980).
26 This was stopped by the "Deposit Law" introduced in October 1982, after which Yugoslavs traveling abroad had to have a deposit of 5,000 dinars in their bank account. Total travel abroad decreased by 69 percent in the month after this measure was introduced. Travel to Italy decreased by 93 percent, to Greece by 94 percent, and to Austria by 42 percent (RFE/RL 11 March 1983).
27 This was the fourth devaluation of the Yugoslav dinar: in 1961 it lost 20 percent of its value, in 1965- 15 percent; in 1971-26.5 percent; and in 1980-30 percent. Its positive effects could be seen in a 32 percent increase in exports and only 7 percent in imports in 1980. As a result, the trade balance deficit decreased by 15 percent compared with 1979. But the devaluation of the currency alone could not bring any further effects without being supported by other measures, on which no agreement could be reached (RFE/RL 29 January 1981).
28 RFE/RL, 7 July 1980.
29 RFE/RL, 2 December 1980.
30 Gligorov was the main creator of the 1965 economic reforms and one of the main economic advisers to Sergej Kraigher and later to Ante Marković. From 1990 and 1999 he was the president of Macedonia.
31 RFE/RL, 7 July 1980.
32 RFE/RL, 20 November 1980.
33 RFE/RL, 7 July 1980.
34 RFE/RL, 6 July 1981.
35 RFE/RL, 15 October 1981.
36 In an interview for this book, Jure Bilić, the Croatian representative in the LCY presidency (1982-86), said Milka Planinc was promoted by Bakarić, but soon she started playing her own game, mostly because Bakarić died in February 1983. "She ended up on the opposite side from what Bakarić expected." Bakarić's widow, Marija, whom I interviewed in summer 1983, praised Milka Planinc for her role in Croatian and Yugoslav politics. However, my impression was that Mrs. Bakarić was only marginally informed about politics after the death of her husband.
37 In his 1985 interview, Županov said that "every prolongation of the crisis would lead to the disintegration of the country's economic and political systems" and that "no one in the world is prepared to give up a monopoly of power if he is not forced to" (RFE/RL 22 April 1985).

38   Slobodan Stanković: "Yugoslav Government Under Domestic Fire," RFE/RL, 16 July 1981. Djuranović simply did not want to discuss issues with members of Parliament, claiming that his report on economic failures had been directed at "some other people" who "were well known-they were the people who really made decisions, who could be found at all levels, and who of late have made the federal government the chief target of their attacks." Djuranović meant republican leaders and ideologues within the federal Party leadership.
39   "LCY Tasks in the Realization of the Economic Stabilization Policy," Resolution of the Twelfth Congress of the LCY (1983:165).
40   Croatian post-1971 leaders (including Milka Planinc, the president of the Croatian League of Communists) were the most outspoken advocates of the policy of high investment, by which they wanted to demonstrate their care for Croatian real (economic and political) interests. In 1983, Croatia faced debt to foreign creditors of US$3 billion. As a consequence of the restrictions introduced by the new federal government, the GDP in Croatia decreased 3.7 percent in 1983 when compared with 1981, and imports fell by 30.4 percent, exports by 5.6 percent. The investment rate fell by 27 percent. As a consequence, foreign currency income decreased by 28.1 percent, and unemployment increased by 24.9 percent (to 124,000 in 1985, from 96,000 in 1981-or to 5.8 percent, from 4.5 percent). In these two years, prices increased 82.9 percent (IP CKSKH 1/1986:13-15).
41   RFE/RL, 12 October 1982.
42   RFE/RL, 26 May 1982.
43   RFE/RL, 21 July 1983.
44   RFE/RL, 13 July 1983.
45   The Party Central Committee discussed the Polish events at its session in July 1983. The main lesson drawn by the president of the LCY presidency, Dušan Dragosavac, was "that our political system of direct Socialist democracy should be consistently developed," since the Polish crisis was a result of "the bureaucratic-technocratic system, which had squeezed the Polish working class onto the periphery." However, "we can only support a Socialist Poland" and not a "bourgeois-clerical and Catholic-nationalist" one, claimed Yugoslav Communists. On Dragosavac's position on the Polish crisis, see my interview with him, quoted in chapter five.
46   The highest GDP growth was realized in 1957-60: 11.3 percent.
47   The RFE/RL report described the chaos in the following words: "Many enterprises, to acquire foreign currency, sold their products abroad at reduced prices, while later other enterprises imported these same products at much higher prices" (29 December 1983).
48   *Nin*, 27 November 1983.
49   In 1981 the Federal Social Council established a Commission for Questions of Economic Stabilization, which was chaired by Kraigher. Over the next two years, the Kraigher commission involved or consulted about 350 leading politicians, economists, and other experts in the field. They produced a long document (more than 1,500 pages) with policy recommendations in 15 fields (such as an anti-inflation program, followed by separate sections on such subjects as unemployment, housing policy, foreign economic relations, and agriculture.)
50   The interviews were published in *Polet*, 31 January and 14 February 1986, and in *Mladost*, February 1988. Here I quote from the minutes of my conversation with Kraigher.
51   "To us there are no other forms, possibilities, or ways to resolve current developmental problems," Kraigher concluded in October 1982 (1985:105). Any possibility

of returning "back to some form of old bourgeois parliamentarism" was ruled out (1983/1985:209).

52 Like Kardelj, Kraigher believed that state Socialism was more likely to be accepted by the general population and political leaders as an alternative to self-management than liberalism was (1983/1985:260). Kraigher opposed all types of statism, regardless of whether they originated at the federal, republican, or even municipal level. To statism, in his view, there was only one real alternative: further development of self-management (1981/1985:62; 1983/1985:176).

53 In an interview I conducted with Milka Planinc in April 1998, she said the Kraigher program was "the best possible" for the time in which it appeared. That means it was not openly hostile to the market, but it was so full of compromises that anyone could interpret it in his or her own way.

54 An increase of trade with COMECON, followed by the rhetoric of radical egalitarianism, was noticed as a bad sign by those who still remembered Kardelj's warning that "state Socialism" represented the greatest danger for post-Titoist Yugoslavia in the long term.

55 For functions of egalitarianism in Yugoslav society, see also Bernik (1989).

56 Josip Županov, *Danas*, 2 August 1983.

57 The gray economy was tolerated, and absenteeism took on massive proportions. According to Yugoslav statistics, about 700,000 people were absent from work every day because of illness; 600,000 a day were on vacation, and 400,000 a day were attending various conferences that kept them from work. "As a consequence, instead of eight hours work a day, after deducting all absences during the year, a Yugoslav worker effectively worked only three hours and six minutes a day." The system itself tolerated this absenteeism which dissipated the energy of the potential conflict between the workers and the elite (RFE/RL 16 August 1983).

58 In return, discontent was growing against this *anarchism*. Only a couple of years later, Slobodan Milošević secured large support against anarchism, which he did not fail to criticize in his public addresses in the 1984-89 period. More on this in chapter six.

59 Plenty of examples to support this conclusion may be found in Duško Doder's book, *The Yugoslavs* (Doder 1978).

60 *Intervju*, 4 January 1985.

61 Radical egalitarianism in Kosovo was the main reason for the support of Enver Hoxha's criticism of Yugoslav "revisionism" and "capitalism." The national movement in Kosovo was led by Hoxhists, whose rhetoric was that of radical egalitarianism (see Maliqi 1998).

62 As Planinc argues, this changed in 1984 when the new Yugoslav Presidency was elected. Its members were now for the first time not Tito's appointees, but representatives of their republics/provinces. Although most of them had been federal politicians under Tito, they now acted more as representatives of their republics than of Yugoslavia.

63 The only exception to this was the possibility of the *Polish scenario* in Yugoslavia, which was energetically denied by the leading Yugoslav politicians.

CHAPTER FIVE

The Political System Reexamined: The Serbian Question and the Rise of the Defenders and Reformers of the Constitution (1974-1984)

> The disintegration of Serbia would be only the first step toward the disintegration of Yugoslavia....The unresolved issue of the constitutional structuring of Serbia is today the only real...root of Serbian nationalism that has not yet been cut.
>
> **Dragoslav Marković, May 1981**

> I have always felt that whenever there was talk of unitarism, people always looked at me in this circle. Because, to judge by old habits, Serbia means unitarism and centralism.
>
> **Petar Stambolić, 1992**

> Serbian nationalism penetrated the highest ranks of Serbian politics with Ranković, and remained there under Draža Marković's and Ivan Stambolić's protection. The 1974 Constitution to us who came from other republics, and especially from Serbia's provinces, was the most powerful tool to defeat it. And we did not want to lose it.
>
> **Josip Vrhovec, interview in 1998**

5.0. Introduction

This chapter examines three attempts to reform the Yugoslav political system from 1974 to 1986 and the reasons for their failure. All three initiatives came from Serbia, the only Yugoslav republic with autonomous provinces in its territory. The disintegrative processes in Serbia followed the decentralization in Yugoslavia after the 1974 Constitution. But while Yugoslavia was a federation with elements of confederalism, Serbia was formally a unitary state whose relations with its provinces were based on political compromises following the 1967-74 constitutional debate. Although Kosovo and Vojvodina did not become republics on their own, in reality their status was in all important elements equal to those of the republics. The constitutional compromise left a space for both sides to interpret the real meaning of the constitution in their own, mutually opposed ways. The interpretation of what the writers of the constitution really meant when regulating the relations in Serbia dominated Yugoslav politics ever after 1974. Already in 1976 the first demand to condemn the unconstitutional practice of autonomy was presented to Tito and Kardelj by the Serbian leaders. From 1976 to 1984, the Serbian leaders unsuccessfully tried twice more (following the 1981 Kosovo protests, and by initiating debate on the political system in 1983) to resolve the problem without rejecting the main ideas of the 1974 Constitution. The Serbian demands met with indifference or with open opposition among the most Kardeljist forces in the party, which had a firm control over the federal institutions and over all other republics and both provinces. They argued that any significant change of the constitutional provisions would mean deviation from Tito's path, which was to be prevented in the first post-Tito years.

This chapter argues that the commitment to the Kardeljist concept among the Yugoslav leaders in the 1970s and 1980s was so strong that it prevented any change in the political system even when it became obvious that the system itself was not functioning. Instead of reexamining the main elements of the concept, the Kardeljists argued that the system had not been implemented in line with Kardelj's recommendations, and that another nonconstitutional practice had been introduced in Yugoslavia. On all three occasions analyzed in this chapter, the Kardeljists successfully blocked demands for serious reforms.

5.1. The Blue Book of 1977

The Serbian question was the core of the political conflicts in Yugoslavia following the 1974 Constitution. The main reason for its revival was the disintegrative process in Yugoslavia that affected Serbia more than the other republics. Bosnia-Herzegovina was a "small Yugoslavia" in an ethnic sense, but Serbia, which in its political structure (having two provinces in its territory[1] without being a federation itself) deserved much more to be called a small Yugoslavia in a political sense. Since ethnic issues, as I argue throughout this book, did not dominate Yugoslav politics in the late 1970s and early 1980s, it was the Serbian (political) question, rather than the Bosnian (ethnic) question, that emerged at the focus of Yugoslav politics.[2]

As demonstrated in chapter three, Serbian leaders originally accepted the confederalized model of Yugoslavia and supported the decentralization of power that occurred in 1967-72. Along with all other republics, Serbia also wanted more autonomy from the federal leadership in deciding on its own internal affairs. She also supported the idea that republics should be treated as states. Although "1974 signified the end of any possibility of Yugoslavia being run by one nation, by its leadership or any too ambitious individual from the Yugoslav elite" (Stambolić 1995), the Serbian leaders now increasingly complained that all other republics were really moving toward autonomy in their internal affairs, but Serbia alone was moving in a different direction. Because the provinces understood their roles as being equal to the republics, they often de facto prevented Serbia from having full control over their territories. Serbia, her leaders felt, remained the only Yugoslav republic that did not gain its statehood by the constitutional changes of 1974.

Whatever has been said about the disintegrative processes in Yugoslavia applies also to Serbia. The "autarkism" of republics in Yugoslavia was paralleled by the closure of the Serbian provinces both toward Serbia and toward others in Yugoslavia. The megalomaniac wave of investment with no control by the federation was duplicated in the Serbian case. The conflict over competencies between the federation and the republics was the same as the intra-Serbian misunderstanding over what the provisions of the constitution really intended. This was emphasized only by compromising formulations in the Yugoslav and Serbian constitutions, by which the provinces were clearly parts of Serbia, but they were also "constitutive elements of the federation."[3]

In the initial post-1974 phase, Serbian leaders did not object to the constitution itself, but to its "selective implementation" and "incorrect interpretation" by the provinces. The first official complaint about the disintegration of Serbia was sent to Tito and Kardelj in the form of the *Blue Book,* as the official document "on the constitutional position of Serbia and its relations to its two autonomous provinces" is now better known. The document was issued after several incidents of symbolic and practical-political character between Serbia and the provinces.[4] The *Blue Book* complained that the provinces considered themselves equal to the republics, which consequently led them to disrespect any authority of Serbia, even in those fields in which only the republic (as the sovereign state) had rights. Serbia listed dozens of examples of such autarkism: in foreign relations, defense, economics, and education policies.[5]

> It was natural, and even compulsory that the provinces participated when the aims and programs of the Serbian prime minister's visits to a foreign country were formulated, and they had always been informed about the results afterward. But to them it seemed perfectly natural that the Serbian prime minister learned from the press about the prime minister of a province's visit to a foreign country-in which he asked for "a million-dollar loan," recalls Ivan Stambolić from his personal experience while in the office of Serbian prime minister. (1995:78)

When Serbia approached the provinces on this issue, Vojvodina rejected the proposal to coordinate international visits (Stambolić 1981/1988:57). The provinces also argued that there could be no social plan for the whole republic, but that three plans should be introduced instead. While Kosovo and Vojvodina had their own social plans, the Serbian plan was implemented only in the territory outside the provinces. "In the volumes and volumes of social plans of the provinces, the words *republic* and *Serbia* were not mentioned even once. Kosovo also denied Serbia any competence to regulate citizenship policy autonomously," said Stambolić (1995:78). The common defense law could not be enacted, since the provinces rejected any cooperation. The ministries of education argued over whether the Serbian writers from Vojvodina should be classified as Serb or Vojvodinan literature (Galović 1981/1989:133). In the Party, democratic centralism was acknowledged on the federal level, but Vojvodina denied any right of the Serbian Party organization to implement the same principle from the level of the republic downward (Galović 1981/1989:133). A few years later, Vojvodina even opposed Serbia, collecting statistical data on the population in the province (Stambolić 1981/1988:25). The terms "narrow Serbia" and "Serbia without provinces" entered the political vocabulary and statistical books, which Serbia found insulting. For all these reasons, the *Blue Book* concluded that the relationship between Serbia and its two provinces "had reached a virtual cul-de-sac." Making states out of provinces was, they argued, against the spirit and the letter of the constitution.

In January 1977, Kardelj agreed with most of the Serbian demands, repeating his firm stand that the provinces-as opposed to the republics-should not be treated as states. Kardelj's position was constructive and supportive, as the three top Serbian politicians of that time confirmed.[6] Kardelj also rejected any notion of the federalization of Serbia, for it would result in a (negative) reaction of the Serb nation. As Ivan Stambolić recalls, Kardelj was "clearly against the disintegration of Serbia....He thought that Serbia ought to be a unitary state with a certain autonomy for its provinces" (Stambolić 1995:72).[7]

However, Kardelj warned Marković not to expect too much from others in Yugoslavia or from Tito himself. Although the others would not be interested in anything but their own "internal affairs," Tito "would be reserved in the beginning" (Marković 28 February 1976; 1987:333). He therefore suggested the Serbians resolve these problems within Serbia, avoiding the Yugoslav level. He also recommended that they be patient, since "this would all be settled through the economic integration of the country anyhow." Kardelj believed that "associated labor" was the formula to integrate the Yugoslavs without denying any rights to their "fully completed" nations. But, as explained in chapter four, associated labor already in 1975 looked like a distant and by no means certain future. On the contrary, the signs of disintegration, which had brought the country to the verge of dissolution in 1971, now reemerged with full strength in both the economic and the political areas.

The Serbs accepted the first of Kardelj's recommendations, but failed to hear the second. At the end of June 1977 a long session of all the relevant leaders in Serbia (including those of Kosovo and Vojvodina) was held, but no compromise between the two positions was possible. The Kosovo leaders even declared that the *Blue Book* was a "Bible of Serbian nationalism," accusing Marković and the two Stambolićs of attempting to undermine the autonomy of the provinces, which was-in their views-unconstitutional. The Kosovars merely repeated their arguments that Kosovo was not only part of Serbia, but also a constitutive element of the Yugoslav federalism itself. Therefore any change in its status was a change to the Yugoslav Constitution and could not be made by Serbia alone. In fact, it could not be made even by a majority or by all the Yugoslav republics acting together unless the Assembly of Kosovo consented.[8] Siding with Kosovo, the Vojvodinan leaders proposed a gentleman's agreement that would put the whole affair *ad acta*, with the continuation of the status quo. What surprised and discouraged Marković and the Stambolićs most was the opposition to the *Blue Book*, which came from their main rival in Serbia Proper, the federal foreign secretary (1972-78), Miloš Minić.[9] Since Minić was Tito's protegé in Serbia, Marković understood that he could not count on Tito's support in any serious clash with the provinces.[10] "Terrible," wrote Marković in his diary on 30 June 1977, concluding that the Serbs again (like the Yugoslavs in general) remained ineffective because they were disunited. But there was only one possible alternative to an open conflict with Tito, which neither of the two wanted: to accept the *ad acta* compromise. Tito, who in his late eighties was much more interested in preventing a new crisis in Serbia and Yugoslavia than in resolving serious economic and political problems, moved in to force the leaders of the provinces to drop their charges against Marković. The debate on the relationship within Serbia was thus pushed under the carpet, but by no means was it resolved. On the contrary, it only increased the distrust between Serbia and its provinces, between Serbia and the other republics, and between the various factions in the Serbian leadership. It also left some Serbs with the bad feeling that Tito himself had prevented them from being a republic equal to all the others in Yugoslavia. Although the whole affair was conducted almost entirely behind closed doors (the news about the *Blue Book* was broken to the general public only in the mid-1980s), it made the Serbian leadership feel somehow discriminated against in Yugoslavia, chained by the unchangeable provisions of the constitution and their *ad voluntatem* interpretations by the provinces. As a result, Serbian politicians became much more critical of the position of Serbia in their public speeches, which were now more direct than before. They argued, as Ivan Stambolić formulated it in July 1979, that "Serbia is lagging behind the others economically and politically" (Stambolić 1979/1988:9).

At the same time, the provinces were once again grateful to Tito for his support, but now more than ever before worried that things would change after him. In the consensus principle, the constitutional principle that gave them the right to veto any change in the constitution by not ratifying it in their assembly, the provinces discovered the best institutional protection against any Serbian attempt at recentralization. When Kardelj died in February 1979 and Tito in May 1980, the Yugoslav leaders mirrored the grief of the largest segment of the population for the deceased leaders. But this sorrow was mingled with fears and expectations of changes in the post-Titoist period. Below the surface, there was a tense atmosphere of expectation and uncertainty. The rhetoric of no changes after Tito, which dominated the public discourse, substantially helped the cause of the provinces. But as Ivan Stambolić described, while they all agreed that there would be "Tito-after Tito," there was still an open question: "Whose *'Tito'* would this be?"

5.2. The Kosovo Crisis

5.2.1. The Background of the Kosovo Crisis (1981)

The death of Tito and Kardelj shifted the focus of the Serbian initiative from "interpretation of the constitution" to "small changes in the constitution." Interpretation had some sense when the "supreme arbiters of meaning" Tito and Kardelj were alive. But the Serbian leaders assumed that the appropriate interpretation of the constitution had become a much less realistic task for Tito's collective successors.

Six months after Tito's death, the president of the Serbian Constitutional Court, Najdan Pašić, sent a public letter to the Yugoslav Party leadership in which he demanded a debate on the political system. Pašić's action was the first post-

Titoist attempt of Serbian leaders to initiate small changes in the constitution, but it was simply ignored by the others.

Things had, however, changed significantly when the Albanian students in Kosovo demanded changes to the constitution in April 1981. From today's perspective, the discontent of the Kosovo Albanians with the 1974 Constitution appears to be a paradox, since this constitution granted them extensive autonomy in Serbia and Yugoslavia. Even more paradoxical is that the Albanian students in Kosovo were motivated by the same feeling as the Serbian leaders in Belgrade: they both felt unequal to the relevant others. Just as Serbian leaders felt that Serbia was unequal to other Yugoslav republics and that it was lagging behind them in economic and political terms, many Albanians in Kosovo felt the same about their status and the status of Kosovo.[11] Although Serbia felt that it could not realize its status of republic without the strict implementation of the 1974 Constitution, many Albanians felt that only if Kosovo became a republic could the inequality they faced vanish. The sense of inequality and demand for equality were the main motives of both the Kosovo events in 1981 and of the Serbian reaction to them. Therefore Županov's theory of radical egalitarianism could equally help us to explain the political as well as the economic crisis of Yugoslavia.

The inequality felt by the Kosovo Albanians had three dimensions: economic, political, and ethnic.

Economically, Kosovo was the least developed area of Yugoslavia. Although it was developing faster than other regions in Yugoslavia, for reasons of its extremely high birthrate (among the highest in Europe), the GDP per capita did not show such a development. In fact, the gap between Kosovo and the most-developed Yugoslav Republic, Slovenia, was widening. Although in 1952 Slovenia had a GDP per capita 4.1 times larger than Kosovo's, in 1981 the ratio was 5.4:1 with a tendency to increase still further.[12] Other economic data showed an even greater difference, approaching an 8:1 ratio. These differences were comparable with those between England and Northern Africa (Horvat 1988:136). Kosovo was lagging behind not only Slovenia, but also all other Yugoslav regions. Although in 1955 its GDP per capita was 43% of the Yugoslav average, in 1984 this fell to 26% (SGJ 1986:417). "In the situation of economic crisis in the country, Kosovo's prospects of reaching the others were even less likely. With a ratio of 6.1:1 and projected annual growth rate of 2%, Kosovo would need 91 years to reach the Slovenian level of 1981," concluded a leading Yugoslav (Croatian) economist Branko Horvat. The unemployment rate in Kosovo was the highest in the country: in 1985 it was 3.33 times higher than the Yugoslav average (SGJ 1986:421). For one available job, 43 unemployed persons were available. In such a situation, it became important that the ethnic structure of employees was not always the same as the ethnic composition of population, although the differences were not drastic. In Kosovo, Albanians made up 74% of the active population, but among employees they made up 65%. The Serbs were 17% of the active population, but 26% of the employed. When a job became a privilege, this could become a problem (Horvat 1988:137).

In 1948 the Kosovo population was 62.2% illiterate. But in 1981, Kosovo had the third largest university (almost 50,000 students) in Yugoslavia. With almost 30 students per 1,000 inhabitants, Kosovo had the highest concentration of students in Yugoslavia. Having 61% of the population under the age of 25 (Stambolić 1988:32), in 1978 every third inhabitant of Kosovo was receiving education (Report 1981[13]:158). Not only did this heavily burden the already weak Kosovo economy, but it also created new social and political problems. Kosovo faced the prospect of having a highly educated mass of unemployed at a time when its economy was collapsing. This would not have been such a problem had not the other Yugoslav republics been undergoing economic crises themselves. Both for the reasons of autarky and for objective economic reasons, they became less and less open for young educated Kosovars (mostly Albanian). Another problem was their feelings that Priština University (opened in 1975) was significantly below the quality level of other Yugoslav universities and were dubious about their degrees.

At the same time, the Albanians themselves did not want to move out of the province to other Yugoslav republics to find jobs; they preferred low-paid jobs in Western Europe instead. They were not alone in this respect in Yugoslavia. An analysis of internal migrations in postwar Yugoslavia shows that economic reasons played a secondary role to ethnic ones when it came to changing one republic for another. The 1981 census revealed that only 1,760,333 out of 23 million Yugoslavs changed their permanent settlements from one republic to another during their lives. Although we might expect that people migrated from heavily underdeveloped Kosovo more than from any other part of the country, the Albanians, whose share in the Yugoslav population was 7.7%, made up only 3.4% of migrants (59,754 people). But the other Yugoslav nations also did not follow economic logic. Although Serbs comprised 36.3% of the population in 1981, they made up 48.8% of the migrants. The Montenegrins twice exceeded their quota: a nation of 2.6% made up 5.6% of the migrants. Although the language barrier can explain the hesitations of Macedonians and Albanians to move out of Macedonia and Kosovo, this argument does not explain why the Croats and Bosnian Muslims remained committed to their territories. The directions of migrations show the same trend: the Croats moved predominantly to Croatia and the Serbs to Serbia. The Albanians stayed in Kosovo, despite the economic hardship and political inequality they felt there (Bilandžić 1986:134-6).[14] All of these data actually show a strong process of ethnolinguistic closure occurring within the republics/ provinces that mirrored the autarkism induced by economic and political reform. Nations, formally declared "completed" by Kardelj, were now consolidating.

In some cases, as with the Albanian students, the Albanians even moved from other areas to Kosovo. The University of Priština was the only Yugoslav institution of higher education where one could study in Albanian. This meant that many Albanians from other republics went to study in Priština. The high level of unemployment only encouraged many young (below 24 years of age) Albanians (who made up 61% of the Kosovo population of 1.7 million) to study at the university nearby. The megalomania of political elites and "personal networks of survival" helped many to realize this dream, and the University, equipped for 15,000 students, now had 50,000. There were only 4,000 beds in the student dormitories, and it was not uncommon for two students to share a bed. This all made a good background for various extreme left and nationalist ideologies among the students, whose expectations rose to high.[15]

Yugoslavia was, however, aware of Kosovo's economic problems, and it recognized its development as a priority. Kosovo (together with Bosnia-Herzegovina, Montenegro, and Macedonia) was treated as an underdeveloped region of Yugoslavia to which money from other republics (including Serbia proper, with a level of development about or just slightly below the Yugoslav average) and Vojvodina was redistributed via federal agencies. The Kosovo share in the total amount of money distributed in this way had been constantly increasing ever since 1966. In the 1966-70 period, it amounted to 30%; in the 1971-75 period, 33.3%; in 1976-80, 37%; and for 1981-85 it reached 42.8% (1981:156).[16] In the 1981-86 plan, it was projected that Kosovo would develop 60% faster than the Yugoslav average (Stambolić 1988:31). The economic strength of Kosovo had enlarged 12-fold since the end of the war, twice as much as the Yugoslav average (Stambolić 1988:32). At the same time, this was not felt in the everyday life of the population. The rhetoric of the Kosovo leaders, who argued that Kosovo was lagging behind the others and who urged the others to spend more and more on Kosovo, sounded much more convincing to the population at large. When Kosovo leaders started arguing that Kosovo was in a disadvantaged position compared with all other Yugoslav regions, they spoke from the hearts of the Kosovars.

Kosovo almost entirely depended on economic help from other Yugoslav regions. It was planned that in the 1981-86 period, almost 136 billion Yugoslav dinars would be spent on various investments in Kosovo, of which only 8.7 billion would come from the Kosovo economy itself (Stambolić 1988:31). The share of federal funds in the Kosovo budget was permanently increasing-to more than 80% in 1976-80, from 53% in 1966-70. From 1952 to 1978, total investment in Kosovo increased 19.1 times, and in Serbia without provinces it was 6.6

times, in Vojvodina 2.6 times, and the Yugoslav average was 7.7 times. But like everywhere else, investments in Kosovo were rarely successful and brought little benefit to ordinary people. The Kosovo political elite, using their autonomy in deciding how to spend money from federal sources, directed a large share to political investments. A huge university library was built in the center of Priština, and the most modern radio-television building in the country was constructed there. These were all symbols of Kosovo's new status in Yugoslavia following the 1974 Constitution and the fall of Ranković in 1966. But the efficiency of investment rate was much lower than anywhere else in Yugoslavia: in 1978 it was 33% lower than the already low Yugoslav average (Stambolić 1988:33). When the economic crisis began, the criticism of "wasted investments" was understood as a criticism of Kosovo's political elite. To many in Kosovo, criticism of the low efficiency rate was seen as criticism of Kosovo's population as such.

A separate problem was Kosovo's high birthrate, the highest in Europe. Although in Yugoslavia the annual population growth was 0.7%, in Kosovo it was 2.5%, three and a half times higher (Horvat, 1988:181). In Kosovo, a woman of child-bearing age on average bore 6.6 children, according to the 1971 census, but in "Serbia without provinces" the number was only 2.7. In this sense, the Kosovo Albanians differed significantly from Kosovo's Serbs and Montenegrins. The number of Albanians in Kosovo doubled in the 20 years from 1961 to 1981 - to 1,227 thousand, from 646. If all of Yugoslavia's nationalities followed the same trend, Yugoslavia would in 1981 have had 50 million inhabitants, rather than 23 million.[17] On the other hand, the number of Serbs in Kosovo decreased to 209,000, from 227,000, in the same period. This meant that the share of the Serbs in the population of Kosovo almost halved in this period: to 13.2%, from 23.6%, but the share of the Albanians rose to 77.5%, from 67.1%.[18]

Not only had this trend changed the ethnic structure in Kosovo, but it also affected the demographic structure of Serbia and Yugoslavia. If the high birthrate had continued, the Kosovo population would have increased to 2.53 million in 2000, from 1.76 million in 1985 (SGJ 1986, Horvat 1988:181).[19] Not only would the share of Albanians in Serbia then have increased to almost 25%, but the Kosovo population would also have become larger than that of three Yugoslav republics (Macedonia, Slovenia, and Montenegro) and the Province of Vojvodina. From 1961 to 1981, the share of Albanians in the Yugoslav population rose to 7.7%, from 4.9%. This happened when all the other Yugoslav nations-except the Bosnian Muslims (who increased their share to 8.9%, from 5.3%) and the Macedonians (to 6.0%, from 5.6%), decreased their percentage. Ethnic nationalists among the Serbs, whose share of the Yugoslav population fell to 36.3%, from 42.1%, over the past 20 years, and the Croats (to 19.7%, from 23.2%) felt especially suspicious about this trend. This is partly because of a significant increase in the Yugoslavs,[20] whose share increased to 5.4%, from 1.7%, of the population in the 1961-81 period. Yugoslavism and the high birthrate of Albanians in Kosovo and among Bosnian Muslims (mostly in Bosnia-Herzegovina) were now placed high on the agenda of the Serb and Croat nationalists, to stay there during the whole war in Bosnia and in Kosovo in the late 1980s and the early 1990s.

These facts played an immense role in further political manipulation, with both the Albanian sense of pessimism about their own future and the Serbian fears of being outnumbered by the Albanian birthrate, which many of them saw as politically motivated. When the economic crisis began in 1981, Yugoslav politicians and economists suggested various measures to be introduced in Kosovo, such as (a) imposing birth control; (b) reducing investments in nonprofitable areas; (c) maintaining strict control over the distribution of money donated or borrowed from other republics; (d) adjusting the number of students to real economic needs; and (e) increasing efficiency. All of these measures, however, were rightly seen as pressure on Kosovo's autonomy and as an attempt to reestablish control over the province. Since Kosovo was becoming increasingly identified with its overwhelmingly Albanian population, the measures were seen as an attack on ethnic Albanians. As soon as this happened, an economic and political debate cleared the ground for an interethnic conflict between the Slavs and the Albanians in Kosovo and throughout the country.

In this context, and bearing in mind the "republicanization" of Yugoslavia after 1974, one can easily understand why the Albanians believed that having their own republic in Yugoslavia was the key to their protection from the others. As long as they did not have a republic, they would feel politically unequal.[21] The demand for a republic of Kosovo, in fact, originated from the intellectual elite and some parts of the political elite of Kosovo itself, and emerged for the first time during the constitutional debate in 1968. The whole debate was kept behind closed doors, and only in the late 1980s were the first documents about it published.[22] They revealed a heated debate within the Kosovo political and intellectual elite on the issue of a republic. In general, the intellectual elite (concentrated at the University) demanded the status of a republic for Kosovo with full rights to self-determination. Their demand was based on historical and ethnic arguments. Historically, the Yugoslav Communists argued that Kosovo decided to join Serbia after the War "of its own free will and on the basis of the right to self-determination." Only because of Ranković's policy of oppression against the Kosovo Albanians did this "right" disappear from the constitutive acts in the first two postwar decades. The removal of Ranković in 1966 and the introduction of the new-Kardeljist-policy on the national question put the Kosovo question again on the agenda. The Albanian intellectuals from Kosovo fully supported Kardelj's concept of the national question, but they argued that the Albanians were a nation like any other in Yugoslavia, and that their non-Slavic origins were not sufficient reason for treating them differently.[23] The argument of the federal leadership, that a Republic of Kosovo would mean the creation of a second Albanian state was rejected: "There are two Korean states and two German states. Why is it impossible to have two Albanian states?" they argued.[24]

The Albanian Communist leaders from Kosovo (some of whom also came from the university, like Mahmut Bakalli, the young leader of the Priština Party Committee), took a middle-of-the-road policy. They knew that the demand for a republic could not be accepted by Serbia or Tito himself, but they in fact used the radical demands of the intellectual elite to extend the autonomy of the province as far as they could. As Dragoslav Marković put it:

> I do not think that all of them are in favor of the weakening of the republic as whole, but it is clear that all are united when it comes to new concessions in the economic, financial, and other fields. (13 January 1968, 1988:48)

The Kosovo leaders demanded a status that would be practically equal to the republics and only nominally different from them. They demanded a constitution (and not a statute) for Kosovo, a separate state holiday, a flag the same as that of the Albanian state flag with the small exception of a five-pointed star, a change of name from Kosovo-Metohija to Kosovo, and equal representation in the federal institutions. But most important, they demanded the redefinition of Yugoslavia in such a way as to incorporate the nationalities on the same terms as nations. Although the Albanian intellectual elite demanded the abolition of the term nationality and the use of the word nation for the Albanians, the political elite found a compromise: Yugoslavia was to be a state of equal nations and nationalities.

These issues, however, split the Albanian and Serb leaders at each level. Members of the Albanian intellectual elite were dissatisfied with the proposals of its political elite, demanding a referendum on them. When they failed to secure one through the institutions, they urged and organized student demonstrations in November and December 1968. The demands of the students were the same as those of their professors: a Kosovo republic. The Communist leadership of Kosovo, however, also split on how to react to such demands. The majority (led by young Mahmut Bakalli and Fadil Hoxha, the doyen of Kosovo politicians and representative of Kosovo in the Belgrade federal leadership) was opposed to harsh measures against them, since this would destroy the Kosovo intelligentsia and recall the worst days of Aleksandar Ranković only two years after his removal.

The Serbs in the Kosovo leadership also split into two groups. While one argued that the demand for a Kosovo republic was nationalistic and counterrevolutionary, the most prominent political representative of the Kosovo Serbs

(Katarina Patrnogić Išma) was of a different opinion. She argued that the issue of republic or province was only secondary to the class dimension of the problem. Although a Serb herself, Patrnogić was seen by Serbian leaders as a promoter of the demand for a Kosovo Republic (Marković, 20 July 1968, 1987:79).

Lastly, the Serbian leaders also differed on how to approach Kosovo's demands. Miloš Minić showed much more willingness to compromise than others. Minić argued that "in the system of self-management, every sociopolitical community has some elements of sovereignty, and thus the provinces have it as well, for which reason we could think of Kosovo becoming a republic" (Marković 2 June 1968, 1988:68). Dobrivoje Radosavljević, a leading Serbian Communist, was also "soft" on the Kosovo issue. He was "obsessed" Marković said, by the "Serbian historical opportunity" to prove that the Serbs did not want to suppress the Albanians and was therefore willing to compromise perhaps even on the issue of a Republic of Kosovo (Marković, 11 May 1968, 1988:66). But most Serbian leaders rejected any possibility of such a prospect. In this they had Tito's support[25] and the tacit agreement of the other Yugoslav Republics, whose interest was only to keep the issue of provinces strictly within Serbia.[26] After a heated debate the Serbian leaders accepted some compromises and came closer to the Kosovo Communist leaders, but on the clear understanding that statehood for Kosovo was out of the question.[27] Kosovo and Vojvodina were declared to be constitutive elements of the federation and were represented in all federal institutions directly, independently of Serbia, but the demand for a republic was swiftly rejected. As with other parts of Yugoslavia, the 1974 compromise left both sides equally dissatisfied (inasmuch as they were equally satisfied) and convinced that they could have got much more but from their "soft" Communist leaders. For Kosovo intellectuals, however, there was one more lesson they learned, that their status in Yugoslavia was not given once and forever and that it could well be changed if there was the political will to do this. As one of the participants in the 1968 constitutional debate in the Kosovo town of Dragaš said, "There will be no republic as long as Tito is alive" (Mišović 1987:162). But everyone knew that this would not be forever. And just like the Serbs, whose *Blue Book* initiative was rejected by Tito, the nationalist Albanians waited for this moment to come. In the meantime, both sides were mobilizing public opinion to support their views (Mišović 1987:187).

5.2.2. The 1981 Protests in Kosovo: the Beginning of the State Crisis of Yugoslavia

It is today widely argued that the Yugoslav crisis began with the Albanian demonstrations in Kosovo in Spring 1981. When analyzing the Albanian public protests, many authors saw them as the first public sign of discontent with the solution of the national question, which was meant to be finally off the agenda following the semiconfederalization of the 1974 Constitution. The Albanian demonstrations are treated as the first demand, if not secessionist, then certainly nationalist, in a long chain of those that followed it in the last decade of Yugoslavia.

This interpretation, however, neglects important social, economic, and ideological dimensions of the protests. Although there should be no doubt that the national question inspired many participants in them, the protests of the Kosovo Albanians in 1981 were not only, and to certain extent not even primarily, motivated by nationalism, but also by egalitarianism, i.e., by a different concept of Socialism from the Yugoslav self-managing and semiconfederalist one. Those who participated in protests (largely the students in Priština) saw in Enver Hoxha's Albania and in the Soviet type of state Socialism a plausible alternative to what they recognized as injustice in the economic, political, and ethnic sense. To Yugoslav political leaders, therefore, their protests looked exactly like the type of danger that Kardelj predicted as possible after his and Tito's death. The egalitarian demands of the Albanian students in Kosovo therefore posed the greatest possible danger for the Yugoslav self-managing project, not only because they could destabilize the fragile balance between ethnic groups in the country, but also because they undermine the narrative that insisted on self-management as a better form of Socialism than any other.

It is in this light that one should understand the reasons why the Yugoslav leaders labeled the organizers of the public protests counterrevolutionaries, and not only ethnic separatists or secessionists. It is also for this reason that the regime decided (unlike in the 1968 Belgrade demonstrations, and even after the 1971 Croatian Spring protests) not to compromise on the students' demands, but to suppress them by all available means.

The social and ideological dimension of the problem may be traced down in the chronology of the actual events. It all began with discontent over bad food and low quality of services in the Student Refectory in Priština on 11 March 1981 and continued in street demonstrations that night.[28] Few others joined the protest, which seemed to be purely socially motivated. However, when a rumor spread that police had arrested a few demonstrators, the students went on the streets of Priština. Together with the people who joined them, there were from three to four thousand demonstrators. Their main slogans were directed against what the demonstrators felt to be injustice in a regime that promised justice: "We want deeds, not words"; "Some sleep in armchairs, and others are without bread"; "We want our friends back from prison" (Report 1981:5). With only rare exceptions, no nationalist slogans were shouted, and ethnic issues seemed not to be on the agenda. The demonstrations ended with police intervention at 2:30 the next morning. About a hundred demonstrators were arrested. The political leadership of Priština, which was summoned next day, concluded that the demonstrations had surprised them, since there "had been no indication of them before they happened (Report 1981:7). Although they recognized that the main demands were about student welfare, they assessed the demonstrations as "politically damaging" (Report 1981:7), since they could be used by "enemies."

It seemed that this was only an episode, since in the next two weeks there were no similar protests. But on 26 March, when it was obvious that some of the detained demonstrators had not been released as expected, the demonstrations were renewed throughout the province. In Priština, several thousand demonstrators clashed with police who prevented them from approaching the central city square where the Relay of Youth (*Štafeta Mladosti*) was expected on its way through the country. Unlike during the previous protests, their demands were now political as well as economic: "We are Albanians, not Yugoslavs"; "Kosova[29] Republic"; "Unity"; "Unity with Albania"; "*Trepča* [the main Kosovo mine industry-a symbol of the Kosovo working class] is working for others"; "*Trepča* works, Belgrade builds"; "Long live Marxism-Leninism, Down with Revisionism." In contrast to the previous protests, the demonstrators now used the ethnic dimension of the problem, claiming that inequality is-at least in part-based on the unfair treatment of Albanians in Yugoslavia. By adding ethnic and ideological dimensions to the already existent social and economic ones, the protests became a potential source of destabilization of the whole system.

This is why the political elite reacted brutally, sparing no force to crush the Kosovo demonstrations. In clashes between demonstrators and police on the first day, 32 demonstrators were injured (Report 1981:11). On 28 March 1981, Aslan Fazlia, president of the Party organization in Priština (Albanian himself) said that the character of the demonstrations was nationalistic and counterrevolutionary. Fazlia announced tough police measures against the demonstrators. Full-scale arrests were launched in Kosovo. This, however, only fueled student protests. Many students saw the wave of coercion as a "return of Ranković's methods" once Tito had gone. Two days later, on 30 March 1981, students of the three largest faculties at Priština University (Law, Economics, and Science-Mathematics) declared a boycott of teaching. On 1 April 1981, the demonstrations swept throughout Kosovo, with new and more radical political demands. When 17 policemen were injured in clashes with demonstrators, the army moved in to secure state institutions. The police did not manage to break up the demonstrations that day. When the reports came that some workers had joined the demonstrations, the Committee for People's Self-Defense of Kosovo (the crisis headquarters of the Kosovo leadership, presided over by Party President Mahmut Bakalli) decided to ask the army to move tanks onto the streets. At the same time, police reinforcements from Central Serbia were stopped by a roadblock near Podujevo. To force the police to withdraw back to "Serbia" (i.e., territory of the republic outside the provinces), the demonstrators took hostages from 34 houses of local Serbs and Montenegrins. Only when additional police came from Priština, were the hostages released. Throughout Kosovo, windows were smashed in many cars, shops, and state institutions. Demonstrators demanded a republic, "unification of all Albanian territories," and "brotherhood among Albanians" (Horvat 1988:140). In Belgrade, an urgent joint meeting of the presidency of Yugoslavia and the presidency of the LCY was convened. The Yugoslav leaders declared a "crisis situation in Kosovo"and a "state of emergency in Priština." They ordered the level of combat readiness to be increased in all army units in Yugoslavia, and the reserve force of the army and police to be mobilized. All republics were asked to send their police troops to Kosovo. The Kosovo Minister of the Interior banned public meetings in the province, and the government of Kosovo (Executive Council of the Province) ordered all schools, the university, and other student institutions (such as halls of residence and refectories) to be closed.

However, on 3 April 1981 the demonstrations reemerged in Vučitrn, Uroševac, Vitina, and Kosovska Mitrovica. New slogans were added: "We don't want our children to be beaten up by the police from outside Kosovo"; "Republic, constitution, by agreement or by force." But the additional police force with full authority (from federal, republican, and provincial institutions) to react immediately and resolutely, prevented these and further demonstrations in Kosovo. The situation was finally under police control. But it was only the beginning of the deep state crisis in Yugoslavia, one that would lead to its dissolution.

5.2.3. The Reaction of the Elite

The Yugoslav leaders, as they publicly admitted, were surprised by what happened.[30] The federal institutions relied on reports by the leadership of the province, which simply painted the situation in the province in bright colors.[31] When the demonstrations occurred in 1981, both the federal leadership and that of Serbia claimed that they had no independent access to the real situation in the Province. What surprised them most was the extent of the violence used by the demonstrators and the relatively large participation. The panic reaction of the Yugoslav leadership (which declared a state emergency in the province and sent the armed forces to crush the demonstrations; an overwhelming campaign to condemn and prosecute demonstrators was also launched) was a consequence of this.[32]

Tito visited Kosovo in 1979 in his last major visit to any republic/province before his death. This is how Dušan Dragosavac, then secretary of the LCY Central Committee, describes Tito's impressions during the interview I conducted with him in April 1998:

> I traveled in the same car with Tito, which enabled me to observe his reaction. He was most fascinated by what we saw. There were thousands and thousands of flags of all types: Albanian, Serbian, Yugoslav, Party, even Turkish, among others. He was also impressed with the folk customs, the well-built villages, and the young girls in jeans. At one moment, he told me: "You see, here it was absolutely impossible to see young girls without a [traditional Muslim] veil immediately after the war, and now they wear jeans!" Then we met a young couple, just married: they had brought flowers to the monument of Boro and Ramiz.[33] All this impressed him very much....He was also pleased to hear an Albanian, the party secretary in Priština, address him in very good, entirely fluent Serbian.[34]

Despite this idyllic reception in Kosovo, Tito was informed about the findings of the Party's special commission on the nationality question, chaired by Dušan Dragosavac. The commission was created in 1978, and presented its report in 1979.

> The main conclusion was that there were no major interethnic problems in Yugoslavia, except as regards two ethnic groups: the Roma population [Gypsies] and the Albanians....We had concluded that the Albanians had developed to a level at which their aspirations rose higher than the opportunities we could offer. This had created economic and potentially political problems that we did not know how to deal with.[35]

Tito was surprised at this finding, but used his visit to warn once again about the necessity to preserve a good relationship between Serbs and Albanians, and invited other republics to help speed up the development of Kosovo.[36]

The Kosovo events were the first sign of public discontent with the constitution of Yugoslavia after 1974. They were particularly unpleasant because they happened less than a year after Tito's death, had a relatively mass character, and may have had an international dimension.[37] In many respects, they reminded the Yugoslav leadership of the 1968 demonstrations in Belgrade and those of 1971 in Zagreb. Having still fresh in their minds the memory of Tito's swift reaction on both occasions, they did not want to fall short of the Titoist formula.

Inasmuch as the demonstrations were a serious threat to the stability of the regime, however, they proved to be a perfect opportunity to launch a new campaign for structural changes in the Yugoslav political system. In this context one should understand why the various groups within the elite did not attempt to remove the event from the agenda as soon as possible, but-on the contrary-even blew it up out of all proportions, taking into account that it was successfully crushed by the police and that neither in its real size (it was localized and with a limited number of victims) nor in its results did it deserve to be given such attention. In the debate that followed, the Kosovo crisis proved to be the perfect case to be exploited by (1) the Serbian leadership-which argued that this was a necessary and unavoidable consequence of the overall disintegration of the country and of the rejection of the 1977 *Blue Book* initiative; (2) the Yugoslav leaders, who argued that Yugoslavia was endangered and that the real threat came, as Kardelj had written, from dogmatist and state Socialist forces; (3) the new leaders in Kosovo,[38] who manipulated them to show that their predecessors were incompetent; (4) the "Belgrade critical intelligentsia," who used it to revive Ćosić's and Ranković's position on Kosovo; (5) the Albanian nationalists themselves, who argued that they had much stronger support among the Albanians than was really so. Later in this chapter, I will map out the official discourses of the first three groups-the Yugoslav, Serbian, and Kosovo political elite, and in the next two chapters I will analyze the reaction of various groups in opposition to the regime, following the protests in Kosovo. I argue that the same ideological commitment, which prevented the Yugoslav leaders from changing the obviously inefficient economic system, now caused the stalemate in their action on the Kosovo issue. It was their commitment to Kardelj's "constitutive concept" that motivated their actions.

5.2.3.1. Discourse One: The Federal Political Elite's Reaction to the Kosovo Protests of 1981

Among the Yugoslav leaders, some differences occurred over the relative importance of the various causes of the crisis.[39] But most of them agreed on four points, which then became the mainstream interpretation of the Kosovo events by the Yugoslav political leaders in the first half of the 1980s, only to be changed with Milošević's rise to power in 1987.

First, the demonstrations were an expression of class struggle (Bakalli 1981:45), and they constituted a counterrevolution (Vlaškalić 1981:90, Krunić 1981:130). As such, they were "directed against all nations and nationalities in Kosovo" (Vlaškalić 1981:90), which therefore should act together to defeat it. They did not constitute a conflict between the nations in Kosovo, but between the minority of discontented nationalists and the large majority of Albanians and Serbs who remained supportive of the Yugoslav system. As a hostile act, the demonstrations did not and could not succeed in involving the masses of any nation or nationality, including the Albanians in Kosovo. On the contrary, "they have nothing in common with the real attitudes of the large majority of working people and citizens of Kosovo, with the interests of Albanians, Serbs, Montenegrins, and members of other nations in SAP Kosovo (presidency SFRY and CC LCY 1981:20). Furthermore, the "enemies and their demonstrations have failed to weaken the unity, brotherhood, togetherness, and mutual respect between all nations and nationalities of Kosovo, for which one should thank the maturity and consciousness of the Albanian nationality...and its activity against Albanian nationalism within its own nation" (Nimani 1981:22).[40] This only confirmed that the Albanian leaders from Kosovo unanimously condemned the demonstrations, arguing in favor of Yugoslav unity. They really did not differ in this respect from their Serbian colleagues-on the contrary, following the Communist logic that Communists should fight against nationalism in their own nation, the Albanian Communists led this campaign.

Second, the main cause of unrest was alleged to be bureaucratic statism, which was much stronger in Kosovo than anywhere else in the country. Speaking about this, the president of the Serbian Central Committee, Tihomir Vlaškalić, said that "socioeconomic development in Kosovo was to a very large extent linked to the political factor...which created conditions in which statism and bureaucratic consciousness were growing, while self-managerial practice was underdeveloped" (Vlaškalić, 1981:91, 94-5). Offering a highly ideological interpretation of the causes of the discontent, Vlaškalić said that workers (and people in general) felt powerless to decide upon the results of their work. The development of self-management was, therefore, seen as the main condition for resolving the problem (Vlaškalić, 1981:94).

Third, the discontent was also inspired by economic factors. This point was emphasized by non-Serbian members of the Yugoslav political elite. In the words of the Macedonian representative with the federal presidency, Lazar Koliševski, the unrealistic ambitions of the Kosovo leaders had contributed to this problem (Koliševski 1981:67). This was especially so regarding the university, which had been developed against the real needs of Kosovo industry (Shukrija 1981:72, Koliševski 1981:68). Such economic unrealism became a heavy burden on the economy and the main source of discontent among the young, educated but unemployed people in the province.[41] The president of the Slovene Central Committee, France Popit, concluded that "economic nationalism" was the main cause of the Kosovo demonstrations (1981:126). Boško Šiljegović (Serbia) went a step further, arguing that economic nationalism would be much harder to beat than "ideological" nationalism (1981:133). "We alone have created the economic basis for our own nationalisms," Šiljegović said. Lazar Koliševski came to the same conclusion: the economic closure of the Yugoslav republics and provinces not only led to economic nationalism, but it also prevented the development of a united Yugoslav working class (Koliševski 1981:66). This all went against Kardelj's idea of the integration of Yugoslavia through the association of free producers. Economic disintegration was therefore seen as the major cause of Albanian nationalism in Kosovo.

Fourth, the influence from abroad (mostly from the neighboring and Communist Albania ruled by Enver Hoxha) was declared to be another important element. At first, the Yugoslav leaders hesitated to accuse Albania of encouraging demonstrations in Kosovo (Dolanc 1981:35). But on 8 April 1981, *Zëri i Popullit,* the main Albanian daily from Tirana, published a commentary on the Kosovo events in which Yugoslavia was criticized for using police force against the demonstrators. The Albanian daily saw in the police intervention a "reappearance of the old spirit of the Karadjordjevićs and the shadow of Ranković," warning Belgrade that it "should not have happened that Serbian militia, armed to the teeth, surrounded Kosovo cities...." (1981:40-1). *Zëri i Popullit* called Kosovo students "brave" and reminded Yugoslavia that "the Albanian population, living as a compact unit on a compact territory, was divided between three republics of the Yugoslav federation," and that "in Bosnia-Herzegovina, in Kosovo, and wherever Albanians live, a Muslim nationality has been created. It has been said that the Muslim nationality was a specificity of Yugoslavia," *Zëri i Popullit* said, arguing that the "Muslim nationality" was invented only to reduce the number of Albanians living in these three republics. The article invited Belgrade to respect "democratic freedoms and political rights," which met with a strong response in a commentary published by *Politika* the next day: "A regime known as a bunker of ultra-Stalinist dogmatism and despotism, known for its police terror against its own citizens, in which the regime has not succeeded in attaining even a similar level of development to that of Kosovo, has tried to present itself as a "defender of human rights," "democracy and freedom," said *Politika,* presenting figures and facts about Kosovo's rapid development. Priština's daily in the Albanian language, *Rilindja,* also criticized Tirana for the commentary in *Zëri i Popullit* (1981:42-4). The polemics continued on 17 May 1981 when an unsigned long article was published in *Zëri i Popullit,* entitled, "The status of a republic for Kosova is a just demand."[42] "Kosova seeks the status of a republic within the Yugoslav Federation. This status represents the aspiration of a great people, who rightly demand the 'status of sovereignty' and not that of a 'national minority,' which it was unjustly allocated at Jajce.[43]" The Albanian official daily then reminded the Serbian leaders (especially Petar Stambolić, whom they called an "incorrigible great Serb") that the Albanians are "one ethnic entity, one people." Repeating the arguments of the Albanian intellectuals of 1968, *Zëri i Popullit* said this:

> There are two Germanies, one in the East and one in the West, just as there are two Koreas, one North and one South. However, nobody doubts that there is a single German people and nation, just as there is a single Korean people and nation (*ZP*: 1981:52).

Naturally, this stand by the Tirana daily encouraged the conclusion that the demonstrations in Kosovo were organized and supported by the most rigid Stalinist regime of the time. At the Session of the Central Committee of the LCY on 6 May 1981, the president of the Serbian presidency, Dobrivoje Vidić, accused Enver Hoxha of inspiring the riot in his speech of 8 November 1978, in which he said that "Albanians in Yugoslavia were more numerous than two Yugoslav republics together, that they were one nation, which was deliberately divided between two republics and one province and that the Albanians in Yugoslavia had no constitutional rights" (1981:125). Macedonian Lazar Mojsov mentioned the clandestine activities of Albanian spies as the main cause of the events (1981:121). Some Yugoslav party leaders admitted their surprise that an ideology and system such as the Enver Hoxha's Albanian Stalinism could have attracted any support among Kosovo Albanians, whose level of freedom and of economic wealth was significantly higher than those of the Albanians in Albania. But to Miloš Minić (one of the leading Kardeljists in the Serbian and Yugoslav political elite), this was just a confirmation of how right Kardelj had been when he claimed that Stalinism was a much more realistic (and therefore more dangerous) alternative than liberalism in Yugoslavia (Minić 1981:140; Koliševski 1981:66). The Yugoslav leaders used this opportunity to reaffirm another postulate of their rhetoric: that both ultraleft and ultraright forces were hostile to self-management. The Albanian Party of Labor (and, naturally, the Albanian demonstrators in Kosovo) was a force that united two such concepts: Stalinism as ultraleft and nationalism as ultraright (Hasani 1981:75). An additional illustration of this left-right cooperation against Yugoslav self-management was found in the political composition of the Kosovo émigrés who supported the demonstrations: the Balists (Albanian wartime Quislings) and the Cominformists (postwar pro-Stalinists) were acting together (Dolanc 1981:31). Paradoxically, Yugoslav leaders succeeded in presenting the Kosovo events as perfect evidence of how farsighted the LCY analysis was.[44]

5.2.3.2. Discourse Two: The Serbian Political Elite's Reaction to the Kosovo Protests of 1981

Although most Yugoslav politicians agreed with these four main points, the differences became unbridgeable on the fifth potential cause of the Kosovo event, which Serbian leaders suggested. Serbian leaders argued that the 1978 compromise on the *Blue Book* was the major reason for the emergence of the 1981 Kosovo crisis. The Serbian position was formulated at the Session of the Central Committee of the LC Serbia on 6 May 1981, to be elaborated at the November 1981 and December 1984 sessions held on the Kosovo situation.

Serbian leaders used the 1981 demonstrations to relaunch a campaign for changes in the relations between the republic and provinces, which had been abruptly stopped by Tito in 1978. Dragoslav Marković, the leading author of the *Blue Book* of 1977, now appeared as the sharpest critic of the Yugoslav refusal to confront the policy of the political closure in both provinces. The events in Kosovo, Marković argued, were the result of a policy that was not to be attributed only to Kosovo, but also to Vojvodina and to the Yugoslav republics in general (1981:99). He reminded members of the CC that the equality of status between Serbia and its provinces was "clearly anticonstitutional." The illusion that this could change (and that provinces could become equal to republics) was the main reason for dissatisfaction in Kosovo. Talking about Kosovo, but thinking also about Vojvodina, Marković said that "Kosovo has its own republic, and that is Serbia."

> The disintegration of Serbia would be only the first step toward the disintegration of Yugoslavia....The unresolved issue of the constitutional structuring of Serbia is today the only real social, the only socioeconomic and sociopolitical root of Serbian nationalism that has not yet been cut. (1981:103)

Opening up (for the first time since Ćosić's debate in 1968) the issue of the exodus of the Kosovo Serbs in the past 20 years, Marković warned members of the Serbian Central Committee that they should not bear any sense of guilt when they raised their voices against such a tragedy.

> It is not a natural matter that the ethnic composition of those who left Kosovo is such that the majority of them were Serbs and Montenegrins.

Marković concluded his speech quoting from Tito's speech in Zagreb in May 1945. Tito then said the following:

> "Many still do not understand what federative Yugoslavia means....It does not mean drawing a borderline between this and that federal unit, so that behind it they can do whatever they want or can, and I am here going to do what I can do. No! These borders, to make a comparison, ought to be like the white bands on one marble pillar. The borders of the federal republics in federative Yugoslavia are not borders of division; they are borders of unification. (quoted by Marković 1981:101)

Marković's speech met with support from three other leading Serbian politicians: Špiro Galović, Petar Stambolić, and Ivan Stambolić.[45] These four, two of whom (P. Stambolić and Marković) were of an older generation and two (Galović and I. Stambolić) of a younger one, formulated the Serbian discourse on the Kosovo crisis in 1981 and on the relationship between Serbia and its provinces from 1981 to 1984.[46]

The main elements of this discourse on Kosovo were:

First, the economic crisis, Kosovo, and its relationship to Serbia are indicators and the outcome of the same problem: disintegration in Yugoslavia. Therefore they should be treated at the same time.

Second, the disintegration is a result of misinterpretation of the constitution (Stambolić 1981/1988:61) and of its obstruction by bureaucratic statism. Nationalism is an anti–self-management action tolerated, supported, and even directly organized by bureaucratic state structures throughout the country. In Serbia, this bureaucratic statism had its base in autonomism in Vojvodina and separatism in Kosovo. Although the bureaucrats based their legitimacy on their endless attacks on enemies, they left the issue of their own responsibility for the political and economic crisis untouched (Galović 1989:80).[47]

Third, self-management remains the main ideological postulate, one that should not be abandoned. It was once again treated as "the basis of democratic solutions of the national question" in Yugoslavia (Galović 1981/1989:130), and as the precondition for the resolution of the economic crisis (Stambolić 1981/1988:50). The society of the future should be an integrated self-managing community of people (Stambolić 1983/1988:63). But inasmuch as self-management was to be developed as a substitute for statism, Stambolić clearly objected to "illusions" that the state itself was an enemy of self-management and to its being equated with statism (1984/1988:90). The autonomists were protecting state functions where they were not necessary and obstructing them when they needed to be protected or developed.

Fourth, just as the state should not be equated with statism, so unity should not be treated as centralism. There is only one working class in Yugoslavia, and it should be united. The idea (Vladimir Bakarić's) of "national economies" had been accepted without serious thought about the consequences. It led to nationalism (Stambolić 1981/1988:23).

Fifth, Serbian Communists continued to oppose any recentralization (Galović 1981/1989:130), but centralism, they argued, was not a realistic danger in the present circumstances. The federal state was so weak that it could not, even if it wanted, encourage or support any idea of the renewal of centralism in Yugoslavia (Galović 1981/1989:81). On the other hand, the decentralized statism in the republics and provinces was a real danger. This it should be noted, was a departure from Kardelj's beliefs that Yugoslavia could be endangered by centralization and not by disintegration.

Sixth, particularism and autarkism were developed not only in Kosovo, but as a general trend also in Yugoslavia. "Without other particularism in Yugoslavia, there would be no Kosovo particularism" (Galović 1981/1989:36). On the issue of autonomy, the two Serbian provinces shared thoughts and practice (Stambolić

1981/1988:57). Particularism led the country to the brink of dissolution. Unrealistic investment was the result of "everybody's closing in on themselves and trying to structure their industry as if Yugoslavia would disintegrate at any moment" (Galović 1981/1989:37). Such a policy simply did not count with Yugoslavia any longer. By doing this, "subjective forces" (including the Party) "expressed their concerns with the interests of their own nation to such an extent and in such a manner that it became difficult to distinguish them from nationalist rhetoric" (Galović 1981/1989:38). This tendency must be stopped. If not, then "Communists would, whether they wanted to or not, find themselves in conflict with one another on a nationalist basis in a dispute in which their arguments and rhetoric would not differ much from those in a bourgeois society" (Galović 1981/1989:38). "Kosovo-Republic" in fact meant "Province = Republic," and this is what should not be tolerated (Stambolić 1981/1988:62). Action should therefore be taken not only against the current Kosovo leadership, but also against all other autonomists and particularists in the country.

Seventh, with regard to Serbian nationalism, Serbian Communists concluded that they would not change their position. In their opposition to Serbian nationalism they could not be mistaken, even when acting too eagerly (Stambolić 1981/1988:22). But nationalism could be defeated only at its root, and, as Marković said, "the only still uncut root of Serbian nationalism was in the undefined relations in Serbia." If the problems in Kosovo were not resolved, Petar Stambolić said, Serbian Communists would face "a serious task in fighting Serbian nationalism" (Report 1981:128). Verbal opposition to nationalist books, plays, and pamphlets should be only a part of the public action against nationalism. It was a necessary but not a sufficient condition for its defeat. By emphasizing only its verbal side, Communists spent too much energy fighting nationalism in an inefficient way: they did not attack "the main reasons for its appearance, which could be found only in bureaucratic statism (Galović 1981/1989:56,68). The focus of antinationalist activities should therefore be shifted to real problems. Instead of being "Socialist apostles," Communists should eliminate the real generators of nationalism. "Criticism of autarky would miss the target if it did not aim at what 'legitimizes' the autarky" (Galović 1981/1989:59).

Eighth, it is true that every nationalism is dangerous and should meet with sincere and strong opposition (Galović 1981/1989:132), primarily by the Communists in the nation in which it appears. But not all nationalisms are equally dangerous at the same time. At this moment, the most dangerous is Albanian nationalism, since this is the one that is active. The danger of Albanian nationalism is still neglected. By talking about nationalism *in abstracto*, one could even encourage the really active nationalists.

Ninth, no one in Yugoslavia has reason to fear a strong and united Serbia, which is a precondition, and not a hindrance, for a strong and united Yugoslavia. The idea that a weak Serbia means a strong Yugoslavia was damaging and should be abandoned (Koliševski 1981:67).

Tenth, the debate on the relationship between Serbia and its provinces in 1977-78 was based on a wrong assessment of the situation, and Communists should "be brave enough to admit it."[48] Ignoring the facts and warnings expressed in this debate (mostly in the *Blue Book*) resulted in the surprise at the 1981 events in Kosovo (Stambolić 1981/1988:56).

Eleventh, in general, Communists should not be hostages of their own regulations and laws. "De-Kardeljisation" would not occur as a consequence of changes, but from a refusal to change laws, which caused inefficiency and disintegration. While Serbian Communists did not propose changes in the Constitution, they started criticizing the Associated Labor Act (ALA). It was true, Galović said, that the ALA had not been fully implemented, but one should ask why this was so (1981/1989:134). "In a normative sense, we have been too optimistic.... In regard to some provisions, we need to start from the beginning," Stambolić argued in 1983 (1988:72). The interests of the working class were still at the focus of Communist rhetoric. But to the Serbian Communists, it had become clear that anything that went against the efficiency and unity of the working class went against its interests (Stambolić 1983/1988:79).

Lastly, the Stabilization Program (Kraigher's Program) was seen as a good first step toward economic reforms. It was welcomed for four reasons: (a) it was an example of a *modus operandi* between politicians and experts; (b) it proved that cooperation on the Yugoslav level was not only possible, but much easier among experts than among "bureaucratic elites"; (c) it demanded a radical reversal of the disintegration of the economy; and (d) it recognized that Serbia was economically lagging behind the other republics (Stambolić 1984/1989:89). But this program met with strong political resistance from statists and was therefore facing failure. Economic reform was thus impossible as long as political issues had not been debated (Galović 1984/1989:60). Political reform was the precondition for the resolution of both the Kosovo and the economic crisis in the country.

By arguing in favor of political reforms and for changes in political practice, Serbian Communists now became the leading reformers within the Yugoslav political elite. Their demand for reforms (for which they were soon named "reformers of the constitution."[49] pushed them into conflict with the most loyal Kardeljists in other republics (especially in Slovenia) and in both Serbian provinces (Kosovo and Vojvodina).

5.2.3.3. Discourse Three: the Provinces

The main position of the provinces (formulated mostly by Vojvodina, which took over the role of the mouthpiece for the weakened Kosovo)[50] can be summarized in the following four points:

First, the core of the problem was in undeveloped self-management and not in the relationship between sociopolitical communities. Integration in Yugoslavia could be successful only as an association of free producers and not as statist integration. The national question and self-management were inseparable processes. Any attempt to deny this would be a diminution of workers' rights to decide on their surplus value (Popović 1982:88). Any attempt by "certain republican leaderships in the League of Communists" to bring the national relationship back to the preconstitutional situation...would result in a conflict with the current level of the development of self-management" (Popović 1982:89). This would be an "unhistorical direction."

Second, self-management and the decentralization of state structure are major achievements of the Yugoslav Communist movement, and as such they should not be abandoned (Popović 1982:86). Provinces were not gifts or inventions by Tito and Kardelj, but expressions of the permanent efforts of the CPY/LCY to resolve the national question in Yugoslavia. Apart from ethnic considerations, there were also historical reasons for their existence. Vojvodina and Kosovo decided to join the Republic of Serbia as separate units in 1945. Vojvodina's status within the party structure was until 1945 equal to that of Serbia. The autonomy of the provinces was guaranteed immediately after the war and is therefore a nonchangeable element of Yugoslav federalism.[51] What happened in the 1967-74 period was only a further development of their autonomy as a consequence of the decentralization of Yugoslavia and not an action against Serbia or anyone else.

Third, the events in Kosovo were being used to promote the recentralization of Yugoslavia. Serbian nationalism was gaining strength, especially in the media and cultural institutions. "The outburst of Albanian nationalism in Kosovo has revived all other nationalisms in Yugoslavia as a whole, and especially greater Serbian nationalism," said Dušan Popović.[52] The main idea of this nationalism was that both autonomous provinces should be abolished. The Serbian leaders had not been sufficiently aware of this danger.

Fourth, by opening up a constitutional debate in such a form, the Serbian Communists did not help the real fight against Albanian nationalism. On the contrary, it was impossible to beat the Albanian separatists if the autonomy of Kosovo and Vojvodina decreased.

The provinces, therefore, insisted that no significant changes in the 1974 Constitution were necessary and that no return to statism should be allowed.

They argued that the "class dimension" of the problem was not understood in Serbia (Krunić 1981:130). The Communists from Vojvodina also opposed the "soft approach" toward liberal intellectuals in Belgrade, arguing that they were in fact Serbian nationalists.[53] They rejected the notion that Serbian nationalism was weaker than Albanian nationalism, even at this particular moment, immediately after 1981. If the Serbian leaders, they argued, showed any sign of abandonment of the Kardeljist concept of Socialism, and especially his concept of the national question, they would come close to the Serbian nationalist opposition. The Communists of Vojvodina-especially the Serbs among them-believed that it was their duty to warn of this possibility. In the early 1980s, they therefore became the most conservative part of the League of Communists, one that distinguished itself by its antidemocratic conservatism and by fighting nationalism wherever any sign of anti-Communism appeared.[54]

5.2.3.4. The Position of Slovenia and Croatia: the "Defenders of the Constitution"

The other Yugoslav republics, still hesitating to change much in the economic and especially in the political system, now found in the Vojvodinan Communists an excellent ally. Their opposition to growing Serbian demands for changes now could not be dismissed as the result of their "anti-Serbian prejudice," since the Vojvodinan Serbs themselves (as well as the Croatian and Bosnian Serbs among the Communist leaders) became the most stubborn opponents of the Serbian leadership.[55] By restricting their action to the support of their colleagues in Vojvodina, the Slovene, Bosnian, and most of the Croatian and some of the Macedonian and Montenegrin members of the Central Committee tried to avoid direct involvement in the sensitive issue of relationships within Serbia. They insisted that Kosovo was primarily a Serbian issue, for which reason the issue of Kosovo was not on the agenda of any federal forum from 1981 to 1985. But just like Tito in 1978, the federal leaders from the republics other than Serbia showed more understanding for Vojvodina's self-management (class) argument than for Serbian statist (nationalist) views. They still insisted on the Kardeljist view that if anything could really endanger Yugoslavia, it was not separatism, but centralism and Serbian nationalism.[56]

The Slovenes, and many others in the Yugoslav political elite, believed that the Serbs were using the Kosovo events to promote their demand for changes, for which reason they (the Serbs) exaggerated the proportions of the Kosovo crisis. The leading Croatian Kardeljist Stipe Šuvar warned his Serbian colleagues that a too-rigid stand toward the Kosovo Albanians following the riots might worsen the situation in the country as a whole, since it would "brand a great number of people (as traitors), that is, future lifelong opponents and unjustified 'national heroes.'" Šuvar was probably speaking for most Yugoslav politicians when he said that "other Yugoslav nationalities also had their own 'greater state' nationalism," not only the Albanians.[57] The solution, said Šuvar, "was not to consider Yugoslavia a sum of states, but rather as several self-managed associations of people, working people, and citizens." The Slovene Party leader Mitja Ribičič also criticized the "draconian" approach shown in the long prison sentence given to the Kosovo teenagers for having demanded a Kosovo Republic. In his interview to the Zagreb daily *Vjesnik* (19 September 1981), Ribičič argued that Kosovo was an economic, political, and self-management problem "rather than a problem to be dealt with by courts and prosecuting attorneys."[58] For him, the main problem was "the functioning of the self-management system in Serbia, that is, things taking place outside this system." He also used this opportunity to conclude that "some people in Yugoslavia would like, for the time being of course, to revise some features in the system, as if they would like to jump into the vacant post of the first theorist of the system," replacing Kardelj in this capacity. But, Ribičič said, "nobody can fill his place." Yugoslav problems, Ribičič argued, could not be resolved outside Kardelj's formulas.

The Kardeljists also differed from the reformers in explaining the causes of the Kosovo crisis. They emphasized much more the economic side, which the Serbia's President Dobrivoje Vidić claimed "was not a cause of the riots." To Vidić, the main reasons lay in the nationalist intentions of the real organizers of the protests, in autarkic tendencies in the country and in foreign (Albanian) interference in Yugoslav (Serbian) domestic affairs.[59]

The arguments of Šuvar (Croatia) and Ribičič (Slovenia) were a clear indication that their two republics had been cautious about the Serbian reaction to the Kosovo events. The argument over the economic and political causes of the events, which started in May 1981, never stopped until the breakup of Yugoslavia. This gap between Serbia and the others only widened in the decade that followed the Kosovo events. Also, the Slovenes insisted on Kardeljism up until late 1988. In 1982 the president of the Slovenian Central Committee, France Popit, denied that Yugoslav self-management was in a crisis. The difficulties Yugoslavia was facing were the result of "opportunism in the LC and a lack of readiness to fight those who are against this policy or this system," he argued, on the lines of the Vojvodina claims that anti-Communism was taking over in the Serbian League of Communists. Popit now said that "Party responsibility must be tightened up," and suggested Yugoslav Party intervention in the Serbian Party's affairs:

> Communal Party committees are responsible to the republican central committees; the republican central committees and their presidiums should be responsible both to the LCY CC and to the CC Presidium. I have the impres-

sion that in this respect, we have been behaving in an opportunistic way, starting with the LCY CC Presidium, which does not dare summon the party leadership of a republic for conferences because it believes that this would be taken as interference in the internal affairs of that particular republic. If it were to be said that something is not right in a republic, we could not consider this to be meddling in other people's business.[60]

Another leading Slovene, young rising star Milan Kučan, favored the revolutionary approach in polemics with his Serbian colleagues in the Yugoslav Central Committee.[61] In October 1982, Kučan was speaking for the majority in the Party when he said that "the abandonment of Marxism turns every revolutionary party into an opportunistic and pragmatic party of the social-democratic type." In reply to his revolutionary statement, the Serbian Party's secretary, Špiro Galović-a representative of the dominant view in Serbia-was much more concerned with the state and its malfunctioning:

> By reducing the relationship between our nations to relations between different countries-which has somehow been the case with us-their democratic and Socialist dimension would be lost.[62]

Kučan was, however, not persuaded by this argument. In 1984, when the Serbs demanded significant changes in the political system, he stated:

> It appears that from time to time we almost forget-both in society and particularly in the LCY-that our main goal is still the creation of a Communist society. In abandoning this idea some people, of course, have also lost the main criterion on which their behavior and decisions should be based.[63]

He also warned that these unnamed individuals could fall into the trap of putting everyday problems before revolutionary goals, thereby changing the revolutionary Communist Party into a "pragmatic Party representing social democratic principles." With such radical revolutionary rhetoric, the Slovene and Croatian Communists rushed into conflict with the intellectual elite, not only in other republics, but also in their own. By supporting the conservative elements within LC Serbia (which were in a minority), they gradually entered into open conflict with the Serbian political elite, which became for the first time visible in the aftermath of the 12th LCY Congress, on 29 June 1982. In the 1982-86 period, this conflict only widened, including economic, internationality and ideological elements.[64] The old divide between liberal and conservative groups within the Party was now becoming institutionalized and accommodated within the new division of power in Yugoslavia, becoming more and more a conflict between various republican leaderships. It is within this general trend that we can understand why the republican leaders moved to secure maximal unity among themselves by eliminating those who represented potential allies of other republics and provinces in their own ranks. The conflict between the defenders of the constitution (conservatives, mostly situated outside Serbia) and reformers of the constitution (recentralizers, mostly from Serbia) became visible already at the 12th LCY Congress, only to be deepened in the next four years until Slobodan Milošević became president of the Serbian Party presidency. These four years (1982-86) were a period of consolidation of the dominant trends in the republican Party organizations by both the promotion of loyal supporters and the removal of those who opposed the dominant trends. At the end of this process, "the coincidence of political cleavages based on the internal divisions of the federal state and the Party and social cleavages based on nationality and levels of economic development" (Burg 1983:27) would occur once again, after it had been suppressed by Tito and Kardelj in 1971-72.

5.3. The First Direct Conflict: The Case of Draža Marković (1982)

Two events at the 12th LCY Congress (26-29 June 1982) demonstrated how deep the conflict was between the "defenders" and "reformers" of the constitution. First, the Serbian delegate Rade Končar[65] proposed an amendment to the LCY Statute, which would-if accepted-strengthen the horizontal links within the Party, helping the self-managing integration of workers and thus introducing a balance to the territorial principle of the Party structure. Končar openly criticized a dominant idea of the 1970s, which he described in these words: "Let us break up everything to reintegrate it in a better way." The only result of this policy was that "we have disintegrated ourselves so far very efficiently without any attempt to reintegrate again" (Končar, quoted by Bilandžić 1986:99).

Končar's proposal met with a swift rejection by Branko Mikulić (Bosnia-Herzegovina), the chairman of the Party Commission for the Statutes, who argued that such a change would lead to the elimination of republican party organizations and thus went against the main trend of Yugoslav postwar history. Mikulić's argument was greeted with standing ovations from the delegates, who rejected Končar's proposal.

But the real conflict between the two factions within the Party happened only a few hours later, at the constitutive session of the new LCY Central Committee, when the Serbian candidate for membership in the LCY Presidency, Draža Marković, failed to secure the two-thirds of the total vote for the support for his candidacy. According to the Party Statute, each republican organization nominated "closed lists" of two candidates for the two positions in the LCY CC Presidency, but the Federal Central Committee was to confirm them only by secret voting. But to be "confirmed," each candidate needed to win a two-thirds majority support from all CC members. It had always been a pure formality. Until then.

Serbia nominated two senior politicians-Dobrivoje Vidić and Draža Marković. Serbia would hold the place of the president in the LCY Presidency a year later (1983-84), and it was known that Marković was its candidate for the post. Marković's nomination met with disapproval in Vojvodina, and also in some other parts of the country, mostly in Croatia and Bosnia-Herzegovina. They preferred Miloš Minić, the leading Serbian Kardeljist and one of the very few remaining defenders of the Constitution among the Serbian leaders. Dušan Dragosavac explains why:

> Tito, Kardelj, and other republics had a very high esteem for Miloš Minić, higher than for any other Serbian politician. This was expressed in the fact that Minić became Foreign Secretary in 1972, at a time when Tito distrusted other Serbian leaders....Also, in October 1979 we had a long meeting with Tito, discussing candidates for the Chairmanship of the LCY Presidency for the next three years. This was at the end of the first one-year term in office of the chairman of the presidency. Mikulić's term was expiring, and Stevan Doronjski (Vojvodina) was about to take the post. Tito wanted to know who the candidates were for the two years after Doronjski, until the next Party congress. Branko Mikulić informed Tito that he had spoken to Petar Stambolić, who proposed Miloš Minić to take the post when it came to Serbia, which was due in the fourth year - 1981/82. Draža Marković was at that time the president of the Yugoslav Assembly, and for this reason he could not be elected to the Party presidency. Additionally, this was a year after the Blue Book, and there was great hesitation about having him in the top Party job. It was thought that he could not take the top position in the Party because of his attitudes toward Albanians and Bosnian Muslims, which were not entirely clear. Tito agreed with this, and it was decided that in 1980/1981 the president would be Lazar Mojsov (Macedonia), and in 1981/1982 Miloš Minić (Serbia). However, Tito died in May 1980, when Doronjski (Vojvodina) was the chairman. In October 1980, Mojsov took over. But when it came to Minić (in October 1981), Serbia changed its mind. This was the year of the Kosovo events, and Serbia wanted a strong advocate of Serbian interests to be elected. It was Draža Marković whom they proposed. This, of course, was unacceptable to all the others. Minić withdrew, arguing that the situation in the country was so difficult that he could not agree to be the president if his own republic was against him. We were facing a stalemate.[66]

However, a compromise was reached when Serbia gave up its one-year term of office in favor of Croatia.[67] But the whole affair was still fresh when the 12th LCY Congress took place, not least because Minić, enormously popular outside Serbia, but equally unpopular in Serbia, seemed to be quietly removed from any list of top executive posts either in the federation or in the republic. However, in a series of clandestine talks with the republican and provincial leaderships, a Bosnian Croat, Branko Mikulić, one of Tito's favorite politicians in his last years,[68] organized the voting out of Marković.[69] Croatian leaders (such as the Croatian Serb Dušan Dragosavac,[70] then president of the LCY Presidency) supported him. Dragosavac explains his reasons:

> I was against Marković because I disliked the whole manipulation with Minić. Many others were also against him. For example, the Party organization in the army, where Dane Ćuić[71] was president, and, of course, Vojvodina and Kosovo. Draža (Marković) proposed a change of legislation on the use of the Albanian flag in Kosovo. I came out against it, saying that the Serbs had the same flag as Serbia in the Austro-Hungarian Empire, and that therefore we could not fall below this historic parallel. In general, the problem was how to treat Kosovo after 1981. The majority in the Party Presidency argued that the rights of republics and provinces guaranteed by the 1974 Constitution should not be reduced, still less withdrawn. Since 1977, some initiatives from Serbia aimed at reducing these rights, which was unacceptable to us.... We argued that Kosovo became a province because the Albanians were a clear majority there, and that there are as many Hungarians in Vojvodina as the total number of Montenegrins, though the Serbs made up only 51% in this province....Additionally, neither Albania nor Hungary was attractive to our Albanians and Hungarians, respectively. We ought to do all we can to preserve the reputation our country had in the eyes of its Albanians and Hungarians. Also, we knew that Enver Hoxha's regime would not be Albanian reality for good, and that we needed to preserve good relations with the Albanians to enable closer links, or maybe even unification with Albania, or at least a "Scandinavization" of the region once Hoxha had gone. We wanted to prove our openness to such a solution.[72]

In a secret ballot at the constitutive session of the new Central Committee of the LCY, Marković secured only 95 votes, 12 short of the two-thirds majority of the 159-member Central Committee (Djukić 1992:34). Such a clear margin surprised even the organizers of this action. The Serbian leaders felt there might be a problem with Marković's election,[73] but now they saw that not only Vojvodina and Kosovo were against them, but also many others in Yugoslavia. The two provinces together had 30 members of the CC LCY. Even if they all voted against, there were still 34 votes missing. When the vote was declared, Chairman Dragosavac simply asked Serbia to nominate another candidate. But the Serbian leaders were outraged. In a passionate and sharp speech, Petar Stambolić attacked "the great plot against Serbia." He could hardly control his reactions. Stambolić situated the whole affair in the wider context of anti-Serbian actions after the *Blue Book* (1977), since others had "constantly interfered in Serbian internal affairs."

Stambolić now directly accused Miloš Minić, saying that he was practically appointed to the LCY Presidency as Tito's personal choice in 1978, against the wish of Serbia. "This time we will not accept such interference," said Stambolić. He announced that he would "consider further action," which many understood as the announcement of his own resignation from the Central Committee. Stambolić, who was then the president of the Yugoslav Presidency, directly accused Dušan Dragosavac, the head of the Party, of being responsible for what had happened.

The resignation of the head of state from the Party Central Committee would certainly have seriously undermined Party credibility, especially if accompanied with a public explanation of the reasons for resignation. Furthermore, Stambolić and Marković were the leading figures in Serbian politics: their example could be followed by some, or even all the members from "Serbia without Provinces," not only on the Central Committee, but also possibly in other federal institutions. Eventually Marković explained that all of this was not a personal matter, but a clash "over the Yugoslav views on Serbia." In protest, Marković resigned from the Central Committee, saying that he "did not want to be a member of the Yugoslav Party Central Committee as long as such views existed." For the first time, the Yugoslav League of Communists faced disintegration. "Interference in Serbian internal affairs," as Stambolić put it, was declared the main reason for this. Party leaders certainly did not want this to happen. The newly elected president of the LCY Presidency, Slovene Mitja Ribičič, said that "this dispute...only a half-hour after the conclusion of the Congress, was a real shame for our country. If this continued, not only would it lead the country into political crisis, but also into complete chaos" (Djukić 1992:38). Nobody was really ready for this. When they realized that they had taken a step too far, the organizers of the plot sought a way out.

In the break of the session, Croatian politicians Milka Planinc (the Yugoslav prime minister) and Jure Bilić (the president of Croatian Central Committee) proposed a new vote, offering "guarantees" that Marković would be elected this time if he withdrew his resignation from the Central Committee and stopped short of making a public scandal. Marković gradually accepted this offer, but only when the Croats agreed to Minić's political elimination. Minić's sin, Marković said to other members of the Central Committee, was that he did not understand the Kosovo crisis.[74] It was now, for the first time after the elimination of Dobrica Ćosić in 1968, that a leading politician was removed because of his misunderstanding of the Kosovo problem. The necessity to strengthen the unity of Serbia was now introduced to purify the Serbian political elite from all defenders of the constitution. The process was finished only five years later, when Slobodan Milošević organized the last round of differentiation between those who "did" and those who "did not" understand the Kosovo question; between those who wanted "a change of the system" and those who wanted "changes within the system"; and between those Serbian leaders who were acceptable and those who were unacceptable to other political leaderships in Yugoslavia.

In a second vote, Marković was elected to the presidency. But in a series of party meetings in the next few months, the Serbian leadership discussed the meaning of this incident and what changes in the Serbian approach toward others in the country it should initiate. Petar Stambolić apologized to his colleagues for how he had reacted to the event, but not for what he had said.

> I underline: I apologize for the way I spoke, but not for what I said. The basic problem is relationships in Serbia and toward Serbia. It has been constantly suggested that the Serbian leadership, as it is now with Draža Marković and Petar Stambolić, is more national [than it should be] and that we are not sufficiently Yugoslav. Second, there is a belief in the provinces that if these two people were not in the main leadership of Serbia, and if Miloš Minić were there, everything would be all right. This policy of trying to find allies among certain people in Serbia proper, which has continued up until now, is very damaging. I have always felt that whenever there was talk of unitarism, people always looked at me in this circle. Because to judge by old habits, Serbia means unitarism and centralism. And I am here, so they look at me. This is what I meant when I said that what happened was a direct interference in Serbian internal affairs. I can prove it: those who have intervened are counting on some other political leadership in Serbia, which would be better than this one. (Djukić 1992:40)

Although Minić had spent the previous ten years (1972-82) as a federal politician, his political destiny was now left to Serbia to decide on. To escape a public scandal, the Serbian leaders allowed Minić to remain a member of the Yugoslav Central Committee, but he was entirely marginalized. In his letter to members of the Serbian Central Committee immediately after the Marković affair, Minić warned that his disagreement with Marković and Stambolić was about political and not primarily personal issues.

> I have been convinced and I remain so that the major reforms of the federation in 1971 and 1974 developed the basis for a solution of the national question in Yugoslavia...[and] that they created long-term guarantees that our federation would further improve as a firm, stable and sound Socialist and self-managing social and state community. In 1971 I rejected as deeply mistaken the conclusion...that Yugoslavia was becoming a confederation, or that the new constitutional reform promoted many elements of confederalism. Today, eight years after the 1974 Constitution, and 11 years after the constitutional amendments, I believe the same. (Djukić 1992:53)

Minić's departure from the front benches of Serbian politics signaled that the position of genuine Titoists, Tito's closest aides in the late 1970s, had weakened in Serbia and Yugoslavia only two years after his death. Furthermore, it showed that Serbia would not accept a replacement of Tito's personal arbitration in political conflicts in Serbia with the arbitration of the post-Tito federal leadership. Serbia wanted to be equal to other republics, which meant to decide fully and alone about its internal affairs. No interference in its own affairs could be tolerated.

The Marković case in 1982 also indicated how complex Yugoslav politics were now becoming. The Yugoslav republics (including Serbia) were much more interested in protecting their sovereignty than in developing a Yugoslav political center as an arbiter in political conflicts in the country. Despite its rhetoric in favor of unity and against autarkism, Serbia was no different from others.[75] The attempts of the other republics to eliminate Marković by a simple federal vote did not succeed-this was a further boost to autarkism and the logic of minding one's own business. The events following it clearly showed that the system had no means to resolve a stalemate. The Serbs, who argued for unity and a majority vote, simply borrowed a confederalist rhetoric whenever they were defeated (however minimally) in majority voting. The others now learned how to play the game, if not for other purposes, then to resist Serbia by rejecting its candidates.[76]

Already in 1982, it was therefore clear that the system of consensus was leading to a stalemate with no solution. But it was also clear that majority votes could have even more damaging consequences: the disintegration of the Yugoslav institutions. Yugoslav players were prepared to play the game as long as they were winners. Inasmuch as they advocated changes, they simply blackmailed others by withdrawal every time the change did not suit them.

5.4. Constructive Criticism and Critical Analysis of the Political System

By 1983 the debate on the economic and political crises had entered the Yugoslav media and academic forums. To some in the academic audience, it became clear that no solution to the economic crisis and no long-term solution for Kosovo could be found without changes in the political system.[77] The political system, they felt, was the core of the problem. But it was almost impossible to change it without serious political conflicts, for which the divided leadership was not prepared. As with the economic crisis, the first initiative to change the political system came from academics who allied with the reformers of the constitution in the Serbian political leadership.

In March 1980 Jovan Djordjević, a top Yugoslav constitutional lawyer and Kardelj's right-hand man during the preparation of all four Yugoslav constitutions, criticized the bureaucratic concepts that followed the 1974 Constitution.[78] But it was another Serbian constitutional lawyer, Najdan Pašić, the president of the Serbian Constitutional Court, who invited political leaders to launch a debate on the system, first in November 1980,[79] then again in September 1982, now as a newly elected member of the Central Committee of the LCY. In his open letter to the Party Presidency, he suggested the establishment of a special commission to study the problems of the functioning of the political system, similar to the one established the year before for the reform of the economic system.[80] He stressed four possible issues of the debate: (1) the still strong political control over the economic system; (2) changes in the electoral system to increase leaders' accountability; (3) the uncontrolled growth of the administrative apparatus (bureaucracy); and (4) the democratic issue, i.e., "the exaggerated use of the state's legal power in all areas." Pašić argued that these four points were the main reasons why the spontaneous action of citizens had disappeared, and why self-management did not show the expected results in practice.[81]

Pašić's proposal was followed by a wave of similar initiatives from Belgrade academics, both those in open opposition to the regime and those who allied with official politics. In May 1983 the Praxis professor, Svetozar Stojanović, proposed democratization of the system in four steps. The genuine reform of the system should begin with the internal democratization of the LCY, including free, democratic, and secret elections with more than one candidate for each position. The LCY should legalize "factions" and "groups" competing within the party. Second, the Socialist Alliance of the Working People (SAWP) should be genuinely reformed to include non-Communist political groups, as had been projected by its own statute. The LCY could still be guaranteed the leading role within the SAWP, providing that the party itself had been democratized. Third, the trade unions should be fully democratized and made independent of any state or party influence to become-together with the SAWP-the basis for grass-roots democracy in Yugoslavia. The democratization of these two organizations would not, Stojanović argued, endanger self-management, social ownership, federalism, or nonaligned foreign policy, the four cornerstones of the Yugoslav political system. On the contrary, it would be a realization of Kardelj's ideas on the "pluralism of self-managing interests." Lastly, the federal structure of Yugoslavia should be preserved, but reformed. Although the administration should be further decentralized (including some federal ministries being allocated outside of Belgrade), the Yugoslav economy should be further integrated.[82] Stojanović's proposal was formally introduced to "official" political space by Mijalko Todorović, the former secretary of the LCY Executive Bureau and president of the Yugoslav Assembly, who was silently ousted from the office in 1974 after his disagreement with Tito's action against the Croatian nationalists and Serbian liberals in the early 1970s. In November 1983, in what was seen as an action supported, if not openly directed, by the Serbian leadership, Todorović promoted Stojanović's program at the session of the Federal Advisory Council, but without any conclusive results.[83]

Pašić's initiative would probably again have fallen on deaf ears with the political elite had it not been supported by several important Yugoslav leaders and (although not overtly) the Serbian Party leadership. Because there was still great resistance to any change, however, only a working team within the Federal Council for Social Order was set up, instead of a special commission at the highest party level to discuss the issues of political system. The team, chaired by Josip Vrhovec (since May 1984 a Croatian member of the Yugoslav presidency), in late 1983 invited the general public and political leadership to an open and democratic debate about the problems the political system was facing. The widest-ever public debate in Yugoslav history lasted for almost a year and a half-until spring 1985, when the Vrhovec Commission offered its "Critical Analysis of the Functioning of the Political System." Only a limited presentation of the main arguments, analyses, and proposals expressed in the course of this debate is possible here.

Among the academic contributions to the debate, the most influential was Jovan Mirić's book, *System and Crisis*, extensive extracts from which had been published as a series in *Borba* (12-25 October 1984). The book, subtitled "a contribution to the critical analysis of the constitutional and political system of Yugoslavia," was a direct response to Vrhovec's invitation. Mirić[84] argued that the 1974 Constitution itself, and not its interpretation or implementation, was the cause of the economic and political crisis. The constitution, he said, was a departure from the principles accepted in 1943 by the Antifascist Council of the National Liberation of Yugoslavia (AVNOJ). Although the AVNOJ Resolution established a federation of five Yugoslav peoples, the 1974 Constitution declared that Yugoslavia was "neither a federation nor a confederation." Although in the AVNOJ Resolution provinces were not even mentioned, they had now become not only "constitutive parts" of the federal structure, but also "sovereign entities." For all these reasons, the 1974 Constitution in fact derogated achievements of the partisan movement, especially when it came to the position of Serbia. By introducing the "consensus principle" for all important federal decisions, the 1974 Constitution also denied the main idea of politics: that there should always be (and always is) a majority and a minority, and that in democratic regimes no one should have the right to permanently blackmail a majority by vetoing its proposals. Mirić argued that the post-1974 Yugoslavia was based neither on democratic nor class principles, but on national principles. Neither citizens nor workers were directly represented in federal institutions, but only as members of their republics/provinces.[85] He said that theoretically constructed on distant dreams of "associated labor" and a self-managing society, which had replaced the principles of parliamentary democracy, Yugoslavia in reality fell below the level of bourgeois society-in a feudalized system that preferred partiality over citizens' equality.

Mirić openly rejected Kardelj's argument that federation was an outdated category of bourgeois legal theory. If federation was an outdated form, the confederation was even more so. Kardelj was wrong, Mirić argued, in confusing forms of state structure (unitary vs. federal, and federation vs. confederation) with types of regime (bourgeois democracy and administrative Socialism vs. self-management). As far as Tito was concerned, Mirić had said that it was the first time that he "failed to recognize" where the changes were leading. He also criticized the leading postwar Croatian politician, Vladimir Bakarić, for advocating national economies, which Mirić saw as the main source of nationalism. The invention of national economies was a typical example of unwillingness to accept any possibility that Yugoslavia might become a community *sui generis*. In the growing share of population who declared themselves Yugoslavs in the 1981 census,[86] Mirić saw such a possibility. The Yugoslavs were not misled or confused products of ethnically mixed marriages, but the best educated part of the Yugoslav population, only a quarter of whom originated from mixed marriages. Nevertheless, the elite panicked at the emergence of Yugoslavs, which they saw as a reemergence of unitarianism. For all these reasons, Mirić said, Yugoslavia was on the verge of dissolution.

Mirić's sharp analysis confused and split party officials and academics into supporters and opponents. Among the academics, Mirić's colleague from Zagreb University, Zdravko Tomac, was the sharpest critic. Tomac argued that the problem lay not in the constitution, but in its slow and selective implementation. It was not the constitutional system, but extra-constitutional and nonconstitutional behavior that produced the crisis in Yugoslavia, Tomac concluded.

> Members of this parallel, informal system of business, executive, administrative, and political structures abused their rights to make implementation of the constitutional system impossible....Instead of criticizing the constitution for our present difficulties, we should analyze the reasons why this parallel system appeared, and why we could not implement the agreements...and resolutely oppose the old system. [87]

Tomac was in fact warning about the dogmatist and statist tendencies that had dominated Yugoslav politics before 1966.

The power balance was objectively such that the forms have changed, but not the real situation. Negative tendencies...which we knew from before we enacted the ALA [1976], have continued. This simply had to result in the destruction of a united market, thus strengthening autarkic tendencies, irrational investment...and stagnation.

Tomac agreed that "technobureaucratism as the political expression of statism has become the main source of nationalism," but his conclusion was entirely opposite to Mirić's: the "problems cannot be resolved by changing the constitutional solutions, but only by resolute action to implement the constitution."[88] Views similar to Tomac's were presented by Ciril Ribičič, a Slovenian professor of constitutional law, who (five years later) succeeded Milan Kučan as president of the Slovenian reformed Communists.[89]

While Mirić's views were welcomed by the Serbian academics and political elite in that republic, Tomac (and Ribičič) were the speech writers of what was to be formulated as the (Croatian and) Slovenian position. The leading Croatian, Slovenian, and Vojvodinan politicians, such as Jure Bilić, France Popit, and Dušan Popović, shared Tomac's view. On the other side, the Serbian media, Macedonian Aleksandar Grličkov and Bosnian Muslim Hamdija Pozderac, welcomed Mirić's appeal for changes. Mirić's book was also welcomed by the Partisan veterans regardless of their ethnic background,[90] and by several free-rider politicians in Slovenia (Mitja Ribičič[91]) and Croatia.[92] It is fair to say that significant support for Mirić's ideas came from all parts of Yugoslavia, though in the most conservative circles of party leadership it was treated as the "worst attack on the Yugoslav Socialist system since Milovan Djilas's articles in 1953."[93] Despite the now increasingly visible match between the dominant attitudes to Mirić's book and republican borders, there were significant and not infrequent exceptions to this "rule."

But although it was a main event among social scientists and with the general public, Mirić's book "did not inspire" Vrhovec.[94] "We argued," he recalled when interviewed for this book in January 1998, "that the republics should continue to have, even to a greater extent, full responsibility for themselves":

> The confederative principles should be fully developed. On this issue I differed not only with Mirić, but with the official Croatian position. Because both in Slovenia and in Croatia many were ready to make concessions to the Serbs regarding Kosovo. Finally, these two republics accepted the new Serbian constitution in 1989 and whatever Serbia did in Kosovo at that time. They believed they could satisfy Serbian frustration by offering major concessions on this issue.

However, if Vrhovec did not pay much attention to Mirić's book, he could not disregard the official position of Serbia, which was formulated at the 18th Session of the Serbian Central Committee on 23 and 24 November 1984. The main message of this session was best summarized in the title of *Politika's* report: "The changes are the condition for the way out of the crisis." This time, the main speaker (Bogdan Trifunović) was more determined than ever to say that "the main problem...of how to implement the constitutional principle that the provinces are part of Serbia...has still not been dealt with. This was still a matter of different interpretations between the republic and provinces, but now these differences occurred with respect to 'almost every single issue on the agenda.'" Trifunović left no doubts that "although the principles of the 1974 Constitution should be better implemented, developed, and defended, we ought not to think that any of its articles were the final and definite word in the formation of our relationships if our practical experience shows that we need to find better and more suitable solutions for existing circumstances." This was, he argued, "especially the case with the Associated Labor Act.[95]

The Serbian demands were formulated in 38 theses for reform of the political system, which were accepted by the Central Committee of LC Serbia. In general, four key demands were put forward by this document: (1) enlargement of economic units by associating several BOALs with larger enterprises; (2) strengthening the executive branch of government (including the federal executive council and other federal institutions); (3) the democratization of the electoral system (by introducing more than one candidate for each post); and (4) uniting Serbia by increasing the prerogatives of the republic in its relations with Kosovo and Vojvodina. Particular attention was given to the fourth point: relations in Serbia. Serbia proposed that the economic and financial aid Kosovo received from Serbia should not go, as it had been, through federal institutions. In this way, Serbia would assume greater control over the economic development of Kosovo. The Serbian proposal also explicitly obliged the leaders of Kosovo to prevent any further exodus of Serbs and Montenegrins from Kosovo and to ensure full equality of the Serbs and Albanians in the province.[96] Such a proposal was accompanied by strong verbal opposition to autonomism, the term reintroduced to the Serbian political vocabulary by Špiro Galović in November 1981 as a synonym for the autarkism of the provinces.[97]

The 18th Session of the Serbian Central Committee for the first time concluded that the rules that were always interpreted in different and opposing ways in Serbia and in its two provinces should indeed be subjected to careful examination. This session also introduced a new type of rhetoric, which now included the possibility of an open clash between members of the Central Committee, for the first time in front of the general public. Probably the most famous of such polemics at the 18th LC CCS Session was the one between the then fairly unknown Belgrade party leader, Slobodan Milošević, and a member of the CC from Vojvodina, Marija Miškolci Zvekić. When Miškolci Zvekić opposed the "38-theses proposal," saying that it reminded her of Mirić's concept of the reform of Yugoslavia and that it would, if accepted, further divide groups in the Yugoslav League of Communists, Milošević replied as follows:

> We have been threatened with a political crisis if we continue to [do nothing more than] discuss these problems. All right, let us enter that political crisis! This crisis is going to produce a great uproar about the question of unity or separatism. In such a crisis separatism will not prevail, because the people have accepted unity. Those leaders incapable of seeing this will and should lose the public's confidence. If separatism is not opposed, our country will have no prospects for the future. It can only disintegrate.

In what happened to be his first prominent public appearance, the young rising star of the Serbian leadership said that "the Serbian Communists have never been in favour of unitarist ideas," and that the others should once and forever cease to accuse them of a policy pursued by the interwar Serbian bourgeoisie. The Serbs were tired of charges of having been oppressors, as a result of which they were constantly having to clear their name and to confirm their acceptance of a united Yugoslavia. "We [Serbs] have no reason whatsoever to bow our heads to anyone," concluded Milošević. Differing in style but not in policy from the majority of the Serbian leaders, Milošević warned the Vojvodinan leaders that their policy of autarkism led to economic and political isolation from Europe and the developed world. The League of Communists, he said, had the opportunity to remove obstacles to the further development of Yugoslavia and its nations. The time was up for those who hesitated to change their behavior quickly (Milošević 1984/1989: 30-8).

In these circumstances, however, Vrhovec's analysis of the functioning of the political system fell short of any adequate proposal on how to resolve the crisis. The problem of this commission was, as Vrhovec admitted in 1985, that "it was just another interrepublican body in which the opinions and proposals could not be accepted without a full consensus of all republics and provinces."[98] Because the majority in the leadership still opposed serious changes in the political system, and also because those who favored changes had entirely different visions of what changes they wanted, the whole debate organized by the Vrhovec Commission fell short of any conclusion. The majority in the leadership, including Vrhovec himself, were still inspired by Kardelj, rejecting any notion of serious changes and talking only of building up the system he projected.[99] In this context, it is easy to understand why the critical analysis offered in fact further devolution of power rather than a recentralization of Yugoslavia.

The critical analysis promoted the idea that the new model should be based on the *confederative* principle, and not on any return to unitarianism, which was hidden behind the *one person, one vote* slogan....I saw this slogan as fatal for Croatia. It would have destroyed the equality of the federal units. This principle would have been acceptable only when and if the national question had been already resolved, when equality had been guaranteed. In our circumstances, this would have blown up Yugoslavia.[100]

"We wanted to preserve Kardelj's concept of the nationality question and his ideas about the relations between federal units," Vrhovec said in the interview.

The main conclusion was that the basic ideas of the constitution should not be put under question. Above all, the right to self-determination, which is a nontransferable historical right. Any denial of the right to self-determination we considered as an attack on the concept of Yugoslavia....Then it was crucial to reconfirm that the sovereignty remains in the republics, and that the Federation has only those competencies on which the republics agreed as common....The republics should be made to an even greater extent responsible for themselves.

Like Šuvar and Ribičič earlier, Vrhovec considered that Serbia was using Kosovo as an alibi for a new recentralization of Yugoslavia. For this reason, the federal leadership, still controlled by Kardeljists, largely ignored the existence of the problem of Kosovo from 1981 to 1985, trying to play down the Serbian attempt to change relations within Serbia by using Kosovo. Vrhovec, as well as his main colleagues in the federal leadership, later (in 1998) argued that the Serbian leadership was already "infected by nationalism" and that Milošević was a consequence, rather than a cause of Serbian nationalism.

Serbian nationalism penetrated the highest ranks of Serbian politics with Ranković and remained there under Draža Marković's and Ivan Stambolić's protection. The 1974 Constitution to the Yugoslav leaders from other republics, and especially from provinces, was the most powerful tool to defeat it. And we did not want to lose it.

Of course this caused endless disputes within the commission on almost every relevant issue. The debate spilled over into the media, which increasingly started promoting the views dominant in their own republics/provinces. The media, still under the control of the political elite in the republics and provinces, now looked increasingly liberalized and freed from political influence. But this was a false image, since they were given the "green light" by the leaders themselves to criticize the views of the leaders in other republics, and (in the Serbian case) in both provinces.[101] Information about political events behind the scenes was leaked to the media directly from the political patrons themselves. The media would never dare to attack their own leaders. This situation, indeed, opened up some space of freedom for the media in Yugoslavia. But it was far from making them independent.[102]

The same was true of the intellectual elite, which was now encouraged to support the views of one or another side. The elite and newspapers gladly accepted this role, with honorable exceptions in each republic. When the media and academics joined politicians in a dispute over the political system, it looked as if Vrhovec's Commission had produced more conflicts than it was capable of resolving. At the same time, its recommendations were no more than just another compromise, condemned in advance to be unsuccessful.[103]

Another megadebate, without results, not only exposed how divided, inefficient, and incapable the elite was, but also eliminated those few credentials it still had in the eyes of the public.

5. 5. Conclusion

By 1984, the two political blocs had already been created and fairly consolidated. The one (led by the Serbian leadership) insisted on reforms of the constitution, and the other (most strongly represented by Slovenia, but also dominant in most other Yugoslav republics, and in the army) firmly defended all provisions of the 1974 Constitutional arrangement and Kardelj's constitutive concept. Although the Kardeljists (the "defenders of the constitution") were stronger in all direct conflicts, successfully preventing any significant change of the political system, the confederalist principles of nonintervening in other republics shielded the reformers of the constitution from being removed from politics. Yugoslav politics in the early 1980s were therefore already in a stalemate.

Although in regard to economic reforms, some agreement between the republics and provinces was made possible after enormous pressure from international factors, the reform of the political system was entirely left to the Yugoslav elite, unwilling and incapable of serious change. The only effective pressure for changes, therefore, could have come from a coalition between the reformers and the dissatisfied segments of the population. This formula was not implemented in the first half of the 1980s, since the elite was still committed to changes from within the system. But the public pressure, channeled and controlled by segments of the elite through the now increasingly open media, played its role and was now, for the first time used as an asset in intraelite conflicts. As the conflict between the groups in republics and between republics increased, the media and masses were mobilized in support of "their" leaders. This all set up the stage for a later phase in which practically a two-party system appeared out of the divided LCY leadership. In this phase, which began in 1986 with the elections of Milan Kučan and Slobodan Milošević as presidents of the Slovenian and Serbian Central Committees, respectively, the political elites now moved closer to the local intellectual elites, widening the gap between themselves and the other republics. Surveys conducted in the mid-1980s showed that the difference between Communists in the various republics was greater than between Communists and non-Communists in the same republic.[104] In these circumstances, any common Yugoslav policy became very unlikely.

Although the debate on economic issues was not structured primarily along the lines of ethnic groups or republics, the political discussion in the early 1980s more closely followed the lines of republics, but not of ethnic groups. By 1985, only the oldest generation of Yugoslav veterans remained untouched by the divisions into republican camps. But their influence significantly decreased after the election of the first post-Titoist LCY Central Committee (1982), in which the most loyal Titoists (such as Miloš Minić, for example) were marginalized, and especially after 1984, when the first representatives of republics/provinces elected after Tito's death replaced Tito's appointees in the federal presidency. However, it was not before the late 1980s that ethnicity became a dividing factor within the Yugoslav political elites. In the mid-1980s the Communist elites within republics/provinces remained united (or disunited), regardless of their ethnic origins, even during the 1981 Kosovo conflict.

The tools used in the last years of the 1980s were thus invented and even tried out during the late 1970s and early 1980s. The "case of Draža Marković" analyzed in this chapter shows that the Yugoslav League of Communists faced a serious danger of splitting up as early as 1982. Although arguments between the republics and provinces permanently characterized Yugoslav postwar politics (for which the analysis of the constitutional debate of 1967-74 offers sufficient evidence), it was only after Tito's departure that the danger of the Party's disintegration became real. The dissolution of the LCY and the Yugoslav state in 1990 and 1991 was therefore not only a simple result of a turning point that happened after the antibureaucratic (1988) or the "velvet" revolutions (1989), but also an outcome of long-existing controversies that became difficult to reconcile once the "supreme arbiters" had gone. These controversies were not, however, the expression either of "ethnic hatred," or of the struggle between democracy and Communism, as is frequently argued. They could not be fully explained by the controversies over economic issues, since the economic debate did not follow ethnic or republican lines, as we have seen in the previous chapter of this book. I argue that the main line of division between the two newly created blocs in Yugoslav politics was about their willingness to remain committed to the ideological picture of the world, most closely expressed by Kardelj, even when it became obvious that the results of its implementation were radically different from what had been intended and expected. It is in the elite unwillingness to abandon the ideology that I find the main reason for the collapse of the regime.

In the final two chapters of this book, I follow the development of the two separate constitutive concepts that emerged out of two different interpretations of Kardelj's concept: in Serbia (chapter six) and Slovenia (chapter seven). These two new concepts, which emerged at the same time and in reaction to one another, ultimately drove Yugoslavia apart in the second half of the 1980s.

Notes

1 Vojvodina in the north of the republic, where Serbs formed 50% of the local population with 22 ethnic minorities and the Hungarian *nationality* of 500,000; and Kosovo in the south, where the Albanians in 1981 made up 77.5% (1,226,736) of the local population (of 1,584,441), together with 209,498 (13.2%) of Serbs, 58,562 (3.7%) Muslims, and 27,028 (1.7%) Montenegrins. Serbia was the only "complex" Yugoslav republic, with provinces within its borders.
2 Only when the discourse shifted from political to ethnic issues did Bosnia-Herzegovina come to the forefront of the Yugoslav crisis.
3 This change was introduced by 1968 amendment 7, which replaced article 2 of the 1963 Yugoslav Constitution (Petranović and Štrbac 1977: III: 95).
4 The "incidents" began in 1975 during Tito's visit to Kosovo, when the Kosovo leaders used this opportunity to emphasize Kosovo's direct links with the federation. "Their obsession with statehood is absolute. By emphasizing 'Yugoslavism' even too much, by linking themselves with Yugoslavia, Tito, and the LCY, they aim to blur the fact that the autonomous provinces are within Serbia," wrote the Serbian leader Draža Marković in his diary on 13 April 1975 (1988:104).
5 For example, the Vojvodinan leaders invited no members of the Serbian leadership to attend Tito's visit to Novi Sad in 1975. Furthermore, in his toast to Tito, Radovan Vlajković, then the president of Vojvodina, failed even to mention Serbia or its League of Communists. The commander of Vojvodinan Territorial Defense on another occasion addressed his colleague-a general from Serbia proper-as a guest from the "neighboring republic," making no difference between him and a Croatian general. Even in foreign policy, the provinces took initiatives without even informing Serbia.
6 Petar Stambolić in Djukić 1992:241; Draža Marković on 12 February 1976 in Marković 1988:328; and Ivan Stambolić 1995:72. As Marković said, the Serbian leaders were "extremely satisfied" with Kardelj's conclusion that "since the republics were sovereign states, it was therefore up to them to decide which part of this sovereignty would be transposed to the federation, and which to lower sociopolitical communities, such as provinces" (1988:328).
7 Kardelj's reaction to the *Blue Book* in 1977 secured him a positive place even in the most recent recollections of events leading to the disintegration of Yugoslavia by his Serbian colleagues.
8 Amendment 18 (December 1968) to replace articles 111 and 112 of the 1963 Constitution.
9 Minić was the military prosecutor in the trial of General Mihailović, the leader of the Yugoslav army in the fatherland (Chetniks) in 1946. This fact made it even more difficult for Marković to attack him, while being already suspected of Serbian nationalism.

The conflict between Marković and Minić was a long-standing one: it originated in the 1968 student demonstrations, about which there is more in chapter three on "constitutional debate 1967-74 (Marković 5 June 1968 and 15 June 1968).

10 This also confirms Ivan Stambolić when he says that Tito took no sides in the conflict, but when they met, "it was clear (from an almost invisible reaction) that he was slightly more supportive of the provinces than of Serbia" (Stambolić 1995:67).

11 The notion of equality occupies the central place in almost all articles discussing Kosovo, whether they present the Serb or Albanian point of view. See Zajmi 1997:98.

12 This actually happened, and already in 1984 the GDP per capita difference between Slovenia and Kosovo was 6.1:1.

13 Here and on several further places I refer to the report "Šta se dogadjalo na Kosovu" (What happened in Kosovo), published by *Politika* in Belgrade immediately after the 1981 demonstrations. I refer to this publication as Report 1981.

14 The issue of migration of the Serbs and Montenegrins from Kosovo will be discussed in detail in the next section of this chapter.

15 As Branko Horvat noticed in an interview I conducted in April 1998, in this sense the situation could be compared with the presence of similar ideologies at Belgrade or Zagreb Universities in the 1930s.

16 Until 1970 federal help was distributed as "nonreturnable loans." After this, 14-year loans, with favorable conditions of repayment, were introduced. Kosovo had additionally 25% better conditions: the loans were for 17 years, and the interest rate was 4.16% instead of 4.5%, among other improved benefits (Report 1981:159).

17 These figures were presented by Stipe Šuvar in his article in *Nin*, 30 August 1981 (RFE/RL 17 September 1981).

18 RFE/RL 18 May 1981. Significantly, the structure of the population in Kosovo did not change much from 1948 to 1961. In 1948 the Albanians made up 68.5 and Serbs 23.6% of the Kosovo population, and in 1961 Albanians were 67.2% and Serbs still 23.6%. This is why many Serbs saw the political changes in the 1960s (especially after 1966) as the main cause of the exodus.

19 In 1981, Kosovo was already the most populous area of Yugoslavia, with 146 inhabitants per square kilometer (0.39 square mile) of territory, almost twice as many as the Yugoslav average of 88.

20 By Yugoslavs here, I mean those citizens who declared themselves Yugoslav in an ethnic sense in the population census.

21 The demand for a republic at first did not seem to be an outrage. Kosovo had changed its status twice within Socialist Yugoslavia; in the AVNOJ Resolution of 1943 it was not even mentioned. During the war and immediately after it, Kosovo was seen as a potential link between Yugoslavia and Albania in a future Socialist Balkan Federation, just as Macedonia was seen as the link between Bulgaria and Yugoslavia. Tito's Partisans announced that Albanian (as well as Macedonian) unification would be the logical consequence of victory of Socialism over nationalist principles. In 1946, however, Kosovo became an "autonomous region" of Serbia, a level below that of Vojvodina, whose status of province was not changed after 1945. But in the 1963 Constitution it was put on a par with Vojvodina, becoming an "autonomous province." In the 1963 Constitution, the Albanians were also given the status of "nationality," which was generally considered to be an improvement compared with the status of "national minority." With the fall of Ranković in 1966 and Ćosić in 1968 (both criticized for their views on Kosovo), there were two more changes in a symbolic sense: instead of being called *Šiptari* [the Alba-

nian word for an Albanian is Shqiptar], which many of them found offensive, the term *Albanci* (Albanians) was introduced.

22 Among them is again Marković's diary (1987) and Miloš Mišović's book *Ko je tražio Republiku Kosovo 1945-85* (Mišović 1987). Additional testimonies on the demands for a Kosovo republic by the main Kosovo leaders in the 1968-81 period were published at this time.

23 The Serbian leaders, however, had problems in accepting this idea of Kardelj's. Marković, for example, writes, "the thesis that South Slav origins have no importance for the character of the Yugoslav community is very suspicious, basically incorrect, and unacceptable" (1 February 1970 1987:237).

24 This argument was heard at the session of the enlarged political leadership (the so-called Political Activ) of Djakovica and Peć (Mišović 1987:133).

25 Dragoslav Marković summarized Tito's position on this issue expressed in their talk on 27 January 1971: "A republic is out of the question, as well as any solution that might suggest a republic, when it comes to the provinces, and especially to Kosovo. It is also out of the question to have a president of the presidency from the provinces (except if he were elected as a Serbian representative); maybe the vice president" (Marković 1987:256). However, Tito later agreed on having presidents from the provinces. Tito told the Kosovo leaders directly that they could not count on his support if they asked for a republic (30 January 1977; Marković 1988:259). But he also "made too many concessions to them," as Petar Stambolić recalls (Djukić 1992:242).

26 The other republics opposed any generalization of the issue of provinces, fearing that this might encourage ethnic groups in their republics to demand the status of provinces. Moreover, Slovenia and Croatia now strictly adhered to a policy of noninterference in other republic's internal affairs.

27 Marković, 1 November 1968 (1987:96).

28 The events are here described using newspaper reports collected in *Šta se dogadjalo na Kosovu*, 1981, as well as from books by the leading Kosovo politicians Sinan Hasani (1986), Horvat (1988), and Mertus (1999). The RFE/RL Reports and analyses are also a helpful source (especially see 7 April 1981 and 28 April 1981).

29 Kosova is the Albanian name for Kosovo. In this book I use this term when the source is translated from Albanian.

30 Dušan Dragosavac in the interview in April 1998.

31 In the interview I conducted for *Polet* in January 1986, Sergej Kraigher (Slovenia), who was vice-president of the Yugoslav state presidency at the time of the Kosovo demonstrations, said that the leaders were surprised because the previous reports indicated no problems, apart from economic ones, in Kosovo. This part of my interview is quoted in Mišović (1987:445).

32 In the interview I conducted in February 1998, one of the leading Belgrade dissidents at that time, Lazar Stojanović, recalled that the regime had tolerated many petitions they had organized, but not the one on Kosovo. The petition protested against the police repression in Kosovo and was signed by 113 students from Ljubljana, Zagreb, and Belgrade. Solidarity between students threatened to undermine the rhetoric of the regime that the demonstrations were nationalistic.

33 Boro (Vukmirović) and Ramiz (Sadiku), Serb and Albanian partisans, were war heroes executed together by the Italians in 1942. In postwar Yugoslavia they symbolized "brotherhood and unity" among Serbs and Albanians.

34 One should here remember what Draža Marković wrote about Tito's visit to Kosovo in 1975-that the Kosovo leadership deliberately wanted to demonstrate the direct link

between them and Tito, and that for this reason they exaggerated the importance and warmth of his reception. Also, this all happened after Tito's 1977 visit to Beijing and Pyongyang, after which the Yugoslavs wanted to repeat the grandeur of the Chinese and North-Korean receptions. And Tito was 87, and everyone knew how much he enjoyed such events.

35   Interview with Dragosavac, April 1998.
36   Which they actually did. Because of increased federal assistance, Kosovo reached 38.9% of the Yugoslav average GDP in 1981 (from 33.8% in 1963), only to fall to 28.2% in the year following the demonstrations (1982). See table 1 in chapter four.
37   A very good overview of the Kosovo events, together with the necessary background information may be found in RFE/RL Reports and Analyses of 7 April 1981 and 28 April 1981.
38   Immediately after the demonstrations, the Party's president of Kosovo, Mahmut Bakalli, and the Kosovo president, Xhavid Nimani, both resigned. In the 1990s, Bakalli reappeared in politics as one of the senior leaders of the "moderate" faction of the Albanian movement in Kosovo.
39   The conflict was over the extent to which external factors played a role in this crisis. Also, the Slovenian and Croatian leaders emphasized "the crisis of self-management and economic crisis, while the Serbian leaders saw the main problem in the "unregulated relations between Serbia and its provinces."
40   This attitude was later criticized by Serbian nationalists as the main illustration of the blindness of the Yugoslav political leaders and their failure to see and admit the reality in Kosovo. But apart from its heavy ideological bias, it was correct: the demonstrations were not massive enough to be treated as an all-Albanian riot in Kosovo, nor did they have (at least originally) predominantly nationalistic demands. Also, the political leadership in Kosovo did not split on national lines when opposing the demands for a republic. The Albanian leaders, with very few exceptions, stood firmly against the demonstrations. In fact, up until the very end of Yugoslavia (until Spring 1990) the main Albanian leaders (such as Vllasi, Kolgeci, Jashari, and Shiroka) distanced themselves from the 1981 protests, treating them as nationalistic and counterrevolutionary.
41   The president of the Yugoslav Party Presidency, the Macedonian Lazar Mojsov, mentioned a tendency to dramatize the real level of underdevelopment in Kosovo. Mojsov said that Kosovo really was the least developed Yugoslav region, but its leaders endlessly repeated this observation to secure more investments for the province. At the same time, however, positive economic results in the province were being neglected (Mojsov 1981:118). Another Macedonian member of the Central Committee of the LCY, Vaska Duganova, said that there could be no "European development with an Asiatic birthrate" (1981:137), alluding to the Kosovo Albanians, whose birthrate was the highest in Europe.
42   The article was then published as a book with the same title. It is widely believed that the Albanian Prime Minister Mehmet Shehu, was the author of this article.
43   Jajce is a town in central Bosnia where the second convention of AVNOJ-the symbol of Communist Yugoslavia-was held on 29 November 1943.
44   However, one member of the Yugoslav Central Committee, Slovene Jože Smole, disagreed on this issue, saying that the international dimension was overemphasized. Even if it existed, he said, it could not have been successful without domestic support (Smole 1981:143).
45   Marković was in 1981 president of the Yugoslav Assembly. In 1982 he was elected a member of the Yugoslav party presidency, in which he held the post of president in

1983-84. In 1986 he retired in protest against the election of Slobodan Milošević as president of the Serbian LC CC. Petar Stambolić was the Serbian representative in the Yugoslav presidency (1974-84), where he was vice president (1981-82) and president (1982-83). Ivan Stambolić, his nephew, was president of the Executive Council of Serbia (Serbian prime minister) in 1978-82, president of the Belgrade Party Organization in 1982-84, president of the Serbian LC Central Committee (1984-86), and president of the Presidency of Serbia (1986-87) before he was forced to resign following his conflict with Slobodan Milošević and the majority of the Serbian CC. Špiro Galović was a member of the presidency of the Serbian Central Committee in charge of ideology (1978-82) and its secretary (1982-84). All four politicians, just like almost all other members of their political generation, have been sharp critics of Slobodan Milošević, at least since 1988. Ivan Stambolić was murdered by members of Serbian special police units in August 2000.

46 By 1984, I. Stambolić had succeeded in decreasing the influence of his three colleagues and promoting himself to be the new leader of Serbia. In Slobodan Milošević (and, to some extent, in Dragiša Pavlović), he found his closest support.

47 The rhetoric against statists and bureaucrats was Kardeljist's.

48 Interestingly, Jože Smole, a Slovenian member of the Yugoslav Central Committee, also said that, unfortunately, the problems had not been resolved in 1977. In 1989 Smole became one of the Slovenian politicians most criticized by the Serbian antibureaucratic revolution.

49 The term *ustavobranitelji* has a historical connotation. It was used to mark progressive (proconstitutional, liberal) forces in Serbian politics in the mid-19th century. One needs to notice here that to defend the constitution now became a position deserving political denunciation in the Serbian political glossary.

50 The leading autonomists and defenders of the constitution within the leadership of Vojvodina were Serbs: Dušan Popović, the ideologue of the Provincial Committee, and Boško Krunić, the president of the Provincial Committee of the LC Vojvodina. This fact only confirms our conclusion that political divisions were not at that time primarily motivated by ethnic issues, nor were they structured along ethnic lines. To a similar extent as with the economic debate, they cut across lines of ethnic groups and even republican borders.

51 The leading Vojvodinan Communist, Boško Krunić, said at the CC LCY Session on 7 May 1981 that the provinces had decided to "enter the Socialist Republic of Serbia" of their own free will. Autonomy was not given to them; it was the "result of our correct policy on the nationality issue"(1981:130-1).

52 For Popović's discussion at the 22nd Session of the LCY Central Committee, see RFE/RL, 17 November 1981.

53 A good example of this rhetoric is given in Dušan Popović's interview to *Polet*, 15 March 1985.

54 One can here perhaps recall Warren Zimmermann's much later warning about the inaccuracy of equating decentralization and democratization. The last U.S. ambassador to Socialist Yugoslavia wrote, "In one of my first cables I cautioned Washington not to equate decentralization with democracy or centralism with authoritarianism. Those equations might have described the Soviet Union, a ruthless dictatorship from the center. But they didn't describe Yugoslavia" (1996/1999:17).

55 The most illustrative documents on how different the views of the Serbian leaders and Serbs were in the leadership of other Yugoslav republics are letters exchanged between the Serbian representative in the SFRY Presidency Petar Stambolić and the

Croatian representative in the LCY Presidency, Dušan Dragosavac (a Serb from Croatia). Stambolić and Dragosavac had been in permanent disagreement on the status of the provinces and the rights of nationalities (as Dragosavac called them) or national minorities (what Stambolić used). (See Dragosavac to Stambolić 20 June 1983 and Stambolić to Dragosavac 27 June 1983; copies of the documents are in my possession.)

56   See speeches by Popović and Krunić at the 26th CC LCY Session, 1982.
57   *Nin*, 30 August 1981. See: RFE/RL, 17 September 1981.
58   RFE/RL, 28 September 1981.
59   RFE/RL, 18 May 1981.
60   RFE/RL, 12 October 1982.
61   Dušan Dragosavac (a member of the LCY presidency together with Kučan in 1982-86) describes Kučan as one who was "endlessly quoting Tito and Kardelj at that time, even in very informal meetings, when this was entirely inappropriate and unnecessary. I think that his turnabout after 1987-88 could, to a large extent, be explained by his earlier hard-line position. He had to prove himself as a democrat after all" (interview with Dragosavac, 15 April 1998). Dragosavac believes the same could explain the behavior of many other Slovene leaders who (like Ribičič and Dolanc) entered politics from the secret police or military. Stipe Šuvar, Kučan's colleague from the 1986-90 LCY presidency, says that many secret police people from Slovenia (like Dolanc) distinguished themselves in the 1966 action against Ranković. Kučan was appointed President of the Slovenian Parliament in 1978, while Kardelj was still the main figure in Slovenian politics. In 1982 he became a Slovenian representative in the federal LCY presidency, where he remained until 1986. He was then elected president of the Slovenian LC CC.
62   Both quotations are taken from the RFE/RL report quoted in footnote 60.
63   RFE/RL, 31 January 1984.
64   In fact it was reminiscent of the 1967-72 intraelite conflict, which is described by Burg (1983).
65   Končar was the only son of the Croatian wartime Communist leader Rade Končar (the only ethnic Serb head of the Croatian Party, with the exception of Stanko Stojčević, elected in 1988), who was killed by the Italians in May 1942.
66   Interview with Dragosavac, 10 April 1998.
67   In fact, Croatia agreed to exchange its term (which was due in two years, in 1983/84) with Serbia (1981/1982) for three reasons: (1) public embarrassment would be avoided; (2) the post would be taken by Dušan Dragosavac, a Serb who opposed the Serbian leadership even more than Minić himself; and (3) Croatia would have more influence at the forthcoming 12th LCY Congress. The others also accepted these reasons, and Dragosavac (unexpectedly) became the president of the LCY Presidency, after being secretary for the two previous years.
68   This is Petar Stambolić's assessment in his interview with S. Djukić (1992:240).
69   In an interview we had in January 1998, the Croatian member of the Party Presidency, Jure Bilić, confirmed that Mikulić's role was crucial in this vote. He said that the Serbian leaders had long-lasting disagreements with the Bosnians, for which Marković's diary (1987 and 1988) is a good source. Mikulić was also one of the leading Titoists in the Yugoslav leadership and thus supported the Vojvodinan leaders rather than Marković.
70   Dragosavac and Marković disliked each other for both political and personal reasons (Djukić 1992:35) The important point here, of course, is that the divisions again did not follow ethnic lines. Minić, Marković, Krunić, and Dragosavac were all Serbs. The lines of republics/provinces were much more important, though the conflict between Minić

and Marković could not be explained by them either. The division was still much more political than territorial: Dragosavac and Mikulić, the most pro-Titoist members of the Yugoslav Party leadership in the last years of Tito's life, preferred Titoist Minić to "nationalist" Marković.

71 General Ćuić was also a Serb. The army supported Minić for his Titoist and antinationalist pedigree.

72 Interview with Dušan Dragosavac, 10 April 1998.

73 Dragosavac recalls that the other LCY Presidency member, Dušan Čkrebić (from Serbia), said in the lobbies before the CC LCY session that "it is good that unity was manifested at the Congress, but now we should confirm our unity in the elections of the LCY Presidency" (interview with Dragosavac, 10 April 1998).

74 Accusing (again for the first time in a speech from a Serbian leader) the others of obstructing the action in Kosovo, Marković identified his destiny with that of Kosovo. "Unregulated relations in Serbia represent a source of manipulation and objectively provide a good opportunity for making various alliances. One should pose the question of the responsibility for Kosovo. One should also pose many other questions. We shall then see what the main attitudes were on our policy toward Albania and who voted against the documents on the Albanian policy toward our country. Who obstructed the building of unity in the League of Serbian Communists and thereby in the League of Yugoslav Communists?," Marković asked rhetorically. The answer was self-evident: the former foreign secretary, Miloš Minić.

75 As explained in chapter three of this book Serbia agreed on the constitutional arrangement on the understanding that Serbia would become equally independent from the federal center as the other republics, which-Serbian leaders felt-was not so before 1966. The provinces and the federal leadership were now seen as the main source of obstruction of this aim.

76 This message was still in their ears in 1989, when the same scenario was implemented against another Serbian member of the LCY Presidency, Dušan Čkrebić. Preventing the outcome of a majority vote in the LCY Central Committee, Slobodan Milošević repeated Petar Stambolić's argument in the Marković case. Since the Central Committee again could not risk a Serbian withdrawal, they simply reinterpreted the vote as nonobligatory and only "morally binding." Čkrebić withdrew his resignation without even repeating the vote. The same situation (but now with a Croat in the main position) occurred with the election of the Yugoslav Presidency President Stipe Mesić in 1991.

77 "A program of economic stabilization conceived under the slogan 'economic reforms yes, political reforms no' cannot yield any serious results because it attempts to deal with the consequences rather than causes of the crisis," said Josip Županov (RFE/RL 22 April 1985). Županov developed the same argument in his 1983 book, *Marginalije o društvenoj krizi*. The most Kardeljist members of the political elite (such as Stipe Šuvar) called Županov a crisologist.

78 *Nin*, 30 March 1980, RFE/RL, 3 April 1980.

79 *Politika,* 6 November 1980.

80 *Politika,* 29 November 1982.

81 RFE/RL, 22 April 1983.

82 RFE/RL, 1 June 1983.

83 RFE/RL, 7 November 1983.

84 Jovan Mirić (Croatian Serb of Yugoslav political orientation) was a professor of political science at Zagreb University.

85 Goati (1989) offers a good explanation of this argument.

86   The number of citizens who declared themselves as ethnically "Yugoslavs/undeclared" rose to 1,209,045 in 1981, from 320,853 in 1971. Some demographic estimations in early 1981 projected a further growth of this population to 5 (about 20%) in 1991. This estimate played some role in fostering fears among the nationalists (Bilandžić 1986). It also enabled Slovenia and Croatia to counter Serbian arguments that the 1974 Constitution destroyed a sense of Yugoslav belonging. The Serbs, however, argued that the growing number of Yugoslavs was a reaction to growing trends of disintegration in the country.

87   Kardelj argued, as explained in footnotes 58 and 59 in chapter two, that extra-parliamentary powers control the capitalist societies of the West. Tomac now argued the same for Yugoslavia.

88   Zdravko Tomac, *Danas*, 13 December 1983. For Tomac's views see Tomac (1984). Before becoming a professor, Tomac was the chief of staff to Croatian President Jakov Blažević (1974-82). In 1990 he became the main ideologue of the reformed Communists in Croatia. As the SDP representative, he was the deputy prime minister in the Croatian wartime coalition government (1991-92). In the 1997 presidential elections, he came in second to Franjo Tudjman with 21% of the vote.

89   On the basis of similar views they held on Mirić's analysis, in 1988 Ribičič and Tomac published a book *Federalism Measured by the Future*, to which Milan Kučan wrote a preface. Mirić, on the other hand, was a referee for Ivan Stambolić's book *Debates on Serbia* (1988). This split within the intellectual elite illustrates the position of the Croatian political elite at that time: even if they had shown much more political ability than they did, the Croatian leaders would have faced enormous difficulties in finding a third way between the Slovenian and Serbian options. The failure of the Croatian political elite to promote its own alternative proved fatal for Croatia itself because it encouraged radical Croatian nationalism, which only helped to close the circle of the disintegration of Yugoslavia.

90   Although the Croat Jure Bilić, for example, strongly opposed Mirić's analysis, Pero Car, a member of Croatian presidency, in his interview with *Danas*, said: "The *fear of unitarism*, in my firm belief, is a creation and a tool of those people whose intention is to destroy Yugoslav togetherness. The time when *unitarism* was successfully used as a scarecrow has gone. There is no danger that togetherness could become unitarism. But there are many things that people who live together need to share. If we call unitarism what happens when people who live together share their responsibility for decisions made in their country, this is a positive *unitarism*. Then we should be for such unitarism" (*Danas*, 10 January 1984). Although Car was not representative of the majority in the Croatian or other political leaderships, it was nevertheless true that these were not only his views. The same division between those supporting and those opposing Mirić's ideas occurred in Slovenia (Mitja Ribičič vs. France Popit) and Serbia (republican leadership vs. Vojvodinan ideologue Dušan Popović).

91   It is interesting that Ciril Ribičič was Mitja Ribičič's son. To explain Mitja Ribičič's behavior in these years, I quote from the interview I conducted with Jure Bilić, April 1998: "He conducted a cold-hot policy; at one moment he would make a most democratic, almost outrageous proposal about something, only to deny or withdraw it a few days later. It seems to me that his past as a UDBA [secret police] officer immediately after the war gave him no peace, so he wanted to go much further in the process of democratization than any of us in the presidency."

92   RFE/RL Situation Report Yugoslavia, 30 November 1984.

93 This was how Milan Rakas, a Croatian Serb in charge of the media in the federal conference of the Socialist Alliance of Working People, described Mirić's book. Rakas was the most appropriate person to react, since he was, like Mirić, a Croatian Serb.
94 In an interview I conducted with him in January 1998, Vrhovec confirmed that he was aware of Mirić's criticism, but that Mirić's position was very different from his.
95 *Politika*, 24 November 1984.
96 RFE/RL, 30 November 1984.
97 It did not need more than three days for the Serbian proposals to meet with criticism from Stane Dolanc (Slovene), the leading Kardeljist in the Yugoslav leadership. Speaking at a public rally in Jesenice, a Slovenian town on the border with Austria on 1 December 1984 (the day when the First Yugoslavia was created in 1918), Dolanc was critical "of those in Yugoslavia who want to change the constitutional provisions concerning the workers' right to control the fruits of their own labor, as well as the provisions guaranteeing national equality, and the right of the republics and autonomous provinces to decide independently about their own development and about the development of the federation as a whole." Repeating the Slovenian Communists rhetoric, Dolanc warned that the politics of opposing the constitution might well favor various "bourgeois-reactionary attempts to restore a system hostile to Socialist self-management" (RFE/RL 20 December 1984).
98 *Nin*, 24 February 1985.
99 Ivan Stambolić recalls the great pressure he came under when the report was published because he proposed "changes of the system" rather than "changes in the system." He even in 1995 admits only that it was a typing error of his secretary, but the federal party leadership was so suspicious of this explanation that he became very unpopular. This would be reflected in their indifference to his removal by Milošević in 1987 (Stambolić, 1995). For this see also Goati, 1989.
100 In an interview, January 1998. Note here that Vrhovec speaks about defending Croatian interests, although he was the chairman of the Federal Commission, and also a member of the Yugoslav State Presidency. A few years later, the Serbian leadership and the Serbian Academy of Sciences and Arts complained that the Slovenes and Croats promoted their views through Kraigher's and Vrhovec's commissions, while Serbian views were underrepresented or even disregarded.
101 The same applies to political conflicts within republics: it was, for example, obvious that Stipe Šuvar controlled *Polet*, and Mika Špiljak patronized *Danas* in Croatia.
102 For this reason, it seems understandable that some leaders believed that the media were pushing the country toward dissolution and civil war (see Dragosavac's letter to Raif Dizdarević, 1987). They did not see (or, better, did not want to see) that the politicians themselves supported the media, pulling the trigger at each other. At the same time as helping openness and democratization, the media became tools of new conflicts, which they would remain during the war in the 1990s.
103 Interview with Milka Planinc, 19 April 1998. In this interview she said that Vrhovec's analysis was "a compromise to an even greater extent than Kraigher's Program of Economic Stabilization."
104 Goati (1989:98). At the same time the survey of the employed population of Yugoslavia (4,460) conducted in November 1985 showed, for example, a drastic decrease in the attractiveness of the LCY among the younger generation. Although in 1974 only 9% of young Yugoslavs said they did not want to become LCY members, in 1985 this number increased to 50%. Although the sharp increase was observable in all the Yugoslav

republics and in both provinces, it progressed faster in the more developed (but most Kardeljist) Yugoslav regions of Slovenia, Croatia, and Vojvodina. Thirty-two percent of young Slovenes in 1974 did not want to become LCY members, but now it was as many as 88%. In Croatia the number rose to 70%, from 13%; in Vojvodina to 54%, from 4%; in Serbia Proper to 40%, from 6%; in Macedonia to 40%, from 7%; in Bosnia-Herzegovina to 36%, from 5%; in Kosovo to 35%, from 4%; and in Montenegro to 18%, from 8%. The data also showed a steep fall in esteem for the Party, again more in the most-developed Yugoslav republics and Serbia proper. In fact, the esteem for the LCY was highest among the Kosovo Albanians (43% of whom said that the LCY enjoy "high esteem") and lowest among the Slovenes (10.2%). The results of the survey mirrored data on the admittance of new members into the LCY: the highest rate of recruiting new members was in Kosovo, the lowest in Slovenia and Croatia. In the first half of 1983, for example, the Slovenian party organization experienced no growth at all.

CHAPTER SIX

The Emergence of Alternative Concepts and the Reaction of the Political Elite in Serbia (1986-1984)

> We made it clear that we were in favor of Yugoslavia, but only if the Serbs were equal to the other Yugoslav nations. We knew the Slovenes and Croats would not accept such a Yugoslavia. But we wanted them to say so and to take responsibility for it. And indeed, it did not take long before the Slovenes and Croats clearly revealed their views on Yugoslavia: they supported it as long as it was a tool for keeping Serbia under permanent surveillance.
>
> **Antonije Isaković**
> **Vice president of the Serbian Academy of Sciences and Arts**

> Accompanied by intolerance and hatred against the Albanian nation, which is the case in some media, this struggle is becoming more and more distanced from Socialist principles and closer and closer to nationalism. The editorial boards and journalists in the media, who do not want to understand that today's struggle against Albanian nationalism means permanent struggle against Serbian nationalism, in effect promote the kindling of nationalist passions as their main policies.
>
> **Dragiša Pavlović**
> **President of the Belgrade LC Committee**

> It is true that we are under pressure from ideological opponents, but the League of Communists must not make the big mistake of reducing its activities only to disputes with them. Because we are also under pressure from a crisis that must be solved. And to be excessively preoccupied with our opponents would put the LC in a defensive position. This is a real, historically confirmed way to lose the leading position in society
>
> **Slobodan Milošević**
> **President of the LC CC Serbia Presidency**

6.0. Introduction

The political monopoly of the LCY was in reality undermined in the first half of the 1980s as the result of economic and political crisis and greater openness of the media. Consequently, two new participants entered Yugoslav politics: (1) various groups of intellectuals, critical of the elite; and (2) spontaneously emergent groups within the population. Both of them centered on Serbia: the former in Belgrade, the latter in Kosovo. By 1986, the elite found itself under heavy pressure from both the critical intelligentsia and popular protests. It became difficult, if not impossible, to ignore their existence.

Gradually, the political elite recognized the need to respond to their demands. This chapter analyzes the reaction of the political elite to these two new participants in Serbian politics in the second half of the 1980s. The first chapter briefly analyzes the emergence of alternative concepts within the critical intelligentsia and the responses of the elite to these challenges. It also examines popular pressure on the leadership, which ignited in Kosovo, and the reaction of the leadership to the actions of the people. It is within this triangle (elite, opposition, popular protests) that one needs to frame the events that unfolded in the four years before the actual disintegration of Yugoslavia.

6.1. Intellectual Dissent in Yugoslavia

As Dragović-Soso points out (2002), the relationship between the Yugoslav regime and its dissidents differed from that between most East European states and their opponents. Although Yugoslav intellectuals frequently criticized the regime, it was only in exceptional circumstances that the state reacted to such criticism by brutal coercion.[1] Unlike their counterparts in the Soviet bloc, the Yugoslav dissidents published at home[2] and in general attracted less attention in the West (with the exception of Milovan Djilas and Mihajlo Mihajlov).[3] There were three main reasons for this.

First, Kardelj's concept promoted the notion of constructive criticism of the regime from within itself. The ideological basis for this was found in the vanguard role of the Party and the scientific character of Marxism. The Party and science (especially the social sciences) were allies (not partners) in building Socialism. Even those whose views were not strictly Marxist (and thus could not be represented within the LCY) were, at least verbally, encouraged to participate in public debate within the Socialist Alliance of Working People. The boundaries of what was socially acceptable were much more flexible than in any other East European country. Thus state action against those who overstepped them was not like that in the Soviet bloc states.

Second, for this reason many more intellectuals in Yugoslavia than in other East European countries believed that the system could be gradually reformed and need not necessarily be overturned by a revolution. Many of them (being-such as the *Praxis* professors-Marxists themselves) restricted their criticisms to deviations from what was officially proclaimed. With growing "constructive criticism," including that originating from various branches of the elite itself, the gap between criticism from outside the regime and from inside the regime was narrowing.

Lastly, some of the most prominent figures among the Yugoslav dissidents had long-standing personal links with political leaders, established during the Partisan struggle or while they themselves still belonged to the Communist establishment. Many of these friendships survived political breakups, providing a certain amount of protection.

In the course of the events followed here, a fourth reason emerged: the political elites-being divided into two blocs (as described in chapter five)-often tolerated, if not openly encouraged, the critical intelligentsia to say what they themselves did not want to state publicly.[4] The dissidents therefore often played the role of "probe balloons" for the elite, which used their existence to push forward their own options in the conflict within Yugoslav politics.

It would be, however, incorrect to assume that opposition to the regime did not exist or that the regime took no action to restrict its activities. This was especially so with those groups of intellectuals whose criticism Kardelj described as potentially the most damaging: the "radical left" groups around the Marxist philosophical journal *Praxis*, as well as those linked to the 1968 Belgrade student protests (such as "the black wave" in Serbian cinematography). As presented in chapter two, Tito and Kardelj had warned that the leftist, statist, and unitarist alternatives to the self-managing concepts would naturally tend to emerge within the largest Yugoslav nation, and in fact, with the high levels of criticism within the Serbian political elite regarding the 1974 Constitution, intellectual dissent was indeed strongest in Belgrade. Tito's personal animosities toward Belgrade intellectual circles (whom he often criticized for their *čaršija* mentality) had forced Serbian leaders to occasionally take unpopular measures against them. Consequently, Tito's departure was awaited among the Belgrade dissidents with more hopes for the future than in any other part of the country.

And indeed, only five months after Tito's death, in October 1980 as many as 36 of the leading Belgrade dissidents addressed an open letter to the Yugoslav Presidency requesting an amnesty for those who had committed the offense of expressing prohibited political views (*Review* 5/1983:412). In December 1980, a total of 102 petitioners proposed an amendment to the Penal Code, requesting that the phrase in article 133, which sanctioned "false description of social and political circumstances in the country with ill intentions," be deleted. The political elite, however, chose to ignore both demands.

But when 120 intellectuals (including now some from Zagreb, Ljubljana, Sarajevo, and Novi Sad) attempted to launch a journal *Javnost* (Public) in November 1980, the elite decided to react, perhaps also because the initiators were Dobrica Ćosić (whose removal in 1968 we followed in chapter three) and Ljubomir Tadić (a *Praxis* philosopher). In their proposal, the two stressed their commitment to democratic Socialism, which was-as explained in chapter two-in itself dangerous for the elite. The democratic Socialism, the proposal for the new journal stated, "would be based on freedom of speech and effective communication, [characterized by] the synthesis of knowledge, experience, and imagination." But the formal application for the registration of Javnost was refused, and its initiators faced public criticism from the federal interior minister, Stane Dolanc, for "attempting to put themselves on a footing with subjective forces and to present themselves as an elite of society." In his speech of 13 December 1980, Dolanc (the leading Kardeljist among the Yugoslav politicians) attacked those small groups who "raised their heads to impose their monopolistic tendencies over the process of understanding the problems of society" (*Review* 5/1983:444).

Instead of gradually opening up to new initiatives, the post-Tito elite (and especially those who remained committed to Kardeljist discourse and were now becoming *defenders of the constitution*) intensified their ideological action. In 1980 the Law on Higher Education was amended, introducing the criterion of "ideological moral and political aptitude" for all teachers, instead of the much less ideological demand for "appropriate social and overall behavior." However, it was only with the Kosovo protests that the regime began to notice and react to initiatives by its dissident "critical intelligentsia."

6.1.1. The Rise of the "Critical Intelligentsia" as a Political Counterelite (1981-84)

6.1.1.1. Political Engagement

The brutal reaction of the elite to the protests of the Kosovo Albanians in March and April 1981 revealed that the Yugoslav leadership was frightened of the possibility of mass protests, not unlike those that seriously threatened to destabilize Poland.[5] For the first time, the dissidents realized that the regime had no such unanimous support as it seemed to have immediately after Tito's death. The Kosovo events therefore sent various signals to all sides: the elite decided to toughen actions against any kind of opposition, and the dissidents saw new possibilities of compromising the regime.

Ensuing events bore out this conclusion. When a month after the publication of his book, *The Woolen Times,* in April 1981, the (Bosnian Serb) poet Gojko Djogo was arrested and charged with "insulting the highest values and symbols of the revolution" (*Review* 5/1983:467-91). Serbian intellectuals organized petitions and other forms of protest against article 133 of the Penal Code. When after a long trial full of controversies Djogo went to prison in March 1983, more than 100 Belgrade intellectuals petitioned Ivan Stambolić (then the Serbian prime minister) and other Serbian senior politicians to release Djogo. When they received no reply, the Writers' Association of Serbia launched Evenings of Solidarity with Djogo, meetings to be held every Wednesday in Belgrade. The sessions were sometimes attended by a couple of hundred Serbian intellectuals and supported by several semiofficial organizations (such as the Serbian Philosophical Society and the Serbian Literary Youth Organization), becoming the main stage for the criticism of the regime. They now demanded that the gap between the letter of the constitution and political practice be eliminated. This joint action resulted in the formation of the Committee for the Protection of Art Freedom in May 1982 within the Serbian Writers' Association. This institution (chaired first by Zoran Gluščević, then by Vuk Drašković[6]) soon became a symbol of democratic resistance to the regime.

Such a strong reaction surprised the political elite and showed up the internal divisions within it. The non-Serbian leaders urged the Serbian Communists to condemn the actions of the Belgrade intellectuals, who were "undermining the stability of the country." It was still expected that the Serbian Communists would act against the Serbian opposition with no interference from outside. But the Serbian leaders felt that the other republics in Yugoslavia (and even more, the provinces) wanted to redirect attention from the causes (the position of Serbia in Yugoslavia) to the consequences (the growing opposition to the regime in Serbia). Having personal links with some of the main dissidents, and being themselves critical toward the implementation of the 1974 constitution, the Serbian leaders hesitated to take firm action. This was confirmed only when in June 1983, after but three months in prison, Gojko Djogo was released on grounds of "poor health."[7] The last "protest evening" by the Serbian Writers' Association was held soon after—in June 1983.

In August 1983, Aleksandar Ranković died, and about 100,000 people in Belgrade attended his funeral, applauding all the way to the cemetery. Ranković's funeral was a demonstration of the discontent of many Serbs with his ousting from office in 1966, but also a sign of solidarity with those who (like Dobrica

Ćosić) criticized the post-Ranković Yugoslavia. Furthermore, it was a demonstration of the growing anti-Albanian atmosphere, which gained much strength in the two years after the protests in Kosovo. The Federal Party Presidency convened to criticize Ivan Stambolić (from 1982 to 1984 the president of the Belgrade Party Organization) for "losing control in Belgrade." Stambolić, already suspected for his role in writing the *Blue Book* (1977) and his actions involving the case of Draža Marković (1982), narrowly survived this criticism, but he never regained the full trust of the other Yugoslav leaders. Serbian political leaders were now slowly, but persistently, slipping toward further isolation within Yugoslavia.

Seeing Stambolić not reacting to the growing opposition in Belgrade, the federal police took further steps. In April 1984 the police raided a session of the "flying university" and arrested 28 of its participants, including Milovan Djilas. All but six were released the next morning, and the trial of these six "New Left" intellectuals was organized later that year. During that time, the trial of the young university lecturer Vojislav Šešelj started in Sarajevo. In an unpublished manuscript commissioned by the Belgrade *Komunist* newspaper (the official newspaper of the LC Serbia), which police found while searching his flat, Šešelj proposed to abolish four of the eight Yugoslav federal units by abolishing the two provinces (Vojvodina and Kosovo) and incorporating Montenegro and Macedonia and the largest part of Bosnia-Herzegovina within Serbia.[8]

The wave of repression by the post-Titoist leadership against the Kosovo demonstrators and opposition throughout the country initiated a new wave of protests by Serbian intellectuals, which alerted the foreign press and governments to the political trials. It was on this occasion that nineteen prominent Belgrade intellectuals (twelve of whom were members of the Serbian Academy of Science and Arts) formed the Committee for the Defense of Freedom of Thought and Expression, chaired by Dobrica Ćosić. In the next five years (1984-89), the committee sent more than 100 letters to political institutions in protest against violations of fundamental rights. Although the committee originally invited Croatian and Slovenian writers to join, they politely refused, already doubtful about the treatment of the national question in the new initiatives of the Serbian critical intelligentsia. The committee nevertheless took an interest in the violation of fundamental rights in other parts of Yugoslavia, protesting against the arrest of Alija Izetbegović and other Muslim intellectuals in Sarajevo (1983), as well as against the long imprisonment of Vlado Gotovac and other Croatian intellectuals associated with the 1971 Croatian Spring. It also organized several petitions in defense of Albanians prosecuted for "hostile propaganda" and "counterrevolution" following the 1981 unrest in Kosovo. In 1986, the committee established a Solidarity Fund that secured financial support for those "whose existence (was) threatened because of their critical views and social activism." By 1986 the Belgrade intellectual dissidents had already created institutions through which they coordinated their actions against the regime. Democratization and regionalization of the media and the overall atmosphere of criticism (both within the elite and from constructive critics of the regime) helped publicize their views. More dependent on international financial support than ever before, Yugoslav political leaders found it much more difficult to ignore protests by foreign institutions about human rights and even-as with the case of the Belgrade Six trial-by their fellow Communists in Western countries.[9] As a result, both the Djogo case and the Belgrade Six trial proved to be a complete disaster for the regime. In the Belgrade case, one of the six defendants was acquitted, two saw their trials indefinitely postponed, and only three received sentences, ranging from one to two years. The Serbian Supreme Court then even acquitted one of these three, while reducing the sentences of the remaining two to eighteen and eight months. At this time, Vojislav Šešelj in Sarajevo (one of the strongholds of the Kardeljist section of the political elite) was sentenced to eight years. This demonstrated the differences within the elite on the issue of reacting to the opposition and the obvious lack of any federal platform regarding the use of coercion.

6.1.1.2. The Literature of Apocalypse

Apart from the openly political activities of the critical intelligentsia in the early 1980s, many of the leading participants in these protests had published literary works in which they undermined the main constitutive myths of Yugoslav Socialism.[10] Four of the main points presented in the literature of the early 1980s were shared by authors of different ethnic backgrounds, and some of them were exclusively argued by Serbian authors. Among those argued by those in all parts of Yugoslavia were:

First, the main argument of Kardelj's concept, that Yugoslavia offered a viable alternative to Soviet experience, was undermined in a series of articles and books on "anti-Stalinist Stalinism." A wave of books on the coercion used against the "Stalinists" in 1948 emphasized these points. The "prison literature" described the inhumane character of Yugoslav Socialism, which was based on the destruction of individual freedoms for the sake of ideological doctrines. Their authors argued that Tito was not substantially different from Stalin, and thus the regime he created was just one of the variants of the Soviet model (Gruenwald 1987). It was clearly argued that Tito became the CPY leader as Stalin's choice and remained a Soviet agent throughout the wartime period (Cenčić 1981).

Second, the Partisans' role in the Liberation War was now reinterpreted. Contrary to the official interpretation that the Partisans were the only antifascist force in the country, several authors now argued that they were just one of many sides fighting the civil war. The bulk of the literature in Slovenia, Serbia, and Croatia argued that the Partisans were perhaps even less sincere about their true political intentions than the others. They came to power by hiding their true intentions both from their own people and from their international allies (the British and the Soviets). Not only did they take power by deliberately misleading the public about the Communist character of their struggle, but they continued to manipulate foreign governments for the whole period of Titoism. The West was misled about the real face of Tito's regime, they argued.

Third, as a consequence of such an interpretation, some authors in Croatia (for example, Franjo Tudjman, later president of Croatia), Slovenia (Spomenka Hribar), and Serbia (Dobrica Ćosić, later the first president of the Federal Republic of Yugoslavia), demanded "national reconciliation" within their respective nations. It was time to end the war, they argued. Instead of further divisions based on the Partisan-Chetniks (in Serbia), Partisan-Ustashas (in Croatia), and Partisan-White Guard (Slovenia) WW II splits, the Serbs, Croats, and Slovenes should "end the last war," primarily because its legacy was still being used to divide the nations into those included and those excluded.

Ultimately, in several accounts published in the early 1980s, Tito's personality and politics were examined in a critical light. The controversies about his prewar life were emphasized even by Tito's personal biographer, Vladimir Dedijer, in his 1981 work entitled *New Contributions to the Biography of Josip Broz Tito*.[11] That Tito remained "the Comintern's agent" was evident, the nationalist stream of the Serbian opposition now claimed, from his political actions that allegedly followed the hostile line the Comintern had taken toward the existence of Yugoslavia. This unprecedented criticism of Tito culminated in Antonije Isaković's public demand for a "reevaluation of Tito's role" in his speech at the Serbian Academy of Science and Arts (SANU) on 27 September 1984.

There was, however, further criticism of Tito and the Communist myths promoted exclusively by Serbian authors.

First, for the first time ever, the Chetniks ("the Yugoslav Army in the Homeland"), the most exclusively Serb fighters in the Second World War, were presented to the Yugoslav public also as antifascists (most notably in Veselin Djuretić's 1986 book *The Allies and the Yugoslav War Drama*). For the reasons explained in chapter two of this thesis (fear of Serbian supremacy and of a "return to the past"), the official ideology treated the Chetniks as the main internal enemies of the Yugoslav Partisans during the war. Serbian writers, such as Vuk Drašković (in his novel *The Knife*), now argued that they were a spontaneous defensive movement created by those patriotic soldiers and officers of the legitimate Yugoslav Army who did not wish to obey their supreme command and surrender to the occupiers after the 17-day war in April 1941. On the other hand, the Partisans were an organized ideological sect, concerned only with their own ideological goals rather than with the fate of their people and their country. It was argued that the Partisans did not start their resistance before 22 June 1941, but only after and as a consequence of Germany's attack on the Soviet Union. They did not care about Yugoslavia (which was, as the Comintern had argued earlier, only an "artificial creation" of world imperialism); only the Soviet Union and the international Socialist revolution were of concern to them.

Second, the Serbian authors now addressed the mass exterminations of the Serbs by Croats and Muslims in the wartime Independent State of Croatia (NDH).[12] One after the other, the authors (such as Drašković, Lubarda, and Radulović), often deeply influenced by tragedies that happened to their own families during the war, accused the Communist Party of trying to cover up these massacres and the postwar tensions between Serbs and Croats in Bosnia and Croatia. Instead of facing the horror of the war and the deep scars that were still fresh in these regions, the elite turned a blind eye on interethnic tensions, doing nothing to prevent their reemergence. Consequently, it was claimed that Titoist Yugoslavia was not much better to its Serbian population than the Ustashas' Croatia.[13]

Third, the Communist interpretation of the Chetnik movement, which equated it with the genocidal Ustasha regime, and the deliberate misinterpretation of the Second World War sufferings of the Serbs in Croatia and Bosnia-Herzegovina, now became symbols of Serbian humiliation in Yugoslavia. The Serbs, being a majority in both antifascist movements, were the only ones who had fought against their occupiers for justice and who in fact had liberated others from their own collaborators. But what did they receive in return? The 1985 best-selling novel, *The Book about Milutin,* by Danko Popović, summarizes the answer: the Serbs gained nothing from Yugoslavia, for which they fought in the First World War and in which they suffered injustice ever after. As the disappointed Serbian *domaćin* Milutin, the main character of the novel, argued, the Serbs had fooled themselves in attempting to live with the others, instead of turning to themselves. Popović's book, which was reprinted a dozen times and sold several hundred thousand copies, became the strongest literary expression of an alternative option for Serbia-to opt out of Yugoslavia in which she had lost "in peace" everything she had won "in wars." Popović's novel, written in simple and accessible language, was the most explicit example of the forthcoming shift of many Serbian nationalist writers from "Yugoslavism" to "Serbianism."[14]

Through both the political and the literary engagement of the Serbian critical intelligentsia, one simple message, formulated in Dobrica Ćosić's 1978 inaugural speech to the Serbian Academy of Sciences and Arts, entered the public discourse:

> In Europe there is no other small nation that in the last two centuries, and particularly in the 20th, has been so burdened by history and has made such sacrifices for the goal of liberation and the improvement of its existence as the Serbian nation....In the same century we survived Austro-Hungarian, fascist, and Ustasha genocides, and in terms of our human losses we have been brought to the limits of biological extinction....What kind of a nation are we, what kind of people, that in wars we die so willingly for freedom and in peace we lose it? (Ćosić, 1982:126-31)

Words such as genocide and ethnic cleansing entered the public debate, making a link between the Serbian past (1941-45) and present (Kosovo) sufferings. Nowhere was this link between the tragic past and present expressed more closely than in Kosovo, the Serbian Academicians argued.

> The physical, political, legal, and cultural genocide of the Serbian population in Kosovo and Metohija is the worst defeat in the battles for liberation that Serbia waged from 1804 until the revolution in 1941. (SANU Memorandum, 1986)

The sense of defeat was underlined only by its being to the Albanians that the Serbs had to surrender. The sense of Serbian spiritual superiority (developed again by the myth of the heavenly people, built on various interpretations of the 1389 Kosovo Polje Battle) was now released again by the nationalist opposition.[15] Again, this was described in Popović's Book about Milutin:

> If God had wanted us to surrender, he would have sent an enemy to whom we could surrender, not Albanians....What would the Germans think of us, and would they respect us if we surrendered to them? Is it not so? We had stronger and more civilized enemies than the Albanians, yet we did not surrender. How could we now become their prisoners? Should we stoop that low? Not that I am a hero, but again, I would be ashamed if I had to surrender to them. Also, I wonder, what do they think of us when they want us to surrender to them? (Popović 1986:26)

"The fate of Kosovo," they claimed, had now become a "matter of life and death for the Serbian people."

6.2. The (Croatian) Political Elite's Reaction: The *White Book* (1984)

When the police action (organized by Dolanc) collapsed in 1983-84, the Croatian party ideologues Josip Vrhovec[16] and Stipe Šuvar[17] took the initiative to launch a political (ideological) counteroffensive against the opposition. Following its 1982

Congress, the Croatian Party leadership organized a series of advisory seminars with its prominent members in various areas of the cultural and public sphere to debate the public criticism of the regime. In preparation for these meetings, the Party administration produced six internal Party books, in which quotes from newspapers contending with various criticisms of the regime were presented.[18]

The seventh Party publication (which would later be named the *White Book* in the opposition press) was used in the preparation for a seminar, "On some ideological and political tendencies in art creativity, literary, theater, and film criticism, and on public speeches by several creative artists in which politically unacceptable messages have been expressed," held in Zagreb in April 1984. The *White Book* was a collection of excerpts from interviews and articles by about 120 authors (ninety of whom were Serbian, one or two dozen Slovene, but only a few Croatian)[19] in the four years following Tito's death. It also presented poems and aphorisms, which the (anonymous) bureaucrats in the Party apparatus found unacceptable. Occasionally, these quotes would be commented on, but usually problematic lines of poems or other texts would simply be underlined.

The document warned about growing opposition to the regime and sought prompt reaction by Communists in cultural institutions and in the media. In introducing the book-against-book method, the conference organizers opposed any action of coercion against the authors and publications and urged ideological action and Communist struggle in public against their opponents. Šuvar argued that although the main danger for the future of Yugoslav Socialism still came from disunity within the Party, the struggle against the growing opposition to the regime should not be neglected. Like Kardelj before him, Šuvar believed that the clarity of the ideas for which the Communists fought was the main precondition for success.

The document concluded that much of the contemporary literary production painted Yugoslav reality in such dark colors that it deliberately misinterpreted it.[20] Šuvar argued that if the trends were not reversed, the country would be led into another civil war, since the ideas expressed destabilized not only Socialism, but also the country's independence in general.

Not surprisingly, Šuvar's initiative met with a sharp reaction from Belgrade and Ljubljana dissidents, who made up almost 80 percent of those quoted in the *White Book*. Appalled by what they saw as a dogmatist attack-or even nationalist-from Zagreb on free-minded intellectuals in Belgrade and Ljubljana, more than 100 writers signed a petition and submitted it to the Yugoslav Party Presidency seeking protection from the emerging Stalinism.[21] Književne Novine and Književna Reč protested against the *Index Librorum Prohibitorum*, calling it "the Black Book of Yugoslav dogmatism in an unprecedented series of antiregime articles. Šuvar's action, which intended to replace police repression by a public dialogue, now faced an opposition as strong as if faced with brutal police coercion itself.

However, what surprised Serbian and Slovene writers much more than Šuvar's ideological offensive was that 150 leading Croatian intellectuals participated in the meeting, but only a few of them disagreed with the methods and contents of the *White Book*.[22] Not all of the participants were Party members, but neither was any of them really an opponent of the regime. This was a demonstration of the unusual closeness between the Croatian Party and a large segment of the Croatian intelligentsia, both of whom were already concerned with what they saw as a Serbian nationalist offensive. But it was also a demonstration of how detailed the purge of independently minded Croatian intellectuals in the decade following the Croatian Spring (1971) actually was. Dozens of Croatian intellectuals, labeled as nationalists, were still entirely out of the public sphere, and those few promoting liberal and democratic Yugoslav ideas flew to Ljubljana and (especially) to Belgrade to publish there, rather than at home.[23] If we consider the dozens of Croatian popular writers in internal exile[24] and others outside the country, as well as the main participants in the Croatian Spring either imprisoned[25] or who had become nonexistent people, the massive attendance of 150 people at Šuvar's debate gave only a partially correct impression of the real situation in Zagreb.

Šuvar himself was surprised when he learned that many within the Croatian Party leadership and most of the Serbian party leaders were equally outraged by his initiative. The Serbian leaders saw it as yet another intrusion into Serbian internal affairs and as a sign of the lack of confidence of the Croatian Communists in their Serbian comrades. What Šuvar had done was a clear violation of the main principle: Serbian nationalism should be fought against by Serbian Communists, and the Croatian Communists were expected to oppose (for any practical purpose—only) Croatian nationalism. Moreover, the *White Book* initiative was seen as another attempt to accuse Serbian leaders of being soft on Serbian nationalism and to redirect public attention from the "main issues" (such as the economic crisis and the constitutional position of Serbia) to "less important ones" (such as ideological struggle). Croatia was now once again accused of ideological vanguardism and lecturing (patronizing) Serbia.[26]

Ivan Stambolić, who became president of the Serbian Party Presidency in 1984, complained about Šuvar's initiative to the new Croatian Party President Mika Špiljak, initiating at the same time a debate within the Federal Party leadership about the whole affair. Špiljak, whose personal animosity toward Šuvar was a consequence of the widespread perception in the Croatian and Yugoslav political elite that he was becoming "the main successor to Bakarić" (Bilandžić 1986)[27] and thus the most serious of Špiljak's contenders for the position of Party President of Croatia, concluded that Šuvar's initiative led Croatia into conflict with the Slovenian and Serbian leadership. He therefore ordered Šuvar to shelve his ideological counteroffensive. To downplay the whole affair, the ideological commissions of the Serbian and Croatian Central committees met twice in late 1984. "The Serbs were furious at these meetings," said Šime Pilić, then the executive secretary to the Croatian Central Committee, in an interview I conducted with him in January 1998:

> They argued that this was a violation of democratic centralism and that their position in Serbia had been significantly weakened by our action. They said that the Serbian public saw the *White Book* as a punch in the face of the Serbian Party. The opposition was now accusing them of not being able to protect the dignity of Serbia and the processes of liberalization within it.

Serbian Party Secretary Špiro Galović was open enough to say that "to talk endlessly about the enemies of Socialism, and at the same time to leave out one's own responsibility for the Socialist content of social trends, was a typical bureaucratic characteristic and one of the means of defending the status quo."[28] The Serbian Communists put Šuvar's initiative into the context of the constitutional debate in which Croatia was, together with Slovenia, the most stubborn opponent of any changes to the 1974 Constitution. In fact, the Serbs believed that the crisis of Socialism could not be resolved by ideological offensives, but only by cutting the roots of the crisis-which they saw in the illogical position of Serbia following the implementation of the 1974 Constitution.

In contrast, Šuvar believed that Yugoslav Communists should not stop their activities in front of the borders of other republics and provinces. In his article in the Party's official review *Socijalizam* (January 1985), Šuvar explained his motives for the *White Book*:

> We need to normalize relations in the whole country. As Communists and as citizens, we need to know what is happening in each corner of our country, in national and social territories in which we do not live, as well as in those where we do. And not only must we know it, but we must also discuss it openly and intervene in it. In this respect, there should be no divisions into "ours" and "theirs," like foreign territories. We are all interlinked by our destiny, and any nationalism should be of equal concern to all of us, because they are all against us, they all work to head us off. The only condition we need to meet before we criticize others is that we ourselves have done the same with regard to our own nation, where we live....And this is not always the case today, and therefore some of us have lost the moral legitimacy to talk about the others. (Šuvar, 1985:48)

Šuvar's criticism was clearly addressed to Serbian leaders and also to Špiljak's group in the Croatian leadership. As one of the leading opponents of Croatian nationalism in and after 1971, Šuvar now warned his colleagues against opportunism and divisions into "our" and "their" matters.

By his open conflict with the Serbian leadership, Šuvar promoted himself as a potential leader of a growing majority in the Yugoslav party elite, dissatisfied with the trends in Serbia. Vojvodina and Kosovo, and also Macedonia and Bosnia-Herzegovina, now began to treat him as the leader of the "third group," a viable alternative to nationalism and opportunism, hoping that he was the right person to keep alight the flame of the revolution while not endangering the basic construct of the 1974 Constitution. This belief was shared by the generation of old Partisans and by the army, the most Titoist segments of the political elite, which were concerned with the growing trends of anti-Communism in Serbia. They were favorable to him not only because Šuvar had built up a reputation as a true Yugoslav and as a follower of Tito, Kardelj, and Bakarić, but also because Croatia (unlike Slovenia and Serbia) was an example of an opposition-free territory. These groups in the Party would bring Šuvar to the position of Yugoslav Party president in 1988, and would subsequently shield him from Serbian demands for his resignation, from Croatian plots against him, and from Slovenian discontent with his refusal to accept a more social-democratic position. But they would not be able to marginalize Milošević's influence in Serbia, well secured by the same confederalist principles that Šuvar implicitly defended while arguing in favor of the constitutional status quo.

Šuvar's action in 1984 aimed at uniting Yugoslav Communists in their fight against the democratic opposition. But it produced rather different results: new divisions within the Party, both within republics and between them. That these divisions became public only further encouraged the opposition, which saw them as yet another of its successes. But most of all, the events following the *White Book* seriously undermined Stambolić's position in Yugoslavia and more notably in Serbia. Already treated as a "Serbian nationalist," a title he inherited from his office predecessors (Petar Stambolić and Draža Marković), Ivan Stambolić was now losing political support. His proposal to reintroduce the post of the president of Yugoslavia (in 1985) was seen as a direct threat to the confederalist rota system of collective leadership. His candidacy for the position of federal prime minister was rejected by a decisive 7-1 vote in the federal presidency in 1986.[29]

6.3. Serbia between the *White Book* (1984) and the *Memorandum* (1986)

Pressed from the federal leadership and other republics, Stambolić moved to demonstrate that he was not soft on Serbian nationalism. In 1984 and 1985, he delivered several antinationalist public addresses that surprised many.[30] In October 1985, he promised he would keep Serbian nationalists out of the public sphere. He sent a clear message to all those who argued that "the Serbian people have not had their own revolution, but have been led by others....[To those who argue] that the Serbs were not Partisans, that the Chetniks were not traitors to the Serbian people, but antifascists, and that the federation was opposed to the historical interests of the Serbian people."

> When it comes to what the Partisans and all Serbian and Yugoslav patriots decided by their blood and their weapons, we shall not accept any dialogue with anyone. The Partisans defeated the Chetniks and Nazis in such a way that between us there is no room for reconciliation, no arguments in any form, not now and never. (Stambolić, 1985/1988:143)

The Serbian Party president invited the Serbian Academy of Science and Arts to dissociate itself from its nationalist members if it did not want to be accused of supporting nationalism. "The League of Communists must not allow any institutional gathering of those who advocate nationalist theses and actions. We shall prevent any attempt by any of our institutions, which survive on workers' money, to transform itself into a seedbed of nationalism," he said as a response to the growing opposition in semiofficial institutions of the system. [31]

But at that time (July 1985) Stambolić also initiated a new debate on Kosovo, this one in the Federal Party leadership. The Yugoslav Party Presidency, surprisingly, had not debated Kosovo since 1981, except in general terms and as a security issue. The main reason, as Stipe Šuvar recalls, was a firm belief that this was a matter of Serbian internal politics in which no one wanted to be directly involved.[32] But by summer 1985 the Kosovo question had become an unavoidable political fact, both because of the activity of the critical intelligentsia and because of the public protests of the Kosovo Serbs and Montenegrins that erupted in the province, only to be spread throughout Serbia.

6.3.1. The Martinović Case and the Emergence of Public Protests in Serbia

The event that sparked the strongest wave of public protests, linking the Serbian dissidents with the Serbs and Montenegrins in Kosovo, happened on 1 May 1985 when an army employee, Djordje Martinović, a Serb from Kosovo, was allegedly attacked by Albanians who "impaled" him with a bottle while he was working in his fields.³³ The story, widely publicized by the Serbian media, was immediately interpreted as the final evidence of Serbian sufferings in Kosovo. Not only had the personal safety of the Serbs and Montenegrins been put at risk, but also their honor had been attacked by "savage" and "violent" Albanians. Martinović himself became a metaphor for the "raped Serbdom." Stories of politically motivated rapes of Serbian girls in the province, as well as of the "politically inspired" high birth rate of the Kosovo Albanians, entered the Serbian media, constructing the image of Albanian violators and Serb victims. Recalling the myths of the Ottoman practice of impalement, the case was used to link the past and present sufferings of the Serbs. It was also used to underline the need for historical revenge on the Muslims for the fate of the Serbs under their rule.³⁴ In the minds of many Serbs, who felt that the high birthrate of the Kosovo Albanians was a deliberate political action aimed at their minoritization in the province, every (male) Albanian was now potentially dangerous.³⁵

The Martinović case was atop the agenda of the Yugoslav media in the following months. The police and army investigated it, but could not agree on the final report. Martinović himself later withdrew his allegations, admitting that there had been no attack on him. But nobody believed him. On the contrary, the narrative of the event was so convincing that the Serbs in Kosovo considered any medical report that denied this narrative as a political attempt to cover the real truth, especially since the main army hospital in Belgrade confirmed what the Kosovo civilian hospitals denied. The Serb and Albanian versions of truth were by now established so firmly that the facts mattered little.

Figures on crime in Kosovo did not support any notion of *genocide*, the word that now replaced *pressure* and *terror* to describe the criminal activities of Albanians against the Serbs. On the contrary, from 1981 to 1987 Kosovo made up 7.5 percent of the Yugoslav population, but only 2.5 percent (in 1982) and 3.5 percent (in 1987) of total (recorded) crimes in Yugoslavia were committed in the province (Horvat 1989:153).³⁶ When the ethnic structure of criminals and victims was analyzed, the extent to which the claims of Serbian intellectuals differed from the facts became even more striking. From 1 January 1981 to 1 November 1986, there were 360 crimes of rape, attempted rape, indecent assaults, and other "acts against honor, morality, and reputation" in Kosovo. In 277 cases, the violators and victims both were Albanians; in 38 cases they were both Serbs. Albanians were violators and Serbs and Montenegrins victims in 58 cases (of which 16 were rapes), and only 7 cases showed opposite situations (Horvat 1989:154). According to these data, Albanians committed relatively fewer crimes of this type than Serbs (when compared with their share of the population), but directed them more often against other national groups. Once the campaign against the interethnic crimes began in 1986, the criminal activities of this type almost entirely disappeared. From the beginning of 1986 to June 1988, the following crimes against Serbs and Montenegrins in Kosovo were registered: no murders, 2 attempted murders, and 4 rapes. There were also 784 charges for physical attacks, 67 for threats, 18 for verbal abuses, 69 for street fights, 56 for damages to fields, 4 for damages to woods, and 2 for water poisoning (Horvat 1989:155).

Still, the perception of the Kosovo Albanians as being *genocidal* against the Serbs and Montenegrins was progressing with almost incredible speed. The relatively low rates of crime registered by official statistics, according to a now ever larger segment of Serbian public, constituted more evidence of the inefficiency and bias of the Albanian courts and police, who simply did not want to take any action against Albanian violence. The judges, Albanians, simply turned their eyes away from these crimes, and the Serbs did not even dare to report them. No arguments helped to change this conclusion. At the Serbian Writers' Association meeting in June 1985, the situation in Kosovo was compared to the "most frightening fascist experiences of the Second World War," and an appeal was made for the personal engagement of all Yugoslav citizens to stop the "hesitations, games, and manipulations undertaken in the name of false social, political, and national interests to cover up the real situation [in Kosovo], the slowness of government action...the impediments to the free flow of information."[37]

Clearly, it was the critical intelligentsia that now took the lead in promoting the Serbian national question, ranking it second to none. What started as an action for the protection of basic human rights by 1985 was almost entirely transformed into an action to end "the tragic fate of Serbia and the Serbs in the twentieth century." Destroying one type of myth, that constructed by the Communist regime, the critical intelligentsia now rapidly promoted another myth, the one of Serbia's "great past and dark present." Showing little concern for either Martinović's right to privacy or indeed for the facts, the Serbian growing opposition now used every tool in its offensive against the regime. If it expected support from anyone in Serbia, it was from the Serbs and Montenegrins from Kosovo. The Martinović case provided an excellent opportunity to bind these two groups of discontented citizens together.

The Martinović case initiated a wave of protests by the Kosovo Serbs, 2,016 of whom signed a petition to the federal government in December 1985. In what the Defenders of the Constitution immediately compared with the 1981 Albanian protests in Kosovo, the Kosovo Serbs demanded the return of Serbian migrants to Kosovo; the abolition of the Albanian flag in Kosovo (in principle, the same as the Albanian state flag); the rehabilitation of politicians ousted for warning about the dangerous consequences of constitutional changes (such as Dobrica Ćosić);

the implementation of Serbian language laws in the province; the removal of the "greater-Albania chauvinists" and the "Serbian opportunists" from all public offices; the deportation of "all 260,000 Albanian immigrants in the province";[38] and the annulment of all sales contracts between Albanian buyers and Serb sellers in the province. The language of the petition was remarkably similar to that used by the Serbian Writers' Association:

> The Serbian nation in Kosovo and Metohija is exposed to genocide....The authorities in Kosovo are masked by Socialist ideology, but in fact do nothing to prevent (the genocide)....This is the last effort to preserve our families' lives in Kosovo in a legal way....[39] To endanger the people in Kosovo means to endanger the Serbs in general.

From the elite's point of view, the Serbs from Kosovo simply demanded the impossible. While Serbian leaders could not remain deaf to their demands, they could even less accept almost any of their demands without a revision of their ideological commitments to the Kardeljist concept. They therefore condemned the petition in the strongest terms, labeling it as yet another act of Serbian nationalists. In return, they further antagonized its signatories, most of whom saw the petition as the last attempt to correct injustice and to stop the inefficiency of the state administration in the province. To the protesters, their claims were not at all anti-Albanian, but aimed at equality between the two ethnic groups in Kosovo. Inasmuch as the Albanians felt unequal in economic, political, and constitutional terms in 1981, the Serbs and Montenegrins now felt the same. Economically, they suffered as much as the Albanians, but more than the Serbs in Serbia and (especially) in Vojvodina. Politically and ethnically they felt unprotected and endangered by the growing majority of Albanians in the Province. Their response to this situation was similar to the Albanian one four years earlier—both of them sought real protection, and both understood that only a republic could grant it. But while the Albanian demonstrators demanded Kosovo as the seventh Yugoslav republic, the Serbs already had their own republic—Serbia. However, this republic, having two provinces within its borders, was not like other Yugoslav republics, and now they wanted to change this. The demand that Serbia should become a republic equal to others was being heard for the first time, only to be repeated by Milošević and other Serbian leaders three years later—as official Serbian policy.

The sense of the inequality of Serbia in comparison with other republics was now paralleled by the sense of inequality between Serbs and Albanians in Kosovo and by the feeling of social injustice in general. The problems of inefficient and corrupt administration, economic hardship, "personal networks of survival"— these all now became *ethnic* problems. To illustrate this, we can quote a certain Čedomir Bojković, a Serb peasant and one of the signatories of the petition:

It has been six years since an electric power transformer was promised to the Serbian village. Then I went to see a doctor to check my knees one day. He told me: "Come again tomorrow." When I came again the next day, he told me the same. The next day-again. Again and again. I complained to his boss, and only then I managed to be examined by this doctor, but only as the last in the queue. When I signed the petition, I wanted to support a public debate about these things; I wanted to say that we should all be equal: Albanians, Serbs, Montenegrins, and all others. I fought for this. Do I need now to leave my land?[40]

Bojković's demand for equality in Kosovo only mirrored similar demands by the Kosovo Albanians, who also felt discriminated against (as explained in chapter five). A general sense of inequality now characterized all participants involved in the Kosovo crisis and-in a broader sense-in that taking place in Yugoslavia. They all believed that the others were more equal than them. But they also claimed that since the others were in fact privileged, their demand for equality was not sincere. This is how the demand for equality became a demand for affirmative action that would reduce the present inequality. Kosovo demanded to be economically supported and politically upgraded to equal other parts of Yugoslavia. Serbia claimed to be given a status equal to other republics, which it did not have because of its two provinces. Finally, the Serbs asked to be additionally protected in Kosovo, to become fully equal in rights to the Kosovo Albanians. Equality understood in these terms was, however, a non-zero-sum game: it could be reached only when the past injustice was reversed by (at least a temporary) positive discrimination. In the eyes of the other side, however, this demand for equality necessarily became a road to discrimination.

The positive discrimination policy was the main reason why the two protests were by no means treated equally by the Belgrade media and official politics. At a joint session of the Serbian state and party presidencies in September 1988, Petar Gračanin, the president of the State Presidency, explained this policy:

For as long as there is a counterrevolution in Kosovo, it is unacceptable to equate those who demand protection of their basic rights on the one hand, and Albanian nationalists and separatists who endanger these rights by destroying the Yugoslav constitutional order and by requesting an ethnically pure Kosovo on the other. (IB CK SKS 8/88:9)

As the Albanians were being accused of counterrevolution, the Serb protests in Kosovo were being treated as justified.[41] Yet it was not Albanians but Serbs who now protested.

While people like Bojković signed the petition for motives that were not exactly purely ethnic, Serbian intellectuals (200 of whom, including 35 members of the Serbian Academy of Science and Arts, supported the petition of the Kosovo Serbs[42]) now poured oil onto the fire of ethnic divisions in Kosovo. In their Letter to the Federal and Serbian Assemblies, they argued that the expulsion of the Serbs from Kosovo had lasted more than three centuries under the Ottoman Empire, Fascist Italy, and Nazi Germany, only to continue with the new violations by the Albanian state and Kosovo leadership.

> Instead of violent Islamization and Fascism [as in the past, we are now facing] Stalinist chauvinism. The only new element in all this is a link between tribal conflict and genocide, disguised in Marxist language.

In almost revolutionary rhetoric, the Serbian intellectuals compared Djordje Martinović to the martyr Avakum in the Serbian epics about the Kosovo Polje battle of 1389. "The case of Djordje Martinović is the case of the whole Serbian nation in Kosovo," they said. The link between "the endangered Serbs of Kosovo" and their supporters in Belgrade was now firmly established.

6.3.2. Stambolić's Initiatives

This link between the Belgrade critical intelligentsia and the Kosovo Serbs became a serious challenge to the Serbian Party. It connected popular discontent with the intellectual elite, which opposed the regime, and the people protesting were Serbs from Kosovo, a category for which the status of victims of the counterrevolution was recognized by official statements after 1981. Moreover, people like Bojković were themselves Partisans during World War II and saw their dreams betrayed by the country they had fought for. Would it then come as a big surprise if they felt nostalgic for the "good old days" of the Ranković period (or even that before 1948), or if they indeed opened their minds to an alternative story, rather than the official interpretation of reality? Was this not then exactly the situation that Kardelj described in his writings as the biggest potential danger for the future of Yugoslav Socialism?

This pressure, created by the common action of the Belgrade opposition circles and the Kosovo Serbs, forced the Serbian leadership to increase its pressure on other republics, its provinces, and the federation to secure more effective control over the situation in Kosovo.

On Stambolić's proposal, in the summer of 1985 the Federal Party Presidency formed a group chaired by Slovenia's representative, Milan Kučan, to conduct talks with all sides involved and to offer conclusions on relations in Serbia. Kučan's report was accepted by the presidency on 29 July 1985 and by the Central Committee on 31 October 1985. It described the situation in Serbia as "tense...full of serious discord and controversies and mutual distrust, which has significantly influenced political life." Kučan's report supported Serbian demands for more unity, saying that "the right of the Serbian people to create its own state in the same way as all other nations in SFR Yugoslavia has not yet been fully implemented because constitutional principles-by which the provinces were within Serbia-have not been always consistently realized in political reality" (Šuvar 1989:120). Kučan's position, shared by other members of the Yugoslav political leadership, was based on the Kardeljist principle that Serbia is a state, but the provinces were not. It was up to the republics to exercise their sovereign rights and to decide freely on their internal matters. It also emphasized that the Party, unlike the state, was not a federalized organization. If the principle of democratic centralism applied to the whole of Yugoslavia, then it should be exercised within Serbia as well. Finally, Stambolić still claimed that the solution could be found within the existing constitution. In other words, despite his criticism of the practice that had emerged because of misinterpretation of the constitution by the provinces, the constitution itself was not yet treated (at least not by the political elite) as the cause of this practice. Since no major constitutional changes were required by the Serbian leadership, it was much easier to reach consensus on supporting the Serbian demands, which would not change the position of others in Yugoslavia.

This statement by the Federal Party Presidency and the Central Committee was the first real political victory for Stambolić. In a way, it was a reaction to his antinationalist rhetoric, which was now "rewarded" by his colleagues from other republics. It was also a sign that perhaps when facing popular protests, Yugoslav leaders could forget their differences, especially if the proposals did not really endanger their own positions or those of their republics. But it also proved to Serbia's leaders that pressure by the Kosovo Serbs did not necessarily need to be a threat to the interests of the Serbian political elite, but could, on the contrary, support their position in the federation. This message would be later fully understood by Slobodan Milošević.

Nevertheless, the support given by his colleagues in the Party leadership now obliged Stambolić to eliminate the influence of nationalists and opposition leaders in Kosovo. When the Serbs from Kosovo organized a protest march to Belgrade, Stambolić, the head of the Serbian Party, flew to Kosovo Polje to stop them. On 6 April 1986, he addressed a group of demonstrators in Kosovo Polje in what was the first direct contact between the elite and the protesters. In what was an obvious allusion to their new links with Serbian dissidents, Stambolić told the crowd that "this was the right place to solve your problems, and any other place is wrong." He urged them "not to leave their homes, not to allow anyone to manipulate [them] or to form any bad and dangerous intentions based on [their] justified discontent" (Stambolić 1986/1988:166). The crowd applauded Stambolić's claims that everyone should be equal before the law and that no one should be allowed to sow hatred between Serbs and Albanians. But although Stambolić was probably referring to several leaders of the Kosovo Serbs arrested just a few days before his speech, the crowd was more likely to associate this demand with the Albanian nationalists. Stambolić's speech was an example of the rhetoric of a Serbian Communist fighting Serbian nationalism:

> I am convinced that in the Kosovo League of Communists, among the Albanians as well as among the Serb and Montenegrin nations, among the whole population of Kosovo, there is enough strength to beat counterrevolution. If we unite and organize, we shall win! Do not allow a bunch of irredentists, regardless of their becoming more violent as we press them harder, to poison relationships between the Serbs and Albanians here, and do not allow a bunch of Serbian nationalists to do the same! (Stambolić, 1986/1988:167)

However, the Kosovo Serbs did not give up their intention to visit Belgrade and talk to federal leaders. On 7 April 1986, the next day, 550 of them arrived in the Yugoslav capital where they spoke to Lazar Mojsov, a member of the federal presidency from Macedonia. Stambolić's speech in Kosovo Polje, it is true, had made them less angry and their criticism of the Serbian leadership less direct. But still, they bitterly repeated their main claims: they were discriminated against, threatened by the counterrevolutionaries, and disappointed by the ineffectiveness shown by political leaders in the capital. Several speakers, in both Kosovo Polje and in Belgrade, threatened public self-immolation, and some of them even suggested talks with Gorbachev (!) if the Yugoslav leaders were incapable of resolving the situation (Stambolić 1986/1988:173). In his speech to the demonstrators, Mojsov again insisted that the main line of division in Kosovo was between revolutionaries and counterrevolutionaries and not between Serbs and Albanians. The meeting in Belgrade was the first of a series of protests by Kosovo Serbs outside Kosovo, in which they tried to initiate solidarity and focus their claims. The rallies of solidarity with Serbs and Montenegrins in Kosovo became a regular practice in the last years of Yugoslavia.

The federal leadership was very worried about the protests of the Kosovo Serbs. When they convened on the day of the demonstrations, Josip Vrhovec, the Croatian representative, asked Stambolić to stop the demonstrators from coming to Belgrade and even accused him of organizing the protests to obtain support for his program of constitutional change. Even Stambolić himself described his visit to Kosovo Polje in dramatic words: "The real situation in Kosovo, in Serbia, and here (in the federation), is much worse than we think and know." The Kosovo Serbs and Montenegrins had no confidence in the Kosovo leadership and were losing confidence in the leadership of the rest of the country. If this were to continue, the Yugoslav leadership would face a mass movement that would link the

Kosovo Serbs with students, workers, and the opposition in Belgrade. "Our main task is to prevent this from happening." Stambolić hinted that the movement of Kosovo Serbs was led by the opposition in Belgrade, and he warned his colleagues that "the elements on which they rely are multiplying, and the chances of their becoming leaders of the masses are high." Stambolić proposed the following action: (1) providing much greater involvement with the masses to prevent their being influenced by the nationalists; (2) continuing "differentiation" in the Kosovo leadership, forcing especially its Serb and Montenegrin members who were not supported by the Serb and Montenegrin population to resign; (3) giving a free hand to the Serbian leadership when it came to Kosovo; (4) using all legal means, including police action, to prevent the Serbian nationalists from Belgrade from spreading their influence in Kosovo. However, the police action should not take place before the Communists had firmly "rooted themselves" among the people in Kosovo. In the meantime, Stambolić opposed those members of the federal leadership who suggested that the Kosovo Polje demonstrators should be treated as nationalists. He told the Federal Party Presidency:

> It is not about concessions to enemies, but about the wishes of the people.... The people believe they have no rights, no freedom, and they react with all enthusiasm to words such as equality and equal rights. They are in favor of Tito, brotherhood and unity, Yugoslavia, and so on....It is true that some unacceptable and counterrevolutionary demands have been heard. But these people are in such a mood that they would sign anything to secure a change in the situation. Should we now treat them as Serbian nationalists? What if it were true that 81,000 signatories live there?[43] Are all of them nationalists? They simply talk about the terrible things to which they have been exposed. Should we call these illiterate women nationalists? I would suggest realism in differentiating between them and real nationalists. (Stambolić, 1986/1988:142-5)

With this speech he challenged certain elements of the ideological discourse constructed immediately after the 1981 Albanian demonstrations in Kosovo. His warning about the widespread use of labels, such as "nationalism," as well as of the need to regain the trust of the people before the opposition leaders were isolated, indicated a more realistic approach.[44]

After his visit to Kosovo Polje in April 1986, Stambolić was facing a decision: either to put himself at the head of the popular discontent and become leader of the Kosovo Serbs and Montenegrins, or to remain committed to the institutions of the system and its ideology. Subsequently, all other Yugoslav leaders faced the same dilemma: Milošević and Kučan chose the former option, while Šuvar in Croatia (as well as leaders of the Montenegrin, Macedonian, and Bosnian LCs) preferred the latter. Stambolić, however, hoped he could avoid the answer by moving to the reserve post of the president of the collective presidency of Serbia, from which he could do more for the changes to the constitution, a task he still saw as the main objective. From such a safe position, he escaped the direct implementation of democratic centralism and increased his autonomy as a political actor. But he was now directly accountable for any use of force in Serbia, including against both the opposition and the Kosovo demonstrators. Stambolić soon found that by escaping one danger, he had moved closer to another-that of being held directly responsible for the repression of these two Serb groups. When faced with another attempt by the Kosovo Polje demonstrators to organize a rally in Belgrade on 21 June 1986, he ordered the police to block all ways to the capital. To them, this was the final sign that he declined to be their leader. This decision would cost him his career in September 1987, when the person he trusted most, Slobodan Milošević, presented himself as the protector of the Kosovo Serbs, trying to do exactly the same as Stambolić announced at the closed Party meeting in June 1986: to strengthen Party influence and isolate the opposition, which was now presenting itself as an evermore viable alternative.

6.3.3. The "SANU Memorandum" and the Reaction of the Political Elite (1986)

In May 1985, when Stambolić urged the Federal Party Presidency to discuss Kosovo for the first time after 1981, the Serbian Academy of Science and Arts (better known by its Serbian acronym, SANU) established a 16-member commission to prepare an analysis of the economic and political situation in the country. The academy's action was a response both to the public invitation given by the Vrhovec Commission on the reform of the political system and to Stambolić's view that the academy should help find a way out of the crisis.[45] It was also a reaction to a meeting between Slovenian dissidents connected to the journal *Nova Revija* and their Serbian colleagues in November 1995 that influenced the writing of the Memorandum. As Ćosić described in his diary (1985/1992:76-9), the Serbian writers realized that the Slovenes had their national program almost ready, though they themselves were disorientated and confused about their national objectives.[46]

The Serbian leaders hoped that the involvement of the academy in public debate would lower tensions between government and opposition and would further support the changes to the constitution proposed by the leadership. The leaders of the academy, being critical of the regime but still somehow close to many Serbian politicians, wanted-as their Vice President Antonije Isaković, the chair of the Commission, explained in 1996-to push them further toward radical constitutional reform.[47]

From May 1985 to September 1986, the Isaković Commission met 15 to 20 times. Their report was, however, only in its draft version when under somewhat suspicious circumstances,[48] on 24 September 1986, the Belgrade daily *Večernje Novosti* published large excerpts of the manuscript and powerful attacks on its main conclusions.[49]

Little was in the draft Memorandum that had not been previously published by the leading members of the Serbian critical intelligentsia. The text itself was more a description of the economic and political crisis, as its authors saw it, than a political program for action, as it was later often described. It was a mixture of Communist (self-management and councils of producers in the federal assembly, and others), democratic (civil rights), and romantic-nationalist ideological elements expressed in a declaratory style.

Retrospectively, Isaković reveals the position the Memorandum had on Yugoslavia, the most controversial point of the debate and the one that could have easily divided the various groups of the opposition and of the political elite itself:

> We made it clear that we were in favor of Yugoslavia, but only if the Serbs were equal to the other Yugoslav nations.[50] We knew the Slovenes and Croats would not accept such a Yugoslavia. But we wanted them to say so and to take responsibility for it. And indeed, it did not take long before the Slovenes and Croats clearly revealed their views on Yugoslavia: they supported it as long as it was a tool for keeping Serbia under permanent surveillance. The 1974 Constitution, written by the Slovene Kardelj and the Slovene-Croat Tito, was the result of this belief. This is why Slovenia and Croatia opposed any change in the constitution. This is also why they kept Serbia under control by using the two provinces, Vojvodina and Kosovo. This is why they divided up the Serbs between various semistates, thus making them unaware of their own national identity. This was the main argument of the Memorandum, the one that we all agreed with.[51]

Developed into a 10,000-word text (the main conclusions of which were expressed in ten specific points), the Memorandum comprised the core of the Serbian dominant discourse in the late 1980s and throughout the 1990s.

One, it demanded radical changes in the economic and political systems to reverse those introduced after 1964. It opposed national (republican) economies (favored by the Croatian leader Bakarić), as well as the ideology that "neglected economic laws...by relying on people's consciousness rather than on their interests." (1995:105)

Two, the Memorandum criticized the political elite for being incapable of "breaking with the illusions that had brought the country to the verge of collapse." (1995:107)

Three, the academicians criticized the unhistorical tendency to transform the Yugoslav federation into a kind of a confederation. The only way out of this paralysis was "to get rid of the ideology that gave priority to the concepts of nationality and territoriality" (1995:112). It was concluded that unfortunately, Slovenia and Croatia, the two Yugoslav republics "which had managed to realize their national programs through this constitution," defended a system that did not deserve to be defended.

Four, the Memorandum argued that the worst of all the crises in Yugoslavia was the moral crisis of Yugoslav society. Corruption had affected the rank and file of the Yugoslav society.

Five, the Memorandum concluded that "parts of the Serbian population, who, in considerable numbers, live in other republics, do not have the right, unlike the national minorities...to organize themselves politically and culturally" (1995:124). The expulsion of the Serbs from Kosovo illustrates this most drastically.[52]

Six, the Memorandum described Serbia's "disastrous position" in Yugoslavia as consisting of three elements: (1) Serbia was lagging behind economically; (2) Serbia was the only republic with provinces and thus was unformed as a state; and (3) the Serbs were undergoing genocide in Kosovo. This situation, the Memorandum concluded, was the result of "consistent discrimination" following the Second World War, which was a consequence of the CPY's belief that Serbia had been privileged throughout the whole interwar period and thus now had to be punished for this. The Serbian leaders had capitulated before Tito and Kardelj and in fact had acted contrary to Serbian interests (1995:131).

Seven, these anti-Serbian policies continued in the post-Tito period, in which politicians from other republics were "lecturing Serbia and the provinces on the fact that the solution could be sought by the strict application of the same constitution" (1995:133).

Eight, the genocide in Kosovo, the Memorandum claimed, was a consequence of this unsustainable position of Serbia. It warned that the goal of Albanian separatists "to ethnically cleanse Kosovo" would be fully accomplished within the next ten years unless something were done quickly. Therefore "the fate of Kosovo remains a matter of life and death for the Serbian nation" (1995:136). If not resolved it would turn into "a European issue with the gravest, unforeseeable consequences" (1995:136). The same urgency should be applied to the position of the Serbs in Croatia, who were "exposed to a subtle but efficient policy of assimilation."

Nine, the Memorandum warned about the "disintegration of the Serbian cultural space." Deliberate action had been taken to divide Serbian culture into

Vojvodinan, Montenegrin, and Bosnian-Herzegovinan[53] literature, while Serb democratic history was ignored or misinterpreted.

The tenth point of the unfinished Memorandum read as an invitation to the Serbs to "divest themselves of their historical guilt" and to "establish their full national and cultural integrity regardless of which republic or autonomous province they live in." The Serbs, it was written, must "become a historical subject" by "regaining awareness of their historical and spiritual being." Although Serbian nationalism was condemned in words, the establishment of Serbia as a state in its entire territory was declared as no longer an impossible option for the resolution of all problems, especially for the "genocide in Kosovo." Favoring a Yugoslav[54] resolution of the crisis, the Memorandum warned that the Serbs "cannot peacefully await their future under such uncertainty," nor should they allow themselves "to be surprised by events" if others decided to separate from Yugoslavia. "The Serbs must not be passive, waiting for the others to speak first, as Serbia has done many times until now" (1995:147). Instead, Serbia should take the initiative. This was possible only if Serbia transformed itself by mobilizing all its democratic potential.

Publication of the Memorandum launched yet another wave of criticism of Serbian nationalism in all parts of the political elite. The Croatian representative in the federal presidency, Josip Vrhovec, whose *Critical Analysis of the Functioning of the Political System* (1985) was sharply criticized by the Memorandum, accused the Serbian leaders of inspiring the most radical nationalism by their proposals for constitutional changes. The sharpest critics of Stambolić were again from the Communist elite in Vojvodina.[55]

Stambolić had all the right reasons to react: he did not share the views of the Serbian nationalists; he felt obliged as a Serbian Communist to condemn them in public; he also wanted to dissociate himself from any action by the academy and to reject accusations of his being a nationalist. On 30 October 1986, speaking at the University of Belgrade, Stambolić labeled the Memorandum as a "chauvinist initiative" aimed at "inflaming conflicts and poisoning relations" among the Yugoslav nations. The authors of the Memorandum, Stambolić said, did not see that it was precisely under his leadership that significant advances had been made in changing the position of Serbia. They even accused him of "Stalinist sins," though they themselves had been members of the elite during the Stalinist period.[56] Moreover, there was a clear difference between "them" and "us": although the Serbian nationalists sought a solution for the Serbian question in the ruins of Yugoslavia, Serbian Communists would "never accept the destruction of Yugoslavia, not only because Yugoslavia is the result of revolution, but also because it is the guarantor of the independence of all its nations." (1986/1988:219)

At about that time, Slobodan Milošević, the newly elected president of the Serbian LC Central Committee, decided to act differently from his patron, Stambolić. He remained surprisingly silent on the Memorandum in public as he launched a Party action against its main authors. Despite direct pressure by Ivan Stambolić, he avoided any public statement on its claims,[57] delegating his authority to other members of the collective Party Presidency. But he chaired the Party Presidency session on 27 May 1987, when an ideological offensive (not unlike Šuvar's earlier initiative) was proposed against several leading cultural and media institutions, including SANU. And indeed, the Party Presidency decided to cut the public funds for "those programs and projects that are not in accordance with social criteria." Blacklisted institutions included the Institute for Social Sciences (especially the Department of Philosophy, where the Praxis philosophers were employed), the Serbian Writers' Association, the Sociological Society of Serbia, the Philosophers' Society, the Serbian Academy of Sciences and Arts, and the Student Cultural Center. The leading opposition media, *Književna reč* and *Književne novine*, were also on the list, and several others, such as *Student, NON, Intervju, Svet, Nin,* and *Duga* were criticized. The Party presidency explicitly asked the Serbian assembly to reassess the criteria for financing SANU. It also invited Communists in these institutions to "make the necessary cadre changes" and to react publicly "to articles in the press and in academic publications, to broadcasts on TV and radio, and to any other public attempts to deny the achievements of the revolution and the leading role of the working class in our society by smuggling historical and scientific lies and by nonobjective interpretation of historical events, occurrences, and personalities" (IB 6/87).

To implement the Party decisions in important cultural and academic institutions, Party Actives were created in December 1987 in professional associations of economists, sociologists, political scientists, philosophers, lawyers, journalists, and writers. A Party activist group was formed in the Serbian Academy of Science and Arts as well (IB 1/88).[58] Following the Operational Program, leading Serbian politicians engaged in public debates, sometimes even by writing unsigned articles in the press,[59] with the noticeable exception of the Serbian Party President.

In later interpretations of these events, it was often assumed that Milošević was by 1987 already an ethnic nationalist and was deliberately avoiding any public statement against the academy. However, as demonstrated by the Operational Program, Milošević was not at all soft on the opposition. There were, of course, pragmatic reasons for him to avoid becoming "a new Stambolić" in annoying both Serbian intellectuals and other Yugoslav leaders. But the reasons for his decision not to engage directly in this public ideological debate would not be fully understood without noticing that he believed that deeds, not empty words, could change the unfavorable situation, and that the Party should be the real generator of these changes in practice, instead of simply verbally. Furthermore, he believed that the opposition should not be treated as a partner, and even less should the Party aim at wasting precious time in debates with the dissidents. Despite his appealing to some Serbian nationalists as a determined protector of Serbian interests in the constitutional debate, Milošević's reasons were originally far from ethnic nationalism. It happened, however—as with so many people in the collapsing Communist systems—that they gradually evolved toward an open flirtation with it.

Before moving on to explain the Milošević discourse in the 1984-87 period, I need to emphasize that by 1987 the critical intelligentsia had transformed themselves into a strong opposition, organized in several institutions and controlling much of the Serbian media and cultural space.[60] Through these institutions (and finally with the 1986 Memorandum) they formulated a new discourse, which consisted of three main demands: (1) democratization of Yugoslavia by rejecting the Communist legacy; (2) changes to the 1974 Constitution to improve the position of Serbia, making it equal to other republics in Yugoslavia; and (3) resolute action against the "genocide against the Serbs in Kosovo" and elsewhere in the country. Although all three demands were present in their rhetoric at all times, the national question and the status of Serbia occupied now the central position. The opposition linked itself to the movement of the Serbs in Kosovo, keeping its finger on the pulse of the enormous pressure put upon the Serbian political elite. In turn, this resulted in a new division within the LCY and LC Serbia. As in previous situations, the elite split on how to react to anti-Communist action by the "opposition." Since the opposition in Serbia now became much more concerned with the national question than with democratic rights, the ensuing divisions in practice split the Party also on the national question.

6.4. Slobodan Milošević's Discourse in 1984-87

To an outside observer, the Serbian Party leadership seemed to be fairly united at its 1986 Congress.[61] The Serbian political leaders (with the exception of those in Vojvodina and some in Kosovo) shared the same strong line when it came to divisions between the defenders and the reformers of the constitution. However, a lot was boiling below the surface of the apparent unanimity. The young generation of technocrats (led by Ivan Stambolić) clashed with the older generation of Partisan veterans who returned to leading positions in Serbian politics following the removal of the liberals in 1972. As in other Yugoslav republics, the young cadres were winning in this conflict. While Petar Stambolić, the leading Serbian Communist of the entire postwar period (with the short exception of 1967-72) retired in 1984, Draža Marković was marginalized to a level at which he decided to resign in 1986.[62]

Milošević became the President in a tight vote within the party leadership, and primarily because he was strongly supported by Ivan Stambolić, who in 1986 moved to chair the Serbian State Presidency. Milošević and Stambolić were, as Stambolić later explained, political twins. One spoke for them both.

But although Stambolić had a longer career in Serbian politics, and thus many opponents both at the federal level and among the dissidents, whom he now openly criticized, Milošević was a newcomer. Being a protégé of Stambolić, whose program he promoted, Milošević distinguished himself as the most radical critic of disunity, inefficiency, and anarchy in Yugoslavia and Serbia. In his programmatic speech in December 1986, he was speaking from the hearts of the whole leadership, when saying as follows:

> Serbia does not seek to be a republic more than any other republic, but—certainly—it cannot accept to be a republic less than the others. Because Serbia has two autonomous Socialist provinces within itself cannot be a reason for it to be reduced to its narrower territory, so-called Serbia without provinces. Neither should the Republic of Serbia be denied political and legal authority over its entire territory or be forced to apply it to only a part of its territory...We shall change everything that stands in our way to end this crisis. (1986:121)[63]

There were four points he often repeated in his public speeches in the 1984-87 period:

First, he was the most outspoken critic of disunity in Serbia and Yugoslavia. To his thinking, unity was the key to all problems in the country.[64] Yugoslavs, Milošević claimed in 1987, thought of themselves as citizens of the world, yet "everything has been done to make them members of their regions, provinces, and narrow communities." Disintegration is against the "spirit of the continent and of this epoch," Milošević had concluded in 1985. The Yugoslav nations, he said, invented the idea of togetherness (*zajedništvo*) a century ago, when still fragmented by foreign empires. "Today, when this idea has conquered Europe and the whole world, we are going back to thoughts and actions that have been abandoned by everyone else, or at least everyone in the developed world. We ought to be worried and we must resist this" (1985:55). The key to the reintegration of Yugoslavia was in the Party. Just like Tito earlier, Milošević insisted that even in a federal state (perhaps precisely because of its federal character) the Party must remain united to prevent disintegrative tendencies from the republics and provinces. For him, just as for Tito and Kardelj, the Party was the key institution, the one that decided the future of the nation.[65] In Milošević's view, the disunity of the Party was the main reason for the growth of the opposition. The political and economic crises, the counterrevolution in Kosovo, and the emergence of nationalist concepts throughout the country were just the results of the Party's inability to act resolutely. This had to be changed.

Second, Milošević demanded "change in the practice," but not in the aims of Party activities. These changes should be "major and urgent" (1984/1989:34), but they should not endanger two supreme values: Socialism and Yugoslavism. Socialism was still "the best and the most progressive idea of our time" (1986:102). To him, Socialism was yet to come, and the revolution was still continuing. (1986:193) But, his description of the society he envisaged did not develop much further than saying that market laws should be implemented, so that "the working people who govern society are not poor, but rich" (1987:136).[66] It is within this context that Milošević indeed became an open advocate of market Socialism, which, as he said, was not "a concession to the capitalist mode of production and is not an abandonment of Socialism and self-management—on the contrary, it is a condition that social ownership of the means of production survives and promotes itself as the optimal form of ownership" (1987:135).[67] Some of Milošević's reformist initiatives, indeed, sounded as threats to "those individuals" and "those territories" whose interests they would endanger. It was perfectly logical for a "reformer of the constitution" to say, for example (in December 1986):

> The stubborn, permanent, and dogmatic opposition to all change, even to that which is unavoidable, at this moment has the same effect as the activity of the anti-Socialist opposition. It can even be more dangerous, because delaying the change presently demanded provokes the justified anger and discontent of the workers, intellectuals, and youth. By refusing economic and political change, we would end up with the absurd situation of the leadership of the League of Communists defending the existing concept of Socialism against workers, intellectuals, and youth—and this would bring Socialism to an end much faster and more efficiently than hoped for by anti-Communists. (1986:122)

Third, seeing again the main problem in the Party and its disunity, Milošević said that the Party should concentrate on its own "positive program" rather than on disputes with the opposition. It was true that between Communists and oppositionists there could be no reconciliation. But:

> Whenever we Communists talk about the activities of anti-Socialist forces, we should have in mind not so much them, but more the arguments with which we have provided them for such activities....It is therefore not a task of Communists in such a situation just to argue with anti-Socialist ideas and their advocates...but above all to offer solutions to the crisis....It is true that we are under pressure from ideological opponents, but the League of Communists must not make the big mistake of reducing its activities to only dis-

putes with them. Because we are also under pressure from a crisis that must be solved. And to be excessively preoccupied with our opponents would put the LC in a defensive position. This is a real, historically confirmed way to lose the leading position in society. (1986:117)

It is this hierarchy of problems and not his sympathies with the opposition or with Serbian nationalism that prevented Milošević from criticizing the academy and the Memorandum in public.[68]

> I see the main problem in the economic and political system.[69] To treat poems, novels, exhibitions, as the main ideological topics-as happens with some leaderships-I consider this to be a lack of consciousness of what the real problems are. (Milošević, 1984:23)

To debate about the past, Milošević said, was futile and counterproductive.

> A society whose eyes are looking at the past instead of the future will have no future. Those who now try to force us to debate the origins of nations and poems, who offer us reconciliation of [past] armies and classes, and who advocate separatism today, at a time when integrative processes have conquered the whole world, they know this even better than we do. (1986:79)

Not only did Milošević (sharing the view of the Party majority) refuse to put opposition activities at the top of the public agenda, but he advocated much closer links with intellectuals than did any of his predecessors by making clear that the Party should rely on them when attempting to formulate its positive program. More than most of his predecessors, Milošević emphasized the role of the intelligentsia, saying (in 1984) that "our relations with the intelligentsia are our relations with our own future" (1984:13). Emphasizing the necessity of distinguishing "honest" intellectuals from the "counterrevolutionaries," Milošević argued that the Party should not forget that a large majority of intellectuals saw their future in Socialism:

> Intolerance toward educated and determined people, who at the same time do not believe that everything is dark and that existing difficulties cannot be overcome successfully-which is still the attitude of some people-should be tolerated no longer. (1986:122)

Milošević was also a more frequent visitor to the university than his two predecessors, Draža Marković and Ivan Stambolić. Although they contacted the university only when asking various faculties to warn their professors about the Party line, Milošević now offered a hand of cooperation. In 1987, he declared that "Balkan dogmatism expressed itself by its almost feudal views on the intelligentsia. The struggle for economic and social prosperity cannot be won if there are no educated, capable, and clever people in the first ranks (of this struggle)" (1987:139). Bearing in mind that his wife, Mirjana Marković, was herself a university professor of sociology with significant influence in the Belgrade University Party Organization,[70] it came as no surprise that many of his closest aides were recruited from among the academics and students.[71]

As the fourth and last point, Milošević introduced into Serbian political rhetoric the notion of "firmness against anarchy" and of "optimism." Milošević believed that Yugoslavia was slipping into anarchy "in which anyone can criticize anyone, without any responsibility for what he does or how he behaves." (1986:101)

> Precisely because of this anarchy, despite all these expansions of the bourgeois consciousness, we are not under the threat of a restoration of capitalism, but much more of the restoration of those dark bureaucratic forces that we have once avoided.[72] (1986:115)

This means, he concluded, that if the processes that led to anarchy continued, "there would be a strong chance that the way out would be found in some version of a totalitarian state and of personal rule." (1986:115)[73] Milošević considered opposition to be dangerous, since it promoted anarchy in society. The "atmosphere of defeatism and pessimism," which had taken over many areas of political and cultural life, was promoted on purpose to spread fear and helplessness (1986:78). Milošević warned that it was entirely illogical that the most pessimistic people led the country, occupying positions from which they could stop or slow down any development. Young people, he said in 1986, should not allow optimism to be pushed aside by the spirit of inferiority, of criticism, and of mourning, which was encouraged by those who were in conflict not only with society, but also with themselves (1986:87). The criticism of pessimists referred not only to the apocalyptic academicians in SANU, but also to those leaders who endlessly criticized one another for the failures they had caused. The rhetoric of optimism that he introduced in his speeches was in sharp contrast to the culture of apocalypse developed in the first half of the 1980s.[74]

As a consequence of all this, Milošević declared "war" on those political leaders who were not ready (a) to accept the necessity to change Party methods; (b) to be optimistic in public; (c) to follow the right hierarchy of problems, among which constitutional changes were an absolute priority; (d) to redirect their attacks from ideological enemies to a "positive program"; (e) to abandon "dogmatism"; (f) to support Party unity in Serbia and Yugoslavia. Milošević soon moved to unite the Party by eliminating all those who did not want to follow these requirements.

6.5. From Divisions to Unity: the Emergence of Institutionalists and Revolutionists within the LCS (April-September 1987)

Three incidents from April to September 1987 set the stage for the conflict within the Serbian leadership, after which unity would be achieved in opposition to anarchy, anti-Socialist tendencies, and pessimism. First, in April 1987 Milošević addressed the Serbian and Montenegrin protesters in Kosovo Polje, creating a new direct link between the elite and the most dissatisfied segments of the Serbian population. Second, in May 1987 he launched an ideological offensive against various attacks on Tito, displaying his determination to stop any further growth of the Serbian opposition movement and any further disunity within the Party. Lastly, after an incident in a barracks in Paraćin in September 1987 when an Albanian soldier killed four and wounded six of his colleagues, Milošević moved on to convince others in Yugoslavia that urgent action was needed. Although the first event (the Kosovo Polje speech) linked the elite with the population, the second (the *Student* case) split the Party into institutionalists and revolutionists, the two groups that would finally drift apart at the Eighth CC LCS Session in September 1987. The third event (the Paraćin case) was used to justify his rhetoric and practice of an emergency situation.

6.5.1. The Kosovo Polje Speech

On 25 April 1987, Milošević faced an angry crowd of about 2,000 Serbs and Montenegrins when he visited Kosovo Polje aiming to prevent yet another protest march to Belgrade. They demanded to talk to him directly, without "representatives" they did not trust. When they pushed forward toward the building where Milošević was holding a meeting with local politicians, police[75] used truncheons. Milošević, informed of the course of events, went out of the building to talk to the demonstrators. Obviously moved by what he saw (people calling the police murderers and claiming they had been beaten by them) Milošević uttered a sentence that would later become a myth: "No one will ever beat you again. No one should dare beat you!" Frightened and confused by what he saw, Milošević moved among the people, inviting as many of them as was physically possible to attend his meeting with the local leadership in Kosovo Polje. During the 13-hour session with the local population, people presented hundreds of cases of maltreatment, injustice, and oppression by local politicians and police. Not only were most of these stories similar to those in the *Book about Milutin* and other novels, but the political demands echoed those of the Serbian Writers' Association and the Serbian Academy of Sciences and Arts. Milošević realized that the opposition to the regime was potentially powerful and that radical action should be taken immediately to prevent the regime's collapse.

At the end of "the night of bitter words" (as the media called this unusual event), Milošević gave a speech of about 2,500 words. In fact, the content of his speech would now perhaps surprise those analysts who tend to focus their historical analyses on the text alone, neglecting the context. What Milošević said did not differ much from what Ivan Stambolić told the same crowd a year before on a similar occasion, but it was said in Milošević's style and heard by a larger number of members of the media. Although Milošević's speech in Kragujevac in December 1986 contained more elements of the new rhetoric of optimism and firmness, it was the Kosovo Polje speech that marked the beginning of the permanent link between the leadership and the Kosovo Serbs and Montenegrins.

Milošević's speech had elements taken from three sources: (1) old Communist ideological rhetoric; (2) notions of (direct) democracy; and (3) patriotic/nationalist programs, including some of those developed in recently published literature and promoted by the critical intelligentsia. He combined claims for "brotherhood and unity" (reviving Tito's catchphrase—after 1974 somewhat forgotten) with invitations to the Kosovo Serbs not to abandon their "fields and yards," since their ancestors would be ashamed and their descendants disappointed. He reminded the Serbs that "it has never been a characteristic of the spirit of the Serbian and Montenegrin people to demobilize when they must fight, to become demoralized when the situation is difficult," and he promised Serbian and Federal support to the population in Kosovo. But he also reminded the demonstrators that things had significantly improved over the past few years and that Kosovo was not the only problem of Yugoslavia. Milošević criticized the state for being bureaucratic, since it had not secured the implementation of laws in the province. But he also warned the Serbs and Montenegrins that a "state of lawlessness" could help no one: neither Albanians nor Serbs in Kosovo. He defended the right of demonstrators to express their opinion and rejected political accusations that their meetings were gatherings of nationalists.[76] But he left no doubt that the Serbs "should not allow the troubles of the people to be misused by nationalists, against whom every honest man must stand." Instead of divisions on ethnic grounds, Milošević proposed unity based on the common interests of Albanians and Serbs to develop the province in both an economic and a cultural sense. The working class, with its "united" interests, was the "bearer of the spirit of brotherhood and unity, justice, and progress." The working class and its Party were the only force that could successfully halt counterrevolution, which demanded that the province should become a republic, a step that would lead to "the break-up of Serbian and Yugoslav territorial unity" (1987:143).

In terms much stronger than any of his predecessors, Milošević warned that the migrations of Serbs and Montenegrins were "probably the last tragic exoduses of the European population"[77] and that could be compared only with those seen in the Middle Ages (1987:142). At this moment, Milošević admitted, it was impossible to recreate the ethnic structure in Kosovo as it was before, but it must be possible to launch a campaign for the return of those who had left the province. "No price should be considered too high to reach this goal" (1987:145).

Although the speech itself left open the possibility of being interpreted also in a nationalistic way, Milošević's messages were still clearly Titoist and antinationalist.

> We must preserve brotherhood and unity like the apple of our eye....We neither wish to nor can we divide people into Serbs and Albanians. But we must make a distinction between those who are honest and progressive, who fight for brotherhood and unity and for national equality on the one hand, and the counterrevolutionaries and nationalists on the other.

In terms that left no doubt, Milošević attacked Albanian nationalism, which wanted an ethnically clean Kosovo. "They count on time, and – of course – time works for them. But they should know that on this soil there will be no more tyranny," he claimed, alluding to Tirana and fears of the long-term victory of the Albanian high birth rate over the existing structure of the Kosovo population. However, he also clearly invited the Serbs to seek allies among the majority of the antinationalistic and progressive Albanian population in Kosovo.

> The Serbs and Montenegrins in Kosovo will surely receive support from many Albanians, Communists, and other Albanian people, among whom they count relatives and friends, and their children their pals. Because it is our common goal here to see the province economically and culturally developed so that people, all the people, can live better and happier. It is around this goal that all working and honest people should gather together: this should be basis of brotherhood and unity in Kosovo.

People in the province, Milošević said, "do not address one another in their everyday life according to their nationality, in the same way that they do not discriminate according to their gender, age, social background, education, and profession." Neither Serbs nor Albanians are a "minority" in Kosovo or in Serbia: the Serbs are a constitutive nation, and the Albanians a "nationality" that enjoys equal rights with other nations. "This part of the Albanian people is streaming toward Europe, toward a modern society, and one should not stop it on its way," Milošević said, reminding his listeners that isolation and nationalism run against the interests not only of the Albanian nation, but also of all other nations in the modern world.

> Nationalism always means isolation from others, closure inside one's own framework, which implies lagging behind others in development: because there is no progress without the cooperation and development of further relations among Yugoslavs, or without cooperation within the wider context. Every nation and nationality that closes itself off and isolates itself from others behaves in an irresponsible way in relation to its own development. This is why we Communists should do all we can to eliminate the consequences of the nationalist and separatist behavior by the counterrevolutionary forces in Kosovo and in all other parts of the country. Our aim is to finally leave hatred, intolerance, and distrust behind us so that all people in Kosovo may live well.[78]

Milošević's firmly Yugoslav/Serbian/South Slavic rhetoric appealed well to his listeners, who enthusiastically welcomed the new leader's determination. Once again, it was not democracy and freedom of speech that they put at the top of their demands. Just like Milošević himself, they demanded an end to anarchy and lawlessness. The Kosovo Serbs and Montenegrins felt that anarchy, not the lack of democracy, was endangering their rights. And they demanded swift and sharp action in a Titoist style. Milošević recognized this demand and offered such action. This is why he had a real chance of redirecting the Kosovo Serbs from Ćosić's promise of a "revolution of burning books" to his own radical rhetoric of antibureaucratic revolution only three years later. And lastly, this is why no other rhetoric, especially rhetoric that would promise a more "liberal democracy," had much chance to do so.

The dramatic context in which the speech occurred contributed much to myths constructed immediately after the event.[79] To Kosovo Serbs, Milošević now increasingly looked like a new Tito. He himself now attempted to repeat the Titoist formula, which included four elements: (1) linking himself directly with the demonstrators; (2) verbally supporting their demands to defuse their discontent; (3) using this new link between the leader and the population to consolidate his own position within the elite by eliminating his opponents; and (4) using the newly established unity of the purged Party to eliminate opposition to the regime.[80] And indeed, he immediately started acting as a new Tito.

6.5.2. The Student Case: "Differentiation" Within the Elite

When Milošević returned to Belgrade from Kosovo Polje, Ivan Stambolić described his arrival as that of a new man. Just like Stambolić a year before, he was worried about the gravity of the situation in Kosovo, but also encouraged by the public support he received both from Serbs and Montenegrins in the province and in the media. And he felt obliged to deliver what he promised. In the five months from April to September 1987, Milošević introduced an "iron discipline" within the Party leadership. He cut out the lengthy meetings and weekly informal consultations between the leaders of the Serbian institutions. Entirely unlike the previous practice of collective leadership within the Party, he now issued orders without asking for advice. It was anarchism he fought against, knowing that, just like Tito, he would be more likely to obtain popular support by showing that he was in full control and determined to make changes than by appealing to others to act. The time for empty talk, he claimed to his colleagues in the Party leadership, was gone. "Opportunistic" behavior for the sake of false unity should be abandoned for good. In a word, Milošević introduced an "emergency situation" within the Party leadership.[81]

Milošević now asked his Party colleagues to be permanently on the alert when it came to opposition. The "positive program" of changes should be accompanied with an "offensive" against all forms of nationalism and anti-Socialist activities. It was in this context that on 2 May 1987, *Student*, the semi-independent newspaper published by the Belgrade University Youth Organization, printed on its cover page an illustration of a vampire with this title: "The Dance of the Vampires." Alert to any opposition, Milošević's ally Dušan Mitević, the ideologue of the Belgrade Party Organization, now immediately recognized in this illustration an attack on Tito and an allusion to the traditional mass celebration of Tito's birthday in a stadium three weeks later. What would in other circumstances have been considered a minor provocation for the regime (compared with much more serious articles and books published at the time), now caused a sharp reaction from Milošević's allies in the Party leadership, who urged immediate Party action, not only against the publisher and editor of *Student,* but also more broadly, against similar "attacks on Tito." However, Dragiša Pavlović, president of the Belgrade Party Organization's Presidency, remained committed to the previous policy of keeping a low profile when it came to opposition and simply said, "There are much more important issues to discuss."

Following the unusual exchange between Pavlović and Mitević at the meeting of the Belgrade Party Presidency, in the next couple of days the media published 35 commentaries, 34 of which either doubted Mitević's interpretation of the *Student* cover page, or even openly rejected his method of analysis as inappropriate to the "new times." In what was an unprecedented show of disagreement among the leading Serbian politicians, the Serbian Minister of Culture Branislav Milošević publicly attacked "dogmatist forces," and above all Mitević, for their "reading" of the *Student* cover page. The conflict between Mitević and B. Milošević came to the forefront of public debate.

On 8 June 1987, Slobodan Milošević used a half-informal but highly influential political institution of "political coordination" to say this:

We are confronted with an offensive of the opposition, and we must strike back forcefully. The opposition has already taken over many associations, and we are now waging a struggle for the press....Wherever differentiation has not been carried out, our offensive is weak...These are not children's games. We are slipping into anarchy. (Milošević, quoted in *Djukić*, 1994:63)

A Party commission was set up in the Belgrade Party Committee to investigate all the circumstances of the *Student* case. But at the same meeting, Milošević for the first time faced criticism from Ivan Stambolić (now president of the Serbian State Presidency), who said that the case caused "a repressive atmosphere, an impression of a permanent conflict." He noticed that Milošević thought it unnecessary to say anything about the SANU Memorandum and that the public tension raised in the *Student* case was much higher than that produced after the Memorandum. Stambolić warned that several statements by the LC Serbia Party Presidency only "added fuel to the fire."

But Stambolić did not find much support for his views even in the most inner circle of Serbian politics. Nikola Ljubičić, the Serbian representative in the federal presidency, concluded that "we have hesitated too much" and that "our side was on the defensive, while the opposition's was on the attack." Listing examples from the press, Ljubičić (the former federal secretary of defense, handpicked by Tito for three consecutive terms in the army's top office) said that "our people" were under much heavier attack than the anti-Communists and that the Memorandum in fact created a new party against the regime. "We should break with this in good time."

Although the conflict over the interpretation of what *Student* really meant and how important it was, and, consequently, what actions should be taken in response to it did not result in any immediate resolution, it was one of the main events preceding the final clash that brought Milošević to full power in Serbia when its political leaders reconvened after the summer break in September 1987.

6.5.3. The Paraćin Case and Its Interpretation

On 3 September 1987, a 20-year old soldier from Kosovo, Aziz Kelmendi, killed four of his soldier colleagues and wounded six more in a barracks in the Serbian city of Paraćin. Among those killed, two were ethnic Muslims (Hazim Džananović and Safet Dudaković), one was a Croat (Goran Begić), and the fourth, Srdjan Simić, from Belgrade, declared himself an ethnic Yugoslav. Among the wounded soldiers, one was from Montenegro, three from Bosnia-Herzegovina, one from Kosovo, and one from Slovenia.[82] Without waiting for any report by investigators, the event was interpreted by the media as yet another action of Albanian separatism against Yugoslavia and its nations.[83] Kelmendi's individual crime was now taken as a demonstration of "what could be the price of further tension and of the neglect of such a delicate and serious problem as counterrevolution in Kosovo." The Serbian press did not fail to use the tragedy as yet another occasion to say once again: the Albanians are not to be trusted, regardless of where they are or how they act.[84] The message was understood throughout Serbia. In Valjevo, Paraćin, Subotica, and other places, kiosks and shops owned by local Albanians were smashed. The members of Kelmendi's family were all arrested and interrogated in Prizren prison. His sister Melihata (aged 16) was expelled from school. The Partisan organization in Kelmendi's village, Dušanovo, asked all the people there to isolate his family.[85] Aziz Kelmendi's high-school tutor, Agish Kastrati, was expelled from the LCY, and five of his teachers got a "final warning" for failing to make a record of Kelmendi's absence from school three years earlier, from 2 and 17 April 1984. Kelmendi spent these 13 days in prison after being caught attempting to "flee to Albania."[86] The atmosphere of emergency spread from Milošević's actions and his speeches all over Serbia and, perhaps for the first time, to the whole of Yugoslavia.[87] The apocalypse described in novels and plays by leading Serbian writers now started unfolding before people's eyes. A pall of fear and uncertainty for the first time began to fall on Kosovo, Serbia, and Yugoslavia.

On 6 September 1987, the funeral of Srdjan Simić took place in Belgrade, which thousands of people attended, shouting "Better grave than slave,"[88] "We want freedom,"[89] "Kosovo is Serbia," "We shall not give Kosovo away," "Enough of resolutions."[90] The situation became so tense that Simić's father personally asked them to stop violating the dignity of the funeral, but in vain. After the funeral, 20,000 participants visited Aleksandar Ranković's grave at the same cemetery, singing the Yugoslav national anthem.

The Party leaders were now facing their most dangerous challenge since Tito's death. Assassination in a barracks, stones thrown at kiosks, inflamed language in the press, and mounting worries throughout Yugoslavia about the situation in Serbia[91] simply forced them to respond. But how?

6.6. Institutionalists vs. Revolutionists-Toward the Last "Palace Putsch" in Yugoslavia

In answering this question, the Serbian political elite split into institutionalists and revolutionists. As in previous cases of intraelite conflicts (for example, in 1967-72, or in 1981 in the Minić-Marković case), this one was also an intra-Serbian division on the issue of reacting to opposition activities. But it involved much broader issues, such as how to approach the Kosovo crisis, whether all nationalisms were equally dangerous, what the internal party principles were for the resolution of conflicts (including the meaning of "democratic centralism"), to what extent should the public be involved in political decision making, how should the achievements of previous Serbian leaders be assessed, and how should one rate the Kosovo issue in comparison with economic problems. Here we map out the main arguments of both sides.

6.6.1. The Institutionalists

An open conflict between the two groups began only eight days after the Paraćin case (11 September 1987), when Dragiša Pavlović, the leader of the Belgrade Communists, held a meeting with the directors, editors, and heads of Communist organizations in the Belgrade media. Obviously worried about the possibility of the situation moving out of control, he attacked them for spreading panic and promoting Serbian nationalism after the Paraćin case.

> The overall situation in Kosovo, which is indeed not improving with the necessary, desirable, or, even less with the lightly promised "urgency," is creating a dangerous atmosphere in which it seems as if every single word against Serbian nationalism is understood as tolerance of Albanian separatist nationalism....The question we are now facing is not only whether we, united in the struggle against Albanian nationalism and separatism, should neither pause nor hesitate; it is also a question of whether we all believe that this struggle should be conducted only within the policy laid down in the program and the statutes of the LCY, through the existing institutions of the system, and on the principles of democratic Socialism.

Insisting that the leadership should not have accepted still less organized populist politics, Pavlović said,

> Unbalanced words only create a hysterical mood, which makes things worse, without resolving any problem. The space for a resolution of the Kosovo problem is now so limited that even the smallest mistake-whatever the intentions of those who made it may be-could only be tragic for the Serbs and for Montenegrins in Kosovo, for the Serbian people, and for overall stability in Yugoslavia. To argue that one can do anything one pleases because of the situation in Kosovo-even make mistakes, which might be corrected later on-is the classic logic of pragmatic and bureaucratic politics on the basis of which we would move from applause today to great troubles as early as tomorrow. The hands of applauding Serbs and Montenegrins in Kosovo are now starting to form into fists, and this is the boundary over which every further step could be drawing us into a tragic development of events. Who today needs blood for our solutions?...What might happen before we understand

that the trigger on a gun is also pulled by unbalanced, hysterical words in the public arena, sometimes even by one single line in a newspaper? (Pavlović, 1988:94-9)

Pavlović then went on to explain what he saw as official Serbian policy toward Kosovo, saying that "the struggle against Albanian nationalism today is a task that should be performed without any wavering or hesitations." However,

> Accompanied by intolerance and hatred against the Albanian nation, which is so in some media, this struggle is becoming more and more distanced from Socialist principles and closer and closer to nationalism. The editorial boards and journalists in the media who do not want to understand that today's struggle against Albanian nationalism means permanent struggle against Serbian nationalism, in effect promote the kindling of nationalist passions as their main policy. (*Borba*, 1987:2)[92]

The idea of Communists fighting nationalism in their respective nations and leaving other Yugoslav Communists to do the same with "their" respective nationalists was widely accepted by all previous Serbian leaders, regardless of their other significant differences. (Perović 1991; Marković 1988) Only when and if Serbian Communists fought Serbian nationalists could Albanian Communists in Kosovo be successful in defying Albanian nationalism.[93] To Pavlović, these were "two halves of the same coin"-there could be no success on only one "front line."

In his speech at the session of the presidency of the LC City Committee of Belgrade on 17 September 1987, Pavlović interpreted his words in the following way:

> Arguing in favor of the toughest action against the Albanian separatists, I advocated also Communist resistance to Serbian nationalism and everything that could cause and encourage it. In certain articles in the media as well as in some public speeches, I have seen such encouragement. I underlined how important constant action against Serbian nationalism was....Every day there are new statements, even among some Communists, [in which it is argued] that Serbian nationalism is only reactive, and that therefore it is less dangerous and will vanish from the scene once the reasons that generated it also vanish. What these statements neglect is that the most successful way of preventing nationalism in Yugoslavia is to prevent it in one's own environment, in one's own nation, and that the clash of one nationalism with another, regardless of the alleged provocation, leads to fratricidal hatred, even to fratricidal war. Ultimately one may raise this question: is it possible to provoke nationalism in someone who is not ready to accept it nor waiting to express such nationalism? (*Borba* 1987:2)

However, Pavlović soon found that the old formulas had lost some of their previous appeal not only among the people and in the media, but also within the political elite. This became clear when the day following Pavlović's meeting with party chiefs and the media a commentary on Pavlović's meeting with the press appeared in the Belgrade daily *Politika Ekspres* under the title "Dragiša Pavlović's Shallow Opinions."[94] The text accused Pavlović of using "complicated sentences, full of allusions, warnings, and unnamed accusations," and of using unbalanced words, such as "arousing passions," "heated words," "hysterical words," and "hysterical atmosphere...inappropriate words that pull the trigger on the gun" (perhaps in the Paraćin barracks?!), and others.[95] But more important, Pavlović was asked "to whom he directed" his criticism of the media: to Serbian nationalists or to the legitimate Serbian Communist leadership? "Who 'lightly' promised a rapid change of the situation in Kosovo?," asked *Politika Ekspres*. For the commentator(s), it was clear that such promises were given "not by Serbian nationalists, but by the Central Committee of the League of Communists, which was supported by all the people." Pavlović's attack was therefore an attack on Serbian Communists, not on nationalists.

The difference in these two interpretations was indeed important. It was legitimate to criticize nationalists, but not to imply that the leadership was soft on nationalism. Milošević's words from December 1986 expressed the beliefs of the Party majority in Serbia:

> If we have been determined and united in anything from the liberation until now in the Serbian leadership, then it is in the struggle against our own nationalism. When nationalism has been on the agenda, we have been neither weak nor selective, we have shown no weaknesses not even to the most distinguished people in science, the arts, politics, and society in general. Neither shall we be selective, as far as the struggle against nationalism is concerned, in the future, whether with institutions or individuals. (Milošević, 1989:127)

To accuse the Serbian leaders now of being weak on nationalism meant supporting those who saddled Serbian Communists with a "complex of greater Serbian nationalism." Serbia wanted to make a final break with this complex.[96]

Furthermore, if Pavlović criticized the legitimate Party leadership, his action amounted to undermining party unity. Since he was president of the Belgrade party organization (230,000 members) and was supported by most of its leadership, his action could restore "factionalism." Because factionalism was not tolerated by Tito, therefore it could not be tolerated by his successors. Pavlović's "attacks on the Serbian party leadership" were therefore an anti-Titoist act that endangered Party unity. It was not only that unity was at the very heart of Milošević's political rhetoric, but this all happened in what was seen as a dramatic moment of economic and political crisis, above all for Kosovo.

And also, bearing in mind Milošević's passionate appeals for the unity of the LCY and his promises given to the Serbs and Montenegrins in Kosovo Polje five months earlier, Pavlović's criticism seemed to be directed precisely at Milošević and the loyalists. This was a clear violation of the "democratic centralism" that Milošević wanted to restore to the Party.

The whole affair became even more serious when Pavlović (now firmly supported by Stambolić, president of the Serbian State Presidency) decided to convene a session of the Belgrade Party leadership to secure support. What started as a conflict over heated words and their interpretation was now clearly shown as a deep split in the interpretation of Serbian political reality. The Eighth Session of the Serbian Central Committee, convened by Milošević to discuss the case of Dragiša Pavlović, was the last palace putsch in Socialist Yugoslavia, to borrow this phrase from Vaclav Havel.[97] Its long-term consequences were so important that many would see them today as the "beginning of the end" of Yugoslavia, a sufficient reason to follow the debate further in this chapter.

6.6.2. *The Eighth Session of the LCS Central Committee (24-25 September 1987): Victory for the Revolutionists*

The Eighth Session of the Serbian Central Committee was characterized by a clash between revolutionists and institutionalists within the Serbian leadership. The revolutionary character of Milošević's supporters was best expressed by Radoš Smiljković, a political science professor from Belgrade, who duly replaced Dragiša Pavlović as the new president of the Belgrade Party organization. In his speech at the Eighth Session, Smiljković opposed Pavlović's appeal for patience and cool heads when debating Kosovo. "What does it mean to invite us to be patient, to wait, to keep cool heads in a situation in which there is blood, and when corpses of sleeping soldiers and bodies of raped girls and women (including old women), are rolling on the ground?" asked Radoš Smiljković, situating Pavlović's words in what he saw as their context. This context was characterized by the Paraćin case.

> Comrade Pavlović said that unbalanced words pulled the trigger, or that they could pull the trigger, with regard to his assessment of the press. The trigger has been pulled in Paraćin....[98]The League of Yugoslav Communists adopted the political stand that there was a counterrevolution in Kosovo, and the crime in Paraćin convinced us once again that the LC conclusions are correct. What does it mean in this context when one emphasizes primarily nonrevolutionary ways of struggle?[99] (*Borba*, 1987:6)

Using metaphors that had not been heard in Yugoslav politics since wartime, Smiljković warned that "in war there were situations when brothers stood against each other, and we shot people for minor mistakes." He reminded Pavlović of an old popular saying: "Vicious herbs for a vicious wound," suggesting that such should be a reaction to counterrevolution.[100] A nonrevolutionary speech, the revolutionists like Smiljković argued, helps counterrevolution and defies Party action. This is how Smiljković (and as will be shown at the end of this debate-most members of the Serbian Central Committee) understood the consequences and meaning of Pavlović's words. A political speech, Smiljković argued, "is not about what is said," but "about what the speech itself produces" (1987:6). Once the "woven form" of Pavlović's words (Sokolović, in his opening speech, 1987:9) was analyzed, it was "clear" that Pavlović "expressed resistance to the course of the League of Communists" (*Borba* 1987:9).

It was on this occasion that the old language of Stalinism suddenly reappeared, indicating that the time of show-trials and unanimous condemnations of leaders that were accused of wrongdoing had not been left entirely in the dark past.[101] Using another (very Stalinist) metaphor, a member of the Central Committee, Radivoje Marinković, said:

> As this debate continues, it seems that the masks are gradually falling away and that the true faces are appearing in front of us. And in fact, the dropping of these masks, at least to me, illuminates and reveals what the real aim was of Comrade Pavlović's performance in front of the editors in chief and party secretaries and the press. (*Borba* 1987:29)

And then, of course, another question arose: was Pavlović one or two personalities, one with a mask and another behind it? What Pavlović wanted to say was not the same as what "went out to the public," said one of the pro-Milošević members (Predrag Živanović). His words might have been comprehensible for Pavlović, but his "allusions...were obvious, and they provoked confusion and anger" (Sokolović 1987:9). And of course, asked Marinković:

> Did Comrade Dragiša Pavlović really act on his own conviction, on his own behalf, or was he, perhaps, only a spokesman, who said only what had already been agreed on elsewhere, who was there only to perform a task given to him? It seems to me that he was there in this latter role. (*Borba* 1987:39)

In revealing Pavlović's "true face" that was hidden by his "mask" in his allusions, the Party justified its existence. It was there to be awake, and awake it was.

But how did they know that Pavlović was criticizing his Party and not the nationalists? Was Pavlović not, as Shefchet Mustafa (member of the CC from Kosovo) said, still alive, sitting among them? Why did they not take Mustafa's advice: "Talk to him, see what he thinks, and don't interpret him as we wish." (*Borba* 1987:23)

The answer to this question should again, I argue, be found in ideology. The Party knew what Pavlović meant because it was, by definition, able to understand what he was really saying better than Pavlović himself. The Party was invited to reveal the "real meaning" because it saw further and knew better than any of its members. Perhaps the best description of this thinking is given by the one who was now accused: Ivan Stambolić, the president of the Serbian State Presidency. Eight years after the 8th Session, he said that even then, back in 1987, for all Communists of his generation, "a conflict with the Party was heresy, hugely so." (1995:247). The supreme ability of the Party to define the project of a perfect world was never to be challenged:

> I only know that as a Party official I was driven by a firm belief that the world would become better when we, Communists, gave life to our ideological project of *making people happy*. And the world, alas, was still organized wrongly only because it happened that we hadn't yet managed to make it to the end. I had not the slightest doubts that despite the world's imperfection, we might not be able to essentially improve the world and man, that we could, on the contrary, maybe even make it worse. (Stambolić, 1995:38)[102]

But although all Communists accepted that the Party had the right to define its "line," many argued that some degree of internal pluralism within should be allowed. Kardelj's notion of "non-Party pluralism" was used to legitimize this position. On the other hand, the revolutionists now argued that there was only one true meaning and that others were false interpretations (revisionism). Smiljković (and of course Milošević) believed that they knew what Pavlović really meant, since the concepts were clearly comprehensible, even when covered by metaphors and allusions.

As a good Communist (indeed one of their most prominent leaders), Pavlović himself accepted, at least initially, that the Party had the final say over what he really meant. Like so many Communists before him, he in fact accepted the rule that any member could be wrong, but the Party itself was always right.[103] This is why this debate between Pavlović and the others was in fact still an intra-Party affair, which did not introduce any methodically new situation in the Yugoslav political space. It was a debate about who the true interpreter of Party policy was, and not only about who the true interpreter was of Pavlović's words. Pavlović argued that his interpretation of Party policy was right and that the media bosses were deviating from the party line. He was not attacking the Party, but, on his understanding, was implementing its policy of rejecting [Serbian] nationalism. He portrayed himself as a true defender of Titoism:

I attempted and will continue to engage all my efforts in the realization of the programmatic goals of the League of the Yugoslav Communists, on the clear road of Tito's revolutionary and realistic policy. (*Borba*, 1987:15)

But his opponents said the same about themselves. It was they who understood what Titoism was, while Pavlović had failed to implement the Party line in defending Tito. He had failed to act against *Student* and its Vampire Dance cover page, and therefore he "blocked the political action, which was launched by the presidency of the Central Committee." (Sokolović 1987:9) This in fact meant that although in words he might have been a true Titoist, in action he was showing opportunism. And the essence of Titoism, they argued, was that words were inseparable from action. For a true Marxist and a revolutionary, such as Tito, it was not about interpreting the world, but about changing it. Words were weapons only when they came into people's possession. Anyone who did not understand this message was not a Titoist.[104] Thus not only was Pavlović not a true defender of Titoism, but he was one of the main obstacles in this struggle.

These two conflicting interpretations of the meaning both of Tito's work and of Pavlović's words made their actors incapable of finding a compromise, even of understanding each other. Stambolić later (in 1995) recalled the situation at and immediately after the 8th Session:

> There was simply no communication any longer. They would have either not understood or ignored it. (Stambolić, 1995:248)[105]

This is how comrades came to the point of a "dialogue of the deaf," in a debate in which they were talking different languages. And it was not surprising that at one moment it looked much more like a talk between "us" and "enemies" than between "us" and "our comrades." Only the enemy speaks a "different language." He does not understand "us," and even less does he attempt to do so. In a revolutionary party, no dialogue can occur between "them" and "us." His words mean nothing to us, since we do not understand them.[106]

> Do not translate [*sic*] this speech as if it were smuggled in here by the enemy, or as if it were written in a foreign language. And [do not] infer from this translation allegations that political forums were attacked, or that some leaders [were attacked], said one of the participants in the debate. (Mitrović, *Borba* 1987: 21)

They were talking different languages because they simply did not share the same meanings regarding the same words. Since words should be inseparable from actions, one needed to achieve unity of understanding first to achieve unity of action. Since ideas became weapons once they were accepted by the masses, it was the struggle for the formulation of the right set of ideas that politics were really about. This was why it was so important to win in a battle over the true meaning of words. This is also why it was so important that in a monolithic society, no alternative explanation of reality was allowed in public.[107]

To undermine unity means to undermine the whole community, because community is not much more than a communicative unity. Being central to his understanding of politics, the notion of unity was placed above all others in Milošević's program. But in defending the principle that there was only one true explanation of Pavlović's words (and that this did not necessarily need to be his own), Milošević did in fact not only renew the monist principle within the Communist part of society, but he also spoke a language many others in society understood as theirs. His message about unity was therefore heard and accepted well beyond the Party itself, and principally by the nationalist and traditionalist ranks of the Serbian nation, which shared the monist understanding of reality too. It was also well received by the egalitarian ranks of society, which now protested against injustice and inequality. From this to the full unity of the nation—without respect to their various political affiliations-—was just one step.

6.6.3. Milošević's Interpretation of Titoism: Return of the Third Concept of Yugoslavia (1945-66)

In promoting the concept of unity and revolution, Milošević in fact presented himself as a real Titoist, and by this he meant the follower of the "original message of the revolution," not of its later (post-1966) interpretation. Milošević now interpreted the post-1974 concept as a betrayal not only of revolution, but of Tito himself. Although Milošević never said this in public, for him the landmark event was the ousting of Ranković in 1966. This is the moment when the "original Tito" was replaced by Kardeljist doctrine, which had very little in common with revolution. Milošević now offered to "bring Tito back in" to "replace" Kardelj.[108]

The best illustration of this rhetorical twist is to be found in Milošević's programmatic speech at a "memorial (Seventh) session" of the CC LCS which celebrated the 50th anniversary of Tito's succession to the post of secretary general of the CPY in 1937. It happened (certainly not as a coincidence) that Milošević convened that session at the same time as the Eighth Session itself. The heated debate at the Eighth Session was therefore interrupted early in the evening to allow Milošević to install himself as the true interpreter of Titoism not only within the party leadership, but also in the eyes of the general public in Serbia.

In his speech, Milošević first said that Tito's opus "did not belong to the past,"[109] and that he "carried in himself a deep and forceful sense of energy, confidence, and optimism."[110]

He did not fear battles, conflicts, enemies, risks. He was not afraid to lose-although he entered every battle to win—perhaps because he was inside deeply convinced that he was fighting for a right, great thing, for the greatest idea of his time,[111] and that this idea would win with him or with someone else later, but win without any doubt....These characteristics of Tito, which were manifested at the worst historical moments of our revolution, must today forge the hearts of a generation that does not live at ease, but that needs to know that life and the future belong to honest and brave people,[112] and that for their ideals they must fight resolutely and without compromise. (1989:166)

An example of such bravery, to which he summoned the new (post-Titoist) generation of Yugoslavs, Milošević found in Tito's "refusal to kneel in front of fascism or to bow down before Hitler's terrible army."

> His dignified and resolute *no* to humiliation, injustice, to all that was not in the interest of his people, Tito voiced again,[113] to be remembered forever by his people and by the whole world.[114]

Milošević then said that Tito showed that "theoretical blueprints and spiritual dogmatism" were foreign to him.

> As a man who had the courage to be free on all occasions,[115] Tito managed to develop Socialist practice and to enrich Marxist theory by bringing new ideas and new solutions at a time when the Marxist idea was exposed to pressure from the dogmatic spirit on one side and from revisionism on the other.

However, the main key to the successes of Tito's Yugoslavia was in the unity of her nations, which Tito promoted his whole life:

> At this moment of Yugoslav reality, unity is the condition for freedom and for peace, the unity that made us winners of battles, which has entered textbooks, history, and the collective memories of the people. The sufferings in fascist prisons, the slaughter by the Chetniks and Ustashas, the Hell of Sutjeska, the almost insane bravery in the battle for the wounded at the Neretva, the apocalyptic killings in Kozara, the cleansing of every single human being who was not an occupier or a traitor in Srem—we survived all this because we were united.[116] The whole horror of the four-year war bears in itself one large, eternal, and imperishable light: the war was survived and brought to a victorious end by the combatants and the whole people, because they were united and unanimous....In this part of the revolution that we are now making [*sic*!], there are new battles waiting for us. To end them victoriously, we need to be together and united as we were then. This is the meaning of Tito's work, this is the essence of the Yugoslav revolution, this is the condition for a future that will nevertheless be beautiful and that is not that far away.

It was by this speech and his subsequent actions that Milošević was recognized as the new (young, revolutionary) Tito by the Kosovo Serbs and many others, who now added his poster to that of Tito's throughout the province, only to remove Tito's three years later.[117] However, the complex subtext that underlined Milošević's assessment of Tito allowed for an alternative interpretation: that he was, as Dobrica Ćosić said, the most deserving Serb for the task of the destruction of the (late, post-1974) Titoist legacy. He was understood in the same way by many other Yugoslav leaders, who were sharply divided when debating his rhetoric and actions in the years to come. These divisions within the elite led to the breakup of the elite consensus and resulted-in 1991-in the disintegration of Yugoslavia.

However, before we come to this point, a question needs to be answered: why did so many of his colleagues in Serbia and also in the Yugoslav leadership support his actions?

6.7. Why Did the Others Support Milošević?

At the end of the 50th anniversary session, which marked Tito's elevation to the party throne, the members of the Serbian Central Committee continued their Eighth Session. However, the stage was set: Milošević's victory was clear. In fact, the vote showed that only eight members of the Central Committee still opposed the proposal of the presidency that Dragiša Pavlović should be expelled from the presidency. Eighteen others, most of whom came from Kosovo and Vojvodina, abstained rather than vote against. Milošević's appeal for unity had worked. But, Milošević said in his concluding speech at the Eighth Session, this did not mean that there would be any unity with Serbian nationalists. In one of the most explicit criticisms of Serbian nationalism in his career, Milošević said:

> Serbian nationalism today is not only intolerance and hatred of another nation or other nations; it is indeed a snake in the bosom of the Serbian nation, which has always in its history tended to be united with other southern Slav nations, and whose most progressive force, the working class, has been the bearer of the spirit of brotherhood and unity, solidarity, and equality with all nations and nationalities on Yugoslav soil-before, during, and after the war. Moving away from this, Serbian nationalists would create the greatest damage for the Serbian nation by what they offered as allegedly their best: isolating it in reality from others to whom we would become intolerant and suspicious. Economically, politically, socially, and culturally-how could the small Serbian nation live alone and on its own and free when even bigger nations cannot do so in this world in which nations and people are more and more interlinked and more and more cannot be free with regard to each other when alone and on their own? (1987/1989:171-2)

This was, in Milošević's opinion, Pavlović's main misunderstanding. Pavlović could not distinguish between the intentions of the Serbian leadership to "solve the problems in Kosovo in the interests of all the people who lived there: Albanians, Serbs, Montenegrins, in the name of their equality, their unity, the unity of Serbia, and the unity of Yugoslavia" (*Borba* 1987:40), and, of course, Serbian nationalism. It is in his plea for unity before the divided Serbian Central Committee that one must start looking for the reasons to support Milošević's success. To many he sounded like a savior. By defending (young) Tito, Milošević's speech sounded very seductive to the older generation of Serbian partisans and to the army officers, many of whom were Serbs or Montenegrins, as Milošević was himself.[118] Stambolić explains:

> He reminded them (the oldest generation in the Party) of a time when they were young, firm, and resolute. They liked his energy, sharpness, the easily recognizable style of a revolutionary.[119]

Moreover, by his resolute and somewhat radical rhetoric, which was in obvious and sharp opposition to the phrases everyone had got used to during the post-Titoist period, Milošević could have quite easily been seen as the hope for Serbs with higher education. To the younger generation he offered immense optimism, a "future that will be beautiful and is not far away."[120] To the workers who organized 75 strikes with 13,000 participants in Belgrade just in the nine months preceding the Eighth Session, Milošević brought big promises and at least some hope of a resolute break with "bureaucracy."[121] To those who were tired of listening to the same phrases and endless description of the situation, he offered a new rhetoric of short and simple sentences.

By opposing bureaucracy (in his antibureaucratic revolution), Milošević became "the People's Prince,"[122] putting himself at the head of the popular discontent. It was not only because of his strong language against the counterrevolution, but also because of his opposition to bureaucracy that he mobilized not only the Kosovo Serbs, but Serbs in general. The point was explained by a Kosovo Serb interviewed by a Slovene researcher in 1989:

> I watch these members of the League of Communists in my commune, for example the president of the Municipality who has two houses and many more, while I ride my bike to go shopping every day. It is like this everywhere else. But now, with the arrival of Milošević, it has become possible for me to overthrow this president of the municipality with his two houses to question whether his property was legally acquired. Hence we have more human rights than ever before since Milošević came to power. This is what is happening in other cities as well, and this is why the people like him. (Gaber and Kuzmanić 1989:251)

A sense of inequality mobilized many.[123] This motive for social action survived even when the ideology of Communism had already collapsed elsewhere in Eastern Europe. In October 1990, it was reported that 30.3 percent of the Serbian population agreed with a typical egalitarian understanding of justice: "The state ought to make sure that everyone in society has about the same and lives in a more or less equal way" (Obradović 1996:495). At the same time, only half of this number (18.3 percent) believed in a libertarian understanding of social justice, that "...the state ought not to limit wealth, but should allow anyone to have as much as he/she is capable of producing and earning," Almost half of the population (49.8 percent), however, felt "betrayed and cheated," since reality was entirely different from what was promised, and 52.2 percent believed that personal links, and not personal qualities, were the main means for success in society. If these were the results of a survey in 1990, one could safely assume that in 1988, at the time when Milošević launched his "antibureaucratic revolution," people felt even more inclined to an egalitarian understanding of social justice and less to a libertarian understanding of it, and they felt even more "helpless" than after three years of his rhetoric of optimism.

To the Serbs in Kosovo, Milošević's sharp action against the bureaucrats demonstrated that their complaints did not fall on deaf ears. To them, Milošević was the first who understood and accepted the sense of the urgency of change that they had been trying to convey to political leaders in the past two decades. Milošević was talking for them when he said in October 1988:

> Almost everyone who speaks about Kosovo accepts that the situation is difficult. But then they immediately warn us that such a situation cannot be resolved overnight. I have been listening to this phrase for at least the past six years. And I ask: should we invite here Yugoslav and world geographers, meteorologists, and astronomers to explain to us how one night can last for six years? The longest night scientists know of is of six months duration and is confined to the Polar areas." (1988/1989:270)

For young politicians in the lower ranks of the party leadership, Milošević's opposition to the Stambolićs,[124] whose influence in Serbian politics had lasted more than 40 years, was a good chance for promotion. For some Serbian politicians, however, the conflict between Stambolić and Milošević was the last chance to extend their political lives.[125] For those Belgrade intellectuals who opposed the 1974 Constitution (such as Mihajlo Djurić), for the Praxis professors (such as Mihailo Marković[126] and Ljubomir Tadić), and even for Milovan Djilas, Milošević was a new chance. In his antibureaucratic revolution they saw the realization of their long-standing claims that Yugoslav society had formed a new class of bureaucratic rulers and had practically abandoned the Marxist vision of a self-managing society. Although he remained critical of his politics, Milovan Djilas later admitted he was "soft on Milošević"; it was under the latter's government that he was allowed to speak in public for the first time since his ousting from office in 1954.

Lastly, although they disliked what they saw as yet another Stalinist intraparty conflict, the Serbian nationalist intelligentsia welcomed the removal of Stambolić and Pavlović, whose attacks on the Memorandum a year before were seen as a betrayal of national interests.[127] Although Serbian nationalists really could not know what to expect from Milošević (for whom nationalism was "a snake in the bosom of the Serbian people"), they certainly welcomed his promises to resolve the Albanian discontent in Kosovo and his appeals for unity. Moreover, Milošević made every effort to convince the academicians that Stambolić met open opposition when he wanted to draw Serbian Communists into an ideological (and even legal) fight with them. His aides simply quoted all those speeches in which Milošević opposed ideological struggles, while hiding his proposals to the Party Presidency earlier in 1987. The opponents of the regime, most of whom had participated in the 1941-45 revolution, now finally became allies in the new, antibureaucratic revolution, which was to annul all the mistakes of the post-Ranković period when they themselves were marginalized and criticized.

The provinces within Serbia and the other Yugoslav republics did not oppose Milošević either. From the position of the provinces, Stambolić's constant attempts to change the Serbian constitution were seen as no less dangerous than Milošević's Titoist rhetoric. Stambolić was, as one of the leading Vojvodinan Communists, Živan Berisavljević said,[128] a prominent participant in post-1981 Serbian politics, which was "centralistic and nationalistic" all the way through. Also, they treated the conflict as an "internal" Serbian matter in which they should not be involved, since they wanted the same autonomy in their internal matters. "Many topics on the agenda were mostly or entirely about Belgrade," explained Boško Krunić, a Vojvodinan politician who was the then President of the Yugoslav Party Presidency.[129]

The Kosovo Communist representatives on the Serbian Central Committee also abstained from taking sides in this conflict. Azem Vllasi, who was then president of the Kosovo Provincial LCY Committee, recalls:

> We in Kosovo differed from the Serbian leadership about the situation in Kosovo a long time before the Eighth Session. Therefore we did not feel invited to help Stambolić's faction. And even if we had wanted to help him, this would have only speeded up his defeat, since the extremists would have taken this as an argument against Stambolić and Pavlović to accuse them additionally.

Vllasi believes that even if Stambolić had won at the 8th Session, "the whole thing would have been delayed only for a month or two, for some other occasion, but the penetration of nationalism, chauvinism, and Stalinism into the political leadership of Serbia could not have been stopped." Vllasi also says that as Albanians, they were simply not a factor in the power struggle in Serbia, and that in this respect Vojvodina was to be blamed more. "In the end, they were Serbs themselves."[130]

The same applied to the other Yugoslav republics. The main Croatian daily, for example, wrote that "the public can hardly see any essential political difference between those who remained in the Serbian leadership and those had left."[131] When Ivan Stambolić was replaced by Titoist General Petar Gračanin as president of Serbia, *Vjesnik* wrote:

> His reputation as a man who has been Tito's soldier all his life, who could have clearly accepted the Titoist vision of the humane Socialist society, his experience as a revolutionary and a long-term party worker, will without any doubt contribute to the stabilization of the situation in Serbia. And without a peaceful and stable Serbia there will be no strong Yugoslavia.[132]

Not only did politicians in other Yugoslav republics refuse to intervene in Serbian politics (the Kardeljist concept suited them in this respect),[133] but some of them saw change as positive. Stipe Šuvar, a Croat member of the Yugoslav Party Presidency, saw it as "a promising awakening of a new generation of leaders who were claiming they were Titoists." Šuvar-who would only a year later become the leading opponent of Milošević's antibureaucratic revolution-thought that even if open Serbian nationalism increased as a consequence of the Eighth Session, this would still be better than "Stambolić's latent nationalism for which he could not be criticized or opposed in the federal leadership," as he said in an interview conducted in October 1997.[134] Šuvar also believed that Kosovo really was the crucial Yugoslav problem, which could "blow up not only Serbia, but also Yugoslavia." He shared Milošević's belief (which was also the official party line) about the "counterrevolution and the secessionist intentions of many among the Kosovo illegal groups. Šuvar also liked Milošević's opposition to attacks on Tito, and saw him as a "Communist who would fight Serbian nationalists."

> I thought that the only way to save Yugoslavia after the Memorandum was to leave it up to the Serbian Communists to clear them up. And in Milošević's Titoism, I saw such an intention.

In another interview conducted in January 1998, Šuvar said:

> My stand on Milošević was also very close to that of the two Montenegrin members of the presidency: Vidoje Žarković[135] and Marko Orlandić,[136]

who later had to withdraw before Milošević's attacks. We concluded that Milošević might really become tough and rough, but that he would not attack Tito and would oppose a wave of Serbian nationalism.

He also saw in Milošević a potential ally in the event of the Croatian intraparty conflict in which he was fighting against Stambolić's Croatian counterpart, Mika Špiljak. Stambolić and Špiljak, Šuvar says, created a "daily alliance" against him.

> After the *White Book*, the Serbian opposition accused me of Croatian nationalism and Stalinism. The Serbian nationalists and their media launched a campaign against me. It was all under the protection of Ivan Stambolić, while Mika Špiljak found a common language with him, not with me.

Šuvar was also convinced that the Stambolić-Špiljak alliance tried to undermine his election to the Federal Party Presidency at the Thirteenth LCY Congress in 1986.[137] Among the political reasons, Šuvar listed Stambolić's interview with *Nin* in 1987.

> He suggested that the president of the Yugoslav Presidency-or even the president of Yugoslavia-should be elected for a four- or five-year term of office.[138] To me, and many others in Croatia, it sounded as if he already saw himself in that position. And I did not like it because I thought that in such a situation, when the Serbian nationalists evidently had become the main promoters of de-Titoization, a president of Yugoslavia on a four- or five-year term should not be a Serb from Serbia. Stambolić's idea came as a surprise to everyone. At that time we were all against any attempted emergence of new Titos. When I analyze this from today's perspective [in January 1998], this was certainly a mistake. Today I think that the five-year term mandate might have been a good idea, but only if the person elected had not been a Serb, Croat, or Slovene. For example, I would have endorsed a Macedonian president elected for a five-year term. But this was entirely impossible, since in Yugoslavia the three main nations were dominant-especially in the army, in the police, and even in the Party. So who then would elect a Macedonian?[139]

But perhaps the most important factor in Milošević's victory at the Eighth Session was the army, symbolically present in the former Yugoslav defense secretary (1970-82), Nikola Ljubičić.[140] Milošević treated him at the Eighth Session as only Tito would have been treated.[141] This is what Ljubičić wanted.[142] Ljubičić was very experienced in "secret and conspirational action" (Stambolić 1995:163), and his control over the military intelligence had never ceased. Being in disagreement with many members of the army (including his successor in the post of defense secretary, Admiral Mamula,[143] who was suspected of being pro-Stambolić[144]), Ljubičić saw the perfect chance to renew his strength. Apart from controlling military intelligence, he had an overwhelming influence over the Serbian state security apparatus. Said Stambolić:

> Ljubičić was safely drawing on instruments of power that he had built up over decades. They proved to be very efficient and decisive for the realization of a state Putsch.[145]

Ljubičić's decision to support the "revolutionist" and "Titoist" Milošević and not the "liberal" Stambolić came at a moment when his opponents (Mamula and others) were speechless-after the Paraćin case. Being worried about the possibility of his removal after Paraćin, Mamula sharpened his position in a speech to the Conference of Communists in the army, which was published on the day of the Eighth Session. His speech had a significant influence on the overall atmosphere that day. *Politika*, now firmly in the control of Milošević, made sure it was published under the title of "Today's Crisis has Endangered the State's Integrity and Its Social System." In their subtitle, the main Serbian newspapers quoted Mamula as saying that 216 illegal terrorist groups with 1,435 members-all Albanians-had been discovered within the army from 1981 to 1987. Mamula was talking about "water poisoning, assassination of officers, and diversions," only as an introduction to a description of the context in which all this was happening. This context was one of nationalism, whose main target was Yugoslavia and its army. It was also a context of political crisis that had not been dealt with properly. He pleaded for resoluteness: "Whatever is feeding our youth with nationalist hatred must be cut out at its root," said Mamula, voicing his views on Yugoslavism.

> Only in a nationalist, deviant, and bureaucratic consciousness do Yugoslavia and Yugoslavism today appear[146] under the guise of unitarism beneath which nationalism is hidden.[147]

Mamula then pledged to ensure "order and implementation of the law" in Kosovo. Otherwise, he said, the conflict in Kosovo would put a question mark over the security of the whole country. Unusually open for an army leader, Mamula accused the Kosovo administration of failing to provide relevant data on the 3,792 Albanian soldiers, including Aziz Kelmendi, the assassin of the Paraćin soldiers. "The army cannot allow itself to sit on such a mine and to fear another Kelmendi setting it off." So Mamula said something should be done, but it could not be done without the resolute action of "others in society." To be successful and safe, the army needed political allies in Yugoslavia. This is when Mamula almost openly supported Milošević's arguments:

> A resolute break with existing practice is unavoidable and urgent....It is a moment for everyone in their own place to show determination and criticism in reexamining their own responsibility. The cadres placed in the main posi-

tions bear a double responsibility: for what they have done and for what they haven't but should have done. The only alternative to this would be continuing the situation as it is: which means sinking into an ever-deeper crisis with entirely unknown consequences....I am convinced that the LCY is the only instrument by which we can find the whole chain of solutions we need.

And these changes were not only "a break with existing practice," but also changes in the social system, which to be successful must be based on what is realistic and not what is a desirable state of consciousness in society.[148]

After concluding that the LCY "is on the margins of society and [its] role is ignored, Mamula offered a solution:

> The LCY must put itself in the vanguard of democratic energy, which is today expressed by the masses everywhere around us, and it must not allow this energy to be diverted in a destructive direction.

In saying this, Mamula in fact explained why the army supported Milošević's action. He saw Milošević as the person capable of controlling and directing the masses, sufficiently strong in his beliefs not to allow them to be misused for destructive purposes, such as nationalism. Milošević, a Yugoslav and a proponent of Yugoslav unity, a strong Communist who sought changes in the system, a forceful critic of Albanian and Serbian nationalism and of Kosovo's and Serbia's inefficient administration, was a logical choice to implement this program.[149]

In the end, it is not surprising that the federal Yugoslav leadership silently and without a single word sanctioned Milošević's victory at the Eighth Session. Not only did the Yugoslav leaders have no real means to stop him, but they actually either agreed with him or ignored what happened. A few days after the Eighth Session of the LC CC Serbia, the Slovenian Party President Milan Kučan asked Milošević to inform the Federal Party Presidency of the results of the session when it ended (under the last item on the agenda: "any other business"). "There is some uneasiness in certain Party organizations in Slovenia about this Session," said Kučan, justifying his question to Milošević, who replied that there was no need for it and continued:

> First, a huge step has been made in accordance with LCY policy. As the majority of participants concluded, this was a fierce battle with our own opportunism, which was making the LC incapable of leading an energetic campaign for the implementation of its own policy. Second, the fears that LC Serbia would split up proved to be unfounded. We have seen that our Central Committee is united and that it shares the views of the people. Third, it has been shown that this was not a question of personal conflict or conflict between two groups, but about some individuals' deviations from LC policy. Fourth, the crucial characteristic of this session was its clear and resolute attitude toward Serbian nationalism. In general, I think that this session, together

with that of the Committee of the LCY in YPA, and especially Comrade Mamula's speech, strengthened the League of Communists' policy in a public and a democratic way. (Djukić, 1994:89)

In a reply to Milošević's explanation, the chairman of the Yugoslav Party Presidency, Boško Krunić (Vojvodina), said only this:

Thank you, Comrade Milošević. Are there any questions, or any suggestions? There aren't. Well, then OK, let us finish. (Djukić, 1994:89)

6.8. The Aftermath: Toward the "Antibureaucratic Revolution"

The victory of the revolutionists at the Eighth Session was followed by consolidation of the Party to secure its unity. The leading revolutionist-Radoš Smiljković- replaced Dragiša Pavlović as Belgrade Party President, and Ivan Stambolić resigned his post of president of the Serbian State Presidency in December 1987. Throughout the Serbian Party and other political organizations, the institutionalists had been removed and replaced by revolutionists.

But the unity of the Party was only a first (necessary, but not sufficient) step toward the final objective: the unity of Serbia and Yugoslavia. Milošević's vision of Yugoslavia included its reintegration on grounds that were similar to the pre-1974 (the "third," as I call it in chapter two) constitutive concept of Yugoslavia. The same determination he displayed in fighting for the unity of the Party, he would soon demonstrate in his actions toward achieving this goal. From September 1987 to June 1988, a new "antibureaucratic revolution" was conceptualized and prepared. In December 1987, the Belgrade Committee summed up the long debates within the Party membership at the Eighth Session: "The members think that we have reached a 'turning point' (*preokret*) with regard to our political life and behavior and that this is a chance for mobilization that should not be missed."[150] Borisav Jović, who became Milošević's main aide, claimed that Party members had to "show revolutionary determination" when fighting inefficiency.[151] This mobilization, they concluded, would not only solve the economic and political crisis, eliminate the Kosovo problem, and democratize political life in Serbia, but it would also change the status of Serbia in Yugoslavia. "Serbia should not be constitutionally undefined....It should be in the same position as other republics. Some individuals do not see this, or do not want to see it," said Slobodanka Gruden, a leading Belgrade Communist.

In a series of speeches, the new leaders of Serbia were optimistically promising fast and radical change as a result of the newly achieved unity. At the same time, their sharp action against "the opportunists" and "bureaucrats" introduced an atmosphere of fear and uncertainty, contrasting sharply with the anarchic situation in which the Yugoslavs had lived not only in the early 1980s, but also during the last decade of Tito's lifetime (Doder, 1978).[152] Living in the culture of apocalypse, feeling the sense of historical injustice presented by the leading members of the opposition movement, being pessimistic about the economic and political crises that were becoming deeper and deeper, the (Serbian) population now became vulnerable to the action proposed by Milošević. To the fears he himself spread, he proposed hopes for a new and brighter future. This combination-fears and hopes-became the main building block of his politics, not only in 1987, but also for longer afterward.[153] Even to those who feared the new revolution," Milošević was now the only alternative to even worse and more radical chage: to open Serbian ethnic nationalism.

Belgrade, once the stronghold of the critical intelligentsia, was now becoming something else, the capital of a new, antibureaucratic, revolution whose first victims had already appeared. The fears forged by this revolution spread fast first throughout Serbia, then throughout Yugoslavia. Already in 1988, physical force by demonstrators (openly supported by the new Serbian leadership) overthrew the political leadership in Vojvodina. When the emergency situation was introduced to Kosovo following a new wave of protests between October 1988 and February 1989, the "unity of Serbia" was finally achieved. In March 1989 the Serbian constitution was finally changed, making Serbia "equal to other republics in Yugoslavia." Any opposition to these changes, and especially to that expressed by Kosovo Albanians in fall 1988/1989, was crushed by the brutal force not only of the Serbian state, but also of the federal state. While he lost a lot of his supporters in other republics, Milošević's actions were still tolerated as long as they remained confined to Serbia and its provinces.

However, in October 1988 Milošević declared that Serbia "did not achieve this victory only to sleep on the wreath of glory." The unity of the Serbian leadership was not achieved so that the leaders could spend their term in office "in harmony and privileges" (IB CK SKS 7/1988:15). On the contrary, as Milošević explained in April 1989, a month after the new Serbian constitution was accepted:

> Those who expect that now, when she has finally become a republic, Serbia would join the defenders of the status quo and oppose changes to the 1974 constitution, are deluding themselves. They will soon have a chance to see how wrong they are. Serbia did not become a state to sleep on the wreath of glory, but-now strong and open toward others-to forcefully initiate democratic changes to make Yugoslavia a strong community of equal nations and nationalities, able to break with the crises, poverty, and humiliation in which she now lives. Of course, those who do not care for Yugoslavia claim that our intentions and plans are "unitarist" and "hegemonistic." But they should

have no illusions that we would-only because of what they say and because they do not agree with us-give up Yugoslavia and Socialism, and democratic processes that no one can stop any longer.[154] We have no time to elaborate our policy to every single person, and especially not to those who are malevolent toward us. The results of our actions will speak for themselves. We can promise them that. (IB CK SKS, 4/1989:10-1)

It was "the unity of Yugoslavia" that Milošević now declared as his goal. Seeing little difference between being a Yugoslav and a Serb, Milošević simply attempted to transpose the means of achieving Serbian unity to Yugoslavia. He demanded unity within the Party to change the constitution, defeat "bureaucracy," and remove "separatists" from all public posts throughout Yugoslavia. It was at this moment that he confronted the others in Yugoslavia. The Defenders of the Constitution, among whom Slovenia had the most prominent position, forcefully opposed such an attempt.

The clash between the two groups (often classified, not sufficiently precisely, as a conflict between Slovenia and Serbia) characterized the final phase of the Yugoslav drama. Unlike the main political conflicts in the Fourth (post-1974) Yugoslavia, the new political conflicts were no longer confined to the political elites, but they involved the masses, and even (formerly) "dissident" segments of population. Instead of the antistate rhetoric of "self-managing Socialism," Milošević now promoted a statist program that had the elements of both the prewar "national unity" and of the pre-1974 conceptions. The state was to be debureaucratized (i.e., cleansed of the old bureaucrats and reideologized), and also reestablished on new grounds. The idea of the "withering away of the state," the main notion of the Kardelj concept, now vanished from the Party's official rhetoric. On the contrary, changes were introduced so that Serbia would become a state "equal to all the others." This "strong Serbia" would be the main pillar of a "new strong Yugoslavia." Instead of the notion of the "completed nation," Milošević now insisted on the unity of Yugoslavia, which would effectively create a Yugoslav nation. Milošević's rhetoric was now openly anti-Kardeljist. His attack on bureaucracy was in fact an attack on the institutional structure of Kardelj's Yugoslavia, defended by the Defenders of the Constitution. Although his predecessors in office, Draža Marković and Ivan Stambolić, had tried to interpret and implement the constitution in a way that suited the interests of Serbia (as perceived by them), Milošević inspired a revolutionary and populist wave of "extrainstitutional pressure." As he explained at the Thirteenth CC LCS Session in October 1988, "institutions should function in accordance with the interests of the people." For the people of Serbia, he said, there was no greater interest than to live united in Serbia and Yugoslavia. Thus, the politics of the present institutions should be changed in order for this main objective to be achieved. "Within the institutions and outside them; by the masses of population or by individuals; with anger or without anger; among the leadership and among the people-but unity [will/should be achieved]-that's for sure!" (IB 9/1988:11)

This shift signified the effective end not only of the Fourth Yugoslavia, but effectively-as it would become obvious only three years after the Eighth Session-of any Yugoslavia.

Notes

1   According to Stipe Šuvar's report at the Seventh CC LCY session in April 1987, in the five years from 1981 to 1985, there were thirty-six bans on publications: ten newspapers, sixteen books, three journals, two calendars, two tourist prospectuses, one geographical map, one bulletin, and one poster. One here needs to take into account that censorship in Yugoslavia did not officially exist, and in practical terms it was easier for a book to be published there than elsewhere in Eastern Europe. Also, this was a period of "counterrevolution" in Kosovo and of the rise of the critical intelligentsia in Belgrade. From 1982 to 1987, a total of 2,443 people were charged for political crimes (including 1,748 for "verbal crimes"). Most of them were from Kosovo (1,020), followed by Croatia (473), Serbia without provinces (306), and Bosnia-Herzegovina (291). In Slovenia 90, in Montenegro 71, in Macedonia 51, and in Vojvodina 37 people were charged with political crimes (Šuvar 1988:131).

2   This does not mean, however, that it was the same situation in all the Yugoslav republics. In the early 1980s, the most tolerant was Serbia, followed by Slovenia. The situation was more difficult for dissidents in the other republics.

3   In this sense, Havel's definition of dissidence (1978/1991:168) could hardly apply to the Yugoslav critical intelligentsia. In a strict sense, the term opposition is as inadequate as dissidents. In the real terms, opposition exists only in parliamentary systems, in which there is freedom of expression. In the Socialist societies of Eastern Europe, the term "opposition" was used by the elite as "the blackest of indictments, as synonymous with the word *enemy*," (Havel 1978/1991:166). The Serbian dissidents themselves rejected both terms and preferred to call themselves the critical intelligentsia. For a debate on dissidence in Yugoslavia, see *Republika*, No. 179-82 (1998).

4   An example of such a link between intellectuals and elite is the polemic between the Serbian writer Dobrica Ćosić and the Slovenian Dušan Pirjevec in 1961. This polemic was encouraged by two groups in the Yugoslav leadership (Pirjevec for the Kardeljists and Ćosić for Ranković's supporters), as explained in Djukić/Ćosić, 1989.

5   The Party leadership debated the situation in Poland on several occasions in 1980 and 1981. According to Dušan Dragosavac, then president of the LCY Presidency, there were two groups in the Yugoslav leadership regarding the situation. As Dragosavac explained to me in April 1998: "One group was for unconditional condemnation of Jaruzelski's Martial Law. The others, including myself, argued that the Russians were already there with 400,000 soldiers and that they had an additional 600,000 on their borders with Poland. They were already intervening in Polish internal affairs, and there was very little we could do to stop them. Second, the United States was also strongly involved, especially via the Catholic Church and the Vatican. Hence we concluded that the most we could do was to condemn any intervention in the internal affairs of Poland and to support Polish independence. We also had to say that we were against bloodshed

and that we would oppose any military intervention or violence. The majority in the leadership accepted this position, and the differences vanished soon afterward. However, some Communist Parties, such as, for example, Carrillo's Spanish Communists, criticized our politics. Carrillo thought this was being too mild toward the Russians. He was somehow anti-Soviet all the way through."

6   Ever since then Vuk Drašković has been one of the leading figures of the Serbian opposition. Although in the 1990 elections he was the leading candidate of the Serbian nationalists, he later evolved toward a much more moderate political position.

7   The Serbian opposition celebrated the decision as a significant political victory. But the Serbian political leaders now came under a new wave of pressure from their colleagues in the federal leadership for being soft on or even sympathetic to Serbian nationalism.

8   The Šešelj trial followed earlier charges against a group of Muslim intellectuals (including Alija Izetbegović) accused of spreading Islamic Fundamentalism in Bosnia. Izetbegović was charged on the basis of his book published twelve years earlier (*Islam Between East and West*) and received a long prison sentence.

9   This was especially obvious when Enrico Berlinguer, the head of the Italian Communist party, supported the six and even announced his wish to attend the trial.

10 Ramet (1985:104-7) argues that five topics were kept out of public debate throughout the whole period of Titoism: (1) criticism of nonaligned foreign policy; (2) Tito's personal role and the official version of the Partisan struggle (including the main enemies of the Partisans, such as the Chetniks and Ustashas); (3) promotion of religious views and of any political activity of churches; (4) criticism of the state's nationality policy; and (5) any discussions of military issues and especially any criticism of the Yugoslav People's Army. By 1984, all these areas had come under either openly political or literary criticism from the dissidents.

11 Dedijer's controversial biography of Tito was published in Rijeka (Croatia) in 1981, and it was sold out in a month. After Vrhovec's criticism, the publishing house refused to publish a second edition. Dedijer, a Montenegrin who supported Djilas in 1954 but then moved back to Tito, lived in Slovenia. He complained that the Federal Police (led by Stane Dolanc) bugged his home, stole some of his documents, and even murdered his son. Vrhovec thinks Dedijer was paranoid. (Interview with Vrhovec, April 1998)

12 It is important to note that the Independent State of Croatia, run by the Ustashas' *Poglavnik* Ante Pavelić, extended to most of today's Croatia (without Istria and the northern part of Dalmatia) and the whole of Bosnia-Herzegovina. The crimes committed by the Croatian Ustashas were now attributed to the whole of the Croatian and Muslim nations. In the Partisan interpretation, the Ustashas were a minority of the Croats who sided with the occupiers (just like the Chetniks were treated as a small part of the Serbian nation that betrayed national interests), and they now became representatives of both Croats and Muslims. The reinterpretation of the World War II role of these two nations had an enormous impact on further events, practically setting the agenda for military conflict between the Serbs on the one hand and the Croats and Muslims on the other in 1992-95.

13 An open statement to this effect was expressed in the 1986 Memorandum of the Serbian Academy of Sciences and Arts, which claimed (1986/1996:327) that "Serbs in Croatia have been exposed to a subtle and effective policy of assimilation."

14 Eight years later, Danko Popović argued that Milošević's attempt to use Serbia's citizens (such as his Milutin) to fight for "another grandiose political project, such as unification with the Bosnian and Croatian Serbs, was in fact one in a line of tragic decisions

by Serbia's politicians in the 20th century." The Serbian peasants, such as he described in his 1985 book, willingly went to war to fight and to die, but were ultimately betrayed by the ludicrous projects of their politicians (see Pavković 1998:517).

15 A good illustration of this feeling was the answer of an anonymous Montenegrin respondent to Slovene sociologists in an opinion poll conducted in 1989. There was still "an inherited belief that they [Albanians] are something of a 'lower race,'" he said. "In fact, they now have an inferiority complex and believe that as soon as they say they are Albanians, I would immediately think of them as lower than I. They believe that we treat them worse because they are Albanians" (Gaber and Kuzmanić 1989:252). One should, however, admit that ethnic prejudice against Albanians did not exist only among the Serbs but also among other Yugoslav nations (as demonstrated by a Slovene public opinion poll, which revealed a strong social distance between Slovenes and Albanians in 1987 (Toš 1987; Pantić 1987).

16 In 1982-83, Vrhovec was a member, and in 1983-84 president, of the Croatian LC CC Presidency. In 1984 he became the Croatian representative in the Federal State Presidency, where he remained until his retirement in 1989. He was also a member of the LCY CC.

17 Šuvar was among the most colorful political figures in Croatia. As one of the most open critics of the Croatian nationalists in 1967-71, he was likened to Croatia's leading politician Vladimir Bakarić. As Croatia's education and culture secretary in 1974-82, Šuvar was associated with the reideologization of schools (introduction of Marxism, destruction of the old school system, and implementation of the Kardeljist concept of self-management in education). In 1982 he became the main ideologue for the Croatian Party, the position from which he moved to the Federal Party Presidency as ideologue (1986-88) and president (1988-89). In 1989 he replaced Josip Vrhovec as Croatia's representative (and vice president) in the Federal State Presidency, to remain there until the election of the CDC majority in Croatia's Parliament in 1990. After 1990 he became one of the most principled critics of Croatian nationalism under Franjo Tudjman. He founded the Socialist Workers Party and remained committed to Marxism until his death in 2004.

18 The topics of these books in 1982 were "Recent criticism of Miroslav Krleža" (25 February 1982), "Goli Otok and the Informbiro" (14 April 1982), "The demythification of the past" (10 May 1982), "The role of the media" (16 July 1982), "Some political, social, and ideological tendencies" (1 February 1983), and "On historiography" in general (May 1983). But it was not until the seventh of these "books" was written that the public knew of their existence.

19 As Lazar Stojanović explains in an interview for this dissertation (1998), the regime showed more tolerance to books than to newspapers and especially to electronic media, since the books were read by a limited number of people and could not really influence public opinion. This is how one can explain the publishing of many non-Communist or even openly anti-Communist authors in Yugoslavia, including leading East European dissidents (Havel and Kundera, among others). The regime even used these books to show the advantages of the Yugoslav model of Socialism, as opposed to its Soviet counterpart. It was also relatively easy to buy and import any book in foreign languages, since the borders were fairly open. Ramet concluded (1985:5) that "in Yugoslavia, one encounters the curious example of a Communist regime that in the past several years has repeatedly allowed its publishing houses to publish highly critical and controversial material, only to subject these same works to vilification in the press for anti-Socialist

views" (1985:5). This openness somewhat changed in 1983 when a deposit for foreign travel was introduced for economic reasons.

20 This was not only the Croatian Party ideologue's conclusion: some Western analysts also spoke about the "apocalypse culture" that had developed in Yugoslav literature (Ramet 1985:2-26).

21 Evidence for Šuvar's "Stalinism" was found when the Czechoslovak ambassador to Belgrade praised his *White Book* in a public interview with Yugoslav Television for criticizing publishing houses that published novels and plays of the Czechoslovak dissidents Kundera and Havel.

22 The meeting was open to the media—and I remember attending it as a journalist for *Polet*. Short and authorized versions of the speeches were later published in *Naše teme*, the official journal of the Croatian LC. Only four out of more than fifty speakers opposed some aspects of the *White Book* material. The summary of the context of *White Book* is here given from reading the document itself. In 1985, a publishing house in Belgrade attempted—unsuccessfully—to publish the White Book. The police prevented it, claiming that, in this case, quotes from Djogo's banned book would be reprinted too. The *White Book* has never been available to the general public.

23 The visible weakness of dissidence in Croatia should be compared with the absence of Slovaks from any common action of the opposition in Czechoslovakia. Among the first 243 signatures collected for Charter 77, only one was that of a dissident living permanently in Slovakia. (Wehrle, 1994:254, quoted in Innes, 1995:125). Czech dissident František Kriegel argued (in 1977) that this was only a reflection of "the Slovak minority exercising power over the Czech majority, though the federation meant to establish parity (Innes 1995:125). The same argument was put forward by the Serbian nationalist opposition in the late 1980s, especially in the SANU Memorandum (1986). They argued that the 1974 Constitution accomplished most of what the Croatian nationalists had been aiming at. For a detailed account of the relationship between the Croatian Spring and the constitutional changes in 1967-74, see chapter three.

24 Authors such as Igor Mandić and Predrag Matvejević were welcome to publish in Belgrade magazines, and *Nova Revija* and *Mladina*, opposition publications in Ljubljana, published even the Croatian nationalists such as Dobroslav Paraga, Vlado Gotovac, and Vladimir Šeks. Throughout the 1980s, the Belgrade media were open to all those who could not publish in their republics. This was exploited by the Serbian nationalist opposition when the Slovene and Croatian writers turned their backs on them in the late 1980s.

25 Leading Croatian poet Vlado Gotovac, historian Franjo Tudjman, economist Marko Veselica, and student leaders Dražen Budiša and Ivan Zvonimir Čičak were all imprisoned following the Croatian Spring. The leading Communists of the period, such as Savka Dabčević Kučar and Miko Tripalo, were forced to abstain from any public activity. "We shall not jail you, but shall not allow any public activity either," Vladimir Bakarić told Miko Tripalo on the day of Tripalo's dismissal following the Croatian Spring in January 1972 (Tripalo 1990). Indeed, no alternative interpretation of the events was allowed until 1990, and police reacted harshly to any sign of Croatian nationalism, even in its most benign form.

26 For similar accusations of "vanguardism" in the late 1960s and before December 1971, see chapter three.

27 In the whole period from 1945 until his death in 1983, Bakarić was the unchallenged leader of Croatia. His support for the controversial Šuvar was a crucial element in

Šuvar's promotion to both Croatian minister of culture and education (1974-82) and ideologue of the Croatian Party (1982-86). Just like Bakarić in earlier years, Šuvar was the most intellectual member of the Croatian leadership. On the other side, Špiljak had a working-class background. Bakarić disliked Špiljak and suspected him of unitarism. For this reason, Špiljak was "sent" to federal positions in Belgrade where he was first the Yugoslav prime minister, then president of a chamber of the Yugoslav Federal Assembly and president of the Yugoslav Unions Federation. As the Croatian politician with the longest federal career, he replaced Bakarić as member of the federal presidency and became its president in 1983-84. Ultimately, in 1984 he returned to Croatia to chair the Croatian Party Presidency, the place of real power. The conflict between Špiljak and Šuvar (i.e., between their protégés) throughout the entire period of 1984-90 was a contributing factor to the now increasingly obvious weakness of the Croatian leadership.

28 *Nin*, 25 November 1984. The same argument was expressed in several speeches by Slobodan Milošević in these years. Milošević remained convinced that the Party should have a "positive program," rather than being focused on the criticism of its opponents.

29 Instead, the Bosnian Croat Branko Mikulić was elected. As demonstrated in chapter five, Mikulić belonged to the closest circle of Tito's confidants in his last years. As a hard-line defender of the constitution, he distinguished himself by his role in the case of Draža Marković (1982), as well as by organizing the Šešelj Trial in Sarajevo (1983) and by effectively undermining the reforms proposed by the Planinc government (1982-86). His candidacy met with public criticism in *Mladina*. Since Mikulić was the fourth Croat in the office of Yugoslav prime minister after the war (the others being Tito, Špiljak, and Planinc, but only one in this office, Petar Stambolić, had been a Serb), the Serbian nationalists later used this as evidence of an anti-Serb coalition in Yugoslavia.

30 For example, the *Times* correspondent Desa Trevisan. Immediately after these speeches, she told Stambolić that she had thought he was a wise politician, but now she was afraid that he was about to "lose his head" by fighting the nationalists. She referred to the opposition that at one time had had some sympathies for Stambolić's isolation from the others, but they (i.e. the opposition) had now lost them after these speeches. (Stambolić, 1995:106).

31 The Serbian critical intelligentsia and especially the Serbian Academy of Science and Arts have never forgotten and even less forgiven this threat. Two years later, when Milošević ousted him from the office of Serbian President, they celebrated his downfall. "He spoke for nobody and nobody listened to him," said Antonije Isaković in April 1996. "He was a traitor to Serbian interests. This is why we welcomed Milošević's action to remove him from office. Especially when we saw that Milošević understood the Serbian situation in a more or less similar way to what we did" (Antonije Isaković in an interview with the author in April 1996).

32 Even when Stambolić initiated a federal debate in 1985, Croatia's representative in the federal presidency, Josip Vrhovec, argued that Serbia should deal with it alone, since "we did not create this problem and cannot accept any responsibility for its resolution." He openly attacked Stambolić for "failing to resolve" Serbia's internal affairs (Interviews with Vrhovec and Stambolić, 1995). See also Meier (1999).

33 For details of this event, see Mertus (1999), and for an analysis of the narratives created in the Serbian "opposition" media on it, see Bracewell (1998).

34 Together, these two elements as permanent reminders of the "Muslim genocide" against the Serbs and the need to protect the Serbs from its repetition, set the context for the future war between the Serbs and Muslims in Bosnia-Herzegovina (1991-95) and in Kosovo.

35 Dobrica Ćosić's letter to Slovenian sociologist Spomenka Hribar, written in November 1986, reveals the extent to which the new image of Albanian sexual crimes had entered the public discourse. Ćosić quotes his friend, a frequent visitor to Kosovo, who told him, "In the village of Klina, there have been more than twenty girls raped this summer, and no word has been said or published about it. These rapes are a form of total war against the Serbian nation, which is planned and systematically implemented by battalions of young people poisoned with ethnic hatred, and who are protected by the law and the government" (Ćosić 1992:87). In his speech at the closed session of the Serbian State and Party Presidencies on 5 September 1988, the president of the state presidency Petar Gračanin said, "In Kosovo, we came to the point at which no girl from a kindergarten, no woman, young or old, if she is of Serbian or Montenegrin nationality, could walk through an Albanian village without being protected and accompanied" (IB CKSKS 8/1988:6).

36 But there was a significant difference in the type of criminal activities in Kosovo when compared with the rest of Yugoslavia. Although in 1980 of all "crimes against the state order," 7.9 percent were committed in Kosovo, in 1987 this share rose to 52.7 percent. More than half of the political convictions in Yugoslavia were confined to Kosovo. Except for industrial criminality (which also included crimes against the economic undermining of the state order), all other types of crime were lower in Kosovo than the Yugoslav average. Crimes against property, human rights, freedom, life, and body, as well as against the honor and reputation of citizens, declined in 1987 when compared with 1980, being three to ten times less frequent in Kosovo than in other parts of Yugoslavia (Horvat 1989:154).

37 *Književne novine*, 1 September 1985.

38 The figure of 260,000 cases of illegal immigration of Albanian citizens into Kosovo was in sharp contrast with the study by the Federal Ministry of the Interior published in July 1986, which found that from 1948 to 1981, only 5,587 people emigrated from Albania to Kosovo, of which only 1,391 actually lived in Kosovo in 1986. Only 31 Yugoslav citizenship applications had been made (*Politika*, 6 July 1986). Nevertheless, an already sky-high figure of 260,000 "illegal immigrants" rose now in the media to 350,000 or even more by 1989 (Gaber and Kuzmanić 1989:252). The enormous difference between the official report of the Federal Ministry of the Interior and claims by the Serbian nationalist opposition may help in understanding the Albanian anger in these years.

39 On several occasions after 1985, the Serbs and Montenegrins from Kosovo threatened collective migration from the province in protest at what they saw as an indifferent leadership. Their marches to Belgrade were therefore seen as unprecedented pressure on the federal and Serbian governments. They created an atmosphere of permanent emergency, which was later exploited by Slobodan Milošević.

40 *Politika Ekspres*, 22 December 1985.

41 From 1981 to 1985, a total of 96 enemy groups were discovered in Kosovo, 1,102 people were sentenced, and 2,657 cautioned for counterrevolution. A total of 176 teachers were "removed from teaching," including 11 university professors, and 511 students were expelled from the university. As many as 1,800 members of the LCY were expelled from the League of Communists in Kosovo, 1,600 of whom were Albanians (*Politika Ekspres*, 1 February 1986). And during that time, an attempt to arrest the leaders of the Kosovo Serbs in April 1986 failed after it brought the Kosovo Party Organization to the edge of splitting on ethnic lines. From then it became clear that the state would not equally treat the two groups of protesters.

42 The full text of the petition was published in *Nova Revija*, 48-49/1986:801-7.
43 Since signatures for the 2,016 petition were collected all the way through, the opposition claimed that 81,000 people signed the petition in the six months from December 1985 to June 1986.
44 What he failed to do, however, was to extend the same demand to the protests of the Albanians in Kosovo. Unfortunately for him, Stambolić was still confined to intraparty debates. Most of his rhetoric would be repeated in public the following year by his successor Slobodan Milošević, who visited Kosovo Polje in April 1987 with the same objective as Stambolić had before him. It was the publicity that made the difference.
45 In line with Kardelj's attempt to see the Party gradually transformed into becoming almost like an institute, rather than being involved in the everyday business of running the state, Ivan Stambolić concluded "that science needs to be more involved in attempts to resolve social, economic, political, and other problems." When he met with the academicians later in 1986 to discuss plans for the centennial celebration of SANU (scheduled for 1 November 1986), he approved their intention to present their vision of possible solutions. (Stambolić 1995:119)
46 More about the Slovene national program in the mid-1980s and about the interaction between the Slovenian and Serbian dissidents in the next chapter.
47 Interview with Antonije Isaković in April 1996. The commission was first chaired by SANU President Dušan Kanazir, who soon resigned his position to Isaković, the vice president of the academy.
48 Isaković believes that the manuscript was given to journalist Aleksandar Djukanović by his father-in-law, Professor Jovan Djordjević, one of the leading experts on constitutional law, who participated both in drafting the 1974 Constitution and in criticizing it after 1977. Djukanović was the official Party commentator for the largest Belgrade daily. He was the last journalist to interview Ranković before his ousting in 1966 (RFE/RL 28 June 1983).
49 For all these reasons, the Memorandum was in fact an unfinished and unofficial paper. The academy refused even to comment on it and especially to condemn it, treating it as a nonexisting document. Nevertheless, the document was attributed to SANU. It was published for the first time in Zagreb in the theoretical journal of the Croatian League of Communists, *Naše Teme* (1989:128-63), and translated in Čović's book: *Roots of Serbian Aggression* (also in Zagreb 1993:289-337). Finally, on the tenth anniversary of the affair, SANU published the entire text of the Memorandum, together with Mihailović's and Krestić's comments. In this book, it is quoted from the SANU edition.
50 As we demonstrated in chapter two, the "only if" approach to Yugoslavia was promoted first by Kardelj himself, only to be continued within Slovenian politics (especially with Kučan) in the late 1980s.
51 Isaković interview in April 1996. For further explanation, see the introductory text by Krestić and Mihailović to the 1996 edition of the Memorandum.
52 It is interesting that the Memorandum did not deny the right of self-determination (including that of secession) to other Yugoslav nations, if Serbs (not Serbia) had the same right. By nations, they understood ethnic groups, which only in the Slovene case largely coincided with the "demos" of existing republics. According to the authors of the Memorandum, only nations, not republics had the right to secede. Republics were provisional and only domestically recognized entities, though the "self-determination of the nation (narod)" was an internationally recognized principle that could not be altered by the domestic "Titoist" constitution.

53 This conclusion indicates that Montenegrin and even Bosnian-Herzegovinan cultures were in fact elements of the Serb culture. In the interpretation of Serbian nationalists, Bosnian Muslims had in fact been Serbs who agreed to accept Islam to obtain privileges from the Ottoman Empire. Tito's Yugoslavia, in fact, sanctioned this historical "loss" of the Serbian nation by recognizing the Bosnian Muslims as a separate ethnic category in the 1960s.

54 The SANU Memorandum explicitly defined Yugoslavia through the AVNOJ 1943 agreement, not through the 1974 Constitution. The criticism of the latter and approval of the former confirm our conclusion that these were perceived as two conceptually different Yugoslavias (see chapter two). It is important that the Memorandum was much more critical of Kardelj than of Tito: all positive examples were taken from before 1964.

55 The leading daily newspaper in Novi Sad (*Dnevnik*) directly linked the Serbian political leaders with the authors of the Memorandum. The journalist Tomislav Marčinko, the ideologue of the Novi Sad Party Committee, wrote that no one could guarantee safety in Vojvodina to those who wanted to ruin the Yugoslav political system (Djukić, 1992:115). In 1990, Marčinko, a Croat from Vojvodina, became the editor in chief of Croatian Television in Zagreb and one of the closest confidants of newly elected Croatian President Franjo Tudjman.

56 A clear allusion to Dobrica Ćosić, Antonije Isaković, and—indeed—many pro-Ranković critics of the 1974 Constitution who now participated in the opposition activities around SANU and the Serbian Writers' Association.

57 An exception being his brief remark at the Belgrade Party Committee meeting in February 1987 on the inactivity of the Communists in the academy who did not find it necessary to distance themselves publicly from the attacks on Tito and the revolution and from the destruction of Yugoslavia. Milošević was expected to offer a platform on the Memorandum at the 5th CC LC Serbia Session in April 1987, but he appointed Milenko Marković to give an introductory speech and decided to close the session to the public (IB 4/1987).

58 However, not much changed after these decisions were taken. The elite soon learned that the old times of 1974 and 1981 had gone and that the ban on all these institutions and papers would be too costly for the regime itself. Ultimately, the Party decision remained just one more unrealized announcement, which left the opposition unaffected.

59 Like Dragiša Pavlović, the president of the Belgrade Party Committee. Pavlović published several articles in the daily *Politika* under a pen name. In 1987 he even published a book against the opposition (Pavlović 1987).

60 More as an illustration of the context of Šuvar's appeal, I quote from Stambolić (1995) selected titles of plays at Belgrade theaters in summer 1987: *The Defeat of the Serbian Tsardom; The Salonika Fighters Speak; The Prince is Assassinated; The Battle of Kolubara; The Memoirs of a Priest; The Secret of the Black Hand; Serbia, Where's Your Shadow?!; Migration of the Serbs; The Rhapsody of St. Andrew.* These were all historical plays in a political theater, almost all of them about Serbian World War I bravery.

61 Not surprisingly, the Serbian Party Congress in 1986 used as its symbol a large fist: the symbol of Party unity and strength.

62 The main reason was the election of Slobodan Milošević, the former president of the Belgrade Party Committee, as president of the Serbian Central Committee. Marković was Milošević's wife's uncle. Stambolić recalls in his book: "Immediately after the election of the new president, Draža told me that history would never forgive me this

choice, that the Serbian nation would never forgive me for my backing of Milošević, and that Milošević would spoil everything....It seemed to me that he said this only because he was a counter-candidate for the position of the CC president....I stood up and left the room" (Stambolić 1995:149). Among those who also opposed Milošević's election was Cvijetin Mijatović, the most prominent politician among the Bosnian Serbs.

63 I happened to have a telephone conversation with Pepca Kardelj, Edvard Kardelj's widow, on the day Milošević's speech was published in the Belgrade daily *Politika*. Pepca Kardelj was very upset with his statement, considering this to be the most outrageous criticism of the 1974 Constitution. When I met her a few days later, she told me how worried her late husband was about the possibility of the reemergence of Serbian nationalism after his and Tito's death. She was convinced that Milošević's 1986 speech was nationalistic.

64 "People can hold their present and their future in their own hands only if they are resolute and remain united," Milošević said in 1984 (1984:21). On the other hand, "lack of unity and disintegration are at this moment the greatest problems of Yugoslav society." (1985:54)

65 As he claimed in April 1987: "The future of Socialism and that of Yugoslavia depend on the unity of the League of Communists of Yugoslavia" (1987:139). Milošević remained committed to this position until the very end of Yugoslavia. In his later speeches (as in Gazimestan, 28 June 1989), he preferred the word concord (*sloga*) to unity (*jedinstvo*). Unlike unity, concord was not directly associated with the Partisans and Tito's Yugoslavia, but more with the Serbian 19th and early 20th century tradition. Concord is one of the key words of the Serbian national slogan: "Only Concord Can Save the Serbs" (*Samo Sloga Srbe Spasava*).

66 Modern Serbia, Milošević said in 1989, would be a Serbia with $10,000 income per capita. (1989:316)

67 In her interview for *Mladina* (27 September 1999), Desa Trevisan recalls that Milošević, visibly annoyed, insisted that he had advocated market reforms before Milan Kučan (Slovenia). Indeed, he did.

68 Lastly, it was his predecessor Ivan Stambolić, who gave the same explanation for his "silence" in polemics with Šuvar about the *White Book* two years earlier. On this occasion, Milošević only repeated Stambolić's old argument that "some people" (sometimes "dogmatist" forces, which opposed political and economic change; sometimes the "opposition") wanted to distract Serbian Communists from the main issues.

69 In the end, as a Marxist, Milošević believed that "cultural questions do not exist independently of economic and material conditions of living" (1984:25).

70 In 1993, Mira Marković described her influence over the cadre policy at the University: "I was pushing through a certain cadre solution very energetically and very successfully (Marković, quoted in *Popov*, 1996:356).

71 Milošević's openness to intellectuals and to the university earned him sympathies among many university professors and students, even from those who had belonged to the opposition to the regime ever since the 1968 student protests and the constitutional debate preceding the 1974 Constitution (like Mihailo Marković, Ljubomir Tadić, et al.). Even Milovan Djilas acknowledges he was soft on Milošević, since it was under his government that he was allowed to speak in public for the first time after his ousting from office in 1954. Although it was certainly not his intention to support dissidents, he seemed to be willing to tolerate them. Support from Belgrade students for Milošević reached its peak with the massive anti-Slovenian and anti-Albanian rally in November

1989 ("the largest since liberation in 1945," as Milošević said), which was organized by the students. The 24-hour rally ended with demands for the arrest of the Communist leader of the Kosovo Albanians, Azem Vllasi, which duly happened three days later.

72   A clear reference to 1948 (the break with Stalin).

73   For a further understanding of the anarchic nature of Yugoslav Socialism, see Doder (1978). If there is any doubt about the link between anarchy and Stalinism, see Tikholaz (1996:131-8). For Kardelj's warnings about the Chilean scenario in Yugoslavia after Tito, see chapter two.

74   So were his rhetorical qualities when compared with his predecessors. By the mid-1980s, people were tired of listening to the same phrases and endless descriptions of the situation. Bureaucratic language could not inspire anyone. Milošević acknowledged this. He spoke a different language, using short and simple sentences, simple but emotionally extensive images (such as heart, children, and snake in the bosom). As Serbian poetess Desanka Maksimović said, praising his book of speeches in 1989: "By his speeches he aroused in many people a desire to fight, shaking out patriotism that had fallen asleep and duties that were neglected." Or, as said by Kosta Mihailović, one of the authors of the SANU Memorandum: "He does not use phrases and empty words from which every trace of content has evaporated. Instead, he expresses his arguments in clear words familiar to everyone" (Milošević 1989, cover page). This was not only recognized by intellectuals, but also by ordinary people. "Milošević's greatest contribution was that he came down to the level at which even children could understand him, even the elderly without any education. This is what matters. He spoke from everyone's heart," said an unnamed Kosovo Serb in an interview with Slovenian sociologists in 1989 (Gaber and Kuzmanić 1989:247). His rhetorical qualities, relatively young age, and the look of a determined Party leader made him a perfect candidate for a popular myth, built with substantial help from his friends in the media. Milošević now became the first person who understood the importance of media "spinning" in post-Titoist Yugoslav politics. Nowhere was this more obvious than in his speech to the Serbs and Montenegrins in Kosovo Polje on 25 April 1987.

75   In later interpretations, it has often been emphasized that the demonstrators assumed that most police were ethnic Albanians. It is, however, very much an open question if this was true, and if it were, how important this element was.

76   Here he only repeated Stambolić's conclusion after his Kosovo Polje visit in April 1986.

77   According to official data presented by the secretary of the Serbian LC CC, Zoran Sokolović, at a joint session of the Serbian state and party presidencies on 2 November 1988, a total of 31,000 Serbs and Montenegrins moved out of Kosovo after 1981. Of the 3,000 households that moved out of Kosovo, about 2,000 sold all their properties in the province. Of 1,445 territorial units in Kosovo, about 700 were already "ethnically pure—Albanian," but in about 300, the number of Serbs and Montenegrins fell below 50. From 1983 to 1987, about 6,500 (i.e., 2,240 households) Croats, Muslims, Romanies, and Turks also left Kosovo. (IB CKSKS 10/1988: 6)

78   Despite this clearly antinationalist rhetoric, authors such as Kaplan (1993:40) today often claim that Milošević made a direct appeal to racial hatred on this occasion. The wide difference between what actually happened and the retrospective interpretation of the events was the result of several methodological mistakes, such as those of the prolepsis and coherence hypotheses; that the texts themselves were not read; and that their contexts were neglected. In Kaplan's book and also in many other accounts of Milošević's policy (see, for example, Bishop's article in the *Daily Telegraph*, 20 January 1999, or

Rose's 1998 book), the ideological dimension of Milošević's motives was neglected, and ethnic hatred was promoted as the explanation of his actions. As I argue here, this is entirely inadequate.

79 Already three days after the event, *Književne novine* published on its cover page a poem, "Hymn in the Fields," by Radoslav Zlatanović: "But a young and handsome speaker arrived/ The Falling Sun cuddles his hair/ I will talk to my people even in the fields, he says/ In School yards and Gardens" (Gojković 1996:373).

80 These four elements, as described in chapter three, were the essence of Tito's personal political technique, which he implemented most successfully after the 1968 student demonstrations.

81 Milošević's rule was one of a "state of emergency," said his critics. Stambolić even hints that "somebody made sure" that at the very moment when Serbia finally agreed with the other republics about the necessity of constitutional change, the SANU Memorandum appeared as a draft in the newspapers with the highest circulation in Serbia, and that the 8th Session occurred when Serbia was about to change its constitution, correcting the mistakes of the 1974 solution. "Well, you know what....Such coincidences, and there are many more, could not occur by chance....Whoever is capable of reading politically could see clearly: to the changes in the federal constitution, one replied with the Memorandum; to the proposal for changes in the Serbian constitution, the immediate shot was the 8th Session; and then you would see clearly the very essence of the global political conflict and who was on which side" (Stambolić 1995:176). Stambolić recalls the old Bolsheviks' logic: "the worse-the better," calling these tactics "a strategy of chaos." One should, of course, take Stambolić's words cautiously, but immediate parallels with Tito's technique of solving political conflicts in the 1967-72 period cannot be avoided. Was Ljubičić (KOS, Army Intelligence) the connection between the two?

82 *Borba*, 4 September 1987.

83 See Tanjug's commentary in *Borba* of 4 September 1987: "Pucnji u Jugoslaviju" (Shots at Yugoslavia).

84 In his book (1992), Slavoljub Djukić quotes from an authorized statement of an unnamed journalist of *Politika* about the immediate reaction of Živorad Minović, the director of *Politika*, to the events in Paraćin: "Minović was lively and excited when he talked about the Paraćin assassination in which "four Serbian soldiers were killed, which was-as he said-"as manna from heaven" in the situation as it was....A few minutes later, he shocked me again when he phoned and told us-now clearly disappointed-that "although not all four of those killed were Serbs, we should give great publicity to this event" (Djukić 1992:150).

85 *Borba*, 10 September 1987.

86 Interestingly enough, the Serbian Writers' Association was among the very few organizations protesting against such ostracism. In a public demarche, they called these proposals barbaric and described their authors as being "deaf to any respect for law and human rights." However, one cannot avoid the impression that the main reason for their protests was to emphasize that the attack on the Kelmendis would be a heavy burden on the "dignity of Serbia and of Yugoslavia," and it might well be used by Albanian nationalists to antedate events so that "an assassin of innocent soldiers would now become a protector of his mother and sister."

87 I quote here from my personal diary on 7 September 1987: "In Zagreb, even those people who were so far defending the Albanians and were strongly against the Serbian nationalist approach to Kosovo, are now ready to boycott Albanian shops here. No one trusts them any longer." On 18 September 1987, I recorded my conversation with

Stipe Orešković, a friend of mine who was then the closest political associate of Stipe Šuvar. "Stipe [Orešković] argues that both Milošević and Stambolić are nationalists, but Milošević is better because his policy leads to a civil war in Kosovo immediately; Stambolić would bring us there in a year or so. He says that if it has to be, let it be now, rather than later, because the Party is rapidly weakening, and the whole system is falling apart. Strange! He is now obsessed with a possibility of war breaking out. In fact, he speaks as if there is no other option at all!" Orešković, at that time a member of the Federal Youth Organization Presidency, was well informed about events within the leadership.

88   This was the most famous slogan of the 27 March 1941 Belgrade demonstrations that overthrew the Yugoslav government two days after the signing of the Tripartite Pact with Germany. A symbol of resistance not only to the world powers, but also to domestic governments cooperating with them. The other famous slogan of 27 March 1941 was "Better War than Pact," ("Bolje rat nego pakt"). Both reappeared among Bosnian Serbs in the 1990s and in Serbia during the NATO attack on Yugoslavia in Spring 1999.

89   Various Communist institutions debated for months before September 1987 on whether this expression was nationalistic, if expressed by Serbs and Montenegrins only, and in Kosovo. Freedom for whom and from whom? Was freedom not secured in 1945 once and for all?

90   In this context, resolutions mean party conclusions that have not been implemented, but remained a "dead letter."

91   In a commentary published in the Zagreb daily *Vjesnik*, Ivkica Bačić asked, "Have we really come to the point that to the madness in Paraćin we react with revenge toward juveniles and entire families?" She warned about ideas of "collective guilt," and "badly thought out actions under sponsorship of the political bodies" that could well "bring us even deeper and lower...to a point without any hope" (*Vjesnik* 12 September 1987).

92   This and many further quotations about the case are taken from the special edition of *Borba* on 28 September 1987 (here and after referred as *Borba* 1987: p.-).

93   An example of this could be found in speeches by Stambolić and Vllasi, leading politicians of Serbia and Kosovo, respectively, in Kosovo Polje in May 1986. Stambolić (a Serb) told a crowd: "Do not let a handful of Serbian nationalists acting from Belgrade manipulate you-they do not do this because of us. Their slogan is: "worse is better"- better of course for them" (Stambolić, *Vjesnik* 06 April 1986). Vllasi said the same, but about the Albanian nationalists: "They pursued a policy of 'the worse for you, the better [for us]'...This is the reason why they permanently seek support from nationalists everywhere to set us against other Yugoslav nations, above all against Serbs and Montenegrins. We must always remember Tito's words, that separated and divided we will be no one and nobody....And this is what the nationalists want: to confront us each against the others, to divide us, to destroy Yugoslavia, and to open the doors to a tragic future for each of our nations and nationalities" (Vllasi, *Vjesnik* 31 May 1986).

94   *Politika Ekspres*, 14 September 1987: "Olake ocene Dragiše Pavlovića." Slavoljub Djukić, in his biography of Slobodan Milošević, reveals that the text was only signed by Milanović, though it was written in Miloševićs' flat the night before. Interestingly enough, Pavlović himself, being the president of the Belgrade Party Organization, previously wrote polemical articles under a pseudonym. In 1991, Borisav Jović, then president of the Yugoslav Presidency, did the same. In his article (under a false name), he attacked the federal prime minister, Ante Marković, using details from private talks and meetings he had had with him (Jović 2 August 1990; 1995:173).

95 One needs to stress here that the whole debate between them concerned what Pavlović meant when he said what he did. The debate was much more like a "philological seminar" than a normal party meeting (Bogdanović 1988). The three most important Party institutions in Serbia (the Central Committee Presidency, the Central Committee itself, and the City Committee Presidency of Belgrade) debated for more than five days (from 17 to 24 September 1987) about the "true" meaning and consequences of Pavlović's words. Paradoxically, in a situation in which the main Serbian intellectuals openly attacked the regime in thousands of "heated words," three words by the Belgrade Party secretary had ultimately brought the Party to an open crisis. But the real power still lay in the Party. And both sides in this conflict firmly believed that the Party was the key to the solution of the Yugoslav crisis.

96 As demonstrated in chapter three, Serbian leaders always felt uncomfortable with accusations of the "Greater Serbian complex." This was one of the main factors in their acceptance of the 1974 constitutive concept.

97 In Havel's words, big social conflicts could not remain forever ignored by the elite. Regardless of the veil the elite drew over them, they continued in the "hidden sphere," growing somewhere under cover to the point where they burst forth onto the political scene. At such moments "life vents itself where it can—in the secret corridors of power, where it can insist on secret discussion and ultimately on secret competition." But the authorities, being unprepared for any recognition of the reality of life, start panicking. "Whereas before every man in authority had spoken the same language, used the same clichés, applauded the successful fulfillment of the same targets, now suddenly the monolith of power breaks down into distinguishable persons, still speaking the same language, but using it to make personal attacks on one another. And we learn with astonishment that some of them, those, that is, who lost in the secret struggle for power, had never taken their targets seriously and never successfully fulfilled them, far from it. Whereas others—the winners—had really meant what they said and are alone capable of achieving their aims" (Havel, 1975/1991:76-7). The whole political history of postwar Yugoslavia was full of palace putsches, such as were, for example, the Djilas case (1954), the Ranković case (1966), the Croatian Spring (1971), the removal of the liberals in Serbia (1972), the Marković case (1982), and the Šuvar-Špiljak conflict (1984-86). This was only the last.

98 Now it is clear why Ivan Stambolić thinks that Paraćin was the crucial moment in Milošević's march to power. (1995:181) "Up until then, we managed somehow to "lean" on the media not to stoop to revenge....[But now] in *Politika* a really hysterical obsession appeared....Even if Milošević himself planned a more convenient motive and moment for a turning point, he could not have thought of anything better than the Paraćin incident. Now he had the Serbian nationalists at his service. Milošević accepted the hand that was offered by Greater Serbian nationalism. His road to unlimited power after this incident was wide open." (Stambolić 1995:189) The Paraćin case also made the army—especially those factions within it influenced by the former defense secretary, Nikola Ljubičić, who was now Milošević's sponsor—much more inclined toward Milošević. For the role of *Politika* in these years, see Nenadović (1996).

99 Smiljković used the dichotomy "revolution-counterrevolution" to express the irreconcilable difference between "us" and "them." If the difference is really unbridgeable, any "relativization" is unacceptable. It is not even important whether the action was taken in a legal way, according to the party statute, or not, as Smiljković emphasized later in discussions. In his words, it was better to make a mistake than to fail to act and be a victim of counterrevolution.

100 In an interview I conducted with him for *Polet* (later reprinted in *Politika*) on 6 March 1989, Smiljković (then already president of the Belgrade Party Organization) said, "Many people simply do not want to take into account a very simple fact: that it was as early as in 1981 that the supreme leadership of this country declared that a counterrevolution had occurred in Kosovo. Could the counterrevolution be suffocated by a cross and flowers? It could not. Then, of course, people react, saying: 'Well, give us weapons then! We are ready to fight against the counterrevolution!' So one should not condemn people, workers, students...."

101 The language of the Eighth Session was analyzed by one of the CC LCS members, the former mayor of Belgrade—Bogdan Bogdanović. In a letter he sent to the CC members after the session, Bogdanović warned that Milošević's faction demonstrated "an almost unbelievable fear, real panic of polysemia, of the pluralist meaning of words and speeches, even in describing obviously pluralist events." (1988:20) This was, Bogdanović said, nothing else but an "obsessive intention to reduce reality itself to *clear* and unilinear occurrences" (1995:20). In Stalinism there were no doubts and no complex situations. Monolithism is the ultimate value. There is no clear line between myth and reality, between death and life, between past and future, he said. Bogdanović concluded that "the cleansing of language precedes effective cleansing (1988:23)," since "oppressive speech" needs to be directed against the other. However, in attacking the other, one heads toward "autodestruction." Serbia, Bogdanović concluded in his letter (later published in his 1988 book, *The Death Knots – the Mental Traps of Stalinism*), was facing "a crisis of its political consciousness, and maybe even a crisis of consciousness in general." (1988:30) Bogdanović's letter caused an outrage in Milošević's camp, not only because it was the first case of a member of a Central Committee rejecting the authority of the CC in "linguistic issues." After failing to attend sessions of the CC for an entire year, Bogdanović was excluded from its membership in June 1988 as "inactive."

102 Stambolić said that his decision not to launch any action in his state function (as the president of the Serbian Presidency) against the Party, which denounced him, was motivated by his still firm belief that it was simply impossible to oppose the Party. He also saw real obstacles to this in his understanding that the state was more about the economy, but the Party was about ideology. Formulating ideology and interpreting it, as I argue, was the main political activity in ideological societies. The state-as an institution projected to wither away-was of subordinate importance to the Party. This explains why both sides in this conflict saw the Party as the main battlefield and not, for example, parliament or the state presidency. It also explains why Milošević wanted to control the Yugoslav party in the first place, rather than the state institutions. Until 1989, he was "only" a Party president, not a state official.

103 Even Khrushchev's interpretation of Stalinism was based on this notion: Stalin might have been wrong, but not the Party as such. The notion of self-criticism originates here: self-criticism is confirmation of the Party's supreme role. True believers in Communism, such as, for example, Bukharin in the purges of the 1930s, Slansky in 1952, and Djilas in 1954, all accepted self-criticism, even when it was clear that it would not "save" them from exclusion or even death at the hands of the Party.

104 Milošević insisted on this message in almost all of his 1984-87 speeches. For him it was clear that words without action had no importance. On the contrary, they might have only negative effects, since they weakened trust in the Party leadership (Milošević 1989:91-4).

105 As an example, Stambolić described his talk with General Gračanin, who replaced him as president of the Serbian Presidency in December 1987. When Stambolić asked him if he did not see that the Chetniks were gaining strength in the media, Gračanin replied: "For God's sake, Ivan, didn't we destroy them 50 years ago?" (Stambolić 1995:248)
106 On the importance of words in what he calls "posttotalitarian systems, see Havel's essay "A Word About Words" (1989/1991:377-389), and his "Power of the Powerless" (1978/1991:125-214).
107 As Havel wrote in his essay "A Word About Words" (1989): "Yes, I do inhabit a system in which words are capable of shaking the entire structure of government, where words can prove mightier than ten military divisions, where Solzhenitsyn's words of truth were regarded as something so dangerous that their author had to be bundled into an airplane and shipped out." (1989/1991:380) This was possible, he argues in "The Power of the Powerless" because in post-totalitarian societies, the ideology forms the glue of the whole political structure. I share this view.
108 The others in Yugoslavia (in my opinion, rightly) saw this as "bringing Ranković back in." As of this moment on, Ranković was *de facto* rehabilitated. By emphasizing the pitfalls of the post-1974 era, Milošević earned respect from Dobrica Ćosić. As explained in chapter three, back in 1968 Ćosić opposed Kardelj's concept and argued in favor of the third constitutive concept of Yugoslavia. Milošević now offered a direct link with this period. His wife, Mira Marković, as well as the Yugoslav Defense Secretary General Kadijević, later openly stated that the Yugoslav problems began in the 1962-66 period. By this "silent" rehabilitation of Ranković, Milošević certainly earned support among many Serbs.
109 Quotes are taken from text of the speech as published in Milošević's book *Godine raspleta* (1989) under the title "Nevertheless, the future will be beautiful and it is not far away" (1989:165-9).
110 As explained earlier, the word "optimism" was one of those most frequently used in his vocabulary at that time.
111 Meaning-Socialism. Milošević explicitly defined Socialism as the "most beautiful and the most progressive idea of our time" in his speech at Valjevo in September 1986 (1989:102-3) and in his toast to Gorbachev in March 1988 (1989:198-200).
112 References to bravery in past historical battles also very often occurred in Milošević's speeches.
113 This is an obvious reference to Tito's refusal to accept Stalin's criticism in 1948. The event is widely known as "Tito's historical *no*," and for a Serbian/Croatian speaker needs no explicit explanation.
114 This interpretation of Tito by Milošević needs to be remembered if one wants to understand why Milošević argued the same regarding international sanctions against the FR Yugoslavia in 1993, and again on the occasion of the NATO bombardment in 1999, and why he was successful in securing support for his policy of "refusal to kneel" in front of the world powers.
115 The idea that one should be courageous to be free should also be remembered. It would have been well understood by a Serbian audience, "bombarded" by novels, plays, and documentaries on the First World War bravery of Serbian soldiers.
116 All the listed examples are from the Partisan struggle in the Second World War. Three notes about them: (1) Milošević continues Tito's and Kardelj's matrix of the Partisan struggle as the basis for Yugoslav unity; (2) as a good Serbian Communist, he mentioned Chetniks first, Ustashas second; (3) the examples are, however, places where the

Serbs suffered most-with the exception of Jasenovac, which was not a battlefield, but a concentration camp in the Independent State of Croatia. Therefore to many Serbs these places were not just empty Partisan symbols, but they bore a heavy emotional reminiscence of the days of bravery and martyrdom that resulted in "victory in wars but defeats in peace." By using this matrix, Milošević in fact did the same as Danko Popović in his "Book About Milutin," using only cases from World War II, rather than from the Great War. This difference is, however, important: Serbian nationalists exploit the myths of a once strong and independent Serbian state, while the Communists show a preference for Yugoslav Partisan myths.

117 Already in 1988, a song was heard: "This time the people are asked/ Who would replace Tito for Us?/ We know who the New Tito is/ Slobodan of the Name of Pride." Yugoslav leaders on many occasions demanded that Milošević oppose this replacement, and he indeed publicly (but not sincerely) asked the population to stop it, but in vain.

118 Milošević's parents were from Montenegro, but he was born in Požarevac (a city southeast of Belgrade, in Serbia). His brother Borislav (a diplomat with a distinguished career as head of the nonaligned countries unit in the Yugoslav Foreign Ministry in the last years of Tito's life, later his brother's ambassador to Russia) considered himself a Montenegrin, unlike Slobodan Milošević, who was a Serb. Nevertheless, his parents' Montenegrin origins played a role in inspiring and realizing closer links between the two republics for which he once (in January 1989) said that they were "two eyes in one head" (1989:324). Milošević did not deny the existence of a separate Montenegrin nation. He even objected when the protests of Serbs and Montenegrins from Kosovo were criticized as "uninational": "One needs to ask the question: to which of these two nations do the critics deny nationhood by claiming these were uninational rallies?" (1988/1989:260) At a joint session of the Serbian state and Party presidencies on 5 September 1988, Milošević used the example of the rallies in Vojvodina to conclude they were not uninational. "If anything is uninational," Milošević claimed, "then it is counterrevolution in Kosovo" (IB CKSKS 8/88: 15). In October 1988, at its 13th Session, the CC LCS issued a statement that clearly classified denial of the existence of the Montenegrin nation as "reactionary" and as an "act of an enemy" (IB CKSKS 9/88:16).

119 Stambolić also said that Milošević was very polite and kind to the generation of revolutionaries. "He remembered, for example, birthdays, and he attended celebrations, of course, with gifts....When he stood for the presidency of the Party, they were all massively with him" (Stambolić 1995:147). A direct link with the 1941-45 period was also something they might have liked, since many of them felt that their ideals had been betrayed and that the state was ever more bureaucratic. Some of them were displeased with the tiny minority of "successful" comrades who-as they saw it-exploited their four war years to keep power for the next forty. The "antibureaucratic revolution," which swept them away, was therefore very much welcomed by the "genuine revolutionaries," even in other Yugoslav republics, such as (for example) Svetozar Vukmanović Tempo (Montenegro) and Jakov Blažević (Croatia). For Tempo's position, see *Nin*, 15 January 1989.

120 One needs to notice here that the Socialist idea, as presented by Milošević, was still attractive to many in 1987 and indeed would be in the next couple of years. Although the 1989 revolutions in Eastern Europe were anti-Socialist and directed against the elites, the Serbian "antibureaucratic revolution" was supportive of Milošević's Socialist rhetoric and directed against the bureaucrats, not against the Party or Socialism as such.

121 According to Šuvar's report at the Seventh CC LCY Session in April 1987, in 1986 there were 927 industrial actions (strikes) with 93,794 participants in Yugoslavia (1988:129).
122 To use James Gow's description of Tito (1997:35-60).
123 More about economic, political and ethnic inequality, especially among Serbs and Albanians in Kosovo, has already been said in previous chapters. One needs to notice that the LCY hesitated to promote equality and openly argued against *uravnilovka* (radical equality in society). As Vesna Pešić points out in her 1988 research on equality, the very term "equality" was mentioned only once in the LCY Program, and not even once in the Resolutions of the Fifth (1948), Seventh (1958), Eighth (1964), Eleventh (1978), and Twelfth (1982) Congresses of the LCY. Only once was the term mentioned in the Resolutions of the Sixth (1952) and Ninth (1969) Congresses, and three times at the 1974 Tenth LCY Congress (Sekelj, 1990:120). This was in sharp contrast to the high acceptance of egalitarian values among the population and also with Tito's frequent use of egalitarian rhetoric in the whole postwar period.
124 The term refers to Petar Stambolić, a Partisan leader in Serbia who became one of the most influential postwar politicians, and his nephew Ivan, but symbolically goes beyond the two and includes the whole generation of post-1972 Serbian leaders. The same meaning in the new post-Eighth-Session Serbian vocabulary is given to the term "dražijanstvo" (origins in Draža, the nickname of Dragoslav Marković), invented by a young Serbian revolutionist-Zoran Todorović Kundak-just before the session.
125 The whole generation of old politicians-such as Dobrivoje Vidić, Dušan Čkrebić, and Nikola Ljubičić-feared an inevitable retirement. By supporting Milošević, they secured a few more years in politics: especially Čkrebić in the Federal Party Presidency (until the end of the LCY in January 1990) and Ljubičić in the Yugoslav Federal State Presidency (until May 1989).
126 Mihailo Marković soon joined the Socialist Party as vice president and chief ideologue. However, following the SPS's close links with Mira Marković's neo-Communists in the Yugoslav United Left, and the ousting of Ćosić in 1993, Marković withdrew from politics. For Mihailo Marković's Praxis engagement and his philosophy, see Crooker 1982.
127 When I asked him in April 1996 to recall the reactions of the Serbian intellectuals in SANU after the Eighth Session, Antonije Isaković said: "Milošević shared our belief that it was no longer possible to accept the situation as it was; he was equally determined to end the period of Serbian inequality in Yugoslavia. I cannot say whether his thoughts at that time were exactly the same as ours, nor to what extent they were the same. But, to be perfectly clear: the Croats and Slovenes conceptualized the constitution in this way because they saw it as the only way of keeping control over the Serbs once Tito had gone. The Serbs needed a very long time to break with this policy. The main responsibility for this lay with the Serbian traitorous politicians. Therefore, of course, we had every reason to be happy seeing someone who was committed to breaking with this practice."
128 Berisavljević (1997): http://www.rferl.org/bd/ss/8.html/ p. 5 of 11.
129 Krunić was a political victim of Milošević's antibureaucratic revolution in October 1988. In his account of the events given to Radio Free Europe in October 1997, he said that Vojvodina "refused to accept the methods of the 8th Session...but abstained from voting, since everything was finished anyway...and their vote would not have changed anything." As president of the Federal Party Presidency, Krunić allegedly

phoned Milošević and told him that "the presidency was worried and disturbed" about the Eighth Session, asking him "to stop it....Of course, they rejected it, both he and Ljubičić, and asked us to leave them alone...." (Krunić, 1997: http://www.rferl.org/bd/ss/8.html; p. 8 of 11). However, when asked, Stipe Šuvar, a member of the same presidency, said he knew nothing about Krunić's alleged phone call. Šuvar said Krunić was certainly not authorized by the presidency to intervene in such a way (interview with Šuvar, January 1998).

130 Vllasi, in his interview with *Radio Free Europe* in September 1997. His comment indicates that for the first time he felt that the ethnic affiliation of members played a significant role. It was certainly true that the public mood in Serbia (as described above) was such that the Kosovo Communists had no other choice but to agree with whatever the majority of the Serbian CC decided or to face a "Ceausescu scenario." In fact, the crowd almost stormed the building of the Vojvodina Provincial Committee during the "Yoghurt Revolution" on 8 October 1988. It was only after they had resigned that the leaders were allowed to leave the building, being stoned by the crowd. To a large extent this was what some members of the federal leadership had in mind when they suggested that the CC should convene in other places, rather than in Belgrade. They knew that the revolutionist Milošević, unlike them, could mobilize the population in his support.

131 Mladen Pleše, *Vjesnik*, 16 December 1987. As Josip Vrhovec explained in an interview I conducted in 1998, Croatian leaders believed that Serbian nationalism was a permanent characteristic of Serbian leaders.

132 The leading article in *Vjesnik*, written by an author who was also the highest party official in the *Vjesnik* publishing house, indicated that this was the semiofficial view of the Croatian party leadership.

133 Boško Krunić said that "some members of the presidency of the CC LCY believed that we had no right to interfere in the work of any republican Central Committee; that we would not be doing the same in any other case, and thus why should we intervene this time; why should we put ourselves on one or another side? [They also believed] that we must leave the Central Committee of Serbia to be responsible to its membership and not to the LCY Presidency" (Krunić, 1997: http://www.rferl.org/bd/ss/8.html; 8).

134 Although many today assume that Milošević's victory at the Eighth Session meant victory for a nationalist, Stambolić himself spoke against such a conclusion: "One should not forget that he (Milošević) was at the beginning of his career, and also at the Eighth Session, not a nationalist. He still was in his ascent to power....He defended Tito from us "liberals" and "nationalists," and this was how the provinces treated us, and how-for example-the Bosnian leadership saw us. So should they then have supported us and not Milošević, after his speech on Tito?" asked Stambolić rhetorically (1995:229). One should also remember that despite nationalist action taken by many participants in politics, not even in 1990 was nationalism the favorite ideology among the Serbian population, as 1990 research demonstrates. As Obradović points out (1996:494), despite a long and aggressive campaign, only 18.5 percent of the population expressed *explicit* nationalist views while the majority remained committed to brotherhood and unity. This is why many Serbs later simply could not understand accusations of them being ethnic nationalists. Milošević was again speaking for them, when (in an interview on the BBC on 25 September 1995) he said: "We wanted to stay in Yugoslavia. It was absurd that in view of such developments, we here were subsequently accused of being nationalists. It turned out that those who had seceded from Yugoslavia forcibly, with a view to establishing their national, or putting it better, nationalist states, were given support by the international community and treated like democrats, while we-who were striving for

the preservation of the multiethnic Yugoslavia, and who have preserved the multiethnic Yugoslavia and remained to live in the country we lived in before-were accused of being nationalists. These two things can in no way go together. That is so obvious....What happened was that those who had seceded from Yugoslavia forcibly were rewarded, and those who had decided to stay in Yugoslavia and preserve it were punished."

135 Vidoje Žarković was a Montenegrin top politician from the late 1960s to 1989. He "survived" Tito's massive attacks on republican leaders in the early 1970s. He was the Montenegrin representative in the Yugoslav state and in the party presidency 1974-84, then president and member of the Yugoslav Party Presidency. He resigned in 1989, since he opposed Milošević's revolutionist supporters (Momir Bulatović and Milo Djukanović) in Montenegro, being closer to (Croatian) Šuvar than to them and to Milošević. For Žarković's assessment of the events, see his interview with RFE/RL, 19 October 1997.

136 Marko Orlandić was a member of the LCY Presidency from Montenegro. He also stood close to Šuvar until he was forced to resign after the January 1989 "antibureaucratic revolution" in Montenegro, together with Žarković and the whole Montenegrin leadership.

137 In what was in fact an unsuccessful attempt to repeat the Marković case with another target, Špiljak's supporters in the Croatian delegation and Stambolić's in the Serbian voted against Šuvar.

138 This idea of Stambolić was much commented on in the media; see *Borba*, 13 May 1987.

139 Interview with Šuvar, April 1998.

140 After serving three terms as federal secretary of defense, Ljubičić in 1982 became president of the Serbian State Presidency, and in 1984 (until 1989) the Serbian representative in the Federal State Presidency. The Ljubičić-Milošević victory-at least for a short time-cemented Ljubičić's influence in Serbia. His comrade-in-arms, General Petar Gračanin, was elected President of the Serbian State Presidency after Stambolić. In 1989 Gračanin became the Yugoslav Interior Secretary in Ante Marković's government. Despite his original plan to be reelected to the federal presidency in 1989, Ljubičić retired in 1989.

141 Ljubičić was the first speaker in the debate. Milošević took up his defense when Pavlović said something against him. Stambolić also quoted from Ljubičić when expressing his views.

142 In Šuvar's view, Ljubičić was so convinced that he would be a new Tito that he even imitated Tito in his gestures and construction of sentences. Slavoljub Djukić, a biographer of Milošević, mentions one episode: "When he once entered a meeting, and no one clapped to support him, he stood in front of the first row and start clapping himself until they responded" (Djukić, 1992:49).

143 On the conflict between Mamula and Ljubičić, see Stambolić (1995). In an interview for this book Šuvar and Vrhovec also confirmed that Mamula and Ljubičić disliked each other and that they had different concepts of defense. Mamula was elected Defense Secretary in 1982 with strong support from Slovenia and Croatia. "This was support against our principles, since in fact Mamula wanted to abandon the Titoist concept of *people's self-defense* and introduce a centralized army. But we played on his conflict with Ljubičić and supported him, only because it suited us to get rid of Ljubičić," said Josip Vrhovec in an interview on 10 January 1998. The Slovenian leadership, media, and public entered into an open conflict with Mamula in 1986, forcing him out of the government in 1988. General Kadijević, Mamula's successor as defense secretary (1988-92), intended to realize his (Mamula's) plan, but it was already too late.

144 After Stambolić's removal Mamula met him in secret and guaranteed his personal safety, offering him protection by army intelligence. He also showed "signs that he supported" Stambolić, but Stambolić said: "I could not have ever accepted such support for any-let's say-counterattack. To be on one side in an armed conflict with my own people? No way!" (Stambolić 1995:244) The duality between pro-Milošević (pro-Ljubičić) and anti-Milošević (pro-Mamula) military staff lasted right up until the end of Yugoslavia, though it was deeply hidden from the public.

145 One may notice here that both sides used the word Putsch to describe the events. The Milošević supporters said that Stambolić's letter to the Party Presidency in support of Pavlović was an attempted Putsch, though Stambolić-as state president-thought that the Party action against him looked like a Putsch. Since Communist reasoning places Party before state, Milošević's interpretation of "Putsch" is more accurate. A Putsch is an overthrow of a real power, rather than a symbolic one.

146 Mamula used the Croatian/Serbian word *prividjati*, which is usually used for ghosts, meaning to appear.

147 Here he refers obviously to the identification of Yugoslavism with greater-Serbianism. In his defense of Yugoslavism, Mamula was speaking Milošević's language and not Kardelj's. At this time, Milošević was very clearly advocating Yugoslavism, which was probably his most visible difference from the "old" Kardeljist vocabulary.

148 This was an important statement in which Mamula basically asked for a new constitution and an entirely new approach-a much more realistic one-in Yugoslav politics. One may ask what he meant by this. Did he mean that the ideological society should come to an end? Did he plead for "representation of what is" instead of "what ought to be"?

149 Stambolić later (in 1995) said that the army itself was developed as an ideological creation: "In the minds of the army, Yugoslavia was cemented as an ideological creation above all, and, ideologically speaking. Milošević was an orthodox Communist.... For the defense of Yugoslavia as an ideological state, Milošević recommended himself as leader" (Stambolić 1995:30). Again, this explains much about the army staying with Milošević to the end. In Borisav Jović's memoirs we can find elements to support Stambolić's conclusion on the ideological elements of the army. The problems appeared when Jović and Milošević proved to be less ideological than the army expected. Still, a different interpretation is also possible: Mamula demanded more realism and fewer ideological dreams in his speech of September 1987.

150 *Politika*, 7 December 1987.

151 Although he became critical of Milošević's policy and retired in 1995 (after publishing his revealing diaries in a book in 1995), Jović persists in maintaining that the Eighth Session was "an escalation of democratism in the Party." He said, "In 1987 we did not talk about Milošević, Jović, Peter, or Paul—we talked about the interest of the Serbs....I do not know what else we should have done....At the Eighth Session we started the process of uniting Serbia; we clearly said that we in Serbia wanted to decide about Serbia, and that no one outside it would decide on it" (Jović, 1997).

152 The depth of the change is nowhere described better than in Richard West's book on Tito (1994). West, himself a frequent visitor to Belgrade since 1945, writes: "For the first time since I had known Belgrade [so, since 1945!], I was warned by friends against careless talk in public places, and still more on the telephone. People were keeping their voices down in the café of the Moskva Hotel. Outside the hotel, one of the dissidents selling student magazines said he had twice been arrested and was now out of a job. This man, who was in his forties, said he was thinking of leaving Serbia for one of

the more enlightened republics, and eighteen months later I met him again in Zagreb, selling his dissident magazines in the tunnel beneath the railway station. When I asked him what were his politics, he once more replied: simply 'Communist.' Friends I had known for thirty years were talking of going to Slovenia or even to the United States to escape what they called a 'Fascist Regime'" (West 1994:345). The loyal supporters of the 1974 constitutional compromise felt especially threatened by the new revolutionary rhetoric of pre-1966 Socialist Yugoslavism and ethnic nationalist rhetoric that spread throughout the media. The Eighth Session marked the beginning of the final defeat for the supporters of the Constitutional compromise in Serbia. In less than a year they would lose their political position and, sunk in fear, cease to be a significant political factor.

153 It is here that one needs to start looking for the background of violence, which looked like pure self-defense to those who committed it. And it is precisely here that one must begin the journey toward understanding contemporary Serbia: the migrations of its antinationalist youth, as well as the almost insane obsession with "global conspiracies," which are believed by too many people in Serbia to be the main reason for their personal and state's tragedy. In October 1990, only 3.1 percent- of the Serbian population felt no worry about or fear for their personal future and that of their families, but 66.4 percent had a Messianic attitude described in a sentence: "I am afraid, but I think we can find a way out, if we are united." This attitude is exactly what authoritarian leaders prefer to hear (Obradović 1996:494). About the role of fears in Serbian politics under Milošević, see A. Djilas (1993).

154 When I interviewed Radoš Smiljković on 6 March 1989 for *Polet*, he told me: "We are not criticized by the workers in [Croatian-based factory] 'Končar,' nor by those in [Serbian-based factory] 'Crvena Zastava.' We have been criticized by the Slovenian and Croatian leaders, and such criticism we shall not take into account…" He was as bitter at the Slovenian and Croatian leadership as Milošević: "I do not want to say that this was the Slovenian or Croatian leadership, but somebody needed the tragedy of the Serbs and Montenegrins in Kosovo." Then he (Smiljković) proceeded: "We must want Yugoslavia. If we do not want it, let us then stop pretending that we do. In this case, one should clearly say: *We do not want Yugoslavia anymore; we Slovenes or we Croats want to live alone!* All right, Comrades! All right! Do only we, the Serbs, need Yugoslavia, damn it!? But we think that there is no other option for us than Yugoslavia." When I asked him whether he was not possibly exaggerating the anti-Yugoslav feelings of others only because they criticized the Serbian leadership, he resolutely replied: "Oh, no, no, not at all! It is not that all of us want Yugoslavia. The forces that would like to destroy Yugoslavia are very strong. They are maybe not dominant in the country, though they are not weak either. But the forces that Yugoslavia does not suit are strong abroad. And if we are disunited from within, in our economic and political system…then a great danger is threatening us."

CHAPTER SEVEN

Slovenia and Serbia: the Final Years of Yugoslavia (1988-1990)

Those who expect that now, when she has finally become a republic, Serbia will join the defenders of the status quo and oppose changes to the 1974 Constitution, are deluding themselves. They will soon have a chance to see how wrong they are. Serbia did not become a state to sleep on the wreath of glory, but–now strong and open toward others–to forcefully initiate democratic changes to make Yugoslavia a strong community of equal nations and nationalities, able to break with the crises, poverty, and humiliation in which she now lives. Of course, those who do not care for Yugoslavia claim that our intentions and plans are "unitarist" and "hegemonistic." But they should have no illusions that we would-only because of what they say and because they do not agree with us-give up Yugoslavia and Socialism, and democratic processes that no one can stop any longer. We have no time to elaborate our policy to every single person, and especially not to those who are malevolent toward us. The results of our actions will speak for themselves. We can promise them that.

Slobodan Milošević, April 1989

When we think about the idea that a majority vote should be introduced in a multiethnic federation, we ask: is this anything else but a denial of the equality of the peoples, a denial of their sovereignty and of their right to self-determination as an inalienable human right?...Yugoslavia is our common state, which we created voluntarily through a democratic agreement with other nations. Nobody accepted us into it, and nobody can discharge us from it. And we shall not give up our right to it...[However,] we do not want to live in a country in which we would be subjugated to political and national suprapower, to economic exploitation, or to forms of political, economic, and cultural and other dictates.

Milan Kučan, June 1989

7.1. Constitutional Changes and the "Antibureaucratic Revolution" (1988-89)

After consolidating his control over the Central Committee in September 1987, Slobodan Milošević declared constitutional changes (both in Serbia and in Yugoslavia) to be his first next goal. Already in January 1987 (thus to a large extent as a result of a decade of Ivan Stambolić's efforts) the federal presidency agreed to open a public debate about constitutional changes. In February 1987, the Party Presidency approved a debate on 130 amendments to the 406 articles of the 1974 Constitution. But the beginning of the debate revealed only deep differences between the republics and provinces, especially over the central issue of Serbia and its two provinces, Vojvodina and Kosovo.[1] It was Milošević's first goal to silence the opposition to his proposals, which originated in the two Serbian provinces, especially in Vojvodina. As has been demonstrated earlier in this book, Vojvodina's leaders opposed any attempts to centralize (or, as Milošević would prefer it, to reunite) Serbia and Yugoslavia, launching a strong campaign against Serbian nationalism and unitarism. The opposition continued after the Eighth Session, and even intensified in the first half of 1988. Milošević and his main aides on several occasions stated their opposition to Serbian nationalism[2] and repeated their guarantees that no substantive rights would be denied to either Vojvodina or Kosovo. However, they warned both provinces that the time for further concessions and negotiations had expired now that the Serbian Central Committee had achieved unity and was supported by the people. "Bureaucratism and dogmatism are today the main obstacles to changes in society and in the League of Communists," said Dušan Ilić, member of the Serbian Party Presidency. The leaders of Vojvodina and Kosovo, as well as the others who opposed the radical changes proposed by the Serbian Party, were these "bureaucrats."

Milošević's criticism of bureaucracy corresponded well to the demand of the rallies of Kosovo Serbs, but also to those of the dissatisfied public in Vojvodina and throughout Serbia. Following the conclusion that "bureaucracy in the provinces" was the main obstacle to the resolution of the Kosovo problem, the Kosovo Serbs organized a series of rallies in Vojvodina and elsewhere in Serbia, trying to "wake up" the local population and organize it against the local "bureaucrats." Just as before, when they went to Belgrade to "raise awareness" of the Kosovo problem, they now went to Novi Sad and other cities in Vojvodina. The leaders of the province, however, considered their demonstrations nationalistic and anti-Socialist and tried to prevent them by all means. They also accused the Serbian leadership of organizing and directing the public protests.[3] In turn, this outraged large segments of the local population, who joined demonstrations against less than popular local political figures. Further encouragement came from the Belgrade media, by then already firmly under the control of Milošević loyalists, who portrayed these events as demonstrations of the people against the bureaucratized leadership of Vojvodina.

In the three-and-a-half months from 9 July to 21 October 1988, the rallies of support for the Kosovo Serbs and Montenegrins turned into demonstrations against the Vojvodinan leaders and a most powerful support for Milošević's new course. It was estimated that 578,000 people participated in 28 rallies in the province. In a survey of participants at some of these rallies, 72% of demonstrators said they were motivated by the desire to change the "untouchable bureaucracy," and 78% assessed the Vojvodina Party organization as "highly bureaucratized." On the other hand, only 9.3% thought the same of the new Serbian Party leadership. They also expressed their dissatisfaction with the Federal Party leadership (led by Stipe Šuvar), of which 59% thought was "highly bureaucratized" (Kerčov 1990:100-1). For 69% of participants, the protests were the way to "express a general revolt against the situation in the country"; 62% came to "fight against the bureaucracy in Vojvodina"; and only 7% demonstrated primarily against the country's economic situation. Significantly, it was an even smaller percentage that demonstrated against the current state of interethnic relations.

The demonstrations in Vojvodina further divided the Yugoslav Party leadership along republican lines. Vojvodina's representatives demanded condemnation of the "pressure of the street." The Slovenian leadership warned Milošević that Vojvodina and Kosovo were not only parts of Serbia, but also constitutive elements of Yugoslav federalism, and that therefore his action undermined the federal character of Yugoslavia. The leaders of Kosovo insisted that demonstrations of Serbs should be treated in the same way as demonstrations of Albanians and therefore should be declared counterrevolutionary and stopped, if necessary by force. The Croatian and Bosnian leaders feared they would worsen interethnic relations in their republics and cause a new wave of anarchy to which the only response could be a "firm hand" by "Stalinist" and "centralizing" forces. For all these reasons, the Party Presidency of Yugoslavia, in which Serbs were again becoming isolated, demanded that all Party leaderships in the republics should act against the demonstrations.

Milošević, however, rejected this demand, and in September 1988 finally publicly endorsed the protests as an expression of democracy at work. They were, he said at the joint session of the Serbian state and Party presidencies (5 September 1988), not only an expression of solidarity with those who were being "terrorized in Kosovo," but they marked an end of people's patience with the inefficiency of the state and their own representatives. They were also "a democratic, honest, and expected reaction" to years of inactivity in regard to Kosovo. Further, they were a realization of many proclamations about self-management and people's rule. Everything that the leadership in many declarations had claimed it represented, Milošević said, was now here: "...the people, democracy, freedom of expression and the public! Yet, all of a sudden, this is labeled as an undesirable and dangerous thing to which we should put an end (Milošević IB 8/88:14). Milošević denied the criticism that the people's protests were in fact destroying the institutional structure of Yugoslavia: people wanted these institutions to work and would stop protesting when the institutions started working properly. He also denied that the protests were uninational.[4] Milošević argued at the joint session of the Serbian state and Party presidencies in September 1988:

> People can gather only on those grounds on which they feel attacked and endangered. They are attacked as Serbs and Montenegrins; they are leaving their homes as Serbs and Montenegrins, and therefore they defend themselves as Serbs and Montenegrins. They cannot defend or gather as Dutch or as Protestants, or as cotton plantation workers, since none of them is threatened for being any of these. (IB, 8/88:14)

In a populist fashion, Milošević now argued that the Communists could not and should not distance themselves from the people-that would be their end.[5] On the contrary, they should always be with the people if they wanted to regain their trust.

By opposing the demand of the Federal Party Presidency, the Serbian leadership put itself in the unique position of being both an opposition (to the bureaucrats at the local and federal levels) and the government (of Serbia). This ambiguity only helped Milošević to establish himself as a powerful alternative to institutions that were losing public support. It was Milošević's League of Communists that now seemed convincing when talking about the "Party's separation from power" and its being a true representative of "the people." Milošević now became both the promoter of a strong and efficient state and an advocate of antibureaucratic revolution by the masses. Although he was pledging strong action against anarchism, he also supported mass rallies, which were-he claimed, a spontaneous action of the people. Being on both sides at once, Milošević in fact offered a platform to many others, both within the political elite and among the population. Members of the elite now followed his example, becoming almost overnight "representatives of the people." On the other hand, by putting himself at the head of the protests, Milošević enabled many of the disappointed, but not anti-Communist members of the public, to join the protests.

On 8 October 1988, a crowd of about 100,000 demonstrators surrounded the Vojvodina Party headquarters demanding the resignations of the entire leadership of the Provincial Committee. The leadership resisted the "pressure from the street" for the whole day, only to finally resign under the combined pressure of stones and yoghurts and Milošević's public support for the demonstrators. The "yoghurt revolution" removed the main opponents of many initiatives by Serbia's leaders from the *Blue Book* of 1977 onward. Radical change now made Vojvodina the most stubborn supporter of Belgrade, changing the balance of power in the Yugoslav federation. The message Milošević sent to the others was clear:

> The refusal of certain leaders and some individuals to respect the voice of the people, so clear and powerful, not only reveals their bureaucratic and undemocratic habits, but it also feeds anger, an escalation of which could result in endangering the safety of all people in the country. (Milošević, Speech at the 13th CC LCY Session, IB 9/88:10)

When it came to "wars between the people and some leaders," it was unimportant whether the change of politics came through institutions or in an extra-institutional manner: what was important was the unity of the people and its leadership.

It was unity, not institutions that Milošević wanted to save. The old Communist slogan, that the place of the party was among the people while the state was "withering away," now came back in his revolutionary actions, which linked populism with Socialism. It inspired both those who demanded radical changes and those who were not excited by them; those who wanted to see Communist leaders finally overthrown and those not ready to abandon Socialism, yet disappointed by existing bureaucratic politics.

A few days after the "yoghurt revolution," similar protests occurred in Montenegro, with the same demands for the "bureaucratic" republican leadership to resign. In October 1988, the leadership managed to defend itself by using police force against the demonstrators, but the protests—supported by the media in Belgrade—continued until January 1989, when the protesters finally succeeded in ousting the whole Montenegrin leadership.

The October protests in Montenegro, however, met with a powerful reaction from the Slovenian Central Committee, which accused Serbia of organizing protests in the other Yugoslav republics. Slovenia's protests were a reaction to Milošević's straying outside of Serbia's borders. As long as the "antibureaucratic revolution" was confined to Serbia (Vojvodina and Kosovo included), the other Yugoslav republics did not actively oppose it. But Montenegro was a sovereign republic within Yugoslavia. The precedent followed in one case could be used in another, and why not in Slovenia?[6]

The Federal Party leadership also supported the Montenegrin leaders, but this only extended the list of bureaucrats whose resignations were demanded by the demonstrators in Serbia and Montenegro. On the other hand, the Serbian Party Presidency declared its public support for the "justified demands of the workers and citizens of Montenegro...their Socialist character and orientation to brotherhood-and-unity" (IB 9/1988:16). The Serbian Party Presidency demanded an investigation of the Slovenian claim that Serbia had organized protests in another republic. They denied that Serbia had any territorial claims on Montenegro, or that it questioned the existence of the Montenegrin nation or republic. But it also pointed out that the history of the two nations was full of examples of cooperation and "common will." The Slovenian attempt to accuse Serbia of organizing protests against the Montenegrin leadership, Milošević said, was yet another attempt to create interethnic problems and destabilize Yugoslavia. In its declaration of 11 October 1988, the Serbian Party Presidency warned Slovenia's leaders that they in fact were accepting the rhetoric of anti-Socialist and anti-Yugoslav groups and that Serbia's population would not seek approval for their rallies from Slovenia's bureaucratic leaders. In a clear message to Slovenia's population, the Serbian leadership emphasized the difference between "the brotherly Slovenian people" and its bureaucratized leaders. It was, however, also an indirect invitation to Slovenes to replace their bureaucrats with real representatives of the people. In other words, to organize an antibureaucratic revolution themselves.

7.2. Slovenia and Serbia: Divisions between the Intellectual Elites

Milošević's criticism of the Slovenian political leadership in the last quarter of 1988 followed a long-lasting public dispute between Slovenian and Serbian intellectuals over the future of Yugoslavia. Since the beginning of the 1980s, Ljubljana and Belgrade had been the two centers of antiregime actions, but they had failed to create a united all-Yugoslav opposition. Despite fairly developed personal links between the Slovene and Serbian intellectuals and the high regard they had for each other,[7] several initiatives by Serbian dissidents (the most famous of which was the meeting between representatives of Ćosić's Committee for the Protection of the Freedom of Artistic Expression and the editors of the Ljubljana-based journal *Nova Revija* in November 1985) ended in failure.[8] Private letters exchanged between several Slovenian and Serbian intellectuals contributed little to their mutual understanding.[9] Public debate between them, also in the form of letters, had an even more negative effect.[10]

It was in this context that another episode showed how deep the disagreements were between Yugoslav intellectuals. In 1986, a Serbian candidate was to be elected to the one-year rotating post of president of the Yugoslav Writers' Association. The Serbian Writers' Association (UKS) proposed Miodrag Bulatović, but his candidacy was rejected by the Slovenian, Kosovan, Montenegrin, and Croatian organizations, who claimed that Bulatović's views were hostile to other Yugoslav nations. The four constitutive members of the Writers' Association managed to block the Serbian appointee, causing a stalemate from which the association would never recover. Serbia saw the Bulatović case not only as a sign of the strong links between these four organizations and their respective Party elites, but also as an example of another humiliation and intervention in its internal affairs. As Dobrica Ćosić argued,

> The national key principle is respected in every case and for everyone, except for the Serbs. Every national donkey can be the Yugoslav president, except the Serbian donkey!

In an open letter that followed the Bulatović case, the Union of Writers of Serbia accused the Slovenian writers of agitating openly and militantly against the Serbs.

> Slovenian writers must know that Serbian writers will never accept any Diktat...and will reject with contempt a language of provincial maliciousness that does not respect their partners....They should know that Serbian history, both ancient and recent, provides...a holy writ and a reminder that the Serbian nation has preserved its national identity and integrity only by resisting aggression.[11]

The Serbian writers also expressed their determination to prevent the Yugoslav Writers' Association from becoming "an instrument by which militant and aggressive minorities might impose their selfish will, which originates in...their nationalist schizophrenia, on the others."

> On this issue [of the election of Bulatović], there will be no compromise, even if the price is the break-up of the YWA....A community of any type can exist only if principles of equality in rights and in duties are respected, and if everyone obeys the rules previously agreed on. Otherwise its existence is not necessary. (*Nova Revija* 1986:811)

The Bulatović case, like the 1982 case of Draža Marković within the LCY (described in chapter five), demonstrated that the Serbs were unwilling to accept defeat, even if this was the result of the procedure they had previously agreed on. The confederalist principle of appointment, not of election, suited them to introduce the candidate they preferred, regardless of how acceptable he was to the others. But once others rejected it, they simply chose not to recognize the legitimacy of the procedure.[12]

The collapse of the Yugoslav Writers' Association (whose acronym, SKJ, in Croatian/Serbian is the same as that of the League of the Communists of Yugoslavia) preceded by four years the dissolution of the Party. Taking into account how much the writers' associations were already influenced by both their local political elites and by ethnic nationalism, this could hardly be surprising. The event, however, had grave consequences, since it in fact demonstrated that not only the institutions of the state and the Party were disunited, but that it was difficult to expect an emergence of an all-Yugoslav opposition movement. The republican/ethnic fragmentation of the opposition, at the same time the LCY was rapidly disintegrating along the same lines, left little space for the democratic transformation of Yugoslavia. It also suggested that the further democratization of the country would in fact go hand in hand with its fragmentation into republican/ethnic components. A democratic and united Yugoslavia was becoming as improbable as a Communist-led united Yugoslavia.[13] As Dobrica Ćosić noticed, "The case of Miodrag Bulatović was…only a new metastasis of the Yugoslav cancer, which had only one possible outcome" (Ćosić 1986/1992:80-3).

7.3. The Slovene National Program (1986-87)

It is today often argued that the Serbs were the ones who started the circle of ethnic nationalism, of which the SANU Memorandum was normally taken as the main example. In most existing literature, however, the role of Slovene nationalism in the disintegration of the Yugoslav Communist ideology is either ignored or treated as almost insignificant.[14] But an explosive mixture of public protests, populism, ethnic nationalism, and even chauvinism did not emerge only in Serbia; they were simultaneously prominent also in Slovenia, only to spread soon to other Yugoslav republics.

The Slovenian opposition scene in the 1980s had two pillars: (1) the civil society concept, promoted by the Association of the Socialist Youth of Slovenia (ZSMS) and its magazine *Mladina*, and (2) the Slovene national program, created by the Slovene intellectuals assembled in the literary review *Nova Revija*. Although the first concept insisted on the demilitarization of society, establishing various NGOs linked to the ZSMS, the latter attempted to formulate the main Slovenian national interests. In 1988 they moved close to each other, seeing the national question and the democratic transformation of Slovenia as conditional on the destruction of the Yugoslav Communist state.

Within the concept of civil society, the national question was treated simply as a part of the democratic question and within the context of the demilitarization of society. It was first raised by Janez Janša, the leading figure of the civil society concept (formerly a member of the ZSMS presidency, resigning after criticizing the army in 1984), who called on the army to make no exception to other federal institutions when it came to equality of the three official languages in Yugoslavia. In a paper written in 1986, Janša reminded the army that the Slovene Partisan units during World War II spoke the Slovenian language, and that Tito himself promised Slovenes that they would never again be forced to speak a foreign language in their military service.[15] Janša argued that the Yugoslav army in fact was violating the federal constitution. In reality, it had never wanted to accommodate to the political trends of decentralization, which started after the fall of Ranković in 1966. The main reason for this was its paternalistic distrust for certain Yugoslav nations, as a result of which it also rejected any idea of having ethnically homogeneous (i.e., Slovene, Serb, Croat, for example) military units. Janša argued that the army had never abandoned its ambition to play the role of the educator of Yugoslavism and that it had never really accepted the existence of republics as states (Janša 1986:263). For most of the civil society authors (such as Gregor Tomc and Tomaž Mastnak, for example) the national question was therefore treated not as a separate issue, it was an inalienable part of the general democratization of the country.[16]

Somewhat different was the approach of those Slovene intellectuals, who in 1981 established the literary monthly journal *Nova Revija*. In 1985, at about the same time the Serbian Academy of Science and Arts started preparing its memorandum, the editors of the *Nova Revija* (Niko Grafenauer and Dimitrij Rupel) invited contributions to a special issue on the Slovene national question. In fall 1986 the issue was ready to be published. But when the Memorandum met with a strong reaction in Serbian and Yugoslav politics, they decided to postpone publication of the issue until January 1987.[17]

The 57th issue of *Nova Revija* was the first publication that debated ways and methods of changing Slovenian public opinion to win support for Slovenian independence. Slovenia was at a crossroads, facing the most important issues of her identity in the new (informational and cybernetic) era. As one of the authors (Tine Hribar) explained, there were three ways ahead, and Slovenia had to make a clear choice among them. First: she could disappear as an autonomous political subject defeated by Yugoslavism or Yugoslavianism[18] of either a Communist or a democratic character. Either of these two "-isms" would make Slovenes only a minority within a unitary state. This choice was clearly unacceptable. The real choice was therefore between the two following options: either Slovenia would preserve its status as a sovereign nation within the modernized Yugoslav federation (which would recognize her sovereignty not only in words, but also in practice), or she should declare full state independence, separating from Yugoslavia.

Debating this dilemma, most of the authors of *Nova Revija* argued in favor of full independence.[19] However, they were aware that not only international political reality, but also Slovene public opinion was not yet ready to accept such a radical solution. True, the public opinion survey in 1987 (SJM 1987) demonstrated that the Slovene population had begun to think that the state independence of Slovenia was not entirely undesirable. More than half (53%) of the respondents in a survey conducted by the University of Ljubljana claimed that outside Yugoslavia, as an independent state, "Slovenia would increase its chances to develop" (in an economic sense); only 18.9% said Slovenia would "have no chance to develop" in such a case (SJM 1987:58). More respondents than ever before (43.2%) claimed that Slovenian politics were "not sufficiently independent," while an additional 7% said "it was not independent at all" (SJM 1987:58). A large majority of Slovenes (65.5%) claimed the Slovenian language was endangered (SJM 1987:59). Much more than half (59.1%) said that the republics and provinces should be "more independent than they are," and only 8.9% were in favor of the "recentralization" of Yugoslavia.

At the same time, however, none of these findings was sufficient to initiate any great dissatisfaction with Slovenia's political leadership, which was "fully supported" by 37.8% of the population, and an additional 42.0% said that "in principle" they trusted them. Nor did they undermine the Socialist orientation of the majority of the population. In 1987, a total of 42% of Slovenes believed in the prospect of Socialism in the world. True, fewer than ever before said that LCY politics "entirely" or "generally" reflected the interests of the majority, but it was still a high percentage (57.2%) that said so (in 1971: 76.2%; in 1976: 66.4%; in 1980: 72.0%; in 1984: 68.5%; and so on). The survey thus confirmed that the Slovenes really faced a crossroads: they no longer ruled out the possibility of being independent; and neither had they lost confidence in the Communist leadership. They opposed the recentralization of Yugoslavia, but they were not yet ready to support anything else but a program that would somehow preserve Socialism while also increasing Slovene national independence. They were less than ever knocking on the doors of the LCY to become members. Yet certainly they did not really believe that developed Socialism, a democratic Yugoslavia, and a highly autonomous Slovenia were incompatible objectives. After all, the main creator of this concept, Edvard Kardelj, was a Slovene himself, and this now became more important than ever before.

In this context, the authors of *Nova Revija* understood their role as one of convincing the Slovenian public that a Slovenian state was a viable option, and should be the primary aim, ranked higher than either Socialism or Yugoslavia. They had to break the "Slovene paradox," which the Slovene philosopher Tine Hribar described as the Slovene lack of desire to have an independent state. "[Slovenes] are afraid of their unconditional sovereignty" and of statehood, "since they are afraid of the very image of a state," he said in his article in *Nova Revija* 57.

> Since we have so far had only the experience of living in foreign states, those that were not ours, we have built a perception that a state is [merely] an instrument of coercion.[20] We do not think of a state as a legal state (*Rechtstaat*) that would be a guardian of the space of liberty and a protector of human rights, but as an enforcer of duties and obligations, an instrument of intrusion, and even as a terminator of our rights. (Hribar, 1987:25)

It was therefore the notion of the state that had to be changed first.[21] Hribar argued that the democratization of the state was a precondition for Slovenes to begin thinking of their own Slovenian state. Furthermore, he argued that the democratization of Yugoslavia would necessarily lead to an independent Slovenia. The main target of democratization was the "ideology of violence in the name of the [Communist] idea." Without changing the ideology on which the state was created, the expression of preferences would not be possible. But, as soon as this ideology was defeated, the very essence of the Yugoslav state came under question.

For the Slovene intellectuals around *Nova Revija* (almost all of whom later played a leading role in DEMOS, the coalition of anti-Communist parties in the 1990 elections), the democratization of Yugoslavia was not an aim in itself, but the independence of Slovenia was. They understood the democratization of Yugoslavia as a means to this end. While Serbian nationalists remained divided between their Yugoslav and (Greater-)Serbian options, the Slovenian nationalists had no other option available-because they never believed they could (or indeed should) even try to control the whole of Yugoslavia. As early as 1986, they established the clear aim of full independence.

However, the Slovenian nationalist intellectuals were also aware of political reality. Even if the whole project of Slovenian independence did not succeed, Hribar argued, and even if the Slovenes freely decided to remain part of Yugoslavia, there was still a bottom line that they should never cross: they should never agree to be treated as a minority, regardless of how small their share of the Yugoslav population was. The Slovenes were a sovereign nation, and as one they had an absolute right to decide about the form of state in which they should live. The existing 1974 Constitution guaranteed this bottom line, and it was therefore absolutely unacceptable to change it for anything but full independence.[22] So if the Slovenes decided to secede from Yugoslavia, argued Peter Jambrek in his article in the 57th issue of *Nova Revija,* this would be perfectly legal. The potential conflict that might follow such a decision would not be between a sovereign state (Yugoslavia) and its secessionist part (Slovenia), but between two independent and sovereign states; thus the right of self-determination would certainly support the Slovene side.[23]

In a series of articles published in Slovenian academic journals and the media, the legitimacy of the Yugoslav state was questioned.[24] "From a strictly legalistic point of view," the Slovene lawyer France Bučar argued, "the Slovene nation was brought into a political system about which it has never had a chance to express its opinion freely" (1987:154). In the past-including the aftermath of World War II-the Slovenes had never had a referendum on Yugoslavia, but were "guided" by the policy of the uncontrollable Communist Party. Only by exercising their right to decide freely on possible links with the other (Yugoslav) nations could the Slovenes legitimize the state they lived in. As the next step of their political activism, the Slovene intellectuals would therefore propose a referendum on self-determination.

Many articles in *Nova Revija* pointed out that Slovenia's independence was neither unrealistic nor impossible. Apart from its historical development,[25] which made Slovenia much stronger and self-confident than it had ever been, the geopolitical position and ethnic structure of its population were (still) favorable to this option. Not only did almost all Slovenes live within the borders of Slovenia, but the borders also separated them from other Yugoslavs in linguistic, cultural, and historical terms. Economic arguments were also used to support the prospects for independence. Slovenia, whose population made up 8% of the Yugoslav total, contributed 15%-17% of the total funds for underdeveloped Yugoslav regions and produced about 15% of total Yugoslav economic output; its share of Yugoslav exports had reached 20% by the mid-1980s. Quoting these figures, the Slovene intellectuals concluded that the "ideology of egalitarianism" (so popular in other parts of Yugoslavia) was certainly not in the interest of Slovenia.

Subsequently to Hribar's demand that the ideological paradigm of the Yugoslav society should be destroyed, several authors in the 57th issue of *Nova Revija* openly criticized the ideological use of concepts, such as, for example, nationalism. In an article that the political elite subsequently criticized more than any other, the Slovene philosopher Ivan Urbančič promoted a Slovene "positive nationalism" that would take the nation out of "entropy, apathy, and fears," developed not only by recent crises, but throughout their history.[26] Without its own nationalism, the Slovene nation was "sentenced to disappearance" because even those who promoted "internationalism" (such as the Yugoslav unitarists) were in fact only "Yugoslav nationalists" themselves.[27]

Although Urbančič accepted that "certain positive changes" had been introduced immediately before the 1974 Constitution,[28] the League of Yugoslav Communists, by the very fact of being the real sovereign of Yugoslavia, still remained the chief promoter of unitarism. Because no mechanisms for conflict resolution between republics and provinces had been provided illustrates that conflicts had not been expected, since they should have always been prevented by the Party in advance. The Yugoslav "federation" was nothing more than the "objectivization" of LCY rule.[29]

> Regardless of the federal character of Yugoslavia and despite rhetorical claims that the 1974 Constitution recognized and even created the statehood of the republics, the federal state still preserves its supremacy in homogenizing society in a political sense. (1987:36)[30]

Ideological and political homogenization under the LCY had produced a de facto unitary state. The army's refusal to promote languages other than Serbo-Croat was only an illustration of this. But the use of the "Serbian"[31] language in the army and state apparatus did not mean, Urbančič said, that the Serbs (as Serbs) really dominated in Yugoslavia. The federal administration was nationless; it was an ideologized instrument of imaginary class interests, not a representative of any nation, including the Serbian nation. The Slovenes, Urbančič said, should never confuse Serbian nationalism with Yugoslav unitarism. While Serbian nationalism was for him a legitimate political doctrine focused on historical interests of an existing nation, Yugoslav unitarism was not-because there was no Yugoslav nation. Urbančič and also many other Slovenian writers expressed some understanding for the claims of Serbian nationalists, but not for those of Yugoslav "unitarists." Subsequently the Yugoslav Army soon became the main target, primarily for its supranational ambitions. For example, Spomenka Hribar (1988b) also concluded that Yugoslavia was not dominated by the Serbs, but by proletarian revolutionaries.

> The Yugoslav army is not a national army, which means-it is not Serbian, either. Even if all its members, to the last one, were Serbs, this would still be primarily an army of the Party. It is a political, "class" army, which a priori disregards nationalities and peoples as nations. This is why the army is convinced that it is logical that its commander in an area does not belong to the nation that has a majority in this area. It is not only logical, but also necessary for Bolsheviks, since the national feelings of the commander should not coincide with the feelings of the population. Of course, it is the same with ordinary recruits, which should be sent to other areas, such as- in our Slovenian case-Kosovo.

Ultimately, on these grounds the Slovene intellectuals showed more understanding for the Serbian nationalists than, for example, the Slovenian Communists. In 1989, at the height of the conflict between the Serbian and Slovenian leadership, France Bučar wrote,

> The Serbs have a right to their national state...In the "AVNOJ Yugoslavia," this right was denied to Serbs, as it was to the other nations. The Republic of Serbia was not shaped as a state of the Serbs, and certainly not by a procedure in which they could participate; a large proportion of Serbs remained outside their nation-state. By the 1974 Constitution, the autonomous provinces of Vojvodina and Kosovo were practically outside Serbian jurisdiction, having-at the same time-sufficient prerogatives to block any law in Serbia. This impossible and irrational situation was unsustainable. (1989:1497)

Not without a sense of solidarity with Serbian demands, Bučar admitted that they had lost Kosovo because of the high birthrate of the Albanians and the real-

Socialist policy of urbanization, which moved them (the Serbs) from Kosovo to the cities, mostly to Belgrade.

> The result of all this was a general national frustration: [the Serbs] are losing their national territories, and their living standards are decreasing. The economy is more or less bankrupt; their real power is much below the power of their total numbers. The Serbs are perhaps the biggest victim of real Socialism in Yugoslavia. (1989:1497)

But while the *Nova Revija* authors did not in general object to Serbian nationalism, they demanded that their Serb counterparts should clearly dissociate themselves from any trace of Yugoslav unitarism. To a large extent, the complex relationship between the two strongest opposition groups in Yugoslavia (as will be demonstrated later in this chapter) was determined by this demand. The SANU Memorandum was, Urbančič concluded, in this respect still a confusing mixture of Serbian nationalism and Yugoslav unitarism, but it was nevertheless "a positive step forward toward an open discussion" (1987:39). On the other hand, it is almost needless to say that Milošević's revolutionary rhetoric of the pre-1966 period, as well as his unitarist Yugoslavism, was entirely unacceptable to the Slovene intellectuals. The new Serbian leader was indeed the embodiment of everything they criticized.[32]

The Slovene nationalist opposition had less consideration for other Yugoslav nations, with the exception of the Croats. As Urbančič explained in his article in the 57th issue of *Nova Revija*, the Yugoslav federation consisted of three types of nations. The Serbs, Croats, and Slovenes belonged to the first category of "old nations." Although they were too weak to remain independent and thus decided to create a common state in 1918, the old nations existed before Yugoslavia. In Yugoslavia they had "grown up" to the point at which they had become mature enough to create their own states. On the other hand, the Bosnian Muslims, Montenegrins, and Macedonians were "new nations" whose separate identities were recognized only after 1945 (for the Bosnian Muslims, even later-in the 1960s):

> These nations were created by the national state-creating force, which was the Communist Party, at the expense of those nations that emerged in its own historical national movement and were therefore also capable of their federal self-sustainability. (Urbančič, 1987)

The third category had only one member, the Kosovo Albanians, who had not been recognized as a nation (but as a "nationality"), though they had formed a genuine national movement and a strong sense of identity (Urbančič 1987:45-6). In Yugoslavia, all nations, old and new alike, had strengthened their identity and increased their chances of survival as independent states.[33] Yugoslavia should simply recognize this change and allow every nation to express a demand for full independence if it wished to do so.

As Urbančič argued, the problem of Yugoslavia was not that the nations wanted to be independent, but that some of them were not confident enough of their ability to sustain themselves. This lack of self-confidence was manifested in the Yugoslavism of the new nations. The newly created nations (and not the Serbs, Slovenes, or Croats) were therefore a pillar of "Yugoslav Socialist patriotism." They were the main allies of the federal state, which found its main *raison d'être* in favoring the least-developed nations at the expense of the most-developed in Yugoslavia. This was also why, even in the 40 years of redistribution, the differences between strong and weak nations in Yugoslavia had not disappeared: it was not in the interest of the Yugoslav Communist elite. In Urbančič's interpretation, if anyone was to be blamed for unitarism, then this should be the new nations, rather than the Serbs. Not only did they make Slovenia less developed than it should have been, but they kept the Yugoslav state functioning.

The existence of such a federal state, in which the weakest nations did not improve their economic situation, created an additional problem for Slovenia: the wave of emigration of ethnic Slovenes from Slovenia to the West and a large immigration to Slovenia from the other nations, predominantly from new Yugoslav nations. Urbančič claimed that 200,000 "members of other Yugoslav nations" had moved to Slovenia since 1945, mostly for economic reasons, and that while (for the same reason) 600,000 Slovenes had left their country in the past hundred years and had never returned.

> This means that the population of Slovenia had not decreased in its size, but only if we neglect the "unimportant" fact that the (ethnically) Slovene population is declining. (Urbančič 1987:55)

The change in the ethnic structure of the Slovenian population is a "time bomb that is ticking in our lands" (Urbančič 1987:55).[34] Among other threats to Slovene national identity, Urbančič included the increasing number of ethnic Yugoslavs in the 1981 census, the notion of Slovenia being a multiethnic society, bilingualism ("which would make Slovenes a national minority in Yugoslavia"), and-again-disrespect for the Slovenian language in the army.[35]

> It must be very clearly stated: we, the Slovenes, did not associate with other Yugoslav nations in the common state to lose our autonomy and national identity, but to preserve it.[36] Therefore we reject all those elements of our common federal state, which would, sooner or later, lead to or support unitarism. And it is up to us, the Slovenes, to autonomously decide what these elements are. (Urbančič 1987:52)

Two years later, Urbančič would conclude that his expectations that the Yugoslav state would democratize in this direction had been naïve.

> Yugoslavia as a state is a historical accident; it is without any indigenous imperative, without an idea of itself. Yugoslavia cannot exist because she does not have any interior necessity....Yugoslavia as a unitary and centralized nation-state is-as has been demonstrated in practice-impossible. (1989:814)

It was impossible because it did not follow "the demands of the epoch." For the Slovenes, the authors in *Nova Revija* argued, there was only one way out: an independent Slovenia.

7.4. Reaction of the Slovene Political Elite

The 57th issue of *Nova Revija* posed a similar challenge to the Slovenian political leadership, as the Memorandum did to the Serbians. Although the new Slovenian Party leadership (since 1986 led by Milan Kučan) engaged in open criticism of the Slovene National Program,[37] following the same pattern as Stambolić and Milošević, these leaders saw potential benefit in a reconciliation with its main authors. Like Milošević, in the criticisms of the *Nova Revija* and *Mladina* (the youth magazine that since 1982 had promoted liberal views, opening its pages to many nationalists, liberals, and others excommunicated in earlier times), they saw themselves coming under pressure. But even though the Serbian opposition criticized political institutions in general (including those in Serbia), the criticism from Slovenia was directed at federal institutions, including the army. It was not other Slovenes, but the dogmatist and *centralist* forces in the Party and state federal leadership that the Slovene elite feared most. This brought a new dimension to the whole problem.

As several opinion polls indicated in the mid-1980s, the discontent with the LCY policy was stronger in Slovenia than in any other Yugoslav republic. Consequently, 38.9% of the Slovenian electorate in the 1986/1987 survey, carried out by Slovene sociologists on a sample representing the entire Yugoslav population, agreed that "the LCY should be only one of the political parties in our society, and it should be up to each individual as to which party he/she would support." The reply from 27.7% was "do not know," which meant that fewer than 25% of Slovenes opposed the introduction of multiparty democracy. The level of acceptance of such a possibility was therefore higher than in any other republic (in Croatia 30.4%, Montenegro 28.3%, Bosnia-Herzegovina 25.6%, Kosovo 25.2%, Macedonia 23.5%, Serbia Proper 22.9%, and Vojvodina 22.8%) (Goati, 1989:96).

On the other hand, however, the same survey showed growing support for the firm-hand policy throughout the country. The proposition by which the level of authoritarian inclinations was tested was this: "A firm hand, which knows what it wants, would be of much more use to our society than any empty talk about self-management."[38] Surprisingly, the acceptance of this statement was again highest in Slovenia (61.1% in favor, 19.6% neutral), while (with the exception of Kosovo) not much difference was found among the regions with regard to their level of economic development. The authoritarian statements were acceptable for about half of the population in all Yugoslav republics: in Serbia Proper 53.4%, Croatia 53.1%, Bosnia-Herzegovina 52.7%, Montenegro 50.3%, Macedonia 48.0%, Vojvodina 46.8%, and Kosovo 24.7%.

These two possible outcomes, multiparty democracy and the firm-hand policy, now appeared as the main alternatives to the crises of leadership. This conclusion could be well supported by a survey of party membership conducted in 1985 by the Party leadership itself. When asked this question, "In your opinion, what is the main value that should be promoted by our Socialist society?" 41% replied: "social equality" and 19% "freedom and democracy." In all the Yugoslav republics, the Communists valued "equality" more than "freedom and democracy," and also in all, the number of those choosing equality rose when compared with previous surveys: in Slovenia 39.1%, compared with 24% in 1978; in Serbia 41.6%, compared with 34% in 1978. But although in Serbia "freedom and democracy" was in 1978 the choice for 13% and in 1985 for 17%, the number of Slovenian Communists who selected it first grew more rapidly: from 16% in 1978 to 28% in 1985 (Goati 1989:69). In general, the survey showed that the Communists in the more-developed regions of Yugoslavia had started shifting their emphases to promoting freedom and democracy from advocating social equality, and those in the least-developed areas remained committed to social equality.

All surveys conducted in Yugoslavia in the mid-1980s showed that the LCY was becoming a heterogeneous organization, whose members differed much more among themselves than with nonmembers in their own republic/province. This was another important indicator of disintegration, and it went against any trends in other countries in crisis, in Poland for example. While in Poland, surveys showed that the gap between members and nonmembers of the Polish United Workers Party was rapidly widening (Wiatr 1988:13, quoted in Goati 1989), in Yugoslavia the gap between the Communists of different republics was growing, and at the same time the differences between Communists and non-Communists in each republic were getting smaller (Goati 1989:82).

Another important conclusion was that the crisis of the system was deepest in Slovenia, where support for the system among the elite was highest. It came as no surprise, therefore, that both percentages of the Slovenes willing to join the LCY and the actual membership of the Party had sharply decreased by the mid-1980s. It was only in Slovenia that less than 10% of the adult population were members of the Party (9.1% in 1981), and in Yugoslavia it was 13.4%.[39] As a consequence, the Slovenes, already underrepresented in the LCY, now rapidly faced a further decrease of their share in the Party. As long as democratic centralism and party unity were the dominant principles of intraparty structure, the Slovenes would need to follow decisions over which they had less and less control. Consequently, this would create a vicious circle in which support for the Party in Slovenia could simply vanish. On the other hand, the Serbs and Montenegrins, whose share in the LCY membership was larger than their share of the population, and also the Muslims and Albanians (whose share was growing rapidly because of demographic trends and other reasons) felt that the share of influence in the Party should follow success or failure in attracting the masses in each republic to join the LCY. Although the state constitution established equal representation of republics in the federal structure, the Party was not meant to be federalized, even less confederalized. Yet the (con)federal principles of organizational structure guaranteed an equal number of Slovenian representatives (twenty) in the Yugoslav Central Committee and in its presidency (three), equal to that of much larger Party organizations. The Slovenes saw no guarantees that the principle of one member-one vote (still implemented when it came to the selection of delegates for the Party congresses) would not make them a small minority in the Party. There were only two ways out of this deadlock: first, to prevent "minoritization" by reforming the Party so as to abolish democratic centralism and transform it into an "alliance of republican leagues of Communists"; and/or as a minimal demand-to legalize "factions" and promote the rights of intra-Party minorities. Without either of these two changes, the Slovene Communists could well be forced to act against their own beliefs and interests in Slovenia, thereby additionally losing their influence in the region. Through democratic centralism, control over the Party mechanism would, in fact introduce firm control over the Slovenian republic. In turn, this would be the final evidence to confirm what the *Nova Revija* authors argued: that Slovenian sovereignty in Yugoslavia was only a form; in reality, somebody else made the decisions. The rejection of the initiatives of the Slovene Youth Organization (ZSMS, the umbrella organization for many newly established nongovernmental organizations and newspapers, such as *Mladina*) at the Federal Youth Organization Congress in June 1986 demonstrated how high the risks of the democratization of Yugoslavia were at that particular moment.[40] The fear of becoming a minority both within the Yugoslav Party and in Slovenia moved the Slovene leaders to start thinking of reforms, which they had so forcefully tried to prevent before 1985. This is how the Slovenes started arguing for changes in the Party. But these changes had a different and opposite direction from the one proposed by the Serbian Communists.

As the pressure for centralization of the Party increased, the Slovenian Party became the main advocate of minority rights.[41] The same principle of minority protection in Yugoslavia made them more tolerant to political minorities in Slovenia. Under the pressure of the "Alternative" (as the Slovene critical intellectuals preferred to call themselves), and faced with the apathy and indifference of the Slovene population toward the Party, the Slovenian leaders started tolerating moderate democratic reforms in Slovenia, while firmly protecting the achieved level of Slovene autonomy in Yugoslavia.[42]

Several reasons facilitated the rapprochement between the Party and some groups within the Alternative. Unlike their colleagues in Serbia, the Slovene leaders faced a relatively heterogeneous network of "alternative" organizations, many of which operated under the umbrella of the official Slovene Youth Organization. To the young Kardeljist Kučan, the development of such a broad and pluralist organization was in fact an implementation of Kardelj's vision of the "pluralism of self-managing Socialist interests." And the Communists, he argued, should be at its head. Furthermore, the Slovene leaders were not exposed to permanent suspicion for their attempts to "dominate Yugoslavia," as the Serbian leaders were. It also took some time until the others realized what was in fact developing in Slovenia under the protection of the youth organization. Newspapers such as *Mladina* that were critical of the regime, regardless of how popular they were in Slovenia,[43] were still accessible only to Slovene-speaking readers (totaling not more than 2 million). Regardless of how strong its criticism of the system was, it could still have only a limited effect on the political situation in Yugoslavia. These reasons (some of which were purely pragmatic, and others were ideological) in fact greatly facilitated the new politics of tolerance between the Slovene leaders and the growing forces of "civil society."

However, even if the Slovene leadership tolerated the ZSMS's initiatives, it did not approve many of them. Kučan often publicly condemned the "extremism" of *Mladina*, and less popular and more critical student publications were even banned. The Slovene public prosecutor did not hesitate to raise charges against leading *Mladina* columnists.[44] But nothing like the trial of the Belgrade Six or the Šešelj trial in Sarajevo ever took place in Slovenia.[45] On the contrary, Matjaž Kmecl, a member of the Slovene Party Presidency, openly declared that the imprisonment of political opponents in other parts of Yugoslavia, such as the Croatian nationalist Vladimir Šeks and others, was something that belonged to the "Middle-Ages," and thus "was not acceptable in a state that is based on self-management and democracy" (*Nova Revija* 1986:1530).

Furthermore, the Slovenian leaders defended the right of the alternative organizations and newspapers, such as *Mladina*, to broaden the scope of the public agenda by addressing issues that were previously restricted to the political elite only. They defended the Slovenian Youth Organization against attacks from Belgrade and other republics. "It does not make any sense to say that these initiatives [of the Slovenian Youth Organization] are almost an antistate activity, and that one should not discuss them. Why would we not discuss them?" the Slovenian member of the LCY Presidency, Franc Šetinc, rhetorically asked.

> Of course, it does not mean that we should immediately agree with them or accept them. But we should have a chance first to see what it is all about, to analyze the good and bad sides, to hear the pros and cons, before we make a decision. When I read various Yugoslav newspapers, I wonder what makes people more disturbed-the actual initiative of the Youth Organization, or the articles in which it is argued that their initiatives are an attack against the system, against the army, that they aim to weaken our defense and to help the enemies of this country, that the peace movement arises from the ashes of the army, and so on. I believe that it is exactly these malignant interpretations of their initiatives that should upset us more. (Šetinc, *Borba* 5 July 1987)

The statements to this effect, made by leading Slovenian politicians led the Slovene leadership into open confrontation with the army and other republics in Yugoslavia. Subsequently, the Slovene leadership in the mid-1980s slowly but surely slipped into an isolation similar to that in which the Serbian leadership found itself, and for similar reasons. The army and the remaining Titoists accused them of tolerating political opposition and ignoring (if not even supporting) Slovenian nationalism. Still, an open attack on the Slovenes was made less viable than the one on the Serbian opposition because an official organization of the system-such as the Slovenian Youth Organization-provided an "umbrella" for and in fact became an organizer of the Alternative. The army was aware that this would only add fuel to the already existing flames. Janez Janša would finally be able to demonstrate what he had already argued-that the army was the real "sovereign of Yugoslavia." A direct confrontation with not only the Youth Organization, but potentially also with the Slovenian Party leadership, would have only increased opposition to the regime in Slovenia.

Kučan understood this position and put himself in between the demands for more liberalization (expressed by the Slovene Alternative, and also within the ZSMS and LC Slovenia) and the army's demands for an effective political action. His program of "Socialism on a human scale" (promoted at the LC Slovenia Conference in 1988) was still arguing against "foreign ideologies" and was in favor of self-managing Socialism. But it was by now much more moderately Socialist in form and moderately democratic in context. His position of a necessary mediator and protector enabled Kučan to remain in full control. But as his close colleague

Sonja Lokar said, when interviewed in 1988, it was "back home" that the Slovene Communists "would fall if [they] had to fall, rather than in Belgrade."[46]

The federal leadership and the army (openly attacked ever since 1986) expected Kučan to "put an end" to the anti-Socialist actions of the Slovene youth. Similarly, as with the Belgrade Six, when the republican leadership declined to stop the "opposition activities," the federal institutions (this time the army itself) took direct action.

7.5. The "Slovene Spring" in 1988: Army vs. Slovenia

The decisive move was taken by the army, which on 31 May 1988 arrested the leading critic of militarism, Janez Janša, and in the next few days a columnist and the editor of *Mladina*, David Tasić and Franci Zavrl, and a YPA noncommissioned officer, Ivan Borštner, charging them with illegal possession of classified army documents. Before the arrests, Tasić and Janša had published commentaries on a heated discussion at the session of the LCY Federal Presidency on 29 March 1988. The debate followed a session of the Military Council four days earlier, at which the army leadership had declared recent events in Slovenia to be counterrevolutionary and psychological warfare. Members of the leadership ordered the commander of the Ljubljana Military District, General Svetozar Višnjić, to approach the Slovene leadership and seek their help in crushing the counterrevolution (Grakalić 1988:24). The general met Slovenian leaders a few days later, claiming that he had been ordered to discuss issues of security in the event of army intervention. At a closed session of the Party Presidency, Milan Kučan sought an investigation into the whole affair, claiming that the Military Council was not authorized to "organize a *coup d'état*" in Slovenia. At the session of the CC LCY Presidency, Kučan said this:

> He [the general] asked [the Slovenian minister of interior] whether we would be able to maintain control of the situation that would follow the arrests, because it was expected that people would protest on the streets and that they would be defending themselves, the barracks, and military personnel, but they were also ready to help us. Our comrades, the minister and his deputy, told him they could not debate these issues without us [political leaders]. Then they found us, and we spoke to them-myself and Stane [Dolanc]. Of course we refused to discuss these issues, since we said we knew nothing about the whole thing. (Grakalić, 1988:27)

Kučan also asked whether it was true that neither the president of the Party Presidency (Boško Krunić, Vojvodina), nor the president of the state presidency (Lazar Mojsov, Macedonia) knew anything about the conclusion of the Military

Council. The minutes from the meeting, which were classified as a "state secret," were leaked,[47] and *Mladina* wrote a comment on the whole affair. An army officer, Borštner (himself also a Slovene), passed on copies of the army's plans related to possible unrest following the action. This is when the army prosecutor raised charges against the author and the editors of *Mladina*, as well as against the military person that forwarded the classified document to them. But the real attack was directed at Kučan himself, since the army (especially after the first "Janša" affair in 1982) suspected the Slovenian leaders of being unreliable when it came to state secrets.

The arrest of the main critic of militarism (Janša) and the editor of *Mladina* (Zavrl) provoked a wave of public demonstrations in front of the army barracks throughout Slovenia. The arrest of civilians by the army intelligence services; the trial of Slovenes in Slovenia by a Serbo-Croat–speaking military court for possessing documents linked to alleged army intervention in Slovenia: this all proved that the danger of unitarism was real.[48] Unexpectedly, even for the *Nova Revija* authors, the arrest was now a practical confirmation that Slovenia's sovereignty (in the 1974 Constitution) was no more than just a "dead letter." The military *coup d'état* was not about marching on the streets, but about military logic having the upper hand over the political, said Spomenka Hribar (1988:1329). The Slovene leadership was now invited to react fast to protect Slovenia's sovereignty, or to admit that there was no sovereignty remaining. But as it was then criticized, the Slovene leadership recorded enormous support for any evidence of its opposition to federal centralism. The Slovenian public identified with its leadership, which was not only clearly uninvolved in the whole affair, but also strongly opposed to federal institutions.[49] To a degree similar to Milošević's, Kučan now styled himself as "opposition" and "government" at the same time.

But unlike its Serbian counterparts, the Slovene leadership was now defending Slovenia from intervention from outside. This was in sharp contrast to the Serbian rhetoric of changing Yugoslavia by introducing the model of antibureaucratic revolution.[50] By defending Slovenia and opening up to the opposition, Kučan reversed the negative trends for the Party in public opinion and, by the end of 1988, had secured a similar level of support to what Milošević had enjoyed in Serbia. According to a survey conducted by Ljubljana University, the support of the Slovene population for Kučan increased in the six months from April to October 1988, to 65.5%, from 26.9%. Although in 1987 he ranked as the third most popular Slovenian politician (behind the president of the Slovene Socialist Alliance, Jože Smole, and a member of the SFRY Presidency, Stane Dolanc) with only 11% of the votes, within 12 months he had multiplied his score almost six times. On the other hand, Dolanc, a representative of the old politics and strongly criticized by *Mladina*, was now the first choice for only 5.1% of the population

(SJM 1988/1989:334). Kučan's main supporters, such as Jože Smole and Janez Stanovnik, also increased their support rates to 53.4% and 58.3%, respectively. Before the arrest of Janša, 26.4% of Slovenes believed that "the present policy of the Slovenian leadership represents people's interests better than before." But after the arrest, this number increased to 57.8%. Moreover, the number of those who considered the Slovene leadership less concerned with the interests of the people had halved (to 12.6% in May 1989, from 24.2% in April 1988) (SJM 1988/1989:336). It was clear that by siding with liberal and nationalist Alternative and by "defending the national interests" the leadership found strong support among the Slovenes.

Slovenian public opinion almost unanimously opposed the trial of Janša and the others: 68.9% said it was "a political show-trial"; 63.3% believed it was unlawful; 86.2% assessed the whole affair as "a limitation of the sovereignty of the Slovene people" (SJM 1988/1989:331-2). Anger was directed against the federal state, the army, and especially against the Serbian leader, Slobodan Milošević. In 1988, Milošević was singled out as the Yugoslav politician whose politics were most unacceptable to 60.7% of the Slovene respondents. No other politician reached even a tenth of his unpopularity (SJM 1988/1989:372).

Slovenian public opinion, however, sent an ambiguous message to Slovenian leaders. On the one hand, they were popular as never before. Were they to be forcibly replaced under the accusation of "nationalism," 18.2% of Slovenes would "oppose this regardless of the consequences," and a further 57.5% would be "outraged and would oppose this as much as [they] could." At the same time, and very much unlike the situation in Serbia, more people than ever before argued that the "LCY has fulfilled its role and needs to exist no longer." In 1986, however, only 18% of Slovenes favored this conclusion, but 49.5% of the population in April 1988 and 53.3% in May 1989 shared this view. For the first time ever, in April 1988 most Slovenes agreed that "the LCY should remain as just one of many political parties, and it should be a matter of personal choice which party should be voted into office." In fact, by May 1989 only 6.9% of Slovenes opposed this idea, while 75.1% supported it (SJM 1988/1989:265). Although the leaders themselves were popular, the Party was losing its appeal.[51]

Three elements that had characterized the Serbian situation in 1987-89 now appeared in Slovenia. First, a homogenization of the Slovenes took place to an extent similar to what had occurred in Serbia. Second, Kučan, the Party leader, was as popular as Milošević was in Serbia. Third, a mixture of fear and hope entered people's hearts and moved them to act together "as one."[52] These fears were not produced via the perception of threat coming from abroad, from some foreign power, as was often the case in previous years. In April 1988, only 1.5% of Slovenes believed Yugoslavia was endangered from the West, and 5.9% saw danger in the East; an additional 25.8% said the potential danger came "from them both." If we take all those who saw any danger from any of these sides together, it was still the case that two thirds (66.2%) of Slovenes saw no danger at all from anywhere outside.[53] The source of fear was inside Yugoslavia, but outside Slovenia-in Belgrade.

To protect the achieved level of freedom and autonomy of Slovenia, an ad hoc Committee for the Protection of Janez Janša was created in May 1988, and in June it was renamed the Committee for the Protection of Human Rights. The committee provided a forum for various branches of the Slovene opposition, representing a new institution of civil society. It was also recognized by the Socialist Alliance of Working People and thus provided a link between the Alternative and the government. The Slovenian media-openly siding with those arrested-whipped up antiarmy sentiments throughout Slovenia. Public protests were held every day in front of the Military Court in Ljubljana. Rallies of support for them were an open provocation to the army and a sign of defiance by Slovenia's population.

Lastly, the Slovene leadership, although not openly supporting the protests, carefully called for "cohabitation" between the opposition and the Party (Rupel 1988:1309). Sharing the same discontent with the army intervention in "internal Slovenian affairs," the Party played the role of mediator between "the radical right" and the federal leadership.[54] It criticized "provocations that are directed against Socialist democracy" and that had an "anti-Yugoslav and anti-Socialist character." But it praised as civilized the actions carried out by the Committee for the Protection of Human Rights and the Youth Organization.[55] Kučan's politics, said Spomenka Hribar, were a politics of equilibrium: in his actions at the federal level, he was "defending the national interests of the Slovenes"; in Slovenia, however, he was a guarantor that "anti-Socialist forces" would ultimately be prevented from taking over (1988a:1332).[56] The politics of "equilibrium" situated Kučan at the center of Slovenian politics. It was around him, with him at its core, that a new Slovenian pluralism was rapidly emerging.

The army sentenced the three civilians mildly: one and a half years in prison for Janša and Zavrl and five months for Tasić; the NCO Borštner was sentenced to four years. But when they came under the authority of the Slovene prisons, the political elite used all available legal means to release them, without violating the existing legal procedure. Although in fact this demonstrated that the army was not a "paper tiger," the whole affair ended as the first political defeat for the Yugoslav Army in one of the Yugoslav republics. The real war, in which the emerging army of Janez Janša-who in 1990 became the Slovene minister of defense-fought the Yugoslav Army until it was ordered-by a decision of the Yugoslav Presidency, based on a compromise between Milan Kučan and Slobodan Milošević-to withdraw from Slovenia three years later (July-August 1991), was only the last battle in the war between Slovenia and the army, which effectively started with the "Janša Affair."

7.6. The Consequences of the Slovene Spring for the LCY

This turnabout of the Slovenian and Serbian Party organizations with regard to their local electorate produced the real preconditions for the disintegration of the LCY. The Kardelj concept was no longer a framework in which the new politics operated. No longer did the Party leaders discuss the meaning of the same concept: there were at least two rival concepts and one nonconcept (that of the *Šuvarites*) that now competed for support. Both in terms of their content and from the methodological point of view, this was a new situation-very unlike anything that belonged to the ideological politics conducted by the LCY in previous years. The unity of the elite was now created at the republican level, not the federal level. But the elite also invited others within their republics to join them. All-Slovene and all-Serbian programs had already been formulated in *Nova Revija* and the unfinished Memorandum of the Serbian Academy of Science and Arts. By 1989, the two republics were highly homogenized, and Kučan and Milošević were their clear leaders.

The two republics now argued against each other, claiming that the other was deviating from the Socialist path by concluding pacts with the nationalist opposition. The Slovenes argued against the "homogenization" of Serbia, but Milošević replied that he saw nothing wrong in this homogenization, since it had been created on Socialist grounds. On the other hand, it was, he argued, anti-Socialism and anti-Yugoslavism that motivated the homogenization in Slovenia. The year and a half from summer 1988 to January 1990 were characterized by endless disputes between Serbian and Slovene leaders about the character of politics in these two republics. Lacking a normal parliamentary space, the two politics clashed at the sessions of the Central Committee of the LCY, which were broadcast live to the Yugoslav public. The shocking experience of Party leaders openly fighting one another, however, only further contributed to the sense of anarchy and fear, already deeply engendered by the Serbian protests, army arrests in Slovenia, and Slovenian unilateral actions in changing the constitution. Moreover, the various segments of the Yugoslav population interpreted very differently what they saw at the sessions of the Central Committee. The Serbian leaders used them as an example of disunity and bureaucratism, of clandestine support for the Albanian counterrevolution, and of a forum for "a nonprincipled coalition" to outvote their republic. The Slovenes saw them as evidence that no united Yugoslav Party was possible any longer and that efforts should be made to transform the LCY into a "League of the Leagues," a loose coalition of republican party organizations. The principle of democratic centralism should be abandoned, and minorities within the Party should be fully protected. To this the Serbs replied negatively, arguing that "no factions within the LCY should be allowed."

However, there was a third group within the Central Committee. It was led by Croat Stipe Šuvar and supported by majority in the army, the Bosnian leadership, and on some occasions by Albanian members from Kosovo, a large section of the Croatian members, and about half of the Macedonian members. This group of "Kardeljists" attempted to eliminate both extremes-the Slovenes and Serbs equally-and to oppose changes in either a confederalist or a centralist direction. But this group of members, though not insignificant in number, was not supported by public demonstrations, nor did it have its own media. It was also internally not as homogeneous as the Serbs and Slovenes. The third group (the "Šuvarites," *šuvarovci*) was strong enough to prevent either of the two combating groups from hijacking the Federal Central Committee. But it was too weak to do much more. In fact, its action caused a permanent stalemate in the Party leadership at the moment when everyone wanted a quick and radical resolution of the conflict. The stalemate in the leadership, however, turned out well for both the Slovenes and the Serbs. Neither group had to fear intervention from the Federal Central Committee, and both could blame it for the growing crisis in the country. However, the stalemate in the Yugoslav Central Committee, the potential vehicle of Milošević's control over the federal institutions and other republics, was acceptable to the Serbian leaders only for as long as they did not secure a clear majority within it. But over the long term, just as he had demonstrated in Serbia, Milošević needed the Party to "unite the country."

7.7. The Final Battle: Changing the Rules of the Game

In spring 1989, the Vojvodina Party organization held its Extraordinary Conference, consolidating the power of the new leadership of the province. In what was a precedent in Party history, the conference demanded a vote of confidence in Yugoslav Central Committee President Stipe Šuvar and initiated an Extraordinary LCY Congress. Though Šuvar survived the (secret) vote of confidence at the Central Committee, the committee could do nothing but accept the proposal for an Extraordinary Congress. According to a highly confederalized Party statute, a congress had to be convened even if only one of the member organizations (any republic or province) demanded it. The tool invented to prevent the domination of any group within the Party (and especially, the greater-statist tendencies linked to Serbia) was now used to change the rules and to oust the 'bureaucrats' and the 'separatists.'

Vojvodina's move was an important step in Milošević's attempt to take over the Federal Party and subsequently the state. Unlike the Central Committee (which had an equal number of members from each republican Party organization), participants in the Congress were elected proportionally to the number of members in each republic. The Serbian Party organization, with more than 850,000 Party members,[57] could therefore safely count on almost 40% of the votes. Together with Montenegro's representatives (who accounted for seven percent of the membership) and with a little help from some Bosnian, Croatian, or Macedonian delegates, many of whom were Serbs, Serbia counted on an easy victory. A majority at the Congress would change the statute of the Party, effectively eliminating any trace of the confederalized structure. The new majority would then be able to impose its decisions on all members, using the principle of democratic centralism. It would also be able to control a fifth vote (in addition to its own, two of its provinces and the Montenegrin one) in the Yugoslav Federal Presidency, whose ninth (ex officio) member was the president of the Party Presidency. In fact, the majority of the Congress would then control all Yugoslav institutions, including the army and the secret police. The whole action was to be legitimized by a simple democratic argument that the majority should rule.[58]

But such an argument would clearly make the Slovenian party a tiny minority in the LCY, taking away from it any possibility to veto decisions. For the Slovenian party, the only way out was to propose further confederalization of the Party. The Slovene Communists therefore proposed an entirely different concept of Party reform-an Alliance of Republican Leagues of Communists. According to Slovenia's proposal, the LCY would follow the state in its decentralization, accepting the autonomy of the republican leagues of Communists, which would be only loosely linked together under the umbrella of the LCY. If this project could not secure support from the others, the Slovene Communists were ready to leave the organization.

Throughout 1989 the conflict between the two programs of reform in Yugoslavia-Slovenian and Serbian-developed both within the constitutional debate[59] and within the Party. It was in this context that on 21 February 1989, a total of 1,350 Albanian miners in Kosovo locked themselves in the largest mine in Kosovo-at Stari Trg, demanding from Serbia the abandonment of the constitutional changes they perceived as being hostile to the autonomy of the province. They also demanded the resignations of three pro-Milošević Albanian leaders: the newly elected president of the Kosovo Party, Rahman Morina, the president of the Priština Committee, Husamedin Azemi, and the Kosovo political veteran, Kole Shiroka. Six days later (27 February 1989), while the miners were still in the mine, the federal presidency declared emergency measures in Kosovo[60]. When

Serbian leaders appeared persistent in their refusal even to talk to the miners, the Slovene Alternative organized public protests in Ljubljana's "Cankarjev Dom" Hall of Culture on 28 February 1989. The entire political leadership of Slovenia, including Milan Kučan, joined the Slovenian opposition on this occasion, which gathered around 2,000 figures from Slovenian public life. Some speakers, including the ZSMS president, Jožef Školč, compared the sufferings of the Albanian miners with the Holocaust, indirectly accusing the Serbian regime of Nazism.[61] The Youth Organization introduced a badge with the Jewish national symbol (a six-pointed star) and the text "Kosovo-My Homeland." Školč had this to say (*Tanjug*, 28 February 1989, in Belić and Bilbija 1989:24):

> Today, the Albanians are excluded from society as "lazy," "violent," and "murderers." Yet tomorrow this could happen to us, the Slovenes, to Croats and Montenegrins, to everyone."

Milan Kučan himself pointed out that the miners in Kosovo should not be treated as "Albanians" or "Serbs," but as workers, "people forced to organize Gandhi-like resistance protests to oppose injustice."

> Yugoslavia, [which guarantees] the equal status of every republic and nation, including Slovenia, is what is now being defended at Stari Trg. This is why we all feel that the tragedy of the miners would be our defeat as well. This would be a very clear announcement that the minority nations and nationalities will first be pushed to the margins, and then out of the country, abroad, or who knows where....We Slovenes are not accidental travelers in AVNOJ Yugoslavia...[and would therefore not allow]...a silent turnabout that would certainly change the very nature and essence of AVNOJ Yugoslavia....Slovenian Communists and LC Slovenia do not want to take part in the creation of such a [new] Yugoslavia....To preserve the SFR Yugoslavia, we should develop democracy and self-management. Because if we lose the federative character of Yugoslavia, together with Socialism, then we shall lose our history, from which we have learned that the freedom of every nation is a condition for the freedom of us all. (Belić and Bilbija 1989:30).

Other speakers in the Cankarjev Dom pointed out that "the politics of greater-Serbian Yugoslavism have brought the country to the edge of civil war" (Franko Juri). Some (like Igor Bavčar) also linked Serbian attempts to change the constitution with the events in Kosovo.

The meeting in the Cankarjev Dom outraged not only the Serbian leaders, but also broad masses of the Serbian population. When a report on the event was shown on Belgrade Television later that day, the students of Belgrade University organized the largest-ever rally in Belgrade since the liberation of the city in 1944, demanding that the Slovene leaders be treated as counterrevolutionaries and "traitors to the homeland."[62] The crowd of more than 700,000 did not respond to Yugoslav State President Raif Dizdarević's promises. It was only when Slobodan Milošević addressed them after more than 24 hours of protests that they agreed to leave for home. On this occasion, 28 February 1989, Milošević promised the arrest of Azem Vllasi "and others who have manipulated with people's lives," and he declared that Yugoslavia would never disintegrate because "the people would not let it disintegrate."[63] The crowd responded, shouting for the first time: "Slobo, the Serb, Serbia is with you!"

As a consequence of Slovenia's solidarity with "counterrevolutionaries," the Belgrade media launched an unprecedented anti-Slovenian campaign. The Serbian Writers' Association immediately cut off any formal relations with their Slovene counterparts for their participation in the meeting at the Cankarjev Dom. One of the leading Serbian writers, Matija Bećković, said:

> For years and years our hand was offered to the Slovenes, only to remain in the air, untaken. We tolerated indifference, suppressed our pride, accepted that it was all only misinformation. Our best efforts produced only the worst results. We are looked down on from their heights and shown a permanent disdain for our truths. It is not noticed how much we desire to have [the Slovenes as] friends. Instead, they do not care if they wound us; they spread Serbophobia and make jokes about Serbian saints and sufferings. Six hundred years after the [Kosovo Polje] Battle we must declare: Kosovo is Serbia, and this fact does not depend on the Albanian birth rate or on the Serbian mortality rate. There is so much Serbian blood in Kosovo that even if no Serb remains there, Kosovo will still be Serbian land. Serbia, the republic that does not exist, can have no aims more important than that it becomes a republic.[64]

In a formal letter to the Slovenian Writers' Association, their Serbian counterparts accused them of "betraying the traditional and historic friendship between our two peoples." At the same time, in protest at the breakdown of the relationship with the Slovenes, the Albanian members left the Serbian Writers' Association. "Serbian writers are not interested in democracy, but in the repression of the Albanian people, against all human norms and values," they claimed. The Serbian Academy of Science and Arts condemned the Cankarjev Dom meeting: "In its entire history, nobody has ever insulted the Serbian people so much," they concluded. Slovenian support for the Albanians in Kosovo is an "unlikely alliance between representatives of a civilized, Central-European society and representatives of oriental violence," they said. At an emergency session of its association on 4 March 1989, the Serbian writers concluded that "anti-Serbism is spreading widely in Kosovo, Slovenia, and Croatia," and that "the Cankarjev Dom meeting is an expression of Slovene Serbophobia that has lasted the whole decade." One of the speakers, Vuk Drašković, went even further, proposing the solution for "anti-Serbism" in changing the borders of Serbia:

> If the division of Yugoslavia occurs, where should be the Western borders of Serbia? Those borders were decided by [Ustashe leader] Ante Pavelić; they are where the Serbian graves are. It is up to the Serbian national program to mark them....The Croats should be aware that if Yugoslavia collapses, its borders will not remain as they were determined at AVNOJ or Brioni, and that-in such case-Jasenovac, Jadovno,[65] and all other graves of us Serbs would get a right to vote. Also, all the Serbs once evicted or forced out of Croatia, Slavonia, Bosnia, Dalmatia, Herzegovina, Kordun, Lika, and Banija[66] after the war will be asked to vote as well. (*Borba* 5 March 1989)

The Slovenian Writers' Association responded with a no less strong condemnation of the Serbs:

> The Serbian political leadership has ignited Greater-Serbian nationalism and has by now occupied half of Yugoslavia by brutal pressure, defamation, blackmailing, and using *coup d'état* methods. The federal leadership has agreed on the Serbian rules of the game. Anti-Albanianism has become the official policy....We find them in a most absurd situation in which the Albanians are declared counterrevolutionaries only because they want to preserve the 1974 Constitution, especially those provisions of this constitution that protect civic and ethnic liberties. Those who demand the overthrow of the constitution and of all the legal institutions of the system have imposed their logic even on the presidency of the state. It is a basic ethical duty to protect the Albanian people from the *pogrom* that is knocking on their doors! (*Nin* 5 March 1989).

Ultimately some Serbian writers (such as the prewar surrealist and Partisan legend Oskar Davičo) asked the Serbian population to boycott all products that come from Slovenia. The media accepted this demand, and soon the boycott took on significant dimensions.[67] The Serbian government declared a ban on importing Slovenian goods into Serbia. An act that was clearly unlawful met with the approval of the Serbian population.

In March 1989 a state of emergency was officially declared in Kosovo, and the units of the federal special police prevented further demonstrations by Kosovo Albanians. The Serbian Assembly was given the rights to direct control over courts, police, and the selection of government officials in Kosovo. And Kosovo was stripped of its veto over Serbian constitutional amendments. Azem Vllasi, the Communist leader of Kosovo, was expelled from the Central Committee of the LCY (by a majority of three votes more than required), arrested, and put on trial for organizing "counterrevolutionary demonstrators"-the Kosovo miners.[68]

On 30 March 1989, the Slovenian Parliament sent an open letter to other republican parliaments, proposing a dialogue to resolve the political crisis. The existing model of Socialism was in deep crisis, and it should be reformed toward "democratic political pluralism," not toward "forced unity." The Slovenian Assembly rejected accusations of Slovenian counterrevolution and its support for "Kosovo irredentism."

> We do not oppose reforms in Serbia that are in accordance with the amendments to the Yugoslav Constitution and with the will of the Serbian people and all other nations and nationalities living in Serbia and its provinces. In Slovenia, there is no organized action to undermine the constitutive role of the YPA or the federative structure of Yugoslavia, explained the Slovenian Assembly. (Belić and Bilbija 1989:151-55)

But it also added that "there is nothing to add to or amend what was said in the Cankarjev Dom."

Following this initiative by the Slovene Parliament, the Slovenian Presidency on two occasions from March to May 1989 invited the Serbian Presidency to discuss problems. But all the Slovenian initiatives met with rejection from Belgrade. Serbian politicians first claimed that any political dialogue concerning the future of Yugoslavia should be conducted within existing federal institutions. They additionally accused Slovenia of issuing ultimatums to others in Yugoslavia and of being intolerant when it came to the position of others, mainly of Serbia. In his speech in Novi Sad on 22 May 1989, Milošević said "the time for empty talks was over," and a "decision on the future of Yugoslavia should be made." This decision (which thus had to be taken with no further discussion), must be "in favor of Yugoslavia, in favor of a new Socialism, of a wealthier and more democratic society that will belong to Europe." He said, however, that Serbia "does not want to enter Europe as a servant, wanting to please Europe by mocking its own country, attacking its own institutions, including the army and insulting other, allegedly noncivilized nations." Slovenian politics, Milošević said, were antidemocratic:

> There is so much talk [in Slovenia] about human rights. Yet they support separatists in Kosovo, who use terror against the Serbs and Montenegrins and violate their human rights. There is so much talk [in Slovenia] about pluralism-but they are aggressive and intolerant toward those who think differently, for example toward us in Serbia. Everyone who opposes them is exposed to threats and pressure....There is no civilized country in the world where such behavior would be treated as democratic. Their vengeful behavior is especially incompatible with the culture of contemporary Europe, which they would like to join. In fact, those fascist-like expressions of irrational hatred tell us only how deep the crisis is and how dangerous it would be if it deepened further. (Milošević, 22 May 1989 in Belić and Bilbija 1989:180-83)

The Slovenian Parliament and the presidency again protested against Milošević's words, again proposing a meeting. Slobodan Milošević replied in his letter of 1 June 1989:

> Our doors are open to you. However, if you are honestly interested in achieving a result, you should be aware that this is possible only if you change your views about Kosovo and if you bring them into line with Yugoslav and LCY politics.[69] We hope you would then stop deliberately underestimating your anti-Serbian and anti-Yugoslav attitudes, such as those expressed in the Cankarjev Dom, which-and especially the view of Yugoslavia defended in Stari Trg-represented the lowest kick in Serbia's back, at a moment when Serbia has introduced constitutional amendments and become a republic, equal to the other Yugoslav republics. Also, we think that our talks cannot really succeed if you continue to misinform the public about the situation in Serbia... and if you continue to shape [and intervene in] Serbia, and especially Kosovo. When you finally realize that you should not be asked about politics in Serbia anymore than we are asked about politics in Slovenia, then we will be happy to welcome you in Belgrade to talk about our common interest, about Yugoslavia as our common homeland. (*Politika*, 2 June 1989)

Milošević's reply was a deliberate public humiliation of the Slovenian leadership. On 2 June, the Slovene Presidency replied:

> SR Slovenia is a sovereign state of the Slovenian people....She has both the right and the responsibility to make decisions on political issues concerning our common life and the future of the country, exactly because we live in our common homeland. This is also the case where the situation in Kosovo is concerned. (*Politika*, 3 June 1989)

The Slovene leaders said that dialogue would not be necessary if the two sides had the same views, and it would be impossible if one side wanted to impose its views on the other. The public dispute between Milošević's and Kučan's presidencies further endangered the functioning of federal institutions. On 15 June 1989, the president and secretary of the Federal Youth Organization, Branko Greganovič (Slovenia) and Anita Bara (Croatia) resigned in protest over the speech of the Kosovo representative, Rexhep Hoxha, who accused the Slovenes of anti-Serbian and anti-Yugoslav politics. On the same day, the Slovenian writers denied the rights of the Yugoslav Writers' Association to represent them abroad, since it had become an instrument of Serbian politics. The Yugoslav institutions were now on the verge of collapse and paralysis.[70] And on 17 June 1989, *Radio Free Europe* reported that "the Yugoslav orientation was still very strong among the population."[71]

On the same day, the Slovenian Parliament proposed a new group of amendments to the constitution, in which the right to self-determination (including secession) was emphasized. Speaking in Tacen (near Ljubljana) that day, Milan Kučan said:

> When we think about the idea that a majority vote should be introduced in a multiethnic federation, we ask, is this anything but a denial of the equality of the peoples, a denial of their sovereignty and of their right to self-determination as an inalienable human right....Yugoslavia is our common state, which we created voluntarily through a democratic agreement with other nations. Nobody accepted us into it, and nobody can discharge us from it. And we shall not give up our right to it....[However] we do not want to live in a country in which we would be subjugated to political and national suprapower, to economic exploitation, or to forms of political, economic, and cultural and other Diktat. (*Borba* 19 June 1989)

In his speech, Kučan said that the individual was at the center of the new Slovenian politics, and that "without the sovereign individual there is no sovereignty of the nation, and no workers' self-management, and these are the main pillars of our Communist movement" (Belić and Bilbija 1989:228). Although he clearly introduced certain elements of political liberalism into his rhetoric, Kučan still remained convinced that the main question was this: "What type of Socialism do we want?" The democracy that the Slovene Communists were introducing was "democracy for all, which means democracy for Socialism." Kučan promised he would never again offer his hand to those who rejected dialogue (the Serbian leadership), saying it was a disgrace that 200 years after the French Revolution there were still political prisoners, and he demanded release for all those "isolated" in Kosovo.

On 21 June 1989, the presidency of the Slovenian Central Committee clearly opposed the one member-one vote principle of voting in the LCY. If at the 14th LCY Congress the principle of majority voting was introduced, the Slovenian organization would "immediately initiate an extraordinary congress and either suspend the principle of democratic centralism, or decide in favor of the full organizational independence of the LC Slovenia." In the programmatic conclusion of this session, the Slovenian Party leadership concluded that "nations can exist without Socialism, but Socialism cannot exist without nations."

The following day, the presidency of the Serbian Central Committee for the first time demanded that "those parts of the nations and nationalities in all our republics [which live outside their own republic] obtain the right to their full national affirmation, and the preservation of their national and traditional characteristics, and also of their national identity." At this moment, the Serbian

Party leadership said, "It is not realistic to expect that Socialism in Yugoslavia could survive without a strong progressive...factor such as the LCY. Equally... the existence of Yugoslavia is also impossible without Socialism based on self-management." The main political battle in Yugoslavia was, the Serbian leaders said, between the national bureaucracies and the progressive forces of self-management. Never before had the Serbian leaders so explicitly said that the AVNOJ principle of "national equality, brotherhood and unity, and federalism" should be preferred to "the model in which Yugoslavia was only what the republics as national states agreed on" (Belić and Bilbija 1989:249). This was a clear rejection of the post-1974 Yugoslavia for the pre-1966 concept.

On 28 June 1989, a large crowd of Serbs gathered in Gazimestan to celebrate the 600th anniversary of the Battle of Kosovo, the central national myth of the Serbs. Slobodan Milošević used this occasion to present himself as the true leader of Yugoslavia. In what was a manifest gesture, he placed himself before the president of the Yugoslav Presidency, Janez Drnovšek (Slovenia), and the LCY Presidency, Milan Pančevski (Macedonia), on all ceremonial occasions.[72] Before a large crowd of Serbs and Montenegrins, he said:

> If we lost the battle, then this was not only the result of the social superiority and military advantage of the Ottoman Empire, but also because of the tragic discord at the head of the Serbian state....The discord and betrayal at Kosovo have followed the Serbian people like an evil fate throughout its entire history. In the past war, this discord and betrayal led the Serbian people and Serbia to agony, the consequences of which were both in a historical and in a moral sense more damaging than those of the fascist [aggression]. And also later, when Socialist Yugoslavia was created, the Serbian leadership remained divided in this new country, always ready to compromise against its own people. The favors many Serbian leaders granted to others while disadvantaging their own people would not be acceptable in either a historical or a political sense to any other people in the world....The disunity of Serbian politicians harmed Serbia, and their inferiority humiliated Serbia. This has been so over decades, for years. We are here today on the field of Kosovo to say that this is not so any longer. There is no better place in Serbia than the field of Kosovo to say that unity in Serbia will bring prosperity to Serbia, and to the Serbian people, and to all its citizens, regardless of their national or religious affiliation. (*Politika* 29 June 1989)

The crowd responded:

Now we know/ now we see/ who is the new Tito/ Slobodan, Slobodan/ a name of pride.[73]

In July 1989, the Serbs in Knin (Croatia) organized their own celebration of the Kosovo battle. The leaders of the newly created anti-Communist Serbian

Democratic Party (SDS) claimed that the Serbs were assimilated, since "every day there are more and more 'Yugoslavs,' and the Cyrillic is underrepresented."[74] They demanded that "the centralist-Comintern cadre in Croatia, including 90% of the Serbian cadres in Split and Zagreb, be replaced," and "that the Croatian people should rise against its own bureaucracy." Simo Dubajić, one of the World War II leaders of the Krajina Serbs, said he would "easily settle these problems with Tudjman, but he would not talk to the Central Committee of the LC Croatia."[75] The Croatian government replied with the arrests of several leaders of the protests in Knin, which in turn caused an outburst of anger in the Serbian media. The issue of the relations between Serbs and Croats in Croatia was now widely open for public debate. The Croats felt seriously endangered by both the Belgrade offensive and the Knin demands for an antibureaucratic revolution against Zagreb. The inability of the Croatian leadership (still divided between pro- and anti-Šuvar factions) to formulate a clear policy for Croatia, now increasingly sandwiched between Slovenia and Serbia, gave rise to Croatian anti-Communist nationalism, which was now represented by newly created parties, most notably by Franjo Tudjman's Croatian Democratic Community.[76] At the 26th Session of its Central Committee, the Croatian Party made a surprising about-face, claiming that "political pluralism is-contrary to what is often argued-not a tool to homogenize, but one to dehomogenize national communities....It is a tool of political segmentation, not of national homogenization. This is why it is in fact a tool against the emergence of monopolist national programs and national mass movements."[77] It was now Croatia, not just Slovenia, that moved toward a pluralist political system.

Ultimately, in October 1989 the Serbian leadership also moved to accept the possibility of party pluralism.[78] In a speech at the Central Committee session, Balša Špadijer finally abandoned the idea of reforming the 1974 Constitution by endless amendments. Serbia now sought "radical changes" based on the "introduction of the citizen as the basis of the system." They demanded a two-chamber Federal Assembly, with a democratic principle of one member-one vote to elect a House of Citizens (as the lower chamber) (IB 10/1989:22-25). The principle of consensus should be still respected, but for a rather limited range of essential issues. Slovenia was again seen as the main obstacle to such reforms.

On 27 September, the Slovenian Republican Assembly amended its constitution to describe Slovenia as "an independent, sovereign, and autonomous state" with the right to self-determination and secession. Before this, the Federal Presidency had asked the Slovenes to withdraw their constitutional amendments, but they failed to obey.[79] On 22 September the Federal Defense Secretary General Kadijević told the vice president of the Federal Presidency, Borisav Jović (Serbia), that he was ready to prevent the Slovenes from proposing their constitutional amendments on the grounds of "the protection of constitutional order," for which the army was authorized by the constitution (Jović 1989/1995:53). However, three days later, Kadijević withdrew on the advice of the army legal experts who thought "the action would be on the edge of legality" (Jović 1989:1995:54). The Serbian leaders now realized that the Army was not a reliable ally and that the Federal Prime Minister Ante Marković was still influential when it came to federal institutions. They concluded that "the historic opportunity" to stop the Slovenes had been missed (Jović 1989/1995:55).

In October 1989, the Serbian leaders decided simply to ignore the Slovenes "as if they did not exist" and to prepare constitutional changes relying on the majority they still commanded in most federal institutions.[80]

On 30 November 1989, the Slovene Ministry of the Interior banned a Serb rally scheduled to take place in Ljubljana on 1 December, the day when Yugoslavia was created in 1918. The Slovenian leaders were not worried that the "export" (as they called it) of the antibureaucratic revolution could succeed in their republic, but they feared incidents between the domestic population and Serb protesters, which could eventually provoke the Federal Army to intervene against Slovenia. On 4 December the Croatian Republican Assembly (Sabor) decided to support Slovenia against Serbia. The demonstrators gave up, but the Serbian leadership decided to cut off all official relations with Slovenia. An economic boycott of Slovenian goods was now official policy. At this time, the Montenegrin League of Communists was supporting Serbia.

In December 1989, Milošević declared the Slovenian leadership to be the "protector of conservatism in Yugoslavia and one of the last defenders of conservatism in Socialist countries in general."

> This conservatism of Slovenia is confronted with the forces of progress in Yugoslavia, and especially with progressive economic and political changes in Serbia, and thus reacts aggressively and brutally....The aggressive reaction of these bureaucratic forces...insults the dignity of other people. And today's politics of Slovenia not only insult our dignity, but they also threaten the very basic human rights of other Yugoslav citizens in the Slovenian part of the Yugoslav state. The bureaucratic, arrogant, and aggressive Slovenian leadership have cut all links with the people in Serbia, and we have taken this decision of theirs seriously. We shall remain consistent in this serious response as long as the forces of conservatism, aggression, and violence are not replaced by a democratic, peaceful, and brotherly attitude in Slovenian politics. (*Borba* 12 December 1989)

At the same time, the newly established Serbian, Croatian, and Slovenian political parties expressed radical views about the future of Yugoslavia. The Serbian Revival Party (led by Vuk Drašković) demanded a restructuring of Yugoslavia toward a confederation of Serbs, Slovenes, and Croats, in which the Serbian state would include Macedonia, Montenegro, and Bosnia-Herzegovina. The Croatian Democratic Community of Franjo Tudjman (initiated on the very day of the Cankarjev Dom meeting and the Belgrade rally against the Slovenes) also demanded more (though not yet full) independence for Croatia. The new Slovenian parties (which appeared in the form of various associations, later to be renamed parties) followed the program of *Nova Revija*. In all three cases, the members of the intellectual elite who opposed the regime now became directly involved in party politics. The LCY, though still the only recognized political party in the country, was far from being in full control of events.

7.8. The LCY Membership Divided

The two political options-Slovenian and Serbian-divided not only the leadership, but the whole membership of the LCY and the population itself. A survey among 5,000 LCY members, commissioned by the Federal Party Central Committee in its preparation for the 14th Party Congress (conducted by Ivan Šiber in November 1989) demonstrated that the LCY had practically split on all the main issues of the debate.

It showed that 67% of members in Slovenia were in favor of decision making by consensus, and 73% of the Serbian Party favored the majority vote. The Croatian and Kosovo organizations were closer to "consensus," and more than 50% supported a majority vote in Montenegro (66%), Vojvodina (65%), Macedonia (57%), and Bosnia-Herzegovina (52%) (Šiber 1989:15).

On further autonomy for republics and provinces, 85% of the members in Slovenia were in favor of "more independence for republics and provinces, but 90% in Vojvodina argued the opposite-for more unity in the federation." Slovenia was, in fact, the only republic in which more members argued in favor of "more autonomy" than "more unity." Even among the Croatian and Kosovan members, 49% and 45%, respectively, favored "more unity," as opposed to 38% and 40% for "more autonomy."

On the direct representation of the two provinces in federal bodies (as it was in the 1974 Constitution), only 30.9% of all respondents in Yugoslavia were now in favor of it, and 61.7% of respondents preferred them to be represented in the federal institutions only as an integral part of the Serbian delegation. The differences were again great between various parts of the LCY: direct representation was favored by 71% of the LC members in Kosovo, 67% in Slovenia, and 48% in Croatia. However, 88% in Serbia, 76% in Montenegro, 74% in Vojvodina (!), 68% in Macedonia, and 51% in Bosnia-Herzegovina were for indirect representation through the Serbian delegation.

The state of emergency in Kosovo, introduced in March 1989, was supported by 81% of the LCY members, but only 28% in Slovenia and 40% in Kosovo. The level of support in other republics and Vojvodina varied from 72% in Croatia to 97% in Serbia outside the provinces.

Mass rallies were supported as the "most suitable form of expressing political views" by 53.3% of LCY members. This was a clear approval of the ongoing demonstrations of the Serbs and Montenegrins that had already forced leaders in Vojvodina, Kosovo, and Montenegro to resign. Not surprisingly, the level of support was highest in Serbia (87%), Vojvodina (76%), and Montenegro (72%), but high support for these protests in Macedonia (56%) indicated that this republic could be next in line for "revolution." Just like their leaders, the LCY members in other republics, however, were much less supportive: in Bosnia the mass rallies were supported by 37% of members, in Kosovo by 22%, in Croatia by 19%, and in Slovenia by 11%.

In another evidence of the relative strength of the Serbian position, 70.1% of the respondents expressed themselves in favor of "democratic centralism" in either the existing (35.1%) or in an even stronger form (35%). In Slovenia, however, 73% of those interviewed demanded that this principle be abandoned in favor of consensual decision making in the Party. In fact, "democratic centralism" had more supporters than the consensus principle in all republics with the exception of Slovenia: in Serbia 81%, Montenegro 78%, Vojvodina 77%, Bosnia-Herzegovina 76%, Macedonia 68%, Kosovo 66%, and Croatia 64% of members were in favor of it. Furthermore, in all these republics except Croatia, more members declared for further strengthening of democratic centralism than for mere preservation of the principle in its existing form.

The centralizing tendencies were to be seen in the demands of 46.2% of LCY members to "abandon any republican/provincial 'key' in the elections to the Central Committee of the LCY." As many as 60% of the members in Serbia supported the conclusion that "the best candidates should be elected, regardless of the republics/provinces they come from." In Slovenia, however, 52% said the elections of the CC members "should be entirely left to each organization in the republic/province," thus not even requiring formal confirmation by the Federal Party Congress. This radically confederalist principle was supported by only 2% of members in Vojvodina and Montenegro, and nowhere outside Slovenia did it secure more than 20% support. Similarly, although 62.7% of the entire sample argued that the Yugoslav Central Committee should have the final say if/when two republican organizations disagreed, 71% of the members in Slovenia refused to accept any arbitration, "since each organization should have the right to its own opinion." The differences were so great that one wondered if it was still the same party.

The survey showed that the Party elites of Serbia and Slovenia enjoyed the almost unanimous support of their respective membership on the issues of the "three reforms": economy, political system, and Party. In Slovenia, 95% of members assessed the Slovene program of economic reform as the best in Yugoslavia, 94% thought the same for the program of political reforms proposed by Slovenia, and 93% for the program of Party reform. Just a slightly lower level of homogeneity was achieved in Serbia: 93% put the Serbian program of economic reform first, 72% favored the Serbian program of democratization, and 79% the Party reforms promoted by Serbian leadership. The same level of support (77%, 63%, and 73%, respectively) for the Serbian program was reached in Vojvodina. There could be no doubt that the Slovenian and Serbian leaders spoke for their members. Consequently, the Serbian accusation against the Slovene leaders of being bureaucrats (i.e., cut off from their members) proved to be unconvincing. The strong support for the Serbian leaders in Vojvodina demonstrated that the "Yoghurt revolution" in this province (unlike the cadre changes in Kosovo) was genuinely supported by the (largely Serb) Party membership.

In other republics, however, many members preferred either the Slovenian or the Serbian programs of the three reforms to those proposed by their local leadership. In Montenegro, 63% of LCY members favored the Serbian program of economic reforms (compared with 19% for the Montenegrin and 13% for the Slovenian). However, the members from Montenegro supported their new leadership more than any other (including Serbia's) when it came to political reforms and the LCY reform (61% and 68%, respectively). In Macedonia, about 40% chose the Macedonian program on all three counts, and about 20% favored the Serbian and Slovenian programs on all three issues. Small deviations from these percentages indicated that more Macedonian members favored the Serbian program of Party reform, at the same time showing more support for the Slovenian program of political democratization.

It is also for this reason that we should be careful when arguing that the conflict followed lines of republics/provinces. The party was in fact still divided on two camps, with many left in between them. The main line of divisions was still the one between the defenders of the constitution and reformers of the constitution, but both now moved further from a compromise and toward constructing their own narratives, rather than debating the one previously existing-the Kardelj concept.

For example, the Slovenian program of economic reforms was favored by 45% of the members in Croatia. The Croatian members were, however, more skeptical about the Slovenian proposal of political reforms (33% ranked Slovenia first) and the Party reforms (23%). However, the Serbian program had no significant support in Croatia. Although almost 25% of the LCY members in Croatia were ethnically Serbs, only 4% to 6% favored the Serbian proposals over all others. Following the pattern of the whole postwar period, political behavior in the LCY did not strictly coincide with the ethnic affiliation of its members. It often did not strictly follow the lines of republics, as the preferences of many Croatian, Macedonian, Montenegrin, and Bosnian members for either the Slovenian or Serbian programs demonstrated even in 1989. However, Serbia, and especially Slovenia, now became exceptions to this rule. The almost exclusive loyalty of the Slovenian members to their own organization, closely followed by the similar level of support for Serbian programs by Serbian members, polarized the Party around two diametrically opposite positions. The others, unwilling or incapable of formulating a third alternative (as the failures of Stipe Šuvar and Ante Marković clearly demonstrate), were driven to support one side or the other. Or to perish.

In some cases, such as in Bosnia-Herzegovina, it was not easy to make a choice. The 1989 survey shows that more members from this republic supported the Slovenian proposals than the Serbian proposals for economic and political reforms (37%:24% and 22%:14%, respectively), although the opposite prevailed with the Party reform (18%:14% for the Serbian program). In others, such as in Kosovo, the choice was less complex. Unlike their new leaders (imposed by Belgrade and shielded by a ban on demonstrations following the state of emergency in the province), the large majority of LCY members in Kosovo supported the Slovenian political (66%), economic (55%), and even Party reform proposals (55%) more than any other on offer. These figures were much higher than those for the Serbian economic (34%), political (24%), and Party (26%) programs of reforms. The survey therefore confirmed that unlike in Vojvodina or Montenegro, the "unity" between Kosovo and Serbia was reached only between the two leaderships, but not among membership of the Party. One could safely assume that support for the Serbian initiatives among the general population in Kosovo was even lower.

In general, the 1989 survey of Party membership showed the following level of support for the Serbian and Slovenian options in the other Yugoslav republics and provinces.

Table 7.1. Acceptance of Serbian and Slovenian programs, 1989.

	Serbian	Slovenian	Difference (Serbian-Slovenian)
Vojvodina	70.9	12.4	Serbian + 58.5
Montenegro	33.7	10.1	Serbian + 23.6
Macedonia	20.5	20.3	Serbian + 0.2
Bosnia-Herzegovina	18.7	24.5	Slovenian + 5.8
Croatia	4.9	33.6	Slovenian + 28.7
Kosovo	28.5	58.6	Slovenian + 30.1
Yugoslavia	40.2	24.3	Serbian + 15.9

Source: Šiber (1989:75).

Thus on the eve of the 14th Extraordinary Congress, the Serbian Party had secured much greater support among the LCY membership than the Slovenes, especially when it came to intra-Party reforms (38.9% in favor of the Serbian approach, 18.0% for the Slovenian). However, it had still failed to secure a clear winning majority of 50% of the votes among the Party members. The support of 24% of Party members in the country as a whole for the Slovene programs exceeded by almost four times the Slovenian share in the LCY membership. It was certainly clear that the Slovene program of reforms was unlikely to win the vote at the 14th LCY Congress. It was, however, less clear whether the Serbian proposals would secure sufficient support for changes of the statute to centralize the organization. From the point of view of both sides, it was crucial to gain the support of Bosnia-Herzegovina and Macedonia on the main issues on the agenda. But the Macedonian and Bosnian Party memberships were split down the middle on every single important issue debated.

The prospects for victory for the Serbian approach on the eve of the 14th Party Congress were further endangered because only 30.7% of the LCY Party membership identified Slobodan Milošević as the person who "expressed political views closest to [their] own." Although the level of personal support for Milošević was five times greater than that of his main competitor, Milan Kučan (6.2%), his personal popularity was almost 10% lower than the popularity of the Serbian programs of reforms. The other two potential candidates for the top post, Stipe Šuvar (former Party president, Croatia) and the newly elected Yugoslav prime minister, Ante Marković (also Croatia), were third and fourth, at 5.2% and

4.9%, respectively. Support for Milošević varied from 0.6% in Slovenia (and only 1.9% in Croatia, despite the large number of Serb members!) to 71.6% in Serbia. Kučan scored 62.8% of the "vote" in Slovenia and 18.5% in Kosovo, but he had no votes at all in Serbia. Two Croatian politicians of different political orientations (the Kardeljist Šuvar and liberal-reformist Marković) fell victims to their refusal to mobilize Croatia behind themselves. Torn apart by deep personal rivalry and led by a Serb, Stanko Stojčević (1986-88) and Party bureaucrat Ivica Račan (1989-2007), the main constructors of the politics of the "Croatian silence," the Croatian Party had no leader to match Kučan and Milošević. Šuvar was the first choice for only 12.5% of the Croatian members, though except in Bosnia-Herzegovina (10.3%) he was only marginally supported elsewhere. Marković was more popular among the general population, but as Yugoslav prime minister he deliberately stood outside Party politics.[81] Marković believed the program of economic reforms he introduced in 1989 would unite Yugoslavia around his government. But the Party was still the main political battlefield. The lack of a Croatian leader was one of the further reasons for polarization within the Party. Having no third partner in traditionally Slovene-Serb-Croat–led Yugoslav politics, neither Kučan nor Milošević were forced to accommodate their claims to a potential coalition partner from Croatia. Yugoslav politics now became polarized, rather than coalition seeking.

The lack of credible Croatian, Bosnian, and Macedonian Communist politicians in this crucial year resulted in the growth of anti-Communist and nationalist leaders in these three republics. The survey revealed that 40.8% of the whole Yugoslav LCY sample did not identify with either of the LCY leaders. These percentages, however, were significantly higher in Croatia (54.8%), Bosnia-Herzegovina (56.8%), and Macedonia (58.3%), the three republics in which the Party finally lost the first democratic elections to the opposition parties less than a year after this survey was conducted. The Croats simply could not wait for Marković and Šuvar to turn nationalist and to homogenize them against Milošević. But Šuvar and Marković refused to become nationalist leaders. As Šuvar said in an interview for this book in April 1998, "It was easy to become a nationalist leader; nothing was more simple. What was difficult was to lead a civil war against each other, if you still believed in Yugoslavia." The leaders of the last generation of the Communist elites in Yugoslavia faced a dilemma they just simply could not resolve while remaining true to their long-standing personal beliefs. They had to "ride the tiger of nationalism if they did not want to be eaten by it," as David Owen (1995:129) metaphorically explained.

In 1989, Milošević and Kučan did not yet command the unconditional and full support of their ethnic groups, not even among Party members, who would, we might think, naturally be supportive of their leaders. One must notice that even in the last months of 1989, the ethnic homogenization behind Milošević and Kučan was still incomplete as far as the members of the LCY were concerned. Although Milošević, for example, was speaking for 54.6% of the (ethnic) Serbs in this survey, the remaining 45.4% of the members of the LCY of Serb ethnic origins did not identify with him first (in fact, 40.3% did not identify with any politician at all). In Kučan's case, he was the first choice for 67.9% of the Slovene members (significantly higher than Milošević among the Serbs), but a third of the members failed to support him. Šuvar and Marković together were favorite choices for only 30% of the ethnic Croat members. The level of ethnic homogenization was thus in all cases (even Slovenian or Serbian) lower than the level of homogenization among members from the same republic.

While Milošević was the first choice for 71.6% of the members in Serbia Proper, only 54.6% of all (ethnic) Serbian members of the LCY voted for him. Considering that 45% of the Montenegrins supported him, as well as (only) 25.2% of those declared "Yugoslavs,"[82] we could safely conclude that the support for Milošević was significantly lower among the Serbs outside of Serbia than in Serbia itself.[83] This explains the gap of more than 15% between the share of the Serbs in the LCY membership (45%) and the vote for Milošević (30.7%). It was precisely because of the uncompleted homogenization of the Serbs in the LCY membership that Milošević could not yet-despite a higher share of the Serbs in the LCY than in the general population-with safety count on an overall and unconditional victory at the Party Congress. He still needed full control over the Kosovo delegation, which seemed very likely to be more defiant in secret ballot than its leadership was in its public endorsement of Serbia's new course. It was also important to discredit the leading Serb members of the Croatian and Bosnian Party leaderships, who were still committed to the old Party line of criticizing nationalism only within their own nation. In the last few months preceding the Party Congress, the Serbian Central Committee, media, and demonstrators launched a strong campaign against Serb Communist leaders from Croatia, such as Dušan Dragosavac,[84] and from Bosnia, such as Bogić Bogićević. In turn, this only inflamed Serbian anti-Communist nationalism in these areas, especially in Bosnia-Herzegovina. Lastly, it was of crucial importance to homogenize ethnic Serbs in the LCY and in the population in general behind Milošević.

7.9. The Last Hours: the 14th (Extraordinary) LCY Congress

The final clash between the two political positions occurred at the 14th Extraordinary Congress of the LCY on 20-22 January 1990, which was in advance considered by both sides to be a potential turning point in the history of Yugoslavia.[85]

The Congress had 1,457 elected members, 564 of whom were from Serbia (333 from Serbia without provinces, 94 from Kosovo, and 137 from Vojvodina), and 114 from Slovenia.[86]

The main aim of the Serbian delegation, as formulated at an informal meeting attended by Slobodan Milošević, Petar Gračanin, Bogdan Trifunović, and Borisav Jović (10 January 1990) was "to preserve the existence of the LCY as an organization and to preserve democratic centralism, at least in the terms of the statute. The aim [was] also that the Slovenes remain isolated, and that Croatia and Macedonia, or even Bosnia-Herzegovina, do not join them (the Slovenes)." The army representatives accepted the role of the front-runners for this policy "so that the Croats and Macedonians are not put off from it" (Jović 1989/1995:88).

In two days of debate, the Slovenian delegation opposed the main tone of the proposed declarations, including the new amended statute of the LCY. However, the delegates of the congress were unwilling to accept any of the Slovenian amendments. The Slovenian proposal that the LCY should be defined as "an organization of republican organizations of the LC, which are equal in rights and associate with one another in the LCY" was rejected 1,156 to 169. Two Slovene proposals, aimed at the immediate suspension of all political trials in Kosovo (including those for "counterrevolutionary endangering of social order; hostile propaganda; and insulting the highest institutions of the state"), were supported by only 236 and 399 members, respectively. The proposal that all economic sanctions introduced by Serbia on Slovenian goods should be immediately lifted was supported by 755 delegates, and 589 voted against it. However, this was still about 70 votes less than the required margin. The amendment proposed by the president of the Slovenian Parliament Miran Potrč, that the Party documents should clearly identify that "the peoples associated in Yugoslavia exercise their sovereignty within republics, having the right to freely decide which of their sovereign rights should be realized through democratically elected institutions in Yugoslavia," was supported by 526 delegates. Moreover, the Serbian amendment that the new federal constitution should clearly define Yugoslavia as a state "with full legal and state subjectivity" was accepted with 955 votes.

Although not all Slovene amendments received the same level of support (ranging from very low support for any confederalization of the Party to higher support when it came to further decentralization of the state), it was nevertheless clear that none of them secured sufficient support at the congress. Almost every Serbian proposal was accepted by a convincing majority, and the Congress was on the verge of becoming a crucial triumph for Milošević's program.

This was the moment when Slovenia's delegation decided to leave the congress, and it declared Slovenia's League of Communists an independent organization, not subject to any democratic centralism by the Federal Party organization. Staying in the LCY under new rules of the game would mean losing any support in Slovenia and subjecting its Party organization to permanent outvoting by the Serbian-led majority. The Slovene Communists simply could not accept this. While they were leaving the stage, the Serbian delegates at the Congress applauded. Milošević immediately proposed that the Congress should establish a new quorum by recognizing that the 114 delegates from Slovenia were no longer part of it and continue as if nothing had happened. This was opposed by the Croatian members, who argued that the LCY without the Slovenes was no longer a Yugoslav organization and warned that they themselves would reexamine their participation in it. The congress therefore postponed its final session, as would become clear, indefinitely.

7.10. The End of the Party and the End of the State

The Serbian Communists, as well as those in the army and most of the other republics, claimed before congress that the existence of the LCY was a *conditio sine qua non* of the existence of the Yugoslav state. Its disintegration was now "the beginning of the end of any possibility for Yugoslavia to function."[87] The same belief was shared by the Slovenian and Croatian opposition. The Slovene Communists, however, claimed that the disintegration of the Party might not inevitably lead to the collapse of the Yugoslav state.

> The disintegration of the LCY is not a fatal event for the future of Yugoslavia. Because the future of Yugoslavia does not depend on the two integrative factors that certain politicians always tend to connect with each other: that is-the Party and the army. The fate of this country depends on the real interests of its peoples, on how we answer the question: should we be able to work and live like the rest of the civilized world....I even think that we are now closer to a democratic solution of the crisis. The LCY was a mechanism that those who created undemocratic politics in Yugoslavia have manipulated. If it is destroyed, then this is certainly a step forward to the faster democratization of society. I would link this process with further pluralization and reforms, which should be even more radical than those proposed by the federal government, said Milan Kučan immediately after the congress. (Kučan, *Danas* 30 January 1990)

Kučan, however, admitted that it was not easy to accept that the LCY had come to an end.

> It was very difficult, although I knew it would happen. All my life, and especially my youth, was linked to the Party. I have been influenced by these ideas through my family, and even if the Party is now clearly not what it once was, it is still not easy to say goodbye. I am perhaps also responsible for this,

since I am still strongly emotionally attached to the Party. (Kučan, *Danas* 30 January 1990)

Although Kučan's emotional attachment to the Party had gone by now, he was still in a state of disbelief when it came to the disintegration of Yugoslavia as a state. In January 1990, he described himself as nonseparatist:

> I can hardly even think about the possibility of Slovenia leaving Yugoslavia. Personally, I have never been for it. I cannot come to terms with this possibility. But, Yugoslavia as it is now is good for no one. If the Helsinki declaration and the way of thinking in Europe, which is now hostile to any amendments of the borders, change-and I am not sure that [Europe] will remain committed to this view after all that has happened in Germany and in the countries of the East-then we Slovenian nonseparatists, would face a very difficult situation. Of course it all depends on what Yugoslavia would look like.

Kučan was still trying to convince others in Yugoslavia that he was the least nationalistic partner in Slovenia. By refusing his proposals, the others in Yugoslavia in fact undermined his position at home. The Slovene Communists felt misunderstood, unsupported, and even humiliated by their Party colleagues from Serbia.[88] Their decision to leave was taken without enthusiasm, but it was clearly seen as necessary.

In Slovenia, the majority clearly supported Kučan's brave decision, but many feared a reaction by the centralizers. Kučan's prediction that separatist ideas would now gain new ground among the Slovenian population proved accurate. Janez Janša, the leading opponent of Belgrade, declared the 14th Congress "the last congress of the Party, but also the end of the Yugoslav state as it is now."[89] Another Slovenian opposition politician, the Christian Democrat Lojze Peterle, also believed that "this is yet another proof that the Second Yugoslavia has come to an end, and that a state should be reestablished on new grounds."[90] These new grounds should be found in the confederal model of a commonwealth of Yugoslav states, said Jože Pučnik. Confederation was now seen as a means to the full independence of Slovenia. It would include full recognition of its statehood and almost entirely destroy the authority of federal bodies.

Similarly, confederalist options became stronger in Croatia, where Franjo Tudjman, the president of the newly established Croatian Democratic Community, commented:

> This is not only the ideological and organizational disintegration of the LCY. The LCY has been identified with the overall construction of the SFR Yugoslavia as a state community. The failure of the LCY is therefore a sign of the ideological and organizational collapse of the existing AVNOJ Yugoslavia. (*Danas,* 30 January 1990)

Tudjman concluded that Yugoslavia should be "thought out again," since it faced not only a state crisis, but a crisis of interethnic relations.

Although the newly established Serbian Renewal Movement (led by Vuk Drašković) proposed a three-member confederation in Yugoslavia, in which the Serbian unit would include Bosnia-Herzegovina, Macedonia, Montenegro, and large parts of Croatia, the confederalist option for the Serbs in fact meant separatism. Similarly to the Czechs in the case of Czechoslovakia, the Serbs felt that confederation was the worst of all options on the agenda. They already felt Yugoslavia was partitioned to the level of disintegration. The new proposals, to them, in fact meant the disintegration of the country. There was therefore no surprise when Borisav Jović concluded:

> The Congress was the last chance for those who sincerely hoped that the course of events in Yugoslavia could be redirected for the better, toward unity and the solution of the constitutional problems....I am afraid that this is the beginning of the end of any possibility of agreement, and also of the functioning of Yugoslavia. A general confusion and uncertainty is created. (Jović, 24 January 1990, 1995:93)

And it was even less surprising that the army felt "totally disappointed," as Defense Secretary Kadijević conveyed to Borisav Jović, the vice president of the Yugoslav State Presidency:

> He [Kadijević] said that many Communists had become scared under the wave of anti-Communism. They had become entirely lost. They do not fight, do not react, as if they do not care about what is happening. And what is happening leads us directly to a civil war, to bloodshed. He analyzed the Western strategy toward Yugoslavia....The tragedy is that they [the West] do not understand that in this way [by introducing multiparty democracy] they are in fact destroying Yugoslavia and pushing it to a civil war. They do not understand that parties like these will not resolve the Yugoslav problem, because they do not understand the national question in Yugoslavia. For Yugoslavia, for its existence and rebirth, it is necessary that the LCY exists and that it is reborn in competition with other parties.[91]

7.11. The Last Hope: Marković's Attempt to Unite Yugoslavia Without the LCY

Immediately after the collapse of the LCY Congress, the federal government of Ante Marković took the initiative to transform Yugoslavia into an economically prosperous and politically viable federation. Just like his predecessors Milka Planinc and Branko Mikulić, Ante Marković faced opposition from the Party in his attempts to reform the Yugoslav economy and political system. This is why he saw the disintegration of the Party as the final chance to take a free initiative.

Marković was elected Yugoslav prime minister on 19 January 1989, when Yugoslavia faced not only political conflicts (such as those in Kosovo or between Slovenes and Serbs), but also annual inflation of about 25,000% (Zimmermann 1996/1999:49). His program of economic reforms, supported and advised by American economist Jeffrey Sachs, was launched in December 1989, showing the first results at the beginning of 1990. The value of the national currency was fixed to the deutsch mark at the 1:7 level. The Yugoslavs were for the first time allowed to buy foreign currency in banks. Inflation sharply decreased, and confidence in the new government rapidly grew. But the new economic program (accompanied by Marković's idea of new Socialism) favored export-oriented companies, most of which were in Slovenia and Croatia. The Serbian leaders saw this as a "robbery of Serbia" in favor of the more developed Western republics.[92] Serbian industry, oriented more to the collapsing market of the Soviet Union, suffered a lot. At the same time, the Slovenes' refusal to agree on a federal budget left federal funds half-empty. The army, already extremely critical of Slovenian politicians, now joined Serbia and the underdeveloped regions against Slovenia and Marković. The federal government, although generally popular among the population, faced enormous opposition from Serbia and Slovenia; on several issues they were joined by other republics and Kosovo.

Trying to find a way out, Ante Marković attempted to rely on the support of the general public (using the media more than any other Communist politician ever had before), Western economic support, and his own cabinet. On all three fronts, however, he faced hurdles. The media were already under the control of his opponents to such an extent that he decided to launch a new Yugoslav TV station. When he did, the local (republican) TV stations, in both Slovenia and Serbia, refused to transmit its program through "their" transmitters. In the West, Marković found a genuine political support, but his financial pleadings remained unanswered. Ultimately, at least two crucial ministers in his cabinet (Interior Secretary Gračanin and Defense Secretary General Kadijević) wavered between loyalty to him and loyalty to Serbia's president.

As the results of a June 1990 survey of 4,232 respondents in Yugoslavia demonstrated, the Yugoslavs were already deeply polarized on the functioning of the federal state and the powers of the federal government.

> The respondents from all republics and provinces were in favor of a market of commodities, capital and labor, a uniform tax system, and an end to the present method of providing aid for underdeveloped regions. On all other topics, the views [were] divided. At one end of the scale, the respondents from Serbia proper, Vojvodina, Montenegro, and to some extent Bosnia and

Herzegovina and Macedonia, would like to see a stronger government with powers to intervene and impose repressive measures: they are in favor of maintaining the current level of expenditure for the Yugoslav People's Army and of promoting investment programs in underdeveloped regions. At the other end of the scale, the public in Slovenia, Croatia, and Kosovo called for a federal government whose functions would be only to take initiatives, maintain coordination, and mediate; they wanted the army budget reduced and were in favor of giving underdeveloped regions professional, cultural, and research assistance, but not monetary aid, or they would even go so far as to abolish all forms of aid.[93]

The differences on this polarized scale are shown in the following table:

Table 7.2. Approval and Disapproval of Marković's Reforms, May-June 1990.

Measure	Yugoslavia approval: disapproval	Highest support	Lowest support
Reforms in general	66% : 7%	Macedonia 81%	Slovenia 32%
Market economy	56% : 2%	Croatia 66% Bosnia 66%	Kosovo 28%
Greater legal powers for the federal government	58% : 21%	Bosnia 72% Vojvodina 72%	Slovenia 26%
Funding a new political party	41% : 28%	Bosnia 65%	Slovenia 23%

Slovenia and Kosovo were the two regions of Yugoslavia in which Marković's government found least support. Whereas 49% of the Yugoslav sample expressed "complete agreement with the policies advocated by Ante Marković," this percentage was as low as 16% in Slovenia and 13% in Kosovo. Even on specifically economic issues, such as Marković's program of market reforms, Slovenia and Kosovo placed themselves next to each other at the two lowest positions on the scale of support. In the most-developed Yugoslav republic, Slovenia, Marković's market reforms were supported by 38% of the population, and in the least developed, Kosovo, by only 28%. In another example, Kosovo and Slovenia were the two least optimistic regions when it came to Marković's anti-inflation program (only 15% in Kosovo and 5% in Slovenia were confident that Marković would succeed in bringing it under full control, compared with 28% on the Yugoslav average.) These data clearly demonstrate how little the economic factors (such as the level of development) influenced political decisions in the last years of Yugoslavia. They also show how difficult, almost impossible, Marković's position was. He was accused by Serbia of favoring the developed Western regions in the country. But it was in Slovenia that he found the greatest opposition to his policy. He was seen as a "cunning non-Yugoslav" by the Serbian leadership-yet in the ethnically heterogeneous regions of the country (such as in Vojvodina, Macedonia, and Bosnia-Herzegovina), he had the most support.

The results of the survey demonstrate that Marković was a much greater threat to Milošević than to Kučan. In Slovenia, the public was already skeptical about Yugoslav initiatives, even when they came from a liberal reformer and a Croat. By contrast, a large share of the Serbian population supported Marković's initiatives, many of which aimed at establishing an effective federal state. Marković's new Socialism was also seen as a veritable alternative to the bureaucratic leadership that sank after the collapse of the LCY. In Serbia proper, 44% of the population was "in full agreement," and an additional 41% was in "partial agreement" with Marković's policies. The survey showed that 56% of the respondents had improved their opinion of Marković when compared with when he was elected six months earlier. It was no surprise, therefore, that Milošević needed to make a great effort to portray Marković as an "enemy of Serbia." Borisav Jović personally contributed to the anti-Marković campaign by writing a long article in *Politika* against Ante Marković, as he explained in his diary on 2 August 1990:

> I wrote a series of three articles, "The Truth about Ante Marković," and sent it to Slobodan. He gave them to *Politika*. They will be published on 5, 6, and 7 [August 1990] under somebody's pen name. We must unmask him because people are under many illusions about who and what he is. Many see him as a savior, but he is just a common cheat and an enemy of the Serbian people. (1995:173)

The articles, subsequently published in the main Serbian daily, were perhaps a unique case of a member (vice president) of the state presidency attacking his prime minister under a pseudonym.

But the most serious threat to Milošević's and Jović's politics came from the popularity Ante Marković enjoyed within the Yugoslav People's Army. Many in the army, including those in the highest positions and-importantly-some Serbian generals, were dissatisfied with Milošević's politics in Serbia. On 26 February 1990, General Blagoje Adžić, the chief of staff of the YPA (himself a Serb) conveyed this dissatisfaction in a conversation with Borisav Jović:

He [Adžić] attacked Serbian politics in the strongest terms. He says Serbia is now isolated and opposed by Slovenia, Croatia, Bosnia-Herzegovina, Macedonia, and half of Montenegro; and that also half of Serbia is against the Serbian leadership....The unintelligent Serbian leadership is responsible for all of this. They [the Serbs] make mistake after mistake. All their actions had played into the hands of the western republics and in fact helped them to realize their aims: anti-Yugoslavism and anti-Communism.

Specifically, Adžić complained to Jović that the Serbian leaders did not need to antagonize the Slovenes by refusing dialogue with them and had to distance themselves from the Greater Serbs in Knin (Croatia). Adžić also criticized Serbian attempts to send 100,000 Serbs to Kosovo as a "provocative and unrealistic" action. In Kosovo, Adžić said, dialogue with the Albanians would give better results than repression. "It was a mistake when Azem Vllasi was removed. He was a suitable person to work with...," he said to Borisav Jović. General Adžić, the highest-ranked Serb in the army's leadership, was not only verbally dismissive of Milošević's politics: in January 1990 he refused to obey the Serbian request to use tanks against demonstrators in Kosovo (Jović 1995:95).

In fact, even General Veljko Kadijević, the federal secretary for defense (himself of mixed Serb-Croat ethnic origins, from Croatia), was for a long time an unreliable ally of Milošević and Jović. He also tried to avoid the involvement of the army in Kosovo, and he stopped short of intervening against the Slovenian constitutional amendments in September 1989. But the main problem the Serbian leaders had with Kadijević in this period was his loyalty to Ante Marković. Although the army and Serbia had "the same objectives," as Jović noticed after spending holidays with Milošević and Kadijević in August 1989 (1995:45), Milošević was aware that "Veljko [Kadijević] might try to convince us to support Ante Marković a little bit more." Milošević warned Jović to "beware of this." For the whole crucial year from August 1989 to August 1990, the Serbian leaders suspected that Kadijević's hesitant behavior in fact originated in his "split loyalty" between them and Marković. In December 1989, Kadijević openly supported Marković's new reforms and tried to convince the Serbs to accept them in exchange for Marković's later support of the Serbian position in changing the constitution.[94] Jović thought this proposal was "naïve" and wondered "how can Veljko not see it" (1995:79). In January 1990, Kadijević saw Marković's program as the potential core for the unification of the country:

> He thinks that Croatia will be with Ante [Marković], that Bosnia will be with Croatia, and that Macedonia would not dare to risk her own future....On these grounds one should make a deal with Serbia....I warned him to think again. I do not share his position. The concept of Ante Marković aims at survival, not a resolution of the problem, and this is what plays into the hands of anti-Yugoslavia forces. (Jović, 1995: 92)

It was only in February 1990 that Kadijević became "disappointed with the federal government."[95] Until then he was, as Borisav Jović had said, "under the obsession that Ante fought for Yugoslavia" (1995:118). It was only on another summer vacation, in August 1990, that Kadijević fully agreed with the three main Serbian leaders (Slobodan Milošević, Borisav Jović, and Bogdan Trifunović) that "Ante Marković is totally unacceptable and unreliable." In a note in his diary of 10 August 1990, Jović described their conversation:

> No one anymore doubts that he is a direct U.S. stooge aiming at the destruction of the system and the removal from power of everyone who even thinks of Socialism....He is playing the dirtiest possible traitors' game....One needs to finish with him, in any case....Veljko [Kadijević] calls him "a son of a bitch." He regrets that he saved him several times from his mistakes that could have compromised him, but he has no intention of repeating it....We should do anything to drive Marković and all others who are destroying the country mad. (1995:177)

Yet even then, Kadijević disagreed with Milošević on ideological and several practical issues. From 1990 to 1991, the army still argued that the existence of Yugoslavia depended on the renewal of the LCY, and it sent this message to various foreign representatives, including the main European armies they visited. For a significantly longer time, the army remained committed to the old ideological paradigm that the existence of Yugoslavia depended on Socialism, whereas the Serbian leaders in November 1989 moved to the argument that "the first problem is the dissolution of the country; the nature of the social order is only a secondary issue." (Jović 16 November 1989, 1995:68). The gap between the two interpretations only widened after March 1990, when the Serbian leaders decided to create a new party out of the Serbian and Montenegrin LCs and Socialist alliances if their attempts to renew the LCY failed. In March 1990, Milošević twice met Dobrica Ćosić. After their first (three-hour) conversation, Milošević was "pleased," though neither he nor Jović shared Ćosić's belief that Yugoslavia was not worth fighting for. However, it was in March 1990 that the Serbian leaders started thinking of Yugoslavia without Slovenia, witnessed in these remarks by Jović.[96]

> We agreed that we need to make a new constitution, regardless of whether the Slovenes agree or not, and that then they should be left with the option of either being in Yugoslavia or out....We fear Croatia-they might leave the whole story and spoil it all. I hope the Croats are aware that this would create problems they could not resolve, and maybe even armed conflicts. (Jović, 21 March 1990, 1995:125).

After the second meeting with Ćosić, Milošević promoted a new Serbian position at the meeting of the "Coordination" Committee in Serbia on 26 March 1990.

> We have concluded that the process of the disintegration of Yugoslavia is under way in a manner similar to that of the LCY. It seems this cannot be halted. Serbia will sincerely try to preserve the federal Yugoslav state, but would also be prepared to live without Yugoslavia. If Yugoslavia disintegrates, we count on unity with Montenegro. We will not beg Macedonia [to join]. If they want to join, they will need to seek forgiveness for what they did to the victims of the First World War, who are still treated as occupiers. Our aim is to avoid bloodshed, to form a territory within which there will be no war. Outside these borders, war will be impossible to avoid, since Bosnia-Herzegovina cannot survive as a state, and it is hard to imagine a struggle for territory without blood. Serbia will not agree to confederation. The only possible way to accept it, but this is impossible to realize, would be contract-like guarantees of the rights of Serbian people in the other Yugo states. Since this would be a provocative demand and unrealistic, and since the Serbs would be cheated even if everyone agreed on this, in reality Serbia has no reason to accept a confederation. No one can impose it on us....Serbia has decided to immediately prepare a new constitution, which would be able to "cover" the new independent Serbian state. (Jović, 26 March 1990, 1995:132)

The results of the first democratic Croatian elections in April 1990, in which Tudjman's CDC secured a majority in the *Sabor* (winning about 42% of the total vote and 56% of the seats), made any future agreement on Yugoslavia very unlikely. Moreover, Tudjman's openly anti-Serb rhetoric only further poured oil onto the (already tall) flames of Serbian nationalism. On his election as president of the state presidency on 15 May 1990, Borisav Jović for the first time mentioned the need to introduce a law on secession to enable any nation to leave Yugoslavia. In June 1990, the Serbian leaders announced that a new Socialist Party of Serbia would be created, following a merger between the League of Communists and Socialist Alliance. This decision "confused and disappointed" General Kadijević. Jović reported Kadijević's reaction:

> He believes that this is the final end of Yugoslavia, and that the Americans have succeeded in their aim in Serbia-removing the LCY from the historical stage. He thinks the Serbs should have preserved the name "Communist." All their plans had now sunk without trace. It will be much more difficult, maybe impossible, to preserve the country....He is especially disappointed that Slobodan Milošević did not tell him about the Socialist Party of Serbia; they had spoken only two days before about further work within the LCY. He cannot recover from this. He has lost his "point of balance." (Jović, 1995:152-4)

In June 1990, Slobodan Milošević still doubted if the army was willing to follow the Serbian plan of "cutting off" all the non-Serbian parts of Yugoslavia in the west of the country.[97] By then the Serbs had already decided to make new borders for the new state. It was then that Milošević and Jović finally left the Yugoslav option behind and favored the "Greater Serbian" alternative instead. Referendums of the local population (especially the Serbs in Croatia and Bosnia-Herzegovina) would in fact draw the new borders.

> He [Milošević] agrees with the "expulsion" of Slovenia and Croatia, but he asks if the army was willing to execute such an order. I told him they have to execute it, and that I have no doubt about this, but the problem is what to do with the Serbs in Croatia and how to secure a majority in the SFRY Presidency for such a decision. Sloba had two ideas: first, to "cut off" Croatia in such a way that the municipalities in Lika and Banija, and also in Kordun, which had created a community, remained on our side and that people later decided by a referendum if they wanted to stay here or to leave. Second, the members of the SFRY Presidency from Slovenia and Croatia were to be excluded from participating in this decision, since they did not represent the part of Yugoslavia that made this decision. If the Bosnians vote in favor, there is then a two-thirds majority. Sloba wants us to make this decision in a week's time if we want to save the state. Without Croatia and Slovenia, Yugoslavia will have 17 million inhabitants, which is enough for European standards. (Jović, 1995:161).

The army was still hesitant to accept the end of Yugoslavia. General Kadijević originally agreed with the Serbian new policy, but then withdrew, showing "an incredible instability" (Jović 1995:163). The army still wanted to "defeat" the Croatian and Slovenian nationalists and to preserve Yugoslavia's unity. On the other hand, the Serbian leaders now accepted Ćosić's argument that this was no more than "plain nonsense that would come back on us like a boomerang" (Jović 1995:169).

In May 1990, more 100 people were injured in fighting between the football supporters of "Dinamo" (Zagreb) and "Crvena Zvezda" (Belgrade) at a Zagreb Maksimir stadium. On 30 May, Franjo Tudjman, the head of the Croatian Democratic Community, was elected president of the Croatian Presidency, and his party formed the first democratically elected Croatian government. The Serbian leaders, and also the Serbs in Croatia, perceived him as "almost insanely anti-Serb."[98] The media in Serbia compared Tudjman's party with the wartime Ustasha regime.[99] On 2 July in a referendum in Serbia, 86% of voters voted in favor of a new Serbian constitution. Furthermore, 114 Albanian members of the Kosovo Assembly then declared Kosovo "an independent republic." On 3 July 1990, the Slovenian Republican Assembly passed a declaration on Slovenian sovereignty. Two days later, Serbia suspended the Kosovo Assembly and seized the radio and TV stations in Priština. On 25 July 1990, the Croatian Assembly (Sabor) approved 12 constitutional amendments, removing the word Socialist from the name of the republic, introducing a new flag with the Croatian checkerboard coat of arms, and "derecognized" the Cyrillic alphabet in areas where it did not predominate. In a last-minute change, several other, more radical proposals (such as to define Croatia as the "nation-state of the Croatian nation" instead of as a state of its citizens) were withdrawn. The former Communists, now renamed the Social-Democratic Party of Croatia, voted for the changes. The Serbs, who had massively voted for the SDP at the April elections, now moved their support to the more radical Serb Democratic Party, whose leaders denounced the changes and declared the sovereignty and autonomy of the Serbian people in Croatia and their right to "determine with whom and under what regime their people would live and how they would integrate with the other nations in Yugoslavia." In August, they held an unofficial referendum on the "Serbian Autonomous Region of Krajina" and took over several police stations and other government offices. The Yugoslav army prevented the Croatian government from intervening, claiming it was only moving between the Serbs and Croats to "protect the villages of the ethnic Serbs from discrimination." Although the army claimed they were only playing a peacekeeping role between the Serbs and Croats, they in fact were marking the new borders of the Serbian unit, just as Borisav Jović and Slobodan Milošević had planned two months earlier.[100] The army was now fully engaged in protecting one ethnic group against the other. What it was no longer protecting, however, was constitutional order as it was defined by the 1974 Constitution: this order simply did not exist any longer.

7.12. Conclusion

August 1990 could be taken as the effective end of the Yugoslav state and the beginning of the war for the territories of the new successor states. By then, no elements of the Yugoslav Federation (as legally established by the 1974 Constitution) had been left intact. The LCY existed no longer, and new parties had been legalized in all republics. Slovenia and Croatia ceased to be Socialist republics and were for the first time run by anti-Communist and largely secessionist parties and coalitions. The borders of the republics were contested, primarily by the Serbs, but also by the Croats (in Bosnia-Herzegovina and Montenegro) and Albanians (in Kosovo and Macedonia). Ethnic homogenization was for the first time taken as the basis of politics in all Republics without exception. Socialism as an ideology was either openly abandoned (as in Croatia and Slovenia) or ranked second to nation-state formations (as in Serbia). No longer did anyone want to "reform" the system, nor did anyone try to convince the others that Kardelj's concept meant something different from what happened in political reality. The Yugoslav institutions had either already collapsed or were completely ignored. New "entities" had been declared in Kosovo, Macedonia (the "Republic of Ilyrida"), and the Serb parts of Croatia (Krajina) and Bosnia-Herzegovina (territories that would soon become the Republic of Srpska, as well as Herceg-Bosna, controlled by ethnic Croats).

Lastly, nothing was left intact of the narrative of the post-1974 (or indeed of any "Titoist") Yugoslavia. In Serbia, just as in Croatia, the new narratives were based on a clear opposition to the previous interpretations of history and identity. These narratives were also incompatible with each other-they blamed the other for the historical injustice done to "us." The internal cohesion of the emerging nation-states was now based on the difference between them and their neighbors. When these differences were small (as with language between Serbs and Croats), they were deliberately enlarged by state intervention. History was reinterpreted in such a way that all examples of cooperation were eliminated and forgotten. "Ethnic hatred" and "ancient conflicts" now emerged as the main preoccupation of new ethnic leaders who argued that their nations should never again live even close to each other.

This, of course, did not have to happen. Had the Yugoslav nations had more responsible political leaders, not only at these crucial moments, but also in previous times, the chain of events might have been quite different. The leaders played the most important decisive role in what happened to Yugoslavia. I argue along the lines of many others[101] that Yugoslavia was destroyed primarily from inside (rather than by some international conspiracy) and from the top down of the social and political pyramids.

To say this, however, we need to understand why the Yugoslav politicians behaved as they did. Why did they behave in an "irrational" and "irresponsible" manner? Why did they take the decisions they did? Were they simply incapable of understanding the real interests of their peoples? Were they simply irrational? The main argument of this book is that they acted on their beliefs in the ideological context in which their actions made perfect sense to them and to many other people who-tacitly or actively-legitimized their actions. To the leading Yugoslav Communist leaders in the 1970s and 1980s, Yugoslavia made sense as long as it was conceptualized as a Socialist self-managing federation of republics and provinces. Once they realized that this concept was no longer viable, or that it was not the best possible, they needed to find another narrative to preserve and reform Yugoslavia, or allow others to do so. To those who found themselves there, it proved impossible to agree on any alternative narrative that would keep Yugoslavia together. Yet, still less did they want to allow "anti-Socialist," "statist," or any other "hostile" forces to replace them. They simply could not allow that, since they still believed in the very narrative they themselves had created. Yugoslavia thus became a victim of its own narrative, whose elements had been collapsing for decades, pulling the Yugoslav institutions after them.

Despite the optimistic predictions of Ante Marković (shared by most Western analysts of the Yugoslav crisis) that the disintegration of the LCY would not necessarily lead to the collapse of the Yugoslav state, but that it would even strengthen democracy in the country, the opposite happened. The League of Yugoslav Communists was not only the ruling party, it was also the core, the essence of Yugoslavia, as defined in the 1974 Constitution and within Kardelj's concept that created it. Furthermore, the concept claimed that Yugoslavia (in the only form in which it deserved to exist) was created by the Party and that it would-as a state—wither away once the Party succeeded in making a stateless, self-managing society. Ultimately, the Party was more important than the state itself. Although the state was to wither away, the Party was expected to lead society toward the final objective: Communist self-management. Without a real state, and now without a Party to replace it, there was little left to bind the Yugoslav republics together.[102]

As a result of a chain of events in Yugoslav history by 1990, no narrative was left to keep Yugoslavia together. And although the common beliefs of the Communist elite made almost impossible compromises (such as that of the 1974 Constitution) viable, the lack of common beliefs now made much more viable options impossible. The fate of the Yugoslav army, a real force that started crumbling once the ideological glue that held it together disappeared, demonstrated that without common beliefs, even the most powerful institutions become powerless. The state, the most powerful of all institutions, now simply collapsed: despite the unwillingness of the great powers to recognize it; despite its powerful law-enforcement agencies; despite even the emotional attachment she commanded from many of its citizens.

Left without its so overwhelmingly important ideology, Yugoslavia now became unsustainable.

Notes

1   The titles of the reports on this decision in the various republican dailies illustrate these differences. *Vjesnik* (Croatia): "The proof of the continuity of the revolution"; "*Nova Makedonija* (Macedonia): "Changes in favor of labor"; "*Rilindja* (Kosovo): "The basic principles not to be touched"; *Politika* (Serbia): "Relations should be resolved resolutely and in a principled manner"; *Dnevnik* (Vojvodina): "The serious work is only beginning." These titles (all published on the same day-20 March 1987-and quoted by *Borba*) revealed how different the expectations of the republics and provinces were regarding the outcome of the constitutional reform. Croatia and Macedonia were concerned with the preservation of the ideological basis of the system. Serbia insisted on changing "re-

lations within Serbia," to which both provinces were opposed. Lastly, Vojvodina openly announced its intention to obstruct any significant change in the constitution.

2   Andjelković, IB CK SKS 9/1987:12-15; Ilić, 5/1988:5-10; Milošević, 7/1988:14-5.
3   In fact, the new Serbian leadership originally tried to prevent the Kosovo Serbs from demonstrating in Vojvodina, but unsuccessfully. When the leaders of the Kosovo Serbs told Milomir Minić, the executive secretary of the Serbian Central Committee, that they would demonstrate regardless of the Party recommendations, the leaders took a neutral stand: they neither prevented nor publicly supported the march (Kerčov 1989:228). This was a demonstration of how much the situation had changed-the leaders could no longer control events at their own will, but had to accommodate themselves to them. Marko Orlandić, the highly popular Montenegrin leader who failed to support the rallies, was immediately put on the "black list" of the demonstrators and was finally ousted together with other Montenegrin leaders in January 1989.
4   This was the main criticism by the other Yugoslav republics. There was no doubt that most of the demonstrators really were Serbs, as Kerčov argued (1989:83). Serbs were 62% of demonstrators, Montenegrins 14%, and together they were 56.5% of the total population of Vojvodina. Among the speakers in these rallies, 75.2% were Serbs and Montenegrins from Vojvodina, 11.7% Serbs and Montenegrins from Kosovo, and 5.6% Hungarians. The Hungarians made up 18.9% of the population of the province, but only 3% of demonstrators. Still, because one of the leaders of the public discontent was Mihail Kertes, an ethnic Hungarian secretary of the LCY Committee in Stara Pazova, his presence was much used to display the multiethnic character of the protests.
5   "The place of Serbian Communists is to be with the people," claimed the leadership of Serbia in September 1988.
6   Slovenian dissident intellectuals, such as Spomenka Hribar (*Nova Revija* 80/1988:1992-8) showed more sympathy for the Montenegrin protests than for Slovenian political leaders. Hribar accused the Slovene Party of supporting the Stalinist leadership of Montenegro, instead of siding with the legitimate claims of the people. "To be perfectly clear," said Hribar, "the demands of the demonstrators in Titograd were entirely legitimate!"
7   Since the early 1980s, many Slovenian intellectuals had joined the Serbs in signing various petitions and publishing articles and interviews in the liberalized Belgrade media. Ljubljana's *Nova Revija* (founded in 1982, at the time *Javnost* was being blocked by the Belgrade politicians), published Serbian authors. This was in sharp contrast to the coldness that opposition activities met with among Zagreb intellectuals, whom both Belgraders and Ljubljaners suspected of "nationalism" and with support for the 1984 *White Book*. The special relations between Serbia and Slovenia were, Dobrica Ćosić argued, forged by "the sameness of our national destinies [in the Second World War] and our brotherhood in suffering and struggle, which did not occur to the same extent with other South Slav peoples" (Ćosić 5-6 Oct 1987; *Književne Novine* 15 November 1987:17). It was the historical suffering and common anti-German sentiments that made the Slovenes a potentially close ally in the eyes of the Serbian intelligentsia. These special links were to some extent acknowledged by Milošević himself. In May 1987, speaking to Slovene painters, he said that the Slovenes and Serbs were divided by their historical destiny, but had created bridges between themselves, forming an example of brotherhood and unity at work. "The past has already entered the national memories of both nations" to be passed from generation to generation and "never to be forgotten" (1987/1989:151). Because Milan Kučan began his life as a refugee in Serbia made him

rather popular in Serbia. But it also deepened the sense of betrayal once Slovenia went independent.

8   The sense of disappointment was described by Dobrica Ćosić (Djukić 1989:268). From Ćosić's later recollections of the meeting, it appeared that the main conclusion of the Slovene intellectuals was that "the Slovenes have nothing to expect from Yugoslavia" (Ćosić 1992:71), and that one should "once and for all reject any internationalism and universalism (1992:72). They also argued that "the Slovenes have always compared [themselves] with Europe, never with Yugoslavia" (1992:72). The Serbs, however, argued that the failure of the Party ideology should not necessarily be the end of the Yugoslav idea, pointing out that the Serbian national question would be widely reopened if Yugoslavia ceased to exist.

9   Following the meeting at Mrak, Dobrica Ćosić exchanged several letters with the Slovene writers Niko Grafenauer, Taras Kermauner, and Spomenka Hribar. In the letter to Grafenauer, Ćosić complained that the Slovenian intellectuals "failed to recognize...the enormous development of Slovenia, which was possible only in Yugoslavia." They also underestimated "the anti-Bosnian, which means anti-Serbian atmosphere in Slovenia." But worst of all was the indifference toward "the humiliating position of the Serbian nation in the existing Brioni Yugoslavia," and especially in Kosovo. "I am saddened by seeing how uninformed you are about the Albanian genocide of the Serb population in Kosovo and Metohija, and how little you care about this, much less than we cared for the Slovenian Coast and Carinthia [after the Second World War]" (Ćosić 23 November 1985/1992:76-9).

10 "Letter to a Serbian friend," by Taras Kermauner was first published in the Serbian literary magazine *Književnost* in 1986, then in *Borba* on 24-26 June 1987. Kermauner accused the Serbs of being anti-Albanian and anti-Slovenian and led by "a blind anger... against anything that is different, anyone who tried to think and behave as he/she liked, against anybody who was not willing to subject themselves to a model of brotherhood and terror." Raising for the first time the issue of separation, Kermauner asked: "Why would it be of any concern to you if I (we) wanted to secede? Civilized behavior is one of the main conditions of civil society. If the partners in a marriage are no longer interested in living together, they can divorce. There is no personal freedom without the possibility of divorce," said Kermauner. He reminded the Serbs that if they felt exploited by the Slovenes (as they had argued in the Memorandum), they should not object to a separation. Kermauner concluded that the Kosovo Serbs, unfortunately, did not demand more democracy and lawfulness, but the renewal of the brotherhood-and-unity policy. This is why the Slovenes could not support them (*Borba* 24-26 June 1987). Commenting on the effect of Kermauner's letter, Dobrica Ćosić said, "This letter, by its Slovenian bias, provoked huge discontent and disappointment in cultural circles in Belgrade and Serbia...It was from Taras Kermauner that the Serbian public realized what Slovenia thought of the Serbs and Serbia, and what Slovenian intentions were: in one word-secessionism" (1992:73).

11 *Nova Revija* 1986:811.

12 In fact, the Yugoslav Writers' Association never fully recovered from the stalemate caused by the Bulatović case, becoming the first Yugoslav organization to effectively disintegrate under the pressure of divisions within Yugoslavia. The official breakup of all links between the two associations (Slovenian and Serbian) happened on 28 February 1989 as a consequence of the Slovenian Writers' Association's participation in a pro-Albanian meeting in Ljubljana (Belić and Bilbija 1989:6). The breakup was unilat-

eral. In its letter to the UKS, the Slovenian association said that they "absolutely and in no way wanted to break relations with the Serbian Writers Association" (*Borba* 2 March 1989).

13 Not many, however, realized this until very late. For example, as the last U.S. ambassador to Yugoslavia (1988-92), Warren Zimmermann, writes, the U.S. government believed that "unity and democracy were the Siamese twins of Yugoslavia's fate...The loss of one meant that the other would die" (1995:6). The same was argued by the Yugoslav prime minister, Ante Marković, the most liberal member of the Yugoslav political elite.

14 An exception being Susan Woodward's book, *Balkan Tragedy* (1995), and to a certain extent James Gow (1992) and Aleksandar Pavković (1996).

15 By the federal constitution, three languages Serbo-Croat, Slovene, and Macedonian, were official in the entire territory of Yugoslavia, though some other languages, such as Albanian, Hungarian, and Italian, were allowed to be spoken in official use in areas with a significant presence of these ethnic groups. Federal documents were issued in all three languages, but Serbo-Croat (spoken by about 16 million Yugoslavs, out of 23 million) was widely used as the lingua franca in oral communication. In the army, Serbo-Croat was declared "the language of command," being therefore singled out as the official spoken language. Although the regulations provided for other languages to be used in the reserve forces of the army (composed of the local population), this rarely materialized. Until 1988, even in Slovenia, for example, the names of the barracks were written only in Serbo-Croat, while Slovene officers and Slovene soldiers were using Serbo-Croat in official communication. Serving my military service in Slovenia (1986-87), under the command of a Slovenian officer, I have personal experience of how damaging this was for the relations between soldiers and the local population.

16 For more on this concept, see Mastnak (1986) and (1990), Fink Hafner (1992), Arzenšek (1986), Jenšterle (1987), and Tomc (1986).

17 It is now widely believed that the Contributions were only a reaction to the Memorandum, which was leaked to newspapers in September 1986. This is, however, incorrect. Spomenka Hribar, one of the editors of *Nova Revija,* said that the special issue was initiated a year and a half before it was actually published. The Slovene and Serbian national programs appeared at the same time independently of each other. The Serbian writers, such as Ćosić, today accept that they started thinking of formulating a national program only after the meeting in Mrak in November 1985. If this is true, we can conclude that the Memorandum was in fact a reaction to an already existing (though unwritten) Slovenian national program, not vice versa. Ćosić says that he was impressed on seeing how well thought out the Slovene concept was.

18 In Hribar's use of these two terms (in Slovenian *jugoslovanstvo* and *jugoslavijanstvo*), they are not synonymous. Yugoslavism is used to describe ethnic affiliation, but Yugoslavianism describes political (civic) affiliation. For Hribar, both are equally unacceptable.

19 Viktor Meier's conclusion (1999: 58) that "in this program, the existence of Yugoslavia was nowhere called into question," was perhaps more a product of his overt sympathies with the Slovenian position, for which he (at that time as correspondent for *Frankfurter Allgemeine Zeitung*) was criticized in an official statement by the Serbian LC CC at its 13th Session, 11 October 1988 (IB 9/88:16), than of his reading of *Nova Revija.*

20 One could perhaps add this explanation to the list of motives for Kardelj's (himself a Slovene) antistatist notion, based also on the concept of the "withering away of the state."

21   In this respect, the Slovenian national program was "statist."
22   The constitution guaranteed the right to self-determination ("including secession," as the Slovene intellectuals often emphasized) by the first article of its basic principles, which declared Yugoslavia to be a federal republic of free peoples equal in rights, whose decision to associate was based on "the right of every nation to self-determination, including also the right to secession" (Jambrek 1987:166).
23   This argument is still used by Slovenia when issues such as succession of the property and rights of the SFRY are debated. Although Serbia (FR Yugoslavia) insists that Slovenia and other republics seceded from Yugoslavia, the Slovenes argue it was partition of the federation, not secession.
24   Kardelj's antistatist concept, which recognized republics as states and Yugoslavia as a "community" of state-republics, was now also used to support this argument.
25   "One should not underestimate the positive national and psychological effects of the recognition of the possibility to secede and become an independent state [provided] by the 1974 Constitution itself" (Urbančič 1987:44).
26   As already mentioned, rarely did any other term have a more negative meaning in the rhetoric of the regime than nationalism. It was what the Communists fought against, not only in the Partisan War, but also throughout the entire period of their 35 years in power. The label "nationalist" would bring on those so labeled a total ban on public appearances, political purges, and, in the most drastic cases, imprisonment. The concept of "brotherhood and unity" was invented as the antipode of (separatist) nationalism and formed one of the main elements of the regime's legitimacy. It was in Urbančič's article that this pillar was undermined.
27   Almost all *Nova Revija* authors shared this conclusion. For instance, Aleš Debeljak (1986) claimed that Yugoslavism was an "outdated" nationalist concept, and, as France Bučar said, belonged to the 19th century (1987).
28   Urbančič analyzes these positive changes in detail in his 1989 text in *Nova Revija* (1989:789-817).
29   Spomenka Hribar pointed out the difference between reality and formal constitutionality in the Yugoslav case in her inspiring article in *Nova Revija* 57 (1987). Paraphrasing her terminology, one could conclude that Yugoslavia was in reality an LCY-ruled unitary state, though in form it was a federation of republics. The difference between rituals and reality in Socialist states is described in Vaclav Havel's essay "Power of the Powerless" (1978).
30   In his article in the 57th issue of *Nova Revija* (1987), France Bučar argued that federation was still only a form of unitary state and that every unitary state develops a state language, state ethnicity, and state identity. As examples, Bučar used the United States and Germany. After the first democratic elections in 1990, Bučar became president of the Slovene Parliament.
31   Serbian writers noticed that the Slovene nationalists deliberately avoided that the Croatian variant of the Serbo-Croat language, and not only the Serbian, was also treated as "official." This was true. Both Tito and the defense secretary at the time, Admiral Mamula, spoke the Croatian variant, rather than the Serbian variant, of the Serbo-Croatian language. Even General Ljubičić, Mamula's predecessor, used many Croatian words, imitating Tito's gestures and speech.
32   It is perhaps here that one should notice that-in this respect-in the brief military conflict during summer 1991, the opposing sides were not Serbs and Slovenes: it was Yugoslavia that the Slovenes fought against. And it was the vote of the Serbian representatives in the federal presidency that in fact brought about Slovenia's independence.

33 Urbančič compared the new nations with the former colonies: "When one gives a form of statehood to somebody, regardless of how this statehood came to be created, it would necessarily lead to nationalist forms of behavior when it comes to the national question, and it would create a nation, even if no trace of any genuine national movement had existed in this place ever before" (1987:47).

34 One can here hardly fail to notice that Urbančič's fear of a time bomb was very similar to the fear of the Serbian nationalist intelligentsia for the fate of the Serbs in Kosovo. The higher birthrate of Albanians in Kosovo was paralleled by the higher birthrate of the Bosnian Muslims, the largest group of immigrants in Slovenia. For the Slovenes' fears of the Bosnians, see Mežnarič, 1986.

35 "There is no military or defense justification for Slovenes to join the army in a foreign environment and under foreign command, as was the case in earlier periods of our non-independence, or for the fact that on their territory there are stationed troops that do not obey Slovenian orders" (Urbančič 1987:56).

36 This argument was heard at the 14th session of the LC CC Serbia in May 1968, when Petar Stambolić argued that Dobrica Ćosić and Jovan Marjanović misunderstood the meaning of Yugoslavism for the other Yugoslav nations. For this debate, see chapter three.

37 For the official position of the presidency of the Slovenian LC CC, see the document "Current ideopolitical situations in society and the LCS," unpublished, 39 pages, typescript. This document was commented on by Rupel in *Nova Revija,* 61-62/1987.

38 The authors of the survey learned that this was a typical statement by an authoritarian person at that moment.

39 For details, see Burg (1987). The Slovenian LC had 126,437 members in 1982. The Slovenes made up 5.2% of the Party, less than any other constitutive nation in Yugoslavia (including the Montenegrins, four times smaller in total population). This share was now further decreasing.

40 The Yugoslav Youth Organization Congress in 1986 rejected all four Slovene proposals put forward by the ZSMS: to stop the *Štafeta Mladosti* manifestations, to propose alternative forms of national service, to abolish the death penalty, and to abolish article 133 of the Penal Code (the "verbal crime"). Of 1,402 delegates, only 72 voted for public debate on the death penalty, while 126 votes were cast for a debate on article 133 (*Politika* 15 June 1986).

41 See Kučan's position on this in 1988. The writers around *Nova Revija,* such as Dimitrij Rupel (1988), criticized Kučan's minority tactics. Rupel saw four problems with this position: (1) Slovenians were not known for tolerating minorities in Slovenia (Italians, Hungarians, Bosnian Muslims, for example); (2) it would not make Slovenia popular in the less developed regions of Yugoslavia; (3) both the Party and Slovenia were minorities-which would enable Serbs to say they were against them both; and (4) the Party formed a minority in society, especially in Slovenia. By promoting the "rights of the minority," Kučan in fact was justifying Party rule in Slovenia. Rupel repeated Tine Hribar's argument that Slovenes should not treat themselves as a minority, but as a sovereign nation. In fact, as Hribar said, Slovenes should never accept the status of a minority in Yugoslavia (1987).

42 By October 1987, as Rastko Močnik, the Deputy Rector of Ljubljana University, said, the Slovene Party leadership "made a move that accommodated the Party to the demands of the time." The Party, Močnik admitted, realized that some of the new initiatives, primarily those coming from "civil society," were not unacceptable, since they did not come from a priori hostile groups, such as they were, for example, the Roman

Catholic Church in the case of Poland. But they were still cautious and very selective when it came to various groups within the opposition. "The new social movements and the Youth Organizations are a much more convenient and open-minded partner when it comes to the Party than the various writers' associations and the *Nova Revija*, "concluded Močnik. *Delo* (17 October 1987, quoted from *Nova Revija*, 1987:1716).

43 The popularity of *Mladina* indeed grew rapidly from 1984 to 1988. Although in 1984 it was read ("regularly," "often," or "occasionally") by 19.7% of the Slovenian population, four years later 49.3% of the population in Slovenia said they read it "regularly" (12%), "often" (11.6), or "occasionally" (25.7%) (SJM 1989:301). In comparison, the official Party weekly, *Komunist*, was "never read" by 79.8% of the population (SJM, 1989: 298).

44 Such as Tomaž Mastnak, for an article published in *Mladina* in which he opposed the election of Branko Mikulić, the new Yugoslav prime minister, in 1986, on the grounds of his ideological rigidity. However, no serious consequences occurred, and Mastnak continued to publish in the Slovenian media.

45 Slovene Interior Minister Tomaž Ertl pointed this out in his 15 July 1986 letter to the Slovene "Alternative" (*Nova Revija* 1986:1529).

46 I interviewed Sonja Lokar, the executive secretary of the CC LC Slovenia in September 1988 for the Croatian Youth magazine *Polet*.

47 In his book *Premiki,* Janša claims that one of his friends, Igor Bavčar, simply took the minutes from the desk of the president of the Slovene Socialist Alliance at that time, Jože Smole, while visiting him on official business. Smole, who was then "a bit drunk," did not even notice it. The army was, however, convinced that one of the three Slovene members of the LCY Presidency (perhaps even Kučan) gave the minutes to *Mladina*. One of the aims of the court case was to prove they were right when saying that the Slovene counterrevolution was in fact organized by the Party leadership of Slovenia (Janša 1993).

48 The essence of the problem was summarized in the diaries of one of the *Nova Revija* editors, Dimitrij Rupel. "1. The military court tries civilians; 2. This military court is in Ljubljana; 3. Neither the presidency nor the parliament of Slovenia have any authority over this court; 4. That means that somebody else is sovereign in Slovenia, not only when military personnel are concerned, but also civilians; 5. The Slovenian leadership invited people to be patient, instead of organizing resistance; 6. This is all happening simultaneously with constitutional changes, which mean more centralization; and 7. The main documents for which Janša and others were imprisoned remain secret. This is not only a conflict between civil society and the military, but also an 'anti-Slovenian intervention' by those who do not even speak Slovene" (1988).

49 On several occasions later, Janša accused Kučan of being in compliance with the army (Meier, 1999). Kučan, in fact, applied the same strategy as Stambolić and Milošević in Serbia: he supported public protests, but also aimed at isolating the opposition. Just like Milošević, he believed he could direct public protests toward his "Socialism on a human scale" (the Slovenian movement against bureaucracy).

50 The defensive character of Slovene nationalism was somehow as natural as the expansive character of Serbian nationalism was. This was the difference between the nationalism of a big nation and that of a small one in Yugoslav circumstances. "Although the Serb nationalists thought of everyone in Yugoslavia as Serbs, the Slovene nationalists argued that no one else was qualified to be a Slovene or even similar to Slovenes," as Stipe Šuvar, the Yugoslav Party President, now caught between the two open fires of Belgrade and Ljubljana, half-jokingly explained the difference. Kučan, who recognized

in the army action (which paralleled the antibureaucratic revolution and the Kosovo protests of the Serbs and Montenegrins) an open great-statist tendency, had very little choice left but to tolerate and try to control the new coalition of the various branches of Slovenia's public, including ethnic nationalists.

51 This trend continued in the following year. In April 1990, Milan Kučan easily won the first free elections for the office of president of the Slovenian Presidency, but his party (renamed the League of Communists-Party for Democratic Reforms) failed to secure a majority of seats in the Slovenian Parliament.

52 The trial of Janša dramatically increased fears among Slovenes. Although in April 1988 (before the trial), 25.4% of Slovenes said they felt "fear and hope at the same time for the future of the country and/or themselves," and 26.1% felt "fear and worry only," these figures had risen to 33.9% and 36.2%, respectively, by October 1988 (after the arrest). "Fear" was therefore the word that 70.1% of Slovenes used to describe their feelings on the eve of 1989 (SJM 1988/1989:132).

53 As public opinion surveys repeatedly showed in the 1969-89 period, Slovenes never really believed Yugoslavia was seriously endangered, especially not by the West. The share of those who sensed danger from the West was highest in 1976 (after the delicate negotiations with Italy over Trieste), 6.4%; in all other 12 surveys conducted in these 20 years, it was lower than 5%. The Slovenes (like other Yugoslavs) always feared the Soviet Union more, but with the understandable exception of 1969 (25.9% in a year after the invasion of Czechoslovakia), it was less than 13% of the Slovenian population that sensed exclusive danger from the USSR. In these two decades, a quarter to a third of the Slovenian population believed Yugoslavia was endangered by "both sides," while from 34% to 55% clearly said they saw no danger at all (SJM 1988/1989:238).

54 Matjaž Kmecl, a member of the Slovenian Party Presidency, told Dimitrij Rupel in June 1988 that there were three factions in Slovenian politics: (1) the radicals around *Mladina* and the committee, and, of course, *Nova Revija*; (2) the moderate Party leadership led by Kučan; and (3) "the monolithists" among Slovenes in the army (General Tominc, Admiral Brovet, and others). Kučan was the natural choice for those who wanted a compromise (Rupel 1988:1298).

55 Milan Kučan's speech at the 20th session of the Slovenian Central Committee, quoted from *Delo* 23 April 1988.

56 Janez Stanovnik, the president of the Slovenian Presidency, used this argument when seeking release for the four at the session of the Federal presidency on 31 May 1989. "If you do not listen to us now, the next time you will find yourself speaking to separatists here," he told members of the presidency (Drnovšek, *Nin,* February 1999).

57 On 31 December 1988, LC Serbia, inclusive of its two provinces, had 855,400 members (Milenko Petrović 26 April 1989; IB 5/1989:7).

58 The Serbian Party ideologue Ratomir Vico said on 12 April 1989: "Taking decisions by majority vote in an organization of similar-minded people, in which a balance between the whole and its parts is achieved, in which the autonomy of these parts does not endanger but strengthens the whole....This is not a domination of the strongest, but a normal procedure in democratic organizations" (IB 4/1989:6).

59 Slovenia amended its constitution on several occasions from 1987 to 1989, always extending the scope of rights she was taking out of federal responsibility. Serbia changed its constitution in March 1989, despite the continuing protests of Kosovo Albanians.

60 Excellent sources for this are memoirs by Raif Dizdarević, who in 1988-89 was president of the Yugoslav State Presidency, and a book by Branko Mamula, then the Yugoslav defense secretary. See Dizdarević (1999) and Mamula (2000).

61 *Nin*, 12 March 1989.
62 Among slogans at the Belgrade rally: Slovenia is lying; Slovenia is a traitor; We don't want divisions; Serbia is Kosovo; Serbia is rising; We will give up our lives, but not Kosovo; Down with nationalists of all colors; Yugoslav peoples are brotherly people; Slobo-the Serb-Serbia is with you; Down with the traitors to Yugoslavia; Arrest [Azem] Vllasi.
63 *Nin* 5 March 1989.
64 Bećković, *Nin* 12 March 1989.
65 Jasenovac and Jadovno are places of concentration camps in WW II Croatia, in which Serbs were the main victims.
66 By dividing Croatia and Bosnia-Herzegovina for this purpose into their historical regions, Drašković in fact implied he would not respect the very existence of these two republics as political entities, at least not in their post-1945 borders.
67 Immediately after Cankarjev Dom, sales by Gorenje, the Slovenian firm producing household equipment, decreased by 28%, and the textile industry Mura lost 20% of its Serbian market.
68 Here, however, one should notice that it was all done with the consent of the federal institutions, and-indeed-with the agreement of the Kosovo representatives in them, including the Kosovo Assembly itself. This fact, which is emphasized by Meier (1999), was much used by Milošević in his later explanations of the situation in Kosovo.
69 In his diary on 1 June 1989, Borisav Jović, the Serbian representative in the Yugoslav Presidency (vice president in 1989-90; president in 1990-91) said: "We had great difficulty in convincing Milošević to mention [in his letter] that this was also the LCY and Yugoslav policy. Privately, he thinks this is our policy and that Yugoslavia and the LCY could not reject it-they would be too ashamed, and he is simply hurt when we mention them. In reality, he is right; but by mentioning Yugoslavia, we are in fact strengthening our political position" (1989/1995:16-7).
70 There was no surprise that the first gaps occurred in the main organization of the opposition (such as the Yugoslav Writers' Association), and in the most liberal organization of the system (the Youth Organization).
71 RFE, 17 June 1989 (Stojan Novak), quoted in Belić and Bilbija (1989:219-20). Indeed, even Slovenian leaders (such as Janez Stanovnik, Jože Smole, and even Milan Kučan) repeatedly stated in their conversations with Meier (1999:68) that they "could not imagine" a Slovenia outside Yugoslavia. The same statements they repeated to U.S. Ambassador Zimmermann, to whom Stanovnik said: "Secession would be suicide for Slovenia…But to survive, Yugoslavia must be democratized, a market economy must be created, and the rights of all nationalities must be respected" (1996/9:32). Kučan even said, "Nobody sees a future here for Slovenia outside Yugoslavia. But Milošević's imperialist arrogance can only make Slovenes wonder whether this is the kind of Yugoslavia they can live in" (1996/1999:31).
72 Borisav Jović described this gesture by Milošević in his diary of 29 June 1989: "Eight in the morning. We are getting ready for going to Gazimestan. Voja Vučićević, the chief of the Federal Protocol came to me to ask if I could use my influence to make a change in the wreath-laying order. The protocol of Serbia wants Serbia first, [then] the federation, [then] the army. He appeals for the federation to be first. I called Slobo, who was at home. He was getting ready for Kosovo. He did not want even to hear about this. He said, "Ask them if the Slovenes would accept anyone else but them to lay a wreath first at their national holiday." But, I managed to persuade him to a compromise, all three wreaths to be laid at the same time: the Serbian in the middle, the federation's on the right, the army's on the left" (Jović 1989/1995:29).

73 *Start*, 8 July 1989.
74 Dragan Dobrota, *Start*, 22 July 1989.
75 Simo Dubajić, *Start*, 22 July 1989.
76 The initiative meeting of the CDC was held on 28 February 1989, the same day the Slovenes organized the Cankarjev Dom meeting, and the Serbs reacted at the mass rally in Belgrade. It held its first congress in February 1990 in Zagreb.
77 Celestin Sardelić, *Start*, 22 July 1989.
78 In private, Borisav Jović argued in June 1989 in favor of legalizing political organizations outside the Socialist Alliance of Working People if these organizations were Yugoslav (and not republican or separatist). "Serbia is the last republic to fear this. The LC in Serbia has wide support, and we do not fear we would lose power....I believe the LCY has had in almost 50 years of power enough time to create its own basis, and that no one is to be blamed if it has failed. Many people accepted my arguments, but it seems to be too early for the final decision" (Jović 1989/1995:36). On 13 October 1989, Jović presented the same arguments to Milošević, who agreed, but said there was also a "state reason" for skepticism. "In this case, an Albanian Party would be created in Serbia. There are almost 2 million of them [Albanians]. Whatever they call their Party, they would win power in almost all areas, and we would lose Kosovo....Our strategy should be to secure, not only in words, but also in practice, full democracy for the Serbian intelligentsia in a non-Party pluralism so that they do not attack us severely....Taking into account the multiethnic character of Yugoslavia, he thinks, the West will understand our country even if we secure democratic nonparty pluralism. This is a much stronger guarantee of the survival of Yugoslavia than the multiparty system, which could partition it" (Jović 1989/1995:62). Jović thought Milošević's arguments did make sense, but was not sure if the West cared so much about the existence of Yugoslavia as it did during the cold war. "They maybe care more about the destruction of the 'regime' than about the existence of Yugoslavia!" he said.
79 See Dizdarević (1999) and Drnovšek (1996).
80 Borisav Jović, on 2 October 1989 (1989/1995:60).
81 Support for Marković was at 15.3% in his own Croatia, but he was popular neither with Slovenian Party members (3.2%) nor in Serbia (1.1%).
82 That only a quarter of the Yugoslavs supported Milošević is significant for two reasons: (1) It shows that the Yugoslavs were not only "reserve Serbs"; and (2) It raises the question of Milošević's Yugoslavism. If those who declared themselves Yugoslavs did not recognize him as the protector of Yugoslavism, how then could the Slovenes, Croats, and others?
83 Subsequently, in all but one of the 14 municipalities with a Serb ethnic majority in Croatia, the (Croatian) League of Communists won elections in April 1990. Only in Knin was the radical nationalist Serbian Democratic Party (SDS) elected. Public opinion polls that my associates and I conducted and published in *Danas* in summer 1990 showed that only when the LC Croatia – Party of Democratic Change supported Tudjman's new Constitution did the Serbs start to support the Serbian Democratic Party. During the summer, the SDS forcibly took over the administration in the municipalities in which the LCC had won elections. More in my article in *Ljetopis* 1996.
84 Dragosavac attacked Milošević's politics at several sessions of the CC LCY in 1989. He later complained that somebody wrote a graffito "Dragosavac-The Traitor" on a street in Belgrade where the CC had its building. Bogić Bogićević, the Serb who since May 1989 represented Bosnia-Herzegovina in the federal presidency, voted against Serbia in

the crucial vote on the state of emergency proposed by the army in March 1991 (Silber and Little 1995). This vote was against Milošević too. In an interview I conducted with him, Bogićević talked about the pressure by Serbian leadership on him.
85 As Borisav Jović described after his talks with Slobodan Milošević on 20 June 1989, "The LCY Congress was the critical moment for changing the constitution. If things were ready by then, the constitution would be changed. If not, everything would remain the same until the next Congress" (Jović, 1989/1990:25).
86 Other republics were represented proportionally to their share in the Party membership: Bosnia-Herzegovina 248, Croatia 216, Macedonia 141, and Montenegro 99; a total of 68 members represented the LCY in the army and 7 in the federal party organizations. The ethnic structure of elected members also closely matched the Party structure: 545 delegates were Serbs, 195 Croats, 137 Macedonians, 128 Yugoslavs, 122 Montenegrins, 114 Slovenes, 95 Bosnian Muslims, 63 Albanians, 21 Hungarians, and so on.
87 Borisav Jović in his diary on 24 January 1990 (1990/1995:93)
88 Sonja Lokar, the secretary of LC Slovenia, cried as she left the congress stage. But her tears met with humiliating applause from her victorious Serbian colleagues. Slobodan Milošević believed the Slovenian action was planned well ahead. As shown earlier in this chapter, the Slovenian LC indeed announced they would leave LCY if outvoted on the main issues.
89 *Danas*, 30 January 1990.
90 Lojze Peterle, *Danas* 30 January 1990.
91 Borisav Jović, in a talk with General Kadijević, 26 January 1990 (1990/1995:94). Although Kadijević remained committed to his Communist vision of Yugoslavia, Jović was soon moved to argue that Yugoslavia could be preserved even as a multiparty democracy.
92 On 12 June 1989, Borisav Jović spoke to Slobodan Milošević and Borisav Srebrić about Marković's program: "We concluded that this was exactly the policy we were afraid of: the policy of redirecting income to Croatia. The bill will be paid by everyone, but to the benefit of the exporters, mainly from the developed regions of the country....Lastly, the benefits for those who export to the USSR, which means mainly the Serbian economy, have been drastically cut-which means that our markets are now limited....The general line of our politics is based on Serbia's inability to survive under this burden, unless new taxes are introduced at the federal level. And it is impossible to introduce new taxes. Thus we must confront this policy, which is very cunning indeed: it reduces the revenue paid to the federation by the more-developed republics and increases contributions from the less developed. On the average, there is indeed, as they claim, some reduction of the budget; but this does not mean anything to those who give more. This policy inevitably will lead to new tensions between republics, and indeed between nations, and is not inspired by good intentions" (Jović 1995:22). On 27 June 1989, Milošević asked Jović to warn Marković that Serbia could "overthrow him much sooner than he could overthrow Serbia" (1995:29). On 2 August 1989, Milošević concluded that Serbia was about to get "robbed" by Marković's economic policy. "This is a deliberate action against the Serbian leadership," wrote Jović in his diary (1995:60). Yet, on 31 October 1989, Jović saw that "Slovenia attacks Marković even more than we do in Serbia" (1995:64). On 17 November 1989, Milošević and Jović concluded that Marković should be replaced by somebody else, preferably by General Veljko Kadijević, the defense secretary. "It is important to have a candidate who is in favor of Yugoslavia and Socialism. Ante is not for either of them" (1995:69). An accommoda-

tion with Marković was reached only from January to March 1990, when Serbia tried to get out of the isolation in which it found itself in Yugoslavia. Soon, however, the Serbian leaders returned to an anti-Marković position.

93 *Yugoslav Survey*, 3/1990: 3-26. The survey was conducted by a consortium of several Yugoslav universities and institutes from 20 May to 26 June 1990 in all Yugoslav republics.

94 In one of his first reports to Washington, Warren Zimmermann concluded that the army was a stabilizing, thus a positive, force (1996/1999:86).

95 The motive for Kadijević's anger at Marković was its ideological commitment: he accused the prime minister of being an agent of Western capitalism. Kadijević was less pragmatic and more dogmatic than Milošević.

96 The shift in Serbian politics was mirrored in the main Serbian media. Milorad Vučelić, the journalist closest to Ćosić and Milošević, wrote in *Nin* (18 March 1990) that LC Serbia decided to move away from the "idea that Yugoslavia is a noncontested project." The last session of the CC LC Serbia, Vučelić said, had come to the conclusion that Yugoslavia was still a rational and desirable project, but that "no one should be begged to be with us in a united Yugoslavia and LCY." On 25 March 1990, the main creator of the new Serbian constitution, Ratko Marković, said that a referendum was the most suitable means to establish whether a nation wanted to remain in Yugoslavia or to leave (*Nin* 25 March 1990). "Serbia should not force anyone to remain in the federation....She must protect her dignity. She must not humiliate herself to save Yugoslavia, since she has the longest state tradition of all the Yugoslav countries; she has the richest constitutional history and the greatest international reputation."

97 Jović, 27 June 1990, (1995:160).

98 Borisav Jović, 22 August 1990, 1995:182.

99 Milorad Vučelić in *Nin,* 25 February 1990. Some statements by Tudjman and his closest political aides only poured fuel on this interpretation. The president of the Croatian League of Communists, Ivica Račan, also warned that the CDC was "a Party of dangerous intentions" (*Nin* 4 March 1990). Croatian journalists, such as Jelena Lovrić (*Danas* 6 March 1990) compared Franjo Tudjman with Vojislav Šešelj. Both expressed their ambitions to extend Serbia/Croatia to the Bosnian territories. The Serbian press and the Croatian press both compared Tudjman not with Milošević and Kučan, but with the Serbian extreme nationalists, such as Vuk Drašković and Vojislav Šešelj. Unlike them, Tudjman won an election in Croatia, becoming the first genuine ethnic nationalist to come to power in a Yugoslav republic.

100 Still, General Kadijević was "appalled" when he saw that the radical Serb nationalists supported him (Jović 1995:179). It seems that he did not see that by then there was little difference left between the official Serbian position and that of the Serbian extreme nationalists.

101 Such as, for example, Zimmermann (1996/9:VII), Perović (1993), Goati (1995), and Sekelj (1990).

102 The army was first to feel the consequences of the lack of a federal state. It soon became, as General Kadijević said in the title of his book-an army without a state.

BIBLIOGRAPHY

1. Primary Sources

1. A. Party and State Documents, Published

Minutes:

26 sjednica Centralnog komiteta SKJ: Aktualna idejno-politička pitanja i aktivnost SKJ. 20 April 1982. Belgrade: Komunist.

Četrnaesta sednica CK SK Srbije (authorised minutes). 29 i 30 May 1968. Belgrade: Komunist.

The Eleventh LCY Congress: Documents. 1978. Belgrade: Komunist.

The Twelfth Congress of the League of the Communists of Yugoslavia. 1982. Belgrade: Komunist.

Reports:

Izvještaj o stanju u Savezu komunista Hrvatske u odnosu na prodor nacionalizma u njegove redove; [The official report, accepted by the Central Committee of the LCC at its 28th Session, 8 May 1972)].

Three decades of the Struggle of Yugoslav Communists for the socialist transformation of society and for new relations in the world. Report. In: *11th Congress of the LCY*. 1978. Belgrade: STP: 107-86.

Programmes:

The Programme of the League of Yugoslav Communists. 1958. Belgrade: Jugoslavija.

Political Platform for Action by the LCY in Developing Socialist Self-Management, Brotherhood and Unity and Fellowship in Kosovo. 1982. Belgrade: STP.

Internal Party Bulletins:

Informativni Bilten CK SK Srbije (all between 1982 and 1990).

Informativni Pregled CK SKH (all between 1982 and 1990).

Foreign Documents Related to Yugoslavia:

Programme CPSU. 1961/1962. *The New Soviet Society: final text of the program of the Communist party of the Soviet Union*. Moscow: CPSU.

The Status of a Republic for Kosova is a Just Demand. 1981. Tirana. 8 Nentori

1.B. Party and State Documents, Unpublished:

Confidential and Internal Party Analyses:

'Reagiranja, istupi i polemike povodom preštampavanja Krležinog *Dijalektičkog Antibarbarusa*,' 25 February 1982. Document, typescript, confidential. Author: Information Department CC LC Croatia.

'Pisanje o Golom Otoku i Informbirou u posljednjih nekoliko mjeseci,' 14 April 1982, Document, typescript, confidential. Author: Information Department CC LC Croatia.

'O nekim napisima i istupima na liniji 'demistifikacije' prošlosti i traženja 'sloboda.'' 10 May 1982. Document, typescript, confidential. Author: Information Department CC LC Croatia.

'O ulozi sredstava javnog informiranja i njihovom utjecaju u društvu, slobodi kritike i različitim devijacijama.' 16 July 1982. Document, typescript, confidential. Author: Information Department CC LC Croatia.

'Neke društvene, političke i idejne tendencije.' 1 February 1983. Document, typescript, confidential. Author: Information Department CC LC Croatia.

'Analiza sadržaja političkog tjednika *Danas*.' 3 February 1983. Document, typescript, confidential. Author: Information Department CC LC Croatia.

'O nekim idejnim i političkim tendencijama u umjetničkom stvaralaštvu, književnoj, kazališnoj i filmskoj kritici, te o javnim istupima jednog broja kulturnih stvaralaca u kojima su sadržane politički neprihvatljive poruke' [*White Book*]. April 1984. Author: Information Department CC LC Croatia. Confidential. 236 pages, typescript.

'Savez komunista Hrvatske u borbi protiv antisocijalističkog djelovanja i antikomunističkih ideologija u razdoblju nakon IX kongresa SKH.' December 1985. Author: Commission for ideo-theoretical work of the LC Croatia Central Committee. Confidential. 277 pages, typescript.

'Aktualne idejno-politične razmere v družbi in v Zvezi komunistov Slovenije.' Summer 1988. Author: Presidency of the CC LC Slovenia. 39 pages, typescript.

Excerpts from Minutes:

Informacija o izlaganju predsednika Savezne Skupštine na proširenoj sednici Predsedništva Savezne skupštine, 17 December 1964: *Jugoslavenski centar*, 1983/II-24 (Document, typescript)

Minutes of the sessions of the Coordinative Commission of all Chambers of the Federal Parliament for the Issues of the Constitution, Brioni (excerpts prepared by the Yugoslav Centre for Theory and Practice of Socialist Self-management *Edvard Kardelj*, Belgrade – Ljubljana); (manuscript, 52 pages):

    21-28 April 1972 (1972/II-8)
    13-22 November 1972 (1972/II-15)
    12-19 December 1972 (1972/II-17)
    17-19 January 1973 (1973/II-2)
    29-30 January 1973 (1973/II-4)

1 November 1973 (1973/II-15)

Dušan Dragosavac at the session of the CC LCY Presidency, July 1984 (under Chairmanship of Draža Marković), 11 pages, typescript, copy in possession of the author.

Letters Between Members of the Political Elite:

Petar Stambolić to Dušan Dragosavac, 20 June 1983; 3 pages, typescript, copy in the author's possession.

Dušan Dragosavac to Petar Stambolić, 27 June 1983 (through the Cabinet of the CC LCY President of Presidency, Document Strictly Confidential 3/25, 27 June 1983, Belgrade, signed by the Chief of the Cabinet Slavko Tošić), 11 pages, typescript, copy in possession of the author.

Dušan Dragosavac to Raif Dizdarević, 13 October 1988, 10 pages, typescript, copy in possession of the author.

Dušan Dragosavac to Aleksandar Bakočević, 18 July 1989. 2 pages, typescript, copy in possession of the author.

2. Memoirs and Diaries by Political Actors:

2.A. Political Elite:

Bilić, Jure. 1988. *1971? Koja je to godina*. Zagreb: Globus.

Čengić, Enes. 1985. *S Krležom iz dana u dan*. Vol I: *Balade o životu koji teče*. Zagreb: Globus.

Dedijer, Vladimir. 1953. *Tito Speaks: his self-portrait and struggle with Stalin*. London: Weidenfeld and Nicolson.

Dedijer, Vladimir. 1953. *Tito*. New York: Simon and Schuster.

Dedijer, Vladimir. 1981. *Novi Prilozi za Biografiju Josipa Broza Tita*. Rijeka and Zagreb: Liburnija and Mladost.

Dedijer, Vladimir. 1984. *Novi prilozi za biografiju Josipa Broza Tita*. Vol:3. Belgrade: Rad.

Dizdarević, Raif. 1999. *Od smrti Tita do smrti Jugoslavije*. Sarajevo: Oko.

Dragosavac, Dusan. 1988. *Zbivanja i svjedočenja*. Zagreb: Globus.

Hasani, Sinan. 1986. *Istine i zablude o Kosovu*. Zagreb. CIP.

Jović, Borisav. 1995. *Poslednji dani SFRJ*. Belgrade: Politika.

Kadijević, Veljko. 1993. *Moje vidjenje raspada*. Beograd: Politika.

Kardelj, Edvard. 1982. *Reminiscences*. London: Blond and Briggs.

Mamula, Branko. 2000. *Slučaj Jugoslavija*. Podgorica: CID.

Marković, Dragoslav Draža. 1987. *Život i politika*. Vol. 1. Belgrade: Rad.

Marković, Dragoslav Draža. 1988. *Život i politika*. Vol: 2. Beograd: Rad.

Marković, Mirjana. 1996. *Answer*. London: Minerva.

Mićunović, Veljko. 1977. *Moskovske godine 1956/1958*. Zagreb: Liber.

Mićunović, Veljko. 1980. *Moscow Diary*. London: Chatto & Windus.

Nenadović, Aleksandar. 1988. *Razgovori s Kočom*. Zagreb: Globus.

Perović, Latinka. 1991. *Zatvaranje kruga: ishod političkog rascepa u SKJ 1971/1972*. Sarajevo: Svjetlost.

Stambolić, Ivan. 1995. *Put u bespuće*. (ed. by Slobodan Inić). Belgrade: B 92.

Tepavac, Mirko. 1998. *Sećanja i komentari*. (ed. by Aleksandar Nenadović). Beograd: B92.

Tripalo, Miko. 1991. *Hrvatsko Proljeće*. Zagreb: Globus.

Speeches and Articles by Members of the Political Elite:

1. Collected Speeches:

Galović, Špiro. 1989. *Govor i pogovor.* Zagreb. Globus.

Jović, Borisav. 1989. *Datum za istoriju: 28. mart 1989.* Belgrade: BIGZ.

Kraigher, Sergej. 1985. *Kako iz krize.* Zagreb and Ljubljana: Globus and Delo.

Milošević, Slobodan. 1989. *Godine raspleta.* Belgrade: BIGZ

Pavlović, Dragiša. 1987. *Pitanjem na odgovore.* Belgrade: BIGZ.

Pavlović, Dragiša. 1988. *Olako obećana brzina.* Zagreb: Globus.

Stambolić, Ivan. 1988. *Rasprave o SR Srbiji.* Zagreb. Globus.

Šuvar, Stipe. 1988. *Vrijeme iskušenja.* Sarajevo: Oslobodjenje.

Šuvar, Stipe. 1989. *Nezavršeni mandat.* Vol 1-2. Zagreb: Globus.

2. Other Major Speeches by Members of the Political Elite:

Andjelković, Zoran. 1989. Speech at the 15th CC LCS Session, 12 April 1989. *IB CKSKS* No. 4/1989:12-16.

Djordjević, Jovan. 1983. 'Stvaranje Ustava Socijalističke Federativne Republike Jugoslavije iz 1974.' *Socijalizam*: 1318-1346.

Djuranović, Veselin. 1985. 'O nekim aspektima politike razvoja koja je prethodila privrednoj krizi.' *Socijalizam.* 28:206-21.

Dolanc, Stane. 1978. 'Introductory Statement at the 5th Session of the CC LCY 09 Feb 1978.' In: *Basic Thesis For the Formulation of Policies....*1981. Belgrade: STP.

Gračanin, Petar. 1988. Speech at the Joint Session of the Presidency of Serbia and the Presidency of the CC LCS, 5 September 1988. *IB CK SKS* No. 8: 5-12.

Kardelj, Edvard Sperans. 1939. *Razvoj slovenskega narodnega vprašanja*. Ljubljana: Publisher unknown.

Kardelj, Edvard. 1955. 'Some Aspects of International Relations in Europe.' In: Edvard Kardelj: *The Nations and Socialism*. 1981. Belgrade: STP: 65-79.

Kardelj, Edvard. 1957. 'The Development of the Slovene National Question. Preface to the second edition.' In: Edvard Kardelj: *The Nations and Socialism*. 1981. Belgrade: STP: 81-135.

Kardelj, Edvard. 1962. 'The Federation and the Republics.' Speech to the National Assembly 20 September 1962. In: Edvard Kardelj: *The Nations and Socialism*. 1981. Belgrade: STP: 137-40.

Kardelj, Edvard. 1965. 'Notes on Social Criticism in Yugoslavia.' In: Edvard Kardelj: *Science and Social Criticism*. 1980. Belgrade: STP: 23-144.

Kardelj, Edvard. 1967. 'Tito and the Communist Party of Yugoslavia.' In: Edvard Kardelj: *Tito and Socialist Revolution of Yugoslavia*. 1980. Belgrade: STP: 5-59.

Kardelj, Edvard. 1967 a. Thirty Years After The Founding Congress of the Communist Party of Slovenia.' In: Edvard Kardelj: *The Nations and Socialism*. 1980. Belgrade: STP: 180-216.

Kardelj, Edvard. 1969. 'Yugoslavia- The Socialist Self-Managing Community of Equal Peoples.' In: Edvard Kardelj: *The Nations and Socialism*. 1980. Belgrade: STP: 217-53.

Kardelj, Edvard. 1970. 'Aktuelni problemi daljeg razvoja našeg političkog sistema.' Speech at the 12th Session of the LCY Presidency. In: Edvard Kardelj: *Izbor iz dela III: Politički sistem socijalističkog samoupravljanja*. 1979. Beograd: Komunist: 259-83.

Kardelj, Edvard. 1972. *Proturječnosti društvene svojine u savremenoj socijalističkoj praksi*. Belgrade: APS. [English translation: *Contradictions of Social Property in a Socialist Society*. 1981. Belgrade: STP].

Kardelj, Edvard. 1973. 'The National Question in Yugoslavia and Its Foreign Policy.' In: Edvard Kardelj: *The Nations and Socialism*. 1980. Belgrade: STP: 275-90.

Kardelj, Edvard. 1974. 'Performance of the Functions of the Federation.' In: Edvard Kardelj: *The Nations and Socialism*. 1980. Belgrade: STP: 291-8.

Kardelj, Edvard. 1975. 'Cultural and Economic Aspects of Relations Among Nationalities.' In: Edvard Kardelj: *The Nations and Socialism*. 1980. Belgrade: STP: 141-77.

Kardelj, Edvard. 1975a. 'National Consciousness and Nationalism.' In: Edvard Kardelj: *The Nations and Socialism*. 1980. Belgrade: STP: 265-70.

Kardelj, Edvard. 1977. 'My First Meeting With Tito.' In: Edvard Kardelj: *Tito and Socialist Revolution of Yugoslavia*. 1980. Belgrade: STP: 209-55.

Kardelj, Edvard. 1977. 'Ways of Democracy in a Socialist Society.' In: Edvard Kardelj: *Self-Management and the Political System*. 1980. Belgrade: STP: 57-281.

Kardelj, Edvard. 1977. *Pravci razvoja političkog sistema socijalističkog samoupravljanja*. Beograd: Komunist.

Kardelj, Edvard. 1979. 'General Remarks on the National Question.' In: Edvard Kardelj: *The Nations and Socialism*. Belgrade: STP: 5-63.

Kučan, Milan. 1985. 'Ostvarivanje ustavne koncepcije jugoslovenske federacije.' Report at the 21st CC LCY Session. *Socijalizam*. 28: 1625-44.

Milošević, Slobodan. 1988. 'Završna reč Slobodana Miloševića, predsednika Predsedništva CK SK Srbije.' Speech at 12th Session CC LCS, 14 July 1988. *IB CK SKS* No. 7:14-5.

Milošević, Slobodan. 1988. 'Završna reč Slobodana Miloševića, predsednika Predsedništva CK SK Srbije.' Speech at Joint Session of the Presidency of SR Serbia and Presidency of the CC LCS, 5 September 1988. *IB CK SKS*, No. 8:14.

Milošević, Slobodan. 1988. 'Završna reč Slobodana Miloševića, predsednika Predsedništva CK CK SKS.' Speech at 13th Session CC LCS, 11 October 1988. *IB CK SKS* No. 9:10-1.

Milošević, Slobodan. 1988. Speech at the Joint Session of the Presidency of Serbia and Presidency of the CC LCS, 2 November 1988. *IB SK SKS*, No. 10/1988. 5-12.

Minić, Milomir. 1988. Speech at the 12th CC LCS Session, 14 July 1988. *IB CK SKS*, No. 7: 5-13.

Minić, Milomir. 1989. Speech at the 18th CC LCS Session, 13 September 1989. *IB CK SKS* No. 8-9: 5-10.

Minić, Milomir. 1989. Speech at the 21st CC LCS Session, 27 November 1989. *IB CK SKS*, No. 11:15-19.

Minić, Milomir. 1990. 'Savez komunista Srbije za mir, slobodu, ravnopravnost, demokratiju i prosperitet Kosova.' Speech at 3rd CC LCS Session, 15 February 1990. *IB CK SKS*, No. 2:5-11.

Petrović, Milenko. 1989. Speech at the 16th CC LCS Session, 26 April 1989. *IB CK SKS*, No. 5: 5-9.

Petrović, Milenko. 1989. 'Predlaganje kandidata za delegate društveno-političkog veća Skupstine SR Srbije iz Saveza komunista Srbije.' Speech at 19th CC LCS Session, 23 October 1989. *IB CK SKS*, No. 10:9.

Raičević, Tomica. 1990. 'Neposredni zadaci Saveza komunista Srbije u sprovodjenju privredne reforme;' opening speech at 2nd Session of the CC LCS. *IB CK SKS*: No. 1: 5-11.

Sekulić, Tomislav. 1989. Speech at the 15th CC LCS Session, 12 April 1989. *IB CK SKS*: No. 4/1989:17-19.

Sokolović, Zoran. 1988. Speech at the Joint Session of the Presidency of Serbia and Presidency of the CC LCS, 2 November 1988. *IB CK SKS* No. 10/1988. 5-12.

Špadijer, Balša. 1989. 'Rasprava o dokumentima za Jedanaesti kongres SK Srbije.' Speech at 19th Session of the CC LCS, 23 October 1989. *IB CK SKS* No. 10:22-5.

Špiljak, Mika. 1986. 'Zadaci SKH u daljnjem materijalnom i društvenom razvoju.' Speech at the 10th Congress of the League of Communists of Croatia. *Informativni Pregled CK SKH*. No. 1: 13-5.

Štambuk, Vladimir. 1988. Speech at the Session of the Commission for ideotheoretical work CC LCS, 2 September 1988. *IB CK SKS*, No. 8: 21-24.

Štambuk, Vladimir. 1989. Speech at the Session of the CC LCS Presidency, 2 October 1989. *IB CK SKS*, No. 8-9: 31-35.

Štambuk, Vladimir. 1989. Speech at the Session of the Commission for ideotheoretical work CC LCS, 16 October 1989. *IB CK SKS* No. 10:17-21.

Šuvar, Stipe. 1985. 'Što je pozitivnog, a što negativnog pružila partijska rasprava.' *Socijalizam* 28:46-55.

Tito, Josip Broz. 1942. 'Nacionalno pitanje u Jugoslaviji u svjetlosti narodnooslobodilačke borbe.' *Proleter 17:3*.

Tito, Josip Broz. 1945. Speech at the Founding Session of the Communist Party of Serbia. In: *Osnivački Kongres KP Srbije (8-12 May 1945)*. 1972. Belgrade: IIRPS.

Tito, Josip Broz. 1978. 'The LCY in the Struggle for the Further Development of Socialist, Self-Managing and Non-Aligned Yugoslavia.' Speech at the 11th Congress of the LCY. In: *11th Congress of the League of Communists of Yugoslavia*. Belgrade: 1978: STP: 7-92.

Tito, Josip Broz. 1978 a. 'Granice federalnih jedinica u federativnoj Jugoslaviji nisu granice razdvajanja, nego granice spajanja.' In: *Nacionalno pitanje i revolucija*, Belgrade: Svjetlost et al: 78-84.

Tito, Josip Broz. 1978 b. 'Bratstvo i jedinstvo je preduslov za jednu snažnu Jugoslaviju.' In: *Nacionalno pitanje i revolucija*, Belgrade: Svjetlost et al: 78-84.

Tito, Josip Broz. 1979. Tribute to Kardelj. In: *Edvard Kardelj*. Zagreb: Globus: 382-5.

Trifunović, Bogdan. 1990. 'Osnovna opredeljenja SK Srbije kao partije koja se bori za demokratski socijalizam.' Spech at the 5th CC LCS Session, 13 March 1990. *IB CKS*, No. 5:5-16.

Vico, Ratomir. 1989. Speech at the 13th CC LCS Session, 11 October 1988. *IB CK SKS* No. 9:5-9.

Vico, Ratomir. 1989. 'Pripreme i sadržina vanrednog kongresa SKJ.' Speech at 15th Session of the CC LCS, 12 April 1989. *IB CK SKS*, No. 4: 5-9.

Vico, Ratomir. 1989. Speech at the 19th CC LCS Session, 23 October 1989. *IB CK SKS*, No. 10: 5-8.

Vico, Ratomir. 1990. Speech at the 4th CC LCS Session, 13 March 1990. *IB CK SKS*, No. 3:5-16.

2.B. 'Dissidents':

Memoirs and Diaries by 'Dissidents':

Ćosić, Dobrica. 1992. *Promene*. Novi Sad: Dnevnik.

Djukić, Slavoljub. 1989. *Čovek u svom vremenu*. Razgovori s Dobricom Ćosićem. Belgrade: Filip Višnjić.

Rančić, Dragoslav. 1994. *Dobrica Ćosić - Predsednik bez vlasti*. Belgrade: Crno na belo.

Speeches, Articles and Books by 'Dissidents':

Arzenšek, Vladimir. 1986. 'Delavsko gibanje in samoupravni socijalizem.' *Nova Revija*, No. 46/47: 370-7.

Bogdanović, Bogdan. 1988. *Mrtvouzice: Mentalne zamke staljinizma*. Zagreb: August Cesarec.

Bučar, France. 1987. 'Pravna ureditev položaja Slovencev kot naroda.' *Nova Revija*, No. 57/1987:150-60.

Bučar, France. 1989. 'Slovenija med Balkanom in Evropo.' *Nova Revija*, No. 91: 1491-503.

Cenčić, Vjekoslav. 1981. *Enigma Kopinič*. Rijeka: Liburnija.

Ćosić, Dobrica. 1982. *Stvarno i moguće: članci i ogledi*. Ljubljana and Zagreb: Cankarjeva Založba.

Ćosić, Dobrica. 1992. *Srpsko pitanje - demokratsko pitanje*. Belgrade: Politika.

Ćosić, Dobrica. 1992b. 'Politics – Challenge and Temptation in Contemporary Serbian Literature.' In: Celia Hawkesworth (ed.): *Literature and Politics in Eastern Europe*. London: Macmillan Press: 17-20.

Debeljak, Aleš. 1986. 'Zastarelost jugoslovanstva.' *Nova Revija*, No. 52/53:1389-1396.

Djogo, Gojko. 1982. *Vunena vremena*. London: Naša reč.

Djuretić, Veselin. 1985. *Saveznici i jugoslovenska ratna drama*. Vol I-II. Belgrade: SANU.

Drašković, Vuk. 1982. *Nož*. Belgrade: Zapis.

Drašković, Vuk. 1985. *Sudija*. Belgrade: Nova knjiga.

Fištravec, Andrej et al (eds). 1989. *Boj za oblast*. Maribor: RK ZSMS.

Hadri, Ali. 1967. 'Kosovo i Metohija u Kraljevini Jugoslaviji.' In: *Istorijski glasnik* (Belgrade), No 1-2: 51-84.

Hofman, Branko. 1982. *Noć do jutra*. Zagreb: Znanje.

Hribar Spomenka. 1987. 'Avantgardno sovraštvo in sprava.' *Nova Revija*, No. 57:75-103.

Hribar, Spomenka. 1988a. 'Samoobramba kot poraz.' *Nova Revija*, No. 77: 1318-32.

Hribar, Spomenka. 1988b. 'Poskus znanstveno fantastične zgodbe.' *Nova Revija*, No. 78/79:1590-604.

Hribar, Spomenka. 1988c. 'Čemu presenečenje?' *Nova Revija*, No. 80:1991-8.

Hribar, Tine. 1987. 'Slovenska državnost.' *Nova Revija*, No. 57:3-29.

Isaković, Antonije. 1982. *Tren I-II*. Belgrade: Prosveta.

Jambrek, Peter. 1987. 'Pravica do samoodločbe slovenskega naroda.' *Nova Revija*, No. 57:161-74.

Janša, Janez. 1988. *Na svoji strani*. Ljubljana: Črt.

Janša, Janez. 1993. *Premiki*. Ljubljana: DZS.

Jenšterle, Marko. 1987. 'Trenutak slovenske mladine.' *Nova Revija*, No. 61/62: 880-8.

Josić Višnjić, Miroslav (ed.). 1984. *Saopštenja, zapisnici i pisma Odbora za zaštitu umetničke slobode pri Beogradskoj sekciji Udruženja književnika Srbije*. Belgrade: Miroslav Josić.

Kljakić, Dragan. 1983. *Dosije Hebrang*. Belgrade: Partizanska knjiga.

Krestić, Vasilije i Kosta Mihajlović. 1995. *Memorandum SANU. Odgovori na kritike*. Belgrade: SANU.

Lubarda, Vojislav. 1991. *Anatema*. Gornji Milanovac: Dečje novine.

Mastnak, Tomaž. 1986. 'Delavsko gibanje in nova družbena gibanja.' *Nova Revija*, No. 46/47: 347-69.

Mastnak, Tomaž. 1990. 'Civilno društvo u Sloveniji: od opozicije do vlasti.' *Sociologija*, No. 4: 439-51.

Matvejević, Predrag. 1986. *Otvorena pisma - moralne vježbe*. Belgrade: Matvejević and Mašić.

'Memorandum SANU.' 1989. *Naše teme* 1989:128-63.

Mihajlov, Mijajlo. 1998. 'Disidentstvo – stvarnost i legende.' *Republika*, No. 181: 1-11 (Internet source: http://www.europe.com/zines/republika/arhiva/98/181/181_19.htm)

Mihajlović, Borislav Mihiz. 1990. *Autobiografija o drugima*. Belgrade: BIGZ.

Mirić, Jovan. 1984. *Sistem i kriza*. Zagreb: Cekade.

'Odprto Pismo Slovenskim Pisateljem' (14 March 1986). *Nova Revija*, No. 50:811.

Popović, Danko. 1985. *Knjiga o Milutinu*. Beograd: Književne novine.

Rupel, Dimitrij. 1988. 'Esej o Janezu Janši.' *Nova Revija*, No. 77:1298-311.

Stojanović, Lazar. 1998. 'Ko behu disidenti.' *Republika*, No. 182: 1-15 (Internet source: http://www.yurope.com/zines/republika/arhiva/98/182/182_11.htm).

Tomc, Gregor. 1986. 'Realno obstaječa gibanja v socializmu.' *Nova Revija*, No. 46/47: 378-92.

Urbančič, Ivan. 1987. 'The Yugoslav 'nationalist crisis' and the Slovenes in the perspective of the end of nations.' *Nova Revija*, No. 57:30-56.

Urbančič, Ivan. 1989. 'Sedamdeset let Jugosalvije.' *Nova Revija*, No 85/86: 789-817.

2.C. Memoirs, Diaries and Books by Foreign Participants

Bildt, Carl. 1998. *Peace journey: the struggle for peace in Bosnia*. London: Weidenfeld.

Holbrooke, Richard. 1998. *To End a War*. Washington: Random House.

Owen, David. 1995. *Balkan Odyssey*. London: Victor Gollancz.

3. Public Opinion Polls and Surveys:

Flere, Sergej. 1988. 'The Ethnic Attitudes of Youth in Yugoslavia.' *Revija za narodnostna vprašanja, razprave in gradivo.* No 21/1988: 133-42.

Goati, Vladimir. 1989. *Politička anatomija jugoslovenskog društva.* Zagreb. Naprijed.

Grdešić, Ivan et al. 1989. *Interesi i ideje u SKJ.* Zagreb. FPN.

Katunarić, Vjeran. 1988. 'Inter-ethnical relations in Contemporary Yugoslavia. Some theoretical notes and empirical findings.' *Revija za narodnostna vprašanja,razprave in gradivo.* No. 21/1988:

Pantić, Dragomir. 1987. 'Karakteristike socijalne distance kod zaposlenih u društvenom sektoru SFRJ.' *Socijalizam* 29:559-602.

'Public Opinion Survey on the Federal Executive Council's Social and Economic Reforms.' 1990. *Yugoslav Survey* No. 3:3-26.

Santrić, Vjeko. 1989. *Vrijeme odustajanja. Prilog razumijevanju omladinskog javnog mnijenja.* Zagreb: CDD SSOH.

Toš, Niko (ed). 1987. *Slovensko Javno Mnenje 1987: pregled in primerjava rezultatov raziskav SJM 69 - SJM 87.* Ljubljana: Delavska Enotnost

Toš, Niko (ed). 1989. *Slovensko Javno Mnenje 1988-1989.* Ljubljana: Delavska Enotnost.

4. Demographic Data:

Statistički bilten No. 1286. 1980. SZS, Belgrade.

Statistički godišnjak Jugoslavije (SGJ). 1986. Belgrade. SZJ

Statistički godišnjak Jugoslavije za 1990/91. 1991. SZJ. Beograd.

5. Interviews Conducted for this Thesis:

5.A. With Academics and Experts:

Dušan Bilandžić, 30 December 1995.

Anthony Giddens, June 1999, parts published in *Feral*, 10 June 1999, the whole text in *Acque e Terre* 4/5/1999:19-24.

Erik Hobsbawm, June 1996, published in *Arkzin*, 21 June 1996.

Branko Horvat, April 1998.

Tolis Malakos, May 1996 – published in *Arkzin*. 7 June 1996.

Jovan Mirić, several occasions 1994-1999.

Ivan Šiber, several occasions 1994-1999.

Josip Županov, December 1995.

5.B. With Political Actors:

Mladen Babun, editor-in-chief of *Polet* (1983-1985), October 1998, Zagreb

Marija Bakarić, widow of Vladimir Bakarić, June 1986

Jure Bilić , January and April 1998, Zagreb

Jakov Blažević, December 1985, August 1987

Bogić Bogićević, March 1996, London

Lord (Peter) Carrington, published in *Arkzin*, June 1996.

Savka Dabčević-Kučar, informal conversations, 1992-1994, Zagreb

Dušan Dragosavac, April 1998, Zagreb

Kiro Gligorov, June 1996, Skopje

Antonije Isaković, April 1996, London

Dara Janeković, December 1997, April 1998, Zagreb

Pepca Kardelj, on several occasions in 1987 and 1988

Sergej Kraigher, January 1986 and February 1988, Ljubljana

Sonja Lokar, September 1988 and informal conversations in 1989, Ljubljana

Andrej Marinc, April 1989, Ljubljana

Stjepan Orešković, informal conversations 1987-1990, Zagreb

Šime Pilić, January 1998, Split

Milka Planinc, April 1998, Zagreb

Radoš Smiljković, March 1989, Belgrade

Lazar Stojanović, February 1998, London

Stipe Šuvar, October 1997, January and April 1998, Zagreb

Miko Tripalo, informal conversation in 1994, Zagreb

Azem Vllasi, telephone conversations, January 1989

Josip Vrhovec, January 1998, April 1998, Zagreb

6. Public Lectures, Unpublished Papers and Dissertations:

Bracewell, Wendy. 1998. 'Rape in Kosovo: Masculinity and Serbian Nationalism,' unpublished paper.

Giddens, Anthony. 20 January 1990. 'Politics After Socialism.' London: LSE (available on the Internet: http://www.lse.ac.uk/Giddens/pdf/20-jan-99.pdf

Dragović Soso, Jasna. 1999. *Between Democracy and Nationalism: The Rise and Fall of the Belgrade Critical Intelligentsia, 1980-1991.,*' Geneve: University of Geneva, PhD thesis.

Innes, Abigail. 1997. *The Partition of Czechoslovakia.* LSE: PhD thesis.

McBride, Cillian. 22 October 1996. 'Meaning and Understanding,' unpublished paper presented at the LSE.

7. The Author's Private Diary (1985-1990, manuscript)

8. Newspapers Articles, Radio Broadcasting and Internet Sources, Quoted:

8.A. Special Editions, News Reports:

Belić, and Djuro Bilbija. 1989. *Slovenija i Srbija od Cankarjevog Doma do Jugoalata i Gazimestana.* Belgrade: Tera.

Šta se dogadjalo na Kosovu. 1991. Belgrade: Politika.

8.B. Other Newspaper Sources, Consulted:

RFE/RL Research Reports, 1974-1990
Danas, 1982-1990
Duga, 1984-1990
Intervju, 1984-1990
Nin, 1974-1990

Secondary Sources:

Allcock, John B. et al. 1994. 'The Fall of Yugoslavia: Symptoms and Diagnosis.' *Slavonic and East European Review.* 72: 686-91.

Allcock, John B et al. (eds). 1992. *Yugoslavia in Transition. Choices and Constraints.* New York and Oxford: Berg.

Banac, Ivo. 1984. *The National Question in Yugoslavia: origins, history, politics.* Ithaca: Cornell University Press.

Bebler, Anton. 1989. 'Sovjetsko *novo razmišljanje* i sigurnost Jugoslavije.' *Politička misao*, No 2/89: 41-60.

Bermeo, Nancy (ed.). 1992. *Liberalization and Democratization, Change in the Soviet Union and Eastern Europe*. Baltimore: The Johns Hopkins University Press.

Bernik, Ivan. 1989. 'Functions of Egalitarianism in Yugoslav Society.' *Praxis International*. 9:425-32.

Bilandžić, Dušan. 1986. *Jugoslavija poslije Tita 1980-1985*. Zagreb: Globus.

Blagojević, Marina. 1997. 'The Other Side of the Truth: Migrations of Serbs from Kosovo.' In: G. Duijzings (ed): *Kosovo – Kosova: Confrontation or Coexistence*, University of Nijmegen: 70-81.

Blagojević, Marina. 1998. 'Kosovo: In/Visible Civil War.' In Thanos Veremis and Evangelos Kofos (eds): *Kosovo: Avoiding Another Balkan War*. Athens: ELIAMEP: 239-310.

Bokovoy, Melissa K et al. (eds) 1997. *State-Society Relations in Yugoslavia 1945-1992*. London: Macmillan.

Breitmann, Richard. 1991. *The Architect of Genocide: Himmler and the Final Solution*. New York.

Bringa, Tone. 1995. *Being Muslim the Bosnian way : identity and community in a central Bosnian village*. Princeton, N.J : Princeton University Press.

Browning, Christopher R. 1992. *The Path to Genocide: Essays on Launching the Final Solution*. Cambridge: Cambridge University Press.

Bunce, Valerie. 1999. *Subversive Institutions*. Cambridge: Cambridge University Press.

Burg, Steven L. 1983. *Conflict and Cohesion in Socialist Yugoslavia: political decision making since 1966*. Princeton, N.J. : Princeton University Press.

Burg, Steven L. 1987. 'New Data on the League of Communists of Yugoslavia.' *Slavic Review* 46:553-67.

Campbell, David. 1998. *National Deconstruction. Violence, Identity and Justice in Bosnia*. Minneapolis and London: University of Minnesota Press.

Clissold, Stephen. 1975. *Yugoslavia and the Soviet Union 1939-1973*. London: Oxford University Press.

Cohen, Lenard J. 1983. *Political cohesion in a fragile mosaic: the Yugoslav experience*. Boulder: Westview Press.

Cohen, Lenard J. 1989. *The socialist pyramid: elites and power in Yugoslavia*. Oakville: Mosaic Press.

Cohen, Lenard J. 1993/1995. *Broken Bonds – The Disintegration of Yugoslavia*. Boulder: Westview Press.

Cohen, Lenard. 1997. 'Serpent in the Bossom': Slobodan Milošević and Serbian Nationalism.' In: Melissa Bokovoy et al.. (eds). *State-Society Relations in Yugoslavia 1945-1992*. London: Macmillan: 315-43.

Čolović, Ivan. 1997. *Politika simbola*. Belgrade: B92.

Čović, Bože (ed). 1993. *Roots of Serbian Aggression: debates, documents, cartographic reviews*. Zagreb: AGM.

Crnobrnja, Mihailo. 1994. *The Yugoslav drama*. Montréal : McGill-Queen's University Press.

Crooker, David. 1982. *Praxis and Democratic Socialism; the critical social theory of Markovic and Stojanovic*. Atlantic Highlands: Humanities Press.

De Koster, Lester. 1964. *Vocabulary of Communism*. Michigan: William B. Eerdmans.

Denitch, Bogdan. 1990. *Limits and Possibilities*. Minneapolis: University of Minnessota Press.

Denitch, Bogdan. 1994. *Ethnic nationalism : the tragic death of Yugoslavia*. Minneapolis: University of Minnesota Press.

Dimitrijević, Vojin. 1992. 'The Absolute Nation State: Post-Communist Institutions.' *Jugoslovenska revija za medjunarodno pravo*. 39:176-7.

Dimitrijević, Vojin. 1996. 'Sukobi oko Ustava iz 1974.' In: Nebojša Popov (ed.): *Srpska strana rata*. Belgrade: Republika: 447-71.

Djilas, Aleksa. 1991. *The Contested Country: Yugoslav Unity and Communist Revolution, 1919-1953*. Cambridge MA: Harvard University Press.

Djilas, Aleksa. 1993. 'A Profile of Slobodan Milošević.' *Foreign Affairs*. 72:81-96.

Djilas, Aleksa. 1993. *Razgovori za Jugoslaviju*. Beograd: Prometej.

Djilas, Aleksa: 1995. *Raspad i nada*. Beograd: Princip.

Djilas, Milovan. 1981. *Tito: The Story from Inside*. London: Weidenfeld & Nicolson.

Djukić, Slavoljub. 1992. *Kako se dogodio vodja: borba za vlast u Srbiji posle Josipa Broza. Belgrade*: Filip Višnjić.

Djukić, Slavoljub. 1994. *Izmedju slave i anateme: politička biografija Slobodana Miloševića*. Beograd: Filip Višnjić.

Doder, Duško. 1978. *The Yugoslavs*. London: George Allen & Unwin.

Dogo, Marco. 1997. 'National Truths and Disinformation in Albanian-Kosovar Historiography.' In: Ger Duijzings (ed): *Kosovo – Kosova: Confrontation or Coexistence*, University of Nijmegen: 34-45.

Dragović-Soso, Jasna. 2002. '*Saviours of the Nation.*' London: Hurst & Comp.

Dubček, Alexander. 1992. *Hope Dies Last*. London: HarperCollins Publishers.

Duijzings, Ger et al (eds). 1986. *Kosovo - Kosova: Confrontation or Coexistence*. Nijmegen. Peace Research Centre.

Dyker, David A and Ivan Vejvoda (eds). 1996. *Yugoslavia and After*. London and New York: Longman.

Dyker, David A. 1996. 'The Degeneration of the Yugoslav Communist Party as a Managing Elite – a Familiar East European Story?' In: Dyker, David A and Ivan Vejvoda (eds). 1996. *Yugoslavia and After*. London and New York: Longman: 48-64.

Ferdinand, Peter. 1991. *Communist Regimes in Comparative Perspective: the evolution of Soviet, Chinese and Yugoslav systems*. Hemel-Hampstead: Harvester-Wheatsheaf.

Filipič, France. 1979. 'Okolnosti i tok nastanka 'Speransa."' In: *Nacionalno pitanje u jugoslavenskoj teoriji i praksi - doprinos Edvarda Kardelja*. Banja Luka: Glas: 149-55.

Filipović, Muhamed. 1979. 'Smisao i domašaj Kardeljeve ispravke i kritike Staljinove definicije nacije za teoriju i praksu socijalističke revolucije.' In: *Nacionalno pitanje u Jugoslavenskoj teoriji i praksi - doprinos Edvarda Kardelja*. Banja Luka: Glas: 157-63.

Gaber, Slavko and Tonči Kuzmanić. 1989. *Kosovo – Srbija – Jugoslavija*. Ljubljana: Krt.

Gagnon, V.R Jr. 2006. *The Myth of Ethnic War*. Ithaca and London: Cornell University Press.

Gellner, Ernest. 1983/1993. *Nations and Nationalism*. Ithaca: Cornell University Press.

Glenny, Misha. 1992. *The Fall of Yugoslavia : the Third Balkan War*. London: Penguin.

Goati, Vladimir. 1997. 'The Disintegration of Yugoslavia: The role of Political Elites.' *Nationality Papers* 25: 455-67.

Gojković, Drinka. 1996. 'Trauma bez katarze.' In: Popov, Nebojša (ed). *Srpska strana rata*. Belgrade: Republika: 365-93.

Gokay, Bulent and Vassilis K. Fouskas. 2005. *The New American Imperialism*. Westport and London: Praeger Security International.

Gow, James. 1992. *Legitimacy and the Military: the Yugoslav crisis*. London: Pinter.

Gow, James. 1997. 'The People's Prince - Tito and Tito's Yugoslavia: Legitimation, Legend and Linchpin.' In: Melissa Bokovoy et al. (eds*): State-Society Relations in Yugoslavia 1945-1992*. London: Macmillan: 35-60.

Gow, James. 1997b. *Triumph of the Lack of Will: International Diplomacy and the Yugoslav War*. New York: Columbia University Press.

Graham, Loren R. 1966/1973. *Science and Philosophy in the Soviet Union*. London: Allen Lame.

Grakalić, Marijan. 1988. *Ljubljanski Proces*. Ljubljana: Emonica.

Gruenwald, Oskar. 1987. 'Yugoslav Camp Literature: Rediscovery the Ghost of a Nation's Past-Present-Future.' *Slavic Review* 1987:513-28.

Havel, Vaclav. 1978. 'Power of the Powerless.' In: Havel, Vaclav. 1992. *Open Letters*. London: Faber and Faber: 125-214.

Havel, Vaclav. 1991. *Open Letters*. London: Faber and Faber.

Hawkesworth, Celia (ed.). 1991. *Literature and Politics in Eastern Europe*. London: Macmillan Press.

Hempel, Carl. 1994. 'The Function of General Laws in History.' In: Michael Martin and Lee C. McIntyre (eds): *Readings in the Philosophy of Social Science*. Cambridge MA and London: A Bradford Book, The MIT Press: 43-53.

Holmes, Stephen. 1996. 'Cultural Legacies or State Collapse? Probing the Postcommunist Dilemma.' In: Michael Mandelbaum (ed): *Postcommunism. Four Perspectives*. New York: The Council of Foreign Relations: 22-76.

Horowitz, Donald. 1985. *Ethnic Groups in Conflict*. Berkeley: University of California Press.

Horvat, Branko. 1988. *Kosovsko pitanje*. Zagreb. Globus.

Horvat, Branko. 1992. 'Lutanja jugoslavenske privrede.' *Ekonomski pregled*, 43:550-77.

Horvat, Branko. 1993. 'Requiem for the Yugoslav Economy.' *Dissent*, 40:333-9

Hoxha, Enver.1982. *The Titoites: Historical Notes*. Tirana: 8 Nentori.

Hudelist, Darko. 1989. *Kosovo – bitka bez iluzija*. Zagreb: CIP.

Hudelist, Darko. 1993. *Novinari pod šljemom*. Zagreb: August Cesarec.

Huntington, Samuel. 1996. *The Clash of Civilizations and the Remaking of World Order*. New York: Simon & Schuster.

Irvine, Jill Al. 1997. 'Introduction: State-Society Relations in Yugoslavia.' 1945-1992. In Melissa Bokovoy et alt. (eds): *State-Society Relations in Yugoslavia 1945-1992*. London: Macmillan: 1-26.

Ivanović, Vane. 1996. *Yugoslav Democracy on Hold*. Rijeka: Dodir.

Jović, Dejan. 2004. 'Communist Yugoslavia and Its 'Others.'' In: John Lampe and Mark Mazower (eds): *Ideologies and National Identities: The Case of Twentieth Century Southeastern Europe*. Budapest and New York: CEU Press: 277-302.

Kaplan, Robert. 1994. *Balkan Ghosts: a Journey through History*. London: Papermac.

Kedourie, Elie. 1960/1993. *Nationalism*. Oxford: Blackwell.

Kedourie, Elie and George Urban (dialogue). 1991. 'What's Wrong with 'Nationalism'? What's Right with the 'Balance of Power'. A conversation.' In: Uri Ra'anan et alt (eds): *State and Nation in Multi-Ethnic Societies*. Manchester. Manchester University Press: 223-54.

Keeler, John. 1993. 'Opening the Window for Reform: Mandates, Crisies and Extraordinary Policy-Making.' *Comparative Political Studies*. 25:435-86.

Kerčov, Sava et al (eds). 1989. *Mitinzi u Vojvodini 1988. godine*. Novi Sad: Dnevnik.

Korošić, Marijan. 1988. *Jugoslavenska kriza*. Naprijed. Zagreb.

Koštunica, Vojislav. 1987/8. 'Transformation of Yugoslav Federalism: From Centralised to Peripheralised Federation.' In: *Praxis International*, 7: 382-93.

Križan, Mojmir. 1989. 'Civil Society - a New Paradigm in the Yugoslav Theoretical Discussion.' *Praxis International*. 9:152-63.

Kullashi, Muhamedin. 1997. 'The Production of Hatred in Kosova (1981-91).' In: Ger Duijzings (ed): *Kosovo – Kosova: Confrontation or Coexistence*, University of Nijmegen: 56-69.

Kuran, Timur. 1991. 'Now Out of Never: The Element of Surprise in the East European Revolutions of 1989.' *World Politics* 44:7-48.

Kuzmanović, Jasmina. 1995. 'Media: The Extension of Politics by other Means.' In: Sabrina P Ramet and Ljubiša S Adamović (eds): *Beyond Yugoslavia: Politics, Economics and Culture in a Shattered Community*. Boulder: Westview Press: 83-100.

Lampe, John R. 1996. *Yugoslavia as History : Twice There Was a Country*. Cambridge: Cambridge University Press, 1996.

Lapenna, Ivo. 1964. *State and Law: Soviet and Yugoslav Theory*. New Haven: Yale University Press

Lendvai, Paul. 1991. 'Yugoslavia Without Yugoslavs: the Roots of the Crisis.' *International Affairs*. 67:251-62

Lees, Lorraine. 1997. *Keeping Tito Afloat: the United States, Yugoslavia and the Cold War*. University Park: Pennsylvania University Press.

Lengyel, Gyoergy (ed.). 1996. *The Transformation of East-European Elites: Hungary, Yugoslavia and Bulgaria*. Budapest: Center for Public Affairs Studies, Budapest University of Economic Sciences.

Lenin, Vladimir Ilich. 1934. *What Is To Be Done? Burning Questions of Our Movement*. London: International Publishers.

Lukic, Reneo and Allen Lynch. 1996. *Europe from the Balkans to the Urals: The Disintegration of Yugoslavia and the Soviet Union*. Oxford: Oxford University Press.

Lukšič, Igor. 1994. *Liberalizem vs Korporativizem*. Ljubljana: ZPS.

Lydall, Harold. 1986. *Yugoslav Socialism Theory and Practice*. Oxford: Clarendon Press.

Magaš, Branka. 1993. *The Destruction of Yugoslavia : Tracking the Break-Up, 1980-91*. London and New York: Verso.

Malešević, Siniša. 2002. *Ideology, Legitimacy and the New State: Yugoslavia, Serbia and Croatia*. London: Frank Cass.

Maliqi, Shkelzen. 1998. 'A Demand for a New Status: The Albanian Movement in Kosova.' In: Thanost Veremis and Evangelis Kofos (eds): *Kosovo: Avoiding Another Balkan War*. Athens: Eliamep: 207-38.

Maliqi, Shkelzen. 1998a. *Kosova: Separate Worlds. Reflections and Analyses 1989-1988*. Prishtina: MM.

Mason, Tim. 1981. 'Intention and Explanation: A Current Controversy about the Interpretation of National Socialism.' In: Gerhard Hirschfeld and Lothar Kettenacker (eds): *Der Fuehrerstaat: Mythos and Realitaet*. Stuttgart: 21-40.

Mastnak, Tomaž. 1990. 'Civil Society in Slovenia: from Opposition to Power.' *Studies in Comparative Communism*. 23:305-18.

Meier, Viktor. 1999. *Yugoslavia : a history of its demise*. [Translated by Sabrina Ramet]. London and New York: Routledge.

Mertus, Julie A. 1999. Kosovo: *How Myths and Truths Started a War*. Berkeley: University of California Press.

Meštrović, Stjepan. 1994. *The Balkanization of the West: The Confluence of Postmodernism and Postcommunism*. London and New York: Routledge.

Meštrović, Stjepan and Thomas Cushman (eds). 1996. *This Time We Knew: Western Responses to Genocide in Bosnia*. New York: New York University Press.

Mežnarič, Silva. 1986. *"Bosanci' - A kuda idu Slovenci nedeljom?'* Beograd: Filip Višnjić.

Mills, John Stuart. 1865. *Considerations on Representative Government*. London: Longman, Green, Longman, Roberts and Green.

Milojković-Djurić, Jelena. 1996. 'Approaches to National Identities: Ćosić's and Pirjavec's Debate on Ideological and Literary Issues.' *East European Quarterly*, 30: 63-73.

Mišović, Miloš. 1987. *Ko je tražio Republiku Kosovo 1945-1985*. Belgrade: Narodna knjiga.

Nečak, Dusan. 1991. 'The Yugoslav Question: past and future.' In: Uri Ra'anan et al. (eds): *State and Nation in Multi-Ethnic Societies.'* Manchester: Manchester University Press: 125-34.

Nenadović, Aleksandar. 1996. ''Politika' u nacionalističkoj oluji.' In: Nebojša Popov (ed): *Srpska strana rata*. Belgrade: Republika: 583-609.

Obradović, Marija. 1996. 'Vladajuća stranka: ideologija i tehnologija dominacije.' In: Nebojša Popov (ed). *Srpska strana rata*. Belgrade: Republika: 472- 500.

Offe, Klaus. 1991. 'Capitalism by Democratic Design? Democratic Theory Facing the Triple Transition in East Central Europe.' *Social Research* 58:865-92.

Oklobdžija, Mira. 1993. 'The creation of active xenophobia in what was Yugoslavia.' *Journal of Area Studies*. 1993:191-201.

Pavković, Aleksandar. 1997. *The Fragmentation of Yugoslavia: Nationalism in a Multinational State*. London: Macmillan Press Ltd.

Pavković, Aleksandar. 1998. 'From Yugoslavism to Serbism: the Serb national idea 1986-1996.' *Nations and Nationalism*, 4: 511-28.

Pavlowitch, Stevan K. 1970. 'Jugoslavia in Perspective.' *Review*, No. 9: 750-67.

Pavlowitch, Stevan K. 1988. *The Improbable Survivor: Yugoslavia and Its Problems 1918-1988*. Columbus: Ohio State University Press.

Pavlowitch, Stevan K. 1992. *Tito: Yugoslavia's Great Dictator*. London: C. Hurst & Company.

Perić, Ivan. 1984. *Suvremeni hrvatski nacionalizam*. Zagreb: August Cesarec.

Perović, Latinka. 1993. 'Yugoslavia Was Defeated from Inside.' *Praxis International*, 13: 422-7.

Perović, Latinka. 1996. 'Beg od modernizacije.' In: Nebojša Popov (ed): *Srpska strana rata*. Belgrade: BIGZ: 119-131.

Petranović, Branko and Čedomir Štrbac (eds). 1977. *Istorija socijalističke Jugoslavije*. Belgrade: Radnička štampa.

Petrović, Ruža and Marina Blagojević. 1992. *The Migrations of Serbs and Montenegrins from Kosovo and Metohija: Results of the Survey Conducted in 1985-1986*. Belgrade: SANU.

Pizzorno, Alessandro. 1984. 'Some Other Kinds of Otherness: A Critique of 'Rational Choice' Theories.' In Alejandro Foxley (ed.): *Development, Democracy and the Art of Trespassing: Essays in Honor of Albert O. Hirschman*. Notre Dame: University of Notre Dame Press: 355-73.

Pleština, Dijana. 1992. 'From 'Democratic Centralism' to Decentralized Democracy? Trials and Tribulations of Yugoslavia's Development.' In: John Allcock et. al (eds): *Yugoslavia in Transition. Choices and Constraints*. New York and Oxford: Berg: 125-68.

Popov, Nebojša (ed). 1996. *Srpska strana rata*. Beograd: BIGZ.

Popov, Nebojša. 1996. 'Univerzitet u ideološkom omotaču.' In: Nebojša Popov (ed): *Srpska strana rata*. Belgrade: Republika: 339-64.

Potts, George A. 1996. *The Development of the System of Representation in Yugoslavia with Special Reference to the Period Since 1974*. Lanham, New York and London: University Press of America.

Przeworski, Adam. 1991. *Democracy and the Market: Political and Economic Reforms in Eastern Europe and Latin America*. Cambridge: Cambridge University Press.

Puhovski, Žarko. 1990. *Socijalistička konstrukcija zbilje*. Zagreb: Cekade.

Ra'anan, Uri et alt (eds). 1991: *State and Nation in Multi-Ethnic Societies*. Manchester. Manchester University Press.

Radošević, Slavo. 1996. 'The Collapse of Yugoslavia – between Chance and Necessity.' In: David A. Dyker and Ivan Vejvoda (eds): *Yugoslavia and After – A Study in Fragmentation, Despair and Rebirth*. London and New York: Longman: 65-83.

Ramet, Pedro. 1985. *Yugoslavia in the 1980s*. Boulder and London: Westview Press.

Ramet, Sabrina P. 1991. 'Serbia's Slobodan Milošević: A Profile.' *Orbis*. 35:93-106.

Ramet, Sabrina P. 1992/1996. *Balkan Babel: Politics, Culture and Religion in Yugoslavia*. Boulder: Westview Press.

Ramet, Sabrina P. and Ljubiša S Adamović (eds). 1995. *Beyond Yugoslavia: Politics, Economics and Culture in a Shattered Community*. Boulder: Westview Press.

Ramet, Sabrina P. 2005. *Thinking about Yugoslavia*: Scholarly Debates about the Yugoslav Breakup and the Wars in Bosnia and Kosovo. Cambridge: Cambridge University Press.

Rawls, John. 1971. *A Theory of Justice*. Cambridge: Harvard University Press.

Ribičič, Ciril and Zdravko Tomac. 1988. *Federalizam po mjeri budućnosti*. Zagreb and Ljubljana: Globus and Delo.

Ricci, David. 1984. *The Tragedy of Political Science. Politics, Scholarship and Democracy*. New Haven and London: Yale University Press.

Ridley, Jasper. 1994. *Tito. A Biography*. London: Constable.

Rose, Michael. 1998. *Fighting For Peace: Bosnia 1994*. London: The Harvill Press.

Rusinow, Dennison (ed): 1989. *Yugoslavia - a Fractured federalism*. Lanham and London. Wilson Centre Press.

Rusinow, Dennison. 1995. 'The Avoidable Catastrophe.' In: Sabrina P Ramet and Ljubisa S Adamovic (eds): *Beyond Yugoslavia: Politics, Economics and Culture in a Shattered Community*. Boulder: Westview Press: 13-38.

Samary, Catherine. 1995. *Yugoslavia Dismembered*. New York: Monthly Review Press.

Schoepflin, George. 1993. *Politics in Eastern Europe 1945-1992*. Oxford and Cambridge MA: Blackwell.

Sekelj, Laslo. 1993. *Yugoslavia: the Process of Disintegration*. Boulder: Social Science Monographs; Highland Lakes: Atlantic Research and; New York, N.Y: Columbia University Press.

Sell, Louis. 2002. *Slobodan Milosevic and the Destruction of Yugoslavia*. Durham: Duke University Press.

Šiber, Ivan. 1989. *Komunisti Jugoslavije o društvenoj reformi 1989*. Belgrade: Komunist.

Silber, Laura and Allan Little. 1995. *The Death of Yugoslavia*. London: BBC Books and Penguin.

Simić, Predrag. 1998. 'The Kosovo and Metohia Problem and Regional Security in the Balkans.' In: Thanos Veremis i Evangelos Kofos (eds): *Kosovo: Avoiding Another Balkan War*. Athens: Eliamep: 173-206.

Skinner, Quentin. 1988. *Meaning and Context: Quentin Skinner and his critics* (ed. by James Tully). Cambridge: Polity.

Sobolevski, Mihael. 1977. *Bombaški proces Josipu Brozu*. Zagreb: August Cesarec.

Srbi i Albanci u XX veku. 1991. Belgrade. Serbian Academy of Sciences and Arts

Stephens, John D. 1986. *The Transition from Capitalism to Socialism*. Urbana and Chicago: University of Illinois Press.

Stojanović, Svetozar. 1997. *The Fall of Yugoslavia : Why Communism Failed*. Amherst, N.Y: Prometheus Books.

Sugar, Peter F and Ivo J Lederer (eds). 1969/1994. *Nationalism in Eastern Europe*. Seattle and London: University of Washington Press.

Šuvar, Stipe. 1995. 'The Demographic Balance of the Second Yugoslavia (1945-1992) and Demographic Aspects of the Future Development of the Successor States.' *Balkan Forum* 1995:137-52.

Sweezy, Paul M and Charles Bettelheim. 1971. *On Transition to Socialism*. New York and London: Monthly Review Press.

Thomas, Robert. 1999. *Serbia under Milošević*. London: Hurst.

Thompson, Mark. 1992. *Paper House: the Ending of Yugoslavia*. London: Hutchinson.

Tikholaz, 1996. 'Could Russia Become a State of Law?' In: Elzbieta Matynia (ed). *Grappling with Democracy: deliberations on post-communist societies 1990-1995*. Prague: Slon: 131-8.

Tomac, Zdravko. 1984. *Ustavna reforma dest godina kasnije*. Zagreb: Zagreb.

Udovički, Jasminka and James Ridgeway (eds). 1997. *Burn this House: The Making and Unmaking of Yugoslavia*. Durham and London: Duke University Press.

Vejvoda, Ivan. 1993. 'Yugoslavia and the Empty Space of Power.' *Praxis International*, 13:64-79.

Vejvoda, Ivan. 1996. 'Yugoslavia 1945-91 – From Decentralisation Without Democracy to Dissolution.' In : David Dyker and Ivan Vejvoda (eds). *Yugoslavia and After – A Study in Fragmentation, Despair and Rebirth*. London and New York: Longman: 9-27.

Veremis, Thanos and Evangelos Kofos. 1998. *Kosovo: Avoiding Another Balkan War*. Athens: ELIAMEP.

Vigor, P.H. 1966. *A Guide to Marxism and its Effects on Soviet Development*. London: Faber and Faber.

Vlajčić, Gordana. 1978. *Revolucija i nacije*. Zagreb: Cekade.

Vlajčić, Gordana. 1984. *Jugoslavenska revolucija i nacionalno pitanje*. Zagreb: Cekade.

Vlajčić, Gordana. 1989. *Kominterna i taktika borbe 'klase protiv klase' (1927-1934)*. Zagreb: Cekade.

Van den Heuvel, Martin and Jan G. Siccama. 1992. *The Disintegration of Yugoslavia*. Amsterdam: Rodopi.

Voegelin, Erik. 1952. *The New Science of Politics: an Introduction*. Chicago: University of Chicago Press.

Von Beyme, Klaus. 1996. *Transition to Democracy in Eastern Europe*. London: Macmillan Press Ltd.

Vučkovic, Gojko. 1997. *Ethnic Cleavages and Conflict: The Sources of National Cohesion and Disintegration*. Aldrshot: Ashgate.

Vujačić, Veljko. 1995. 'Serbian Nationalism, Slobodan Milošević and the Origins of the Yugoslav War.' *The Harriman Review*, 4: 1-15.

Vujović, Sreten. 1996. 'Nelagode od grada.' In: Nebojša Popov (ed). *Srpska strana rata*. Belgrade: BIGZ: 132-158.

Wachtel, Andrew Baruch. 1998. *Making a Nation, Breaking a Nation*. Stanford: Stanford University Press.

Waller, Michael. 1972. *The Language of Communism: A Commentary*. London: Bodley Head.

Warner Neal, Fred. 1962. 'Yugoslavia at the Crossroads,' reprinted, available on Internet: http://www.theatlantic.com/atlantic/atlweb/flashbks/balkans/nealf.htm, 30 July 1997.

West, Richard. 1994. *Tito and the Rise and Fall of Yugoslavia*. London: Sinclair-Stevenson.

Wilczynski, Jozef. 1981. *An Encyclopedic Dictionary of Marxism, Socialism and Communism*. Berlin and New York. De Gruyter.

Williams, John. 1998. *Legitimacy in International Relations and the Rise and Fall of Yugoslavia*. Houndmills, Basingstoke : Macmillan Press.

Wilson, Duncan. 1978. 'Self-management in Yugoslavia.' *International Affairs*. 54:253-63.

Winch, Peter. 1958/1990. *The Idea of Social Science and Its Relation to Philosophy*. London: Routledge.

Woodward, Susan L. 1995. *Balkan Tragedy – Chaos and Dissolution After the Cold War*. Washington: The Brookings Institution.

Woodward, Susan L. 1996. 'The West and the International Organisations.' In: David A. Dyker and Ivan Vejvoda (eds): *Yugoslavia and After – A Study in Fragmentation, Despair and Rebirth*. London and New York: Longman: 155-76.

Zajmi, Gazmend. 1996. *Kosova's Constitutional Position in the former Yugoslavia*. in: Ger Dujzings (ed): *Kosovo/Kosova - cooperation or co-existence*. Nijmegen. Peace Research Centre.

Žanić, Ivo. 1998. *Prevarena povijest*. Zagreb: Durieux.

Zimmermann, Warren. 1995. 'The Last Ambassador.' *Foreign Affairs*. No. 2: *2-21*.

Zimmermann, Warren. 1996/1999. *Origins of a Catastrophe: Yugoslavia and Its Destroyers*. New York: Random House.

Zukin, Sharon. 1975. *Beyond Marx and Tito*. London: Cambridge University Press.

Županov, Josip. 1983. *Marginalije o društvenoj krizi*. Zagreb: Globus.